THE POLITICS OF THE PRESIDENCY

THE POLITICS OF THE PRESIDENCY

FIFTH EDITION

JOSEPH A. PIKA
University of Delaware

JOHN ANTHONY MALTESE
University of Georgia

NORMAN C. THOMAS
University of Cincinnati

CQ PRESS

A DIVISION OF CONGRESSIONAL QUARTERLY INC.
WASHINGTON, D.C.

CQ Press
A Division of Congressional Quarterly Inc.
1255 22nd Street, N.W., Suite 400
Washington, D.C. 20037

(202) 822-1475; (800) 638-1710

www.cqpress.com

Typeset and designed by Sheridan Books, Ann Arbor, Michigan.

Cover design by Karen Doody

Printed and bound in the United States of America

05 04 03 02 01   5 4 3 2 1

LIBRARY OF CONGRESS CATALOGING-IN-PUBLICATION DATA

Pika, Joseph August, 1947–
    The politics of the presidency / Joseph A. Pika, John Anthony
Maltese, Norman C. Thomas.— 5th ed.
        p. cm.
    Rev. ed. of: The politics of the presidency / Norman C. Thomas,
Joseph A. Pika. Rev. 4th ed. c1997.
    Includes bibliographical references and index.
    ISBN 1-56802-419-3 (alk. paper)
    1. Presidents—United States.   I. Maltese, John Anthony. II.
Thomas, Norman C. III. Thomas, Norman C. Politics of the presidency. IV.
Title.
    JK516 .P53 2001
    352.23'0973—dc21
                                                    2001005976

TO MARY, ANNA, AND MARILYN

CONTENTS

TABLES AND FIGURES

TABLES

FIGURES

PREFACE

AFTER MORE THAN TWO CENTURIES of change and development, the presidency stands not only as the nation's preeminent public office but also as its most problematic. Because presidents today are far more important for peace and prosperity than were their nineteenth-century counterparts, ensuring the selection of qualified candidates and enhancing the winner's effectiveness in office are major concerns of specialists and citizens alike. In the post–World War II period, however, few presidents have left office with a record of unqualified success. In fact, academic and media observers have labeled most presidents since Lyndon Johnson as "failures," although reputations sometimes improve with the passage of time.

Johnson enjoyed unparalleled success in getting his Great Society legislative program through Congress, but he could not extricate himself or the country from the Vietnam War. Richard Nixon managed to bring the war to an end and initiate new relationships with the Soviet Union and China, but Watergate cost him the confidence of the country. Gerald Ford and Jimmy Carter failed to convince voters that they could exercise effective leadership. Like Johnson, Ronald Reagan convinced Congress to approve his program of economic reforms, but the budgetary consequences of those policies and his mishandling of the Iran-contra affair tarnished his reputation—a tarnish that is receding as time goes by. George H. W. Bush and Bill Clinton were threatened by the same difficulties that beset Ford and Carter—a perception of ineffectiveness. Clinton also came to be viewed as possessing a severely flawed character, committing errors in his personal life that prompted an unsuccessful effort to have him removed from office. Given the inflated expectations of performance held by the public and political elites, it is reasonable to wonder if any president can be considered a success, but these executives also contributed to widespread disappointment through their own actions.

Our focus in *The Politics of the Presidency* is on how presidents govern—in the country and in Washington. The book views the presidency as essentially a political office; that is, the chief executive must govern more through skilled political leadership than through the assertion of constitutional prerogatives. We examine how effectiveness in office varies with the character, personality, and political style of the incumbent. Major developments in society, the U.S. political system, and the international arena also affect how well or how poorly a president does in office. By examining this full range of influences, *The Politics of the Presidency* provides a comprehensive treatment of the nation's most important political office.

Part I begins with an analysis of the origins and development of the presidency as well as an examination of the changing conceptions of the office. It then explores the president's relations with the public in electoral politics and in the process of governing. Next, it examines the kinds of people who have become president and the interactions between them and the office. Part II analyzes the president's relations with other government elites—members of Congress, the bureaucracy, and the judiciary. In Part III the focus shifts to how presidents formulate and implement domestic, economic, and national security policies. The book concludes with a case study of George W. Bush's first half-year in office— a particularly critical period for any administration—and a brief discussion of how the terrorist attacks on September 11, 2001, transformed his presidency.

A new author joins the fifth edition of *The Politics of the Presidency,* and a founding author departs. Norman C. Thomas, coauthor of all four previous editions, collaborated with Richard Watson on the original volume, and their influence remains present throughout. John Anthony Maltese, the new member of the team, is primarily responsible for Chapters 1, 3, 7, 8, and 11. Joseph Pika updated and accepts major responsibility for Chapters 2, 4–6, 9, and 10.

This edition includes extensive discussions of Bill Clinton's second term, the historic election of 2000, and the equally historic balancing of the federal budget. With a new party controlling the White House, we had expected to describe the novel arrangement of unified *Republican* government, but once again events overtook scholarship with the dramatic party switch of a single senator, James M. Jeffords of Vermont. From impeachment to the first electoral college misfire in more than a century, to the resumption of budget wars with a decidedly new flavor, to the war on terrorism provoked by attacks on the World Trade Center and the Pentagon, we have chronicled the twists and turns of the past decade while incorporating findings from a wide range of scholarship. At the same time we have sought to retain a strong appreciation for historical development, starting with an expanded discussion of the constitutional foundations.

We wish to thank Philip Mundon and Thomas Langston as well as four anonymous reviewers for their helpful comments on the previous edition and on drafts of revised chapters. Their reflections helped our own thinking, even if we did not always follow their advice.

We are grateful to Brenda Carter, Charisse Kiino, Michelle Tupper, and Belinda Josey of CQ Press for their encouragement and contributions to this edition. Jarelle Stein improved the book with her fine copyediting. We also appreciate the research assistance provided by Mark Cutrona, Julia Kohen, and Josh Templet and the clipping services contributed by Frank Langr.

1 THE CHANGING PRESIDENCY

The White House—nerve center of the executive branch and home of its chief.

FOR MOST AMERICANS THE PRESIDENT is the focal point of public life. Almost every day, they see the president on television newscasts interpreting current events, meeting with foreign dignitaries, proposing policy, or grappling with national problems. This person appears to be in charge, and such recurrent images of an engaged leader are reassuring. But the reality of the presidency rests on a very different truth: presidents are seldom in command and usually must negotiate with others to achieve their goals. It is only by exercising adroit political skill in winning public and elite support and knowing how to use it that a president can succeed in office. For more than three decades this lesson has dominated scholarly accounts of the presidency, but it has not always been fully appreciated by either the public or the presidents themselves.

The Scope of Presidential Power

In some respects, presidents in the last half of the twentieth century were stronger

1

than ever before. Presidents at the beginning of the century had embraced new, expansive views of presidential power that by midcentury were accepted as normal. They used the power of the "bully pulpit" to shape public opinion. With the advent of radio and television, they became the leading voice in government. Congress added to the power of presidents by requiring them to submit annual federal budgets for congressional approval—an action that made presidents policy leaders in a way that they had never been before. Staff support for presidents increased dramatically. And by leading the United States to victory in two world wars and playing for high stakes in the cold war, presidents took center stage on the world scene.

And yet, since World War II, we have witnessed a string of "failed" or otherwise abbreviated presidencies. Of the ten presidents serving from 1945 through the end of the twentieth century, only three (Dwight D. Eisenhower, Ronald Reagan, and Bill Clinton) served out two full terms of office. Despite a strong rally of public support when they were thrust into the presidency, Harry S. Truman and Lyndon Baines Johnson left office repudiated by their own parties after they involved the country in controversial military conflicts abroad. Both could have run for another term, but neither chose to do so. John F. Kennedy was assassinated before completing his first term. Richard Nixon resigned in disgrace two years after his landslide reelection. Nixon's vice president, Gerald R. Ford, failed to win the presidency in his own right after completing Nixon's term, and Jimmy Carter lost his reelection bid after seeing his public approval ratings plummet to a record low of 21 percent in the face of the Iranian hostage crisis and runaway inflation. George H. W. Bush, whose approval rating skyrocketed to 89 percent during the Persian Gulf War, lost reelection the next year when faced with an economic recession and criticism of his domestic agenda. Even Ronald Reagan and Bill Clinton were distracted by scandal in their second terms. Reagan faced congressional investigations and an independent counsel probe into the Iran-contra affair (leading to guilty pleas and convictions of a number of administration officials). Clinton also faced an independent counsel probe and became the first president since Andrew Johnson in 1868 to be impeached by the House of Representatives (like Johnson, Clinton was ultimately acquitted by the Senate). Moreover, both Reagan and Clinton were constrained in their second terms by a Congress controlled by the opposition party.

Like such recent presidents as Kennedy, Nixon, and Clinton, George W. Bush entered office in January 2001 with less than 50 percent of the popular vote. But unlike any president since Benjamin Harrison in 1888, Bush also came in *second* in the popular vote to his Democratic rival, Al Gore.[1] Bush won the electoral college vote only after the U.S. Supreme Court refused to allow a manual recount of the bitterly contested votes in Florida.[2] In Congress, the newly elected president found himself with only a slim majority of fellow Republicans in the House of Representatives and a Senate evenly divided between Democrats and Republicans for the first time since 1883. As a result of the questions about the legitimacy of his electoral victory and the closely divided Congress, Bush, like his immediate predecessors, may face an uphill battle as president. This seemed even more likely after the Democrats regained control of the Senate in June 2001. The bumpy road encountered by many recent presidents reminds us that presidential power is not a fixed commodity. Formal powers mean little if presidents cannot convince others to follow their lead. As Richard Neustadt so succinctly put it: "Presidential power is the power to persuade."[3]

Dramatic changes in presidential fortunes are not new to American politics, nor are "failed" presidencies. Indeed, for a variety of reasons, only about 20 percent of all our presidents have served out two full terms. The very fact that they are the focal point of public life exposes presidents to intense scrutiny and allows them, as Stephen Skowronek puts it, to become "the lightning rod of national politics."[4] Through both success and failure, though, one might think that constitutional provisions would serve as a constant source of presidential power. As the following sections demonstrate, however, those provisions not only were a source of great debate at the Constitutional Convention but also have been subject to widely different interpretations by presidents and others ever since then. Quite simply, both the scope of presidential power and the conceptions of the office have changed dramatically over the years.

Inventing the Presidency

Those who invented the presidency in 1787 did not expect the office to become the nation's central political institution. In fact, Article II of the Constitution, which deals with the executive branch, is known for its brevity and lack of clarity, particularly in comparison with the carefully detailed description of the legislative branch in Article I. But within the presidency's vague constitutional description lay the seeds of a far more powerful position, one that has grown through elaboration of its explicit, *enumerated* powers as well as interpretation of its *implied* and *inherent* powers. Moreover, through the years Congress and the public have caused the range of responsibilities associated with the presidency to expand, particularly in response to changes in society and America's position in the world. What has developed over two centuries is the office that now stands at the center of American government and American politics.

The office of the presidency gained stature and a set of precedents from its initial occupant, George Washington. During the nineteenth century, however, the office languished, so much so, in fact, that Lord Bryce, the British chronicler of American government, felt compelled to explain in 1890 that great men do not become president because of the institution's weaknesses. Government during this period centered on Congress and political parties (an American invention that the Founders did not anticipate). A few presidents—most notably Thomas Jefferson, Andrew Jackson, and Abraham Lincoln—seemed to foreshadow strong presidents of the future, but most receded quickly from history. How, then, did the presidency come to assume its exalted position? The answer is complex and involves a variety of factors. At one level, the original design of the office—its structure, mode of selection, and powers—continues to exercise

This is James Hoban's original architectural drawing of the White House from 1792. Like the building itself, the office of the presidency has changed over time.

important influence on its operation today. The office has changed over time, however, partly in response to the influence of its occupants, partly in response to changing expectations in Congress and by the public, and partly in response to internal dynamics of institutional development.

Constitutional Design

In the wake of the events leading to the American Revolution, the colonists disparaged anything that resembled a monarch. Thomas Paine's enormously influential pamphlet, *Common Sense,* published in January 1776, sharply dismissed the institution of monarchy, calling it "the most prosperous invention the Devil ever set on foot for the promotion of idolatry."[5] Paine went on to call for a new government that had no executive. Some 120,000 copies of *Common Sense* were sold in just the three months following its publication.[6] The pamphlet's rallying cry against monarchy and executive power had hit a nerve.

In the weeks leading up to the Declaration of Independence, the Continental Congress urged the colonies to adopt new constitutions in anticipation of statehood. The resulting state constitutions that were drafted in 1776 and 1777 "systematically emasculated the power of the governors."[7] Pennsylvania's constitution, drafted by Benjamin Franklin, went the furthest. It provided for a unicameral legislature and no chief executive at all. Those states that did create chief executives made them subordinate to the legislature. Most governors served one-year terms, were elected by the legislature, and had little or no appointment or veto powers.[8] Even where governors were not chosen by the legislature (such as in Massachusetts), their powers were checked by a privy council.[9] New York stood out as the exception to this practice of weak governors and strong legislatures.[10]

As a result, most state legislatures became all powerful. This led to something of a backlash against strong legislatures by other participants and observers of the political process. For example, after serving as governor of Virginia for two years, Thomas Jefferson strongly criticized the concentration of power in the Virginia legislature. Although the Virginia constitution explicitly called for the separation of the three branches, the executive and judicial branches were so dependent upon the legislative that their powers had been eviscerated. Mindful of the fear of executive power, Jefferson nonetheless wrote that his experience with the Virginia legislature had convinced him that "173 despots would surely be as oppressive as one."[11] If an unchecked executive could lead to tyranny, so too could an unchecked legislature. These experiences would inform the delegates to the Constitutional Convention in 1787 and make them more willing to accept a strong executive than they would have been immediately after the Revolution.

Experience with the Articles of Confederation also would inform the delegates. The Articles were a compact among the thirteen states that the Continental Congress endorsed in 1777 and that all of the states finally ratified by 1781. The Articles of Confederation not only avoided the creation of anything resembling a president but also failed even to create an independent executive branch. Over time, this omission proved problematic. Attempts to administer laws through ad hoc committees, councils, or conventions were unsuccessful, and Congress found it necessary to create several permanent departments in 1781 (including treasury, foreign affairs, and war). Although Congress appointed eminent men such as Robert Livingston, John Jay, and Robert Morris to head them, the departments nonetheless remained mere appendages of the legislature.[12] Since the Articles of Confederation did not create a federal judiciary either, the resulting government revolved around a single legislative body. In the zeal to ward off monarchy, the principle of separation of powers had been ignored. However, because the states had not delegated much power to the national government under the new scheme, Congress had nonetheless remained impotent. Indeed, the national government had so little power to control the states that the confederation seemed to be but a "cobweb."[13] Congress did not even have the authority to regulate commerce among the states. This led to a dire economic situation in which states fought with each other for economic advantage. Protective tariffs and trade barriers became routine weapons used by one state against another. Trade was further complicated by the fact that states had different currencies. Some states went so far as to pass legislation canceling their debts. With no federal judiciary to turn to, those affected by such legislation sometimes had no legal recourse. The resulting chaos was so great that it became a driving force for the Constitutional Convention.

Riots and mob actions in various states, culminating in Shays's Rebellion in Massachusetts, also signaled the need for change. Shays's Rebellion—an uprising in 1786–1787 by more than 2,000 farmers who faced foreclosures because of high property taxes and economic depression—underscored the chaos. Massachusetts had to rely on a volunteer army to stop the rebellion because the Confederation Congress was powerless to act. This failure of the Confederation Congress highlighted the need for a strong national government to maintain public order and prompted several states to vote to send delegates to the proposed Constitutional Convention. Even more significantly, it helped to legitimize the idea of a strong *executive*. As Forrest McDonald has written: "Shays' Rebellion stimulated many Americans, especially in New England, to talk openly of monarchy as a safer guardian of liberty and property than republican institutions could be, particularly in a country as large as the United States."[14]

As a result of these various experiences and events, delegates to the Constitutional Convention came to Philadelphia agreed that the power of the national government had to be increased, though they disagreed over *how* to increase it and how *much* to increase it. Virtually all agreed that the new constitution should impose some form of separation of powers with a distinct executive branch at the national level. But delegates disagreed fundamentally about what that executive branch should look like and just how strong it should be. Despite that disagreement, it is striking that in the eleven years since the Declaration of Independence, support for an executive (and even support for a *strong* executive) had increased dramatically because of recent experiences at both the state and the national level. In short, the delegates brought with them to the task of designing an executive office two conflicting attitudes: a healthy skepticism for executive power and a new appreciation of its necessity.

Initial Convention Debates. James Madison, the thirty-six-year-old Virginian commonly credited as the chief architect of the Constitution, was the first delegate to arrive in Philadelphia. He was convinced that the national government had to be dramatically refashioned, especially to increase its power over the states, but he had given little thought to the issue of executive power. In a letter that he wrote to George Washington two weeks before arriving in Philadelphia, Madison admitted that "a national Executive must . . . be provided," but confessed, "I have scarcely ventured as yet to form my own opinion either of the manner in which it ought to be constituted or of the authorities with which it ought to be cloathed."[15]

The "Virginia Plan"—written mostly by Madison but introduced on the first working day of the convention by his fellow Virginian Edmund Randolph—reflected this uncertainty. The plan called for an executive of unspecified size and tenure, selected by the legislature, and with unclear powers.[16] Indeed, the executive did not appear to be a matter of high importance to Randolph. His opening speech on May 29, 1787, included a lengthy analysis of the defects of the Articles of Confederation, but he failed to include the lack of an executive as one of them.[17]

When the convention began its executive branch deliberations on June 1, Randolph revealed his preference for a weak executive by arguing strongly for a plural executive. More than a quarter of the delegates agreed.[18] Although we now take a single president for granted, the question of whether there should be a singular or plural executive (one president or multiple presidents) was an open question for the delegates. Benjamin Franklin, for one, had long argued for a plural executive.[19] When Franklin's fellow delegate from Pennsylvania, James Wilson, moved that the executive should be singular, a "lengthy embarrassed silence ensued."[20] Franklin broke the silence by encouraging the delegates to express their views on the matter. The debate that followed was the first of many between advocates of a strong executive and those of a weak one.

Roger Sherman, a delegate from Connecticut, took the most extreme view for a weak executive. He saw no need to give the executive an explicit grant of power in the Constitution. As far as Sherman was concerned, the executive should be completely subservient to the legislature. Not only should the executive be "nothing more than an institution for carrying the will of the Legislature into effect," but the executive should "be appointed by and accountable to the Legislature only."[21] Rather than using the Constitution to settle whether the executive should be singular or plural, Sherman argued that Congress should be able to change the size of the office at will. Wilson's motion for a singular executive—a first step toward creating a strong one—eventually won on June 4. But Sherman's suggestion for legislative appointment—something that Wilson and other proponents of a strong executive vigorously opposed—had won on June 2. On yet another issue, presidential veto power, the delegates steered a middle course. After voting for a single executive, the delegates gave the executive a qualified veto power, subject to an override by a two-thirds vote of the legislature.

This, however, proved to be just the beginning of the debate over the position. On June 15, William Paterson introduced the "New Jersey Plan," which proposed simply amending the existing Articles of Confederation rather than replacing them with a new constitution. The plan reintroduced the idea of a plural executive and embraced the idea that the executive should be elected by Congress for a single term.[22] Although the primary motivation of the New Jersey Plan was to protect the power of small states (the Virginia Plan apportioned representation in the national legislature according to population; the New Jersey Plan called for equal representation regardless of size), it is clear that those favoring the New Jersey Plan preferred a weak executive.

Since the first debates on executive power in early June, Gouverneur Morris, a delegate from Pennsylvania, had joined the convention. Morris, who had spent most of his life in New York, became—along with James Wilson—one of the most influential proponents of a strong executive. He stood out because of his appearance—he had a wooden leg as a result of a carriage accident and a crippled arm as a result of a scalding as a child—but, as Richard J. Ellis has noted, "it was his rapier wit, infectious humor, and brilliant mind that set him apart and drew others."[23] On July 17, he began his offensive. Attempting to free the executive from its dependence on the legislature, Morris called for popular election by freeholders. Sherman vigorously objected, and Morris's motion was quickly defeated by a resounding margin. But the battle lines were drawn, and the debate over presidential selection was far from over.

Heated and sometimes confused debate over presidential selection continued for the next week, but when the delegates finished their debate on July 26, the plan for an executive that had been agreed upon in early June remained unchanged: legislative appointment of a single executive for one unrenewable seven-year term. Thereupon, the delegates turned their resolutions over to a five-member Committee of Detail chaired by James Wilson. Its task was to take the resolutions passed by the Committee of the Whole and turn them into a draft of the Constitution.

Committee Work and Final Action.   One of the most notable contributions of the Committee of Detail was its decision to employ the word *president* to identify what the delegates had simply referred to as "the Executive." The word *governor*—suggested by John Rutledge of South Carolina—was rejected by the committee because of the negative connotations associated with the royal governors who ruled the colonies. The committee chose *president* because it was an innocuous term. Derived from the Latin word *praesidere* ("to sit in front of or at the head of" and "to defend"), president had historically been used to denote passive guardianship rather than strong executive power. The presiding officer of Congress under the Articles of Confederation was called its president. George Washington, who performed a mostly ceremonial function at the Constitutional Convention, served as its president.[24] Arguably, this choice of a term helped to sugarcoat executive power and make it more palatable.

In its draft of the Constitution, the Committee of Detail followed the convention's wishes and gave the president relatively little power. But the fact that it gave the president a specific constitutional grant of power at all was significant. The alternative would have been to follow Sherman's suggestion and allow Congress to dictate presidential powers. The Committee of Detail followed the convention's recommendation for a single executive elected by Congress to one unrenewable term, subject to impeachment, and with a qualified veto power. The draft also gave the president the power to appoint executive officers, to grant pardons, and to receive ambassadors. But many powers traditionally associated with the prerogative of the executive—such as raising armies, making war, making treaties, appointing ambassadors, and coining money—were all withheld from the president and given to the legislative branch.[25]

Convention debate resumed on August 6. When the delegates took up the article dealing with the president, it was obvious that they remained dissatisfied. But there seemed to be no agreement on how to improve things. When convention

George Washington presides over the signing of the Constitution by members of the Constitutional Convention in Philadelphia on September 17, 1787. This depiction of the event was painted by Howard Chandler Christy and hangs in the U.S. Capitol.

debate ended on August 31, the president remained largely unchanged. At that point, the convention sent unresolved issues to the Committee on Postponed Matters. The committee, chaired by David Brearly of New Jersey, consisted of one member from each state (including, significantly, Gouverneur Morris). It was in that committee that the final constitutional vision of the president took shape.

One of the most significant accomplishments of the Committee on Postponed Matters was its cobbling together of a compromise plan for presidential selection. This had been a major focus of debate throughout the convention. Various proposals had been introduced either for popular election of the president or selection by some sort of electoral college. But the delegates had always reverted back to selection by Congress. The Committee on Postponed Matters revisited this issue and offered a novel twist on an earlier suggestion that had been made by James Wilson. The committee proposed that a president—and a *vice president* (the first time this position had been recommended)—be chosen by an electoral college consisting of electors from each of the states. Each state would be free to choose its electors (equaling that state's combined number of senators and representatives in the U.S. Congress) as its state legislature saw fit. Electors would meet and vote in their respective states. Each elector would have two votes, only one of which could be cast for a candidate from that elector's state. When the votes from all states' electors were counted, the candidate with the most votes would be elected president and the runner-up would be elected vice president. If no candidate received a majority in the electoral college, the Senate would choose from among the five candidates who had received the most electoral votes. (Later the convention changed this provision so that the House of Representatives, with each state delegation having an equal vote, would decide the outcome in such cases.)

The committee's proposed electoral college seemed to resolve the problems that had stymied previous debate on presidential selection. First, it placated both large and small states. Basing the number of electors on the combined number of a state's senators and representatives served as a compromise between equal and proportional allocation of electors. Large states could support the plan with the hope that they would dominate the electoral college. At the same time, small states were placated by the fact that each elector could cast only one vote for a home-state candidate. Small states were further assured that if the election was thrown to Congress, each state would have an equal vote (this was true under both the committee's plan for Senate selection and the eventual constitutional provision for House selection). Second, the compromise plan satisfied proponents of an independent president and proponents of congressional selection of the president. Proponents of congressional selection argued that a presidential candidate would seldom get a majority of votes in the electoral college. Thus, they believed that Congress would ultimately choose the president most of the time anyway, with the electoral college acting simply as a nominating convention. Advocates of an independent president, on the other hand, saw the electoral college as an explicit rejection of congressional selection. They discounted the argument that presidential candidates would seldom get a majority in the electoral college.[26] Even on those occasions when a candidate did not get a majority, Congress was limited in its choice to the five candidates with the most votes in the electoral college.[27] Clearly this limited Congress more than the original plan, in which congressional choice was unrestricted. Finally, the proposal for both a president and a vice president resolved concerns about succession if presidents did not complete their terms.

In addition to its plan for an electoral college, the Committee on Postponed Matters made a few other significant decisions. It shortened the president's term from seven to four years and made the president eligible for reelection to an unlimited number of terms. And—of great import to advocates of a strong executive—it gave the president a number of executive powers that the delegates had previously given to the Senate, including expanded appointment power and the power to make treaties. The resulting language was again a compromise. The president could *nominate* ambassadors and other public ministers, Supreme

Court justices, and all other officers whose appointments were not otherwise provided for. Actual *appointment* would come only with the "advice and consent" of the Senate. And though the president could make treaties, they could be ratified only by a two-thirds vote of the Senate.[28]

The convention as a whole spent several days in early September scrutinizing the proposals of the Committee on Postponed Matters. The only major change came on September 6, when the convention gave the House of Representatives the power to choose the president if no candidate received a majority in the electoral college. The change was the result of fear among the delegates that the Senate was becoming too powerful. When voting for president, each state delegation in the House would have one vote. This guaranteed that each state would have an equal vote (a counterbalance to the electoral college itself, which gave large states an advantage).

On September 8, the delegates created a five-member Committee of Style, chaired by Gouverneur Morris, to write a final draft of the Constitution. This committee was responsible for the opening words of Article II of the Constitution: "The executive Power shall be vested in a President of the United States of America." As we shall see, the ambiguity of this sentence continues to be the subject of debate, and it stood in marked contrast to the opening words of Article I, which seemed to explicitly limit Congress's powers to those listed in the Constitution: "All legislative powers *herein granted* shall be vested in a Congress of the United States." Ironically, the opening of Article II, the meaning of which has been debated so often in subsequent years, was accepted by the whole of the Constitutional Convention without any debate over its specific language.[29] Thus, the end result of the constitutional language regarding the presidency was compromise, although it was a compromise that ultimately favored the strong executive model more than the weak one (see Table 1-1). Credit for this usually goes to a small group of delegates (chief among them, James Wilson and Gouverneur Morris) who used their strategic positions within the convention's working committees to further their goal of a strong executive.

Interpreting the Constitutional Language

The ambivalence over executive power exhibited by the convention has become a permanent feature of American political culture. Like the delegates in 1787, Americans have had to confront the trade-off between tyranny and effectiveness—the one to be feared and the other to be prized. The antifederalists, who opposed ratification of the Constitution, frequently pointed to the risks inherent in a national executive, a post that some considered even more threatening than its British counterpart. As George Mason, a delegate from Virginia who ultimately refused to sign the Constitution, had argued: "We are not indeed constituting a British monarchy, but a more dangerous monarchy, an elective one."[30] But others, such as Alexander Hamilton, saw the newly created presidency as essential to effective government, the source of energy, dispatch, and responsibility in the conduct of domestic and foreign affairs.[31]

Table 1-1   Models of Executive Considered by the Constitutional Convention

Elements of executive	Weak-executive model	Strong-executive model	Decision by convention
Relation to Congress	To put into effect will of Congress	Powers independent of Congress	Powers independent of Congress but with checks and balances
Number of executive	Plural or single individual checked by council	Single individual with no council or only advisory one	Single individual with Senate advisory on some matters
Method of choosing	By Congress	By means other than congressional selection	Electoral college
Tenure	Limited term; not renewable	No limitation	Unlimited
Method of removal	By Congress during term of office	Only for definite, enumerated reasons after impeachment and conviction by judicial body or Congress	For treason, bribery, high crimes and misdemeanors, by impeachment by majority of House and conviction by two-thirds of Senate
Scope and source of powers	Limited powers delegated by Congress	Broad powers from Constitution, not subject to congressional interference	Broad powers delegated by Constitution
Appointment and foreign policy and war-making powers	None—province of Congress	Would appoint judicial and diplomatic officials and participate in foreign policy and war-making powers, including making of treaties	Appoints executive and judicial officials with consent of Senate; shares foreign policy and war-making powers with Congress; Senate must approve treaties negotiated by president
Veto	None	Veto over legislation passed by Congress, exercised alone or with judiciary	Qualified veto, may be overridden by two-thirds vote of House and Senate

Source: Joseph E. Kallenbach, *The American Chief Executive: The Presidency and the Governorship* (New York: Harper and Row, 1966), chap. 2.

This ambivalence has been reflected over the years in differing interpretations of constitutional language concerning presidential power. As we have seen, Article II of the Constitution opens with the words "The executive Power shall be vested in a President of the United States of America." The language drafted by Morris and the Committee of Style has proven to be, as presidential scholar Charles C. Thach Jr. put it in the 1920s, the "joker" in the game of presidential power.[32] Constitutional language limits both legislative and judicial power. Article I limits legislative powers to those "herein granted." Article III uses the phrase "the judicial power shall extend to," followed by an enumeration of those powers, which suggests the same sort of limitation of power as the one contained in Article I. But Article II contains no such limit. Whether this was intentional or not is unclear since the full convention never even debated the language. But Thach points to letters that Morris wrote in which he admitted how much impact small, seemingly inconsequential changes of phraseology could have on the meaning of constitutional clauses. Although Morris did not refer explicitly to presidential power in these letters, his advocacy of a strong executive is well known, and Thach suspects that Morris embraced the language of Article II with "full realization of its possibilities."[33] By failing to limit executive power to those "herein granted," Article II suggests that the scope of presidential power is not confined to those powers that are enumerated in the Constitution. Carried to its extreme, this view gives the president unlimited powers. The ambiguity of the first sentence of Article II has led to three widely divergent theories of presidential power: the constitutional theory, the stewardship theory, and the prerogative theory.

Proponents of the *constitutional theory,* such as William Howard Taft, argue that presidential power is strictly limited. According to the constitutional theory, presidents have only those powers that are either enumerated in the Constitution or granted by Congress under its constitutional powers. As Taft put it in his book *Our Chief Magistrate and His Powers:*

The true view of the Executive function is, as I conceive it, that the President can exercise no power which cannot fairly and reasonably be traced to some specific grant of power or justly implied and included within such grant as proper and necessary to its exercise. Such specific grant must be either in the Federal Constitution or in an act of Congress passed in pursuance thereof. There is no undefined residuum of power that he can exercise because it seems to him to be in the public interest. . . . [Presidential power] must be justified and vindicated by affirmative constitutional or statutory provision, or it does not exist.[34]

In contrast, the *stewardship theory* holds that the president can do anything that is not explicitly *forbidden* by the Constitution or by laws passed by Congress under its constitutional powers. Theodore Roosevelt embraced this view as president and explained it in his *Autobiography:*

My view was that every Executive officer and above all every Executive officer in high position was a steward of the people bound actively and affirmatively to do all he could for the people. . . . I declined to adopt [the] view that what was imperatively necessary for the

Nation could not be done by the President, unless he could find some specific authorization to do it. My belief was that it was not only his right but his duty to do anything that the needs of the Nation demanded unless such action was forbidden by the Constitution or by the laws. Under this interpretation of executive power I did and caused to be done many things not previously done by the President and the heads of the departments. I did not usurp power but I did greatly broaden the use of executive power. In other words, I acted for the common well being of all our people whenever and in whatever measure was necessary, unless prevented by direct constitutional or legislative prohibition.[35]

Taft, who had served as Roosevelt's vice president and later ran against Roosevelt for president, took direct issue with the stewardship theory in his book:

My judgment is that the [stewardship theory], ascribing an undefined residuum of power to the President, is an unsafe doctrine and that it might lead under emergencies to results of an arbitrary character, doing irremediable injustice to private right. The mainspring of such a view is that the Executive is charged with responsibility for the welfare of all the people in a general way, that he is to play the part of a Universal Providence and set all things right, and that anything that in his judgment will help the people he ought to do, unless he is expressly forbidden not to do it. The wide field of action that this would give the Executive one can hardly limit.[36]

The *prerogative theory* is the most expansive of these three theories of presidential power. John Locke defined the concept of prerogative power in his *Second Treatise of Government* as the power "to act according to discretion for the public good, without the prescription of the law, *and sometimes even against it.*"[37] Thus, the prerogative theory not only allows presidents to do anything that they are *not* forbidden to do but allows them to do things that *are* explicitly forbidden when in the national interest. Abraham Lincoln exercised such prerogative power at the outset of the Civil War. During the almost twelve weeks from the outbreak of hostilities at Fort Sumter, South Carolina, on April 12, 1861, to the convening of Congress in a special session on July 4, Lincoln stretched the executive's emergency powers further than ever before. This period has been described as a time of "constitutional dictatorship."[38] Lincoln unilaterally authorized a series of drastic actions: He called up the militia and volunteers, blockaded Southern ports, expanded the army and navy beyond the limits set by statute, pledged the credit of the United States without congressional authority to do so, closed the mails to "treasonous" correspondence, arrested persons suspected of disloyalty, and suspended the writ of habeas corpus in areas around the nation's capital. Admitting that most of these matters lay within the jurisdiction of Congress rather than the president, Lincoln asserted that they were done because of popular demand and public necessity, and with the trust "that Congress would readily ratify them." But he deliberately chose not to call the national legislature into special session until he was ready to do so, and then he presented it with faits accomplis.

Although Lincoln's presidency was most dramatic in those early days of hostilities, he continued to exercise firm control over the war during the entire time he was in the White House. He controlled the mails and newspapers, confiscated property of people suspected of impeding the conduct of the war, and even tried civilians in military courts in areas where the regular courts were operating. To justify such actions, he appealed to military necessity, asserting that the Constitution's commander-in-chief clause (requiring command of the armed forces) and its take-care clause (that the laws be faithfully executed) combined to create a "war power" for the president that was virtually unlimited. Lincoln's success in defending that position is demonstrated by the fact that neither Congress nor the courts placed any significant limits on his actions.

A century later, Richard Nixon pointed to Lincoln's actions in an attempt to justify illegal covert actions that he had taken as president. In fact, Nixon went so far as to claim that if a president chooses to do something illegal because he believes it to be in the national interest, it is—by definition—no longer illegal. As he explained in a televised interview with David Frost in 1977:

When the President does it, that means that it is not illegal. . . . If the President, for example, approves something because of the national security, or in this case because of a threat to internal peace and order of significant magnitude, then the President's decision in that instance is one that enables those who carry it out, to carry it out without violating the law. Otherwise they're in an impossible position.[39]

In short, the ambiguity of the opening sentence of Article II, Section 1, has allowed individual presidents to expand significantly the power of the office. As constitutional scholar Edward S. Corwin wrote in 1957, "Taken by and large, the history of the presidency is a history of aggrandizement."[40] By the 1970s, Arthur Schlesinger Jr. had coined the phrase "the imperial presidency" to describe the current conception of the office.[41]

Presidents have also relied on ambiguities in their specifically enumerated powers, in Sections 2 and 3 of Article II, to further that aggrandizement. Together, the enumerated powers have created at least five presidential roles that have evolved and expanded over time.

Commander in Chief. This role is specifically enumerated in Article II, Section 2 ("The President shall be Commander in Chief of the Army and Navy of the United States, and of the Militia of the several states, when called into the actual Service of the United States"). But did this language merely confer a title on the president or imply wide-ranging powers in times of emergency? Lincoln, of course, believed the latter. From this germ of constitutional power has grown the enormous control that modern presidents exercise over a permanent military establishment and its deployment. The Constitution stipulates that the legislative and executive branches share the war power, but the pressure of events and the presidency's institutional advantages in taking decisive action have led Congress to give greater discretion to the executive. Nor was this delegation of power completely unexpected. Recognizing the need to repel attacks when Congress was not in session, the Constitutional Convention altered language describing the role of Congress in armed hostilities from "make" war to "declare" war (Article

I, Section 8, Paragraph 11), thereby expanding the president's realm of discretionary action.[42] Over time, presidents have invoked the commander-in-chief clause to justify military expenditures without congressional authorization, emergency powers to suppress rebellion, the internment of American citizens of Japanese descent during World War II, and the seizure of domestic steel mills during the undeclared armed conflict in Korea in the 1950s.[43] Moreover, presidents have initiated the use of force far more frequently than they have awaited congressional authorization.

Chief Administrator. This role for the president is more implicit than explicit as set forth in the Constitution. It rests on the executive power clause (Article II, Section 1, Paragraph 1) as well as passages dealing with the right to require opinions from the heads of government departments (Article II, Section 2, Paragraph 1) and the power to make personnel appointments subject to whatever approval Congress may require (Article II, Section 2, Paragraph 2). As the national government has grown, so too has the significance of these powers, but Congress has jealously guarded its own appointment and oversight powers, thereby denying the president anything approximating a monopoly of administrative power.

Chief Diplomat. When combined with the president's expanded war power, constitutional primacy in the conduct of foreign affairs establishes the office's claim to being the government's principal agent in the world if not its "sole organ." Presidents are not only authorized to make treaties "by and with the Advice and Consent of the Senate" but are also empowered to nominate ambassadors, subject to Senate approval (Article II, Section 2, Paragraph 2) and to receive diplomatic emissaries from abroad (Article II, Section 3). Presidents have varied in how closely they have collaborated with the Senate in making treaties, most waiting until after negotiations have been concluded before allowing any Senate participation. More significant, the conduct of foreign affairs has come to rely on executive agreements between heads of state in place of treaties. These agreements are not subject to Senate approval.[44]

Chief Legislator. A nascent constitutional role that stressed negative leadership (the veto) rather than positive leadership, this feature of the job did not fully develop until the twentieth century. Today, the president's power to provide leadership for Congress rests primarily on the ability to shape the legislative agenda. Now considered a task for all presidents to fulfill, it stems from language in Article II, Section 3, that obliges the president to give "the Congress Information of the State of the Union" and to recommend such other measures for its consideration as deemed "necessary and expedient." Presidents now routinely develop extensive legislative agendas and present them to Congress and the nation at the beginning of each year. Moreover, the development of an activist national government has led presidents, their aides, and cabinet secretaries to submit detailed proposals for legislative consideration rather than await congressional reaction to their ideas.

Chief Magistrate. Perhaps the least clearly recognized area of presidential activity, but one that was important to the Founders' conception of executive power, was the general charge that "he shall take Care that the Laws be faithfully executed" (Article II, Section 3). Eighteenth-century conceptions of executive power did not draw sharp distinctions with judicial power: each type of official interpreted and applied the laws in the process of enforcing them. In addition, relations between these two branches of the new government were less distant during the 1790s than is the case today.[45] Now presidents play a complementary role to that of the courts in the enforcement of federal laws; the executive branch helps by apprehending criminals and exercising responsibility for prosecution.

Although these presidential responsibilities are enumerated in the Constitution, what is most striking about them is their ambiguity. As a consequence, their effect on behavior—*what* presidents should do and *how* presidents should behave—is limited. Multiplicity provides presidents with the opportunity to select among a range of activities, and ambiguity gives them maximum flexibility in deciding how to go about the job. The constitutional job description is permissive rather than confining, providing presidents with great freedom in deciding how to invest energy but leaving them open to criticism for failing to fulfill tasks of lesser interest.

Expansion of the Presidency

Students of the presidency commonly divide the office's development into two major periods: traditional and modern. In the traditional era, presidential power was relatively limited, and Congress was the primary policymaker. The modern era, on the other hand, is typified by presidential dominance in the policymaking process and a significant expansion of the president's powers and resources. The presidency of Franklin D. Roosevelt was the turning point into the modern era. Political scientist Fred Greenstein argues that the modern presidency is distinguished by four features: (1) the president is expected to develop a legislative program and to persuade Congress to enact it; (2) presidents regularly engage in direct policymaking through actions not requiring congressional approval; (3) the presidential office has become an extensive bureaucracy designed to enable presidents to undertake points 1 and 2; and (4) presidents have come to symbolize the nation and to personify its government to such an extent that the public holds them primarily responsible for its condition and closely monitors their performance through intensive media coverage.[46]

A number of factors have contributed to this expansion of the American presidency. Several individual presidents, culminating in FDR, helped to precipitate the change. In addition, changes in the presidency have been established by Congress through statute; as a result of presidential actions that later became customary practices; and through institutional development. We will examine each of these in turn.

Expansion by Individual Presidents

Several early presidents—including George Washington, Thomas Jefferson, Andrew Jackson, and Abraham Lincoln—are often credited with providing their successors with an institutional legacy that left the office more powerful than before.[47] Although this is true to a certain extent, it is three twentieth-century presidents who are largely responsible for expanding presidential power and creating the modern presidency: Theodore Roosevelt, Woodrow Wilson, and, of course, FDR.

Theodore Roosevelt. As president, Theodore Roosevelt helped to spur the emergence of the United States as a world power. Concerned over the rise of Japan as a threat to American interests in the Pacific, Roosevelt sought and obtained a major role in negotiating the Portsmouth treaty, which terminated the Russo-Japanese War of 1905. Closer to home he intervened in the affairs of neighbors to the south when he considered it vital to the national interests of the United States, sending troops to the Dominican Republic and Cuba. Even more blatant was Roosevelt's role in fomenting the rebellion of Panama against Colombia so that the United States could acquire rights to build a canal. An avowed nationalist with the desire to expand U.S. influence in international affairs, Roosevelt ordered the navy to sail around the world as a symbolic demonstration of American military might. The image of mighty U.S. naval ships sailing off their shores would serve as a potent reminder to other countries that the United States was now a major world power. When Congress balked at the expense, he countered that there were sufficient funds to get the navy halfway there; if the lawmakers wanted the fleet back home, they would have to provide the money for the return trip.

Roosevelt also responded vigorously to the rapid industrialization of American life. He had charges pressed against corporations that violated antitrust laws, and he pushed legislation through Congress that gave the Interstate Commerce Commission power to reduce railroad rates. When coal mine operators in Colorado refused to agree to arbitration of a dispute with their workers, Roosevelt threatened to have troops seize the mines and administer them as a receiver for the government. He was the first American chief executive to intervene in a labor dispute who did *not* take management's side. Roosevelt also championed major reclamation and conservation projects, as well as meat inspection and pure food and drug laws.

Perhaps most important, Roosevelt did much to popularize the presidency after three decades of lackluster leaders. (Of the eight men who served between Lincoln and Roosevelt, only Grover Cleveland is considered at all significant.) A dynamic personality, an attractive family, and love of the public spotlight enabled Roosevelt "to put the presidency on the front page of every newspaper in America."[48] Considering himself the "steward of the people" and seeing the office as a "bully pulpit" from which the incumbent should set the tone of American life, Roosevelt was the first president to provide meeting rooms for the members of the press and to hold informal news conferences to link the presidency with the people. His style of leadership depended upon extensive use of popular rhetoric, a distinctive reinterpretation of statesmanship that ushered in the era of the "rhetorical presidency."[49] In keeping with his stewardship theory of presidential power, Roosevelt was also the first president to rely on broad discretionary authority in peacetime as well as in crisis.[50]

Woodrow Wilson. Although Theodore Roosevelt laid the groundwork for use of popular appeals during his presidency (1901–1909), it was Wilson (1913–1921) who linked inspirational rhetoric to a broad program of action in an effort to address domestic and foreign affairs in much the same way as a British prime minister. Jeffrey Tulis has argued that this effort rested on a systematic, ambitious reinterpretation of the president's role in the constitutional order.[51] A skilled public speaker, Wilson was the first president since John Adams to go before Congress in person to give his State of the Union message, a practice we now take for granted.[52] Like Jefferson, he was a powerful party chief who worked through congressional leaders and the Democratic caucus to influence legislation. He also did not hesitate to take his case to the people, casting himself as the interpreter as well as the representative of their interests.

During his first term in office, Wilson pushed through a vast program of economic reform that lowered tariffs, raised taxes on the wealthy, created a central banking system, regulated unfair trade practices, provided low-interest loans to farmers, and established an eight-hour day for railroad employees. When the United States became involved in World War I during his second term, Wilson went to Congress and obtained authority to control the economic as well as the military aspects of the war (rather than prosecuting it through unilateral executive action). This grant gave him the power to allocate food and fuel, to license trade with the enemy, to censor the mail, to regulate the foreign language press of the country, and to operate railroads, water transportation systems, and telegraph and telephone facilities. At the end of the war, he made a triumphant trip to Europe, where he assumed the leading role in the writing of the Versailles peace treaty.

Wilson also provided a lesson in how *not* to work with Congress: his adamant refusal to accept any reservations proposed by the Senate for the League of Nations Covenant of the Treaty of Versailles ensured that the United States would not participate. Wilson's archenemy, Sen. Henry Cabot Lodge, R-Mass., calculated that the president's intransigence and personal hatred of him would be so intense that the president would reject all compromises proposed to the treaty. Lodge was right: Wilson, spurning the advice of his wife and of close friends such as Col. Edward House, avowed it "better a thousand times to go down fighting than to dip your colors to dishonorable compromise." A trip to win popular support for the league ended in a physical breakdown (Wilson suffered a stroke) and failure. As a result, the country whose leader proposed the League of Nations ended up not belonging to the organization at all.

Franklin D. Roosevelt. Confronted by enormous domestic and international crises, Franklin Roosevelt began a program of action and innovation unmatched by any chief executive in our history. In most respects, his service is now used as a yardstick against which the performance of his successors is measured.[53] When he came into office in March 1933, business failures were legion, 12 million people were unemployed, banks all over the country were closed or doing business under restrictions, and Americans had lost confidence in their leaders as well as in themselves. Counseling the nation in his inaugural address—the first of four—that "the only thing we have to fear is fear itself," the new chief executive swung into action: a four-day bank holiday was declared, and an emergency banking bill was prepared within a day's time. During Roosevelt's first hundred days in office, the nation witnessed a social and economic revolution in the form of his New Deal. Congress adopted a series of far-reaching government programs insuring bank deposits; providing crop payments for farmers; establishing codes of fair competition for industry; granting labor the right to organize; providing relief and jobs for the unemployed; and creating the Tennessee Valley Authority, a government corporation, to develop that region. With these measures and others such as Social Security, public housing, and unemployment compensation, Roosevelt established the concept of the "positive state" in America—a government that has the obligation to take the lead in providing for the welfare of all the people.

Internationally, Roosevelt extended diplomatic recognition to the Soviet Union, embarked on the Good Neighbor policy toward South America, and pushed through the Reciprocal Trade Program, which lowered tariffs with other nations. In his second term, FDR began the slow and difficult task of preparing the nation for its eventual entry into World War II: He funneled aid to the Allies; traded fifty "over-age" destroyers to Britain for naval and air bases in the British West Indies, Argentia (Newfoundland), and Bermuda; and obtained the passage of the nation's first peacetime draft. After Pearl Harbor, in his own words, "Dr. New Deal" became "Dr. Win-the-War." He took over the economic control of the war effort granted him by Congress and established the victorious strategy of concentrating on defeating Germany before Japan. While hostilities were still going on, he took the lead in setting up the United Nations. Unfortunately, he died before he could see the organization established in 1945.

Roosevelt was an innovator whose actions reshaped the presidential office. He was not only an effective legislative leader but also a skilled administrator responsible for a thorough reorganization of the executive branch, including the creation of the Executive Office of the President *(see chapter 6)*. Even more important, FDR was probably the most effective molder of public opinion the nation has ever known. He pioneered the use of "fireside chats" over radio to explain his actions to the people. In addition, he raised the presidential press conference to new heights as a tool of public persuasion. As a man who could take idealistic goals, reduce them to manageable and practical programs, and then sell them to Congress and the American people, Roosevelt has no peer.

Expansion Through Statute

Congress is another major source of change in the presidency. Legislators have mandated activities that earlier presidents exercised on a discretionary basis or have formally delegated responsibility for activities that traditionally resided with Congress. One of the contemporary presidency's major responsibilities—serving as the nation's economic manager—is suggested nowhere in the Constitution.[54] Congress foisted this power on the president. In 1921, Congress passed the Budget and Accounting Act as part of an effort to increase the fiscal responsibility and efficiency of government. The act created the Bureau of the Budget as a part of the Treasury Department and required the president to use the expert advice of the bureau to propose annual fiscal policy to the government. Quite simply, the legislation compelled the president to take an active role in domestic policy formulation. As James Sundquist has written:

Before 1921, a president did not have to have a program for the whole of the government, and none did; after that date he was compelled by the Budget and Accounting Act to present a program for every department and every bureau, and to do it annually. Before 1921, a president did not have to propose a fiscal policy for the government, and many did not; after 1921, every chief executive had to have a fiscal policy, every year. That made the president a leader, a policy and program initiator, and a manager, whether he wished to be or not.[55]

There were, of course, strong presidents who exerted policy leadership before 1921, but nothing had compelled presidents to act. Likewise, it is wrong to assume that the Budget and Accounting Act automatically produced strong presidents. The first three presidents affected by the act—Warren Harding, Calvin Coolidge, and Herbert Hoover—dutifully submitted proposals to Congress but seldom exerted strong leadership to secure enactment.[56] That changed during the presidency of Franklin Roosevelt, who used the crisis of the Great Depression as a rallying cry for policy enactment.

Over time, Congress further expanded presidential power. It created the Executive Office of the President in 1939 as a source of expert advice to help presidents in the formulation of policy. And Congress added to the president's economic responsibilities by passing the Employment Act of 1946. As Sundquist explains, the act "compels the president to maintain a continuous surveillance of the nation's economy, to report on the state of its health at least annually, and if there are signs of pathology—inflation, recession, stagnation—to recommend corrective action."[57] Despite giving the president new tasks to fulfill, Congress did not surrender its traditional right to alter presidential proposals, thereby ensuring that tax rates and spending proposals would remain a mainstay of partisan politics as well as legislative-executive relations. (The politics of economic policymaking are examined in detail in chapter 9.)

Congress has taken comparable action in other areas as well. In 1947, Congress charged the president with the task of coordinating national security policy—foreign policy, intelligence collection and evaluation, and defense policy—through the creation of the National Security Council (NSC). Harry Truman resisted the newly created NSC as an intrusion on his powers and was slow to use it. In fact, no president can be *required* to use such a structure, but the more conflictive setting of the cold war saw one president after another establish administrative machinery designed to achieve the same goal of coordination of American foreign policy *(see chapter 10)*. Thus, we find that Congress may encourage presidents to provide leadership in areas that are wholly absent from the original constitutional design or encourage executives to devise new ways to exercise their traditional responsibilities.

Expansion Through Custom and Practice

Across a wide range of presidential activities, "action based on usage may acquire legitimacy."[58] Nowhere in the Constitution did it say that presidents would serve as leaders of their party, but that task has been associated with the office since Thomas Jefferson first established his dominance of the Democratic-Republicans' congressional caucus. Enormous variation may be found in how presidents have pursued such activities and in how successful they have been. Some, like Jefferson, have had a close relationship with their party, while other executives have been virtually abandoned by their partisan allies (Rutherford B. Hayes). At other times, presidents have sought, and seemed to derive, greater influence by appearing to serve "above" party (Eisenhower). If the political parties continue to weaken or have difficulty reasserting themselves as structures vital to democracy, this informal part of the president's job description could disappear.

A second example of precedent and custom can be found in Theodore Roosevelt's attempt to mediate a labor-management dispute. Earlier presidents had intervened on the side of company owners, but Roosevelt put his prestige on the line when he sought to resolve the anthracite coal strike of 1902, a struggle that had paralyzed a vital industry. Other presidents followed suit: Wilson intervened in eight major disputes, Harding in two, FDR in eleven, and Truman in three.[59] The response of one president to emergency conditions had become an accepted precedent for his successors, if they wished to pursue it.

Institutional Sources of Change

Finally, it needs to be recognized that the modern presidency is no longer a one-person job—a reality that may have significant consequences for the office's evolution. Although designed to be unitary rather than plural, the modern presidency has become a working collectivity in order to dispatch the many responsibilities placed at the president's door. This shift toward what has been called the "institutional presidency"—a twentieth-century phenomenon—is partly a result of changing customs and practice, but it is also something that was furthered by statute. During Franklin Roosevelt's first term, the average number of full-time White House staffers was 47. By Richard Nixon's second term some thirty-five years later, that number had grown to well over 500.

Congress spurred along this increase in staff by creating the Executive Office of the President (EOP) in 1939 and then passing subsequent legislation to create additional staff units within that structure (such as the Council of Economic Advisers and the National Security Council). At the same time, presidents unilaterally created their own specialized staff units within the White House itself. These include the Congressional Liaison Office (to help secure congressional passage of presidential initiatives), the Office of Communications (to help communicate the president's agenda to the American people and to coordinate the flow of information from the many departments and agencies within the Executive Branch), and the Office of Public Liaison (to maintain support from interest groups). By some counts, the president's full-time executive staff under Nixon (including presidential advisers in the Executive Office of the President) grew to more than 5,000. Under FDR's first term, comparable executive staff (including groundskeepers and the White House police force) numbered only 103.[60]

Presidential Culture

Understanding the presidency's institutional development provides an important perspective on roles played by the office, but one also needs to address a less concrete question: What does the presidency *mean* to Americans? The final section of this chapter focuses on the development of the office's emotional and psychological significance.

Despite the Framers' ambivalence toward executive power, the office of president quickly acquired mythic dimensions when it was filled by the country's first true hero. George Washington, argues Seymour Martin Lipset, supplied the virtues of a charismatic leader who serves as "symbol of the new nation, its hero who embodies in his person its values and aspirations. But more than merely symbolizing the new nation, he legitimizes the state, the new secular government, by endowing it with his 'gift of grace,'" the near magical qualities such leaders supposedly possess.[61] A cult of personality grew up around Washington so that well into the nineteenth century citizens displayed his likeness in their homes, named their children after him, and paid him endless tributes.

In the process of contributing stability and identity to the new nation, Washington also endowed the presidential office with a special meaning that has become part of our collective heritage. Bruce Buchanan refers to this as *presidential culture*, "widely held meanings of the presidency, derived from selected episodes in the history of the institution and transmitted from one generation to the next by political socialization."[62] Buchanan explains that families, teachers, and the media sustain this view of the presidency as an office with the ability to deliver the nation from danger as a result of its occupants' greatness. Somehow, it is widely believed, the institution "has the potential to make extraordinary events happen" and the incumbent "should be able to realize that potential."[63] Occupants of the position, then, are expected to live up to these levels of performance and are roundly criticized when they fall short.

Why have such unrealistic expectations taken hold? One reason is that we have glorified the memories of past presidents. The "great" presidents, particularly those who took decisive action and bold initiatives, and even some of the "not so great" are treated as folk heroes and enshrined in a national mythology—figures whose births we celebrate, whose virtues we are urged to emulate, whose achievements we memorialize, and whose sex lives continue to interest us long after their deaths. Schoolchildren throughout America are regaled with stories of Washington and Lincoln every February while looking at bulletin boards featuring their silhouettes. Every summer, thousands of vacationers make the pilgrimage to visit shrines located along the Potomac in Washington, D.C., or scattered throughout the nation in presidential libraries and museums. But historical and popular glorification does not constitute the full story. The presidency has always been important in American civic life, but it may have assumed even greater proportions in the modern era, assisted by new technologies and resting on new conceptions of the office.

A number of political scientists have pointed to the importance of the presidency in meeting the emotional and psychological needs of the populace. In particular, it is argued that citizens have expressive needs for confidence, security, reassurance, and pride in citizenship.[64] In the view of Murray Edelman, citizens suffer from a "general sense of anxiety about the comprehensive function played in human affairs by chance, ignorance, and inability to comprehend, plan, and take responsibility for remote and complicated contingencies." The natural response is to seek emotional comfort through attachment to reassuring symbols, "and what symbol can be more reassuring than the incumbent of a high position who knows what to do and is willing to act, especially when others are bewildered and alone?"[65] We know that American children develop a highly idealized image of presidents that emphasizes both their power and their benevolence, a source of reassurance that may be transferred from childhood to adulthood.

Fred Greenstein suggests additional psychological needs that are met through the presidency. Citizens seeking to sort through the complexity of political life turn to presidents for cognitive assistance. Presidents personify the government and make it possible to become engaged by what would otherwise be an impersonal abstraction. By following the president's activities, citizens may also experience a sort of vicarious participation in public affairs, giving them a sense of power and control that ordinarily would be unavailable. As a symbol of stability, predictability, and national unity, the president soothes fears and enables us to proceed with our daily lives.[66]

Symbols, in fact, are central to the character of the presidential office, which has become particularly "potent as a symbol of the public welfare, built-in benevolence, and competence to lead."[67] Barbara Hinckley points out that "symbols evoke ideas the society wants to believe are true. . . . [They] can substitute for something that does not exist otherwise."[68] In fact, Hinckley argues that because the Constitution failed to clarify the presidency's nature and responsibilities, symbols have become enormously significant: "The office is undefined; thus presidents become what people want them to be."[69] And the people want them to be many things. The list of desirable personal attributes is impressive, as Ray Price, an aide to Richard Nixon during the 1968 presidential campaign, pointed out in a memo to the staff:

People identify with a President in a way they do with no other public figure. Potential presidents are measured against an ideal that's a combination of leading man, God, father, hero, pope, king, with maybe just a touch of the avenging Furies thrown in. They want him to be larger than life, a living legend, and yet quintessentially human; someone to be held up to their children as a model; someone to be cherished by themselves as a revered member of the family, in somewhat the same way in which peasant families pray to the icon in the corner. Reverence goes where power is.[70]

The problem for candidates (and incumbents) is how to project an image that matches these public expectations. Theodore Lowi has argued that "the expectations of the masses have grown faster than the capacity of presidential government to meet them."[71] According to Lowi, modern presidents resort to illusions to cover failures and seek quick fixes for their flagging public support in foreign adventures. As we shall see in chapter 3, advances in the means of communication have increased the ability of presidents to do this. Such behavior—portrayed by Lowi as rooted in the presidential institution, not in individual presidents' personalities—is ultimately self-defeating because it does nothing more than further inflate expectations and ensure public disappointment. This may help to explain the string of failed presidencies described at the outset of this chapter.

Conclusion: The Changeable, Political Presidency

There can be little doubt that today's presidency is a far cry from the office designed by the Constitutional Convention. Responsibilities have grown enormously as have means to fulfill them. So have the mythic dimensions of the office. Unlike the office that was launched in 1789, today's presidency is firmly rooted in the national consciousness as the consequence of childhood socialization and a secular mythology whose idealized images are magnified with the passage of time. There is no way to determine whether today's office means more to Americans than it did two centuries ago in terms of the emotional and psychological needs it meets, but certainly it occupies a more central—some would argue excessive—place in the public consciousness.

The contemporary presidency is not a static construct, however. As this overview of institutional development demonstrates, Americans' perceptions of the office and what they want from it can and will change over time. This has been true even over the past thirty years. All too often, observers of the presidency treat temporary conditions as if they were permanent—mistaking a snapshot for a portrait.

To summarize, the presidency is variable for several reasons. First, in no other public office do the personality, character, and political style of the incumbent make as much difference as in the presidency. As an institution, the presidency exhibits important continuities across administrations, but the entry of each new occupant has an undeniably pervasive effect on the position's operation. The presidency is also heavily influenced by changes outside the office and throughout the U.S. political system—whether in the formal political structure (Congress, the executive branch, the courts), in the informal political institutions (political parties and interest groups), in society at large, in the mass media, or in conditions surrounding substantive issues, particularly national security and the economy. Because of their extensive responsibilities, presidents must contend with all of these influences. Furthermore, although the Constitution and historical precedents give structure to the office, the powers of the presidency are so vague that incumbents have tremendous latitude to shape the office to their particular desires.

The presidency is not only highly *changeable* but also essentially *political*. Although on occasion, especially in times of crisis, presidents rule by asserting their constitutional prerogatives, they usually are forced to govern by political maneuvering—by trying to convince and persuade the many participants in the political process. This is a very complex task. Not only must they perform on the public stage of mass politics, but they must also master the intricacies of elite politics, a game played among skilled insiders. In the following chapters, we first examine "public politics" (chapters 2, 3, and 4) and then turn to the skills that presidents bring to relations with other public elites (chapters 5, 6, and 7). These separate dimensions are linked in discussions of major policy areas (chapters 8, 9, and 10).

NOTES

1. In fact, Gore won the popular vote by a margin of some 539,947 votes. This is almost five times the size of John Kennedy's 1960 popular vote margin of 114,673 votes over Richard Nixon and almost 30,000 votes more than Nixon's 1968 margin of 510,645 votes over Hubert Humphrey. In addition to Bush and Harrison, John Quincy Adams in 1824 and Rutherford B. Hayes in 1876 won the presidency without winning the most popular votes.

2. *Bush v. Gore*, 121 S.Ct. 525 (2000).

3. Richard Neustadt, *Presidential Power: The Politics of Leadership* (New York: Wiley, 1960), 26.

4. Stephen Skowronek, *The Politics Presidents Make: Leadership from John Adams to George Bush* (Cambridge: Harvard University Press, 1993), 20.

5. Quoted in Forrest McDonald, *The American Presidency: An Intellectual History* (Lawrence: University Press of Kansas, 1994), 127.

6. McDonald, *The American Presidency,* 126.

7. Richard J. Ellis, ed., *Founding the American Presidency* (Lanham, Md.: Rowman and Littlefield, 1999), 1.

8. McDonald, *The American Presidency,* 132–133.

9. Richard M. Pious, *The American Presidency* (New York: Basic Books, 1979), 23.

10. Sidney M. Milkis and Michael Nelson, *The American Presidency: Origins and Development, 1776–1993,* 2d ed. (Washington, D.C.: CQ Press, 1994), 5. One of the drafters of the New York state constitution, Gouverneur Morris, later played an important role in the creation of presidential power at the 1787 Constitutional Convention.

11. Thomas Jefferson, *Notes on the State of Virginia,* quoted in Ellis, *Founding the American Presidency,* 4.

12. Charles C. Thach Jr., *The Creation of the Presidency, 1775–1789: A Study in Constitutional History* (Baltimore: Johns Hopkins University Press, 1923), chap. 3.

13. Pious, *The American Presidency,* 22.

14. McDonald, *The American Presidency,* 151.

15. Quoted in Ellis, *Founding the American Presidency,* 6.

16. Milkis and Nelson, *The American Presidency,* 2d ed., 13–14.

17. McDonald, *The American Presidency,* 163.

18. Ibid.,164.

19. Ellis, *Founding the American Presidency,* 31–32.

20. McDonald, *The American Presidency,* 164; see also Max Farrand, ed., *The Records of the Federal Convention* (New Haven: Yale University Press, 1913), 1:65.

21. Farrand, *Records,* 1:65.

22. Ibid., 1:244.

23. Ellis, *Founding the American Presidency,* 13.

24. This paragraph is based on McDonald, *The American Presidency,* 157.

25. Ibid., 171.

26. Ellis, *Founding the American Presidency,* 112–113.

27. We use the term *Congress* loosely here. As we have pointed out, the original recommendation of the Committee on Postponed Matters called for the *Senate* alone to choose from among the top five presidential candidates. As finally ratified, the Constitution called for the *House* alone to choose from the top five candidates. After the ratification of the Twelfth Amendment in 1804, the Constitution called for the House to choose from among the top *three* presidential candidates.

28. This account of the Committee on Postponed Matters is drawn largely from McDonald, *The American Presidency,* 176–178; see also Milkis and Nelson, *The American Presidency,* 2d ed., 21–22.

29. Edward S. Corwin, *The President: Office and Powers,* 4th ed. (New York: New York University Press, 1957), 12.

30. Quoted in Michael Nelson, ed., *Guide to the Presidency,* 2d ed. (Washington, D.C.: CQ Press, 1996), 30. Although this sort of hostility toward a strong executive was common among antifederalists, Herbert J. Storing has pointed out that there are greater differences of opinion among them than one might expect. Although some antifederalists continued to argue for a plural executive or an executive council, many agreed that a unitary executive was necessary. Storing points out that among antifederalists there was even "a fair amount of sympathy for a strong (even, under some circumstances, a hereditary) executive to resist the aristocratic tendencies of the legislature; and some of the Anti-Federalists objected that the President would be too weak to stand up to the Senate and would become a mere tool of aristocratic domination." Herbert J. Storing, ed., *The Complete Anti-Federalist,* Vol. 1 (Chicago: University of Chicago Press, 1981), 49.

31. Alexander Hamilton, *Federalist* No. 70.

32. Thach, *The Creation of the Presidency,* 138.

33. Ibid., 139.

34. William Howard Taft, *Our Chief Magistrate and His Powers* (New York: Columbia University Press, 1916), 139–140.

35. Theodore Roosevelt, *Autobiography* (New York: Macmillan, 1913), 388–389.

36. Taft, *Our Chief Magistrate,* 144–145.

37. Quoted in Corwin, *The President,* 4th ed., 8 (emphasis added).

38. Clinton Rossiter, *Constitutional Dictatorship* (Princeton: Princeton University Press, 1948).

39. Interview with Richard Nixon by David Frost, televised May 19, 1977; quoted in Craig Ducat, *Constitutional Interpretation,* 7th ed. (Belmont, Calif.: West, 2000), 206.

40. Corwin, *The President,* 4th ed., 30.

41. Arthur M. Schlesinger Jr., *The Imperial Presidency,* 2d ed. (Boston: Houghton Mifflin, 1989).

42. McDonald, *The American Presidency,* 173–174.

43. Louis Fisher, *Constitutional Conflicts between Congress and the President,* 3d ed. (Lawrence: University Press of Kansas, 1991), chap. 9.

44. Ibid., chap. 8.

45. Robert Scigliano, "The Presidency and the Judiciary," in *The Presidency and the Political System,* 3d ed., ed. Michael Nelson (Washington, D.C.: CQ Press, 1990), 473–476.

46. Fred Greenstein, "Change and Continuity in the Modern Presidency," in *the New American Political System,* ed. Anthony King (Washington, D.C.: American Enterprise Institute, 1978), 45–46.

47. See, for example, Corwin, *The President,* 4th ed., chap. 1.

48. Clinton Rossiter, *The American Presidency,* rev. ed. (New York: Harcourt, Brace, 1960), 102.

49. Jeffrey K. Tulis, *The Rhetorical Presidency* (Princeton: Princeton University Press, 1987), chap. 4.

50. Milkis and Nelson, *The American Presidency,* 2d ed., 208.

51. Tulis, *The Rhetorical Presidency,* chap. 5. Also see Jeffrey K. Tulis, "The Two Constitutional Presidencies," in *The Presidency and the Political System,* 6th ed., ed. Michael Nelson (Washington, D.C.: CQ Press, 2000).

52. Thomas Jefferson had discontinued the practice as an undesirable indication of monarchist tendencies.

53. William E. Leuchtenberg, *In the Shadow of FDR: From Harry Truman to Ronald Reagan,* rev. ed. (Ithaca: Cornell University Press, 1985).

54. James L. Sundquist uses the term *economic stabilizer,* and earlier Clinton Rossiter had used the term *Manager of Prosperity.* See Sundquist, *The Decline and Resurgence of Congress* (Washington, D.C.: Brookings, 1981), chap. 4.

55. Sundquist, *The Decline and Resurgence of Congress,* 39.

56. Ibid., 33.

57. Ibid., 66–67.

58. Fisher, *Constitutional Conflicts,* 24.

59. Corwin, *The President,* 4th ed., 175–177.

60. Gary King and Lyn Ragsdale, eds., *The Elusive Executive: Discovering Statistical Patterns in the Presidency* (Washington, D.C.: CQ Press, 1988), Table 4-1, 205. The precise size of presidential staff, though, is hard to calculate. For a discussion of this and an overview of the debates over how to count presidential staff, see John Hart, *The Presidential Branch: From Washington to Clinton,* 2d ed. (Chatham, N.J.: Chatham House, 1995), 43–45, 112–125.

THE CHANGING PRESIDENCY **29**

61. Seymour Martin Lipset, *The First New Nation: The United States in Historical and Comparative Perspective* (New York: Norton, 1979), 18.

62. Bruce Buchanan, *The Citizen's Presidency: Standards of Choice and Judgment* (Washington, D.C.: CQ Press, 1987), 25.

63. Ibid., 28.

64. See especially Murray Edelman, *The Symbolic Uses of Politics* (Urbana: University of Illinois Press, 1964); and Fred I. Greenstein, "What the President Means to Americans: Presidential 'Choice' between Elections," in *Choosing the President*, ed. James David Barber (Englewood Cliffs, N.J.: Prentice-Hall, 1974).

65. Edelman, *The Symbolic Uses of Politics*, 76–77.

66. Greenstein, "What the President Means to Americans," 142–147. It should be noted that in this essay Greenstein de-emphasized the likelihood that children socialized to a positive feeling about the president as an authority figure would extend this reliance on an "unconscious symbolic surrogate of childhood authority figures" into adulthood.

67. Murray Edelman, "The Politics of Persuasion," in *Choosing the President*, 172.

68. Barbara Hinckley, *The Symbolic Presidency: How Presidents Portray Themselves* (New York: Routledge, 1990), 5.

69. Ibid., 8.

70. As cited in Michael Novak, *Choosing Our King: Powerful Symbols in Presidential Politics* (New York: Macmillan, 1974), 44.

71. Theodore J. Lowi, *The Personal President: Power Invested, Promise Unfulfilled* (Ithaca: Cornell University Press, 1985), xii.

SUGGESTED READINGS

Corwin, Edward S. *The President: Office and Powers, 1789–1984*, 5th ed. New York: New York University Press, 1984.

Ellis, Richard J., ed. *Founding the American Presidency*. Lanham, Md.: Rowman and Littlefield, 1999.

Farrand, Max, ed. *The Records of the Federal Convention of 1787*. New Haven: Yale University Press, 1911.

Heclo, Hugh, and Lester M. Salamon, eds. *The Illusion of Presidential Government*. Boulder, Colo.: Westview Press, 1981.

Lowi, Theodore J. *The Personal President: Power Invested, Promise Unfulfilled*. Ithaca: Cornell University Press, 1985.

McDonald, Forrest. *The American Presidency: An Intellectual History*. Lawrence: University Press of Kansas, 1994.

Milkis, Sidney M., and Michael Nelson. *The American Presidency: Origins and Development, 1776–1998*, 3d ed. Washington, D.C.: CQ Press, 1999.

Nelson, Michael, ed. *The Presidency and the Political System*, 6th ed. Washington, D.C.: CQ Press, 2000.

Neustadt, Richard E. *Presidential Power and the Modern Presidents: The Politics of Leadership from Roosevelt to Reagan*. New York: Free Press, 1990.

Skowronek, Stephen. *The Politics Presidents Make: Leadership from John Adams to George Bush*. Cambridge: Harvard University Press, 1993.

2   ELECTION POLITICS

THE FOCAL POINT OF AMERICAN POLITICAL life is the presidential election. More citizens participate in this process than in any other aspect of civic life, and their choice has enormous significance for the nation and, indeed, for the world. Historians use presidential terms to break history into four-year blocks of time, and policymaking at the federal level follows the same rhythm. The election also serves as a unifying event, a collective celebration of democracy coming at the conclusion of an elaborate pageant replete with familiar rituals, colorful characters, and plot lines that capture attention despite their repetition every four years.

Today's selection process bears little resemblance to what the Founders outlined in the original Constitution. Most of the changes have been extraconstitutional; that is, they have resulted from the evolution of political parties, coverage by the media, and citizen expectations rather than constitutional amendments. There has been almost constant tinkering with

Modern presidential election campaigns center on sophisticated media advertising, but campaign rallies remain a traditional way to generate community attention and enthusiasm replete with balloons, ticker-tape, and excited supporters like those surrounding Richard Nixon when he successfully campaigned for re-election in 1972.

the rules governing presidential elections, with the movement c toward greater democratization. Even before the 2000 election, most tion with the process centered on the remnants of indirect democrac, ... per- sist, particularly the national party conventions and the electoral college. The most recent election gave new life to the debate about rules as the nation waited thirty-six days for the final results in Florida. Bush was declared the winner by a margin of 537 votes out of nearly six million ballots. During the prolonged period of uncertainty that followed election day, Americans relearned the arcane workings of the electoral college and discovered the fallibility of voting methods and tally rules.

At the conclusion of this chapter, we review recommendations for reform intended to improve system performance and provide for a greater degree of direct democracy. To appreciate the current selection process and suggestions for reform, it is necessary to gain an understanding of the major transformations in both the nomination and the general election phases of the process.

Evolution of the Selection Process

In 1789 and 1792, electing a president was simple. Each member of the elec- toral college cast two votes, one of which had to be for a person outside of his state. Both times George Washington was elected by unanimous votes.[1] And both times John Adams received the second highest number of votes to become the vice president. In 1789, the process took only three months to complete: there was no campaign, electors were chosen on the first Wednesday of January, they met in their respective states to vote on the first Wednesday in February, and the votes were counted on April 6. In 1792, the procedure took even less time. The contrast with today's process could not be sharper: candidates now launch nomination campaigns up to two years before the general election, spending millions of dollars in pursuit of the office, and party nominees expect a winner to be declared on election night.

Consensus support for Washington ensured smooth operation of the selection procedure during the first two elections: there was widespread confidence that the nation's wartime hero would govern in the interest of all the people. The ero- sion of consensus triggered the development of a separate nomination proce- dure. Policy differences in Congress created the basis for an important institution not mentioned in the Constitution—the political party. By the early 1790s, the Federalist Party had formed around the economic policies of Secretary of the Treasury Alexander Hamilton, and his supporters in Congress backed his pro- grams.[2] Resigning as secretary of state in 1793, Thomas Jefferson joined James Madison, then serving in the House of Representatives, as a critic of Hamilton's policies, and they formed the rival Republican Party.[3] By the mid-1790s, cohe- sive pro- and antiadministration blocs had formed in Congress, and congres- sional candidates were labeled either Democratic-Republicans or Federalists.[4]

Washington's retirement at the end of his second term opened the presidential election to party politics.

Political parties had an almost immediate impact on the electoral college. Electors became party loyalists, whose discipline was apparent in 1800, when Jefferson, the Democratic-Republicans' candidate for president, and Aaron Burr, the party's candidate for vice president, tied in the electoral college vote. Loyal to their party, the electors had cast their ballots for both candidates, but the Constitution had no provision for counting the ballots separately for president and vice president. Jefferson and Burr each received seventy-three votes to President Adams's sixty-five. The election was decided in the House of Representatives, where Jefferson won after thirty-six ballots. Hamilton broke the tie by throwing his support behind Jefferson, his longtime rival. Party loyalty, with infrequent exceptions, has prevailed in electoral college balloting ever since. (The Twelfth Amendment to the Constitution, ratified in 1804, provided for separate presidential and vice presidential balloting in the electoral college to prevent a similar deadlock.[5])

The rise of parties also fundamentally altered presidential selection by creating a separate nomination stage: the parties had to devise a method for choosing their nominees. Influence over presidential selection shifted from the local notables who had served as electors to party elites, whose character would evolve continually over time. In 1796, the Federalists' leaders chose their candidate, John Adams, and the Democratic-Republicans relied on their party members in Congress, the *congressional caucus*, to nominate Jefferson as their standard-bearer. Four years later, the Federalists adopted their opponents' idea, and the congressional caucus became the nominating mechanism for both parties, a practice that continued until 1824, when the system broke down.

The congressional caucus allowed members of Congress, already assembled in the nation's capital and facing minimal transportation problems, to select a nominee. Because legislators were familiar with potential presidential candidates from all parts of the new country, they were the logical agents for choosing candidates for an office with a nationwide constituency. Caucuses provided a peer review of candidates' credentials, with one group of politicians assessing a fellow politician's skills, abilities, and political appeal. But the congressional caucus had serious flaws. It violated the constitutional principle of separation of powers by giving members of the legislative body a routine role in choosing the president rather than an emergency role, assumed only in the event of an electoral college deadlock. The caucus also could not represent areas in which the party had lost the previous congressional election, a problem quickly encountered by the Federalists. Moreover, interested and informed citizens who participated in grassroots party activities, especially campaigns, had no means to participate in congressional caucus deliberations.

The 1824 election brought an end to nomination by congressional caucus. First, the Democratic-Republicans in Congress insisted on nominating Secretary

Although media coverage of party nominating conventions has been severely reduced, party luminaries still attract attention like former Senate Majority Leader Trent Lott shown at the 2000 Republican National Convention in Philadelphia with Nic Lott (no relation), the first African American student body president at the University of Mississippi.

of the Treasury William Crawford, who had suffered a debilitating stroke. Then, in the general election, Andrew Jackson, proposed by the Tennessee legislature, won more popular votes and more electoral votes than any other candidate but failed to achieve a majority in the electoral college. The election had to be decided by the House, where John Quincy Adams emerged victorious after he agreed to make Henry Clay, another of the five contestants, secretary of state in return for his support. These shenanigans permanently discredited King Caucus, as its critics called it. Favorite sons nominated by state legislatures and state conventions dominated the 1828 campaign, but this method proved too decentralized to select a national official. A device was needed that would represent party elements throughout the country and at the same time facilitate the nomination of a candidate.

National Party Conventions

What developed was the *party nominating convention,* an assembly made truly national by including delegates from all the states. Rail transportation made such meetings feasible, and the expanding citizen participation in presidential elections made the change necessary. Influence over selection of the party nominee therefore shifted to state and local party leaders, particularly those able to commit large blocs of delegate votes to a candidate.

Two minor parties with no appreciable representation in Congress, the Anti-Masons and the National Republicans, led the way with conventions in 1831.[6] To rally support in 1832, the Democrats, under President Andrew Jackson (elected in 1828), also held a convention. Major political parties have nominated their presidential and vice presidential candidates by holding national conventions ever since. National committees composed of state party leaders call the presidential nominating conventions into session to choose nominees and to adopt a platform of common policy positions.[7] Delegates are selected by states and allocated primarily on the basis of population.

Although today's conventions in some ways resemble those of 170 years ago, the nomination process has undergone drastic revision, especially since 1968, when Democrats introduced reforms that diminished the importance of conventions. Just as influence over selection of the party nominee shifted from Congress to party leaders, it has moved within the party from a small group of organization professionals to a broad base of activists and voters. The origins of this shift can be traced to the development of presidential primary elections early in the twentieth century (Florida passed the first primary election law in 1901).

Under the system that operated from roughly 1850 to 1950, party leaders from the largest states could bargain over presidential nominations. Most influential were those who controlled large blocs of delegates and would throw their support behind a candidate for the right price. These power brokers—hence the term *brokered conventions*—might seek a program commitment in the platform, a place in the president's cabinet, or other forms of federal patronage in return for support. To be successful, candidates had to curry favor with party and elected officials before and during the national convention. An effective campaign manager might tour the country selling the candidate's virtues and securing delegate commitments prior to the convention, but about half the conventions began with no sense of the likely outcome. Protracted bargaining and negotiation among powerful state and local party leaders were often the result. In 1924, for instance, the Democrats needed 103 ballots cast over seventeen days to nominate John W. Davis, an effort that must have seemed pointless later when he attracted only 29 percent of the popular vote. Nevertheless, the convention was a deliberative body that reached decisions on common policy positions as well as on nominees. Providing a way to accommodate the demands of major elements within the party established the base for a nationwide campaign.

In this respect, modern conventions are quite different. Not since 1952, when the Democrats needed three ballots to nominate Gov. Adlai Stevenson of Illinois for president, has it taken more than one ballot to determine either party's nominee.[8] Raucous floor battles over procedures and delegate credentials have given way to a stream of symbols and speakers whose appearances are carefully choreographed to appeal to a prime-time television audience. Today, modern conventions serve as ratifying assemblies for a popular choice rather than deliberative bodies, and candidates with popular appeal have the advantage over those whose appeal is primarily with party leaders.

Although much of the convention's business is still conducted in backroom meetings, the most important business—determining who the presidential nominee will be—already has been decided through the grueling process used to select convention delegates. Compared with their forerunners, modern conventions conduct their business in a routine fashion, adhere to a set of enforceable national party standards for delegate selection and demographic representation, and are more heavily influenced by rank-and-file party supporters than by the party organization's leaders.[9] These changes, however, appeared gradually through a process often fraught with conflict that centered on the rules governing delegate selection.

Recent Reform of the Selection Process

The pace of change accelerated when the Democratic Party adopted a set of internal reforms following its loss of the presidency in 1968. In addition to the actions already noted, rules adopted by a variety of actors—100 state political parties and fifty legislatures, the national political parties, and Congress—reformed the process. Sometimes individuals even turned to the courts to interpret provisions of these regulations and reconcile conflicts among them. In addition, the rules were adjusted so drastically and so often that, particularly in the Democratic Party, candidates and their supporters found it difficult to keep up with them.

Reform has been especially pervasive in the nomination process. Following their tumultuous convention in 1968, when Vietnam War protesters clashed with police in the streets of Chicago, the Democrats adopted a set of guidelines that reduced the influence of party leaders, encouraged participation by rank-and-file Democrats, and expanded convention representation of previously underrepresented groups, particularly women and African Americans. The result was a pronounced shift of influence within the party from *party professionals* toward *amateurs*, a term encompassing citizens who become engaged in the presidential contest because of a short-term concern such as an attractive candidate (candidate enthusiasts) or an especially important issue (issue enthusiasts).

States, seeking to conform to the party's new guidelines on participation, adopted the primary as the preferred means to select delegates to the national convention. Primaries allow a party's registered voters—and in some states independents—to express a presidential preference that is translated into convention delegates. In most states, voters cast ballots for specific presidential candidates, but in some places only delegate names appear on the ballot. In sharp contrast is the party caucus, an alternate means of selecting delegates. The caucus is a local meeting of registered party voters that often involves speeches and discussion about the candidates' relative merits. A caucus is more social, public, and time-consuming (often requiring two hours to complete) than a primary, where voters make choices in the traditional voting booth. Ultimately, the caucus also produces delegates to the national convention, but it usually requires multiple stages. For example, delegates from the local caucuses go to a county convention that selects delegates to a state convention that in turn selects the national delegates. In 1968, only seventeen states chose delegates through primaries, the remainder using caucuses that were dominated by party leaders; in 2000, forty-one states and the District of Columbia held primaries, and even the remaining caucuses provided for far greater participation than in the past.[10] Because of these changes, nominations are more apt to reflect the voters' immediate concerns, winners are known well before the convention is held, and the influence of party leaders has declined.

But abandoning the convention's traditional deliberative role, some argue, has come at a heavy cost. By transferring power to amateurs and by sacrificing the peer review exercised by professionals, many Democrats, in particular, fear they have been weakened organizationally and chosen less capable nominees, such as those who lost throughout most of the 1970s and 1980s. Moreover, the changes have enhanced the importance of the media. By operating as the principal source of information about the candidates and by emphasizing the "horse race"—who is ahead—the media have become enormously influential during the delegate selection process. So not everyone has been satisfied with the general movement toward a more democratized selection process, as evidenced by several counterreforms that appeared during the 1980s.

The Contemporary Selection Process

Now that the historical context has been set and some of the current concerns about the nomination process have been previewed, the discussion focuses on how the contemporary selection process operates. Despite the seemingly perpetual flux that characterizes presidential elections, it is possible to identify four stages in the process: (1) the pool of eligible candidates is defined; (2) following the primaries and caucuses, the parties nominate their candidates at the national conventions; (3) the general election campaign is waged, culminating in election day; and (4) the electoral college validates the results.

No two presidential election cycles are identical, but the customary time line is relatively predictable (see Figure 2-1). Potential candidates maneuver for position during the one or two years preceding the election. Selection of convention delegates begins in January and February of the election year, with conventions typically scheduled first for the out party (the one seeking the White House), then for the party that currently controls the presidency: in 2000, July 31 through August 3 in Philadelphia for the Republicans, and August 14 through August 17 in Los Angeles for the Democrats. Traditionally, the general election campaign begins on Labor Day and runs until election day, the first Tuesday following the first Monday in November, but modern campaigns really begin once the identity of major party nominees becomes clear, usually in March and April. Unlike the situation in 2000, voters usually know the winner on election night and the mid-December balloting by electors in their state capitals is automatic. Finally, the electors' ballots are officially tabulated during the first week in Jan-

Figure 2-1   The 2000 Presidential Contest Time Line

1999

Stage 1 Defining the pool of eligible candidates		
2000	**Jan.**	Federal matching funds provided to qualified candidates (1/2/00) Iowa, first caucus (1/24/00)
Stage 2 Nomination	**Feb.** **Mar.**	New Hampshire, first primary (2/1/00) Titanic Tuesday (3/7/00) Super Tuesday (3/14/00)
(delegate selection, caucus-conventions, and primaries	**Apr.** **May** **June**	Last primaries (6/6/00)
	July **Aug.**	Republican convention, Philadelphia (7/31–8/3/00) Democratic convention, Los Angeles (8/14–8/17/00)
Party conventions		
	Sept. **Oct.** **Nov.**	Labor Day (9/4/00) Election day (11/7/00)
Stage 3 General election campaign		
Stage 4 Validation in electoral college	**Dec.**	Electoral college balloting, state capitals (12/18/00)
2001	**Jan.**	Electoral college results, joint session of Congress (1/6/01) Inauguration day (1/20/01)

uary during a joint session of the U.S. Congress, which is presided over by the incumbent vice president. The duly elected president is inaugurated on January 20, a date set in the Twentieth Amendment to the Constitution.

Defining the Pool of Eligibles

Who is eligible to serve as president? The formal rules relating to the candidates' qualifications are minimal and have been remarkably stable over time. Individuals need to meet only three requirements, which are set forth in Article II, Section 1, of the Constitution. One must be a "natural-born" citizen, at least thirty-five years of age, and a resident of the United States for fourteen years or longer.[11] In 2000, approximately 125 million Americans met these constitutional requirements, but the pool of plausible candidates is far smaller than that of possible candidates.[12]

The informal requirements for the presidency are less easy to satisfy than the formal. People who entertain presidential ambitions must have what is generally called *political availability;* that is, they must have the political experiences and personal characteristics that make them attractive to political activists and to the general voting public. Potential candidates accumulate these credentials through personal and career decisions made long before the presidential election year.

However, there is no explicit checklist of job qualifications for the presidency. The closest that one can come to determining what particular political experiences and personal characteristics put an individual in line for a presidential nomination is to look at past candidates. Even this approach poses some difficulties because the attitudes of political leaders and the American public change over time.

Political Experience of Candidates

Who is nominated to run for president? Overwhelmingly, the answer is people with experience in one of a few civilian, elective, political offices. Nominees' backgrounds have changed very little since the last half of the nineteenth century.[13] Since 1932, with only two exceptions, nominees have been drawn from one of four positions: the presidency, the vice presidency, a state governorship, or a U.S. Senate seat.[14] *(See Appendix B.)* Candidates with other backgrounds are seldom successful. For example, in 2000, five aspirants who lacked experience in elected office unsuccessfully sought the Republican nomination. In 1992, H. Ross Perot, a billionaire businessman, sought election without a party nomination and did so again in 1996 as nominee of the Reform Party. Before retired general Colin Powell withdrew from consideration in November 1995, considerable speculation also centered on whether he would seek the presidency either as a Republican or as an independent.

Presidents and Vice Presidents. Since 1932, the party controlling the presidency has turned to the presidency or vice presidency for candidates, while the out party has turned primarily to governors and then to the Senate. In only one of the eighteen elections from 1932 to 2000 has the name of an incumbent president or vice president not been on the ballot. Thirteen times, the incumbent president was renominated, and in four of the five instances when the incumbent president was either prohibited by the Twenty-second Amendment from running again (Dwight Eisenhower in 1960, Ronald Reagan in 1988, and Bill Clinton in 2000) or declined to do so (Harry S. Truman in 1952 and Lyndon Baines Johnson in 1968), the incumbent vice president won his party's nomination. The exception occurred in 1952, when Truman chose not to run for reelection, and Adlai Stevenson became the nominee rather than the vice president, seventy-five-year-old Alben Barkley.

There are no guarantees that an incumbent president will win the party's nomination, but it is enormously difficult for the party in power to remove these leaders from the national ticket. Incumbents have considerable advantages when it comes to winning renomination, as demonstrated by Gerald Ford in 1976, Jimmy Carter in 1980, and George Bush in 1992. Party leaders are reluctant to admit that they made a mistake four years earlier; incumbents can direct federal programs toward politically important areas or make politically useful executive branch appointments; and presidents enjoy far greater media exposure than others seeking the nomination. As a result, even unpopular presidents tend to be renominated. The Republicans chose Ford again despite an energy crisis and slow economy; the Democrats renominated Carter when both inflation and unemployment were high, Americans were being held hostage in Iran, and Soviet troops occupied Afghanistan; and Bush was renominated despite a weakening economy and charges that he broke a campaign pledge not to raise taxes.

Incumbent vice presidents are more likely to win their party's nomination today than in the past.[15] Recent presidential candidates have chosen running mates who are arguably more capable than their predecessors, which makes these individuals more viable prospects for the presidency. Moreover, presidents now assign their vice presidents meaningful responsibilities, including political party activities (especially campaigning in off-year elections), liaison assignments with social groups, and diplomatic missions to foreign countries. As the position's visibility and significance have increased, so have the political chances of its occupants improved.[16]

If it was an asset in securing the party's nomination, the vice presidency seemed to be a liability in winning the general election until George Bush's victory in 1988 broke a 152-year-old tradition of losing campaigns. Richard Nixon and Hubert Humphrey lost as incumbent vice presidents in 1960 and 1968, and Al Gore suffered a similar fate in 2000, despite winning a popular vote plurality.

Senators and Governors. From 1932 through 2000, the party out of power nominated ten governors, four senators, two former vice presidents, one general (Eisenhower), and one businessman (Wendell Willkie). (See Table 2-1.) Both major parties have looked to governors as promising candidates, except for the period from 1960 to 1972, when Sens. John Kennedy (D-1960), Barry Goldwater (R-1964), and George McGovern (D-1972), as well as former vice president Nixon (R-1968), won the nomination. Governorships later regained prominence with the nomination of former governors Carter (D-1976) and Reagan (R-1980) as well as sitting governors Michael Dukakis (D-1988), Bill Clinton (D-1992), and George W. Bush (R-2000). Only twice in the past seven elections did the party out of power not turn to a governor: former vice president Walter Mondale was the Democratic nominee in 1984, and Senate majority leader Robert Dole was the Republican nominee in 1996.

It is possible to argue that these patterns understate the importance of the Senate as a recruiting ground for president. Certainly, many senators have sought their parties' presidential nomination since the early 1950s. Senators share the political and media spotlight focused on the capital, enjoy the opportunity to address major public problems and develop a record in foreign affairs, and usually can pursue the presidency without giving up their legislative seat. Nonetheless, only twice in American history have senators been elected directly to the White House (Warren Harding in 1920 and Kennedy in 1960).[17]

Instead of serving as a steppingstone to the presidency, the Senate has often been one to the vice presidency, which then gave its occupants the inside track either to assume the presidency through succession or to win nomination on

Table 2-1   **Principal Experience of In- and Out-Party Candidates Before Gaining Nomination, 1932–2000**

Election year	In party	Out party
1932	President (R)	Governor (D)
1936	President (D)	Governor (R)
1940	President (D)	Businessman (R)
1944	President (D)	Governor (R)
1948	President (D)	Governor (R)
1952	Governor (D)	General/educator (R)
1956	President (R)	Governor (former) (D)
1960	Vice president (R)	Senator (D)
1964	President (D)	Senator (R)
1968	Vice president (D)	Vice president (former) (R)
1972	President (R)	Senator (D)
1976	President (R)	Governor (former) (D)
1980	President (D)	Governor (former) (R)
1984	President (R)	Vice president (former) (D)
1988	Vice president (R)	Governor (D)
1992	President (R)	Governor (D)
1996	President (D)	Senator (R)
2000	Vice president (D)	Governor (R)

their own. This role of the Senate can be seen in the careers of Vice Presidents Truman, Nixon, Johnson, Humphrey, Mondale, and Gore, who served as senators immediately before assuming their executive posts. (Interestingly, Gerald Ford, who succeeded to the presidency when Nixon resigned in 1974, had moved into the vice presidency from the House of Representatives. Dick Cheney, who was elected vice president in 2000, had served in the House before becoming secretary of defense and then becoming a businessman.) Service in the Senate, therefore, has been an important source of experience for presidents since 1932, but almost all have needed seasoning in the vice presidency.

Historically, governors seeking the presidency confronted major obstacles. It was difficult for them to gain national publicity unless they served in states with large cities that functioned as national media centers. Nor did governors have responsibilities of consequence in foreign affairs; instead, they were more closely tied to their home states, particularly when the state legislature was in session, than were senators. Laws often imposed term limits or governors were defeated for reelection because of public disappointment at their failure to solve major domestic problems without increasing taxes. Becoming sufficiently well known to be a viable presidential candidate was a major task.

Today, governors seem to have a competitive advantage over senators. Two of the last five presidents—Clinton and George W. Bush—moved directly into the Oval Office from a governor's mansion. Two others—Carter and Reagan—were former governors who were free to devote themselves full time to the demanding task of winning the nomination, an opportunity not available to the senators who sought the presidency in both of those years. Governors can claim valuable executive experience in managing large-scale public enterprises and thousands of state government employees in contrast to a senator's essentially legislative duties and direction of a small personal staff. Moreover, the public's concern with foreign affairs has declined since 1976 and been replaced by anxiety over the domestic economy, taxes, the budget, education, and health care. This shift in public attitudes was evident in 1992 and 2000, when Clinton and George W. Bush benefited from the cold war's reduced prominence during their successful election campaigns.

Among those who pursued the 2000 Republican presidential nomination, senators outnumbered governors by three to two. Three Republican senators—John McCain (Ariz.), Robert Smith (N.H.), and Orrin Hatch (Utah)—announced their candidacies during the first half of 1999. The two governors were George W. Bush, who had won reelection in Texas in 1998 and was the sole sitting chief executive to pursue the nomination, and Lamar Alexander, a former governor of Tennessee. In addition to these five candidates, six others launched campaigns: Patrick Buchanan, a political commentator and former White House speechwriter; Alan Keyes, a talk-show host; Malcolm (Steve) Forbes Jr., a wealthy magazine publisher; Elizabeth Dole, former secretary of labor and of transportation and former director of the American Red Cross; and Gary Bauer, a Reagan administration appointee. Only former senator Bill Bradley (N.J.) challenged Vice President Gore for the Democratic nomination.

Personal Characteristics of Candidates

Although millions meet the formal requirements for president, far fewer meet the informal criteria that have guided choices in the past. Most constraining have been the limits imposed by social conventions on gender and race. So far only males of European heritage have been nominated for president by either of the two major parties, although several women and African Americans have waged national campaigns since 1972, and former representative Geraldine Ferraro of New York was the Democrats' 1984 nominee for vice president. Presidential aspirants also have had to pass other "tests" based on personal characteristics, although these informal requirements have undergone change in the past three decades.[18]

Until 1960, it seemed that candidates had to meet unspoken demographic and religious requirements: that they hail from English ethnic stock and practice a Protestant religion. These tests have weakened in the intervening years. The successful candidacy of John Kennedy, a Roman Catholic, in 1960, challenged the traditional preference for Protestants. (Alfred Smith, also a Catholic, was nominated by the Democrats in 1928 but lost the general election.) Today, little is made of the fact when Catholics pursue the nomination. The Republican senator Barry Goldwater was the first nominee from a partly Jewish background, and Sen. Joseph Lieberman joined the Democratic ticket in 2000 as an Orthodox Jew. Other recent candidates have come from Irish, Norwegian, and Greek heritage, suggesting that the traditional preference for English stock has weakened.

Representing an idealized version of home and family life also seemed to be essential to winning a party's nomination. These criteria have undergone modest change, but other considerations may have taken their place. Nelson Rockefeller's divorce in 1963 from his wife of more than thirty years and his rapid remarriage virtually ensured the failure of his efforts to win the Republican nomination in 1964 and 1968. The marital status of several later candidates was an issue as well, but then in 1980, Reagan became the country's first president to have divorced and remarried.

Public attitudes about other moral and ethical questions have become important. Gary Hart's widely reported extramarital affair ended his presidential hopes for 1988, even though he began the campaign as the clear front-runner. Bill Clinton's alleged extramarital relationships and drug use also became issues in 1992. However, allegations of prior drug use and an admission of alcohol abuse did not damage George W. Bush in 2000. Although traditional moral and ethical tests regarding divorce may have changed, it is not clear which standards will continue to receive media attention and elicit public response, particularly in an era when religion and political activism seem to mix more readily than in the past.

Thus, several of the informal qualifications applied to the presidency have altered with the passage of time, probably in response to changes in the nomination process itself as well as broader currents in U.S. society. One observer suggests that the proliferation of presidential primaries "provides a forum in which prejudices can be addressed openly."[19] The vice presidential nomination offers a way to confront traditional social views indirectly, as was the case with Ferraro and Lieberman. We might expect something similar to happen with an African American candidate in the near future.

The development of a more common culture and the nationalization of American life in general, brought about by modern communication and transportation, have reduced the importance of parochial concerns—the candidates' religious, ethnic, or geographical background—and increased the emphasis on their experience in the national political arena and their association with national issues. Moreover, as other groups that are still socially or politically disadvantaged—African Americans, women, and immigrants from Asia, Mexico, and eastern and southern Europe—begin to occupy governorships and seats in the U.S. Senate, they will enhance their chances of becoming serious candidates for the presidency.[20]

Competing for the Nomination

Once the pool of eligible candidates is established, the selection process begins. This phase has two major components: choosing delegates to the two parties' national conventions and selecting the nominees at the conventions. By far the more complicated of these steps, the selection of delegates has been the principal focus of party reform efforts since 1968. Prior to the conventions, candidates crisscross the country to win delegates, who then attend the convention to select the party's nominee.

The first presidential primary of 2000 was held in New Hampshire on February 1. Delegate selection extended into June, when five states held primaries, the last of forty-two Republican and thirty-nine Democratic primary contests that chose convention delegates, including those from the District of Columbia. Through this complex process, the Republicans chose 2,065 delegates to attend their national convention, and the Democrats selected 4,334 for theirs. Consistent with post-1968 reforms, most of these delegates were chosen through primaries. Millions of Americans participate in primaries: in 2000, for example, 14.66 million voted in Democratic primary elections, and another 20.71 million in Republican primaries.[21] Caucus participation is less easily calculated, but in 1996 nearly 200,000 attended seven Republican caucuses.[22]

In truth, the nomination contest begins much earlier than January of the election year. For example, in pursuing the 1988 nomination, former Delaware governor Pierre "Pete" DuPont officially declared his candidacy in September 1986; thirteen others followed suit in 1987, nine before the Fourth of July. By starting their campaigns early, candidates hope to amass the financial backing, attract the media attention, and generate the popular support necessary to ensure eventual victory. Although Sen. Robert Smith was the first to announce his candidacy in February 2000, Steve Forbes ran tax-reform issue ads in Iowa as early as 1997 and Lamar Alexander followed suit in 1998.[23]

The Nomination Campaign

The nomination campaign is a winnowing process in which each of the two major parties eliminates from the pool of potential candidates all but the one who will represent the party in the general election. As the political scientist Austin Ranney points out, the nomination phase of the campaign is more important than the election stage because "the parties' nominating processes eliminate far more presidential possibilities than do the voters' electing processes."[24] A nomination campaign is long, arduous, and relatively unstructured: Aspirants typically do not know how many opponents they will face or who they will be; candidates start two or more years early and drop out along the way; and, instead of a simultaneous nationwide campaign, the competition takes place in weekly stages with candidates hopscotching the nation in pursuit of votes. Planning and conducting such a campaign are enormously difficult tasks. Most first-time candidates must organize a nationwide political effort, a chore that dwarfs the campaign required to win a Senate seat or governorship in even the largest states.

Preliminary planning is essential, and presidential hopefuls spend considerable time before January of the election year laying the groundwork for their effort. The journalist Arthur Hadley called this period the "invisible primary," a testing ground for the would-be president waged behind the scenes to determine whether his or her candidacy is viable.[25] Candidates must assemble a staff to help raise money, develop campaign strategy, hone a message, and identify a larger group of people willing to do the advance work necessary to organize states for the upcoming primaries and caucuses. Visits are made to party organizations throughout the country, but especially in pivotal states such as Iowa and New

Hampshire, to curry favor with activists. Competition often takes on the trappings of a full-fledged campaign, with candidates broadcasting television ads, engaging in debates, and seeking to finish well in prenomination popularity contests known as straw polls.

Because the media's coverage provides name recognition and potentially positive publicity, developing a favorable relationship with reporters and commentators is crucial during this phase of the contest. Those hopefuls who are ignored because the media do not regard them as serious contenders find it almost impossible to become viable candidates. Adverse publicity can seriously damage a candidacy. Most candidates' campaigns are scuttled during the "invisible primary" stage.

Financing Nomination Campaigns

It is now more important than ever that candidates for the nomination begin raising funds early. Candidates can qualify to receive federal funds that match individual contributions of $250 or less if they can raise $100,000 in individual contributions, with at least $5,000 collected in twenty different states. By checking a box on their federal income tax forms, taxpayers authorize the government to set aside $3.00 of their tax payments for public financing of campaigns—a system introduced in the 1976 election. Candidates who accept public financing—and since 1976 only John Connally, Steve Forbes, Maurice Taylor, Orrin Hatch, and George W. Bush, all Republicans, have chosen not to do so—must also accept limitations on total expenditures and a cap on spending in individual states that is based on population. For 2000, the national expenditure ceiling for the prenomination campaign was $45.6 million, up from $37.1 million in 1996.[26]

By providing partial funding of nomination campaigns, congressional reformers in the 1970s sought to establish a system based on citizen contributions, replacing the financial support of a small number of "fat cats," who previously bankrolled candidates.[27] In 2000, ten candidates qualified for $57.74 million in matching funds, up from $55.95 million in 1996.[28] The federal government also provided $13.512 million to the Democratic and Republican Parties to finance their nominating conventions.[29] The Federal Election Commission (FEC), a bipartisan body of six members nominated by the president and confirmed by the Senate, oversees the administration of these provisions.

Personal money played an unprecedented role in the prenomination stage of the 1996 campaign. Steve Forbes loaned his campaign $37.5 million, and Maurice Taylor spent $6.5 million of his own resources. Neither was ultimately successful, but Forbes dramatically influenced the Republican nomination process by outspending his rivals in several early contests. Because he received no public funds, Forbes was not subject to the state spending limits imposed on his competitors. He launched a $12.5 million media blitz during the last three months of 1995 that concentrated on Iowa, New Hampshire, and other early events. Even Bob Dole, who led all candidates in fund raising, could not match such expenditures since he had to observe federal limits.[30] This experience partly shaped Bush's strategy in 2000. Anticipating that Forbes would pursue a similar tactic this time around, Bush raised a record $94 million in private funds, double that of Forbes and McCain, his closest competitors, and therefore had to observe none of the spending limits associated with public funding.[31]

Most candidates continue to raise funds from a large number of individual contributors, often through direct mail solicitation.[32] In 2000, for the first time, contributions made through the Internet were important, especially for McCain and Bradley. Public funds open the door for candidates who formerly could not afford to mount a nomination campaign because large contributors would not support them. Even some third-party candidates, such as Pat Buchanan and John Hagelin of the Reform Party and Ralph Nader of the Green Party, qualified for federal funds at the nominating stage in 2000. Although public funds reduced financial disparities among candidates, their financial resources are still highly unequal. In 1988 and 1992, George Bush easily outdistanced the financing of his Republican competition, and Bob Dole did the same in 1996. Eventual nominees Michael Dukakis and Bill Clinton led the Democratic fields in fund raising in 1988 and 1992, 1996, respectively.[33] George W. Bush used fund raising as a way to demonstrate his superiority over the rest of the field in 2000.

Superior financial resources enable candidates to compete in more of the early nomination contests, help them extend their fund-raising lead, make it possible to survive poor results (such as Bush's loss of New Hampshire in 2000), and make them stronger in later primaries. Failing to do well in early caucus and primary contests means more than losing delegates to opponents; it also means that contributions stop. Moreover, under the campaign finance law, federal matching funds must be cut off within thirty days if a candidate receives less than 10 percent of the votes in two consecutive primaries. Leading Republican candidates in 1995 worked aggressively to reach the target of $20 million in contributions by year's end, the consensus target among political consultants on what it would take to run a "serious" campaign.[34] Bush's record fund raising in 2000 may have dramatically raised that threshold for the future.

Candidates must decide not only how to raise funds but also how to spend them. In the face of overall campaign spending limits as well as expenditure limits in each state, money must be carefully allocated. Because they want to win the first primaries and caucuses, candidates are inclined to spend heavily in the very early stage of the campaign, which can create problems in later competition. This was an especially pressing problem for Dole in 1996, when he nearly reached the spending limit by April, fully three months before the convention.

Dynamics of the Contest

Candidates who begin the election year as leaders in the public opinion polls frequently go on to win nomination. This pattern prevailed from 1936 through 1968, was interrupted in four Democratic contests between 1972 and 1992, but returned in the 1990s.[35] In the last two elections, early leaders won the nomination in both parties, Bill Clinton and Bob Dole in 1996 and Al Gore and George W. Bush in 2000. Leaders in the polls must guard against verbal slips, personal indiscretions, and the assumption that early popularity is permanent.

When deciding which contests they should emphasize in their nomination campaigns, candidates take into account the premium placed on competing in as many locations as funds will allow. This is especially true for Democrats, whose rules call for proportional allocation of delegates: as long as candidates achieve at least 15 percent of the vote, they are awarded a share of delegates proportional to the vote share.[36] The earliest contest, traditionally the New Hampshire primary, attracts most of the major contenders because it is the first test of rank-and-file voter sentiment. Although the number of New Hampshire delegates is small, victory ensures immediate attention, as it did for Kennedy in 1960 and Carter in 1976. Pat Buchanan was the surprise winner in 1996, with a slim 1 percent victory margin over Dole, and McCain defeated George W. Bush in 2000 by the wide margin of 48.5 to 30.4 percent. As was the case for McCain, the relatively small New Hampshire electorate enables candidates with more modest financial resources to conduct labor-intensive campaigns.

A new twist in the 1988 campaign was the large number of primaries held on Tuesday, March 8—a day consequently known as Super Tuesday. Twenty states selected delegates, sixteen through primaries and four through caucuses. In 1992, only eleven states participated in Super Tuesday, but the Democratic designers accomplished their goal of boosting the chances of a moderate candidate when Clinton won all six of the southern primaries and two caucuses, while Paul Tsongas, his principal rival, claimed victories in just two primaries and one caucus. George Bush, who swept all sixteen of the 1988 Super Tuesday primaries, repeated this success in March 1992. Likewise, Dole won all seven Super Tuesday primaries in 1996.

The competitive situation was more complex in 2000. Super Tuesday was March 14, when the focus was on southern contests, but March 7 was an even bigger prize—dubbed Titanic Tuesday by the media—when eleven states, including California and New York, held both Republican and Democratic primaries. (Many states had moved their contests forward in the calendar, producing a *front-loaded* schedule.) Gore defeated Bradley in all contests on both days, clinching the nomination. The real showdown between Bush and McCain occurred in South Carolina, nearly three weeks after the New Hampshire primary but before the March contests. Both Republican candidates targeted the state as crucial, and the campaign turned negative. Bush emerged with a 53 to 42 percent victory. Although McCain scored several later victories, Bush won the larger contests on Titanic Tuesday, prompting McCain to withdraw from the race even before Super Tuesday, resulting in a clean sweep for Bush in the southern primaries.

Primaries held later in the election calendar once played an important role in nomination contests. Until 1996, California scheduled its primary on the final day of delegate selection, giving Golden State voters the chance to determine a party's nominee, as with Goldwater in 1964 and McGovern in 1972. With the early selection of a nominee in 1996, new Republican rules were adopted that encouraged states to schedule their primaries later in 2000 by providing them with bonus delegates.[37] But the schedule was only slightly less front-loaded in 2000, and the contests were concluded earlier than ever—March 9, when both McCain and Bradley discontinued their campaigns. Another effort by Republicans to revise their rules for 2004 was defeated at the Philadelphia convention, so the nation will once again contend with a compressed, front-loaded schedule in 2004.

State caucuses operate in the shadow of the primaries, although they remain important for candidates able to mobilize an intensely motivated group of supporters who can exert greater influence than in a primary. The Iowa caucus, long the initial delegate selection contest, has diminished in importance as a launching pad for presidential contenders. McCain sidestepped Iowa altogether in 2000 to focus on New Hampshire. When primaries do not produce a clear victor, candidates devote more attention to delegates chosen in caucus-convention states, as in the 1976 Republican contest and the 1984 Democratic race, but the role of the caucus has been declining.

Media Influence and Campaign Consultants

The media play an enormous role in the nomination campaign. "For most of us, the combination of media coverage and media advertising *is* the campaign; few voters see the candidates in person or involve themselves directly in campaign events."[38] As the nomination process has grown in complexity, the influence of the media also has grown. Candidates who must campaign in a score of states within two weeks, as they did in 1992, 1996, and 2000, necessarily rely on the media to communicate with large numbers of potential voters. Televised advertisements, network- and station-sponsored debates, and prime-time news coverage are critical to candidates' efforts. Even talk-show appearances became an important communication link in the 1990s.

The media tend to focus on the game aspects of the preelection-year maneuvering and the early contests. As candidates begin to emerge, journalists concentrate on the race for financial contributions, the quality of professionals enlisted to work on a campaign, and speculations about the candidates' relative chances of success based on polls and nonbinding straw votes in various states. Once the delegate selection contests begin, the media focus on political tactics, strategy, and competitive position more than on the candidates' messages and issue stands, particularly in coverage of Iowa, New Hampshire, and the compressed schedule of contests in March. In general, the media use a winner-take-all principle that, regardless of how narrow the victory or the number of popular votes involved, gives virtually all the publicity to the victorious candidate. In the 1976 Iowa caucuses, for example, Carter was declared the "clear winner" and described as leading the pack of contenders even though he received only about 14,000 votes, 28 percent of the 50,000 cast; he actually trailed the "uncommitted" group.[39] Gore defeated Bradley in the 2000 New Hampshire pri-

mary by a mere 49.7 to 45.6 percent, but Bradley's narrow loss was a less important story than Gore's victory.[40] A surprise showing by a runner-up, however,
may garner the most attention: after winning a mere 16 percent of the votes to
finish an unexpected second in the Iowa caucuses in 1984, Hart got as much
publicity as Mondale, who captured three times as many votes.[41]

As the fate of presidential candidates has passed from a small group of party
professionals to rank-and-file voters, media-based appeals have grown in importance. Voter attitudes evolve during the course of the nomination contest, in
large part because of the media's influence. The media help determine who the
viable candidates are, label the "winners" and "losers," and influence the results
of future contests as voters, as well as contributors, gravitate toward the winners
and desert the losers. Public opinion polls reflecting voters' presidential preferences are a fixture of media coverage. Favorable polls impress media representatives as well as political activists and many rank-and-file voters, leading to
more victories for the poll leaders in both nonprimary and primary contests. The
result of this reinforcement process is that by the time the delegates gather for
their party's national convention, one candidate usually has enough delegates to
receive the nomination.[42] The last remaining hurdle for the front-runner to
overcome is for the most part automatic—the party's national convention.

The National Convention

No part of the selection process has undergone more dramatic change than
the presidential nominating conventions. Long the province of party leaders,
today's conventions are largely media extravaganzas carefully choreographed to
project images designed to reawaken party loyalty, appeal to contemporary public concerns, and project the most desirable aspects of the newly anointed presidential ticket. In short, the national convention is important to presidential candidates for two reasons. First, whatever may have happened during the long
search for delegates, the actual nomination occurs at the convention. Second, a
well-run convention can help candidates win the general election.

Nominating the Ticket

Since the early 1950s, conventions have offered little drama about the choice
of the presidential nominee. In the twenty-eight conventions held by the two
major parties since World War II, only two nominees—Thomas Dewey in 1948
and Adlai Stevenson in 1952—failed to win a majority of the convention votes
on the first ballot. In all other cases, victory has gone to the candidate who
arrived at the convention with the largest number of pledged delegates.
Nonetheless, there is a dramatic air of excitement that still surrounds the traditional balloting by state delegations on who the presidential nominee will be.

Selecting the vice presidential nominee is the convention's final chore and the
only chance to create any suspense. Although in theory the delegates make the
choice, it has been a matter of political custom since 1940 to allow presidential

nominees to pick their own running mates after conferring with leaders whose judgment they trust. Parties traditionally attempt to balance the ticket—that is, broaden its appeal by selecting a person who differs in certain ways from the presidential nominee. George Bush's links to the eastern establishment and moderate wings of the Republican Party complemented the conservative, western Reagan in 1980. Ferraro balanced the 1984 Democratic ticket geographically and in other ways: the first woman to serve as a major party candidate in a presidential contest, she was also the first Italian American.

In 1988, Dan Quayle brought generational balance to the ticket, and he was enthusiastically supported by the party's conservative wing. But the media raised questions about Quayle's ability to perform as president should the need arise, his service in the National Guard during the Vietnam War, and his modest academic performance. Quayle remained on the Republican ticket in 1992 despite speculation about his replacement. Clinton violated political tradition by selecting Al Gore, a fellow southerner and baby boomer, rather than balancing the ticket, but the choice was well received by the party faithful and probably helped Clinton erode Republican support in this crucial region. For the 1996 election, Dole chose Jack Kemp as his running mate, a one-time presidential candidate who was highly popular with Republican activists. Clinton retained the faithful Gore. In 2000, George W. Bush asked Dick Cheney to join the ticket. Although a fellow western conservative, Cheney brought extensive Washington and White House experience to offset Bush's own inexperience. In what the media described as a "bold" move, Gore added Joseph Lieberman to the ticket, thus breaking a long-existent barrier to having a practicing Jew on a national ticket. Lieberman's early criticism of Clinton's personal conduct also helped Gore to further distance himself from the incumbent president.

The final night of the convention is devoted to acceptance speeches. The presidential nominee tries to make peace with former competitors and to reunite various party factions that have confronted one another during the long campaign and the hectic days of the convention. Major party figures usually come to the stage and pledge their support for the winner in the upcoming campaign.

Conducting Party Business

Parties continue the writing and adopting of a convention platform, although participants acknowledge that winning presidential candidates may disavow planks with which they disagree. Because delegates, party leaders, and major groups affiliated with the party have strong feelings about some issues, the platform provides an opportunity to resolve differences and find a politically palatable position.[43] Civil rights and the Vietnam War once prompted major disagreements within the Democratic Party; civil rights, foreign policy, and abortion have been major bones of contention among Republicans.

Despite intraparty differences, conventions provide strong incentives for compromise, to bring back to the fold a disgruntled segment of the party that might otherwise offer only lukewarm support during the fall election or launch a third-party effort. To avoid such damage, almost every presidential candidate decides to provide major rivals and their supporters with concessions in the platform and a prime-time speaking opportunity during the convention. At the Republican convention in 1992, Pat Buchanan was given an opportunity to address a national audience, but his address proved so controversial that the invitation was not extended four years later. John McCain and Elizabeth Dole addressed Republicans in 2000, and Bill Bradley and Jesse Jackson spoke to Democrats.

National nominating conventions have become so predictable that network television coverage was dramatically reduced in 1996 and 2000. To obtain the traditional "gavel to gavel" coverage that ushered in the television age, viewers had to follow proceedings on cable networks such as CNN or on the Internet, where more than fifty outlets had a presence at the conventions. Parties may have become so adept at scripting these quadrennial gatherings that their very existence is jeopardized.[44]

The General Election

With nominees selected, the nation moves into the general election period. Candidates must develop new political appeals for this stage of the process, which is a one-on-one contest that pits the nominees of the two major parties against each other (although a strong independent candidate such as Ross Perot in 1992 and 1996 may also run). The campaign's audience increases greatly: more than twice as many people vote in the general election as participate in the nomination process. Candidates and staff members therefore must decide how they can win the support of these new voters as well as appeal to people who identify with the other party and partisans who backed losing candidates for the nomination. A further complication is time: this nationwide phase of the presidential contest is compressed into a mere ten weeks, traditionally running from Labor Day to election day.

The general election phase differs from the nomination phase for two reasons: the way the electoral college works and the distinctive provisions of the campaign finance laws. Compared with changes effected in the nomination stage, the constitutional requirements surrounding the president's election have been remarkably stable over time, but campaign finance laws have undergone significant change since 1972. Both the college and the laws are critical considerations in how the campaign is waged.

The Electoral College

To understand how candidates plan and carry out their general election strategies, it is necessary to keep in mind the ultimate goal, which is to win a majority of electoral college votes (those cast by state electors in their respective capitals in mid-December). At first, electoral votes were determined by congressional districts: the winner of a popular vote plurality in each district would receive the associated electoral vote, with the statewide winner of the popular vote getting the two electoral votes representing senators. However, legislatures soon began to adopt the "unit" or "general-ticket" rule, whereby all the state's electoral votes went to the candidate who received the plurality of the statewide popular vote. This rule benefited the state's majority party and maximized the state's influence in the election by permitting it to throw all its electoral votes to one candidate. By 1836, the district plan had vanished and the unit system had taken its place. Since then, two states have returned to the old plan: Maine began following the district plan in 1969, and Nebraska in 1992.

The final product is a strange method for choosing a chief executive. Although most Americans view the system as a popular election, it is not. When voters mark their ballots, the vote actually determines which slate of electors pledged to support the party's presidential candidate will have the opportunity to vote. In a few states, electors' names appear on the ballot either with or without the presidential candidate's name. The electors are party loyalists, chosen in primaries, at conventions, or by state committees. In mid-December, the electors associated with the winning candidate meet in their state capitals to cast ballots. (About one-third of the states attempt by law to bind the electors to vote for the winner of the popular vote, but there is some question whether such laws are constitutional.) The electoral votes are transmitted to Washington, D.C., and counted early in January of the following year. Next, the presiding officer of the Senate—the incumbent vice president—announces the outcome before a joint session of Congress. If, as usually happens, one candidate receives an absolute majority of the electoral votes, currently 270, the vice president officially declares that candidate to be president. Because the winner of the popular vote usually wins in the electoral college as well, we call this final stage of the selection process the "validation" of the popular vote outcome. For candidates who win without a popular vote plurality, such as George W. Bush in 2000, the electoral college may validate a victory but not necessarily provide legitimacy.

Financing the General Election

The financial resources needed to mount a nationwide campaign are significantly greater than those required to win the nomination. For the general election, complete public financing is provided to nominees of the major parties; any party that won 25 percent or more of the popular vote in the last presidential election is considered a major party. In the 2000 presidential election, the federal government gave each major party candidate $67.56 million, up from $61.8 million in 1996.[45] Candidates of minor parties, those that won between 5 percent and 25 percent of the vote in the previous election, receive partial public financing and can raise private funds up to the major party limit. Candidates whose parties are just getting started or did not win at least 5 percent of the vote in the previous election receive no help, a major disadvantage. Ross Perot sought no federal funds in 1992 but spent an estimated $63 million of his own money to mount a major campaign effort. In 1996, however, he accepted $29 million in federal funds and was limited to using only $50,000 of his own money in the general election. As the official Reform Party nominee in 2000, Pat Buchanan received $12.6 million as a result of Perot's 8.4 percent share of the vote in 1996. But the party will be ineligible for public funding in 2004 after Buchanan's poor showing of .43 percent. Candidates of parties that won less than 5 percent of the vote in the previous election can be partially reimbursed after the current election if they receive at least 5 percent of that vote. Ralph Nader of the Green Party came closest to this goal with a 2.7 percent share of the national vote in 2000, achieved with $3.3 million in private contributions.

Campaign expenditures other than those from public funding may be paid by two sources. There is no limit on *independent campaign expenditures,* which are made by individuals or political committees that advocate the defeat or election of a presidential candidate but are not made in conjunction with a candidate's campaign. In addition, state and local party organizations may spend money for any purpose except campaign advertising and the hiring of outside personnel. Until 1996, these funds, commonly called *soft money,* had largely been used for grassroots activities such as distributing campaign buttons, stickers, and yard signs; registering voters; and transporting voters to the polls. Spending from both these sources has varied: between 1988 and 1992, independent expenditures declined from $10.1 million to about $4 million, and soft money expenditures remained steady at $42.5 million.[46] But in 1996, the Democratic and Republican parties enormously expanded their use of soft money to fund *issue advocacy* campaigns, media advertisements that do not expressly support or oppose a candidate but ostensibly educate the public about an issue or a candidate's position on an issue. The Democratic National Committee launched an aggressive series of such ads in mid-1995, designed to help Clinton even before the nomination contests began. When Dole ran short of money in late spring 1996, the Republican National Committee stepped in with a similar campaign to help their expected standard-bearer. The two parties spent a combined total of more than $65 million in these efforts. In 2000, these activities grew even larger: the national parties spent more for television advertising in the presidential election than did the candidates.[47] Most of these efforts were targeted on a short list of key "battleground states," including California, Tennessee, Pennsylvania, Ohio, Michigan, and Missouri. In Florida, the key to Bush's victory, pro-Bush expenditures exceeded those for Gore by about $4 million. In 2000, independent expenditures by political groups favored Gore by a wide margin of seven to one, with Planned Parenthood leading the way.[48]

Until recently, the system of public financing introduced in the 1976 election was viewed as a success: major party candidates no longer depended on wealthy contributors and other private sources to finance their campaigns; expenditures of the two major party candidates were limited and equalized, an advantage for Democrats who were historically outspent by their opponents.[49] The 1996 and 2000 experiences with soft money have called into question the adequacy of current regulations and their future for both presidential and congressional elections. These concerns gave rise to the McCain-Feingold bill, which seeks to ban soft money altogether, and other reform efforts in Congress.

Targeting the Campaign

As in the nomination process, presidential candidates must decide which states will be the focus of their efforts in the fall campaign. By far the most important consideration is the electoral college. The candidate's task is clear: to win the presidency, he or she must win a majority—270—of the 538 electoral votes.[50] This fact places a premium on carrying the states with the largest number of electoral votes (see Figure 2-2). In 2000, by winning the eleven largest states—California, New York, Texas, Florida, Pennsylvania, Illinois, Ohio, Michigan, New Jersey, North Carolina, and Georgia or Virginia—a candidate could win the presidency while losing the other thirty-nine states and the District of Columbia. Naturally, candidates from both major political parties concentrate their personal visits and spending on the most populous states.

Another element that affects candidates' decisions on where to campaign is the political situation in a particular state—that is, whether the state generally goes to one party's candidate or whether it swings back and forth from one election to the next. Distinctly one-party states are likely to be slighted by the major party candidates; both will think it a waste of time, although for different reasons. Swing states with large populations naturally draw a good deal of attention from presidential candidates of both parties.

In formulating campaign strategy, therefore, candidates and their advisers start with the electoral map as modified by calculations of probable success. The electoral college creates fifty-one separate presidential contests—fifty states plus the District of Columbia—primarily following the winner-take-all principle, the goal of which is a popular vote victory in each, no matter how small the margin of victory may be. The winner in a large state benefits from the unit or general-ticket system by getting all of the state's electoral votes. In 2000, Bush won Florida by a margin of 537 votes of the 5.94 million legitimate ballots cast.[51] Nonetheless, he won all 25 of the state's electoral votes, giving him a one-vote margin of victory in the electoral college, 271–267.

Bush's victory in Florida was not finalized until a controversial 5–4 Supreme Court decision that resolved legal challenges to countywide vote counts was handed down two hours before midnight on December 12. Confusion had reigned on election night as television anchors first called Florida a victory for Gore, later withdrew it, and then awarded it to Bush. This led Gore to phone his opponent with his concession. But hours later, Gore withdrew the concession, triggering weeks of tense hand recounts of paper ballots, court arguments over ballot tallies, and hours of television discussion filled with talk of "hanging chad," butterfly ballots, and undercounts. The suspense finally came to an end on December 13, when Gore conceded for the final time.

Electoral votes will be reapportioned for the 2004 presidential election, reflecting the results of the 2000 census. Early projections released by the Cen-

Figure 2-2   State Size by Number of Electoral Votes, 1992, 1996, and 2000

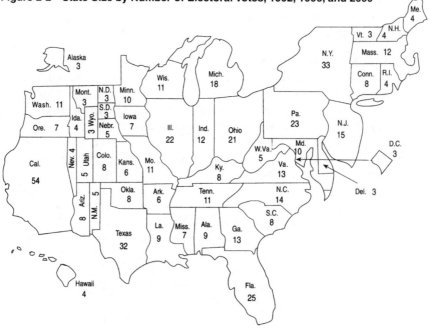

sus Bureau in December 2000 indicate that New York and Pennsylvania will each lose two House seats. Connecticut, Illinois, Indiana, Mississippi, Missouri, Ohio, Oklahoma, and Wisconsin will each lose one. The biggest gainers will be Arizona, Florida, Georgia, and Texas, with two seats each, while California, Colorado, North Carolina, and Nevada will each gain one seat.[52]

The regions that have been important in recent presidential contests are the Middle Atlantic states of New Jersey, New York, and Pennsylvania and the Midwest states of Illinois, Michigan, Missouri, and Ohio. These seven industrial states controlled 143 electoral votes and also tended to be highly competitive, which means that campaign efforts there can be very important in deciding which candidate prevails. Because these states are so often the focus of campaign efforts, analysts refer to them as the "battleground" states. Although they will have fewer votes over the next decade, they are likely to remain critical.

In formulating a strategy likely to produce victory during the 1980s, Democratic candidates confronted a difficult strategic problem, most of which can be traced to the historic realignment of the South in presidential politics. For many decades, southern voters were a bastion of solid Democratic support and critical to their candidates' success. Until 1992, no Democrat had ever won the White House without carrying a majority of southern states, but southern voters had not supported the party's nominee since 1976, when they helped to elect Jimmy Carter. Carter was the first southern presidential nominee (other than Lyndon

Johnson, who had succeeded to the office) since before the Civil War. Southern support evaporated in 1980, when only Georgia supported its favorite son. No southern state voted for the Democratic ticket in 1984 or 1988. The Solid South was a Republican stronghold until Clinton cut into Bush's support in 1992 by winning four states: Arkansas, Georgia, Louisiana, and Tennessee. Clinton added support from the West, the Midwest, and the Mountain States to the Democratic strongholds in the Northeast. In 1992, the Democrats won each state that had voted for Dukakis in 1988 and added all but one of the twelve where the previous Democratic nominee had won at least 45 percent of the vote, a significant part of the thirty-two states carried by Bill Clinton.[53] Clinton won twenty-nine of the same states in 1996 and added two longtime Republican strongholds— Florida and Arizona. The tables were turned in 2000. George W. Bush won the entire South, including Gore's home state of Tennessee and Clinton's of Arkansas. All together, eleven states switched columns from 1996, including West Virginia, a Democratic stronghold, Florida, and New Hampshire. In the latter two states, it can be argued that votes cast for Ralph Nader cost Gore the election. Nader's vote came predominantly from liberal Democrats. With his strength in the Northeast, in the upper Midwest, and on the West Coast, Gore could have won the election with either the Granite State's four votes or Florida's twenty-five.[54] (For 2000 election results, see Appendix A.)

Appealing for Public Support

Presidential campaigns spend millions of dollars and untold hours of effort pursuing two goals: motivating people to vote on election day and winning their support for a particular candidate. Several factors other than campaign appeals determine who votes and how. Voters' choices depend on their long-term political predispositions, such as political party loyalties and social group affiliations, and their reactions to short-term forces, such as the particular candidates and issues involved in specific elections. Candidates and their teams of campaign professionals try to design appeals that activate these influences, attract support, and counter perceived weaknesses.

Because the audience is larger and the time is shorter during the general election period than during the nomination period, presidential candidates use their resources primarily for mass-media appeals. Advertising expenditures have risen accordingly, with campaigns spending half their public funding on radio and television advertising, primarily the latter. Since 1952, television has been the chief source of campaign information for most Americans. In addition, polls indicate that people are more inclined to believe what they see on television than what they read in the newspapers or hear on the radio. Increasingly, however, advertising is targeted on selected markets in key electoral college states rather than being national in scope, a pattern especially apparent in 2000.

Long-Term Influences. Students of elections have categorized influences on voter decisions as either long-term or short-term. Long-term influences include partisanship and group membership, while the short-term ones include issues, candidate image, and campaign incidents.

Partisan loyalty, although still important for a large part of the public, has become less significant as a determinant of election outcomes. Conditions have changed considerably since a group of researchers studying presidential elections in the 1950s concluded that the single most important determinant of voting at that time was the *party identification* of the voter.[55] This general psychological attachment, shaped by family and social groups, tended to intensify with age. For the average person looking for guidance on how to vote amid the complexities of personalities, issues, and events of the 1950s, the party label of the candidates was the most important reference point. At that time, partisanship was also fairly constant: about 45 percent of Americans in 1952 and 1956 said they thought of themselves as Democrats, and about 28 percent viewed themselves as Republicans, for a combined total of nearly three-fourths of the electorate. When asked to classify themselves further as "strong" or "weak" partisans, both Republicans and Democrats tended to divide equally between those two categories. Independents in 1952 and 1956 averaged about 23 percent of the electorate.

In the mid- to late 1960s, however, partisan affiliation in the United States began to change (see Table 2-2). Beginning with the 1968 election, the number of independents started to increase, primarily at the expense of the Democrats; by 1972, independents constituted one-third of the electorate. Even those voters who stayed with the Democrats were more inclined than formerly to say they were weak rather than strong party members. This trend progressed one step further in 1988, when some polls found that independents outnumbered Democrats for the first time. Since 1968, more people also identify themselves as independents than as Republicans. The rise in the number of independents has occurred primarily among younger people, particularly those who entered the electorate in 1964 or later. Voters who have come of age since that time are much more likely to be political independents than are voters of earlier political generations, a development that has been linked to the influence of Vietnam and Watergate.

Total partisanship—the combined percentage of citizens declaring themselves to be Democrats or Republicans—fell to its lowest level between 1972 and 1976, rebounded slightly in the 1980s, and sank again to that level in 1992, with another modest uptick in 1996. (Republicans had scored modest gains of roughly 5 to 10 percent after 1980 gains that offset Democratic losses of the same size. Republican identification rose during the period of their startling success in winning control of Congress in 1994, but then receded to previous levels.) The picture then became stable through 1998, with just under two-thirds of citizens expressing a party identification.[56] Although the trend away from party affiliation seems to have stopped, the parties have been unable to lure the public back. The percentage of independents has remained strong for nearly three decades. Going into the 2000 election, the Gallup Organization (using a different polling question from that used by the National Election Studies in Table 2-2) found

Table 2-2   Party Identification, 1952–1998 (Percent)

Party	1952	1956	1960	1964	1968	1972	1976	1980	1984	1988	1992	1994	1996	1998
Strong														
Democratic	22	21	20	27	20	15	15	18	17	18	18	15	18	19
Weak														
Democratic	25	23	25	25	25	26	25	23	20	18	18	19	19	18
Total	47	44	45	52	45	41	40	41	37	36	35	34	37	37
Strong														
Republican	14	14	16	11	10	10	9	9	10	14	11	16	12	10
Weak														
Republican	13	15	14	14	15	13	14	14	15	14	14	15	15	16
Total	27	29	30	25	25	23	23	23	25	28	26	31	27	26
Independent	22	24	23	23	30	35	37	34	34	36	38	35	35	36

Sources: Data drawn from National Election Studies, Center for Political Studies at the University of Michigan's Institute for Social Research; *The NES Guide to Public Opinion and Electoral Behavior*, Table 2a, www.umich.edu/~nes/nesguide.

independents composed 38 percent, Democrats 34 percent, and Republicans 28 percent of the overall electorate.[57] Because partisanship remains an important factor for so many voters, campaigns seek support from their own identifiers by activating traditional loyalties, yet they also attempt to lure identifiers of the other party by blurring traditional themes, a tightrope act that can confuse the general public.

Social group membership is another potentially important influence on voting that candidates try to tap. Patterns of group support established during the New Deal have persisted during succeeding decades, although with decreasing vibrancy. In the 1940s, Democrats received most of their support from southerners, blacks, Catholics, and people with limited education, lower incomes, and a working-class background. Northerners, whites, Protestants, and people with more education, higher incomes, and a professional or business background supported Republican candidates. Table 2-3, which is based on Gallup polls, shows the support of various groups on the eve of presidential elections from 1952 through 2000. The support of many groups for their traditional party's candidates declined over the forty-eight-year period. The most significant drop for the Democrats came in the southern white vote: in 1988, only one in three white votes in the South went to Dukakis, and only 26 percent of white males supported the Democrat.[58] The only group that significantly increased its support for its traditional party candidate over this period was nonwhites, whose support for Democrats strengthened between 1964 and 1988 but then returned to the 1952 level.[59] In the 2000 election, both election-eve polls and exit polls showed that the racial and gender gaps were especially large. Bush won 53 percent among men but only 43 percent among women compared with Gore's 42 and 54 percent, respectively. African American support for Bush was among the lowest for any Republican presidential candidate since 1960, and Gore won two-thirds of

Table 2-3 Group Voting Patterns in Presidential Elections, Selected Years (Percent)

Group	1952 Stevenson	1952 (R) Eisenhower	1960 Kennedy	1960 (R) Nixon	1964 Johnson	1964 (R) Goldwater	1968 Humphrey	1968 (R) Nixon	1968 Wallace	1972 McGovern	1972 (R) Nixon
Sex											
male	47	53	52	48	60	40	41	43	16	37	63
female	42	58	49	51	62	38	45	43	12	38	62
Race											
white	43	57	49	51	59	41	38	47	15	32	68
nonwhite	79	21	68	32	94	6	85	12	3	87	13
Education											
college	34	66	39	61	52	48	37	54	9	37	63
high school	45	55	52	48	62	38	42	43	15	34	66
grade school	52	48	55	45	66	34	52	33	15	49	51
Occupation											
professional, business	36	64	42	58	54	46	34	56	10	31	69
white collar	40	60	48	52	57	43	41	47	12	36	64
manual	55	45	60	40	71	29	50	35	15	43	57
Age											
under 30	51	49	54	45	64	36	47	38	15	48	52
30–49	47	53	54	46	63	37	44	41	15	33	67
50 and older	39	61	46	54	59	41	41	47	12	36	64
Religion											
Protestant	37	63	38	62	55	45	35	49	16	30	70
Catholic	56	44	78	22	76	24	59	33	8	48	52
Region											
East	45	55	53	47	68	32	50	43	7	42	58
Midwest	42	58	48	52	61	39	44	47	9	40	60
South	51	49	51	49	52	48	31	36	33	29	71
West	42	58	49	51	60	40	44	49	7	41	59
Members of labor union families	61	39	65	35	73	27	56	29	15	46	54
National	45	55	50	50	61	39	43	43	14	38	62

Sources: Excerpted from *Gallup Report,* November 1988, 6, 7; *The Gallup Poll Monthly,* November 1992, 9; 1996 data provided by Gallup Organization from poll conducted November 3 to November 4, 1996; 2000 data released Nov. 6, 2000, and posted on Web site, www. gallup.com.

Note: NA = Not available.

Table 2-3   (Continued)

1976		1980			1988		1992			1996			2000		
	(R)		(R)			(R)	(R)				(R)				
Carter	Ford	Carter	Reagan	Anderson	Dukakis	Bush, G.	Bush, G.	Clinton	Perot	Clinton	Dole	Perot	Gore	Bush, G.W.	Nader
53	45	38	53	7	44	56	37	39	19	45	39	11	38	53	5
48	51	44	49	6	48	52	36	48	10	53	34	6	48	43	4
46	52	36	56	7	41	59	40	40	15	44	41	9	39	52	4
85	15	86	10	2	82	18	12	76	4	78	9	4	78	12	4
42	55	35	53	10	42	58	39	43	14	44	44	6	42	49	5
54	46	43	51	5	46	54	37	45	12	52	30	11	46	44	4
58	41	54	42	3	55	45	35	43	15	NA	NA	NA	NA	NA	NA
42	56	33	55	10	NA	NA	NA	NA	NA	NA	—	—	NA	NA	NA
50	48	40	51	9	NA	NA	NA	NA	NA	NA	—	—			
58	41	48	46	5	NA	NA	NA	NA	NA	NA	—	—			
53	45	47	41	11	37	63	44	38	14	54	27	13	43	45	9
48	49	38	52	8	45	55	35	43	17	49	36	10	41	50	5
52	48	41	54	4	49	51	37	46	11	48	39	6	46	46	3
46	53	39	54	6	42	58	NA	NA	NA	NA	—	—	NA	NA	NA
57	42	46	47	6	51	49	NA	NA	NA	NA	—	—	45	45	5
51	47	43	47	9	51	49	33	47	15	59	26	9	52	38	6
48	50	41	51	7	47	53	35	45	13	47	39	8	43	47	4
54	45	44	52	3	40	60	42	40	13	45	39	9	36	56	3
46	51	35	54	9	46	54	36	43	15	48	38	8	43	47	6
63	36	50	43	5	63	37	NA	NA	NA	NA	—	—	NA	—	—
50	48	41	51	7	46	54	37	44	14	49	36	**9**	43	47	5

the Hispanic vote, although Bush's share was 10 percent higher than that of the 1996 Republican candidate.[60]

Table 2-3 also shows that group preferences can vary greatly from election to election. In 1964, when the very conservative Barry Goldwater was the Republican standard-bearer, all of these groups, including those that typically support the GOP, supported the Democratic candidate, Lyndon Johnson. In 1972, the opposite occurred; when the very liberal George McGovern ran on the Democratic ticket, all the groups that usually sympathize with that party, except for nonwhites, voted for Richard Nixon, the Republican candidate. In 1992, Bush's support declined from 1988 levels in virtually every category, but the decline was especially marked among men, the college-educated, and baby boomers, the voters between thirty and forty-nine. Dole rebounded among men and the college-educated but not enough for victory in 1996, whereas George W. Bush's victory in 2000 was built on solid support among men, an overwhelming lead among southerners, and substantial improvement among older voters from 1996.

The weakening of party loyalties means that candidates must target many groups. Organized labor, far from a monolithic entity, has been seriously divided in recent elections, and both camps have openly courted ethnic groups. Moreover, new groups have emerged as critical factors: women, fundamentalist Christians, young voters, and Hispanics have attracted particular attention. But because many American voters have lost their partisan anchor, short-term influences—such as candidates, issues, events—and presidential performance are now more important to them.

Short-Term Influences. Voters look for many qualities in a president. During the 1984 campaign, for example, the Michigan Center for Political Studies found that Reagan was favored over Mondale on leadership (commands respect, inspires) and integrity (decent, moral), and Mondale was preferred on competence (hard-working, intelligent) and empathy (compassionate).[61]

In a 1988 election day poll, voters concerned with experience and competence overwhelmingly supported Bush, while those who wanted a more caring president and one more likely to introduce change disproportionately supported Dukakis. Those who saw Dukakis as too liberal predictably supported Bush, but those worried about dirty campaigns leaned toward Dukakis.[62] In a 1992 exit poll that asked voters what qualities mattered most in deciding how they voted, more than one-third cited the ability to bring about change, with Clinton winning 67 percent of those votes. Clinton also led among voters concerned about which candidate had the best plan for the nation, cared about people, and had the best vice presidential candidate. Bush led among voters concerned with experience, trustworthiness, and good judgment in a crisis.[63]

In 1996, Dole won 84 percent of those mentioning honesty and trustworthiness (20 percent of respondents), but Clinton won 72–89 percent of those who mentioned caring, having a vision for the future, and being in touch with the 1990s—more than one-third of the voters.[64] In 2000, honesty was the trait mentioned most by voters (24 percent), and 80 percent of those who mentioned it voted for George W. Bush, who was also perceived as the stronger leader and more likeable. Gore was regarded as more experienced, better able to deal with complexity, and more caring about people.[65]

Because the public focuses so much attention in a presidential campaign on the candidates themselves, the personality and character the aspirants project are particularly important. Each campaign organization strives to create a composite image of its candidate's most attractive features. To do this sometimes means transforming liabilities into assets: age becomes mature judgment (Eisenhower); youth and inexperience become vigor (Kennedy). Alternatively, a candidate can direct attention to the opponent's personal liabilities, a move that has proved beneficial even though some voters see such an effort as dirty campaigning and beneath the dignity of the office.

The 1988 and 1992 campaigns provide good examples of how candidates try to shape each other's image. Pollsters working with presidential campaigns try to project their candidate's most attractive features and direct voter attention to the opponent's least attractive features. Bush succeeded in creating a negative portrait of Dukakis in 1988. Dukakis enjoyed a largely favorable image before the summer conventions, but Bush's pollsters discovered it was based on very little information.[66] Interviews conducted with small groups of Democrats who had supported Reagan in 1980 and 1984 shaped the Bush campaign's charges that the Democratic nominee was sympathetic to criminals, weak on defense, opposed to saying the pledge of allegiance in school, and a liberal who favored high taxes and big government.[67] Bush launched a similar effort against Clinton in 1992. First he tried to picture Clinton as the failed governor of a crime-filled state with environmental problems and as an unpatriotic antiwar activist. Then Bush focused on the issues of trust and taxes in the final weeks of the election. But these negative tactics proved less successful against Clinton than they had against Dukakis for at least two reasons. Since 1988, observers have demanded more supporting evidence for campaign charges. And unlike Dukakis, Clinton met all negative charges with broadcast rebuttals and attacks of his own that focused on Bush's role in the Iran-contra incident, the pro-Iraq actions of his administration prior to the Persian Gulf War, and Bush's violation of 1988 campaign promises. By leaving no charge unanswered, Clinton succeeded where Dukakis had faltered.[68]

Issues are the other major short-term influence on voting behavior. University of Michigan researchers in the 1950s suggested that issues influence a voter's choice only if three conditions are present: the voter is aware that an issue or a number of issues exist; issues are of some personal concern to the voter; and the voter perceives that one party represents his or her position better than the other party does.[69] When the three conditions were applied to U.S. voters in the 1952 and 1956 presidential elections, researchers found that these criteria existed for relatively few voters. About one-third of the respondents were unaware of *any* of the sixteen principal issues about which they were questioned. Even the two-

thirds who were aware of one or more issues frequently had no personal concern about them. Finally, many of those who were aware and concerned about
issues were unable to perceive differences between the two parties' positions.
The analysts concluded that issues *potentially* determined the choice of, at the
most, only one-third of the electorate. (The proportion who *actually* voted as
they did because of issues could have been, and probably was, even less.)

Studies of political attitudes in the 1960s and 1970s demonstrate a change:
the number and types of issues of which voters were aware increased.[70] Voters
during the Eisenhower years had exhibited some interest in traditional domestic
matters, such as welfare and labor-management relationships, and in a few foreign policy issues, such as the threat of communism and the danger of the atomic
bomb. Beginning with the 1964 election, however, voters' interests broadened
to include concerns such as civil rights and the Vietnam War. The war in particular remained an important consideration in the 1968 and 1972 contests and
was joined by new matters, such as crime, disorder, and juvenile delinquency—
sometimes referred to collectively along with race problems as "social issues."
Naturally, the issues that are salient vary from election to election. For example,
the economy and jobs led the list in 2000, followed by education, social security,
taxes, world affairs, health care, and prescription drugs.[71]

Incumbency. Incumbency may be viewed as a candidate characteristic that
also involves issues. Service in the job provides experience that no one else can
claim. Incumbency also provides concrete advantages in conducting a campaign:
an incumbent already has national campaign experience (true for all incumbents
in U.S. history except Gerald Ford), can obtain media coverage more easily, and
has considerable discretion in allocating benefits selectively. As noted earlier,
incumbency has been especially important since World War II because of the pattern of recruitment. Until the elder Bush's victory in 1988, incumbency seemed
to provide advantages solely to presidents and not to incumbent vice presidents.
Gore's loss in 2000 reestablished the historical pattern.

Of the five incumbent presidents who ran for reelection between 1976 and
1996, only Reagan and Clinton succeeded, and of the past four incumbent vice
presidents who sought the presidency, only Bush was elected. The defeats of
Ford, Carter, and Bush demonstrate the disadvantages of incumbency, particularly if service in the presidency coincides with negative economic developments
such as a recession and high inflation or an unresolved foreign crisis for which a
president is blamed, even if erroneously. Experience in the job, then, is not a
political plus if a sitting president's record is considered weak or national conditions seem to have deteriorated under the incumbent's stewardship. The president may be held accountable by voters who cast their ballots *retrospectively*
rather than *prospectively;* in other words, these voters evaluate an administration's past performance rather than try to predict future performance.

Retrospective voting has been suggested as the major explanation for Carter's
defeat in 1980 and Bush's in 1992. To illustrate the problem, one can contrast

what many perceived as Carter's failure to resolve the hostage crisis in Iran with the respect that many believed the nation enjoyed after Reagan's first term. Bush's foreign policy success in the Persian Gulf War made his apparent inaction in dealing with the slowing economy all the more vivid. In the 1996 election, Clinton benefited from the conditions of peace and prosperity during his first term, but this record was not transferred to his chosen successor. Al Gore failed to highlight these accomplishments during the campaign as he tried to distance himself from Clinton in order to avoid association with the president's questionable personal conduct. In doing so, he also distanced himself from the administration's achievements.[72]

Presidential Debates. Voters have the opportunity to assess the issue positions and personal characteristics of presidential and vice presidential contenders during nationally televised debates. Debates, first staged in 1960, have been held each election year since 1976; they quickly became the most important and most widely watched campaign events. Candidates recognize the danger of making a mistake or committing an embarrassing gaffe on live television, a particular danger for incumbents. Ford misspoke in 1976, when he suggested that countries of Eastern Europe were not under Soviet domination; Reagan appeared to be confused and out of touch during his first debate with Mondale in 1984 but rallied in the second encounter. Challengers try to demonstrate their knowledge of issues and their presidential bearing to a nationwide audience. Kennedy in 1960, Reagan in 1980, and George W. Bush in 2000 seem to have benefited the most from debating a more experienced opponent, in part because they exceeded performance expectations and dispelled negative impressions. Most candidates prepare carefully prior to the meeting and follow a conservative game plan of reemphasizing themes already made prominent during the campaign. As a result, the exchanges often seem wooden rather than extemporaneous, an impression heightened by the cautious rules approved by the respective camps. Bush surprised many by holding his own in 2000, while Gore appeared both overaggressive and given to exaggerating his own accomplishments. Bush met a credibility threshold that was more important than scoring on debating points.

In 1992, the first three-way presidential debates in history included Ross Perot, who met the two party nominees in three different formats: questions posed by the traditional panel of journalists, by citizens at a town meeting, and by a single moderator. The formats allowed for greater interaction and extemporaneous exchange among the contestants rather than triggering the patented responses that have characterized so many of these meetings in the past. Perot did not get the same chance in 1996, nor did Pat Buchanan or Ralph Nader in 2000. The Commission on Presidential Debates, a joint venture sponsored by the Democratic and Republican Parties, concluded that these candidates could not win the election, and they were excluded from participating.

Single vice presidential debates were held in 1988, 1992, 1996, and 2000. Dan Quayle's performance was the focus of the first two encounters. Much younger than Lloyd Bentsen, his 1988 opponent, Quayle was repeatedly asked what he would do if forced to assume the duties of president. When Quayle compared himself to former president John F. Kennedy, Bentsen pounced with withering directness: "Senator, I served with Jack Kennedy. I knew Jack Kennedy. Jack Kennedy was a friend of mine. Senator, you're no Jack Kennedy." Quayle never recovered.[73] In 1992, Quayle debated Al Gore, the Democrat, and James Stockdale, Perot's running mate, who watched as his younger opponents struggled to dominate one another. Gore's encounter with Jack Kemp in 1996 previewed some of the problems he would experience in 2000. Gore was so focused on the campaign message that he appeared even more wooden than usual. The Cheney–Lieberman debate in 2000 was a more cordial and mature exchange than the presidential series, suggesting to some viewers that the vice presidential candidates should have been leading the tickets.

Televised debates enable even the least engaged citizen to develop an impression of the major party contenders. However, candidates have become more adept at staging, and the public may now expect more than just a polite exchange of policy challenges as candidates try to display assertiveness, empathy, humor, or "character."

Election Day

One of the ironies of U.S. presidential elections since 1960 is that, although more citizens have acquired the right to vote, a smaller proportion of them have exercised that right. As Table 2-4 indicates, the estimated number of people of voting age has more than doubled since Franklin Roosevelt was first elected in 1932. After reaching a peak in 1960, however, the percentage of people who voted declined in the next five presidential elections and resumed its decline in 1988 after a modest increase in 1984. Only 50.1 percent of the eligible voting age population went to the polls in 1988, a pattern that was unexpectedly reversed in 1992, when 55.2 percent of the eligible voters went to the polls.[74] But the resurgence was short-lived; only 49.1 percent of eligible voters showed up in 1996, the lowest turnout since 1924. There was an uptick in 2000 to 51.2 percent, a modest gain but at least movement in the desired direction.[75]

The decline in voter participation runs counter to most theories of why people do not vote. Laws pertaining to registration and voting, said to prevent citizens from going to the polls, have been eased in most states. Federal laws made it much easier for a person to register and to vote for president in 1996 than in 1960. A person's lack of education is often put forward as a reason for not voting, but the level of education of U.S. citizens rose as participation declined. Lack of political information is yet another frequently cited explanation, but more Americans than ever are aware of the candidates and their views on public issues, thanks to media coverage and the debates. Finally, close political races are supposed to stimulate people to get out and vote because they think their ballot will make a difference in the outcome. Pollsters predicted that the 1964 and 1972 elections would be landslides and that the 1968, 1976, and 1980 elections would

Table 2-4   Participation of General Public in Presidential Elections, 1932–2000

Year	Estimated population of voting age (in millions)	Number of votes cast (in millions)	Number of votes as percentage of population of voting age
1932	75.8	39.7	52.4
1936	80.2	45.6	56.0
1940	84.7	49.9	58.9
1944	85.7	48.0	56.0
1948	95.6	48.8	51.1
1952	99.9	61.6	61.6
1956	104.5	62.0	59.3
1960	109.7	68.8	62.8
1964	114.1	70.6	61.9
1968	120.3	73.2	60.9
1972[a]	140.8	77.6	55.1
1976[a]	152.3	81.6	53.6
1980[a]	164.6	86.5	52.6
1984[a]	174.5	92.7	53.1
1988[a]	182.8	91.6	50.1
1992[a]	189.0	104.4	55.2
1996[a]	196.5	96.46	49.1
2000[a]	205.8	105.4	51.2

Sources: U.S. Bureau of the Census, *Current Population Reports*, Series P-25, No. 1085 (Washington, D.C.: U.S. Government Printing Office, 1994). 1996 and 2000 data from Federal Election Commission Web site, www.fec.gov, and U.S. Census Bureau Web site, www. census.gov.

[a]Elections in which persons eighteen to twenty years old were eligible to vote in all states.

be close contests, but a smaller percentage of people voted in 1968 than in 1964, and participation also declined in 1976 and 1980 despite close contests. In 1984, there was a slight (0.5 percent) increase in participation, even though the outcome was hardly in doubt, while participation declined in 1988, a closer contest. From early in 1996, polls showed Clinton comfortably ahead, and many reports suggested voters expected the eventual outcome.

Why did voting decline in recent years, surge in 1992, decline again in 1996, and recover in 2000? Paul Abramson, John Aldrich, and David Rohde link the long-term decline to the erosion in political party identification and to lower political efficacy—the belief that citizens can influence what government does.[76] But these authors note that neither party identification nor political efficacy changed significantly in 1992 and 1996. There is evidence that Ross Perot's presence contributed to the 1992 turnout increase; 14 percent of Perot voters (which translates into nearly 3 million voters, a substantial portion of the increased turnout) indicated in exit polls that they would not have voted if the Texan had not been on the ballot. Neither major party made a concerted effort in 1992 to register new voters, although there were some nonpartisan turnout efforts, including MTV's "Rock the Vote" feature aimed at youth voters, the group with the lowest turnout rates. By 1996, the "Motor Voter" bill, which requires states to provide voter registration opportunities through driver's license agencies, among other public offices, had increased registration, and Democrats made a concerted effort to register newly naturalized citizens. Thus, we cannot be certain what caused the changes. It is important to note, however, that even the 1992 turnout was still well below that for 1960 and that neither of the long-term causes of the voting decline noted above has been reversed.[77]

Validation

Translating the popular vote into the official outcome is the final stage of the selection process, in which the electoral college produces the true winner. Until 2000, it had been more than a century since the constitutionally prescribed process failed to do so or produced a winner who was not also the "people's choice," though we had been dangerously close to such an electoral college *misfire* on a number of occasions.

Despite the separation of the presidential and the vice presidential balloting in 1804, three possible ways for a misfire to occur remain. First, the electoral college does not ensure that the candidate who receives the most popular votes wins the presidency: John Quincy Adams in 1824, Rutherford B. Hayes in 1876, and Benjamin Harrison in 1888 became president even though they finished second in total popular vote to their respective political opponents, Andrew Jackson, Samuel Tilden, and Grover Cleveland. For the first time in the twentieth century, the same thing happened in 2000, when Gore won a national plurality of 539,898 votes over Bush but lost in the electoral college.[78] This had nearly happened in 1976, when Ford would have won if some 9,000 voters in Hawaii and Ohio had cast different ballots.

Second, candidates may fail to win an electoral college majority, thereby throwing selection into the House of Representatives. This situation occurred in the elections of 1800, 1824, and 1876. In 1948, Harry S. Truman defeated Thomas Dewey by more than 2 million popular votes, but if some 12,000 people in California and Ohio had voted for Dewey rather than the president, the election would have been thrown into the House of Representatives. The same thing could have happened in 1960, 1968, and 2000 with the shift of a few thousand votes in close states.

The 1968 election illustrates a third danger of the electoral college system: an elector need not cast his or her ballot for the candidate who wins the plurality of votes in the elector's state. This problem of the *faithless elector* has occurred seven times in the twentieth century, most recently in 1988, when an elector from West Virginia cast her vote for Bentsen as president rather than Dukakis. It is not particularly dangerous when isolated electors refuse to follow the result of their state's popular vote, but the possibility of widespread desertion from the popular choice would be another matter.[79]

The electoral college as it operates today violates some of the major tenets of political equality that are central to our contemporary understanding of democracy. Each person's vote does not count equally: one's influence on the outcome depends on the political situation in one's state. For the many Americans who support a losing candidate, it is as though they had not voted at all, because under the general-ticket system all the electoral votes of a state go to the candidate who wins a plurality of its popular votes. Thus, although Perot received 19,741,048 votes, 18.9 percent of the total votes cast nationally in 1992, he won no electoral votes because he finished first in no states nor in any of the House districts in Maine and Nebraska. Citizens who live in populous, politically competitive states have a premium placed on their vote because they are in a position to affect how large blocs of electoral votes are cast. Similarly, permitting the House of Representatives, voting by states, to select the president of the United States is not consistent with the "one person, one vote" principle that has become a central tenet of modern American democracy.

Proposals to reform the electoral college system attempt to remove the possibility of system failures and uphold a more modern understanding of democracy. They range from the rather modest suggestion of prohibiting faithless electors— votes would be cast automatically—to scrapping the present system altogether and moving to direct popular election. Intermediate suggestions would nationalize the congressional district plan used in Maine and Nebraska, divide electoral votes proportionally between (or among) the contenders, or provide the popular vote winner with 100 bonus votes, enough to ensure his or her victory in the electoral college. No proposal is foolproof, and most have to develop the means to guard against new problems. Moreover, any change requires passage of a constitutional amendment by Congress, which is problematic because national legislators will calculate how the new system would affect their state's influence on the outcome (or affect their own chances to pursue the office) and vote accordingly.

Is the electoral college a constitutional anachronism that should no longer be preserved? In the aftermath of the 2000 election, attention once again focused on this eighteenth-century process, with many people stressing its inadequacies and others praising its genius. Defenders of the current system note that the most serious misfires occurred during periods of intense political divisiveness (for example, 1824 and 1876), when alternative selection systems would have been just as severely tested. Several of the close calls in the twentieth century, such as in 1948 and 1968, occurred when political parties were suffering serious internal divisions. An examination of the historical conditions surrounding the misfires shows that only 1888 and 2000 offer clear examples of a popular-vote winner who lost the general election.[80] If popular vote rules had been in place in 2000, the chaos would have been even more widespread since the results would have been challenged in many states with close outcomes, not just in Florida.

Defenders of the present system argue that far from having performed badly, the system has been remarkably successful in producing peaceful resolutions even in years of unusual turmoil. The system's virtues include the requirement that candidates not only receive sufficient popular support but also that support is sufficiently distributed geographically to enable the winner to govern. George W. Bush, for example, won thirty states in 2000, including eleven that had voted for Clinton in 1996. Even more significantly, because of Bush's strength in the South and the West, "[h]ad the 2000 presidential election been conducted using the new numbers [from the 2000 census] rather than the numbers based on the 1990 census Texas Governor George W. Bush would have defeated Vice President Al Gore by a more comfortable 278-260 margin."[81] Ethnic minority groups, it is argued, receive special leverage under the present system because they are concentrated in states with large electoral vote totals and receive attention because their support might make the difference between a candidate's winning all of the electoral votes or none of them. Finally, there is concern that a system of direct election would encourage the development of minor parties based on regional or ideological interests that might organize in hopes of denying any candidate a majority or winning plurality and thereby force a runoff. Two-party stability, it is suggested, would be threatened.[82]

Analysts of the American political system differ over the wisdom of retaining the present electoral system, and even the recent brush with electoral crisis did not produce a uniform response. Maintaining legitimacy is a widespread concern, but some people believe that is achieved through continuity while others believe it is achieved through adherence to popular control.

Transitions to Governing

For the individual and election team that prevail in this long, grueling process, victory requires a change in focus. Successful candidates suddenly realize that winning the election is the means to an end, not an end in itself. Making that transition is sometimes difficult. It involves putting together a team of political executives to staff the new administration as well as establishing a list of program and policy priorities. Much of this is accomplished during the transition, the period between election and inauguration. Many other tasks are tackled during the first six months of the new administration. Governing, however, offers a new set of problems. Frequently, the techniques that proved successful during the election are simply transferred over to help meet the new challenges, but such methods are seldom sufficient to ensure success. In the modern presidency, governing involves some of the same activities as getting elected, but the two are far from identical, a lesson that some incumbents are slow to learn.

The burning question for everyone is how effective will the president be in leading the nation. Presidents vary along a wide range of dimensions—abilities, interests, personality—even as the office exhibits certain commonalities over time. In chapter 4, we turn to the problem of understanding the ways that a president's personal characteristics influence performance in office, and subsequent chapters focus on presidents' political success. First, however, we examine their relationship with the public between elections, a relationship that has grown increasingly important in modern times. In chapter 11, we offer a case study of George W. Bush's assumption of power and his first hundred days in office.

NOTES

1. Besides George Washington, James Monroe is the only candidate to approach this distinction; he won all but one electoral college vote in 1820. *Guide to the Presidency,* 2d ed., vol. 2, ed. Michael Nelson (Washington, D.C.: Congressional Quarterly, 1996), 1638.

2. William Chambers, *Political Parties in a New Nation: The American Experience, 1776–1809* (New York: Oxford University Press, 1963), chap. 2.

3. In the early 1820s, the Republican Party became known as the Democratic-Republicans and in 1840 was officially designated as the Democratic Party. Paul David, Ralph Goldman, and Richard Bain, *The Politics of National Party Conventions* (New York: Vintage, 1964), chap. 3.

4. Joseph Charles, *The Origins of the American Party System* (New York: Harper Torch, 1956), 83–94.

5. Other constitutional amendments dealing with presidential selection have expanded participation (Amendments 15, 19, 24, 26), set the term of office (20, 22), or sought to cope with death or disability (20, 25).

6. David, Goldman, and Bain, *National Party Conventions,* 50. The National Republican Party was soon to give way to the Whigs, with many Whig supporters joining the Republican Party when it was formed in the 1850s (57–59).

7. Ibid., 61.

8. First-ballot convention decisions have been surprisingly prevalent. Through 2000, the two major parties selected their candidates on the first ballot at fifty-five of eighty-one conventions. Many of the multiballot conventions were held from 1840 to 1888, when sixteen of the twenty-two went past the first ballot. What distinguishes the post-1952 era is that *none* of the twenty-four conventions went past one ballot.

9. Richard C. Bain and Judith H. Parris, *Convention Decisions and Voting Records,* 2d ed. (Washington, D.C.: Brookings, 1973), 1–6.

10. Thirty-nine states and the District of Columbia held primaries for both parties and eight states held caucuses for both. Michigan and South Carolina held caucuses for the Democrats and a primary for the Republicans, while Virginia held a Republican primary and a Democratic caucus.

11. Naturalized citizens (such as former secretary of state Henry Kissinger, who was born in Germany) do not meet this requirement. There is some question whether persons born abroad of American citizens (one such is George Romney, former governor of Michigan and 1968 presidential contender, who was born of American parents in France) are also legally barred from the presidency by this stipulation.

12. Estimated by the author based on data from the U.S. Census Bureau. See especially Bureau of the Census, *The Foreign-Born Population in the United States* (Washington, D.C., March 2000), Figure 4.

13. John Aldrich, "Methods and Actors: The Relationship of Processes to Candidates," in *Presidential Selection,* ed. Alexander Heard and Michael Nelson (Durham: Duke University Press, 1987).

14. The two exceptions were Wendell Willkie, the president of a public utility company, who was nominated by the Republicans in 1940, and Dwight D. Eisenhower, a career military man and World War II hero, who became the successful GOP candidate in 1952.

15. Before Richard Nixon's selection in 1960, the last incumbent vice president to be nominated was Martin Van Buren in 1836.

16. Joseph A. Pika, "Bush, Quayle, and the New Vice Presidency," in *The Presidency and the Political System*, 3d ed., ed. Michael Nelson (Washington, D.C.: CQ Press, 1990). Also see Joseph A. Pika, "The Vice Presidency: New Opportunities, Old Constraints," in *The Presidency and the Political System*, 6th ed., ed. Michael Nelson (Washington, D.C.: CQ Press, 2000).

17. Ronald D. Elving, "The Senators' Lane to the Presidency," *Congressional Quarterly Weekly Report*, May 20, 1989, 1218.

18. For a statement of informal expectations from three decades ago, see Sidney Hyman, "Nine Tests for the Presidential Hopeful," *New York Times*, January 4, 1959, Sec. 5, 1–11.

19. Michael Nelson, "Who Vies for President?" in *Presidential Selection*, 144.

20. For example, Jesse Jackson finished third behind Walter Mondale and Gary Hart for the 1984 Democratic nomination and second for the 1988 nomination. Jackson was again mentioned prominently in 1995 as a possible nominee, as was Colin Powell, another African American.

21. Federal Election Commission Web site, www.fec.gov.

22. Harold W. Stanley, "The Nominations: Republican Doldrums, Democratic Revival," in *The Elections of 1996*, ed. Michael Nelson (Washington, D.C.: CQ Press, 1997), 22.

23. William G. Mayer, "The Presidential Nominations," in *The Election of 2000*, ed. Gerald M. Pomper (New York: Chatham House, 2001), 20.

24. Austin Ranney, "Changing the Rules of the Nominating Game," in *Choosing the President*, ed. James David Barber (Englewood Cliffs, N.J.: Prentice-Hall, 1974), 71.

25. Arthur Hadley, *The Invisible Primary* (Englewood Cliffs, N.J.: Prentice-Hall, 1976). For a valuable update see Emmett H. Buell Jr., "The Invisible Primary," in *In Pursuit of the White House*, ed. William G. Mayer (Chatham, N.J.: Chatham House, 1996).

26. Anthony Corrado, "Financing the 2000 Elections," in *The Election of 2000*, 98.

27. Normally about 30 percent of the prenomination funding comes from public sources. Individuals are limited to contributions of $1,000 to a presidential candidate for each election (the nomination and general election are considered separate contests), $5,000 to a political action committee (a group that contributes to more than one candidate), $20,000 to the national committee of a political party, and a total contribution of no more than $25,000 a year. Presidential candidates are free to spend an unlimited amount of their own and their immediate family's money on their campaigns, but if they accept public financing, their contributions to their own campaigns are limited to $50,000 per election.

28. This constituted only 17 percent of the prenomination funding, largely the product of efforts by George W. Bush and Steve Forbes to operate free of spending limits. Anthony Corrado, "Financing the 2000 Elections," in *The Election of 2000*, 97.

29. *FEC Record*, 26:4 (Washington, D.C., April 2000), 10.

30. Anthony Corrado, "Financing the 1996 Elections," in *The Election of 1996*, ed. Gerald M. Pomper (Chatham, N.J.: Chatham House, 1997).

31. Corrado, "Financing the 2000 Elections," 98.

32. Not all individual contributions are small, and it is legal for political action committees to help finance nomination campaigns, but their contributions are not matched by federal funds as in the case of individuals. Vice President Bush, for example, received $1,000 contributions (the maximum) from 16,500 individuals in 1988 for a total of $16.5 million. Cumulatively, PACs contributed $3.114 million during the 1988 prenomination campaign, but that sum represented only 1.4 percent of total funding. Herbert E. Alexander and Monica Bauer, *Financing the 1988 Election* (Boulder: Westview, 1991), 23, 25.

33. Bush raised $18.7 million in 1988 to Dole's $14.0 million and Pat Robertson's $14.0 million. Dukakis raised $10.6 million, with Richard Gephardt ($4.4 million), Al Gore ($3.8 million), and Paul Simon ($3.8 million) trailing badly. Alexander and Bauer, *Financing the 1988 Election*, 20.

34. Richard Berke, "In G.O.P. Presidential Field, a Race to Raise Money Is On," *New York Times*, February 2, 1995, 1.

35. The exceptions were that George McGovern defeated front-runner Edmund Muskie (1972), Jimmy Carter surpassed Hubert Humphrey (1976), Michael Dukakis bested the early leader Gary Hart (1988), and Bill Clinton came from far behind to win in 1992.

36. In 1984, the minimum was 20 percent, a rule that favored the front-runner, Walter Mondale. Complaints from the defeated candidates Jesse Jackson and Gary Hart resulted in lowering the qualifying level to 15 percent for the 1988 contest, and that rule was continued in 1992, 1996, and 2000. Most Republican contests have been conducted under "winner take all" rules, although some states use proportional rules for both parties.

37. Alan Greenblatt and Rhodes Cook, "Nominating Process Rules Change," *Congressional Quarterly Weekly Report*, August 17, 1996, 2299. For the 2000 election, see Andrew E. Busch, "New Features of the 2000 Presidential Nominating Process: Republican Reforms, Front-Loading's Second Wind, and Early Voting," in *In Pursuit of the White House 2000*, ed. William G. Mayer (New York: Chatham House, 2001).

38. Marjorie Randon Hershey, "The Campaign and the Media," in *The Election of 2000*, 47.

39. C. Anthony Broh, *A Horse of a Different Color: Television's Treatment of Jesse Jackson's 1984 Presidential Campaign* (Washington, D.C.: Joint Center for Political Studies, 1987), 4.

40. For discussion of the primary contests in 2000 and election results, see William G. Mayer, "The Presidential Nominations," in *The Election of 2000*.

41. Broh, *A Horse of a Different Color*, 44.

42. Exceptions to this pattern can be found when two candidates end the preconvention period fairly even, which Ford and Reagan did in 1976, McGovern and Humphrey did in 1972, and Mondale and Hart did in 1984; in each case, however, the preconvention leader took the nomination.

43. Judith Parris, *The Convention Problem: Issues in Reform of Presidential Nominating Procedures* (Washington, D.C.: Brookings, 1972), 110.

44. Edwin Diamond, Gregg Geller, and Chris Whitley, "Air Wars: Conventions Go Cable," *National Journal*, August 31, 1996, 1859.

45. *FEC Record* 26:4 (Washington, D.C., April 2000), 10. Nominees receiving full funding may accept other direct contributions only to meet legal and accounting fees. So George W. Bush's enormous fund-raising advantage during the prenomination phase in 1999–2000 could not be repeated for the general election phase.

46. Alexander and Bauer, *Financing the 1988 Election*, Table 2-1. Herbert Alexander and Anthony Corrado, *Financing the 1992 Election* (Boulder: Westview, 1995), chap. 5, Table 5-1; Federal Election Commission, *The Presidential Public Funding Program* (Washington, D.C., 1993), 31.

47. Corrado, "Financing the 2000 Elections," 107.

48. Ibid., 109.

49. Although presidential candidates are free to refuse public funds, no major party nominee has done so in the general election, perhaps because the maximum contribution limitations have made raising money from individuals and groups more difficult. Candidates may also think the public favors the use of public rather than private funds.

50. The Twenty-third Amendment, ratified in 1961, gave the District of Columbia the right to participate in presidential elections. Previously, District residents were excluded. Their inclusion accounts for there being three more electoral votes (538) than the total number of senators and representatives (535).

51. For election results and a brief account of the events surrounding the Florida outcome, see Pomper, "The Presidential Election," in *The Election of 2000*, 125–135. For an in-depth journalistic account of the Florida situation, see *Deadlock: The Inside Story of America's Closest Election*, comp. Political Staff of the *Washington Post* (New York: Public Affairs, 2001).

52. Reapportionment was complex following the 1990 census. Because of widespread criticism, the Census Bureau agreed to conduct a post-census survey to determine the extent to which some population groups had been undercounted. The results of that study would have called for further changes in congressional representation. However, the secretary of commerce recommended following the initial census findings rather than the adjusted figures. A similar debate followed the 2000 census, and Utah filed suit to have its residents serving as missionaries abroad included in the count, which would give it the additional seat awarded to North Carolina. For a valuable source on reapportionment, see www.electiondataservices.com.

53. Dukakis won electoral votes from the District of Columbia and ten states in 1988: Hawaii, Iowa, Massachusetts, Minnesota, New York, Oregon, Rhode Island, Washington, West Virginia, and Wisconsin. He won 45 percent or more of the vote in California, Colorado, Connecticut, Illinois, Maryland, Michigan, Missouri, Montana, New Mexico, Pennsylvania, South Dakota, and Vermont. Of these states, only South Dakota did not support Clinton in 1992. That year, Clinton won only four southern states plus Kentucky and trailed Bush in the region's popular vote as well.

54. Gore lost New Hampshire by 7,300 votes, while Nader garnered 22,200. Nader also received 97,500 votes in Florida, thousands more than Gore needed for victory. Pomper, "The Presidential Election," in *The Election of 2000*, 134, Table 6-1.

55. Angus Campbell et al., *The American Voter*, abr. ed. (New York: Wiley, 1964).

56. Figures for the 2000 election were unavailable at the time of writing this edition but will be posted on the National Election Studies Web site, www.icpsr.umich.edu.

57. Lydia Saad, "Independents Rank as Largest U.S. Political Group," April 9, 1999, www.gallup.com/poll/releases.

58. Gerald M. Pomper, "The Presidential Election," in *The Elections of 1988: Reports and Interpretations*, ed. Gerald M. Pomper (Chatham, N.J.: Chatham House, 1989), 136.

59. Offsetting gains in nonwhite voting, white fundamentalist Christians have gained significance in national politics. This group has become solidly Republican and in 1988 composed nearly as large a proportion of the voting population as blacks (9 percent versus 10 percent). See poll results reported in Pomper, "The Presidential Election," in *The Election of 1996: Reports and Interpretations*, ed. Gerald M. Pomper (Chatham, N.J.: Chatham House, 1997), 134.

60. Pomper, "The Presidential Election," in *The Election of 2000*, 137. The reported data are based on exit polls rather than the final Gallup survey.

61. J. Merrill Shanks and Warren Miller, "Policy Direction and Performance Evaluation: Complementary Explanations of the Reagan Elections" (paper delivered at the annual meeting of the American Political Science Association, New Orleans, Aug. 29–September 1, 1985), 60, 69.

62. Pomper, "The Presidential Election," in *The Election of 1988*, 143. The results of this CNN/*Los Angeles Times* poll also can be found in *National Journal*, November 12, 1988, 2854.

63. Voter Research and Surveys exit polls as reported in Paul J. Quirk and Jon K.

Dallager, "The Election: A 'New Democrat' and a New Kind of Presidential Campaign," in *The Elections of 1992,* ed. Michael Nelson (Washington, D.C.: CQ Press, 1993), 81.

64. Exit poll conducted by Voter News Service and reported in Michael Nelson, "The Election: Turbulence and Tranquility in Contemporary American Politics," in *The Elections of 1996,* ed. Nelson, 57.

65. Pomper, "The Presidential Election," in *The Election of 2000,* 146.

66. Marjorie Randon Hershey, "The Campaign and the Media," in *The Elections of 1988,* 78.

67. Ibid., 80–83; Paul J. Quirk, "The Election," in *The Elections of 1988,* 76.

68. Nelson, "The Election: Turbulence and Tranquillity," 58. Marion R. Just, "Candidate Strategies and the Media Campaign," in *The Elections of 1988,* 91–96.

69. Campbell et al., *The American Voter,* chap. 7.

70. For 1960s data, see Gerald Pomper, *Voters' Choice: Varieties of American Electoral Behavior* (New York: Dodd, Mead, 1975), chap. 8. For 1970s data, see Norman Nie, Sidney Verba, and John Petrocik, *The Changing American Voter* (Cambridge: Harvard University Press, 1979), chap. 7.

71. Pomper, "The Presidential Election," in *The Election of 2000,* 146.

72. Ibid., p. 142.

73. See the transcript of this debate and others at www.pbs.org/newshour/debatingourdestiny.

74. The 1992 turnout represented an increase of about 13 million voters over the 1988 total. Twenty-three candidates shared the votes, although only four—Bush, Clinton, Perot, and the Libertarian Party candidate, Andre Marrou—were on ballots in all fifty states. Federal Election Commission, press release, January 14, 1993.

75. The FEC Web site reports 105.405 million votes were cast in the presidential election. The voting age population in 2000 was estimated by the Bureau of the Census at 205.814 million. U.S. Census Bureau, Public Information Office, press release, March 14, 2001. The resulting calculation is 51.21 percent turnout. This was also the figure reported by the Committee for the Study of the American Electorate.

76. Paul R. Abramson, John H. Aldrich, and David W. Rohde, *Change and Continuity in the 1980 Elections* (Washington, D.C.: CQ Press, 1982), chap. 4.

77. Paul R. Abramson, John H. Aldrich, and David W. Rohde, *Change and Continuity in the 1992 Elections* (Washington, D.C.: CQ Press, 1994), 120.

78. Pomper, "The Presidential Election," in *The Election of 2000,* 134, Table 6-1.

79. In 1960, 1968, 1972, 1976, and 1988, single electors in Oklahoma, North Carolina, Virginia, Washington, and West Virginia failed to cast their ballots for the candidate receiving the popular vote plurality in their state. For complete results of electoral college voting, see Nelson, ed., *Guide to the Presidency,* 1634–1658; see 1634 for a list of faithless electors.

80. Kimberling, "Electing the President," 16.

81. Sean Scully, *The Washington Times* December 29, 2000, A12. Gore carried all but two of the states that lost House seats, and Bush won all of the states that stood to gain seats except California.

82. Ibid., 19–20.

SUGGESTED READINGS

Abramson, Paul R., John H. Aldrich, and David W. Rohde. *Change and Continuity in the 1980 Elections.* Washington, D.C.: CQ Press, 1982.

___. *Change and Continuity in the 1984 Elections.* Washington, D.C.: CQ Press, 1986.

___. *Change and Continuity in the 1988 Elections.* Washington, D.C.: CQ Press, 1990.

___. *Change and Continuity in the 1992 Elections.* Washington, D.C.: CQ Press, 1994.

___. *Change and Continuity in the 1992 Elections, Revised Edition.* Washington, D.C.: CQ Press, 1995.

___. *Change and Continuity in the 1996 Elections.* Washington, D.C.: CQ Press, 1998.

___. *Change and Continuity in the 1996 and 1998 Elections.* Washington, D.C.: CQ Press, 1999.

Alexander, Herbert E., and Anthony Corrado. *Financing the 1992 Election.* Boulder, Colo.: Westview, 1995.

Bartels, Larry M. *Presidential Primaries and the Dynamics of Public Choice.* Princeton: Princeton University Press, 1988.

Campbell, Angus, Philip Converse, Warren Miller, and Donald Stokes. *The American Voter,* abr. ed. New York: Wiley, 1964.

Heard, Alexander, and Michael Nelson, eds. *Presidential Selection.* Durham: Duke University Press, 1987.

Mayer, William B., ed. *In Pursuit of the White House: How We Choose Our Presidential Nominees.* Chatham, N.J.: Chatham House, 1996.

___. *In Pursuit of the White House, 2000: How We Choose Our Presidential Nominees.* Chatham, N.J.: Chatham House, 1999.

Nelson, Michael, ed.*The Elections of 1996.* Washington, D.C.: CQ Press, 1997.

___. *The Elections of 2000.* Washington, D.C.: CQ Press, 2001.

Pomper, Gerald M., ed. *The Election of 1996: Reports and Interpretations.* Chatham, N.J.: Chatham House, 1997.

___. *The Election of 2000: Reports and Interpretations.* Chatham, N.J.: Chatham House, 2001.

Rose, Gary L., ed. *Controversial Issues in Presidential Selection.* 2d ed. Albany: State University of New York Press, 1994.

Shafer, Byron E. *Quiet Revolution: The Struggle for the Democratic Party and the Shaping of Post-Reform Politics.* New York: Russell Sage Foundation, 1983.

Wayne, Stephen J. *The Road to the White House 1996: The Politics of Presidential Elections.* New York: St. Martin's Press, 1997.

___. *The Road to the White House, 2000, The Post-Election Edition: The Politics of Presidential Elections.* Boston: Bedford, 2001.

3 PUBLIC POLITICS

Woodrow Wilson throws out the first ball on opening day of the baseball season in 1916. Wilson helped to usher in the modern public presidency.

FOR MORE THAN A CENTURY, STUDENTS OF the presidency have argued that the chief executive's continuing relationship with the American public is a major factor in governing the nation. Writing in 1900, Henry Jones Ford concluded that only presidents can "define issues in such a way that public opinion can pass upon them decisively."[1] Woodrow Wilson, anticipating his own approach to the office, echoed that sentiment: "His [the president's] is the only national voice in affairs. Let him once win the admiration and confidence of the country and no other single force can withstand him; no combination of forces will easily overpower him."[2]

As discussed in chapter 1, this preeminent position was strengthened during the last half of the twentieth century. In 1960, Richard Neustadt explained how the presidents' "public prestige" (their "standing with the public outside Washington") influences the decisions of other government officials and nongovernmental elites, such as members of Congress, the bureaucracy, state governors, military commanders, party politicians, journalists, and foreign diplomats.[3] By the mid-1980s, Samuel Kernell argued that "going public"—issuing campaignlike appeals for citizen support—rather than the traditional strategy of bargaining with other elites, had become the key to presidential success in the modern era.[4] For the past few decades, the most powerful tool for going public has been television. Kernell and Matthew A. Baum suggested in 1999, however, that the rise of cable television has made such appeals more difficult: hundreds of channels of alternate programming mean that presidents are losing the captive audiences that they used to command when all three major networks preempted their regular schedules to carry presidential appearances.[5] No matter the means or the difficulty involved, presidents cannot afford to stop courting voters after the returns are in on election day; modern chief executives must woo the American public between elections just as they do during elections.

Despite a president's best efforts, maintaining public support is often a difficult task. Approval ratings can change quickly and can be influenced by the state of the economy and crises abroad—events that are sometimes unrelated to specific presidential action. George W. Bush's shot up 35 points in one week after terrorist attacks on the World Trade Center and the Pentagon. But George H.W. Bush enjoyed a similarly high 89% approval rating during the Persian Gulf War, only to have it dwindle to 32%—largely because of a faltering economy. After defeating Bush in 1992, Bill Clinton failed to generate high levels of public support during his first three years as chief executive but left office in 2001 with the highest approval rating of any departing president since the advent of public opinion polls.[6] Even in the face of impeachment, Clinton had maintained high job approval ratings—a factor that some attributed to the strong economy, and one that may have aided his acquittal in the Senate.[7] Interestingly, Clinton's high approval ratings did not help his vice president, Al Gore, secure electoral victory in the 2000 presidential election. Indeed, political scientist Charles O. Jones has argued that Clinton's efforts to boost his own popularity may actually have hurt Gore.[8]

This chapter begins with an analysis of enduring public attitudes toward the presidency and then considers the ways chief executives try to hold the support of the American people. This includes the use of public appeals, targeted communications to interest groups and party activists, and efforts to use the media to the president's advantage. We conclude the chapter by arguing that these tactics have helped to create a "permanent campaign" that is waged by presidents between elections.

Public Attitudes Toward the Presidency

Citizens relate to the presidency on many levels. At the conscious level, people develop attitudes toward three major components of a political system: the political community of which they are a part; the regime, or formal and informal "rules of the game" followed in the constitutional system; and the authorities, or public officials who hold positions in the government structure.[9] If these attitudes are sufficiently strong and positive, the public may follow its leaders even if it does not like a particular incumbent or the policies that leader advocates.

The president, it can be argued, is the focus of public attitudes in each of these three areas. Like the British monarch, the U.S. chief executive is the symbol of the nation, a personification of government capable of inspiring feelings of loyalty and patriotism, particularly in times of crisis when the leader becomes the rallying point for national efforts. For example, Franklin D. Roosevelt's political friends and foes alike turned to him for leadership when the Japanese attacked Pearl Harbor in December 1941. The same support arose when Ronald Reagan decided to invade the Caribbean island of Grenada in 1983 and Bill Clinton directed that cruise missiles strike Iraq in 1993. Calls to support the president quickly drown out critical voices.

Because presidents are central figures in the constitutional system, they can benefit from upholding the accepted rules of the game or suffer from violating them. Many Americans felt that Richard Nixon violated his constitutional obligations as well as basic democratic values by placing himself above the law during the Watergate scandal; evidence indicated that he participated in a cover-up designed to hide the truth about an illegal break-in directed by White House aides. The Monica Lewinsky scandal, however, showed that many Americans seemed to make a distinction between the types of abuses of power that Nixon engaged in and Clinton's efforts to cover up a sexual affair with Lewinsky. Most viewed Clinton's affair as a private matter that had nothing to do with his job as president.[10] On the other hand, his pardon, on the last day of his presidency, of fugitive financier Marc Rich caused a furor that may do more long-lasting damage to Clinton's image.[11]

Finally, presidents are major actors in the policymaking process; the positions they adopt elicit support or opposition, and their overall performance in office becomes the object of citizens' evaluations. Again, Clinton showed that Americans could make a distinction between job performance and personal approval. On leaving office in January 2001, a Gallup poll (taken before the Rich pardon) showed a 65 percent job approval rating but only a 41 percent personal approval rating. An earlier, April 2000, Gallup poll was even more striking: 59 percent job approval but only 29 percent personal approval.

Fred Greenstein has suggested that presidents meet a variety of psychological needs of the citizenry. As a *cognitive aid,* the president can make government and politics comprehensible; by focusing on the president's activities, citizens simplify a distant and complex world. The president also provides an *outlet for feelings* experienced by supporters and opponents, giving citizens the opportunity to develop and express emotions about politics. On the subconscious level, some citizens may seek *vicarious participation,* a desire to identify with a powerful political figure much as people do with fictional figures and entertainment personalities. Presidents symbolize *national unity* as well as *stability* and *predictability,* providing citizens with psychologically satisfying feelings that may meet fundamental needs for membership and reassurance. Finally, presidents serve as a *lightning rod* within the political system, figures to blame for bad times and to credit for good times.[12] Because presidents play a central role in the nightly dramas communicated on television news—not to mention the round-the-clock cable news outlets such as CNN, Fox News, and MSNBC—their importance as objects of psychological feelings may be greater today than ever before.

Beyond basic beliefs and psychological needs, the public also has views about the day-to-day operation of the political system—in particular, the major issues of the day and the policies the government should follow in dealing with them. These views, which are generally assumed to be less stable and enduring than beliefs about the political culture, are often described as matters of "public opinion." A citizen's attitudes on policy issues and presidential performance depend on his or her identity with a particular group, such as a political party, and his or her social, economic, and geographical background. As the nation's leading political figure, the president is expected to develop and help put into effect controversial policies that are binding on the entire populace. People respond favorably or unfavorably to each chief executive's particular personality and political style and to the events that occur while a president is in office. People also assess presidents by the way they relate to particular groups—political parties as well as social (religious, ethnic, racial), economic (business, labor), and geographical divisions of the population.

Thus, many diverse factors affect public opinion of the president. At times, people see the chief executive as the embodiment of the nation; on other occasions people link the president with a particular issue or policy they favor or oppose. After examining the symbolic importance accorded the presidency, we turn to political socialization and how people develop their attitudes toward the presidency. We then look more closely at public opinion polls.

Symbolic Dimensions of the Presidency

The Ronald Reagan Presidential Library opened on November 4, 1991, a day marked by speeches from five presidents (Nixon, Ford, Carter, Reagan, and Bush—the largest number of former and current chief executives alive at the same time since 1861) and appearances by six first ladies (including Lady Bird Johnson) as well as offspring of Franklin D. Roosevelt and John F. Kennedy. It was perhaps the largest assemblage of presidents and presidential families in history.[13] The library, located in Simi Valley, California, cost $60 million to construct and devotes 22,000 of its 153,000 square feet to exhibits commemorating the Reagan years. Every president since Herbert Hoover has had a library erected in his name to house the papers of his administration and his pre-presidential career, explain his record to the public, and define his legacy to the nation. President Clinton's will be in Little Rock, Arkansas, and may be open to the public as early as 2003. It will contain nearly 80 million pages of documents, 9 million photographs, and 75,000 artifacts—more material than has been collected for any other presidential library. (For a National Archives Web site offering an overview of the presidential library system and links to each of the individual libraries, go to www.nara.gov/nara/president/address.html.) All presidential libraries combine commemoration with facilities for research. Most visitors choose only to view relics from a president's life, items drawn from childhood through retirement, and to reexperience personal memories and moments of drama through museum-like displays, many of which are interactive.

The presidential libraries, therefore, have a significance that extends beyond their ostensible purposes. In many respects, they can be viewed as shrines constructed to commemorate the lives and achievements of the most recent heroes in the nation's collective memory, a veritable presidential pantheon whose most sacred shrines, the Washington Monument and Lincoln Memorial, are located in Washington, D.C. Presidents stand at the center of what might be termed an "American mythology," a collection of stories and interpretations loosely linked to historical events but serving larger purposes in our collective experience: to celebrate basic values held in common, extol national virtues, and maintain unity in the face of enormous national diversity. In addition to the commemorative sites, Americans have created national holidays, public rituals, and icons, as well as a collection of stories, some of them apocryphal, which are passed on to our children. All attest to the presidency's symbolic importance.

Ceremony and pomp surround the presidency, another indication of the importance of the office in national life. A presidential inauguration resembles the coronation of a king, complete with the taking of an oath in the presence of notables and "the hailing by the multitudes."[14] Public appearances are accompanied by a display of the special presidential seal and the playing of "Hail to the Chief" as the president arrives. News conferences are conducted under a set of rules designed to communicate deference and respect as much as elicit hard news.

Particular occasions have been elevated to ritualistic status. The State of the Union message, for example, allows the president to outline an agenda for Congress and the nation. Woodrow Wilson resurrected this ceremony after a century of disuse; today it is an annual occasion for high drama and solemn pronouncements aimed as much at the prime-time television audience as the political elites in attendance. Members of Congress, the cabinet, and the diplomatic corps as well as distinguished visitors gather in the House chamber and chatter expectantly until the sergeant-at-arms solemnly announces the president's arrival, at which point the audience respectfully rises to its feet and applauds. Following a formal introduction from the Speaker of the House, there is another standing ovation. After the speech, a phalanx of congressional leaders accompanies the president as he leaves the hall, and members reach out along the way to shake hands or just to touch the presidential person.

These outward manifestations of respect, made part of recurrent governing rituals, indicate the near reverence accorded the position of president. Respect for the *presidency* as distinct from the *president*, the current officeholder, is deeply ingrained in American political culture. George Washington and his advisers gave the office dignity by enhancing its ceremonial functions and designing a set of "republican rituals" for which no direct precedents existed, based on their exclusive experience with monarchy.[15] But Washington's major contribution to the presidency was to imbue the office with nearly mythical stature. At one time, Washington's likeness was so widely displayed that it became a virtual icon, the picture of a venerated saint displayed by fervent believers in hopes of deriving blessings.[16] The hero worship lavished on Washington during his lifetime and the subsequent cult that developed in commemorating his service to the nation ensured that the presidency will always be associated with the nation's own sense of moral virtue and collective destiny.[17]

In the late nineteenth century, Washington's birthday became a day of national celebration second only to the Fourth of July. In many states, Abraham Lincoln's birthday, too, came to be celebrated as a holiday. Eventually, the two were combined into Presidents' Day. Every February, American schoolchildren are taught stories about these presidents whose youthful endeavors illustrate the fundamental virtues of truthfulness ("Father, I cannot tell a lie"), honesty (walking miles to return change), and hard work (wilderness surveyor and rail-splitter). In like ways, we celebrate the lives of Washington's successors, but we also expect them to live up to the heroic qualities of their predecessors during service in this most sacred of America's political positions.

Consistent with this symbolic role, the nation routinely turns to the president to perform a variety of ceremonial chores, many of which are minor, such as lighting the national Christmas tree and issuing proclamations on the observance of special days. But Americans also call upon presidents to perform more important symbolic tasks, such as helping citizens deal with their collective grief when disaster strikes. For example, President Bush expressed the feelings of millions when he publicly mourned the thousands of deaths caused by the terrorist attacks on September 11, 2001, and President Clinton provided solace and reassurance in the face of sudden, inexplicable death after the bombing of the federal building in Oklahoma City on April 19, 1995.

The presidency, more than any other aspect of political life, links Americans with both the past and the future. In focusing on the current White House occupant, citizens simultaneously derive a sense of fulfillment from past accomplishments and reassurance about the future. Presidents often help to evoke such feelings of continuity through symbolism. When President Clinton gave his farewell address on January 18, 2001, he was flanked with busts of Abraham Lincoln and Franklin D. Roosevelt. When George W. Bush took the oath of office two days later, he used the same 1767 Bible used in the inauguration ceremonies of George Washington, Warren Harding, Dwight D. Eisenhower, Jimmy Carter, and his father, George Bush. As the newest chief executive gave his inaugural address, former presidents Carter, Bush, and Clinton sat behind him. (Gerald Ford, who had suffered a minor stroke the previous summer, did not attend.)

Barbara Hinckley has argued that presidents and their speechwriters are highly attuned to the public's expectations of a chief executive. In turn, the White House projects "a symbolic presentation of the presidential office" expressed through the chief executive's public actions and statements.[18] Her study (tracing the Truman through Reagan administrations) showed that, with remarkable consistency, the picture portrayed to the public emphasized several common themes: The president, the American people, and the nation were presented as indistinguishable from each other and as together carrying out most of the work of "government"; Congress, when mentioned, was usually dismissed rather than recognized as an equal branch of government; identifiable population groups were pictured as sharing in the larger purposes that unite the nation; political and electoral activity was far less prominent in presidential discourse than references to religious objects such as God and the Bible; presidents were presented as being without peers and enjoying a unique relationship with the public.[19]

As Hinckley suggested, there is always the possibility that the public might be able to reshape the presidency and its position in the constitutional order by altering expectations of the office and its occupants. After the Democrats' humiliating defeat in the 1994 midterm elections, for example, it looked as though Congress might be able to assert itself as a prime force through the Republicans' "Contract with America." Although House Speaker Newt Gingrich, R-Ga.—the chief architect of the contract and the leader of the "Republican revolution"— dominated the headlines during his first hundred days as Speaker, he quickly lost his momentum.[20] Then, in the famous budget battle of 1995–1996, President Clinton reasserted himself. Republicans called for sharp budget cuts that would affect major entitlement programs such as Medicaid, Medicare, and Social Security. Clinton called such cuts irresponsible and rallied the opposition to the Republican plan. Deadlock over the budget led to government shutdowns in November 1995 and again in December and January 1996. The public blamed the Republicans for the shutdowns by a margin of two to one, and Clinton emerged victorious from the budget battle. One poll showed Gingrich's approval rating plummeting to 25 percent, while Clinton's had risen to 52 percent. Had Congress won instead, the stage might have been set for a more long-term shift in the balance of power between Congress and the president—one that might have undermined the president's symbolic position as the nation's leader.

Such a scenario, though, is very unlikely. Even if Congress had won, it is hard to imagine the presidency itself being displaced from its preeminent position—at least for long. Individual presidents may face periods of weakness and defeat, but the power of the presidency itself endures. As we have seen, enormous pressures for continuity have developed around the presidential office. Even in the wake of the Clinton scandals, expectation of heroic performance and belief in the identity between presidents and the nation are attitudes that are deeply embedded in the political culture. Collectively, these beliefs about the presidency provide the incumbent with a remarkably durable base of popular support.

Developing Attitudes Toward the Presidency

Not surprisingly, the president is the public official most likely to be correctly identified in surveys. Traditionally, presidents have also enjoyed general respect

and admiration. In Gallup polls asking Americans to name the man, living anywhere in the world, whom they most admire, the president of the United States
has almost always been the first choice.[21] Neither Whitewater nor Monica
Lewinsky managed to topple President Clinton from the top of that list: he
remained the most admired man in the world in every Gallup poll from 1993
through 2000 (although he tied with Pope John Paul II in 2000, a year when
there was relatively little consensus among Americans about what man they
most admired). Similarly, Hillary Clinton—like most first ladies—topped the poll
of most admired women every year of her husband's presidency.

Often, favorable attitudes are expressed toward the "generalized abstract"
president rather than toward any specific incumbent.[22] The initial basis for these
attitudes is formed in childhood through a process social scientists call "political
socialization." Political scientist Paul Beck has argued that there are three conditions necessary for an "agent" of political socialization (such as an individual or
an institution) to shape one's attitudes: exposure, communication, and receptiv-
ity. In other words, one cannot be influenced unless one is exposed to that agent,
unless one actually receives communication from that agent, and unless one is
receptive to that agent's views. Parents are the most important agent of socialization for young children. School is another significant agent. As children get older,
peers become more important in shaping attitudes.[23] So, too, do the media.

Early work on the development of childhood attitudes toward the president
showed that children viewed the president as both powerful and benevolent.[24]
In the *cognitive* (knowing) world of the young child, the president personified the
government. Until they were teenagers, most children were not even aware that
the president shared the running of government with Congress and the Supreme
Court. In addition to children's awareness of the president's importance, these
studies also underscored the *affective* (emotional) dimension of children's attitudes toward the president. Thus, they thought of the president as a "good" person who cares about people, wants to help them, and wants to "get things done."

There are several explanations for why young children developed these
favorable attitudes about the president. Parents who viewed the president favorably might have passed on these views to their children; those who did not,
might have suppressed their unfavorable views for fear of undermining the
child's respect for authority. Children's favorable attitudes toward other authority figures, such as teachers, might also have carried over into their respect for
the president.[25] Yet another explanation for children's favorable views emphasized their vulnerability: they wanted to believe the president is a good person
who will protect rather than threaten them.

Other research, however, found that not everyone experienced the same
socialization. Poor children in Kentucky were found to be much less favorably
disposed toward the president, regarding him as less honest, less hard working,
less caring, and less knowledgeable than had the urban middle-class children of
previous studies.[26] Nearly a quarter of these children viewed the president as a
malevolent rather than a benevolent leader. Moreover, after revelations of the

Watergate scandal in the early 1970s, a study of middle-class children found that they were less likely to idealize the chief executive than were their earlier counterparts; nor did they assign the president as important a role in running the country or making the laws.[27] Within just a few months of President Nixon's resignation, however, these views began to moderate.[28] Indeed, evidence suggests that children are able to distinguish between the person temporarily occupying the office and the presidency itself. They therefore can respect the institution without respecting the incumbent, an attitude that can carry over into their adult years and provide a solid basis of support for the U.S. political system.

Political scientists have continued to study childhood socialization,[29] although recent studies have not tended to focus on the specific question of childhood attitudes toward the president. However, a CNN–Gallup poll of children ages eleven to seventeen conducted February 4–9, 1999 (during the impeachment trial of President Clinton), sheds interesting light on the question. The poll showed that children had a considerably lower opinion of the president than did adults surveyed at the same time. Although 65 percent of the adults approved of Clinton's handling of his job, only 42 percent of the children did. Even more striking, when the children were given a list and asked, "Please tell me whether each of the following are people you, personally, look up to as role models in your life," in last place was "The President" (at 34 percent), behind "Your parents" (94 percent), "Your teachers" (77 percent), "Your friends" (72 percent), "Sports stars" (65 percent), "Music, TV and movie stars" (61 percent), and "Other elected officials" (41 percent). When asked more specifically, 65 percent of the children stated that they did *not* look up to "The President." Only 26 percent of the children said that they would like to grow up to be president of the United States someday, and only 45 percent of adults said that they would like for their children to grow up to be president.

Tracking Public Opinion

Since the end of World War II, the Gallup organization periodically has polled a cross section of Americans on whether they approve or disapprove of the way the president is handling the job. The emphasis of the question is on performance in office rather than personal qualities, a virtual "continuing monthly referendum" on how the president is handling the job.[30] Up-to-date results of these polls can be accessed online at www.gallup.com. In recent years, many other organizations have also conducted polls, including ones measuring presidential approval ratings. These, too, can be accessed online by going to www.govspot.com and clicking on "Polls/Opinion."

Independent pollsters are not the only ones keeping a finger on the pulse of public opinion: every president since Richard Nixon has retained his own polling consultants.[31] These White House pollsters go far beyond simple tracking of presidential approval. As political scientist Diane Heath has written, presidential pollsters "helped their administrations isolate constituencies by focusing on what linked individuals to the president and the administration's policies."[32] Thus, the

White House has highly specific polling data on everyone from homeowners to born-again Christians. At the height of the energy crisis in the 1970s, President Carter's pollsters even created polling categories based on the type of home heating used by the respondent.[33] By focusing on specific demographic groups and identifying issues that resonate with them, presidents are able to engage in highly targeted public appeals.

Presidents also use polling and focus groups to test language that they plan to use in speeches.[34] For example, the Reagan administration used focus groups in 1987 and 1988 to help plan the president's State of the Union address, his speech to Congress about the summit meeting with Soviet leader Mikhail Gorbachev, and his response to the Iran-contra affair. Using such focus groups helped the White House to fashion messages that were both appealing and believable.[35] Similarly, Bill Clinton made extensive use of polls and focus groups in formulating his agenda. Some have described the Clinton White House as driven by polls.[36] Molly Andolina and Clyde Wilcox have noted that President Clinton often frustrated opponents by his "ability to cut right or left, depending on prevailing sentiments." They point out that in his second term he adeptly embraced issues that enjoyed popular support so that even in the face of a Senate impeachment trial in February 1999, 69 percent of the respondents of a Pew Research Center survey liked Clinton's policies.[37] Thus, despite the scandals and the impeachment, Clinton is the only president since polling began whose average Gallup job approval rating was higher for his last year in office (60 percent) than for his first (48.8 percent). No doubt the upward trajectory of Clinton's job approval ratings was also buoyed by a surging economy. This is an exception to the general rule that presidents deplete their public support as time goes by.

Paul Brace and Barbara Hinckley have called this depletion of public support a "decay curve."[38] This decay can be attributed to the deflation of unrealistically high expectations of performance, and the curve typically bottoms out near the thirtieth month of an initial term. Brace and Hinckley suggest that this decay normally occurs "irrespective of the economy, the president, or outside events." If a president is fortunate enough to be reelected, an uncertain prospect at best, the decline usually begins earlier and follows a steeper path. Beyond this cycle, though, Brace and Hinckley recognize that events that capture the public's attention may increase or diminish presidential support. In general, events that "dramatize conflict in the nation," even if the president has taken no action to trigger them, are likely to reduce support. Events that "unify the nation around its symbols"—for example, an international crisis or an assassination attempt on the president—are likely to increase support. Some presidents may simply have better luck than others; domestic or international events beyond their control conspire to increase public support. Others may be responsible for their own good or bad fortune by taking actions that trigger positive or negative public responses.[39]

To the extent that presidents rely on public support for policy success, the decay curve suggests that they are well advised to "hit the ground running" and accomplish as much as they can as early as they can in their administration.[40] Along with public support, other pieces of political "capital," such as a mandate from a strong electoral margin and congressional support, are also likely to be strongest at the outset of a president's term.[41] David Gergen, an adviser to Presidents Nixon, Ford, Reagan, and Clinton, recognized this early on. As a member of Reagan's transition team in 1980, he wrote a detailed memorandum comparing the first hundred days of every administration since that of Franklin D. Roosevelt. In it, he showed that the successful presidents were those who immediately established a clear and simple agenda and used their capital to achieve it.[42] Reagan followed Gergen's advice and framed his entire legislative agenda around just four major issues that the administration carefully promoted (and implemented). In contrast, both Jimmy Carter and Bill Clinton—despite a Congress controlled by their own party—largely squandered their first years in office.

Like Reagan, George W. Bush charted a clear-cut legislative agenda for his first hundred days in office. For Bush, those days were especially important. He came to office without a clear electoral mandate (indeed, he lost the popular vote to Al Gore), without strong support in Congress (although enjoying a small Republican majority in the House, the Senate was evenly divided between Republicans and Democrats), and his initial Gallup job *dis*approval ratings were, at 25 percent, the highest of any new president since polling began. Success at selling his legislative agenda—with a tax cut as its centerpiece—became a way to win public support and build political capital.

With low expectations from the public, Bush gave an address to a joint session of Congress on February 27, 2001—a de facto State of the Union address, although it was not officially billed as such. The speech was a resounding success. In the first half of the speech he threw Democrats one applause line after another—reserving core Republican issues for the end—and he played the crowd masterfully when discussing his tax cut. "Some say my tax plan is too big," he said, with Democrats interrupting to applaud. "Others say it is too small," he continued, with a group of Republicans interrupting to applaud. "I respectfully disagree," he concluded. "The plan is just right." That led to the biggest applause of all. Bush's ploy skillfully made him look like he was embracing the compromise position.

Among those that Bush recognized during the speech was Mayor John Street of Philadelphia—a liberal Democrat and an African American. "Mayor Street has encouraged faith-based and community organizations to make a significant difference in Philadelphia," Bush said. "He's invited me to his city this summer to see compassion in action." He then praised Street and poked fun at himself for losing Pennsylvania in the 2000 election. "I'm personally aware of just how effective this mayor is. Mayor Street is a Democrat [applause]. Let the record show, I lost his city—big time [laughter, applause]. But some things are bigger than politics, so I look forward to coming to your city to see your faith-based programs in action [applause]." Frank Luntz, a Republican pollster monitoring the reactions of a group of Philadelphians to the speech, was ecstatic. Luntz found that Philadelphia Democrats, who at the outset of the speech were skeptical, were won over by the president: by the end, they approved of the speech almost as much as Republicans.[43] President Bush had taken a big step toward mobilizing public support for his agenda—and toward laying the groundwork for winning Pennsylvania in 2004.

A Gallup poll taken immediately after the speech found that 66 percent of those polled had a "very positive" reaction to the speech, and an additional 26 percent had a "somewhat positive" reaction. Quite simply, an overwhelming 92 percent viewed the speech in a positive light. Only a minuscule 1 percent had a "very negative" reaction, with a mere 6 percent having a "somewhat negative" reaction. The same poll showed that 84 percent felt that Bush's policies were taking the country in the right direction.[44] Even before the speech, Bush's job approval rating had jumped from 57 percent to 62 percent.[45]

Figure 3-1 shows results of the Gallup poll on presidential performance from Eisenhower through the second George Bush. An examination of the figure shows evidence of the decay curve for every president except Clinton. It is also clear that starting in the mid-1960s it became common for presidential approval ratings to fall below 50 percent. Even incoming presidents have confronted lower ratings in recent years. Eisenhower and Johnson both had approval ratings of 78 percent when Gallup first gathered information about them as president, and Kennedy had an approval rating of 72 percent—even though he received only 49.7 percent of the popular vote in the 1960 election.[46] No president since Carter, however, has had an initial job approval rating of more than 58 percent. There has been a similar decline in average first-year ratings (from 69.9 percent for Eisenhower's first year to 48.8 percent for Clinton's). Some of this decline may be attributable to cynicism borne of Vietnam, Watergate, Iran-contra, and Whitewater. Television may also have helped to demystify the presidency. And, the decline may reflect a persistent trend toward tighter presidential elections (often coupled with a lack of enthusiasm for either candidate) and "divided government" (in which one party controls the White House and another controls Congress). Neither George W. Bush in 2000 nor Bill Clinton in 1992 or 1996 received 50 percent of the popular vote. Even Ronald Reagan's "landslide" in 1980 amounted to only 50.7 percent of the popular vote (although he won 90.9 percent of the electoral vote). For whatever reason, Americans seem warier of new presidents than in times past—less willing to give them the benefit of the doubt and more apt to withhold support until they prove themselves.

Rallying Public Support

Presidents are not passive objects of public attitudes. Rather, presidents and their aides take the initiative in shaping public perceptions. Over time, the White House has developed several specialized staff units devoted to maintaining favorable public relations and for promoting its agenda on Capitol Hill, with interest

Figure 3-1   Presidential Approval, 1953–2001

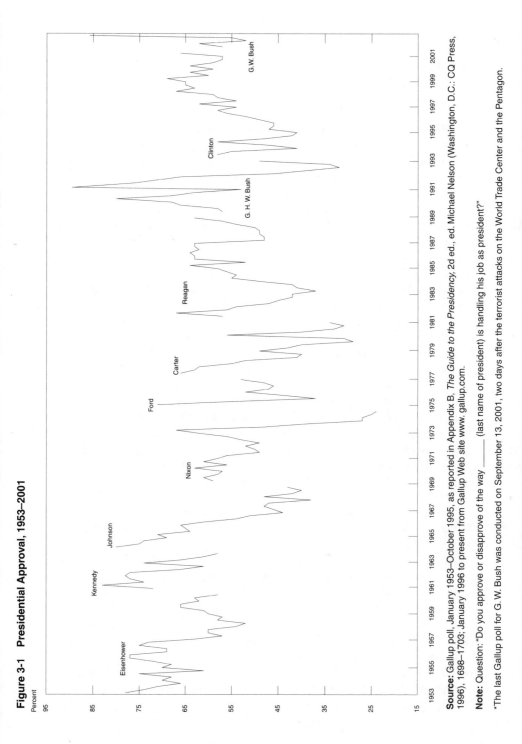

Source: Gallup poll, January 1953–October 1995, as reported in Appendix B, *The Guide to the Presidency*, 2d ed., ed. Michael Nelson (Washington, D.C.: CQ Press, 1996), 1698–1703; January 1996 to present from Gallup Web site www. gallup.com.

Note: Question: "Do you approve or disapprove of the way _____ (last name of president) is handling his job as president?"

*The last Gallup poll for G. W. Bush was conducted on September 13, 2001, two days after the terrorist attacks on the World Trade Center and the Pentagon.

groups, and with members of the president's own party.[47] In performing these tasks, aides take actions and fashion appeals designed to win the support of different kinds of audiences, including other elites, the public at large, and specific constituencies.

The Rise of the Public Presidency

We now take public appeals by the president for granted, but, as noted in chapter 1, scholars such as Jeffrey Tulis argue that the rise of the "rhetorical" presidency is really a twentieth-century phenomenon.[48] Arguably, the now commonplace practice of presidents "going public" to build public support for specific legislative initiatives is one of the most significant changes of the modern presidency.[49] As presidents have embraced public appeals, the source of presidential power has expanded from narrowly defined constitutional underpinnings to a broader plebiscitary base.[50]

Tulis argues that presidents avoided the widespread use of public appeals in the nineteenth century because they adhered to a fundamentally different understanding of our political order than the one commonly held today. Their avoidance of public appeals reflected the Founders' distrust of "pure" or "direct" democracy. Although the Founders felt that public *consent* was a requirement of republican government, they nonetheless felt that the processes of government should be insulated from the whims of public *opinion*. Thus, they attempted to instill "deliberation" in government through such things as indirect elections, separation of powers, and an independent executive. In such a system, public appeals by the president were proscribed because they were thought to "manifest demagoguery, impede deliberation, and subvert the routines of republican government."[51] Policy rhetoric by presidents—to the extent that it existed—was primarily written and principally addressed to Congress (as opposed to modern-day policy rhetoric, which is primarily spoken and principally addressed to the people). Thus, it was "*public* (available to all) but not thereby *popular* (fashioned for all)."[52]

Presidents avoided "going public" (which is specifically designed to whip up public opinion) because it went against the existing interpretation of the constitutional order. That is not to say that other sorts of popular appeals were never made. Government-sponsored partisan newspapers flourished in the early part of our history and were clearly a means of generating public support—often by ridiculing the opposition with highly inflammatory articles.[53] The Federalist Papers themselves are another early example of public appeals. Indeed, Federalists made a point of befriending key printers, thus forming a network for the distribution of information favorable to the Federalist cause.[54] Once in power, Federalists were accused of thwarting the circulation of opposition papers through control of the post office.[55] But arguably these early examples were designed primarily to build public consent for broadly based structures—partisan newspapers for emerging political parties, and The Federalist Papers for a new form of government—rather than as a more direct tool used by presidents to mobilize public opinion for congressional passage of specific policy initiatives. Securing legislation remained an elite process of bargaining.

Nineteenth-century presidents did not maintain total public silence. They made occasional speeches to the people and even made some tours around the country (called "swings around the circle"). But public speeches were not as important as public appearances on those tours. President Washington, for example, initiated a "grand tour" of two months' duration by visiting the South in 1791, a region where suspicions of central authority had run strong during the constitutional ratification campaign. Washington himself emphasized the importance of "seeing and being seen" on the tour, and though the president gave public remarks, Tulis emphasizes that they contained only "general articulations of republican sentiment, not even a clear enunciation of principle."[56]

Indeed, the overall character of eighteenth- and nineteenth-century presidential speeches was very different from those given today: they were largely ceremonial and usually devoid of policy content. They were also much less frequent. Tulis calculated that from George Washington through William McKinley presidents averaged thirteen public speeches a year—of which 80 percent or more were very brief "thank you" remarks. The first eleven presidents averaged three public speeches a year.[57] In comparison, Clinton averaged one public speech almost every other day during his first three years in office.[58] To underscore the very different nature of rhetorical "common law" that existed in the nineteenth century, Tulis points out that Andrew Johnson was the first president to engage in a full-scale popular appeal over the heads of Congress for the passage of legislation and that he had an article of impeachment brought against him for doing so.[59]

Tulis identifies Theodore Roosevelt and Woodrow Wilson as catalysts for the new rhetorical presidency. He cites Roosevelt's public campaign to win passage of the Hepburn Act (legislation that gave the Interstate Commerce Commission authority to regulate railroad shipping rates) as the first example of a president securing legislation with the help of going public.[60] Use of the "bully pulpit" dovetailed neatly with Roosevelt's broad "stewardship theory" of presidential power (*see chapter 1*). Like TR, Wilson believed that presidents had powers beyond those specifically enumerated in the Constitution, and he saw public opinion as an important source of that additional power.[61] Thus, he expanded the use of rhetoric and used it in new ways. He was the first elected president to have engaged in a full-scale speaking tour as part of the general election campaign.[62] Then once in office, Wilson changed the norms of presidential rhetoric. He was the one largely responsible for the shift to policy rhetoric that was primarily spoken and principally addressed to the people. When Wilson delivered his State of the Union report orally—the first president to do so since John Adams—the message was clearly fashioned for the people even though it was presented to Congress. One of Wilson's most dramatic appeals for public support—his whistlestop train tour to promote the League of Nations—was cut short by the stroke he suffered in Colorado on September 26, 1919.

Presidential Appeals

Appeals for public support are now a routine part of presidential governance. Presidents use that support as a bargaining chip with Congress—a way to convince (or coerce) it to follow his lead. George W. Bush, for example, spent his first week in office promoting his proposed education reforms. He and others in his administration stayed "on message" so that what they said about education reform would be the major topic in the news. The White House spent subsequent weeks promoting other aspects of the president's agenda. Bush used his address before Congress on February 27, 2001, to mobilize public support for his plans. He then followed up the address with speaking tours to promote the centerpiece of his agenda: a proposed $1.6 trillion tax cut. In just the two days following his address to Congress, Bush gave speeches touting his tax cut in Pennsylvania, Nebraska, Iowa, Arkansas, and Georgia. The explicit purpose of these speeches was to urge the American people to put pressure on Congress to pass the president's initiatives. When the House of Representatives approved the president's tax cut on March 8, Bush was still on the road—visiting states where Democratic senators who opposed the plan would be facing tight reelection battles in 2002. In Fargo, North Dakota, the president urged a cheering, flag-waving crowd to put pressure on their senators: "If you like what you hear today, maybe e-mail some of the good folks from the United States Senate from your state," Bush said. "If you like what you hear, why don't you just give 'em a call and write 'em a letter."[63]

Likewise, President Clinton used his State of the Union addresses to build public support for his policies—and himself. His 1998 State of the Union came just one week after the Monica Lewinsky story broke. In the firestorm of media coverage that immediately followed the news of the Lewinsky affair, many media commentators predicted that Clinton would be forced to resign or would be impeached. Even Clinton's former communications director, George Stephanopoulos, predicted resignation or impeachment if the story proved to be true.[64] Initial public opinion polls showed a drop of five percentage points in Clinton's job approval rating. Many advisers counseled him to postpone his State of the Union address or to use it as a forum for responding to the allegations and apologizing to the American people.[65] Instead, Clinton gave the address as planned and never mentioned the Lewinsky affair. Fifty-three million Americans watched him give one of the best speeches of his presidency. In it, he outlined his policy goals. Public reaction was overwhelmingly positive, and his Gallup approval rating surged to 67 percent (the highest of his presidency to date) and stayed high for the rest of his term. The speech arguably did much to save his presidency. He gave a State of the Union address at a similarly awkward time—and with equal success—during his Senate impeachment trial a year later. When weighing whether to convict Clinton, senators must have been mindful of his soaring job approval ratings (which, according to Gallup, had reached another new high of 73 percent just after the House voted to impeach).

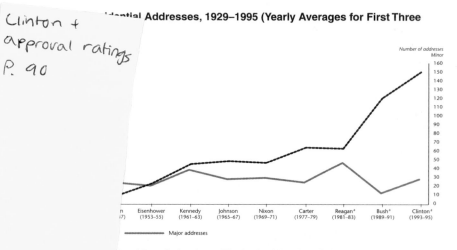

·······ial Addresses, 1929–1995 (Yearly Averages for First Three

Clinton + approval ratings P. 90

ll and Gary C. Jacobson, *The Logic of American Politics* (Washington, D.C.: CQ

ılic activities inspired by concerns of reelection rather than governing, only the first ␣␣␣␣␣␣␣ ı tabulated. For this reason, Gerald Ford's record of public activities during his two and one-half years oı office has been ignored.

ªIncludes television addresses only.

In addition to major prime-time television speeches such as the State of the Union, presidents give many minor speeches to groups around the country. Presidents ration their major speeches out of fear that the tactic will lose effectiveness if overused. In the face of competition from rival cable channels, the major networks have even begun to refuse airtime to the president if they feel the speech is not important enough. Even when the networks do cover a speech, viewers with cable or satellite channels can easily tune the president out by choosing alternate programming.[66] Minor speeches allow the president to target appeals to specific constituencies. When given on the road, they can also generate considerable local media coverage. As you can see from Figure 3-2, these speeches have increased dramatically in recent years.

Corresponding with this increase in "going public" is a similar increase in presidential travel (see Figure 3-3). This dramatic increase in travel began under Reagan and reflects the "permanent campaign" for public support that presidents now wage while in office.[67] Even Clinton's inability to run for a third term did not deter him from campaign mode. George W. Bush followed suit, crisscrossing the country during his first hundred days to stump for his tax cut and education reform. Although most presidential travel is domestic, modern presidents have significantly increased their foreign travel as well. Political scientist Richard Rose has dubbed this "going international." As Rose puts it, presidents can no longer do their job simply by staying in the United States. "Whereas Herbert Hoover spent only three days abroad in his term of office and Franklin Roosevelt spent

Figure 3-3   Days of Political Travel by Presidents, 1929–1995 (Yearly Averages for First Three Years of First Term)

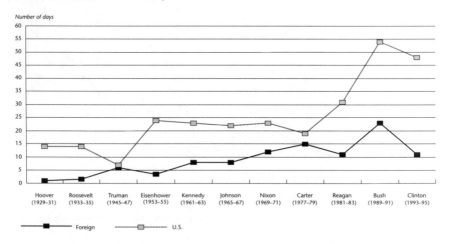

Source: Samuel Kernell and Gary C. Jacobson, *The Logic of American Politics* (Washington, D.C.: CQ Press, 2000), 243.

Note: To eliminate public activities inspired by concerns of reelection rather than governing, only the first three years have been tabulated. For this reason, Gerald Ford's record of public activities during his two and one-half years of office has been ignored.

only nine days abroad in his first term, Richard Nixon spent fifty-nine days abroad in his first four years in office, and Jimmy Carter fifty-six days."[68] Such trips highlight the president's role as head of state and can paint a picture of the president as diplomat and peacemaker. Nixon's dramatic trips to China and the Soviet Union in 1972 (an election year) were beamed back live to American television with newly developed satellite technology. Reagan's trips abroad provided many memorable television moments, including his emotional visit to the Normandy beaches of France (which became the backdrop for dramatic reelection ads in 1984).

Aside from foreign travel, "going international" has also come to include efforts by presidents to monitor and build public opinion abroad. Reagan was the first to do this in a systematic way.[69] The Reagan administration made a concerted effort to reach an international audience in 1981–1982 to deflect criticism of the president's decision to deploy nuclear weapons in Europe. This included an extensive public relations campaign in western Europe. President Reagan kicked off the campaign with a speech that the White House transmitted live by satellite to Europe—timed so as to air prime time on European television.[70]

Appeals by Surrogates

Presidential surrogates, ranging from the vice president and members of the Cabinet to party officials and political consultants, also promote the president's agenda through speaking tours, satellite interviews with local media outlets, and nationwide television appearances on the Sunday morning talk shows and cable outlets such as CNN, MSNBC, and Fox News. Nixon was one of the first presidents to aggressively choreograph the use of these surrogates as part of a broader strategy of going public. He sought to build, as his chief of staff, H. R. Haldeman, put it, "a stable of television personalities from within the Administration."[71]

Nixon was also one of the first presidents to use late-night talk shows and other entertainment outlets to promote himself and his agenda. He appeared on the popular Jack Paar television talk show in 1963 to chat, play the piano, and help rebuild his image after his stinging loss to Pat Brown in the 1962 California gubernatorial race. He made a one-line ("sock it to me") cameo appearance on *Rowan and Martin's Laugh-In* during the 1968 presidential campaign. Once in the White House, Nixon hired a full-time staffer named Al Snyder (a former television executive from New York) to book television appearances for administration officials. Snyder sent Vice President Spiro Agnew on the *Tonight Show with Johnny Carson*, Attorney General John Mitchell on the *Dick Cavett Show*, and even arranged for the White House communications director, Herb Klein, to cohost the Cavett show. Snyder also booked more traditional appearances on programs such as *Meet the Press* and arranged local media appearances by administration officials along with advising them where and how to get the best media exposure when they traveled around the country.[72] Another Nixon staffer, Virginia Savell, coordinated speaking tours by administration surrogates. In Nixon's first year in office, she arranged for surrogate speakers to crisscross the country promoting everything from Nixon's proposed family assistance plan to postal reform.[73]

Surrogates—be they traveling around the country on speaking tours or appearing on television—now follow a carefully scripted "line of the day" that is part of the broader message that the administration is trying to convey at that point in time. Thus, when George W. Bush focused on education reform during his first week in office, his surrogates followed suit. Education secretary Roderick Paige made the rounds on the morning shows and cable news outlets, as did Vice President Dick Cheney and White House chief of staff Andrew Card. Republican members of Congress joined in, as did other proponents of education reform. In everything from public speeches to background interviews with reporters, administration surrogates stressed education reform. At the same time, the White House arranged for photo opportunities, such as the president reading to children at a local school.

The point of such activities is to convey a carefully orchestrated message that is reinforced by different people in a variety of contexts. Such coordination was clearly on display on December 19, 1998, the day the House of Representatives voted to impeach President Clinton. In a morning statement to reporters, White House press secretary Joe Lockhart three times decried "the politics of personal destruction." House minority leader Richard Gephardt repeated the line that morning in a speech on the floor of the House. So, too, did the president in his Rose Garden speech after the impeachment vote.

One advantage of surrogates is that they can be used to target very specific constituencies. Another way of targeting specific constituencies is through links with interest groups, as we see in the next section.

Targeted Communications: Presidents and Interest Groups

Presidents have come to recognize the value of targeting appeals to organized interests and mobilizing interest groups to support presidential policy. Liaison with such groups is now an important part of governance. As Mark A. Peterson has written, "Working with (as well as working against) interest groups to piece together support among the public and in Congress played a large role in the [Clinton] administration's political and policy strategies."[74] People who organize to advocate a particular interest are highly attentive to public issues that affect their members. These groups also have ongoing links with Congress and the bureaucracy that provide them with policymaking influence. It is not surprising, therefore, that they are a prime target of presidential communication. For example, presidents give major public addresses on business to conventions of the National Association of Manufacturers or the Chamber of Commerce of the United States and on labor relations to meetings of the American Federation of Labor–Congress of Industrial Organizations (AFL–CIO). Chief executives also dispatch surrogates to meet with these groups and to promote the administration's programs. White House aides serve as a channel for private communications with group representatives and will sometimes arrange meetings with the president.

Interest groups want to hear about current matters of public policy, but they also want to be reassured that the president is sympathetic to the problems group members face. Not surprisingly, chief executives pay particular attention to the groups that helped them get elected. They hope to convert their electoral coalition into one that helps them govern, as well. Democratic presidents typically have focused on labor unions and civil rights organizations; Republicans have concentrated on business and professional organizations. Presidents also know that as the leader of the nation, they are supposed to represent *all* the people, not just those who supported their election. Chief executives cannot afford to ignore prominent interest groups, even those that are politically opposed to them.

Presidents also have established channels for routine communication with particular groups through systematic White House liaison. Truman used David Niles, formerly on FDR's staff, as a liaison with blacks and Jews.[75] Eisenhower, who cultivated an image of being above politics, de-emphasized, but did not completely ignore, group relations, and the Kennedy and Johnson administrations designated White House staff members to work with Jews, Catholics, and other groups. Gradually, however, the range of group ties became more predictable. Presidents since Nixon have assigned aides to work with eight population groups: business, labor, Jews, consumers, blacks, women, Hispanics, and the elderly.[76] Most of these ties are pursued through the Office of Public Liaison, a White House staff unit first conceived and implemented in the Nixon administration (under the direction of Charles Colson) and officially consolidated and named an independent staff unit under Gerald Ford.[77]

The Office of Public Liaison has continued to be a part of each subsequent administration and has sometimes played an important role in promoting administration policies. Thus, the official representation of interest groups in the White House has become institutionalized in the administrations of both political parties. People who serve in the liaison office articulate the demands of interest groups inside White House circles and rally the support of interest groups behind the president's programs. Despite this dual purpose, there is little doubt that the office exists primarily to further the president's wishes rather than those of interest groups; aides who reverse these priorities encounter difficulties.[78]

Although many regularities in relations between the White House and interest groups carry across administrations, significant differences still occur. George W. Bush, for example, maintains close ties with groups traditionally associated with Republicans, such as big business and the oil industry. Bill Clinton, on the other hand, was far more responsive to the goals of groups that had recently joined the Democratic coalition.[79] One of President-elect Clinton's first public policy statements in 1992 was a commitment to change the government's policy on gays in the military. After both the military and influential members of Congress opposed such changes, the president retreated to a policy of "don't ask, don't tell," which angered gay groups at the same time that it made him appear weak. Clinton was more successful in opposing the policy goals of two powerful groups, the AFL–CIO and the National Rifle Association (NRA). Organized labor had been a member of the Democratic Party's core coalition since Franklin Roosevelt's New Deal, but Clinton found himself opposing it when he sought congressional approval of the North American Free Trade Agreement (NAFTA). Ultimately, Clinton triumphed with substantial Republican support in the House but created dissension within his own coalition of support, and many liberal Democrats joined labor in opposing the new treaty. Clinton also won the battle against the NRA when the Brady bill, which required a waiting period before the purchase of a handgun, and limits on assault weapons were passed by Congress. In contrast, powerful organized groups were successful in their opposition to the president's proposal for universal health care. One coalition of insurance interests financed a $60 million ad campaign featuring a middle-class couple, Harry and Louise, pondering the impact of Clinton's reforms. Although the administration may have made many mistakes that contributed to the demise of health care reform, it clearly was never able to create a stable coalition of groups favoring reform.[80]

Targeted Communications: Presidents and Political Parties

Outreach to political parties is also an important part of the modern public presidency. Presidents since Harry Truman have assigned staff to serve as liaison with their political party.[81] As early as Richard Nixon, this staff was referred to as the Office of Political Affairs, although it did not become a freestanding entity listed in the *U.S. Government Organization Manual* until the Reagan administration.[82] As political scientist Kathryn Dunn Tenpas has noted, the precise functions of the office have changed a good deal from president to president, but there are at least three core functions. First, the office serves as a formal liaison to national, state, and local party organizations, as well as to congressional campaign committees. Such liaison is a two-way street. On the one hand, it allows the White House to monitor the actions of relevant political actors and receive input from them. On the other hand, it provides an opportunity for the White House to mobilize political support from these actors. Thus, Harry S. Dent—head of Nixon's Office of Political Affairs—mobilized state Republican chairs to lobby U.S. senators from their state to vote for Nixon Supreme Court nominee Clement Haynsworth in 1969 and to orchestrate a grassroots letter-writing campaign on behalf of the nomination.[83] The office made similar efforts on behalf of George Bush's Supreme Court nominees, David Souter and Clarence Thomas, in 1990 and 1991. The office also uses such ties to promote the president's legislative agenda. This includes building support *for* presidential initiatives and mobilizing *opposition* to programs the president does not support. For example, the office may use pressure from party activists to help gain votes for cloture and help guard against veto overrides, and it may also apply grassroots pressure on members of Congress to vote against legislation. Creating a groundswell of grassroots opposition can also make it easier for the president to oppose certain policies. The first George Bush used the Office of Political Affairs very effectively to help stop campaign finance reform.[84]

Second, the office serves as liaison with major supporters of the president. This includes private citizens who have donated money to support the president's political activities. If such a supporter requests a signed photo from the president or a White House tour, the Office of Political Affairs arranges it. Some alleged that the Clinton administration went beyond this simple sort of constituent service and improperly used the office to raise funds and reward donors. A 1998 report by the House Committee on Government Reform and Oversight, chaired by Rep. Dan Burton, R-Ind., pointed to efforts by members of the Office of Political Affairs under Clinton to create a computerized White House database to identify potential donors. This was part of a broader effort to share information on White House databases with the Democratic National Committee. "This is the President's idea and it's a good one," Marsha Scott, a member of the office, wrote in a draft memorandum to White House chief of staff Mack McLarty in 1994. She wrote that the database would be used to "identify and contact key supporters in all fifty states" and would allow the White House to identify, by early 1995, "key financial and political folks in each state who can work with us."[85] Another memo, dated October 25, 1994, noted that the president wanted the database to correlate contributions from individuals and their invitations to and attendance at White House events.[86] In other words, the Office of Political Affairs used the list to reward donors with invitations to meet the president, attend White House functions, or sleep over in the Lincoln Bedroom.

Finally, the office engages in what Tenpas calls "electioneering." This includes planning early reelection strategies for the president (in the first term) and using presidential resources to help elect members of Congress from the same political party as the president. To help reelect the president, the office looks for ways to expand the president's electoral base. Thus, Tim Kraft engaged in early reelection strategy for Jimmy Carter while working in the office and later became Carter's campaign manager. Similarly, Ed Rollins and Lee Atwater worked in the office before moving over to the Reagan–Bush campaign headquarters.[87] It was especially important for Clinton to expand his electoral base in anticipation of a reelection bid, because he won the White House in 1992 with just 43 percent of the popular vote. George W. Bush—winning the White House with roughly 48 percent of the popular vote—is in a similar situation. To help elect members of Congress, the office arranges presidential appearances in the candidate's home state or congressional district, coordinates photo opportunities with the candidate at the White House, and maintains liaison with House and Senate campaign committees.

Presidents, of course, are eager to influence the outcome of midterm congressional elections (those held between presidential elections) in hopes of minimizing the loss of seats that the president's party customarily experiences in such elections.[88] Nonetheless, there are limits to what a president can accomplish, especially in elections for the House of Representatives. For one thing, the sheer number of contests (435 every two years) precludes participation in many of them. For another, there is good evidence that the off-year House elections are primarily local, not national, events. Scholars who have examined off-year congressional elections report the same basic finding: how people vote has more to do with their evaluations of the congressional candidates than with their assessment of the president.[89] Moreover, incumbency is a valuable asset for congressional candidates; they benefit from previous campaign experience, close relationships with voters, greater knowledge of issues, and superior financial resources, which give them a considerable advantage over their opponents.[90] Presidents who attempt to campaign against sitting members of Congress therefore face almost insurmountable odds.

Senatorial midterm elections offer a somewhat more encouraging opportunity for presidents who wish to influence results. Approximately one-third of the Senate's 100 seats are at stake every two years, so the chief executive can concentrate on these contests in a way that is not possible for House races. Although sitting senators are in the same position as House members in being able to bring their name to the attention of constituents, incumbency is not as advantageous for a senator as it is for a House member. Senators represent an entire state rather than a small district, and the prestige associated with being a senator means races are hard fought. Challengers are much more visible to the electorate than are those who run against House incumbents. Popular presidents, therefore, are better able to help candidates who challenge incumbent senators of the opposite party by increasing the challengers' visibility through public association.

Midterm election outcomes depend on the condition of the national economy and the president's standing in public opinion polls at the time of the elections.[91] Voting in these contests tends to be *negative;* that is, those who disapprove of the president's performance in office are more likely to cast their ballot in such elections than those who approve.[92] Gary Jacobson contends that the president's role in congressional elections is essentially indirect: the state of the economy and the president's ratings in the public opinion polls influence the caliber of candidates who run in congressional elections. If, for example, these are not favorable, the opposition party will be able to field an unusually large proportion of formidable challengers with well-financed campaigns, and the president's party in Congress may lose a considerable number of seats.[93] Democrats fared miserably in the 1994 midterm elections when Bill Clinton's Gallup approval ratings came near their lowest point—fluctuating between 39 percent on September 6 and 48 percent on October 22, 1994. On the other hand, Democrats fared unusually well in the 1998 midterm elections when Clinton's approval ratings remained consistently high, hovering near 66 percent despite the looming threat of impeachment. (See Table 3-1.)

Despite the efforts of modern presidents to secure electoral victory for their party's candidates and their desire to reach out to party regulars, it is important to note that they are far less reliant on political parties than were presidents of even 40 or 50 years ago. For the first 150 years or so of our history, political parties were the central structure in the presidential selection process. They nominated candidates, helped diverse social and economic interests to coalesce under a common banner, mobilized voters, organized campaigns, raised funds, recruited personnel to staff the winning administration, mediated relations with interest groups, and helped to develop programmatic appeals. In modern times—especially since the advent of television—responsibility for most of these activities has been transferred elsewhere. The emphasis has increasingly shifted to "personalized politics." As electoral competition has come to concentrate more on individual candidates than traditional party loyalties, the link between presidents and their political parties has changed. Presidential campaign staffs are personal constructs almost wholly independent of party structures, and televised ads are the principal means of mobilizing voters. Once in office, presidents use White House aides to recruit personnel, maintain liaison with interest groups, and develop program ideas. In short, presidents are now less dependent on their parties both for winning elections and for governing and have largely preempted the services traditionally performed by party leaders.[94] A key to success in this new environment is the president's own ability to communicate appeals through the media, the subject of the following section.

The President and the Media

Historically, the most important link between the president and the American public has been the press. In the early years of the Republic, the press was as

Table 3-1   Losses by President's Party in Midterm Elections, 1862–1998

Year	Party holding presidency	President's party: gain/loss of seats in House	President's party: gain/loss of seats in Senate
1862	R	−3	8
1866	R	−2	0
1870	R	−31	−4
1874	R	−96	−8
1878	R	−9	−6
1882	R	−33	3
1886	D	−12	3
1890	R	−85	0
1894	D	−116	−5
1898	R	−21	7
1902	R	9[a]	2
1906	R	−28	3
1910	R	−57	−10
1914	D	−59	5
1918	D	−19	−6
1922	R	−75	−8
1926	R	−10	−6
1930	R	−49	−8
1934	D	9	10
1938	D	−71	−6
1942	D	−55	−9
1946	D	−55	−12
1950	D	−29	−6
1954	R	−18	−1
1958	R	−48	−13
1962	D	−4	3
1966	D	−47	−4
1970	R	−12	2
1974	R	−48	−5
1978	D	−15	−3
1982	R	−26	1
1986	R	−5	−8
1990	R	−8	−1
1994	D	−52	−8
1998	D	5	0

Source: Harold W. Stanley and Richard G. Niemi, *Vital Statistics on American Politics, 1999–2000* (Washington, D.C., CQ Press), 2000.

Note: Each entry is the difference between the number of seats won by the president's party in that midterm election and the number of seats won by that party in the preceding general election. Because of changes in the overall number of seats in the Senate and House, in the number of seats won by third parties, and in the number of vacancies, a Republican loss is not always matched precisely by a Democratic gain, or vice versa.

[a]Although the Republicans gained nine seats in the 1902 elections, they actually lost ground to the Democrats, who gained twenty-five seats after the increase in the overall number of representatives after the 1900 census.

partisan as it is in many European countries today. The partisan press reached its peak during the presidency of Andrew Jackson, when federal officeholders were expected to subscribe to the administration organ, the *Washington Globe,* which was financed primarily by revenues derived from the printing of official government notices.[95]

The partisan press began to decline during the presidency of Abraham Lincoln. The establishment of the Government Printing Office in 1860 destroyed the printing-contract patronage that had supported former administration organs.[96] The invention of the telegraph led to the formation of wire services, which provided standardized and politically neutral information to avoid antagonizing the diverse readerships of the various subscribing newspapers. Advertising provided newspapers with a secure financial base independent of the support of presidential administrations. By the end of the nineteenth century "news about the White House was transmitted to the public by independent, nonpartisan news organizations," a factor that continues to affect relationships between the president and the press today.[97]

Not until 1896, though, did the White House become a regular beat for reporters. Not surprisingly, given their role in establishing the public presidency, both Woodrow Wilson and Theodore Roosevelt formalized innovative ties with those reporters in the early part of the twentieth century. Roosevelt began the practice of meeting with them (often during his late afternoon shave). In 1902, he had a pressroom built in the new West Wing of the White House and began having an aide, William Loeb, give daily press briefings. Wilson continued the practice of daily press briefings (conducted by Joseph Tumulty) and became the first president to hold regularly scheduled press conferences. He held his first in the East Room of the White House on March 15, 1913—just eleven days after his inauguration—for 125 reporters.[98]

In the twentieth century, several media took their place beside newspapers as important channels between the president and the people. Radio became a dominant force in communications in the 1920s, as did television in the 1950s. By the end of the century, cable and satellite technology had dramatically increased the number of potential sources of news and commentary, and the Internet had revolutionized the way people communicate and gather information. The emergence of broadcast technology, coupled with the array of "new media" (cable, satellite technology, and the Internet) by century's end, allowed presidents to communicate messages directly to the people rather than having their messages relayed (and interpreted) by journalists.

The Presidential Media

Today, the words and actions of the U.S. president are covered by an enormous variety of media. These media differ in the way they deal with executive branch developments and in their target audience. They also vary in importance to chief executives and their programs. Over the past fifty years, the way Americans get information has undergone a fundamental change. In 1959, 57 percent of the public claimed to get most of their news from newspapers and 51 percent from television (more than one response was allowed in the survey); only 19 percent claimed to get their news from television alone. By 1997 only 37 percent cited newspapers as a principal source and 69 percent cited television; 47 percent claimed to get their news only from television.[99] This pattern developed with the spread of television ownership: only 9 percent of households had television sets in 1950, a figure that grew to 87 percent by 1960 and 98 percent by 1980.[100] As one would expect, White House attention to television coverage rose over the same period.

In addition, the White House must be attentive to the most influential media figures—a select group of columnists, elite reporters, anchors of the broadcast news, and executives of the media organizations. Indeed, there is substantial evidence that the stated views of news commentators and experts have a greater impact on citizens' policy preferences than the president's own comments.[101]

Syndicated columnists earn White House attention because they reach powerful audiences outside government, including business and labor leaders, lobbyists, and academics, as well as top officials in government—members of Congress, members of the bureaucracy, judges, governors, and mayors. These columnists influence views on the political feasibility of a president's proposed programs. They deal in matters of opinion rather than just factual developments affecting the presidency. "They are guaranteed space, they have no assigned topics, they are freed from the pressure of breaking news stories at deadline, and they have the opportunity to introduce their own perspectives into their stories."[102] George Will epitomizes this sort of columnist, and he appears regularly on television.

Television anchors such as Dan Rather, Peter Jennings, and Tom Brokaw are important to the president because of the size of the audience they reach—more than 26 million people each weekday night[103]—and the respect they command. They are joined now, of course, by the twenty-four-hour cable news networks and their coterie of anchors and commentators. Because far more people watch television than read newspapers, the information the ordinary citizen receives about the presidency depends on what is included in the evening news and covered on outlets such as CNN and Fox News. At the same time, television coverage of the presidency has serious limitations: Newscasts devote very little time to the most important stories (about seventy-five seconds on the average); emphasis is placed on events that are visually exciting; a focus on the president personalizes complex developments; and broadcasts usually lack in-depth reporting and analysis.[104] Sound bites of the president speaking on the evening network newscasts have shrunk from an average of forty-two seconds in 1968 to less than seven seconds in 1996.[105]

Cable provides some additional television outlets for presidents. C-SPAN carries many presidential speeches in their entirety, as well as White House press briefings. Cable news channels also offer a degree of expanded coverage, though actual news stories are similar to those on the evening newscasts. Most significantly, cable has given presidential surrogates many more venues to state their case. When Fox and MSNBC joined the cable news lineup in 1996, they relied heavily on talk shows to fill their airtime. Such shows are cheap to produce and require limited resources. They are also popular with viewers—so much so that CNN followed suit and expanded its number of talk shows in 2001.

Helping to shape both print and broadcast coverage are the bureau chiefs and other media executives who determine which stories are covered, how they are handled, which reporters will cover the White House, and who should be represented in "pools" that travel with the president to cover significant events. The White House press corps is also an important determinant of what will be reported and how it will be reported. These are the reporters assigned to the White House itself. They attend the daily press briefings, travel with the president, and have as their primary responsibility the task of reporting what the president is doing. Some members of the press corps are especially influential. Reporters for the *New York Times* and the *Washington Post* are examples because of the readership of their papers—in addition to public officials and important people in the private sector, their readers are the other Washington reporters.[106] The *Times*, in particular, is known to influence network news decisions about which stories to cover.[107] Also significant are the reporters for the wire services— Associated Press (AP) and United Press International (UPI)—because they provide coverage of the president for newspapers across the country. Collectively, the press corps frames most of what we read and see about the president.

Presidents pay a price for alienating the press corps, as Bill Clinton found out in the early days of his first term. One of the first decisions of his communications director, George Stephanopoulos, was to restrict the access of the press corps: he closed off the upstairs foyer in the West Wing, where he and the press secretary had their offices. For more than twenty years, members of the White House press corps had been free to wander that foyer in search of news. They could chat informally with communications officials or poke their heads into the press secretary's office to get a quick answer to a question. It was a clear symbol that reporters and officials were on an equal playing field. For Stephanopoulos, giving so many reporters access to such a cramped space might have seemed like a burden to him and his staff. But the decision to restrict access to the area infuriated the press corps. As reporter Ann Compton put it, the foyer had become a "no-fly zone" symbolizing the hierarchical relationship between reporters and officials.[108] In the new arrangement, reporters had to wait downstairs to be spoon-fed. Reporters felt that the White House was not even making much of an effort to do that. Calls from downstairs were not returned in time for reporters to meet their deadlines, and some felt that when they were invited upstairs, they were not treated with respect.[109] As a consequence, President Clinton started out his presidency by losing the goodwill of the White House press corps. "Put it this way," said Karen Hosler, Washington correspondent for the *Baltimore Sun* and president of the White House Correspondents Association, "we're not going to cut them any breaks."[110]

This question-and-answer session on MTV is an example of candidate Bill Clinton using "narrowcasting" in the 1992 presidential election to transmit direct, targeted messages to young voters.

One reason why Clinton and his aides felt they could get away with such treatment of the White House press corps was because of the rise of the new media.[111] Cable, satellite technology, and the Internet all provided an unparalleled opportunity for direct communication with the American people. In the 1992 presidential campaign, Clinton very effectively followed a strategy of "narrowcasting"—using media outlets such as MTV, the *Arsenio Hall Show, Phil Donahue,* and Don Imus's radio talk show to transmit direct, targeted messages to particular constituencies. Once Clinton was elected, he and his advisers planned to continue that strategy and expand their use of the new media to bypass the critical filter of the White House press corps. This included innovative use of the Internet and extensive use of cable outlets, talk radio, and local media. Sidney Blumenthal, who later joined the Clinton White House as a communication strategist, touted such possibilities for unmediated communication in an article in the *New Yorker.* There he wrote that the "Old Media," such as the White House press corps and the three network news shows, were "anachronistic" and were "no more likely to return than are the big bands."[112] By the time Clinton left office, swing dancing was the rage and the White House had learned to appreciate the old media. A 1998 Gallup poll showed that Americans continued to get most of their news from the old media and, even more important, *trusted* it more than the new media.[113] In the new environment, narrowcasting and circumvention of the White House press corps had its place. But that symbiotic relationship between the White House and the old media continued to exist, and that worked only if the White House courted the press corps and fed it information instead of snubbing it. In contrast, President George W. Bush and his aides seemed to recognize how to balance the two when they entered the White House in 2001. Bush carefully cultivated relations with the press corps, while at the same time taking advantage of narrowcasting and circumvention.[114]

We turn next to the two White House staff units that deal most directly with the press and communications planning: the Press Office and the Office of Communications.

The White House Press Office

Franklin Roosevelt officially created the White House Press Office in 1933. As we have seen, a routinized White House relationship with the press had been in place since Theodore Roosevelt directed William Loeb to provide daily briefings for reporters. Every president after TR assigned a member of his staff to deal with the press, with Herbert Hoover being the first to hire an aide for whom the press was the *sole* responsibility. That man, George Akerson, served from 1929 to 1931 and was the equivalent of a modern day press secretary, although that post was not formally created until FDR came to office in 1933.

The Press Office maintains day-to-day contact with the reporters assigned to cover the White House. It is housed in the West Wing. The Briefing Room and space for reporters are located downstairs in an area that used to house a swimming pool (President Nixon converted the area during his first term). Junior staff has space next to the Briefing Room in what is called the Lower Press Office. Senior staff members, including the press secretary, have their offices upstairs. All together the Press Office consists of about twenty people, some of whom specialize in a certain issue area (such as foreign affairs). These include several deputy press secretaries, as well as the junior staffers who write press releases and do other sorts of research. The most visible (and most senior) member of the Press Office is the press secretary.

The press secretary is the most important person in the executive branch for day-to-day contact with the presidential media. Typically holding two daily briefings, the press secretary provides routine information on executive branch appointments and resignations, on presidential actions and policies, and on the president's schedule—visits, meetings, and travel plans. By the end of an administration there may have been more than 2,000 such briefings. In addition, the press secretary holds private meetings with select reporters to provide background information to explain the president's actions on a particular problem or program.

Press secretaries serve three constituencies. They try to balance serving the interests of the president, members of the White House staff, and members of the media.[115] The secretary can perform well only if granted continuous access to and the confidence of the president so that journalists may assume that the news comes from the chief executive. If presidents try to be their own press secretary, as may have been true of Lyndon Johnson, even a capable and influential person such as Bill Moyers will not succeed in managing the message.[116] When secretaries are excluded from White House decisions, as appeared to be the case with Clinton's first press secretary, Dee Dee Myers, their credibility suffers.

The modern era's press secretaries have varied in effectiveness. Among those considered successful are Stephen Early (for FDR), James Hagerty (for Eisenhower), Jody Powell (for Carter), and Mike McCurry (for Clinton). Some, such as Hagerty and Powell, benefited from the fact that their presidents kept them informed on virtually everything that was going on in the White House. But sometimes even well-informed press secretaries do not want to know everything. After leaving office, Mike McCurry admitted that he purposely stayed out of the loop so that he could truthfully respond that he did not know all the answers to the Monica Lewinsky affair.[117] On the other hand, Nixon's press secretary, Ron Ziegler, was so out of the loop that he, like Dee Dee Myers, lost credibility with reporters. This was true even before the Watergate affair when, after months of denying any White House involvement, Ziegler was forced to declare those denials "inoperative." Indeed, Nixon purposely diminished the importance of the press secretary when he became president. White House reporters considered Nixon's choice of Ziegler—who was only twenty-nine years old and had no background in journalism—a slap in the face.[118] Another secretary who never had a particularly good relationship with reporters was Larry Speakes, who became Reagan's press spokesman when James Brady was shot and incapacitated in the assassination attempt on the president. After leaving office, Speakes provoked cries of outrage when he admitted in his memoirs that he had manufactured presidential quotes during Reagan's Iceland summit meeting with Soviet leader Mikhail Gorbachev in November 1985. Fearing that Reagan was being upstaged, Speakes created a public relations solution to the problem, and the fabricated quotes were given prominent attention back home.[119]

The White House Office of Communications

Richard Nixon created the White House Office of Communications in 1969.[120] Its functions are quite different from those of the Press Office. As originally conceived, the Office of Communications had four primary goals: (1) long-range communications planning; (2) the coordination of news from all the many departments and agencies of the executive branch; (3) outreach to local media; and (4) oversight of presidential surrogates. Thus, while the Press Office is largely *reactive* (responding to the questions and needs of the White House press corps), the Office of Communications is primarily *proactive* (responsible for setting the public agenda and making sure that all the players on the presidential team are adhering to that agenda). This includes setting the "line of the day" and choreographing presidential photo opportunities.

The precise jurisdiction of the Office of Communications has varied some from administration to administration. Outreach to local media, for example, has sometimes been subsumed by a subunit of the Press Office. In fact, the Press Office itself has sometimes been a subunit of the Office of Communications (and vice versa). For at least part of the administrations of former presidents Reagan, Bush, and Clinton, the Office of Communications became an umbrella term for a variety of offices that fell under the supervision of the communications director. At various times, this included the Press Office, as well as the offices of Planning, Speechwriting, Advance, Public Liaison (outreach to interest groups), Media Affairs (outreach to local media), Political Affairs (outreach to members of the president's political party), and Public Affairs (liaison with public information officers throughout the executive branch).

For Nixon, a primary motivation in creating the office was to install a mechanism for bypassing the critical filter of the White House press corps. Outreach to local media, the coordination of surrogate speakers, and using venues such as television, radio, and mass mailings to communicate directly with the people were all a part of that effort. For presidents since Reagan, the emphasis has been on long-range communications planning (although tactics of circumvention are often part of that plan).

In George W. Bush's administration, the Office of Communications falls under the supervision of Karen Hughes, whose official title is counselor to the president. She is one of Bush's most trusted advisers, having served as his communications director during the 2000 presidential campaign, and she is largely responsible for communications planning in the White House. Two people lead the Office of Communications: a special assistant to the president and deputy communications director for planning and a special assistant to the president and deputy communications director for production. In addition to heading the Office of Communications, Hughes oversees the Speechwriting Office and the Office of Media Affairs. Several other people in the second Bush White House also play a major role in communications planning and execution. Carl Rove, Bush's former campaign manager, is senior adviser for strategic initiatives and oversees the Office of Public Liaison. Mary Matalin is assistant to the president and counselor for the vice president. She is, in effect, the senior communications adviser to Vice President Cheney. And, of course, there is White House press secretary Ari Fleischer.

Vice President Cheney himself had considerable experience with communications planning as White House chief of staff for President Ford. As vice president, he quickly became Bush's point man on television and radio talk shows, and he established a pattern of giving weekly interviews to selected regional media commentators outside of Washington.[121] In an interview, Cheney stressed that it is essential for the White House to manage presidential news. "That means that about half the time the White House press corps is going to be pissed off," Cheney admitted, "and that's all right. You're not there to please them. You're there to run an effective presidency. And to do that, you have to be disciplined in what you convey to the country. The most powerful tool you have is the ability to use the symbolic aspects of the presidency to promote your goals and objectives." That means the White House has to control the agenda. "You don't let the press set the agenda," Cheney emphasized. "They like to decide what's important and what isn't important. But if you let them do that, they're going to trash your presidency."[122] Responsibility for controlling the communications agenda rests with the Office of Communications and a variety of other communications advisers—some of whom are not officially members of the White House staff.

Such sharing of communications responsibilities is not unusual. For example, in his first term, President Reagan benefited greatly not only from the skill and experience of communications director David Gergen (who had also served in the Nixon and Ford administrations and came back as a communications adviser to President Clinton in 1993) but also from that of James A. Baker III and Michael Deaver, other members of the White House staff who carefully managed the president's media and public image. This team was especially adept at selecting the "line of the day" (often as part of a broader "theme of the week") and creating "photo opportunities" featuring the president to highlight it. As Donald Regan later wrote: "[Deaver] saw—designed—each presidential action as a one-minute or two-minute spot on the evening network news, or picture on page one of the *Washington Post* or the *New York Times,* and conceived every presidential appearance in terms of camera angles. . . . Every moment of every appearance was scheduled, every word was scripted, every place where Reagan was expected to stand was chalked with toe marks."[123] Reagan, the former Hollywood actor, followed the script masterfully.

Clinton also had a great deal of duplication and overlap of communications functions. In his first term, this led to turf wars and diminished the ability of the White House to control the public agenda. In his second term, division was used more strategically. For example, the White House created a special communications team to deal with nothing but the Monica Lewinsky story. In part, that reflected the seriousness of the story. But it also reflected a strategy of putting the story on a "separate track"—to have the rest of the White House go on with business as usual rather than becoming consumed with damage control.

Presidential Press Conferences

Presidents, of course, do not leave all press interactions to their staff. They, too, cultivate ties with reporters—often through off-the-record sessions when traveling on *Air Force One* and during other informal gatherings. Presidential press conferences are one of the best-known avenues for interaction between presidents and reporters. Franklin Roosevelt perfected the art of the press conference. He held a total of 998 while president—an average of almost 7 a month. His were informal gatherings—usually held in his office—and there was strict control over how reporters could use material from the press conferences (as there had been since President Wilson first began the practice of regular press conferences in

1913). Nonetheless, FDR's system—as Samuel Kernell has pointed out—was one of "hard news, openly conveyed."[124]

The emergence of broadcast media and their desire to cover press conferences eroded the intimacy of these interactions between presidents and reporters. It also reduced the White House's dependence upon reporters to communicate the president's views to the public. Radio and television became ways to reach the masses directly. Indeed, press conferences came to be used more to meet the people than to meet the press when President Kennedy began the practice of televising them live in 1961 (Eisenhower had allowed filming, but the White House controlled which clips could be broadcast). As President Nixon's chief of staff bluntly put it in a 1970 White House memo: "The President wants you to realize and emphasize to all appropriate members of your staff that a press conference is a TV operation and that the TV impression is really all that matters."[125] Nixon also began the practice of prime-time televised news conferences. Kennedy's were almost always held at either 11:00 a.m. or 4:00 p.m. Lyndon Johnson never held one after 4:50 p.m. Nixon changed that. He preferred 9:00 p.m. Back in the age when the networks preempted regularly scheduled programs to cover such conferences, that time guaranteed a large audience. It was also just late enough that it was difficult for the morning newspapers to dissect the president's performance. And by the next evening's network news programs it was already "old" news. The first George Bush and Bill Clinton both returned to more informal exchanges with the media and held most of their sessions during midday rather than prime-time evening hours. As a result, their press conferences were less widely viewed (CNN was the principal source of coverage), but the two presidents earned points with the press for their accessibility.

Without the strict ground rules that earlier presidents had used to control what information reporters could use from press conferences, presidents facing live coverage of their press conferences have sought other ways to minimize risks. Members of the president's staff have drawn up a list of questions likely to be asked by reporters, together with suggested answers and supporting information. Some presidents have held full-scale mock news conferences for practice. Reagan, for example, liked two-hour practices, dividing the time between foreign policy and domestic policy. Errors would be pointed out, and the president's performance critiqued by staff. On the day of the news conference, photos of the reporters expected to attend were fixed to their likely places on a seating chart, and difficult questions were reviewed.[126] The emphasis, in short, shifted to performance.

President Nixon liked to emphasize the appearance of risk that he was taking in such performances. He likened himself to "the man in the arena" facing hostile adversaries when he confronted the press. To symbolize his lack of fear of these adversaries, he sometimes held press conferences with no podium to shield him from reporters. But, overall, presidents control the interchange at these conferences. At times, the White House limits questions to domestic policy or foreign policy, and presidents can always refuse to answer certain questions on the grounds that the subject matter is too sensitive for public discussion, a frequent response to foreign and military questions.

The success of a press conference depends on the skills of the president. President Eisenhower came across badly in them. He appeared to have trouble expressing himself clearly and grammatically and displayed meager knowledge about many vital issues of the day. Revisionist accounts have suggested that he may have used this as a tactic to avoid sensitive issues.[127] President Johnson also came across poorly in formal televised press conferences. On the other hand, FDR and Kennedy were masters of the press conference. Roosevelt had a keen sense of what was newsworthy and even suggested reporters' lead stories to them. He also prepared members of the press for actions he took on controversial problems by educating them initially with confidential background information; consequently, reporters tended to support his decisions because they understood his reasoning. Kennedy, who had served a brief stint as a newspaperman and enjoyed the company of reporters, used his press conferences to great advantage; his ability to field difficult questions impressed not only the members of the press but also the public. Clinton did not have the close relationship with reporters that Roosevelt and Kennedy enjoyed, but he also performed well in press conferences.

Most people who have studied or been involved in modern-day press conferences have concluded that they serve primarily the interests of the president rather than those of the media. As George Reedy, press secretary to Lyndon Johnson, has pointed out, a president rarely receives an unexpected question on an important issue in a conference, and, should that happen, the president could respond with a witty or a noncommittal remark.[128] Michael Grossman and Martha Kumar summarize the president's advantage as follows: "The President decides when to hold a conference, how much notice reporters will be given, who will ask the questions, and what the answers will be."[129]

In managing their relationships with the media, presidents must take into account their particular strengths and weaknesses. Nicknamed the Great Communicator, Reagan benefited enormously from his previous professional experience in radio, films, and television. To take advantage of those skills, the president frequently addressed the nation on prime-time television and used a series of Saturday radio broadcasts to explain and justify his administration's policies. The administration also avoided or restricted its use of other media formats that President Reagan did not handle as well as prepared speeches, specifically those that required him to give spontaneous answers to questions. He did not participate in call-in shows and seldom invited reporters to the White House for informal, on-the-record question and answer sessions. Reagan seldom would answer impromptu questions from reporters at photo sessions, and he held fewer press conferences in eight years than President Carter did in four. Nationally televised speeches were Reagan's best vehicle for communicating his views to the American people. If early indications are correct, that will also be true for George W. Bush.

Relations Between the President and the Media: Conflict or Collusion?

It is common for presidents to view the press unfavorably. George Washington, whom journalists treated rather well, was inclined not to run for a second term because of what he considered a critical press.[130] Since then, virtually all presidents have expressed outrage, indignation, resentment, or consternation over their treatment in the media. In turn, members of the press have criticized the way presidents have handled media relations. Typically, chief executives are accused of "managing" the news and, as their terms in office progress, of becoming increasingly isolated from the media and the American people. Some, such as Lyndon Johnson and Richard Nixon, also were charged with deliberately lying to the media and the public.

There is little question that a built-in conflict exists between the president and the media. Chief executives want to suppress information they feel will endanger the nation's security or put their administrations in a bad light. Members of the media are eager for news, however sensitive it may be, and they have an interest in criticizing the president and the president's associates as a means of getting the public's attention—thereby creating a demand for the journalists' services. They have also had an increasing penchant for what might be called "attack journalism": stories focused on scandal.[131]

Despite the potential for conflict, there is a basis for cooperation between presidents and the press that ultimately produces a collusive relationship.[132] Quite simply, the two are mutually dependent: neither presidents nor the press can perform their jobs without the assistance of the other, and cooperation is, therefore, mutually beneficial. The president must be able to communicate with the public through the media, and the media must have the administration's cooperation if they are to cover the most important official in the national government and give the public an accurate assessment of presidential activities. Moreover, the White House offers a range of media services designed to seduce reporters into favorable coverage. The product is an *exchange relationship,* a set of negotiated terms for the interaction between the media and the president that favors the White House and disadvantages the public.[133] As David Broder has argued, "We have been drawn into a circle of working relationships and even friendships with the people we are supposed to cover. The distinction between press and government has tended to become erased."[134]

Grossman and Kumar have argued that the general relationship between the president and the media goes through certain predictable phases.[135] During the initial period of "alliance," both parties agree that the focus should be on the new administration's appointees and its proposed goals and policies—the presidency is "open"; reporters are likely "to have their phone calls answered, to be granted interviews, and to get information that has not been specifically restricted."[136] During the second phase, "competition," the president wants to concentrate on portraying members of his administration as part of a happy team, committed to common goals and policies, while the media focus on conflicts among personalities in the administration and controversies over policies.[137] Presidents restrict access to themselves and others in the administration and may even go on the attack against especially critical reporters or organizations. The final phase of presidential-media relationships is "detachment." Surrogates manage the news, and presidents appear only in favorable settings scheduled to coincide with major events. The media, in turn, engage in more investigative reporting and seek information from sources other than the White House.

The Clinton administration's relationship with the press did not seem to follow the typical phases identified by Grossman and Kumar. There was an unusually brief period of "alliance," relations becoming obviously strained within a matter of months. As we have seen, Clinton got off to a rocky start with the White House press corps by pointedly circumventing them and restricting their access. The period of "competition" set in early, and Clinton exacerbated it by offering outspoken criticism of the press on several occasions, including a bitter public exchange with Brit Hume of ABC News on June 12, 1993, and a first-year-ending interview with *Rolling Stone* magazine that blamed the media for giving a false impression of his administration.[138] Moreover, one study found that television news coverage provided, on balance, more negative than positive comments for all but one of the administration's first sixteen months in office. In fact, nearly three-quarters of all network reporters' assessments of Clinton were found to have been negative.[139] Administration spokespersons quickly latched on to the report as a way to explain why the president was getting no credit for the good economic conditions (Lichter found that 60 percent of the network stories on the economy were negative),[140] and there was an upsurge in stories considering whether the press had been harsh in its treatment of the president. Although the precise content of coverage may be debated, it is clear that Clinton was the darling of neither establishment nor nonestablishment (such as talk radio) media.[141]

Many people in the executive branch help presidents deal with the media, but the media also have their share of resources. A large number of reporters cover the White House, many of whom have expertise in substantive areas such as law, science, welfare, and defense policy.[142] Nonetheless, members of the media may not use their skills to full advantage. Journalists covering the presidency generally lack confidence in dealing with the substance of policies and consequently focus their coverage on four areas where they feel most comfortable: administration scandals, internal dissension, a public gaffe or tactical blunder, and the ebb and flow of electoral contests and public opinion polls.[143] The result is unintended collusion between the presidency and the media that keeps the public less rather than more informed about American government. This line of criticism, focused on journalistic norms and practices, goes beyond those who believe that particular presidents received less vigorous scrutiny than they deserved. For example, some have suggested that Reagan's vaunted "Teflon coating" (a term commonly used during his presidency to suggest that negative stories did not seem to stick to Reagan) was the product of poor journalism.[144]

The ever-increasing speed with which news is reported—and the emergence of a never-ending news cycle—has arguably made the media less careful in what they convey about the president and other political figures. In their haste to keep up with the opposition, news organizations often pick up and report breaking news stories without independent corroboration. As Bill Kovach and Tom Rosenstiel have written: "Information is moving so fast, news outlets are caught between trying to gather new information and playing catch-up with what others have delivered ahead of them. The result for any news organization is a set of flexible standards that are often bent beyond recognition as the organization relies on another's reportage."[145] The Internet, in particular, has altered the way that news is reported. The traditional old media had served as a gatekeeper of what news was reported. With the Internet, however, virtually anyone can post a story. Thus, the "Drudge Report" broke the Monica Lewinsky story on the Internet, and the Internet came to shape the way that the media covered the story of the scandal.

Before the Monica Lewinsky story erupted in 1998, the major media outlets had an unwritten rule that they would not use Web sites to break a story.[146] That changed with the Lewinsky scandal. With news organizations struggling to stay ahead of the competition, Web sites became important. After the "Drudge Report," the first mainstream coverage of the Lewinsky scandal appeared on the *Washington Post* Web site, followed by the *Newsweek* Web site. (*Newsweek* had been investigating the story for a year and had not previously published it because Kenneth Starr, the independent counsel investigating the president, had asked the magazine not to do so.)[147] In the ensuing drive to scoop the competition, errors were made. The *Dallas Morning Herald*, for example, posted an erroneous story on its Web site saying that a Secret Service agent was an eyewitness to a presidential tryst. The editors pulled the story, but not before other news outlets, such as ABC, had reported it.[148]

A study by the Committee of Concerned Journalists examined 1,565 statements and allegations contained in media reports of the Lewinsky scandal in the first six days after the story broke. It found that the press "routinely intermingled reporting with opinion and speculation—even on the front page."[149] Among the specific findings of the study:

- Four in ten statements (41 percent of the reportage) were not factual reporting at all—here is what happened—but were instead journalists offering analysis, opinion, speculation or judgment.
- Forty percent of all reporting based on anonymous sourcing was from a single source.
- Only one statement in a hundred (1 percent of the reporting) was based on two or more named sources.[150]

Such situations prompted CNN senior analyst Jeff Greenfield to express concern about what he called an "echo effect": news organizations picking up and repeating without independent corroboration a story from a single source. He expressed concern that even unreliable stories gained credibility through the simple act of repetition in various news venues.[151] The constant chatter of talking heads on twenty-four-hour cable networks further exacerbated the echo effect. Another report by the Committee of Concerned Journalists suggested that these talking heads were responsible for the most blatant errors and distortions in the coverage of the Lewinsky scandal. For example, rumors of Clinton liaisons with other interns that would never have merited coverage by a responsible news organization were fair game on these talk shows.[152] This continues to be a cause of concern as talk shows proliferate. In 2001—facing falling ratings and stiff competition from Fox News and MSNBC—CNN, as noted above, expanded its number of talk shows and decreased its coverage of hard news.[153]

Conclusion: The Permanent Campaign

The rise of the public presidency corresponds with the development of "the permanent campaign." Sidney Blumenthal popularized that phrase in a 1982 book of the same name (although the phrase had been used before—notably in a transition memo from adviser Pat Caddell to President-elect Jimmy Carter in 1976).[154] Blumenthal noted that the traditional distinction between *campaigning* and *governing* had broken down and that the resulting permanent campaign had remade government "into an instrument designed to sustain an elected official's popularity."[155] More recently, Hugh Heclo described the permanent campaign this way:

[P]ermanent campaign is shorthand for an emergent pattern of political management that the body politic did not plan, debate, or formally adopt. It is a work of inadvertence, something developed higgledy-piggledy since the middle of the twentieth-century. The permanent campaign comprises a complex mixture of politically sophisticated people, communication techniques, and organizations—profit and nonprofit alike. What ties the pieces together is the continuous and voracious quest for public approval.[156]

The presidency of Bill Clinton is a quintessential example of the permanent campaign in action.[157] Charles O. Jones noted that Clinton remained in full campaign mode even in his eighth year in office—unable because of the Twenty-second Amendment to the Constitution to run for a third term. "Here was a prime example of the campaigning style of governing, practiced by a virtuoso," Jones wrote.[158]

The White House staff units discussed in this chapter are important tools for waging that campaign. The problem with such tactics is that campaigning—by its very nature—is *adversarial*, while governing is—or at least should be—largely *collaborative*. As Heclo puts it, "campaigning is self-centered, and governing is group-centered."[159] When the permanent campaign becomes the predominant governing style, however, collaboration becomes difficult. Not surprisingly, recent years have seen a breakdown of the elite bargaining community that used to collaborate to produce policy. Samuel Kernell has noted that this bargaining community is neither as isolated from public pressure nor as tightly bound together by established norms of elite behavior as it used to be.[160] He contends that presidents used to promote their programs primarily by negotiating with other political elites in Congress and the executive branch, but today they more often choose to "go public" by circumventing those elites and appealing directly to the American people for support.[161] Presidents do this through the means we have discussed in this chapter: public speeches, public appearances, and political travel, coupled with targeted outreach using White House staff units such as the Office of Communications and the Office of Public Liaison.

Although these new developments undoubtedly have affected the presidency, the fact remains that there are limits to a president's ability to transform public opinion into public policy.[162] If presidents want to see their programs adopted and implemented, they must also use the powers and institutional arrangements of their office, and they must work with Congress, the executive branch, and the courts to accomplish their purpose. In chapter 4, we examine the personality traits and skills that presidents bring to this task.

NOTES

1. Henry Jones Ford, *The Rise and Growth of American Politics: A Sketch of Constitutional Development* (New York: Macmillan, 1900), 283.

2. Woodrow Wilson, *Constitutional Government in the United States* (1908; reprint, New York: Columbia University Press, 1961), 68.

3. Richard Neustadt, *Presidential Power: The Politics of Leadership* (New York: Wiley, 1960), 86–107.

4. Samuel Kernell, *Going Public: New Strategies of Presidential Leadership*, 3d ed. (Washington, D.C.: CQ Press, 1997).

5. Matthew A. Baum and Samuel Kernell, "Has Cable Ended the Golden Age of Presidential Television?" *American Political Science Review* 93 (March 1999): 99–114.

6. The numbers in this paragraph are based on Gallup polls. See Appendix B in Michael Nelson, ed., *Congressional Quarterly's Guide to the Presidency*, 2d ed. (Washington, D.C.: CQ Press, 1996), 1698–1703, for Gallup presidential approval ratings from 1949 to 1995. The latest Gallup polls can be found on the web at www.gallup.com. Summaries of polls from a variety of polling organizations can be found at www.pollingreport.com.

President Clinton's final Gallup job approval rating (based on nationwide surveys taken on January 5–7, 2001—before Clinton pardoned Marc Rich) was 65 percent. Other polls showed similar results: CNN/*Time* showed Clinton's job approval rating at 64 percent, CBS showed it at 68 percent, and NBC/*Wall Street Journal* showed it at 66 percent. Ronald Reagan came closest with his final Gallup job approval rating of 63 percent.

For an account of Clinton's early low poll ratings, see George C. Edwards III, "Frustration and Folly: Bill Clinton and the Public Presidency," in *The Clinton Presidency: First Appraisals*, ed. Colin Campbell and Bert A. Rockman (Chatham, N.J.: Chatham House, 1996).

7. Molly W. Andolina and Clyde Wilcox, "Public Opinion: The Paradoxes of Clinton's Popularity," in *The Clinton Scandal and the Future of American Government*, ed. Mark J. Rozell and Clyde Wilcox (Washington, D.C.: Georgetown University Press, 2000), 171–194.

8. Charles O. Jones, "Preparing to Govern in 2001: Lessons from the Clinton Presidency," in *The Permanent Campaign and Its Future,* ed. Norman J. Ornstein and Thomas E. Mann (Washington, D.C.: American Enterprise Institute, 2000), 206–207.

9. David Easton, *A Systems Analysis of Political Life* (New York: Wiley, 1965), chaps. 10–13.

10. Andolina and Wilcox, "Public Opinion," 189; for example, a CBS/*New York Times* poll conducted on September 22–23, 1998, showed that 65 percent of all those surveyed felt that the affair was a private matter (83 percent of Democrats thought it was a private matter, as opposed to 67 percent of independents, and 40 percent of Republicans). See also Robert J. Spitzer, "The Presidency: The Clinton Crisis and Its Consequences," in *The Clinton Scandal and the Future of American Government,* 3–4.

11. A Fox News/Opinion Dynamic poll conducted February 7–8, 2001, found that 55 percent of those polled considered the pardon to be an "abuse of power" and 68 percent felt that Clinton gave the pardon in return for "contributions and favors from Rich's friends and family." A poll conducted by the same organization on February 21–22, 2001, found that 71 percent considered the Rich pardon to be "justice denied," while only 9 percent considered it "justice done."

12. Fred I. Greenstein, "What the President Means to Americans: Presidential Choice between Elections," in *Choosing the President,* ed. James David Barber (Englewood Cliffs, N.J.: Prentice-Hall, 1974), 144–146.

13. *New York Times,* November 5, 1991.

14. Joseph E. Kallenbach, *The American Chief Executive: The Presidency and the Governorship* (New York: Harper and Row, 1966), 275.

15. Barry Schwartz, *George Washington: The Making of an American Symbol* (Ithaca: Cornell University Press, 1987), 58–63.

16. Schwartz's discussion of the various public portrayals of Washington and their iconography is especially valuable. It may be of interest to students to note which figures' portraits appear on the most widely circulated coins and currency of the time.

17. Schwartz, *George Washington,* esp. part 2.

18. Barbara Hinckley, *The Symbolic Presidency: How Presidents Portray Themselves* (New York: Routledge, 1990), 130.

19. Ibid., 131–133.

20. Colin Campbell, "Demotion? Has Clinton Turned the Bully Pulpit into a Lectern?" in *The Clinton Legacy,* ed. Colin Campbell and Bert A. Rockman (New York: Chatham House, 2000), 56.

21. Findings of the Survey Research Center at the University of Michigan in the mid-1960s indicated that of all the occupations in the United States, including "famous doctor," "president of a large corporation like General Motors," "bishop or other church official," "Supreme Court justice," and "senator," more than half the adults named the president as the most respected.

22. Samuel Kernell, Peter Sperlich, and Aaron Wildavsky, "Public Support for Presidents," in *Perspectives on the Presidency,* ed. Aaron Wildavsky (Boston: Little, Brown, 1975), 148–181.

23. Paul Allen Beck, "The Role of Agents in Political Socialization," in *Handbook of Political Socialization: Theory and Research,* ed. Stanley Allen Renshon (New York: Free Press, 1977), 117–118.

24. Fred Greenstein, *Children and Politics* (New Haven: Yale University Press, 1965); Robert Hess and Judith Torney, *The Development of Political Attitudes in Children* (Chicago: Aldine, 1967); David Easton and Jack Dennis, *Children in the Political System: Origins of Political Legitimacy* (New York: McGraw-Hill, 1969).

25. Jerry L. Yeric and John R. Todd, *Public Opinion: The Visible Politics,* 3d ed. (Itasca, Ill.: Peacock, 1996), 54.

26. Dean Jaros, Herbert Hirsch, and Frederick J. Fleron Jr., "The Malevolent Leader: Political Socialization in an American Subculture," *American Political Science Review* (June 1968): 564–575.

27. Jack Dennis and Carol Webster, "Children's Images of the President in 1962 and 1974," *American Politics Quarterly* (October 1975): 398.

28. Christopher Arterton, "Watergate and Children's Attitudes towards Political Authority Revisited," *Political Science Quarterly* (fall 1975): 477–496. Cf. Christopher Arterton, "The Impact of Watergate on Children's Attitudes towards Political Authority," *Political Science Quarterly* (June 1974): 269–288.

29. For example, David O. Sears and Nicholas A. Valentino, "Politics Matters: Political Events as Catalysts for Preadult Socialization," *American Political Science Review* (March 1997): 45–65.

30. Paul Brace and Barbara Hinckley, *Follow the Leader: Opinion Polls and Modern Presidents* (New York: Basic Books, 1992), 19.

31. Diane J. Heath, "Presidential Polling and the Potential for Leadership," in *Presidential Power: Forging the Presidency for the Twenty-first Century,* ed. Robert Y. Shapiro, Martha Joynt Kumar, and Lawrence R. Jacobs (New York: Columbia University Press, 2000), 382.

32. Ibid., 384.

33. Ibid., 387.

34. Ibid., 392.

35. John Anthony Maltese, *Spin Control: The White House Office of Communications and the Management of Presidential News,* 2d rev. ed. (Chapel Hill: University of North Carolina Press, 1994), 213–214.

36. Carl M. Cannon, "Hooked on Polls," *National Journal,* October 17, 1998, 2438 ff.

37. Andolina and Wilcox, "Public Opinion," 183.

38. Paul Brace and Barbara Hinckley, "Public Opinion Polls: The New Referendum," in *Understanding the Presidency,* ed. James P. Pfiffner and Roger H. Davidson (New York: Longman, 1997), 125. See also Brace and Hinckley, *Follow the Leader.* An earlier study that made a similar finding about the decay of presidential support was John Mueller, *War, Presidents, and Public Opinion* (New York: Wiley, 1973).

39. Brace and Hinckley, *Follow the Leader,* 23–24, 32, 24.

40. James P. Pfiffner, *The Strategic Presidency: Hitting the Ground Running,* 2d ed., rev. (Lawrence: University Press of Kansas, 1996).

41. Paul C. Light, *The President's Agenda: Domestic Policy Choice from Kennedy to Clinton,* 3d ed. (Baltimore: Johns Hopkins University Press, 1999).

42. Maltese, *Spin Control,* 180.

43. Ann McFeatters, "Tax Cut, Other Proposals Well Received," *Pittsburgh Post–Gazette,* March 4, 2001, A9.

44. Gallup News Service, Poll Release, February 28, 2001, "Instant Reaction: Speech Viewers Give Bush High Marks," www.gallup.com.

45. Gallup poll conducted February 19–21, 2001.

46. Johnson's first approval ratings came just after President Kennedy was assassinated in 1963. On taking office in January 1965, after being elected in his own right, Johnson's approval rating was 71 percent.

47. Bradley H. Patterson Jr., *The White House Staff: Inside the West Wing and Beyond* (Washington, D.C.: Brookings, 2000). See also Charles E. Walcott and Karen M. Hult, *Governing the White House: From Hoover through LBJ* (Lawrence: University Press of Kansas, 1995), chaps. 3 and 10.

48. Jeffrey K. Tulis, *The Rhetorical Presidency* (Princeton: Princeton University Press, 1987).

49. Kernell, *Going Public,* chap. 2.

50. Jeffrey Tulis, "The Two Constitutional Presidencies," in *The Presidency and the Political System,* 6th ed., ed. Michael Nelson (Washington, D.C.: CQ Press, 2000), 115–116.

51. Tulis, *The Rhetorical Presidency,* 95.

52. Ibid., 46; see, generally, chaps. 1 and 2.

53. See, for example, Richard L. Rubin, *Press, Party, and Presidency* (New York: Norton, 1981); Culver H. Smith, *The Press, Politics, and Patronage* (Athens: University of Georgia Press, 1977).

54. Robert A. Rutland, *The Newsmongers* (New York: Dial Press, 1973), 58.

55. Frank Luther Mott, *American Journalism* (New York: Macmillan, 1941), 119–120.

56. Tulis, *The Rhetorical Presidency,* 69.

57. Based on Table 3-1 in Tulis, *The Rhetorical Presidency,* 64.

58. Samuel Kernell and Gary C. Jacobson, *The Logic of American Politics* (Washington, D.C.: CQ Press, 2000), 242.

59. Tulis, *The Rhetorical Presidency,* 91–93.

60. Ibid., 106.

61. James W. Caesar, *Presidential Selection: Theory and Development* (Princeton: Princeton University Press, 1979), 181–184.

62. Tulis, *The Rhetorical Presidency,* 182.

63. "Bush Tax Cuts Clear First Hurdle," *World News Tonight,* American Broadcasting Company (ABC), March 8, 2001.

64. George Stephanopoulos, *Good Morning America,* ABC, January 22, 1998, transcript no. 98012217-jl4. See also John Anthony Maltese, "The New Media and the Lure of the Clinton Scandal," in *The Clinton Scandal and the Future of American Government,* 198.

65. Kernell and Jacobson, *The Logic of American Politics,* 239.

66. Baum and Kernell, "Has Cable Ended the Golden Age of Presidential Television?"

67. For a discussion of the permanent campaign and its impact on presidential governance, see Norman J. Ornstein and Thomas E. Mann, eds., *The Permanent Campaign and Its Future* (Washington, D.C.: American Enterprise Institute, 2000).

68. Richard Rose, *The Postmodern President,* 2d ed. (Chatham, N.J.: Chatham House, 1991), 38.

69. Maltese, *Spin Control,* 195.

70. Mark Hertsgaard, *On Bended Knee: The Press and the Reagan Presidency* (New York: Farrar Straus, 1988), 273.

71. Memo, H. R. Haldeman to Herb Klein, March 20, 1969, in "Memos/Herb Klein (March 1969)," Box 49, H. R. Haldeman Files, Nixon Presidential Materials Project. For a thorough discussion of the use of presidential surrogates from Nixon through Clinton, see Maltese, *Spin Control.*

72. Maltese, *Spin Control,* 34, 222.

73. Ibid., 35.

74. Mark A. Peterson, "Clinton and Organized Interests: Splitting Friends, Unifying Enemies," in *The Clinton Legacy,* 147.

75. Joseph A. Pika, "Interest Groups and the White House under Roosevelt and Truman," *Political Science Quarterly* (winter 1987–1988): 647–668.

76. Joseph A. Pika, "Interest Groups and the Executive: Presidential Intervention," in *Interest Group Politics,* ed. Allan J. Cigler and Burdett A. Loomis (Washington, D.C.: CQ Press, 1983), 318. Also see Mark A. Peterson, "The Presidency and Organized Interests: White House Patterns of Interest Group Liaison," *American Political Science Review* (September 1992): 612–625; Joseph A. Pika, "Opening Doors for Kindred

Souls: The White House Office of Public Liaison," in *Interest Group Politics*, 3d ed., ed. Allan J. Cigler and Burdett A. Loomis (Washington, D.C.: CQ Press, 1991); Martha Joynt Kumar and Michael Baruch Grossman, "Political Communications from the White House: The Interest Group Connection," *Presidential Studies Quarterly* (winter 1986): 92–101; Walcott and Hult, *Governing the White House*, chap. 6; and Bradley H. Patterson, *The Ring of Power: The White House Staff and Its Expanding Role in Government* (New York: Basic Books, 1988), chap. 14.

77. For a discussion of Colson and his tactics as Nixon's liaison with interest groups, see Maltese, *Spin Control*, 38, 82–84.

78. Kumar and Grossman, "Political Communications," 98.

79. Graham Wilson, "The Clinton Administration and Interest Groups," in *The Clinton Presidency: First Appraisals.*

80. In addition to the essay by Wilson, "The Clinton Administration and Interest Groups," see Barbara Sinclair, "Trying to Govern Positively in a Negative Era: Clinton and the 103rd Congress," and Paul J. Quirk and Joseph Hinchliffe, "Domestic Policy: The Trials of a Centrist Democrat," in *The Clinton Presidency: First Appraisals.*

81. Patterson, *The Ring of Power*, 230.

82. Kathryn Dunn Tenpas, "Institutionalized Politics: The White House Office of Political Affairs," *Presidential Studies Quarterly* (spring 1996): 511.

83. John Anthony Maltese, *The Selling of Supreme Court Nominees* (Baltimore: Johns Hopkins University Press, 1995), 77.

84. Tenpas, "Institutionalized Politics," 514.

85. House Committee on Government Reform and Oversight, *Investigation of the Conversion of the $1.7 Million Centralized White House Computer System, Known as the White House Database, and Related Matters*, 105th Cong., 2d sess., 1998, H. Rept. 105 828 (available online at www.house.gov/reform/neg), 43–44.

86. Ibid., 44.

87. Tenpas, "Institutionalized Politics," 512.

88. Losses by the president's party in midterm elections have been remarkably predictable. In the thirty-five midterm elections from 1862 through 1998, the president's party lost seats in the House of Representatives in thirty-two (1902, 1934, and 1998 are the exceptions) and in the Senate in twenty-one of the elections. Harold W. Stanley and Richard G. Niemi, *Vital Statistics on American Politics, 1999–2000*, 5th ed. (Washington, D.C.: CQ Press, 2000), Table 1-16, 48.

89. Thomas Mann presents his findings on the 1974 elections in *Unsafe at Any Margin: Interpreting Congressional Elections* (Washington, D.C.: American Enterprise Institute, 1978), 92; Lyn Ragsdale presents her findings on the 1978 elections in "The Fiction of Congressional Elections as Presidential Events," *American Politics Quarterly* (October 1980): 375–398.

90. David Leuthold, *Electioneering in a Democracy: Campaigns for Congress* (New York: Wiley, 1968).

91. Edward Tufte, "Determinants of the Outcomes of Midterm Congressional Elections," *American Political Science Review* (September 1975): 812–826.

92. Samuel Kernell, "Presidential Popularity and Negative Voting: An Alternative Explanation of the Midterm Decline of the Presidential Party," *American Political Science Review* (March 1977): 44–66.

93. Gary Jacobson, *The Politics of Congressional Elections* (Boston: Little, Brown, 1983),138 ff.

94. See the discussion by Sidney M. Milkis, "The Presidency and Political Parties," in *The Presidency and the Political System*, 4th ed., ed. Michael Nelson (Washington, D.C.: CQ Press, 1995). See also Thomas E. Patterson, *Out of Order* (New York: Knopf, 1993).

95. James Pollard, *The Presidents and the Press* (New York: Macmillan, 1947), chap. 1.

96. William Rivers, *The Opinion-Makers* (Boston: Beacon Press, 1967), 7.

97. Michael Baruch Grossman and Martha Joynt Kumar, *Portraying the President: The White House and the News Media* (Baltimore: Johns Hopkins University Press, 1981), 19.

98. Elmer E. Cornwell, *Presidential Leadership of Public Opinion* (Bloomington: Indiana University Press, 1965), 17; Stephen Hess, "Press Relations," in *Encyclopedia of the American Presidency,* ed. Leonard W. Levy and Louis Fisher (New York: Simon and Schuster, 1994), 1230.

99. *TV Dimensions 2000* (New York: Media Dynamics, 2000), 245.

100. Harold W. Stanley and Richard G. Niemi, *Vital Statistics on American Politics,* 5th ed. (Washington, D.C.: CQ Press, 1995), Table 2-1, 47.

101. Benjamin I. Page, Robert Y. Shapiro, and Glenn R. Dempsey, "What Moves Public Opinion?" *American Political Science Review* (March 1987): 23–43; and Donald L. Jordan, "Newspaper Effects on Policy Preferences," *Public Opinion Quarterly* (summer 1993): 191–204. Page, Shapiro, and Dempsey examined television reports, whereas Jordan concentrated on newspaper effects.

102. Grossman and Kumar, *Portraying the President,* 209–210.

103. Stanley and Niemi, *Vital Statistics on American Politics,* 5th ed., Table 2-2, 48–49.

104. There are some notable exceptions to this rule. The *NewsHour with Jim Lehrer,* broadcast nightly by the Public Broadcasting Service (PBS), takes an hour to examine two or three topics in depth; ABC's *Nightline* looks at one topic for half an hour. PBS's *Washington Week in Review* uses major political reporters to analyze the significant news developments of the previous week; CNN provides continuing coverage as well as expanded focus on Washington, as on *Inside Politics.*

105. Baum and Kernell, "Has Cable Ended the Golden Age of Presidential Television?" 99.

106. Stephen Hess, *The Washington Reporters* (Washington, D.C.: Brookings, 1981), chap. 2; Leon Segal, *Reporters and Officials* (Lexington, Mass.: D. C. Heath, 1973), chap. 1.

107. Hess, *The Washington Reporters,* 31.

108. Quoted in Burt Solomon, "How a Leak-Loathing White House Is Putting the Press in Its Place," *National Journal,* February 13, 1993, 416.

109. Tom Rosenstiel, *The Beat Goes On: President Clinton's First Year with the Media* (New York: Twentieth Century Fund, 1994), 10.

110. Quoted in Leslie Kaufman, "The Young and the Relentless," *American Journalism Review* (March 1993): 30.

111. For a discussion of this, see Richard Davis and Diana Owen, *New Media and American Politics* (New York: Oxford University Press, 1998).

112. Sidney Blumenthal, "The Syndicated Presidency," *New Yorker,* April 5, 1993, 42.

113. Frank Newport and Lydia Saad, "A Matter of Trust," *American Journalism Review* (July–August 1998): 30.

114. For an early account of Vice President Cheney's role in circumventing the press corps, see Eric Schmitt, "Talk Show Debut Suggests Cheney Role," *New York Times,* January 29, 2001, A18.

115. Grossman and Kumar, *Portraying the President,* chap. 5.

116. M. L. Stein, *When Presidents Meet the Press* (New York: Messner, 1969), 166.

117. John F. Kennedy Jr., "Mike McCurry's About-Face," *George* (March 1999): 78.

118. Maltese, *Spin Control,* 24, 29.

119. Larry Speakes, *Speaking Out: Inside the Reagan White House* (New York: Scribner's, 1988), 136, 153.

120. For a full account of the office and its precursors, see Maltese, *Spin Control.*

121. Schmitt, "Talk Show Debut Suggests Cheney Role."

122. Interview with John Anthony Maltese, March 10, 1989, Washington, D.C., quoted in Maltese, *Spin Control*, 2.

123. Donald T. Regan, *For the Record* (New York: Harcourt Brace Jovanovich, 1988), 248.

124. Kernell, *Going Public*, 63.

125. Quoted in Maltese, *Spin Control*, 44.

126. Patterson, *The Ring of Power*, 174.

127. Fred I. Greenstein, *The Hidden-Hand Presidency: Eisenhower as Leader* (New York: Basic Books, 1982), 66–70.

128. George Reedy, *The Twilight of the Presidency* (New York: New American Library, 1970), 164.

129. Grossman and Kumar, *Portraying the President*, 244.

130. Pollard, *The Presidents and the Press*, 14.

131. Larry J. Sabato, *Feeding Frenzy: Attack Journalism and American Politics* (New York: Lanahan, 2000).

132. Grossman and Kumar, *Portraying the President*, chap. 1.

133. Michael Grossman and Francis Rourke, "The Media and the Presidency: An Exchange Analysis," *Political Science Quarterly* (fall 1976): 455–470. Also see Timothy E. Cook and Lyn Ragsdale, "The President and the Press: Negotiating Newsworthiness at the White House," in *The Presidency and the Political System*, 6th ed.

134. David Broder, quoted by Patterson in *The Ring of Power*, 170.

135. Grossman and Kumar, *Portraying the President*, chap. 11.

136. Ibid., 178.

137. This tendency first became apparent during the second year of the Reagan administration when reporters began to ask him more embarrassing questions (for instance, why he did not set an example by making more generous donations to private charities). They also appeared not to take seriously the president's statement that members of his administration were one big happy family.

138. Martha Joynt Kumar, "President Clinton Meets the Media: Communications Shaped by Predictable Patterns," in *The Clinton Presidency: Campaigning, Governing, and the Psychology of Leadership*, ed. Stanley A. Rehshon (Boulder: Westview, 1995), 167–171.

139. Study conducted by Robert Lichter of the Center for Media and Public Affairs as reported in Howard Kurtz, "The Bad News about Clinton," *Washington Post*, September 1, 1994, D1.

140. James Risen, "Clinton Gets Little Credit for Economic Turnaround," *Los Angeles Times*, September 5, 1994, A2.

141. Godfrey Sperling, " 'Clinton Bashing' and the Liberal Press," *Christian Science Monitor*, September 20, 1994, 19.

142. Stephen Hess showed that in 1978, 73 percent were college graduates and 33 percent had graduate degrees (*The Washington Reporters*, 83); Leo Rosten reported that in 1936, 51 percent were college graduates and 6 percent had an advanced academic degree; see *The Washington Correspondents* (New York: Harcourt, Brace, 1937), 159–160.

143. James Fallows, "The Presidency and the Press," in *The Presidency and the Political System*, 3d ed., ed. Michael Nelson (Washington, D.C.: CQ Press, 1990).

144. Hertsgaard, *On Bended Knee*.

145. Bill Kovach and Tom Rosenstiel, *Warp Speed: America in the Age of Mixed Media* (New York: Century Foundation Press, 1999), 51.

146. David Noack, "Clinton Sex Story Forces Print Media Changes," *Editor and Publisher*, January 31, 1998, 62. The remainder of this section is drawn from John

Anthony Maltese, "The Presidency and the News Media," *Perspectives on Political Science* (spring 2001): 81–82.

147. Howard Kurtz, *Spin Cycle: How the White House and the Media Manipulate the News* (New York: Touchstone, 1998), 291.

148. Dan Trigoboff, "The 'Source' Heard 'Round the World," *Broadcasting and Cable* February 2, 1998, 62.

149. Kovach and Rosenstiel, *Warp Speed,* 99 (the study is reproduced in Appendix 1 of their book).

150. Ibid.,100.

151. Trigoboff, "The 'Source' Heard 'Round the World," 62.

152. Alicia C. Shepard, "White Noise," *American Journalism Review* (January–February 1999): 20.

153. John Cook, "CNN's Free Fall," *Brill's Content* (April 2001): 1. Instead of hard news, the spring 2001 prime-time lineup on CNN consisted of the talk-show oriented programs *Wolf Blitzer Reports, The Point with Greta Van Susteren, Larry King Live,* and *The Spin Room.* Interspersed at 10:00 p.m. was a half-hour newscast anchored by Bill Hemmer.

154. Sidney Blumenthal, *The Permanent Campaign* (New York: Simon and Schuster, 1982); see also Ornstein and Mann, eds., *The Permanent Campaign and Its Future,* vii.

155. Blumenthal, *The Permanent Campaign,* 7.

156. Hugh Heclo, "Campaigning and Governing: A Conspectus," in Ornstein and Mann, eds., *The Permanent Campaign and Its Future,* 15.

157. George C. Edwards III, "Campaigning Is Not Governing: Bill Clinton's Rhetorical Presidency," in *The Clinton Legacy,* 33.

158. Jones, "Preparing to Govern in 2001," 185.

159. Heclo, "Campaigning and Governing," 11.

160. Kernell, *Going Public,* 23.

161. Ibid., 2.

162. Brandice Canes-Wrone, "The President's Legislative Influence from Public Appeals," *American Journal of Political Science* (April 2001): 313–329.

SUGGESTED READINGS

Brace, Paul, and Barbara Hinckley. *Follow the Leader: Opinion Polls and Modern Presidents.* New York: Basic Books, 1992.

Cornwell, Elmer E. *Presidential Leadership of Public Opinion.* Bloomington: Indiana University Press, 1965.

Edwards, George C., III. *The Public Presidency: The Pursuit of Popular Support.* New York: St. Martin's Press, 1983.

Grossman, Michael Baruch, and Martha Joynt Kumar. *Portraying the President: The White House and the News Media.* Baltimore: Johns Hopkins University Press, 1981.

Hinckley, Barbara. *The Symbolic Presidency: How Presidents Portray Themselves.* New York: Routledge, 1990.

Kernell, Samuel. *Going Public: New Strategies of Presidential Leadership,* 3d ed. Washington, D.C.: CQ Press, 1997.

Maltese, John Anthony. *Spin Control: The White House Office of Communications and the Management of Presidential News,* 2d ed., rev. Chapel Hill: University of North Carolina Press, 1994.

Ornstein, Norman J., and Thomas E. Mann, eds. *The Permanent Campaign and Its Future.* Washington, D.C.: American Enterprise Institute, 2000.

Patterson, Bradley H., Jr. *The White House Staff: Inside the West Wing and Beyond.* Washington, D.C.: Brookings, 2000.

Shapiro, Robert Y., Martha Joynt Kumar, and Lawrence R. Jacobs, eds. *Presidential Power: Forging the Presidency for the Twenty-first Century.* New York: Columbia University Press, 2000.

Tulis, Jeffrey K. *The Rhetorical Presidency.* Princeton: Princeton University Press, 1987.

4 PRESIDENTIAL CHARACTER AND PERFORMANCE

In a dramatic moment intended to halt media reports and rumors, President Bill Clinton publicly denied in January 1998 having had a sexual relationship with "that woman," Monica Lewinsky, but was later forced to publicly apologize for lying about the relationship and to defend himself against impeachment charges.

PRESIDENT WILLIAM JEFFERSON CLINTON left office at noon on January 20, 2001, at the completion of a controversial, eight-year roller-coaster ride on the national scene. A man of uncommon intellectual ability and verbal facility, Clinton left behind many lingering questions centered on his personal character and judgment. Retrospective evaluations of his legacy recognized the mixed nature of his performance as president, a record of "striking strengths [and] glaring failures."[1] Foremost among the latter was his relationship with former White House intern Monica Lewinsky. When word of the alleged affair swept the nation in January 1998, Clinton publicly denied having any sexual relationship with "that woman," a position he also took in providing a legal deposition in a civil suit for sexual harassment that had been filed against him by Paula Jones, a former Arkansas state employee. But after a sustained grand jury investigation into whether his testimony constituted perjury, Clinton grudgingly admitted the relationship had been "not appropriate" and "wrong" in a nationally televised speech on August 17, 1998. This brief, 10 P.M. address concluded a day in which the president had answered questions for four hours before Kenneth Starr, the independent counsel appointed to look into allegations of wrongdoing.[2] Ultimately the Republican House impeached Clinton on charges of perjury and obstruction of justice, but the Senate did not find him guilty, and he completed his term in office. (*See Chapter 5.*)

Could we have predicted Clinton's performance in office? Did we know enough about his personal background and previous experience in elected office to have anticipated his record of dramatically alternating highs and lows? The presidency invites such speculation because its occupants wield enormous power in a one-person office rather than as part of a collective institution. Moreover, during the last third of the twentieth century, enormous attention was devoted to the psychological makeup of chief executives. Many analysts attributed the conduct of the Vietnam War (1965–1973) and the Watergate scandal (in which White House aides covered up illegal activities committed to help the president get reelected) to the unique emotional needs of Presidents Lyndon Baines Johnson and Richard Nixon.[3]

In this chapter we look more closely at what kinds of people have served as president and how their personal qualities may have shaped their conduct. We are especially concerned with the backgrounds, skills, psychological traits, and management styles of presidents and how these factors influence their performance in office. We therefore examine the abilities and attitudes that presidents develop before entering office, ways in which their personalities affect how they do the job, and habitual modes of working. We also look at the way presidents interact with their staffs, those assistants whose positions were created to extend presidents' personal capabilities. To conclude, we take a closer look at Bill Clinton to understand the factors that shaped his performance in office, and we offer a preliminary sketch of George W. Bush.

Determinants and Evaluations of Performance

For generations, historians and political scientists have argued among themselves about just how important a leader's characteristics are for understanding and explaining events. Does one, for example, place great significance on the intelligence, stature, and wisdom of Abraham Lincoln in explaining the Union's ultimate victory over the Confederacy? Or was victory the product of forces beyond Lincoln's control, such as the changing nature of modern warfare in an industrial age, which favored the North? Did America and the Soviet Union avert nuclear war during the Cuban missile crisis of 1962 because of the decision style adopted by John F. Kennedy? Or was the outcome the result of organizational routines for crisis management and other random occurrences perhaps not even intended by either side during the confrontation? The larger questions, then, are, just how much importance should one ascribe to the president's personal characteristics, and are these elements powerful predictors of performance in office?

Specialists have not reached agreement on the importance of these factors, although there is widespread belief that it does indeed matter—and probably a great deal—just who is president. As Fred Greenstein argues, "If some higher power had set out to design a democracy in which the individual on top mattered, the result might well resemble the American political system."[4] Every four years the nation devotes enormous effort and resources to selecting a leader, and this confidence in the difference that an individual can make is revealed when citizens proudly explain that they "voted for the person, not the party." Public attention focuses on the presidency, with the mass media personalizing the solution to public problems and portraying presidents as the embodiment of the larger political process. Moreover, presidents and their media advisers encourage personalization when they highlight traits that the public regards as desirable, such as decisiveness and strength of character.

Not everyone agrees that presidents' individual characteristics are critical to understanding their accomplishments in office. The alternative is to stress the environment within which presidents operate as the truly significant determinant of outcomes. The most influential interpretation in this tradition is the work of Stephen Skowronek, whose analysis rests on comparison of presidents in decidedly different time frames and centuries. Thus, Thomas Jefferson, Andrew Jackson, Lincoln, Franklin Roosevelt, and Ronald Reagan shared common "leadership tasks" associated with the decline and reconstruction of the links among societal interests and the political parties essential to a political order. Similarly, James Monroe, James K. Polk, Theodore Roosevelt, and Lyndon Johnson had more in common with each other—the position they inherited in relation to the dominant political order—than with their immediate predecessors and successors in office. Although the title of Skowronek's principal work—*The Politics Presidents Make*—emphasizes the role of leadership, the unfolding evolution of larger forces in American social and political life defines the tasks presidents confront and severely limits the possibilities they enjoy at the outset of their terms in office.[5]

Nonetheless, there is broad consensus among students of the presidency that each chief executive brings to the job a combination of attitudes, skills, strengths, and shortcomings that will influence his or her performance in office and may at times have an enduring effect on the nation's history. There is still disagreement on the relative significance of these causal factors and exactly how they are related to job performance and policy outcomes. A number of analysts have suggested ways to conceptualize these issues; a modified, considerably simplified diagram based on two of the most prominent treatments is presented in Figure 4-1.

All presidents bring to the job enduring personality traits as well as attitudes and beliefs toward a wide range of political structures, institutions, and relationships. These personal characteristics and attitudes take shape within a distinctive social context—their family situation, place in the community, educational

Figure 4-1 Relationship of Background to Performance

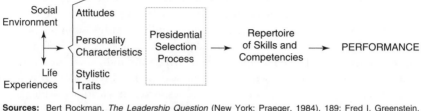

Sources: Bert Rockman, *The Leadership Question* (New York: Praeger, 1984), 189; Fred I. Greenstein, *Personality and Politics* (New York: Norton, 1975), 27.

experience, and so on. In addition, their adult professional experiences prior to entering office, particularly as they relate to role demands of the presidency, produce a personal style that may be more or less congruent with the demands of serving as chief executive. The presidential selection process filters out those personal styles, skills, and competencies that will be brought to the office. Ultimately presidents may be more or less likely to produce successful outcomes as these individual traits interact with the situations they confront. In concentrating on the importance of leaders' individual characteristics, one recognizes that presidents are in the position to have potentially decisive impacts on political events. Even if the environment, forces beyond the control of the individual leader, has a determinative effect on events, "environments are always mediated by the individuals on whom they act."[6]

Just as analysts disagree over the determinants of presidential behavior, there is no consensus on how to evaluate a president's performance, although the general public and professional presidency watchers engage in evaluations all the time. Polls provide current, short-term assessments of public approval *(discussed in Chapter 3)*, and journalists are constantly assessing the administration's record in dealing with Congress or in addressing particular areas of public policy. Certain evaluation points have become institutionalized: the end of an administration's first one hundred days in office (a carryover from Franklin Roosevelt's first term) always produces a spate of articles. Other evaluation points are at midterm (the end of two years) and on departure from office.[7] In other words, the public, journalists, and academics are constantly engaged in *contemporary evaluation* of presidential performance.

Scholars and others use a variety of criteria in reaching these evaluations. Bruce Buchanan has drawn broad distinctions between subjective and objective criteria. Judgments based on subjective grounds emphasize the "appearance and demeanor" of leadership, including success in projecting the image of integrity and charisma; the "moral desirability of a president's means or ends;" and the pragmatic test of self-interest—the extent to which the president contributed to a citizen's well-being. Objective criteria, on which professionals make their evaluations, focus on presidential skill in making things happen, especially short-term successes, or on the lasting results produced for the nation.[8] For example, in reflecting on the record of achievements by the administration of Ronald Reagan, a number of works adopted the long view in assessing the administration's legacy. As Bert Rockman put it, politicians can "leave greater or lesser footprints. Assessing the depth and durability of those marks is hazardous while the administration under evaluation is still in power. The real answers will come later—much later."[9]

Bill Clinton's conduct has reawakened public and professional concern with "presidential character," a term with many contradictory meanings. James Pfiffner seeks to help the public address this murky area: how should Americans assess the personal failures of presidents when they fail to tell the truth about trivial or important matters, violate marriage vows, or intentionally seek to deceive the public?[10] Pfiffner reviews numerous instances of presidential untruths in terms of the teller's intent and the seriousness of the lie, a recognition that evaluation of this conduct depends heavily on the context in which it occurred. Although "telling the truth . . . is an important ethical imperative for presidents," Pfiffner accepts the possibility of a "justified lie."[11] Thus, lies to protect the national security, concerning trivial matters (for example, describing one's personal history or illustrating a point), or to prevent embarrassment and preserve political viability are less serious than those used to cover up important facts or deceive the public on policy matters. Pfiffner's discussion of Clinton's marital infidelity is placed in the context of Franklin Roosevelt, Dwight Eisenhower, John Kennedy, and Lyndon Johnson, other presidents known or suspected to have committed similar acts.[12]

Efforts to evaluate presidential performance and conduct are not new. Since 1948 various scholars, primarily historians, have been asked on several occasions to "rate" American presidents. In essence they were to assess the "depth and durability" of presidential footprints and provide a *historical evaluation*. The results from six of these efforts are reported in Table 4-1. Each poll was structured a bit differently and surveyed a different panel of "experts."[13] Even so, one finds considerable consensus among participants on the top ten and the bottom ten, with the exception of Richard Nixon, whose reputation has undergone a marked resurgence since his death in 1994. Because of the similar results across polls, Robert Murray and Tim Blessing concluded that historians "had in mind more than vague and uncritical generalities when they evaluated presidential performances."[14] Assessments of recent presidents are particularly susceptible to change with the passage of time. Note how Dwight D. Eisenhower moved up from twentieth place in 1962 to ninth in both the *Chicago Tribune* poll in 1982 and the C-SPAN poll in 2000. Harry S. Truman's standing among professionals was already strong by 1962 and has remained so. The most recent survey included Bill Clinton, who finished in the middle of the pack at number twenty-one, just behind George Herbert Walker Bush.

In addition to analyzing 846 completed surveys, Murray and Blessing conducted sixty in-depth interviews with historians to determine their evaluative criteria. The most important personal trait contributing to presidential achieve-

Table 4-1   Ratings of U.S. Presidents

Schlesinger poll (1948)	Schlesinger poll (1962)	Maranell-Dodder poll (1982)	*Chicago Tribune* poll (1982)	Murray-Blessing poll[a] (1982)	C-SPAN poll (2000)
Great	Great	Accomplishments of administration	Ten best presidents	Great	Overall leadership
1. Lincoln	1. Lincoln		1. Lincoln (best)	1. Lincoln	1. Lincoln
2. Washington	2. Washington	1. Lincoln	2. Washington	2. F. Roosevelt	2. F. Roosevelt
3. F. Roosevelt	3. F. Roosevelt	2. F. Roosevelt	3. F. Roosevelt	3. Washington	3. Washington
4. Wilson	4. Wilson	3. Washington	4. T. Roosevelt	4. Jefferson	4. T. Roosevelt
5. Jefferson	5. Jefferson	4. Jefferson	5. Jefferson		5. Truman
6. Jackson		5. T. Roosevelt	6. Wilson	Near great	6. Wilson
	Near great	6. Truman	7. Jackson	5. T. Roosevelt	7. Jefferson
Near great	6. Jackson	7. Wilson	8. Truman	6 Wilson	8. Kennedy
7. T. Roosevelt	7. T. Roosevelt	8. Jackson	9. Eisenhower	7. Jackson	9. Eisenhower
8. Cleveland	8. Polk	9. L. Johnson	10. Polk (10th best)	8. Truman	10. L. Johnson
9. J. Adams	Truman (tie)	10. Polk			11. Reagan
10. Polk	9. J. Adams	11. J. Adams		Above average	12. Polk
	10. Cleveland	12. Kennedy	Ten worst presidents	9. J. Adams	13. Jackson
Average		13. Monroe	1. Harding (worst)	10. L. Johnson	14. Monroe
11. J. Q. Adams	Average	14. Cleveland	2. Nixon	11. Eisenhower	15. McKinley
12. Monroe	11. Madison	15. Madison	3. Buchanan	12. Polk	16. J. Adams
13. Hayes	12. J. Q. Adams	16. Taft	4. Pierce	13. Kennedy	17. Cleveland
14. Madison	13. Hayes	17. McKinley	5. Grant	14. Madison	18. Madison
15. Van Buren	14. McKinley	18. J. Q. Adams	6. Fillmore	15. Monroe	19. J. Q. Adams
16. Taft	15. Taft	19. Hoover	7. A. Johnson	16. J. Q. Adams	20. G.H.W. Bush
17. Arthur	16. Van Buren	20. Eisenhower	8.. Coolidge	17. Cleveland	21. Clinton
18. McKinley	17. Monroe	21. A. Johnson	9. Tyler		22. Carter
19. A. Johnson	18. Hoover	22. Van Buren	10. Carter (10th worst)	Average	23. Ford
20. Hoover	19. B. Harrison	23. Arthur		18. McKinley	24. Taft
21. B. Harrison	20. Arthur	24. Hayes		19. Taft	25. Nixon
	Eisenhower (tie)	25. Tyler		20. Van Buren	26. Hayes
Below average	21. A. Johnson	26. B. Harrison		21. Hoover	27. Coolidge
22. Tyler		27. Taylor		22. Hayes	28. Taylor
23. Coolidge	Below average	28. Buchanan		23. Arthur	29. Garfield
24. Fillmore	22. Taylor	29. Fillmore		24. Ford	30. Van Buren
25. Taylor	23. Tyler	30. Coolidge		25. Carter	31. Harrison
26. Buchanan	24. Fillmore	31. Pierce		26. B. Harrison	32. Arthur
27. Pierce	25. Coolidge	32. Grant			33. Grant
	26. Pierce	33. Harding		Below average	34. Hoover
Failure	27. Buchanan			27. Taylor	35. Fillmore
28. Grant				28. Reagan	36. Tyler
29. Harding	Failure			29. Tyler	37. W. H. Harrison
	28. Grant			30. Fillmore	38. Harding
	29. Harding			31. Coolidge	39. Pierce
				32. Pierce	40. A. Johnson
					41. Buchanan
				Failure	
				33. A. Johnson	
				34. Buchanan	
				35. Nixon	
				36. Grant	
				37. Harding	

Sources: Harold W. Stanley and Richard G. Niemi, *Vital Statistics on American Politics* 1999–2000 (Washington, D.C.: CQ Press, 2000), Table 6-2, 244–245; and C-SPAN Survey, February, 2000, http: //www.americanpresidents .org/survey/historians/overall.asp.

Note: These ratings result from surveys of scholars and range in number from 49 to 846.

[a] The rating of President Reagan was obtained in a separate poll conducted in 1989.

ment, in the view of these participating historians, was decisiveness; intelligence, particularly the capacity for growth, and integrity were close behind.[15] Greatness, many seemed to feel, is achieved by those leaders able to exercise moral, inspirational leadership, who have "a capacity for creative innovation and an imagination that was fired by a clear vision of the future."[16] James MacGregor Burns's discussion of leadership emphasizes similar abilities as the source of "transformational" leadership, by which presidents appeal to the higher goals and motives of followers to achieve true change.[17] Fred Greenstein suggests that a president's job performance is shaped by six qualities: proficiency as a *public communicator; organizational capacity* to rally colleagues and structure activities; *political skill* insofar as it is linked to a *vision* of public policy; *cognitive style* in processing advice and information; and *emotional intelligence,* by which he means the ability to manage one's own emotions for constructive purposes.[18]

As Greenstein makes clear, it is now necessary to factor in an additional consideration in assessing performance: modern presidents no longer govern alone. Since the 1930s they have been assisted by a large number of aides appointed to serve in the Executive Office of the President, who may prove a genuine asset in helping presidents exercise their responsibilities. Aides have the capacity to amplify a president's personal capabilities; mobilizing such efforts is a new dimension of the job just as public communications have taken on a much greater significance than they had prior to the 20th century.

In examining the importance of individual characteristics, we turn first to a discussion of the backgrounds from which presidents have been drawn. As depicted in Figure 4-1, a president's life and occupational experiences are distant from the actual service in office and should therefore have only limited power to explain performance. Nonetheless, the patterns uncovered tell us something about leadership in America.

What Manner of Person?

Each president brings to the office a cumulation of life experiences derived from a position in American society and previous professional experience. The selection process, rather than producing a random sampling of Americans, favors some backgrounds over others. After reviewing the historical pattern for social background and education, scholars have found, not surprisingly, that presidents have disproportionately been drawn from traditionally dominant groups in American society. It is less clear, however, just what this has meant for their performance in office.

Social Background

Although there is no single indicator of social status on which all Americans would agree, occupation is probably the most important criterion for social ranking in the United States.[19] Moreover, the occupation of a person's father provides a reasonably accurate picture of his or her class origins. By analyzing such origins, one can determine the extent to which presidents have achieved their positions

Table 4-2   Pessen's Analysis of Presidential Social Class

Social Class	President
Upper-Upper	G. Washington, T. Jefferson, J. Madison, J. Q. Adams, W. H. Harrison, J. Tyler, Z. Taylor, B. Harrison, T. Roosevelt, W. H. Taft, F. D. Roosevelt, George H. W. Bush*, George W. Bush*
Middle-Upper	J. Polk, J. Kennedy
Lower-Upper	J. Adams, J. Monroe, W. Wilson
Lower-Upper/ Upper-Middle	F. Pierce, R. Hayes, G. Cleveland, W. Harding, C. Coolidge, H. Truman
Upper-Middle	A. Jackson, M. Van Buren, J. Buchanan, U.S. Grant, C. Arthur, W. McKinley, H. Hoover, L. Johnson, G. Ford, J. Carter
Middle	A. Lincoln, D. Eisenhower, R. Reagan, W. Clinton*
Lower-Middle	M. Fillmore, J. Garfield, R. Nixon
Upper-Lower	A. Johnson
Lower-Lower	None

Source: Edward Pessen, *The Log Cabin Myth: The Social Backgrounds of the Presidents* (New Haven: Yale University Press, 1984), 68.

*Presidents not rated by Pessen.

of power as a result of their own ability or thanks to the advantages of family background.[20] The presidency has long been cited as an example of how ability can enable individuals to overcome disadvantages and rise to positions of power. But the reality of presidents' personal histories, argues Edward Pessen, contradicts "the log cabin myth" and demonstrates that "the political race here as elsewhere has usually been won by those who had the advantage of starting from a favorable position."[21] Pessen characterized the family background of each president through Reagan in terms of six basic groupings: upper-upper and lower-upper, upper-middle and lower-middle, upper-lower and lower-lower.[22] In making his evaluations, Pessen compared the presidents' family backgrounds with the economic and social conditions that existed at the time rather than using a permanent yardstick.

Five distinguished American families have produced ten American presidents, more than one-fifth of the total. Included were John Adams and his son John Quincy Adams; James Madison and Zachary Taylor, who had grandparents in common; William Henry Harrison and his grandson Benjamin Harrison; cousins Theodore and Franklin Roosevelt; and George H. W. Bush, father of George W. Bush (unranked by Pessen). All five families meet Pessen's criteria for upper-class status as depicted in Table 4-2. It is also not uncommon to find that presidents come from politically prominent families, a background that, more often than not, is also upper class. John Tyler was the son of a Virginia governor; William Howard Taft's father served as secretary of war, attorney general, and ambassa-

Having Presidents Ford, Nixon, Bush, Reagan, and Carter together in 1991 for the dedication of the Reagan Presidential Library highlighted the distinctive attitudes, experiences, skills, and psychological dispositions that each occupant brings to the office of president.

dor to Austria and Russia; and John Kennedy's father was the chairman of the Securities and Exchange Commission and ambassador to Great Britain. Franklin Pierce's father was governor of New Hampshire, but Pessen locates the family between the lower-upper and upper-middle classes. The father of George H. W. Bush and grandfather of George W. Bush accumulated a considerable fortune working on Wall Street before he was elected to the Senate from Connecticut.

Other chief executives from upper-class origins but whose fathers did not hold high political office include George Washington, Thomas Jefferson, James Monroe, James K. Polk, and Woodrow Wilson. Pessen ranks Chester Arthur as upper-middle class. There are also a number of presidents, including Pierce, Rutherford B. Hayes, Grover Cleveland, Warren G. Harding, Calvin Coolidge, and Truman, in a special bridge category between upper-class and middle-class origins. Altogether, Pessen considers sixteen presidents to be drawn from upper-class roots (the Bushes would make eighteen) and six more as bordering on this exclusive group—a total of twenty-four, more than half of all those who have served in the White House.

Ten presidents fall within Pessen's upper-middle category, leaving only seven who can be regarded as drawn from middle- or lower-class roots, and Bill Clinton would make an eighth. The presidents who were most socially disadvantaged include Andrew Johnson, whose father held a variety of jobs, including janitor and porter at an inn; Millard Fillmore, who was probably the only president truly born in a log cabin as the son of a dirt farmer; and James Garfield, whose father pulled the family into prosperity through manual labor as a canal worker in the Midwest. Despite the many schoolbook stories about Lincoln's modest background, his father owned more property and livestock at the time of Abraham's birth than did the majority of his neighbors, and his prominence in the community continued to grow.

Three more recent presidents—Eisenhower, Nixon, and Reagan—were the sons of poor men who tried numerous jobs without much success. Eisenhower's father was a mechanic in a creamery for a time after an investment failed; Nixon's father was a streetcar conductor in Columbus, Ohio, before trying his luck as a painter, carpenter, glass worker, and sheep rancher; and Reagan's father worked on and off as an itinerant shoe salesman. Bill Clinton's father, a traveling salesman, died before his son was born, and Clinton's mother became a nurse anesthetist. His grandfather, with whom he lived until age six, was first the town iceman and later a neighborhood grocer, and his stepfather was a car salesman. The fathers of three recent presidents—Johnson, Gerald Ford, and Jimmy Carter—met mixed success in business: Johnson's father traded in commodities and livestock; Ford's stepfather (the president was born Leslie King and adopted as Gerald R. Ford Jr.) operated a paint and lumber business; and Carter's father founded a successful peanut warehouse.

Although presidents have come from diverse backgrounds, those with upper-class origins have been the most prevalent, while most others were drawn from prosperous and socially respected backgrounds. Even so, one can discern some changes over time. The first six chief executives came from socially, and in many cases politically, prominent families. Not wholly by coincidence, they served during the period when presidential candidates were nominated by congressional caucus. After both political parties adopted the national nominating convention in the early 1830s, the picture changed, with some presidents continuing to come from prominent families (John Tyler and Zachary Taylor, for example), while others from less-privileged backgrounds also began to make it to the White House. Fillmore, Lincoln, Andrew Johnson, and Garfield—four presidents with humble origins—are concentrated in the period 1850–1880. Few generalizations can be made, however, about twentieth-century presidents, who come from distinctly upper-class families (the two Roosevelts, Taft, Wilson, Kennedy, and the two Bushes) as well as more modest circumstances (Eisenhower, Nixon, Reagan, and Clinton).

Education

Education is often closely correlated with social class, a pattern that holds true for the presidency. Most U.S. presidents have been well educated. Only nine of the forty-two individuals (Cleveland served two, nonconsecutive terms, making

George W. Bush the forty-third president) did not have any formal instruction at a college or university. Moreover, the trend has been toward chief executives with greater college training. Of the nineteen who have occupied the presidency in this century, only one, Harry Truman, did not attend an institution of higher learning.[23] The universities and colleges that presidents attended are among the most highly regarded in the nation. Harvard University leads the list with five chief executives as alumni—the two Adamses, the two Roosevelts, and Kennedy (George W. Bush also has an M.B.A. from Harvard). Alma maters of other presidents include major private universities such as Princeton (Madison and Wilson), Yale (Taft and the two Bushes; Ford and Clinton also have Yale law degrees), Stanford (Herbert Hoover), Georgetown (Clinton), and a wide variety of prestigious, smaller private colleges, such as Allegheny (William McKinley), Amherst (Coolidge), Bowdoin (Pierce), Dickinson (James Buchanan), Hampden-Sidney (W. H. Harrison), Kenyon (Hayes), Union (Arthur), and Williams (Garfield). Although less prevalent than private institutions, well-known public universities also figure among the alma maters of the presidents: Miami University of Ohio (Benjamin Harrison), the University of Michigan (Ford), the University of North Carolina (Polk), William and Mary (Jefferson, Monroe, and Tyler), and the two service academies, Annapolis (Carter) and West Point (Ulysses S. Grant and Eisenhower). Twentieth-century presidents hailing from families with more modest social standing attended less prestigious institutions: Johnson attended Southwest Texas State Teachers College; Nixon graduated from Whittier College in California before attending Duke University Law School; Reagan majored in economics and sociology at Eureka College in Illinois.

The fact that so many presidents attended prestigious institutions of higher learning probably has less to do with their innate abilities or career aspirations than with family status or their desire to improve their economic and social positions through education. A classic example is James Garfield, the son of a canal construction worker, who died when Garfield was two. Garfield managed, after a long struggle for education, to graduate from Williams College and then become the principal of a church school before being admitted to the bar and eventually going into politics. More presidents attended private than public schools because private schools were established earlier, particularly in the northeastern states, such as New York and Massachusetts, which have produced ten presidents, and the midwestern states, such as Ohio, which has produced six presidents. Several postwar presidents, including Eisenhower, Johnson, Ford, and Carter, attended public institutions, a trend that may become more pronounced in the future. The selection of more presidents from states in which there are more public than private universities (such as the western states) would contribute to this trend. Although most citizens today would probably agree that a college education is essential if presidents are to understand the many complex problems confronting the nation, there is no direct correlation between quality of institution or years of training and performance.

Career Experience

Although the family occupational backgrounds of the presidents are fairly broad, their own careers prior to and outside politics have been much less diverse. Twenty-five of the forty-three chief executives practiced law at some time in their lives. Other occupations include the military (W. H. Harrison, Taylor, Grant, and Eisenhower), education (Wilson and Lyndon Johnson), journalism (Harding and Kennedy), engineering (Hoover), and entertainment (Reagan). Two presidents, Washington and Madison, were gentleman farmers. Carter combined farming with his family peanut business after he gave up his career as a navy engineer to return home to Georgia when his father died. George W. Bush was an oilman and managing general partner of a baseball team. Two presidents who pursued less prestigious careers before entering public life were Truman, who, in addition to trying his hand at farming, was a haberdasher and a railroad timekeeper, and Andrew Johnson, who was a tailor. It is not surprising that so many presidents were lawyers because that profession is closely linked with a political career. Law is a prestigious occupation, rewards skill in interpersonal negotiation and conciliation as well as verbal and argumentative facility, and enables its practitioners to return to private life more readily than is true of medicine or engineering, for example.[24] Although the law is a natural profession for presidents, in recent years fewer chief executives have come from that occupation. Of the ten presidents since World War II, only three—Nixon, Ford, and Clinton—were lawyers. As increasing numbers of people from nonlegal backgrounds—business and teaching, in particular—become senators and governors, the positions from which today's presidents often are recruited, still more presidents without legal training may occupy the White House.

Only three presidents, career military officers, have not held previous public office before becoming president. Zachary Taylor, Ulysses S. Grant, and Dwight D. Eisenhower were thrust into the vortex of presidential politics because of heroic exploits in the Mexican War, Civil War, and World War II, respectively. Not only did these three presidents lack experience in civilian office, but as professional military men they also had not even been involved in partisan activities. Taylor, elected as the Whig candidate in 1848, had never voted before in a presidential election and had no party affiliation.[25] Grant, the Republican Party candidate elected in 1868, had voted for James Buchanan, the Democratic standard-bearer in 1856, and had political views that have been described as "obscure."[26] Even more perplexing for party leaders was Eisenhower, the Republican Party candidate in 1952 and 1956, whom a number of liberal Democratic leaders had tried to draft for their party's nomination in 1948.[27]

For most U.S. chief executives, the road to the presidency involved a long apprenticeship in public office with careers usually beginning at lower levels of the political system when they were in their twenties or thirties. Andrew Johnson and Calvin Coolidge began their public careers as city aldermen or councilmen. Others were first elected to county offices: John Adams was a highway surveyor; Harry Truman was a member of the county court, an administrative, not a judicial, position. Some presidents, including Andrew Jackson, James Buchanan, Grover Cleveland, William McKinley, and William Howard Taft, entered public service as prosecuting or district attorneys; others, such as Rutherford B. Hayes and Benjamin Harrison, served as city solicitors or attorneys. Bill Clinton began his career in 1976 as Arkansas's attorney general. Several chief executives—Jefferson, Lincoln, and the two Roosevelts among them—began their public careers as state legislators.

The typical career pattern for these presidents was to move up the political ladder by winning offices representing progressively larger constituencies. Approximately two-thirds of the presidents served in either the House of Representatives or the Senate or both. There are, of course, exceptions. Woodrow Wilson spent most of his adult life as a professor of government and later as president of Princeton University; in 1910, at age fifty-four, he was elected governor of New Jersey, just two years before he won the presidency. Ronald Reagan was primarily a radio, movie, and television performer until his fifties, when he became active in national politics in the 1964 presidential campaign in behalf of Barry Goldwater. In 1966 he was elected to the first of two terms as governor of California; in 1980 he was elected president. George W. Bush became governor of Texas in 1994 at age forty-seven and was reelected in 1998. Neither William Howard Taft nor Herbert Hoover held any elective office before being chosen as president. Taft served as a judge at the county, state, and federal levels, and later became governor general of the Philippines and secretary of war. Hoover chaired the Commission for Relief in Belgium after World War I; oversaw prices, production, and distribution of food during World War I as U.S. food administrator; and later served as secretary of commerce in the Harding and Coolidge administrations.

Most presidents come to the White House directly from another high public office. (*See the discussion in Chapter 2.*) Typical positions include the vice presidency, state governorships, Senate seats, and appointive executive office. From one era to the next in U.S. political history, these offices have varied in the extent to which their occupants have been favored or disfavored in their pursuit of the presidency.

How is experience related to performance? Most observers assume that experience can make a president more or less familiar with the problems confronting the nation as well as with the institutions and people who must collectively address these problems. Moreover, an earlier career in elective office may enable individuals to develop the skills necessary for exercising leadership—bargaining skills, facility in public speaking, and the capacity to persuade or inspire others. Candidates, therefore, usually argue that their particular blend of experience—whether in state, national, or nonpublic sectors—has made them best qualified for the position.

Background-Performance Links

How have scholars linked these biographical characteristics to presidential performance? Are there systematic patterns that would enable the public to predict which candidates will enjoy greatest success in office? Unfortunately, there are no simple answers.

Our review shows that most presidents achieved political success with a substantial boost from their family circumstances, advantages that included political and social standing as well as educational and professional opportunities unavailable to most of their fellow citizens. "The common characteristic [of presidents] . . . for all their dissimilarities in other respects, has been the essential conservatism of their social, economic, and political beliefs . . . all of them were champions of the prevailing order, said Pressen."[28] Because the selection process is not neutral toward social class, it seems likely that most presidential aspirants will sustain the status quo.

Two sociologists, E. Digby Baltzell and Howard G. Schneiderman, have more specifically sought to link class origin with performance in office. They correlate Pessen's analysis of class origins with a ranking of presidential performance based on the Murray-Blessing survey of American historians described earlier.[29] Their conclusion challenges some of the myths surrounding the presidency. "There has been . . . not only a high correlation between high social origins and getting to the presidency, as Pessen clearly has shown, [but] once elected to office, men of privileged origins have performed far better than those of lower social status."[30] Of the eight presidents ranked by historians as great or near great, five were from upper-class families (Washington, Jefferson, Theodore Roosevelt, Wilson, and Franklin Roosevelt), two from the upper-middle class (Jackson and Truman), and only one from the middle and lower classes (Lincoln, who is generally ranked number one). In contrast, no presidents drawn from the upper class are found among those regarded by historians as failures (Andrew Johnson, Buchanan, Nixon, Grant, and Harding). Overall, Baltzell and Schneiderman find that eleven of the fifteen upper-class presidents included in their study (73 percent) were judged to have performed above average in office, while only six of the twenty-one presidents drawn from below the upper class (29 percent) were comparably rated.[31] Although they do not provide a clear explanation for how background is translated into success, this analysis suggests that an upper-class background does make a difference: "Our best aristocratic traditions have stressed *doing* a better job rather than the prevalent, middle-class ideology which has always stressed *getting* a better job."[32]

Richard Neustadt is probably the foremost advocate of electing an experienced politician to the presidency. As he has argued since 1960, when the first edition of his influential book, *Presidential Power and the Modern Presidents*, appeared, "The Presidency is no place for amateurs."[33] This seemed an apt aphorism to capture the difficulties experienced by Dwight Eisenhower in the presidency, although evaluations of his performance as president have risen with the passage of time. As articulated in some of Neustadt's later editions, experience enhances presidents' self-confidence, which in turn makes it easier for them to make the choices about power that are critical to success. Yet, "the quality of experience" may count "more than the quantity," an admission that Neustadt had to make after two highly experienced presidents, Lyndon Johnson and Richard Nixon, seemed to fail in office. He ultimately concluded that "the variety of experience is such that none of it can be applied predictively with confidence."[34] Bert Rockman reaches a similar conclusion after looking at the length and types of government experience in relation to performance. In comparing the government experience of the top ten and bottom ten presidents as ranked by an expert panel, the bottom ten actually had modestly *greater* government experience than did the top ten (16.9 mean years versus 15.1) and more than twice as many years of congressional experience (7.6 mean years versus 3.7).[35] Experience, it appears, offers no guarantee of success.

We are left with fundamental uncertainties about how life experience may have a bearing on performance. In addition to social class and career experience, there has also been considerable interest in the psychological traits that presidents bring to the office, the subject of the next section.

Psychological Characteristics of U.S. Presidents

In October 1972, just before voters were to choose between Richard Nixon and George McGovern, the political scientist James David Barber drew attention to the inherent shortcomings of evaluating a candidate's life experience when deciding how to vote. Barber made a prediction. The person who would win had grown up as part of a Republican family in a small town. He had excelled in school, studied piano, had a younger brother rowdier than himself, and had been elected president of his college class. Following military service during World War II, he had attended graduate school and followed an uncertain career path until gaining election to Congress in a contest marked by anticommunist appeals. After two terms in the House and service in the Senate, he was considered a member of his party's liberal wing and respected for hard work and independent thinking. The description fit both Nixon and McGovern. Despite the similarities in life experiences, few doubted that the two would make very different presidents.[36]

The degree of similarity between the major party candidates in 1972 was uncanny even in light of the broadly similar backgrounds from which presidents are drawn. Yet no two people, regardless of how similar their life circumstances, will bring identical personalities to the office. They inevitably bring a set of distinctive psychological characteristics, features that may loom large under the intense pressures that concentrate on the presidency. Psychological traits are more proximate to presidential behavior than are life experiences, but that does not make them easier to study or evaluate. Fred Greenstein points out that psychologists view personality as a complex phenomenon, involving diverse factors such as how people adapt to the world around them by screening reality (cognition), how they express their feelings (affect), and how they relate to others (identification).[37] These structures are likely to be deeply rooted, making it even more necessary to "infer" their existence rather than to observe them directly. Analysts, in short, introduce personality as a construct to account for the regularities in a person's behavior. For these reasons, examinations of psychological characteristics are more uncertain and subjective than are examinations of professional experience and social backgrounds.

Despite these problems, political scientists and historians have used psychological concepts to help explain why political figures behave as they do, a field of study that has come to be known as *psychobiography*. Several presidents, including Wilson, Lyndon Johnson, Nixon, Carter, and Clinton, have been the subjects of such biographies.[38] These studies tend to concentrate on the childhood experiences of the subjects, particularly their relationships with their parents, and how such experiences shaped their perceptions of themselves, their self-confidence or lack of it, and their psychological needs.

Even with the upsurge in interest, analysts remain divided on precisely how to conduct these studies and the theoretical framework within which they should be conducted. Two broad approaches can be adopted: single-subject case studies seek to develop a comprehensive analysis of the full array of behaviors manifested by one person, with particular attention paid to explaining the origins of recurrent patterns; multicase studies also rely on close examination of biographical materials but seek to draw conclusions from similarities found among several actors' behavior.[39] An example of a single-subject case study is Alexander George and Juliette George's highly acclaimed, comprehensive work on Woodrow Wilson, which attempts to explain his strikingly complex and contradictory behavior. James David Barber's study *The Presidential Character* has identified similarities between Wilson's conduct and that of three other presidents—Hoover, Lyndon Johnson, and Nixon—so that they may be treated as examples of a similar personality type.

Practitioners of these two styles of inquiry disagree, sometimes quite strongly, on how analysis should proceed.[40] There are multiple, competing theories of personality and a lack of established rules on how such research should be conducted. Although the research remains controversial, it would be unrealistic to overlook the importance of personality in trying to understand the presidency because this office imposes fewer constraints on the occupant's behavior than does any other in American government. In other words, there is enormous opportunity for presidents to be themselves in performing their day-to-day responsibilities.[41] Consequently, their emotional fitness for the job is enormously important.

Barber's Approach to Studying Personality

In addition to his prediction of the 1972 election already noted, Barber made a more famous forecast that brought considerable attention to himself and to the study of presidential personality. Barber predicted that Nixon would be susceptible to the same "danger" as were Wilson, Hoover, and Johnson, namely, "adhering rigidly to a line of policy long after it had proved itself a failure."[42] Given the right set of circumstances, Nixon was likely to pursue a self-defeating plan of action even in the face of mounting evidence of its likely failure. The

Figure 4-2 Barber's Typology of Character

		Affect	
		Positive	Negative
Activity Level	Active	**Adaptive**, self-confident, power used as means to achieve beneficial results	**Compulsive**, power as a means to self-realization; "driven"; problem managing aggression
	Passive	**Compliant**, seek to be loved; easily manipulated; low self-esteem	**Withdrawn**, respond to sense of duty; avoid power; low self-esteem

Source: James David Barber, *The Presidential Character: Predicting Performance* in the White House, 4th ed. (Englewood Cliffs, N.J.: Prentice Hall, 1992).

causes were rooted in his personality—his emotional needs—no less than they had been for the other three presidents Barber cited. Nixon's conduct during Watergate, the extended investigations conducted by Congress during 1973 and 1974 into questionable campaign practices of the 1972 election, seemed to validate the prediction and the method on which it was based.

How did Barber arrive at such a conclusion? Was his prediction lucky, or had he uncovered the secret of how to predict presidential performance in office based on systematic personality analysis? If so, the next step would be to make such insights available to voters before an election to produce more informed decisions.

Barber attempts to identify broad character patterns that will predict general patterns of presidential conduct in office. Central to his analysis are three personal characteristics—*character, world view,* and *style*—and two environmental conditions—*power situation* and *climate of expectations.* Together, these elements determine the likelihood of presidential success. Character, the most important of Barber's analytic constructs, develops during childhood and is expressed in two analytic dimensions: energy and affect. Presidents may be active or passive in terms of the effort invested in their job; they also may be positive or negative about their position. Both dimensions influence performance.

The resulting four-cell typology is presented in Figure 4-2, with the principal personality trait identified by Barber for each type. *Active-positives* evidence personal growth and adaptability; they enjoy their work and find it a challenge to use power productively as a means to pursue goals beneficial to others. Their success rests on a fundamental sense of self-confidence expressed in goal-oriented behavior. Nonetheless, they are flexible in their pursuit of goals and willing to change or abandon them altogether rather than suffer a costly political defeat. In short, they are pragmatic politicians. Barber's active-positives include Franklin Roosevelt, Truman, Kennedy, Ford, Carter, George H. W. Bush, and Clinton.[43]

Active-negative presidents also invest a great deal of energy in being president, but unlike their active-positive counterparts, they do not appear to derive enjoyment from serving in the office. Rather than exercising political power for the benefit of the citizenry, active-negative chief executives seem to seek power for its own sake, exhibiting compulsiveness as if they are driven to pursue a political career rather than doing it because the career gives them pleasure. This behavior arises from a poor self-image and lack of self-confidence, traits caused by painful childhood experiences; they seek power and domination over others as compensation for their own lack of self-esteem. In this pursuit, active-negatives may come to believe that the policies they favor are morally right, vital to the nation's interest, and impossible to compromise. They may pursue a course of action even if it obviously is not working, exhibiting a pattern of "rigidification" that can ultimately cause their own political failure. Thus, they constitute a great danger to the nation. Barber classifies four twentieth-century presidents as active-negatives: Wilson, Hoover, Johnson, and Nixon.

Passive-positive presidents are not in politics to seek power either for the betterment of the American people or to compensate for their own sense of inadequacy. Rather, they choose politics because they are, in Barber's terms, "political lovers." They genuinely enjoy people and want to help them by doing small favors; in return, they get the feeling that they are wanted and loved. Barber suggests that passive-positive presidents have low self-esteem combined with a superficial optimism about life; they tend to let others set goals for them and find it difficult to make decisions. The danger they pose is one of drift, leaving the affairs of state undirected. Barber uses three presidents to illustrate passive-positive chief executives: Taft, Harding, and Reagan.

Passive-negative presidents combine two characteristics one would *not* expect to find in the person who attains the nation's highest office: an unwillingness to invest much energy in that office and a lack of pleasure in serving. Such persons pursue public service because they believe it is something they *ought to do*. Passive-negative presidents have a fundamental sense of uselessness and compensate for that feeling by dutifully agreeing to work on behalf of their fellow citizens. Two presidents who exemplify passive-negative chief executives are Coolidge and Eisenhower.

Barber also examines two other personal factors that influence presidential behavior but play a smaller role in his analysis than does character. *World view* consists of a president's "politically relevant beliefs, particularly his conceptions of social causality, human nature, and the central moral conflicts of the time."[44] Rather than dealing with specific policy issues, these attitudes are general in nature and are therefore more likely to have wide applicability. Barber sees them as developed primarily during adolescence.

Style is the president's "habitual way of performing three political roles: rhetoric, personal relations, and homework."[45] In other words, style focuses on how presidents typically work with words, people, and substantive problems. These patterns are developed largely during early adulthood, particularly in conjunction with the president's "first independent political success," which usually occurs in college or in a first elective or appointive office. *Character* "colors" both world view and style but does not determine them in any direct way.

Figure 4-3   Barber's Characterization of Modern Presidents

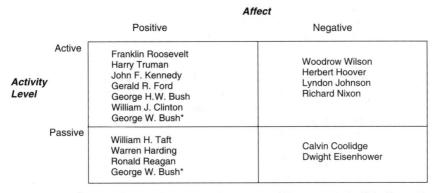

		Affect	
		Positive	Negative
Activity Level	Active	Franklin Roosevelt Harry Truman John F. Kennedy Gerald R. Ford George H.W. Bush William J. Clinton George W. Bush*	Woodrow Wilson Herbert Hoover Lyndon Johnson Richard Nixon
	Passive	William H. Taft Warren Harding Ronald Reagan George W. Bush*	Calvin Coolidge Dwight Eisenhower

Source: James David Barber, *The Presidential Character: Predicting Performance in the White House*, 4th ed. (Englewood Cliffs, N.J. : Prentice Hall, 1992). For Barber's views on Clinton, see the *News Observer* (Raleigh, N.C.), January 17, 1993.

*Possible characterization (not evaluated by Barber).

Barber analyzed the life histories of all presidents from William Howard Taft through George Herbert Walker Bush, thereby covering all but three of the twentieth-century presidents (his discussion of Clinton was very preliminary). These analyses are summarized in Figure 4-3. Some of his classifications have been highly controversial, but after 1972 journalists sought out his views of each candidate during presidential elections, and he offered inauguration-eve predictions of how the new president would perform in office.

Views of Bill Clinton

Unlike his thorough analyses of other recent presidents, Barber's analysis of Bill Clinton as an active-positive was only tentative.[46] Another analyst, Stanley A. Renshon, offered a "preliminary assessment" based on events of the presidential campaign and Clinton's first year in office that illustrated the difficulties of analyzing presidential character more generally.[47] Renshon agreed that "on initial impression," Clinton would appear to be an active-positive. Throughout his academic and political career, Clinton was a prodigious worker, training himself in college to function on five hours of sleep and repeatedly reacting to setbacks with even higher levels of personal activity. Moreover, Clinton's efforts were dedicated to accomplishing purposes beyond simply advancing his own personal ambition.[48]

Renshon, however, noted that Clinton's frenetic activity is "closer to the driven investments of energy of active-negative Lyndon Johnson" than to the behavior of other active-positives like Kennedy or Truman.[49] Nor is it uniformly obvious that Clinton enjoyed the experience. Although he apparently thrived on long days of interpersonal contact and campaigning, Renshon offers evidence of how intensely Clinton resents the limited appreciation he received in the press and from the public. This resentment was dramatically manifested by an outburst at the conclusion of an interview conducted by two journalists from *Rolling Stone* near the end of his first year in office. When asked about a young supporter who wanted to know what issues Clinton was "willing to stand up for and die on," the president exploded:

But that's the press's fault, too, damn it. I have fought more damn battles here for more things than any president has in twenty years, with the possible exception of Reagan's first budget, and not gotten one damn bit of credit from the knee-jerk liberal press, and I am sick and tired of it, and you can put that in the damn article.

I have fought and fought and fought and fought. I get up here every day, and I work till late at night on everything from national service to family leave to the budget to the crime bill and all this stuff, and you guys take it and you say, "Fine, go on to something else, what else can I hit him about?" So if you convince them I don't have any convictions, that's fine, but it's a damn lie. It's a lie. . . . .

I have fought my guts out for that guy, and if he doesn't know it, it's not all my fault. And you get no credit around here for fighting and bleeding.[50]

Linking this outburst to other features of the president's personality, Renshon suggested that Clinton could be a hybrid type within Barber's framework, a borderline active-negative with a "strong need to be validated."[51] Clinton, argued Renshon, had developed an idealized view of himself—his skills, his accomplishments, and his motives. "Most people wish to think well of themselves but Bill Clinton appears to have come to believe the *best* of himself and to have discounted evidence from his own behavior that all is not as he believes it to be."[52] In this view, when Clinton's self-idealized image collides with criticism and refusal to acknowledge his accomplishments, anger and hurt emerge. Unlike active-negatives who use power to overcome low estimates of themselves, Renshon suggests that "it is also possible that political leaders might well use power to validate high estimates of themselves," something that Barber had not anticipated and that Clinton might embody.[53] Fred Greenstein, writing toward the end of Clinton's term and therefore with the full record in front of him, agreed with Renshon's assessment: "The ever-smiling, hyperactive Clinton has all of the outward signs of an active-positive character. Yet his actions, particularly his astonishing recklessness in the Monica Lewinsky affair, reveal him to be as emotionally deficient as any classically active-negative president."[54]

Greenstein's final assessment of Clinton was somewhat different from his initial one. In an earlier assessment, he had pointed out one quality of Clinton's that makes him unlike active-negatives: the "capacity (in spite of his thin-skinned tendencies) to admit his own failings" and make self-correcting adjustments. Thus, unlike the compulsive tendency of Woodrow Wilson, Herbert Hoover, Lyndon Johnson, and Richard Nixon to pursue even self-destructive policies, Clinton appears "incapable of sustained error."[55] Greenstein acknowledges, however, that "much of what is puzzling about him [Clinton] stems from inner complexities that do not figure in Barber's (and perhaps any other) classification."[56] Indeed, Barber's effort to study presidential personality has attracted extensive commentary, examined in the next section.

Reactions to Barber

Because Barber's work was widely popularized in the press, it is important to assess its analytic quality. Academics have been especially critical, suggesting it suffers from the fundamental problem common to all studies in the field—reductionism, paying "insufficient attention to the full range of possible psychological and non-psychological determinants of behavior."[57] Insufficient attention is given to the impact of the environment on presidents, including the nature of the problems they confront, the political support they enjoy, and the constraints within which they operate.

Barber's classification of presidents also has been questioned. The behavior patterns associated with his character types fit some presidents grouped into the same cell better than others. For example, evidence on Eisenhower published after Barber completed his analysis suggests that Ike was really a more active president than was generally recognized when he was in office.[58] Hoover's reluctance to use extensive federal aid to restore the economy might better be understood as arising from his worldview rather than from his unresolved emotional needs.[59] Another study, using markedly different methods, finds Ronald Reagan's personality to be most similar to those of Franklin Roosevelt and Kennedy, although Barber considered Reagan a passive-positive and the other two active-positives.[60] In fact, Barber acknowledges that no president fits any of the types perfectly and that each is a mixture of all four types.[61] Nonetheless, he argues that it is possible to identify a dominant pattern.

Is Barber guilty of positing an ideal personality type that may also conceal a partisan bias? When Barber's study first appeared, all the active-positives were liberal Democrats. Republicans Ford and Bush were subsequently added. The approach may, however, favor the heroic model of presidential leadership that assigns principal responsibility for solving national problems to the White House. Barber recognizes that not all active-positives will be successful in office and may pose risks for the political system; their "hunger for and attention to results" may lead them to challenge structures and norms that the public believes are better preserved than overturned.[62] Franklin Roosevelt's effort in 1937 to alter the structure of the Supreme Court by increasing its membership to as many as fifteen posed a challenge to the tradition of checks and balances and illustrates this possible danger.[63]

Can types other than active-positives achieve substantial success in office? Jeffrey Tulis argues that in Barber's terms Abraham Lincoln should be considered an active-negative, but few would argue that Lincoln's stewardship of the nation during the Civil War was not successful.[64]

In sum, Barber's work does not represent a panacea to a nation searching for effective leaders. Like most of social science, Barber's work is best thought of in terms of probabilities rather than certainties. In the long run, Barber aspires to present voters with the kind of information on candidate backgrounds and records that would improve the likelihood of informed electoral choices, but the kind of research necessary for personality analysis is difficult to undertake at any time and perhaps most difficult in the heat of an electoral contest. Journalists may be able to improve their coverage of candidates' records and identify behavior patterns of concern, but the chance of conducting a complete study of candidates' personalities in the midst of a campaign is negligible. Nor is it clear who in our society should be given such inordinate influence as to declare some personalities "fit" and others "unfit" for office. Therefore, the practical value of Barber's work remains a controversial and open question.

Despite these criticisms of Barber, it is important to reaffirm the critical importance of continuing to study the personalities of presidents and their emotional fitness for the position. Perhaps the most compelling justification comes from those who have experienced the power of presidential personalities firsthand. Clark Clifford, a longtime Washington power broker who served in the Truman and Johnson administrations, colorfully voiced the prevailing wisdom among government veterans: "The executive branch of our government is like a chameleon. To a startling degree it reflects the character and personality of the president."[65]

Management Styles of Modern Presidents

Presidents do not govern alone. Traditional presidents—those serving before Franklin Roosevelt—drew heavily on the assistance of cabinet secretaries and the bureaucracies they headed. Since the Roosevelt administration, another source of advice and assistance has emerged to supplement more traditional sources of help. The modern presidency has become a collectivity of political and policy specialists whose expertise is placed at the president's disposal. To what extent do presidents avail themselves of these institutional sources of assistance? How do they structure their advisory systems and make decisions? This section provides a brief discussion of the development of presidential staffing and the management styles presidents use with these assistants.

Just as important as attitudes drawn from life experiences, and skills developed in previous careers, is a president's aptitude for management. Aides have the potential to magnify whatever skills presidents bring to the office and to compensate for their shortcomings. Moreover, it is possible that having a layer of advisers between the president and his performance will reduce the impact of undesirable personality traits on the operation of the office.

The Development of Presidential Staffing

The presidential staff has grown substantially since Congress authorized its modern structure in 1939. Today, the Executive Office of the President houses a wide range of expert staff units, including the well-known Office of Management and Budget, Council of Economic Advisers, and National Security Council (all discussed more fully in later chapters), as well as the lesser-known Office of U.S. Trade Representative and Office of Science and Technology Policy. Perhaps best known, and certainly most notorious in Washington circles, is the White

House Office, a unit that has traditionally emphasized the president's personal and political concerns.

Like other presidents before him, Franklin Roosevelt had a limited number of aides working on his behalf, many in clerical positions who were borrowed from other parts of the federal bureaucracy. Looking for a justification to expand these resources, in 1936 he appointed a blue-ribbon group of public administration professors, headed by Louis Brownlow, to study the management needs of the modern president. The resulting structure, based on recommendations from that group but reorganized many times since, has always been viewed as a response to the Brownlow Commission's defining sentence: "The President needs help." As Roosevelt and others recognized, the president required additional "eyes and ears" as well as brains to help him discharge the ever-growing list of responsibilities placed at the White House door. Presidential staffing, therefore, is an attempt to help presidents avoid the danger of "overload," the possibility that demands of the job will exceed the capacity of any individual whose time and ability are finite. While the staff is a way to *amplify* the capabilities brought by one person to the presidency, it also may be seen as a structure that can *buffer* the direct impact of a president's personality on performance. Presidents have been given great latitude in their use of staff resources, a flexibility that ensures responsiveness to new problems and perceived needs.

Staff size, although a recurrent political issue, is difficult to monitor with precision. Best estimates place the size of today's Executive Office at approximately sixteen hundred employees.[66] Moreover, the percentage of positions at higher levels of policymaking responsibility appears to have increased substantially over the years.[67] Staff growth has been accompanied by a shift in influence, with one analyst going so far as to suggest that the new structure constitutes a "presidential branch" of government distinct from the larger executive branch.[68] Clearly, presidents can draw on a wide range of assistance located both outside and within the presidency.

Presidential Management Styles

Style is no doubt an overused term in describing characteristic patterns of presidential behavior, but a number of analysts have focused more narrowly on how presidents structure and use their advisory systems in making decisions. We term these behavior patterns a president's *management style*. Alexander George identifies three personality factors that determine a president's management style: the executive's habitual ways of dealing with information (acquiring, storing, retrieving, evaluating, and using it); the president's sense of competence in dealing personally with problems, which in turn determines the tasks delegated to others; and the president's orientation toward conflict, particularly the tolerance for competition and dissent among advisers.[69]

Because it reflects personality characteristics and distinctive traits, each president's management style is unique. However, most analysts agree that recent presidents have chosen to operate within one of three broad advisory structures (described by R. T. Johnson), with multiple variations consistent with their management style.[70] The *formalistic* pattern emphasizes clear division of labor among staff assistants, well-defined procedures, and a carefully controlled flow of information to the president, usually through a chief of staff, who tries to deflect problems not worthy of presidential attention. Truman, Eisenhower, and Nixon constructed and operated such systems, although differences in operation reflected the unique combination of needs and contributions each of these men brought to the presidency. The *competitive* pattern, typified by Franklin Roosevelt, encouraged conflict among advisers and thrived on diversity of opinion, with the president reserving ultimate judgment to himself. Conflict is endemic to decision making within the American government, but Roosevelt encouraged even more of it. Under a *collegial* system, emphasis is on group problem solving, teamwork, and shared responsibility for outcomes, with the president participating in the process and choosing among identified options. Kennedy, particularly in his decision making during the Cuban missile crisis, typified this style.

Johnson's three models are a starting point for describing how the systems work. Presidents may follow more than one pattern or construct hybrid combinations. Ford followed a collegial pattern in domestic policy but was more formalistic in foreign policy.[71] Carter's system has been described as a mixture of collegial and formalistic elements.[72] Reagan constructed a variant of the formalistic and collegial models during his first term, and this system drew considerable praise from many observers, particularly when its successor in the second term became less collegial and proved notably less successful.[73] Clinton's style, discussed later in the chapter, has evolved from a highly undisciplined, sometimes collegial style to a somewhat more disciplined collegial pattern. George W. Bush seemed to adopt a formal style with considerable delegation from the outset. It is also important to note that the size of government as well as the number and complexity of issues that confront modern presidencies probably "forces every modern president to rely at least to some extent on formalistic procedures."[74]

In general, formalistic structures seem to place more modest demands on presidential time and knowledge. Delegating a larger range of tasks to others conserves time and may increase the probability that experts will deal with the problem. Because much of the work in a formal system is processed in written form, the formal style is less appropriate for presidents who prefer to rely on group interaction, discussion, and even argument as part of the decisionmaking process. Both competitive and collegial structures place heavier demands on the president, who not only must rely largely on his own substantive knowledge in making choices among competing alternatives but also must be able to monitor a policymaking process that is inherently political in nature. Advisers and the policy areas they represent push hard for the president to adopt their solution to a problem, and the maneuvers used to gain an advantage during such policy struggles are believed to be the keys to success. Unfortunately, winning such battles may come at the expense of good decisions.

In the modern era Democratic presidents, using Franklin Roosevelt as a model, often have adopted a different, more interactive advisory system, sometimes described as a "spokes-in-a-wheel" system, with the president at the center of several principal aides in and out of the White House. Such a system encourages dispute and argumentation. Republican presidents, with few exceptions, have operated within a more highly structured system, in which the chief executive interacts with a single chief of staff or a very limited number of advisers and relies more heavily on systematic review processes. This approach is thought to be less susceptible to political maneuvering by those surrounding the president. George W. Bush seems to be following in this Republican tradition— limiting his reliance to a small number of principal aides.

Is one pattern more conducive to success than the others? Each has strengths and weaknesses, but unfortunately analysts disagree on the criteria to be used in evaluating the styles, and they even disagree on how the systems perform. There are no reliable measures of which systems produce decisions of higher quality or greater political responsiveness, within reasonable spans of time.[75] Moreover, if the advisory systems ultimately reflect the kind of personality variables identified by Alexander George, it would be impossible to identify one as preferable because it might be inappropriate for the particular president asked to use it.

Multiple Advocacy: Learning a Decision Process

The best-known effort to prescribe a specific decision process for presidents to follow is Alexander George's system of *multiple advocacy*.[76] In essence, George has suggested that presidents should be able to learn a set of techniques to follow in managing advisers and making decisions. Although recognizing that a given president may find this style "uncongenial to his cognitive style and work habits," George nonetheless believes that the advantages would make it worthwhile for a president to consider.[77] For example, Richard Nixon found it painful to be the object of direct, face-to-face argument among his advisers, but he might have modified the system advocated by George to derive its benefits.[78]

George defines multiple advocacy as a *mixed* system that tries to ensure that presidents benefit from a wide review of policy options and hear a variety of viewpoints before making a final policy decision. It tries to build on the inevitable conflict that arises among individual advisers and bureaucratic agencies by channeling that conflict in productive ways. The overall process must be structured so that every relevant viewpoint receives a fair hearing. One of the major tasks, then, in operating such a system is to monitor the breadth of options being considered and the opportunities that advocates of such views have to be heard. To operate such a system, the president requires a full-time assistant, a "custodian-manager" who acts as an "honest broker" among the advisers pushing their positions on the president.

George's hope is that systematic review of options, one of the claimed benefits of a formalistic system, also can be achieved under multiple advocacy, with the added benefit of the open debate and discussion that are encouraged by competitive and collegial systems. The president should act as a magistrate—"one who listens to the arguments made, evaluates them, poses issues and asks questions, and finally judges which action to take either from among those articulated by advocates or as formulated independently by himself after hearing them."[79] Consistent with this role, presidents need to suppress the urge to announce their own preferences early in the process and ensure that they remain faithful to the premise on which the system rests, which is the guarantee of giving an equal hearing to all views.

Such a process can be time-consuming, and George recognizes that presidents would have to decide when it should be used. There may be times when presidents feel that they already know the policy they wish to pursue. Nothing will prohibit them from exercising such discretion. As George recognizes, even though advisers may have become indispensable to modern presidents, constitutional responsibility in the American executive remains unitary, not collective. Only two names appear on the election ballot—the president's and the vice president's— and because vice presidents have virtually no independent powers, presidents are singularly responsible for the discharge of executive responsibilities.

Even George does not believe that use of a multiple advocacy system and the magistrate presidential style that accompanies it can ensure good decisions. Rather, he urges its adoption as a way to improve the quality of information made available to presidents and to prevent the bad decisions that result from faulty procedures.[80] There are no guarantees of success.

Understanding Presidents: The Cases of Bill Clinton and George W. Bush

Explaining presidential behavior and linking its determinants to performance is much like putting together the pieces of a puzzle, but a puzzle whose final shape is uncertain. One way to illustrate how background, experience, personality, and management style shape behavior and performance is to take an in-depth look at individual cases. It is still too soon to provide a final evaluation of Bill Clinton's full effectiveness in office, but we can at least trace major features of his life and explore ways in which these potentially affected his performance as president. The sketch of George W. Bush is necessarily more uncertain but offers a starting point for thinking about these relationships.

Clinton and Bush offer strikingly contrasting personal portraits. Clinton's ambition to be president can be traced to his teenage years, and he systematically set about to accomplish his goal. Bush was the classic "late-bloomer" and speaks openly of a life-changing event at forty. He did not even enter politics until he was forty-seven. Clinton was elected to office as a "new Democrat" seeking to move his party toward more moderate positions, but he encountered scathing criticism during his first year for being a vintage liberal. Bush ran as a "compassionate conservative" and a "different kind of Republican" but may have been so attentive to his conservative base during his first six months in office that his future effectiveness was threatened. Although a product of the 1960s, an era known for its revolt against established power structures and social norms, Clinton, the first "baby boomer" president, has been consistently criticized for compromising with power centers, first in Arkansas and later in Washington. Bush, the heir to one of the great political family traditions in American life, was always the iconoclast who challenged traditional authority but resisted the lure of 1960s-style rebellion. A booster of family values and a devout Baptist, Clinton confronted repeated charges of marital infidelity throughout his political career, charges that culminated in the Lewinsky scandal. Bush is a born-again Christian who acknowledges an earlier problem with alcohol and making unspecified mistakes during his "irresponsible youth." Filled with nostalgic pride for his small-town roots, Clinton burned with ambition to succeed on larger stages—Georgetown University, Oxford University, Yale University Law School, Arkansas politics, and the presidency. Bush claims small-town Texas as his adopted home despite the ready access he has always had to larger stages. Here are snapshots of their lives.

Clinton's Early Life

Bill Clinton entered life in the wake of tragedy. Shortly before the birth of William Jefferson Blythe III, his original name, Clinton's natural father drowned in a roadside ditch following a car accident while driving from Chicago to Hope, Arkansas. The newly widowed Virginia Blythe, a wartime bride, completed her training as a nurse anesthetist in New Orleans, leaving her young son behind with her parents for his first two years. Although his grandmother doted on Bill, her hot temper offset his grandfather's universal friendliness, traits later displayed by the adult Bill Clinton.

When Bill was four, his mother married Roger Clinton, a car dealer also known to deal in bootleg liquor who had been divorced by his first wife for abuse. The new family settled in Hot Springs, Arkansas, a resort town where gambling and prostitution were openly pursued. For the next twelve years, the future president lived in two very different worlds: a public world centered on school and church, where he earned plaudits as a model citizen, and a private, turbulent world in which his stepfather had become an abusive alcoholic. The situation was stormy: after repeated episodes of abuse, Virginia divorced her second husband in 1962, with Bill providing testimony in the trial, only to remarry him three months later. During the interlude, Bill Blythe took it on himself to change his last name to Clinton so that it would be the same as that of his younger half brother, Roger Clinton.

Inevitably, Bill Clinton's personality was heavily influenced by this unhappy family life. As his most authoritative biography argues, Clinton assumed the role of "family hero," one of the characteristic roles found among children of alcoholics. Not only does this child assume responsibility for protecting the family, but he may also serve as its redeemer to the outside world by winning awards and praise.[81] Clinton did both. He intervened in one instance to stop his stepfather from abusing his mother, and he tried to protect his half-brother. Through his high school successes, he brought glory to the family: he was fourth in his graduating class, junior class president, band major and all-state band member, and a delegate to Boys' State and Boys' Nation; as a Boys' Nation delegate, in a memorable moment captured on film, the sixteen-year-old shook the hand of John F. Kennedy. Other accounts note that children of alcoholics have an "exaggerated need to be agreeable."[82] Such children, sharing the concern of alcoholics that they are not worthy of being liked, decide that personal accomplishments will make people like them.[83] It has also been suggested that "as a child of addiction," Clinton was predisposed to develop an addiction of his own, in this case a sexual addiction.[84]

Clinton went to Georgetown University's School of Foreign Service and succeeded in becoming a campus leader. "His political skills, his ability to think on his feet, to build coalitions and networks, were unrivaled on campus; but perhaps they were a bit too much, and he was too smooth," said Maraniss resulting in a senior-year defeat for student president.[85] Clinton's lesson from the experience seemed to be played out later in life: work harder next time, talk to every possible voter, listen more carefully. Clinton assiduously built networks of acquaintances and potentially helpful contacts through an internship on Capitol Hill, work in political campaigns, and selection as a Rhodes Scholar. The latter delayed the onset of his own political career, exposing Clinton to a much wider world but posing the dilemma of how to avoid being drafted for military service in Vietnam. Like other male college students of the Vietnam era, Clinton developed a strategy to avoid military service. On returning from one year in Oxford, he arranged to enter the Reserve Officers Training Corps (ROTC) unit at the University of Arkansas, where he promised to enroll in the law school in the fall of 1969. This arrangement persuaded his draft board to cancel his induction, which had been scheduled for late July. Instead of entering law school, however, Clinton returned to England and was saved by the new lottery system for selecting inductees—Clinton's high number was never called. These stratagems, plus a letter Clinton wrote to the University of Arkansas ROTC commander, formed the basis for charges that he dodged the draft.

When he returned to the United States in 1970, Clinton chose to enter the prestigious Yale University Law School. The school's lax attendance policies enabled him to gain valuable campaign experience in a Connecticut Senate campaign and in Texas as state coordinator for the presidential candidate George McGovern in 1972. These campaigns widened his network of contacts to a new generation of political activists, heavily motivated by antiwar sentiments and the desire to reform the American political and economic systems. The other lasting effect from his time at Yale was a romance with Hillary Rodham, a no less brilliant and far more focused law school classmate.

Clinton's Pre-Presidential Political Career

Throughout college Clinton confided to many of his friends his intention to pursue a political career in his home state. After serving for less than a year on the faculty of the University of Arkansas Law School, which he had earlier spurned for Yale, Clinton challenged the incumbent U.S. representative John Paul Hammerschmidt in what appeared to be a hopelessly one-sided contest. Instead, Clinton surprised the state's political establishment by running an aggressive, imaginative campaign, even though he lost by four thousand votes. As the campaign was coming to a close, Hillary Rodham left the House Judiciary Committee's Watergate investigation team, also joined the law school faculty, and became a major figure in Clinton's campaign. They married soon after. His unexpected competitiveness made another election contest inevitable, and in 1976 he easily won election as Arkansas's attorney general and served as Jimmy Carter's state campaign chairman at the same time.

Clinton's meteoric rise now assumed an air of inevitability, and he won the governorship in 1978 with 63 percent of the vote, making him the youngest governor in the United States in four decades.[86] Just before the election, however, the Clintons joined another young politico, James McDougal, in an unsuccessful real estate venture, later to become famous as Whitewater. Clinton's first two-year term as governor was not unlike his first two years as president. He pursued an overly ambitious, highly idealistic agenda of initiatives intended to reform Arkansas's education system and protect the environment from the timber industry. His young staff ruffled feathers in the Arkansas establishment and was unable to discipline Clinton's "loose, free-ranging management style," which included off-the-cuff comments to the press, an inability to adhere to a schedule, and excessive accessibility to any and all comers.[87] Successes were scarce, and the governor's ratings slipped; he narrowly won the 1980 primary against a weak opponent (Arkansas governors then served two-year terms) as voters protested newly raised automobile license fees and public safety crises that were triggered by protests of the Cuban refugees housed at Fort Chafee.

Clinton lost badly in the general election, making him the youngest defeated governor in American history. The experience was reportedly devastating, triggering months of soul-searching about what had gone wrong as Clinton unenthusiastically entered private law practice. Clinton regained the governorship in 1982 and secured reelection in 1984, 1986, and 1990, after the term was lengthened to four years.

Clinton's return to power was eerily similar to later chapters in his political career. As he planned his return, Clinton turned for help in his comeback to Dick Morris, a political consultant, the same adviser to whom Clinton turned in 1995 after the devastating Republican victories in the 1994 midterm elections. Then, as later, Morris urged Clinton to moderate his positions, to become more pragmatic and less idealistic. Another feature of that comeback is familiar. To regain public support, Clinton apologized to Arkansans for mistakes he had made as a young governor, essentially admitting that he had become "too big for his britches." A similar drama of apology and personal penance was played out in 1998–1999 as the Monica Lewinsky scandal produced his initial nonapologetic televised address to the nation in August, followed by gradually increasing statements of regret. The pattern was unmistakable.

Clinton's return to power in Arkansas was far different from his first gubernatorial term. Seasoned veterans replaced his youthful aides; the idealistic program of reforms was replaced with a more modest agenda of achievable reforms; compromises were struck with the state's most powerful economic interests.[88]

Clinton pursued his most ambitious goal of restructuring public education by providing a major increase in funding while requiring that teachers pass a competency exam, something the education union, a onetime supporter of the governor, vigorously opposed. Again, there are remarkable similarities between Clinton's return to power and his record as president from 1994 onward.

Clinton's next career step was designed in Arkansas. He became chairman of the National Governors' Association in 1986, where he built networks and developed a new set of issue positions on job creation, welfare reform, and education for an expanded audience. He addressed the 1980, 1984, and 1988 Democratic National Conventions, delivering a long-winded nominating speech at the last. In fact, Clinton had come within minutes of running for the 1988 nomination himself, agonizing for weeks over whether to run and then disappointing a gathering of friends who had come to Little Rock anticipating an announcement that would not be made for another four years. Clinton's ambition collided with the reality of modern campaigns. He was reportedly dissuaded from announcing by a female aide who confronted him with a long list of women whose past relationships with him would be probed by the press.[89]

Clinton reversed a campaign promise to Arkansans that he would finish out his full term as governor and announced his candidacy in the fall of 1991, a decision that surprised few of his closest friends. As David Maraniss observes, Clinton had always performed well against the toughest competition: "In settings where he found himself among high-powered peers, whether with the Rhodes Scholars at Oxford or, much later, with the governors of other states, Clinton rose quickly to prominence, outpacing others with his ambition, affability, appetite for ideas and deal making."[90] Clinton has always exuded supreme self-confidence in his own skills and capacities, and throughout his life others had assured him of his presidential potential—his mother, his classmates, his fellow Rhodes scholars, and his wife. The election, described in Chapter 2, demonstrated his effectiveness as a campaigner and a political strategist.

Evaluating Clinton's Performance

The Clinton presidency is over, and we now know the end of the story. Many questions will never be answered. The most troubling are those surrounding his relationship with Monica Lewinsky, nicely summarized by Maraniss:

Why would someone who had achieved his lifelong dream needlessly jeopardize it? Why would an inherently cautious politician with an obvious need for public affirmation follow such a careless private path? . . . Why would someone with a deep distrust of his political enemies give them so much ammunition with which to attack? Why would someone with a near photographic memory, who could immediately recall a telephone number that he had not dialed in thirty years, seem so incapable of remembering and learning from history and his own mistakes?[91]

Speculation on these and related questions gripped the nation for fourteen months as the drama of the president and the intern unfolded. Clinton has been

[handwritten margin note: Clinton's imperfections 53]

evere lack of self-discipline" and "defective impulse control,"[92]
delusion of invincibility" that fed his recklessness and could be
ng traits in his character."[93]

s these questions may be, we will never have definitive answers.
reaffirms, however, the importance of trying to avoid presidents
ionally handicapped," as Greenstein describes Johnson, Nixon,
ton. As he points out, "in the real world, human imperfection is
some imperfections are more disabling than others."[94] Although
nt to great lengths to show the nation that he was effectively dis-
ties throughout the ordeal of his investigation and impeachment,
avoidable suspicion that the nation's life and business were dis-
at his own legacy would have been greater had he not had to
hours to his legal defense.

we draw more confident conclusions about Clinton's service as
ton was the first president born after World War II, the first "to live
real-time media culture that magnified his every mistake," and the
resident to be impeached.[95] He was a man of contradictions: "con-
siderate and calculating, easygoing and ambitious, mediator and predator"; "sin-
cere and deceptive at the same time"; "indecisive, too eager to please, and prone
to deception" but also "indefatigable, intelligent, empathetic, and self-deprecat-
ing."[96] He projected "relentless optimism" and "great resilience" in the face of
repeated setbacks inflicted on him by the media, his political opponents, and himself.[97] His political skills were prodigious, acknowledged even by some of his
harshest critics, who recognized a "talent for language that is rare in politicians"
and an "extraordinary gift for intimacy" revealed in his capacity to relate to people, to listen to their concerns, and to empathize with their problems.[98] Newt Gingrich, a longtime adversary, described Clinton as " 'the best tactical politician, certainly of my lifetime.'"[99] Fred Greenstein describes him as "political to the core,"
much like Franklin Roosevelt, Lyndon Johnson, and Richard Nixon.[100] There
was, as well, near universal praise for his native intelligence and natural abilities,
as well as his energy.[101] A seasoned academic observer of presidents declared that
Clinton is that "rare combination of a complex policy thinker and a sophisticated
thinker about politics."[102] Perhaps it is precisely because of Clinton's prodigious
talents that disappointment was widespread about his performance in office.

Some of Clinton's greatest problems seemed to flow from his most notable
skills. A major example is his ability to relate to others, a tremendous asset for
someone who must win support through inside bargaining and public persuasion but a talent triggering doubts about his sincerity. He was described as dis-
playing a "chameleon-like quality," a "plastic political identity" that reflected the
president's "habit of adapting to the people around him and trying to present to
them the version of himself he thought each would most admire."[103] Even his
most authoritative biographer is unsure whether this pattern arose from his mastery of the political art of dissembling or from a deep-seated need to avert conflict and be liked.[104]

Because of his virtuoso skills, people came to distrust his honesty and to question whether he held any strong beliefs. Clinton seemed to adjust too readily to each new audience he addressed. Throughout his political apprenticeship, Clinton displayed a knack for "speaking the idiom, wherever he was," whether Capitol Hill, the halls of Oxford, an Arkansas roadhouse, or a country store.[105] To one observer, such verbal facility caused him to suffer from an "almost pathological inability to tell the whole truth."[106] His reversals on policy were legendary, and his tendency to play word games heightened the impression of deception; instead of admitting to reporters during the 1992 presidential election campaign that he had smoked marijuana, for example, he denied having inhaled or having broken any laws. The central issue in the charges of perjury leveled at Clinton in the Lewinsky matter concerned his legalistic parsing of the phrase "sexual relations." Clinton maintained that the absence of intercourse meant that sexual relations had not occurred, despite the fact that he later acknowledged having had oral sex with the intern.

Even when his honesty was not in question, Clinton's verbal skills were sometimes out of control. Although an unusually gifted extemporaneous speaker, Clinton made numerous mistakes. During his first two years as president, "Clinton too often thought out loud, too frequently seemed to promise things he either could not or chose not to deliver, and thus too frequently could not be taken at his word."[107] Not until later in his term of service were Clinton's speaking skills used to their full strategic advantage. At first, Clinton found "it all too easy to deluge the public with details, and it appear[ed] to be difficult for him to transcend policy mechanics and convey the broad principles and values behind his programs . . . the antithesis of Ronald Reagan, who was notoriously innocent of policy specifics, but gifted at evoking larger themes."[108] His presentations of the 1998 and 1999 State of the Union messages, however, were extraordinary given the pressure-packed circumstances of speaking in the midst of a media-frenzy over his relationship with Lewinsky and while the Senate was deliberating on impeachment.

Confusion over Clinton's larger goals raises another issue: did Clinton offer the public, the press, and politicians a consistent policy vision? His harshest critics questioned whether he had any lasting principles that directed his activity: "Clinton means what he says when he says it, but tomorrow he will mean what he says when he says the opposite. He is the existential President, living with absolute sincerity in the passing moment."[109] A careful reading of his political history suggests that Clinton believes in an activist government and, more than any other policy area, has supported intervention in civil rights. Yet even that lifelong commitment was sorely tested in 1995 when he ordered a review of government-sponsored affirmative action programs (ultimately ordering few changes) and supported welfare reform before the 1996 election. His initiative to improve race relations, launched in 1997 and intended as a centerpiece of his second term, floundered on the national fascination with impeachment.[110]

Clinton's reversals and waffling on policy matters were explained as a personal fault as well as a political reflex: "President Clinton vacillates . . . partly because he cannot make up his own mind and partly because he wants to please the last group to have spoken to him."[111] Others suggested the problem lay in the sophistication of his mind, making him "an indecisive person partly because he has the capacity to look at matters from a variety of angles and partly because he cannot, in the end, decide exactly what his political identity is and what he is willing to fight for."[112] Still others suggested it flowed from his frequent efforts to reconcile contradictory positions.[113]

It is clear that ideological consistency was never a hallmark of Clinton's political career. Over the years he frustrated numerous allies by reversing his position on what others had thought were commitments. This was true with organized labor, environmentalists, and teachers while he was governor; congressional Democrats felt betrayed on many occasions by his shifts in strategy. Clinton had difficulty articulating a clear vision of his current goals and frustrated many in his zigzag course on some policy issues, a course frequently dictated by the needs of political survival. Observers will continue to argue whether his achievements measured up to those expected from an eight-year term and whether he may actually have diminished the role of the president in national politics, reducing the "bully pulpit" to a mere "lectern."[114]

Although coherence may have been minimal, there was no dearth of action. Like Jimmy Carter, Clinton was accused of failing to set priorities among his many first-year initiatives, resulting in a serious overload of the congressional and public agendas. This overload is reminiscent of the problems encountered during his initial year as governor. As Clinton explained, "I'm the most impatient person on earth. If there is a legitimate criticism about me, it is that I have thrown myself against the wall this year. I've tried to do so many things that sometimes when I do things, no one notices."[115] That self-description, of course, puts the problem in its best light, the product of trying too hard and not getting sufficient credit. A review of Clinton's life makes it clear that the tendency is deep-seated. As noted earlier, Clinton trained himself to function on fewer hours of sleep while a student at Georgetown so that he could accomplish more; as a professor, he "always seemed to be juggling too many things at the same time"; and he has admitted to feeling "an urgent sense to do everything he could in life as quickly as possible" because of his father's death at the early age of twenty-eight.[116]

Clinton's capacity to bounce back from adversity was much in evidence. This became part of his presidential campaign following the 1992 New Hampshire primary, when Clinton labeled himself the "Comeback Kid," a candidate who overcame damaging stories about marital infidelity, draft dodging, and marijuana use to finish a surprising second in the nation's most-watched primary. He has demonstrated the same resilience throughout his life. Maraniss suggests that Clinton engaged in extended periods of introspection following three major pre-presidential crises: the suicide of fellow Rhodes scholar Frank Aller, which came on the heels of Clinton's own personal torment over the Vietnam draft; his crushing defeat when he sought reelection after his first term as governor; and the arrest of Roger Clinton, his brother, for cocaine dealing. The latter episode produced an extensive round of counseling and the family's first open discussion of how it had been affected by his stepfather's alcoholism. During this period Clinton reportedly recognized how his own dislike of personal conflict and his desire to please were linked with his family experience.[117] All reports indicate that he faced two additional periods of reflection during his presidency: the months following the Democrats' loss of a congressional majority in November 1994 and the time of the extended inquiry that led to his impeachment in 1998. These were difficult periods for the young adult, the promising politician, and the older brother, as well as for the president and husband. The first four were navigated successfully; the last remains in question.

This capacity for introspection and self-correction probably helped him as president. Even when he was wrong he had the laudable ability "to admit his own failings" and make pragmatic adjustments.[118] Clinton seems to have learned about the job while serving as president; one would hope he also learned about himself.

George W. Bush's Life[119]

If Bill Clinton's lifetime challenge was to overcome the absence of a father, the challenge for George W. Bush was to escape his father's shadow. Born in Connecticut, where his father was completing college at Yale after returning from World War II, George W., as the family has always called him, adopted Texas as his home. Midland was the site of his childhood and his career in the oil industry, though he also spent time in Houston. Bush is the eldest of four sons and one daughter. His closest sibling died of leukemia at age four, an especially traumatic time for Bush (then seven) and his parents. In fact, this event has been portrayed as a critical moment in his life. Barbara Bush, his mother, slipped into an extended period of depression after her daughter's death. With his father often away on business, George W. took it on himself to keep her company and cheer her up, an effort leading to his habitual clowning and role as the family's "ebullient cutup."[120] As a result of the close bond between Bush and his mother, family members suggest he possesses more of her "blunt outspokenness," "irreverence and readiness with a joke," and spontaneity than he does his father's "guarded, dignified" personality.[121]

Descriptions of Bush's childhood in Midland sound like vintage Americana. Little League, picnics, and adventures with brothers and friends with Bush in the lead characterize the president's memories of those years. Bush attended public schools through seventh grade, spending one of those years in Houston, where he later attended an exclusive private school for two years. At that point his life took on a shadowlike quality, retracing the footsteps of his illustrious father. Bush entered his father's prep school alma mater, Phillips Exeter Academy in Andover, Massachusetts, to complete his high school years before moving on to Yale. He was an indifferent student at Andover, falling far short of his father, who had been senior class president and captain of the baseball team. George W. worked his way onto the baseball and basketball teams but was much more of a social leader, expressing opinions on everything (hence his nickname "Lip").[122] Although mediocre grades meant he was concerned about getting into Yale, where his grandfather and uncles also had attended, Bush entered as a legacy in 1964. Again, academics were not his major concern—he became president of his fraternity, known on campus as the "party fraternity," and like his father he was selected for membership in Skull and Bones, Yale's most elite secret society, where members pledge not to disclose the content of conversations held behind closed doors. Bush's grades have not been released, although they were not sufficiently strong to gain him admission to the University of Texas Law School, where he applied two years after graduating from Yale. Classmates recall Bush as fun loving, lacking pretense, and outspokenly supporting the Vietnam War in the face of overwhelming campus opinion and activity to the contrary.

Like Clinton who graduated from college in the same year, Bush confronted the draft and pursued an avenue that kept him out of direct fire. This decision has become one of the more controversial features of Bush's early life, with charges leveled that he received favorable treatment as the son of a member of Congress. Two weeks before his college graduation, the point at which his draft deferment would run out, Bush applied to the Texas Air National Guard and was immediately sworn in despite a waiting list. Some allege that strings were pulled; Bush argues that he wanted to follow in his father's footsteps and be a fighter pilot.[123] What followed were two years of training and a four-year commitment to part-time service. His unit was not sent overseas, and Bush completed his military obligation while working in a variety of jobs back home, none of them with much gusto, while he partied in Texas with considerable gusto. Both Bush and his family refer to these as his "nomadic" years, when he seemed to lack direction or purpose.

Bush chose at this point to prepare for a career in business and attended Harvard Business School, graduating in 1975. He is remembered for his iconoclastic behavior at Harvard—pinching snuff, dressing shabbily, disdaining those aspiring to a career on Wall Street—but even after graduation he seemed to lack direction, holding several entry-level jobs in the Midland oil business. At age thirty-one he showed the first indication of political ambition. Over the years, he had worked in three of his father's campaigns and two Republican senatorial campaigns. When an unexpected retirement opened the House seat in West Texas, Bush, once again following in his father's footsteps, declared his candidacy and won the Republican nomination in a June 1978 runoff against a Reagan-backed conservative.[124] In the midst of the campaign, he married Laura Welch, a librarian who had known Bush in elementary school but had had no contact with him until a blind date put them together. His Republican adversary set the groundwork for the Democratic opponent, who charged Bush with being a privileged product of the eastern establishment and out of step with bedrock values of West Texas. Bush won 47 percent of the vote but lost the election. Reportedly, he concluded that his own political career would have to be delayed until his father was out of politics, a long wait since at that point George H. W. Bush was preparing to seek the Republican presidential nomination.

Perhaps in preparation for the day he could turn to a career in public service, Bush looked to business as a way to create financial security, thus freeing himself to run for political office. Like his father, he entered the oil business in Midland, establishing a small independent oil drilling company that was renamed and reorganized several times between 1979 and 1986. Bush no doubt benefited from his name and family contacts in winning the support of investors for such a high-risk venture. (It did not hurt to be the son of the vice president of the United States.) The business was not successful, limping along from year to year without any major finds and suffering from depressed oil prices. This was all part of a "nagging pattern that marked his life until past the age of forty: once again, he had followed his father's path but failed to achieve his father's success."[125] At a critical time when losses were mounting and his corporation was millions in debt, the corporate assets were bought out, the debts assumed, and Bush was given stock and options of Harken Oil and Gas, a large Dallas firm whose board Bush joined. Again, the suggestion has been made that this success was not so much earned by Bush as the result of his name and special contacts. Even more controversial was Bush's sale of his entire stock holdings in the company in 1990, eight days before the announcement of major losses reduced the stock price by 25 percent. The Securities and Exchange Commission conducted an investigation into whether Bush had engaged in "insider trading," profiting from the privileged information available to a board member. No impropriety was found, although Bush's opponent in the 1994 Texas governor's race alleged otherwise.[126]

Bush's sudden turn in fortunes coincided with the turning point in his life highlighted by Bush himself: his foreswearing of alcohol on the morning after a boisterous fortieth birthday party in 1986 and his increasing spirituality on the heels of a 1985 conversation with the Reverend Billy Graham.[127] As the *Washington Post*'s close study of the president's life concludes, Bush was abusing alcohol though he was not an alcoholic—more a fraternity binge drinker than someone with an addiction. But alcohol had begun to cause problems for him, including a charge of DUI (Driving Under the Influence) in Maine ten years earlier.[128] Bush sought to seize control of his life. "By doing so he would finally begin to close the gap between what was expected of him and what he had achieved."[129] Moreover, his decision to take control of his affairs provided evidence of the personal discipline that had largely eluded him.

His major independent success followed the 1988 presidential election, when George W. worked in the presidential campaign headquarters of his father, serving as principal liaison with evangelical Christian leaders and groups.[130] Bush put together an investment group that purchased the Texas Rangers baseball team and began the process of fashioning an identity distinctive from his father's. Bush served as the managing partner, the public face of the team. He handled public relations, built and maintained consensus among members of the management team he assembled, and used baseball as the way to become "a man of the people."[131] He oversaw the financing and planning for a new ballpark that ushered in a new era of team success and greatly enhanced the value of the franchise. When the partnership sold its interest in 1998, Bush's original investment of $606,302 was worth more than $15 million.[132] By then, however, he had already reaped other benefits, riding his newfound identity to the Texas governorship.

Bush's Pre-Presidential Political Career

This part of the Bush story is much shorter than the preceding one. Although he unsuccessfully ran for Congress in 1978 and worked in numerous campaigns (including his father's 1988 presidential campaign), Bush had never held elected or appointed public office until he became Texas's governor in 1995. He had considered running for the position in 1990, finally agreeing with advice from his mother and principal strategists that the time was not right, particularly with his commitment to the Rangers.[133] With his father's defeat in 1992, however, Bush was able to run for office with less fear of the criticisms he had encountered in the congressional campaign. Moreover, his success with the Rangers had established a separate persona for him as a Texas businessman.

His race against Ann Richards, the incumbent governor who had memorably parodied his father at the 1988 Democratic nominating convention, was remarkably similar to that against Al Gore six years later. Like Gore, Richards seemed intent on provoking Bush into an undisciplined verbal mistake. Bush never took the bait and remained tightly "on message" throughout the campaign, focused on the issues he chose to emphasize and sticking with broad themes rather than policy details. Richards had difficulty defending her record, and none of the rumors about Bush's wrongdoing in his youth or his questionable business dealings ever produced a major embarrassment. Bush won, 53 percent to 46 percent.

In 1998 Bush became the first Texas governor to be reelected to a four-year term (most governors had served for two years) when he defeated a weak opponent, 69 percent to 31 percent. The election was particularly noteworthy for the strong support Bush received from Hispanic voters and women, taken as an indication that he would run a strong national campaign if nominated for president. In fact, there had been open discussion about Bush's national ambitions during the campaign, and the governor explained that he would wait to make a decision on his future until after the election.[134] His presidential aspirations, however, were relatively recent. "Unlike almost any other serious presidential candidates in modern memory, no one who knew him [earlier in life] envisioned George W. Bush in the White House."[135]

What Kind of President Is Bush Likely To Be?

George W. Bush brings a diverse set of skills and experiences to the White House. On a personal level, he appears to be gregarious, unpretentious, persistent, and highly adaptable. His interpersonal skills appear to be outstanding.

There is universal acknowledgment of how well he relates to a wide range of people, using humor and warmth as a way to make them comfortable and win their support. This has been a central feature of his success in business and politics. No less than Bill Clinton, Bush has moved through life creating networks of contacts that have later played a key role in both his financial and political success. In this connection, he seems to elicit considerable personal loyalty. For example, his chief political adviser, Karl Rove, first joined him in the unsuccessful 1978 congressional race, and his closest financial advisers are longtime friends and associates.[136] His humor prevents him from personalizing battles or taking himself too seriously; nonetheless, he is a determined competitor in politics, no less than in sports.

By acknowledging that there are some skeletons in his closet (particularly his partying as a youth) and by changing his behavior, Bush has demonstrated a capacity for self-reflection and personal growth. (Of course, he was fairly old when the changes occurred.) There is no reason to expect a repeat of the marital problems experienced by his predecessor. In terms of Barber's typology, Bush appears best described as an active-positive. He exudes strong self-esteem, invests reseasonably high levels of energy in discharging his duties, and appears to enjoy the position of president.

Bush's pedigree connotes privilege—Andover, Yale, Harvard—yet his manner is decidedly populist. This could arise from discomfort with his own roots or the trappings of elitism, either conservative or liberal in origin.[137] He does not appear to agonize over decisions—if anything, he has a tendency to be impulsive, a potential weakness in the past, partially managed by his wife.[138] There is some evidence that he is likely to be impatient with policy details,[139] and while critics have questioned his intellectual ability, others agree that he has not always applied that ability to its fullest. In that respect, Bush resembles Ronald Reagan, an instinctive politician more comfortable with themes than specifics and always ready to delegate. Bush brings the same CEO style to the presidency that Reagan did, a style honed during his period as managing partner of the Texas Rangers, but Bush's higher energy levels will probably make him less susceptible than Reagan to the danger of not monitoring subordinates closely enough. Much like Reagan, Bush also seems to keep the presidency in perspective; he enjoys the job but also enjoys his time away from the job. A president's ability to relax is probably underrated by both journalists and academics.

Close your eyes, listen to speeches of George W. Bush and his father, and you will immediately note the similarities—the broken syntax, the occasionally labored delivery, the mangled vocabulary. Nonetheless, both men demonstrated they could rise to the occasion when it was important to perform well with a set speech, and George W. gained far more experience in working with the media and the public in the baseball business than his father did in his many government posts. Will George W. Bush possess the communication skills necessary for modern presidents to be successful? Will the content of his speeches provide more "vision" than was found in his father's? The knock on the elder Bush was the "vision thing," as he once dismissed it. George W.'s worldview is still a bit of a mystery, a montage of traditional conservative themes, evangelical Christian overtones, and rejection of the liberal excesses found in the baby boom genera-tion. "Compassionate conservatism," Bush's own term for his philosophy, will come to be defined through his proposals and positions in the upcoming years.[140]

Has Bush had enough political experience to be a successful president? His political activity has been far broader than the nearly six years he spent as Texas governor. His ground-up view of elections, gained through work in numerous campaigns, should provide him with the confidence to make independent polit-ical judgments. It is less clear whether he has sufficient grasp of the broad range of policy issues that confront the president or the commitment to develop the knowledge base that he needs. Although he has no experience at the federal level and the Texas governorship is notoriously "weak" when its powers are compared with those of other state executive offices, Bush has gathered a team of advisers who are intimately familiar with the ways of Washington. (*See Chapter 6.*)

Conclusion: Seeking Presidential Success

Paul Quirk has posed a deceptively simple question: what does a president need to know? Quirk identifies a list of presidential competencies that could serve as the basis for making decisions about how best to allocate the president's time, energy, and talent as well as that of the White House staff and the inner-most group of presidential advisers.[141] In Quirk's view, presidents require a min-imal level of *substantive familiarity* so that they can make intelligent choices among policy options. Moreover, presidents need a degree of *process sensibility* that reflects familiarity with how government decisions are made and carried out as well as with how such systems might best be designed. Finally, presidents need the capacity for *policy promotion,* the means that make it possible to achieve their goals through bargains with other Washington elites and through appeals for broad public support. Every president brings a different mix of personal com-petencies to the job and needs to compensate for personal weaknesses or to com-plement strengths with the help of others. In Quirk's view, it is critical that each president have a well-designed strategy for how to succeed, what he terms *strate-gic competence.* This strategy will involve decisions on how to allocate time, energy, and talent in relation to mastering substantive issues, delegating tasks, and establishing the prerequisites for successful delegation—for example, select-ing personnel.[142]

How are these competencies developed? Implicitly, Quirk seems to suggest that experience in government at the federal level is a critical qualification for presidents to bring to the position. Without it, they have difficulty developing adequate levels of process sensibility and substantive familiarity. But Quirk's advice is directed more to presidents than to voters. Above all else, Quirk urges presidents to approach the office self-consciously with an eye to developing a management strategy—know yourself and take the steps necessary for effectiveness. Only in this way can presidents hope to achieve some measure of success. It is not clear how readily presidents will accept such advice. Are they likely to be sufficiently self-critical to recognize their own shortcomings? One might expect that any newly elected president, imbued with ambition and flush with success, will proceed to the task of governing filled with self-confidence. Moreover, one might expect that those presidents whose personalities drive them to pursue achievement will be least likely to undertake self-analysis.

In many respects, this chapter has explored a question similar to the one posed by Quirk. *What personal qualities make a successful president?* As we have seen, there are no simple answers to that question. Competencies may be part of the solution, but so are temperament and attitudes. As this chapter demonstrates, we have little sense of how the qualities necessary for success are derived from family background, career experience, personality, and beliefs. This is true in no small measure because success is the product of these personal qualities interacting with the constraints and opportunities of situations. Despite this fundamental uncertainty, there remains a pervasive confidence that the president's personal qualities have the utmost effect on performance in office, and, therefore, the American people are likely to continue their search for men and, certainly one day, women, with heroic qualities.

NOTES

1. Todd S. Purdum, "Striking Strengths, Glaring Failures," *New York Times*, Dec. 24, 2000, A1.

2. For a detailed analysis of the speech on Aug. 17, 1998, in light of Clinton's life, see David Maraniss, *The Clinton Enigma* (New York: Simon and Schuster, 1998). Jones's lawyers had been informed that secret tape recordings existed of telephone conversations between Monica Lewinsky and Linda Tripp that described the affair. They were then able to probe the relationship and elicit the president's denial. Lewinsky had been working in the White House during the fall of 1995. One evening, a flirtatious relationship with the president turned into a sexual encounter in the Oval Office suite, followed by nine others over the next eighteen months. Excruciating details of these encounters were provided in the report of Special Counsel Kenneth Starr to the U.S. House of Representatives in September 1998. This report formed the basis for Clinton's subsequent impeachment.

3. The most influential of these interpretations was offered by James David Barber, *The Presidential Character: Predicting Performance in the White House*, 4th ed. (Englewood Cliffs, N.J.: Prentice Hall, 1992).

4. Fred I. Greenstein, *The Presidential Difference: Leadership Style from FDR to Clinton* (New York: Free Press, 2000), 3.

5. Stephen Skowronek, *The Politics Presidents Make: Leadership from John Adams to George Bush* (Cambridge: Harvard University Press, 1993). For another work that deals with the importance of a president's environment, defined in a different way, see Bert A. Rockman, *The Leadership Question: The Presidency and the American System* (New York: Praeger, 1984).

6. Fred I. Greenstein, "Can Personality and Politics Be Studied Systematically?" *Political Psychology* 13, no. 1 (1992): 109. For a general discussion of studying person-

ality and politics with special attention to the presidency, see Fred I. Greenstein, *Personality and Politics: Problems of Evidence, Inference, and Conceptualization*, 2d ed. (New York: Norton, 1975); and Bert Rockman, *The Leadership Question: The Presidency and the American System* (New York: Praeger, 1984).

7. See, for example, *The Clinton Legacy*, ed. Colin Campbell and Bert A. Rockman (Chatham, N.J.: Chatham House, 2000).

8. Bruce Buchanan, *The Citizen's Presidency* (Washington, D.C.: CQ Press, 1987), 102–104. Buchanan proposes a set of "competent process standards" that are more susceptible to empirical verification. See *Citizen's Presidency*, 108–134.

9. Bert Rockman, "Conclusions: An Imprint but Not a Revolution," in *The Reagan Revolution?* eds. B. B. Kymlicka and Jean V. Matthews (Chicago: Dorsey, 1988), 205. Other works in this vein, important because of the significance attributed to the Reagan experience, include the following: Larry Berman, ed., *Looking Back on the Reagan Presidency* (Baltimore: Johns Hopkins University Press, 1990); Sidney Blumenthal and Thomas Byrne Edsall, eds., *The Reagan Legacy* (New York: Pantheon Books, 1988); Charles O. Jones, ed., *The Reagan Legacy: Promise and Performance* (Chatham, N.J.: Chatham House, 1988); and John L. Palmer, ed., *Perspectives on the Reagan Years* (Washington, D.C.: Urban Institute, 1986).

10. My thanks to Professor Pfiffner for sharing an advance copy of his book with me. Hence, quotations are cited by chapter rather than by page. See James P. Pfiffner, *Character and the Modern Presidency* (Washington, D.C.: Brookings, 2001), chap. 1.

11. Ibid., chap. 2.

12. Ibid., chap. 4. Pfiffner's conclusion is that Clinton was reckless and irresponsible in his behavior and that he extended the effect of his lies by repeating them to cabinet members and White House staff aides whom he knew would repeat the untruths. But the lies "did not constitute the same level of institutional threat to the polity that Watergate and Iran-Contra did." See chap. 6.

13. Arthur Schlesinger's initial effort polled fifty-five scholars, and his second included seventy-five, with historians constituting the greater part of each group. Maranell and Dodder included results from 571 historians, and the *Chicago Tribune* poll focused on forty-nine scholars who had studied individual presidents. The Murray-Blessing poll was based on 846 responses to a nineteen-page, 180-question survey that was sent to 1,997 Ph.D.-holding American historians with assistant professor rank (an additional 107 responses were returned late). Finally, the C-SPAN survey included 58 historians. For information on poll samples, see Henry J. Abraham, *Justices and Presidents* (New York: Oxford University Press, 1985), appendix B. For discussion of these efforts as well as their own, see Robert K. Murray and Tim H. Blessing, *Greatness in the White House: Rating the Presidents, Washington Through Ronald Reagan*, 2d updated ed. (University Park: Pennsylvania State University Press, 1994), chaps. 1 and 2. The ranking of Ronald Reagan was completed in 1988–1990 and is reported in Murray and Blessing's updated edition.

14. Murray and Blessing, *Greatness in the White House*, 24.

15. Ibid., 41–43, and appendix 8, 139. The personal traits conducive to success also were examined in terms of how they changed for different times. For the modern era, 1945 to the present, respondents ranked intelligence first and integrity second, with other qualities in declining order: sensitivity to popular demands, charisma, previous political experience, pleasing physical appearance, intense patriotism, and an aristocratic bearing.

16. Ibid., 63.

17. James MacGregor Burns, *Leadership* (New York: Harper and Row, 1977).

18. Greenstein, *Presidential Difference*, 5–6.

19. Donald Matthews, *The Social Background of Political Decision Makers* (New York: Random House, 1954), 23.

20. Edward Pessen, *The Log Cabin Myth: The Social Backgrounds of the Presidents* (New Haven: Yale University Press, 1984), 56–57.

21. Ibid., 171.

22. Ibid., 56–63. Pessen views a family's class as a combination of wealth and possessions, income and occupational prestige, lifestyle, status, influence, and power. He recognizes, moreover, that analysts' characterizations are subjective.

23. Truman attended night classes at the Kansas City Law School, but it was a proprietary institution not then affiliated with a university. It is now part of the Law School of the University of Missouri—Kansas City.

24. Max Weber, "Politics as a Vocation," in *Max Weber: Essays in Sociology,* eds. H. H. Gerth and C. W. Mills (New York: Oxford University Press, 1946), 85.

25. Hugh Montgomery-Massingberd, ed., *Burke's Presidential Families of the U.S.A.* (London: Burke's Peerage, 1975), 250.

26. Ibid., 320.

27. Robert Donovan, *Conflict and Crisis: The Presidency of Harry S Truman, 1945–48* (New York: Praeger, 1977), chap. 40. It should also be noted that military officers have demonstrated leadership skills and may be called on to develop substantial political skill while building careers or in dealing with foreign leaders. Eisenhower, for example, did both.

28. Pessen, *The Log Cabin Myth,* 171.

29. E. Digby Baltzell and Howard G. Schneiderman, "Social Class in the Oval Office," *Society* 26 (September/October 1988): 42–49. The ranking of presidential performance used in this study was conducted by Robert K. Murray and Tim H. Blessing and was first published in the *Journal of American History* 70 (December 1983): 535–555.

30. Ibid., 47.

31. W. H. Harrison and Garfield were not rated because of the brief time they served in office.

32. Baltzell and Schneiderman, "Social Class in the Oval Office," 49.

33. Richard Neustadt, *Presidential Power and the Modern Presidents* (New York: Free Press, 1991), 151.

34. Ibid., 205.

35. Rockman, *Leadership Question,* 212. Rockman uses a performance ranking compiled by the *Chicago Tribune* in 1982.

36. We are indebted to Leonard P. Stark for this account and continuing stimulation on the subject of presidential personality. See his senior honors thesis, "Personality and Presidential Selection: Evaluating Character and Experience in the 1988 Election," University of Delaware, June 1991, 47–48. Barber's article was "The Question of Presidential Character," *Saturday Review,* September 23, 1972, 62–66.

37. Fred I. Greenstein, *Personality and Politics,* 3.

38. Alexander George and Juliette George, *Woodrow Wilson and Colonel House: A Personality Study* (New York: John Day, 1956); Doris Kearns, *Lyndon Johnson and the American Dream* (New York: Harper and Row, 1976); Bruce Mazlish, *In Search of Nixon: A Psychohistorical Inquiry* (Baltimore: Pelican, 1973); Betty Glad, *Jimmy Carter: In Search of the Great White House* (New York: Norton, 1980); and Stanley A. Renshon, *High Hopes: The Clinton Presidency and the Politics of Ambition* (New York: NYU Press, 1996). For an excellent biography of Clinton that provides psychological insights but is not informed by psychological theory, see David Maraniss, *First in His Class: A Biography of Bill Clinton* (New York: Simon and Schuster, 1995).

39. For an extended discussion, see Greenstein's treatment of these issues in *Personality and Politics,* chaps. 3 and 4, as well as the introduction.

40. See, for example, Alexander George's discussion of Barber's book *The Presidential Character: Predicting Performance in the White House* in George, "Assessing Presi-

dential Character," *World Politics* 26 (January 1974): 234–282. This essay is reprinted with several related essays in *Presidential Personality & Performance*, Alexander L. George and Juliette L. George (Boulder, Colo.: Westview, 1998), 145–197.

41. Although the call of conservatives during the Reagan years was "let Reagan be Reagan," Clinton's aides had begun the practice during his gubernatorial years of "protect[ing] Clinton from Clinton." See David Maraniss, *Clinton Enigma*, 60.

42. Barber, *Presidential Character*, 34.

43. James David Barber, "Predicting Hope with Clinton at Helm," *Raleigh* (N.C.) *News Observer*, January 17, 1993. Barber has not offered a preliminary evaluation of George W. Bush.

44. Barber, *Presidential Character*, 5.

45. Ibid.

46. Barber, "Predicting Hope."

47. Stanley A. Renshon, "A Preliminary Assessment of the Clinton Presidency: Character, Leadership and Performance," *Political Psychology* 15, no. 2 (1994). Also see a slightly revised version of the paper in *The Clinton Presidency: Campaigning, Governing, and the Psychology of Leadership*, ed. Stanley A. Renshon (Boulder, Colo.: Westview, 1995), 57–87.

48. David Maraniss, *First in His Class*.

49. Renshon, "Preliminary Assessment," 382.

50. Jann S. Wenner and William Greider, "The Rolling Stone Interview: President Clinton," *Rolling Stone*, December 9, 1993, 81.

51. Renshon, "Preliminary Assessment," 381.

52. Ibid., 380.

53. Ibid., 382.

54. Greenstein, *Presidential Difference*, 255.

55. Fred I. Greenstein, "The Two Leadership Styles of William Jefferson Clinton," *Political Psychology* 15, no. 2 (1994): 357. Also see Greenstein's essay "Political Style and Political Leadership: The Case of Bill Clinton," in *Clinton Presidency: Campaigning, Governing, and the Psychology of Leadership*, 137–147.

56. Greenstein, "Two Leadership Styles," 358.

57. Greenstein, *Personality and Politics*, 19.

58. Fred I. Greenstein, *The Hidden-Hand Presidency* (New York: Basic Books, 1982). Barber, however, has responded that the new evidence confirms his original analysis even more fully. See Barber, *Presidential Character*, 522–525.

59. See George, "Assessing Presidential Character"; and Michael Nelson, "The Psychological Presidency," in *The Presidency and the Political System*, 4th ed., ed. Michael Nelson (Washington, D.C.: CQ Press, 1995).

60. Dean Keith Simonton, *Why Presidents Succeed: A Political Psychology of Leadership* (New Haven: Yale University Press, 1987), 151–152.

61. Barber, *Presidential Character*, 487.

62. Ibid., 298.

63. Ibid., 296–299.

64. Jeffrey Tulis, "On Presidential Character," in *The Presidency in the Constitutional Order*, eds. Jeffrey Tulis and Joseph M. Bessette (Baton Rouge: Louisiana State University Press, 1981), 283–313.

65. Clark Clifford, "The Presidency As I Have Seen It," in *The Living Presidency*, ed. Emmet John Hughes (New York: Coward, McCann and Geoghegan, 1973), 315, cited by Fred I. Greenstein in *Presidential Difference*, 189.

66. Harold W. Stanley and Richard G. Niemi, *Vital Statistics on American Politics 1999–2000* (Washington, D.C.: CQ Press, 2000), 250–251.

67. Joseph A. Pika, "Management Style and the Organizational Matrix: Studying White House Operations," *Administration and Society* 20, no. 1 (May 1988): 11.

68. John Hart, *The Presidential Branch: From Washington to Clinton* (Chatham, N.J.: Chatham House, 1995).

69. Alexander George, *Presidential Decisionmaking in Foreign Policy* (Boulder, Colo.: Westview, 1980), 139–168.

70. The three basic structures were identified in the early 1970s by R. T. Johnson and have been the object of much discussion. See Richard Tanner Johnson, *Managing the White House* (New York: Harper and Row, 1974). Also see Johnson, "Presidential Style," in *Perspectives on the Presidency,* ed. Aaron Wildavsky (Boston: Little, Brown, 1975).

71. Roger Porter, "A Healing Presidency," in *Leadership in the Modern Presidency,* ed. Fred I. Greenstein (Cambridge: Harvard University Press, 1988), 218.

72. George, *Presidential Decisionmaking,* 159.

73. Colin Campbell, *Managing the Presidency: Carter, Reagan, and the Search for Executive Harmony* (Pittsburgh: University of Pittsburgh Press, 1986), 93–111; James Pfiffner, *The Strategic Presidency: Hitting the Ground Running* (Chicago: Dorsey, 1988), 30–37; and Buchanan, *Citizen's Presidency,* 124–133.

74. Alexander L. George and Eric Stern, "Presidential Management Styles and Models," in *Presidential Personality & Performance,* 263.

75. Pika, "Management Style," 9.

76. Alexander George, "The Case for Multiple Advocacy in Making Foreign Policy," *American Political Science Review* 66 (September 1972): 751–785. Also see George, *Presidential Decisionmaking,* chap. 11.

77. George, *Presidential Decisionmaking,* 203.

78. Ibid., 203–204.

79. Ibid., 201.

80. Ibid., 204.

81. Maraniss, *First in His Class,* 38.

82. Greenstein, "Two Leadership Styles," 358.

83. Michael J. Kelly, "A Man Who Wants to Be Liked, and Is: William Jefferson Blythe Clinton," *New York Times,* November 4, 1992, A1.

84. Jerome D. Levin, *The Clinton Syndrome: The President and the Self-Destructive Nature of Sexual Addiction* (Rocklin, Calif.: Prima, 1998), 5.

85. Maraniss, *First in His Class,* 88.

86. Ibid., 357.

87. Ibid., 362.

88. Michael J. Kelly is highly critical of the last pattern, arguing that Clinton betrayed his populist roots and cozied up to the traditional centers of Arkansas power. See Michael J. Kelly, "The President's Past," *New York Times Magazine,* July 31, 1994.

89. David Maraniss, *Clinton Enigma,* 14.

90. Maraniss, *First in His Class,* 340.

91. Maraniss, *Clinton Enigma,* 42–43.

92. Greenstein, *Presidential Difference,* 174, 199.

93. Maraniss, *Clinton Enigma,* 43.

94. Greenstein, *Presidential Difference,* 200.

95. Todd Purdum, "Striking Strengths, Glaring Failures," *New York Times,* December 24, 2000, A1.

96. Maraniss, *First in His Class,* 124, 199, 355.

97. Purdum, "Striking Strengths," A13.

98. Kelly, "A Man Who Wants to Be Liked," A1; and Kelly, "President's Past," 25.

99. Quoted in Purdum, "Striking Strengths," A1.

100. Greenstein, *Presidential Difference,* 174.

101. Wenner and Greider, "Rolling Stone Interview," 40.

102. Bert A. Rockman, "Leadership Style and the Clinton Presidency," in *Clinton Presidency: First Appraisals*, 347.

103. Kelly, "President's Past," 25; Campbell and Rockman, introduction to *Clinton Presidency: First Appraisals*, 9; and Maraniss, *First in His Class*, 169.

104. See, for example, the alternative explanations in Maraniss, *First in His Class*, 323, and Maraniss, *Clinton Enigma*, 58–59.

105. Maraniss, *First in His Class*, 98.

106. Kelly, "President's Past," 40.

107. Rockman, "Leadership Style," 342.

108. Greenstein, "Two Leadership Styles," 356–357.

109. Kelly, "President's Past," 45.

110. Jason DeParle and Steven A. Holmes, "A War on Poverty Subtly Linked to Race," *New York Times*, December 26, 2000, A1.

111. Graham K. Wilson, "The Clinton Administration and Interest Groups," in *Clinton Presidency: First Appraisals*, 220.

112. Rockman, "Leadership Style," 355.

113. Maraniss, *First in His Class*, 72, 74, 367; and Renshon, " Preliminary Assessment," 386.

114. Colin Campbell, "Demotion? Has Clinton Turned the Bully Pulpit into a Lectern?" in *Clinton Legacy*, 48–69.

115. Wenner and Greider, "Rolling Stone Interview," 80.

116. Maraniss, *First in His Class*, 293, 349.

117. Ibid., 422.

118. Greenstein, "Two Leadership Styles," 357.

119. Two multipart series on the life and preparation of George Bush, originally published in the *Washington Post* in 1999 and 2000, provide the background for this sketch. Both can be found on the paper's Web site, http://www.washingtonpost.com/wp-dyn/politics/news/postseries/. Separate installments are cited where appropriate.

120. Lois Romano and George Lardner Jr., "Part 2: Tragedy Created Bush Mother-Son Bond," *Washington Post*, July 26, 1999, A1.

121. Ibid.

122. Romano and Lardner, "Part 3: A So-so Student but a Campus Mover," *Washington Post*, July 27, 1999, A1.

123. Romano and Lardner, "Part 4: At Height of Vietnam, Bush Picks Guard," *Washington Post*, July 28, 1999, A1.

124. Romano and Lardner, "Part 5: Young Bush, A Political Natural, Revs Up," *Washington Post*, July 29, 1999, A1.

125. Romano and Lardner, "Part 6: Bush Name Helps Fuel Oil Dealings," *Washington Post*, July 30, 1999, A1.

126. Ibid.

127. The reawakening of Bush's spirituality can also be traced to his participation in a weekly men's Bible study group organized in Midland. See Hanna Rosin, "Applying Personal Faith to Public Policy," *Washington Post*, July 24, 2000, A1.

128. This incident was revealed late in the 2000 campaign by a Fox-affiliate news reporter in Maine, temporarily throwing the Bush campaign off-balance. Bush admitted to having had too many beers at a local bar in Kennebunkport and to having been pulled over for driving erratically. He was fined $150 and had his driving privileges suspended in Maine for thirty days, though they were not restored until 1978 because he was unable to attend a required rehabilitation program. Bush explained that he had not revealed the incident earlier because he sought to protect his daughters from learning of their father's dangerous behavior. See Dan Balz, "Bush Acknowledges 1976 DUI Arrest," *Washington Post*, November 3, 2000, A1; and Steven

A. Kurkjian and David Armstrong, "Bush Downplayed Drinking: '78 Comments Got License Back," *Boston Globe,* November 4, 2000, A11.

129. Romano and Lardner, "Part 1: Bush's Life-Changing Year," *Washington Post,* July 25, 1999, A1. Bush has resolutely refused to answer reporters' questions on whether he engaged in illegal drug use. He has unequivocally declared his faithfulness to his wife but has not assumed a similar position on drug usage. Needless to say, this stance spurs media curiosity. For an extensive examination of this question and how it became an issue in the 2000 election, see Felicity Barringer, "When an Old Drug Question Becomes New News," *New York Times,* August 22, 1999.

130. Hanna Rosin, "Applying Personal Faith," A1.

131. Dana Milbank, "Dispelling Doubts with the Rangers," *Washington Post,* July 25, 2000, A1.

132. Romano and Lardner, "Part 7: Bush's Move Up to the Majors," *Washington Post,* July 31, 1999, A1.

133. Ibid.

134. Exit polls showed Bush winning 46 percent of the Hispanic vote, an all-time high for a statewide Republican candidate. See R. G. Ratcliffe, "Election 98: Bush Leads Statewide GOP Blitz," *Houston Chronicle,* November 4, 1998, A1.

135. Romano and Lardner, "Part 1: Bush's Life-Changing Year," A1.

136. Lois Romano, "A Fierce Loyalty Marks Bush's Inner Circle," *Washington Post,* July 26, 2000, A1.

137. Hanna Rosin, "Bush's Resentment of 'Elites' Informs Bid," *Washington Post,* July 23, 2000, A1.

138. See the story of Bush deciding to run for governor in Romano and Lardner, "Part 7: Bush's Move Up to the Majors," A1.

139. See the experience of Joseph Allbaugh, his campaign manager in 1994, as reported in Ibid.

140. For a thoughtful discussion of the generational and Christian influences on Bush's thinking, see the two articles by Hanna Rosin published in the *Washington Post* (cited in notes 127 and 137).

141. Paul Quirk, "Presidential Competence," in *The Presidency and the Political System,* 6th ed., ed. Michael Nelson (Washington, D.C.: CQ Press, 2000), 171–198; and Paul Quirk, "What Must a President Know?" *Transactional Society* 23 (January/February 1983).

142. Quirk, "Presidential Competence."

SUGGESTED READINGS

Barber, James David. *The Presidential Character.* 4th ed. Englewood Cliffs, N.J.: Prentice Hall, 1992.

George, Alexander, and Juliette George. *Woodrow Wilson and Colonel House: A Personality Study.* New York: John Day, 1956.

___. *Presidential Personality & Performance.* Boulder, Colo.: Westview, 1998.

Greenstein, Fred I. *Personality and Politics: Problems of Evidence, Inference, and Conceptualization.* New York: Norton, 1975.

___. *The Presidential Difference: Leadership Style from FDR to Clinton.* New York: Free Press, 2000.

Hargrove, Erwin. *Jimmy Carter as President: Leadership and the Politics of the Public Good.* Baton Rouge: Louisiana State University Press, 1988.

Kearns, Doris. *Lyndon Johnson and the American Dream.* New York: Harper and Row, 1976.

Maraniss, David. *First In His Class: The Biography of Bill Clinton*. New York: Simon and Schuster, 1995.

Mazlish, Bruce. *In Search of Nixon: A Psychohistorical Inquiry*. Baltimore: Pelican, 1973.

Pessen, Edward. *The Log Cabin Myth: The Social Backgrounds of the Presidents*. New Haven: Yale University Press, 1984.

Pfiffner, James P. *Character and the Modern Presidency*. Washington, D.C.: Brookings, 2001.

Renshon, Stanley A. *High Hopes: The Clinton Presidency and the Politics of Ambition*. New York: New York University Press, 1996.

Rockman, Bert A. *The Leadership Question: The Presidency and the American System*. New York: Praeger, 1984.

5 LEGISLATIVE POLITICS

HIGH DRAMA FREQUENTLY CHARACTERIZES relations between the president and Congress. Three examples are presented below to highlight the centrality of this institutional relationship. Twice during the winter of 1995–1996, the federal government shut down because Bill Clinton and the Republican-controlled Congress could not reach agreement on a new budget. No less dramatic was the winter of 1998–1999, when Clinton became only the second president in American history to be impeached by the House and also the second to survive a trial in the Senate. On a markedly different note, his successor, George W. Bush, signed a massive tax-cut bill into law on June 7, 2001, fulfilling a campaign pledge and reversing within a few short months one of Clinton's major legacies. But this success may have come at the cost of a Republican majority in the Senate.

Despite his best efforts, President George W. Bush was unable to persuade Sen. Jim Jeffords (I., Vt.) to remain a Republican rather than become an Independent and switch his voting support to the Democrats, thereby giving them a Senate majority in June 2001.

The Budget Battle, 1995–1996

The saga of the government shutdowns stretched over several months.

On November 17, 1995, the Republican-controlled 104th Congress enacted a comprehensive reconciliation bill (see chapter 9) designed to produce a balanced budget in 2002. The bill would have reduced the growth of federal mandatory spending for several major programs (Medicare, Medicaid and other welfare programs, and agriculture subsidies) as well as discretionary spending in education, job training, and environmental protection. The bill also would have cut taxes by $245 billion during the same period and transferred responsibility for caring for the poor to the states. In two votes, largely along party lines, the legislation passed the House 237–189 and the Senate 52–47.[1] President Clinton, while supporting the goal of a balanced budget, attacked the bill as unfair to the poor and the elderly. After he vetoed it, his negotiations with Republican leaders of Congress failed to produce a comprehensive agreement on how to balance the budget. Six of the thirteen major appropriations bills required to fund the government in fiscal 1996, which began on October 1, 1995, were not finalized. Moreover, congressional Republicans refused to raise and extend the limit on the national debt when the government's authority to borrow funds to meet its financial obligations lapsed in November.

At the heart of this confrontation was a philosophical disagreement over the future role of the federal government. Clinton proposed a ten-year plan to balance the budget (later reduced to seven years) based on economic assumptions and data provided by the Office of Management and Budget (OMB). Republicans insisted on following a seven-year plan based on Congressional Budget Office information. The two sides differed over the size of tax and spending cuts. By mid-January 1996, Clinton and the Republicans had moved toward each other's position and appeared ready to split the monetary differences between them. They could not, however, resolve the philosophical conflict over how to restructure Medicaid and Aid to Families with Dependent Children (AFDC), two major welfare programs.

As a result of the impasse, two government shutdowns occurred: 800,000 federal employees were furloughed November 14–20 and 280,000 December 16–January 5. Although the Republican Congress had passed continuing resolutions temporarily extending funding to cover the agencies' operations, Clinton vetoed them because they contained unacceptable budget conditions—ones seeking to reduce funding for the environment, education, Social Security, and Medicare. Eventually, temporary funding agreements ended these episodes (workers later collected back pay), but permanent appropriations were not finalized until late April 1996.[2] In their struggle with Clinton, congressional Republicans had used continuing resolutions and the debt limit extension bill as leverage to try to force his hand. They reasoned that he would rather accept their terms than allow the government to shut down or default on its obligations. To everyone's surprise given his earlier eagerness to compromise in legislative negotiations, Clinton proved to be resolute. Secretary of Treasury Robert Rubin was able to use certain trust funds under his control to prevent default. And Clinton's media campaign successfully painted the Republicans as extremists intent on damaging average citizens. The public placed more of the blame for the shut-downs on Congress than on the president.

The Impeachment Battle, 1998–1999

The high-stakes game of fiscal chicken played in 1995–1996 was an early bat-tle on the rocky road of Clinton's relations with Congress, but the stakes were raised considerably on December 19, 1998, when the House of Representatives approved two articles of impeachment against President William Jefferson Clin-ton. By a vote of 228–206, the House accused Clinton of lying under oath while giving testimony to a grand jury in August 1999 and, by a vote of 221–212, accused him of obstructing justice by hiding his improper relationship with a young White House intern. (Two other articles of impeachment that had been rec-ommended by the House Judiciary Committee failed to be adopted by the full House.) These votes came at the end of a lengthy investigation by Independent Counsel Kenneth Starr. Originally named to investigate the president's possible involvement in a failed land development project in Arkansas (known as White-water), Starr's investigation was expanded at several points to include other sub-jects of alleged wrongdoing.[3] The last of these was Clinton's testimony in con-nection with a civil suit brought against him by Paula Jones, a former state employee who charged him with making unwanted sexual advances in 1991, while he was governor of Arkansas. To document a pattern of sexual harassment with other state or federal employees, Jones's lawyers posed questions to the pres-ident about his relationship with a former White House intern destined to become a national celebrity, Monica Lewinsky. When Clinton denied the existence of that relationship in a court deposition and subsequently misrepresented it to both the public and a grand jury, the ground was set for a constitutional confrontation.

Starr conducted a grand jury investigation throughout most of 1998. In the course of the investigation he subpoenaed President Clinton and desposed him by closed-circuit television on August 17, 1998, the first instance of such testi-mony by a sitting president. In September, the independent counsel filed a report with Congress (also released to the public replete with salacious details) that formed the basis for the House Judiciary Committee's recommendation, in a straight party vote, that the House conduct an impeachment inquiry. Starr testi-fied before the committee on two occasions in November, and President Clinton responded to an extensive list of written questions. Throughout this period, the public's approval of the president remained surprisingly high and interest in the scandal surprisingly low. Several factors may explain this pattern. Observers sug-gested that the public had entered a period of "scandal fatigue" and merely wanted federal officials to return to business.[4] In addition, the public may have had greater tolerance of presidential misbehavior during a period of peace and prosperity. The White House may also have been successful in making the scan-dal appear to be nothing more than a question of sex and adultery, sources of concern but falling far short of impeachable offenses. In fact, throughout this saga, the meaning of "high crimes and misdemeanors," the constitutional grounds for removing a president, remained a central question. Advocates of removal believed that undermining the "rule of law", enforced by the courts met that test; defenders of the president believed that personal misconduct did not constitute a threat to the republic.[5] "Clinton turned the struggle into a question of whether a president who was performing well should be removed for actions unconnected to his official duties."[6]

Following the December House vote on impeachment, the Senate began the impeachment trial of President Clinton on January 7, 1999. It was the first such proceedings since 1868, when President Andrew Johnson avoided removal by a single vote. In the modern version, thirteen Republican members of the House served as managers and had three days to present their case; the president's legal team responded over three days. The House managers were distressed that their fellow Republicans in the Senate seemed less committed to removal than they were. Majority Leader Trent Lott insisted on steering a path that would maintain the dignity of the Senate, a strategy that reflected a realistic assessment of how difficult it would be to generate the two-thirds majority needed for removal of the president when the Democrats held forty-five seats. A motion to dismiss the case, even though it failed by 44–56, revealed that the Democrats were relatively united: only one Democrat had crossed party lines rather than the dozen needed for conviction. And when the House managers sought to conduct a very public trial with a long list of witnesses testifying to the president's immoral behavior, the Senate instead approved a short list of witnesses deposed in private, their videotaped testimony available only to members of the Senate.[7] In the end, neither article of impeachment received even a majority vote on February 12, when the Senate finally concluded its consideration. Article I failed by a 45–55 vote, with ten Republicans joining all Democrats in opposition. Article II failed as well by a vote of 50–50, with five Republicans joining all the Democrats. Although the president survived, impeachment will always help define his place in history.

Clinton's relations with Congress had not always been so stormy. During his first two years as president, the Democratic 103d Congress passed most of his legislative program, usually with little support from Republicans and some opposition from conservative Democrats. He relied on Republican support to pass two international trade bills opposed by organized labor and liberal Democrats in the House. Of the major bills he proposed during this early period, only health care reform and welfare reform failed to be enacted. In stark contrast, the pattern of Clinton's legislative relations following the Republican takeover of Congress in 1994 is comparable to the experiences of Presidents Richard Nixon, Gerald Ford, Ronald Reagan in his last two years in office, and George Bush. Like these predecessors who confronted a Congress controlled by the opposition party, Clinton was engaged in protracted conflict about the direction of public policy, institutional prerogatives, and ultimately his political survival.

Bush's Tax-Cut Victory and Senate Setback, 2001

George W. Bush entered office with something that no Republican president had enjoyed since 1955—a Republican majority in both the House and the Senate. Despite repeated success in winning presidential elections and controlling the White House for two extended periods (1969–1977 and 1981–1993), the Republican Party had not controlled both elected branches of government since the two years following Dwight D. Eisenhower's first electoral victory in 1952. But Bush's working majorities were small: a mere nine votes in the House and an even smaller one-vote advantage in the evenly divided Senate, a vote to be cast by the vice president in the event of a tie.[8] Bush's hotly contested electoral victory might have translated into a difficult working relationship with Democrats in Congress, and Bush made well-publicized efforts early in the administration to consult with the opposition to promote bipartisanship and to project a less confrontational tone. The media dubbed this outreach effort the "charm offensive."[9] Ultimately, however, the president put forward a relatively aggressive agenda that would rise or fall based largely on Republican unity. In short, Bush sought to "hit the ground running" with a focused legislative agenda that could be accomplished while his political influence remained high.[10]

House Republicans were especially unified during the early months, adopting the president's budget proposals and his $1.6 trillion tax-cut proposal with only modest changes. Senate Republicans proved less cooperative when two moderates refused to support the proposed budget because of the large tax cut, and Sen. John McCain of Arizona, Bush's opponent for the Republican nomination in the primary races, continued to assert his independence.[11] Nonetheless, with the support of several moderate Democrats, President Bush was able to deliver on his primary legislative priority and his signature campaign promise of tax relief. The size of the cuts was close to the original proposal ($1.35 trillion) as were many of the details. Bush stressed the historic nature of the moment when he noted at the signing ceremony, "Tax relief does not happen often in Washington. . . . In fact, since World War II, it has happened only twice: President Kennedy's tax cut in the 60's and President Reagan's tax cuts in the 1980's."[12]

But many Republicans worried about the long-term consequences of this victory. Sen. James M. Jeffords, R-Vt., announced on May 24, just two days before the House and Senate approved the tax-cut bill, that he would become an independent and vote with the Democrats for organizational purposes. This meant the Republicans would lose control of the Senate and Democrats would have an opportunity to define the agenda, block nominations, conduct investigations, and derail administration-sponsored legislation. The stakes, in other words, were enormous. Jeffords gave his word to the president that he would not try to undermine the tax bill (in fact, he ultimately voted for it) and would not leave the party until June 5 or until the tax bill became law, whichever came later.

Why had Jeffords, just reelected to a third term in November 2000, taken this drastic, though not unprecedented, step? Rumors and possible explanations swirled through Washington. Some blamed the bullying tactics taken by the White House and Republican leaders to make Jeffords adhere to the party line in critical votes. It was also suggested that he had fought with the White House concerning large and small differences over education. The president had rejected Jeffords's insistence that more money be spent for special education, a program of particular concern to him as chair of the Health, Education, Labor, and Pensions Committee. It was also rumored that the White House had angered Jeffords by excluding him from a social function when a Vermont teacher was chosen teacher of the year.[13] Jeffords mentioned neither of these in his public statement but pointed to the growing distance between the Republican Party's national agenda and his own moderate Republicanism, which stressed the principles of "moderation, tolerance, and fiscal responsibility."[14] Bush, many argued, had placed such emphasis on maintaining support from the conservative wing of the party that moderates such as Jeffords felt their views on abortion, the environment, energy, judicial appointments, and missile defense were already being ignored and would not be respected in the future. During blunt discussions among Senate Republicans, the strategy of "governing from the right" was questioned by some and defended by others.[15]

This incident signaled the end of Bush's brief honeymoon period in relations with Congress and illustrates the complexity of legislative–executive relations.[16] *Intraparty* disputes can prove just as important as *interparty* conflicts, and presidents must worry about the strategic logic of their program as well as the tactical nuances of working with individual legislators. Like his predecessors, Bush discovered that the skills and techniques of leadership that enabled him to capture his party's nomination and win the election do not always match those needed to sustain his public and legislative support. Nomination and electoral politics require the ability to raise money, to build an organization composed of election professionals, to project an attractive and engaging image, and to sense the concerns of the public. But the politics of governing—that is, legislating and administering—requires talents that can move a complex, cumbersome government to get things done. These talents include persuasion, personal and organizational leadership, and managerial skill.

Americans judge presidents by their performance in office, and their ability to persuade Congress to pass their legislative program is central to that evaluation. The solutions to most national problems require congressional action, but Congress is seldom a fully cooperative partner. The stage is thus set for the kind of dramatic confrontations detailed above. This chapter places the president's relations with Congress in a larger context. It begins by tracing the development of the chief executive's legislative role in the twentieth century and then presents an analysis of the constitutional relationship between the president and Congress. A discussion of the president's formal legislative powers and a description of presidential strategies to influence legislation follow. The chapter then analyzes what factors contribute to the success and failure of presidents in gaining their legislative goals.

Development of the President's Legislative Role

The Constitution, in Article 1, Section 8, grants Congress seventeen powers that cover a wide range of subjects—for example, levying and collecting taxes, borrowing money, and regulating foreign and interstate commerce—as well as the power to choose the means to execute the specifically enumerated powers. Quite clearly, the Framers expected that Congress, not the president, would have primary responsibility for formulating national policy and that the president's legislative role would be minor. Until the twentieth century, most presidents did limit their involvement in the congressional process. Even Thomas Jefferson and Abraham Lincoln, who were most inclined to try to lead Congress, encountered strong opposition, and their activism did not alter the pattern of congressional supremacy.[17]

The presidency acquired a greatly expanded legislative role early in the twentieth century as the national government responded to the problems of industrialization and urbanization under the leadership of Theodore Roosevelt and Woodrow Wilson. Roosevelt worked closely with congressional leaders and sent several messages to Congress that defined a legislative program. He saw it as the duty of the president to "take a very active interest in getting the right kind of legislation."[18] Wilson, who as a political science professor had argued that strong presidential leadership of Congress was needed if the nation were to cope with its growing problems, actively participated in the legislative process.[19] He took the lead in defining the goals of his program, helped formulate bills, reinstated the practice abandoned by Thomas Jefferson of personally delivering the State of the Union message to Congress, used members of his cabinet to build congressional support for bills, and personally lobbied for some of his most important measures, such as the Federal Reserve Act and the Clayton Antitrust Act. (*See the discussion in chapter 1.*)

Franklin D. Roosevelt undertook the next major expansion of the president's legislative role. Taking office in 1933, when the economy was mired in the depths of the Great Depression, FDR called Congress into a special session that lasted for a hundred days. During that period, the new president proposed, and Congress passed, legislation designed to meet the economic crisis. Together they overhauled the banking system, authorized a program of industrial self-government under the National Recovery Administration, buttressed farm income through passage of the Agricultural Adjustment Act, regulated financial markets under the Truth in Securities Act, and created the Tennessee Valley Authority, a program of comprehensive development of one of the nation's most depressed areas. This period of unprecedented activity established the practice of assessing a new president's first one hundred days in office.

During the remainder of his first term, FDR continued to develop a series of measures designed to help farmers, industrial workers, and individual citizens. The legislation promoted soil conservation and restricted excess agricultural production; it guaranteed labor the right to organize and bargain collectively; and it established a system of social insurance to protect people against the loss of work due to economic slowdowns, physical disability, or old age. FDR established the expectation that the president would be actively involved at all stages of the legislative process by submitting a legislative program to Congress, working for its passage, and coordinating its implementation. Thus, today's presidents behave much like FDR: They send Congress messages that analyze a problem and outline the presidents' proposed solution, assign aides to monitor the bills and lobby for their passage, ensure adherence to a common legislative program for the executive branch enforced through a central clearance process monitored by OMB,[20] and threaten to veto legislation that fails to meet presidential demands or that they regard as unwise or contrary to their purposes. Harry S. Truman and Dwight Eisenhower, FDR's two immediate successors, institutionalized the president's legislative role by creating structures and processes to assist in carrying it out on a regular, systematic basis with help from the Bureau of the Budget (which later became the Office of Management and Budget) and the White House staff.[21]

By the mid-1960s, it appeared to some observers that the presidency had come to dominate the legislative process. Writing in 1965, Samuel P. Huntington remarked that "the congressional role in legislation has largely been reduced to delay and amendment." Such tasks as taking the initiative in formulating legislation, assigning legislative priorities, generating support for legislation, and determining the final content of legislation had "shifted to the executive branch," which, in Huntington's view, had gained "at the expense of Congress."[22] Others argued, however, that although congressional and presidential roles in the legislative process had changed substantially, Congress remained vitally important by constantly modifying and altering policy through appropriations, amendments, and renewals of statutory authorizations.[23]

Moreover, Congress and the president are not engaged in a zero-sum game in which the power of one necessarily decreases as the power of the other increases. In an absolute sense, since 1933 Congress has increased its power as an instrument of government by vastly expanding the subjects on which it has legislated. During this time, however, presidents have assumed greater responsibility as innovators of public policy. In three brief periods of intense legislative activity—1933–1937, 1964–1965, and 1981—activist presidents (FDR, Lyndon Johnson, and Reagan) led responsive Congresses in the adoption of major changes in domestic policy. Congress also responded to presidential leadership in establishing the role of the United States in world affairs during and immediately following World War II.

Nevertheless, there have also been periods in which Congress substantially increased its authority vis-à-vis the president. During the 1970s, for example, Congress expanded its control over the executive branch through increased use of the legislative veto (*see chapter 6*), curbed presidential use of military force abroad through passage of the War Powers Resolution of 1973 (*see chapter 10*), and strengthened its ability to determine the amount of federal spending by redesigning the congressional budget process (*see chapter 9*).

All presidents since FDR, with the possible exception of Eisenhower, have aspired to lead Congress as a way to lead the nation. Some have succeeded temporarily; others have been totally unsuccessful. For example, in 1981, Reagan quickly took command of bipartisan conservative congressional majorities, which passed his taxing and spending proposals and sharply altered the course that domestic social and economic policy had been following since the 1930s.[24] But Reagan's period of dominance was short-lived; congressional critics of his policies regrouped in 1982, support among Republican legislators sagged, and legislative concerns shifted as budget deficits soared to unprecedented levels. Reagan discovered, as had Roosevelt in 1937 and Johnson in 1966, that congressional approval of a president's program is not automatic. Congressional support must be cultivated and maintained and can rapidly disappear when the conditions that created it change. Reagan's immediate successor, George Bush, offered very modest, rather than sweeping, initiatives, but he, too, was unable to develop sustained congressional support from a Democratic-controlled Congress. In contrast, as previously noted, congressional Democrats enacted much of President Clinton's initial legislative agenda with only limited help from Republicans.[25] But when Republicans won control of Congress in 1994, Clinton's agenda and strategies changed drastically, and the nation watched the prolonged battles described earlier. For his first 123 days in office, President George W. Bush advanced a notably conservative legislative agenda that reflected Republican control of Congress. The consequent dramatic party shift of Senator Jeffords forced a reexamination of both the agenda and the tactics of winning congressional support.

The Presidential–Congressional Relationship

By its fundamental design, the Constitution creates inherent tension between Congress and the presidency. Yet cooperation between the two institutions is necessary if the government is to act in a significant way. Institutional competition arises from the separation of powers, but the Constitution also mandates a sharing of powers: joint action by the president and Congress is required to authorize programs, appropriate money to pay for them, and levy taxes to provide the funds. Neither branch can achieve its goals or operate the government without the participation of the other. However, since 1970, presidential–congressional relations have become competitive because of the distrust between the branches and intensified party differences between presidents and members of Congress.[26] Charles O. Jones describes the relationship as one in which "these separated institutions often *compete* for shared powers."[27]

The Separation of Powers

James Madison's *Federalist* No. 51 makes it clear that the Framers had intended presidential–congressional conflict:

To what expedient . . . shall we finally resort, for maintaining in practice the necessary partition of power among the several departments, as laid down in the constitution? The only answer that can be given is . . . by so contriving the interior structure of the government as its several constituent parts may, by their mutual relations, be the means of keeping each other in their proper places. . . .

In order to lay a due foundation for that separate and distinct exercise of the different powers of the government, which to a certain extent is admitted on all hands to be essential to the preservation of liberty, it is evident that each department should have a will of its own. . . .

But the great security against a gradual concentration of the several powers in the same department consists in giving to those who administer each department the necessary constitutional means and personal motives to resist the encroachments of the others. . . . Ambition must be made to counteract ambition. The interests of the man must be connected with the constitutional rights of the place.[28]

Since 1789, the task of governing the United States has been to overcome the constitutional dispersion, and simultaneous sharing, of power among competing institutions. The most important division of power, from the standpoint of making and implementing national policies, is that between the president and Congress.

The pattern of the presidential–congressional relationship has not been static. A cyclical pattern of power aggrandizement by Congress or the presidency and resurgence by the other institution has operated from the beginning of the Republic.[29] In the nineteenth century, the institutional surges and declines oscillated evenly within well-defined boundaries and returned at the end of each cycle to the balance envisioned in the Constitution. However, U.S. economic, social, and technological transformations and emergence from international isolation during the twentieth century created problems and conditions that called increasingly for executive rather than legislative decision making. The president can act more quickly, more decisively, and more consistently than can Congress, which has difficulty ascertaining its institutional will and coherently pursuing its goals. Presidential surges have resulted in permanent expansions of executive power and presidential aggrandizements, such as Johnson's use of the war powers to involve the United States in the Vietnam War (*see chapter 10*) and Nixon's sweeping claims of executive privilege and his extensive impoundments of appropriated funds (*see chapter 6*). Although Congress managed to reassert its constitutional authority during the 1970s,[30] the cycle turned again in the 1980s toward increased reliance on presidential power. The nation found that it needed presidential leadership to deal with difficult problems such as severe inflation, economic interdependence, and international terrorism.

Most recently, Republicans sought to follow their surprise victory in the 1994 elections with a new collective assertiveness that might have reversed presidential ascendancy or at least undermined the leadership of President Clinton. Under the aggressive, ideologically conservative leadership of Speaker Newt Gingrich, House Republicans hoped to take action on the ten priorities outlined in the Contract with America, an election manifesto that most Republican candidates for the House had endorsed. In fact, the House acted on all ten proposals within the first hundred days of the new Congress, but even this novel strategy to seize the legislative initiative did not restore congressional ascendancy as Senate Republicans pursued more moderate priorities and Clinton developed effective defensive tactics.[31]

Sources of Presidential–Congressional Conflict

In addition to institutional competition born of the separation of powers, conflict stems from the difference in the constituencies of the members of Congress and the president and from the fragmentation of power within Congress. The 535 members of Congress represent constituencies that vary in geographical area, population, economic structure, and social composition. Each congressional constituency is but a part of the nation. Every member of Congress depends for reelection on constituency-based political forces, making all members somewhat narrow-minded at times in their policy orientations. When members claim to be acting in behalf of the national interest, they must be judged in the context of their constituency interests.

Because congressional parties lack the power to command the votes of their members, there is only a limited basis for the elected party leaders of either house to speak in the institution's behalf. The only way the national interest emerges in Congress is through bargaining between members and blocs of members responsive to particular interests. This practice results in the formation of temporary majority coalitions to pass specific measures. Congressional policymaking is thus deliberate, incremental or piecemeal, and reactive. Congress often is unable to maintain consistency in its actions in different policy areas or cohesiveness within those areas. Speed, efficiency, consistency, and cohesiveness usually are lacking, except in a crisis.

In contrast, presidents claim the entire nation as their constituency. Only they can claim to speak authoritatively on behalf of the national interest or to act for various inarticulate and unorganized interests who are not adequately represented in Congress. Presidents can resist the demands of well-organized particular interests by posing as champions of the national interest (even though there may be times when they, too, respond to such pressures).

Changes in electoral politics also have widened the gap between presidents and Congress. Members of Congress are political entrepreneurs who routinely seek reelection through constituency-based electoral coalitions that are largely independent of party membership.[32] (Since 1946, more than 90 percent of House and 75 percent of Senate incumbents who have sought reelection have been successful.)[33] They are nominated in direct primaries, their campaigns are financed heavily from nonparty sources, and they sustain electoral support through activities unrelated to their party, such as providing service to constituents. Presidents can exert little leverage on members of Congress through appeals to party loyalty or the exercise of party discipline. Moreover, presidential coattails—votes won by the congressional candidate because of support for the presidential candidate—have nearly disappeared, and there has been an increase in the number of constituencies supporting a presidential candidate of one party and electing members of Congress from the opposition.

This separation of presidential and congressional electoral coalitions has resulted in a divided government that has reduced pressures on members to sup-

Table 5-1   Partisan Control of the Presidency and
Congress, 1933–2001

Dates	Presidency	Congress
1933–1946	Democratic	Democratic
1947–1948	Democratic	Republican
1949–1952	Democratic	Democratic
1953–1954	Republican	Republican
1955–1960	Republican	Democratic
1961–1968	Democratic	Democratic
1969–1976	Republican	Democratic
1977–1980	Democratic	Democratic
1981–1986	Republican	Senate-Rep. House-Dem.
1987–1992	Republican	Democratic
1993–1994	Democratic	Democratic
1995–2000	Democratic	Republican
2001 (1/20–6/6)	Republican	Republican
2001 (6/7–)	Republican	Senate-Dem. House-Rep.

port even their own party's president. Under the best of conditions, when a president's party controls both houses of Congress, party loyalty is a weak link, but even this connection is not available to a president faced with a Congress controlled by the opposition party. Since 1933, Democratic presidents have had to deal with an opposition Congress in 1947–1948 and 1995–2000, while Republican occupants of the White House have confronted full opposition control in all years except 1953–1954, 1981–1986, and 2001–2002 (see Table 5-1).

Analysts are sharply divided in their assessments of the consequences of divided partisan control of the government. The critics of divided government argue that it renders unworkable the already cumbersome and inefficient separation-of-powers structure established in the Constitution.[34] Critics blame the large federal budget deficits of the late 1980s and 1990s on divided government, where each branch has a stake in the failure of the other.[35] These critics also charge that divided government undermines electoral accountability because it is impossible for voters to hold either party responsible for the policies adopted and the results achieved since the last election.

Other researchers draw different conclusions. David Mayhew concluded, after a systematic empirical analysis of legislation and congressional investigations since World War II, that it does not make "much difference whether party control of the American government happens to be unified or divided."[36] Morris Fiorina, while acknowledging that divided government results in more "conflictual" presidential–congressional relations, asks whether its consequences are "necessarily bad."[37] Although divided government may limit the potential for social gain through public policy, it also limits potential loss through government action,[38] and divided government is the American electorate's way of establishing the coalition governments that are common in multiparty systems.[39] Without question, divided government dominated presidential–congressional relations for most of the last quarter of the twentieth century and unexpectedly reemerged early in the twenty-first century.

A fragmented internal authority structure also makes Congress no match for the decisiveness, cohesion, and consistency of the presidency as a national policymaking institution. Among Congress's oft-mentioned weaknesses are loosely structured congressional parties, the limited power of party leaders, the absence of party discipline in congressional voting, the presence of strong committees and subcommittees, and the ambitions of individual members to enhance their reelection chances and to advance to higher office.[40] The short-lived experiment with party government under Speaker Gingrich in 1995 is a case in point: many party members, worried about reelection, defied party leadership and moved to the center in 1996.

Even an internally fragmented Congress can be assertive, but its thrust is to negate or restrain presidential action rather than direct it. As presently constituted, Congress values the function of "representation" over that of "lawmaking."[41] This means that Congress is responsive primarily to constituency interests and to well-organized interest groups. It also means Congress is more comfortable with distributive policies and programs, which provide benefits on a widespread basis, than with redistributive policies, which change the allocation of wealth and power in society. Ironically, presidents have assumed responsibility for exercising the lawmaking function that translates electoral mandates into policies with broad societal impact.

Patterns of Presidential–Congressional Policymaking

To make national policy, the president and Congress must cooperate and resolve numerous conflicts. Some analysts have identified patterns in this relationship, which vary according to issues, presidential leadership styles, and political context. Presidential domination tends to prevail in foreign and military policy and those issues to which presidents attach high priority, such as Lyndon Johnson's Great Society program in 1964 and 1965.[42] Congressional domination of domestic policy is the norm and was the prevailing pattern in the 1970s, when Congress passed major legislation on the environment, consumer protection, and occupational safety; Congress also has always prevailed on public works. Stalemate, where differences prevent policy from moving forward, characterized much of the energy legislation proposed by presidents in the 1970s, as well as proposals for reducing the federal budget deficit in the 1980s and 1990s. Occasionally, a proposal may be stalemated for years and then move rapidly to passage as conditions change or a new president takes office. Medicare provides a good example. Proposals for national health insurance had languished in Congress since first advanced by President Truman in 1946. The political climate turned favorable for liberal social legislation in 1964 and 1965, following the assassination of John F. Kennedy. Responding to Johnson's forceful leadership,

Congress enacted legislation authorizing national health insurance for the elderly (Medicare) in 1965.

Presidential ambition and leadership style are potentially important causes of conflict. An activist president who is committed to an extensive legislative program, such as FDR or Lyndon Johnson, normally tries to dominate Congress, whereas a president who is more restrained and less active, such as Eisenhower or Ford, may be more inclined to cooperate with Congress or accept considerable congressional initiative in program development. Establishing good relations with Congress is so important that none of the modern presidents has sought policy stalemate and some have even been willing to share leadership. For example, Reagan was an activist with a conservative agenda that did not require extensive new legislation. To achieve his primary goals of reducing the role of the federal government and strengthening the armed forces, he attempted to dominate Congress. On issues of less importance to him, such as farm policy and Social Security financing, he was willing to share responsibility with Congress. When he disagreed with Congress, as he did over reducing the federal budget deficit, he was willing to settle for the status quo. Reagan's successor, George Bush, a conservative with a limited agenda, sought congenial relations with Congress, but many crucial issues—the deficit, taxes, and civil rights—remained unresolved because of irreconcilable differences on which neither the president nor Congress was willing to compromise.

Bill Clinton, a moderate with an ambitious reform agenda, initially attempted to dominate Congress through the Democratic majority and its more liberal leaders, thereby angering a small but important group of moderate and conservative Democrats.[43] After Republicans gained congressional majorities in 1995, Clinton portrayed their proposals as dangerously extreme but also established distance from liberal Democrats. This independence (called at the time a strategy of "triangulation" as he positioned himself as the moderate force between liberal Democrats and conservative Republicans on Capitol Hill) enabled him to make alliances with any group of legislators. For example, Clinton and congressional Republicans fashioned a major reform of national welfare policies in 1996 that angered many Democrats. Nonetheless, Democrats rallied to the president's defense during the impeachment controversy of 1998–1999.

George W. Bush entered office with a more ambitious legislative agenda than many had expected, given his narrow electoral victory. On some matters, most notably education reform, Bush sought common ground with Democrats, but on most issues (developing national energy and environmental policies, reforming Social Security, cutting taxes, reviewing national defense) he relied on support from conservative Republicans and a few conservative to moderate Democrats.[44] After Senator Jeffords's party switch, there were extensive discussions about how Bush's strategy would have to moderate, but initially no one knew how the changed political setting would shape the administration's actions.

Presidents have two sets of tools at their disposal to accomplish legislative goals: (1) the formal powers vested in the presidency by the Constitution and by statute, and (2) the informal resources inherent in the office through which a president may influence the congressional agenda. The chief executive uses both sets of tools simultaneously and in conjunction with each other. In the next two sections, each is examined separately.

The President's Formal Legislative Powers

The Constitution outlines the president's legislative role. Article II, Section 3, authorizes him to call Congress into special session and requires that he "from time to time give to the Congress information of the state of the Union, and recommend to their consideration such measures as he shall judge necessary and expedient." Article I, Section 7, makes presidents direct participants in the legislative process by providing for their approval or disapproval (through the veto) of "every bill" and "every order, resolution, or vote to which the concurrence of the Senate and House may be necessary." These formal legislative powers are augmented by statutory delegations of authority to the president and to administrative agencies.

Special Sessions

The president's power to call Congress into special session is less important today than it was in the past, primarily because Congress, since the 1930s, has remained in session for much of the year, taking periodic short recesses. The expansion in government activity, the complexity of the budgetary process, and the change from indefinite to specific term authorizations of federal programs that must be periodically renewed have so increased the congressional workload that early adjournments have all but disappeared. In an earlier age, the president could call Congress back to Washington to consider specific proposals, thereby placing responsibility for action on the nation's legislators.

FDR made perhaps the most effective modern use of this power in March 1933, shortly after his inauguration. The famous "hundred days" was a special session that enacted the first stage of the New Deal program of economic recovery and social reform statutes. A dramatic exercise of the special session power occurred in July 1948, when President Truman called the Republican-controlled Congress back to Washington from its summer recess to give it the opportunity to enact several major planks in the party's 1948 platform. When Congress failed to act, as Truman had anticipated, he made the "do-nothing Congress" a major focus of his successful reelection campaign.

Messages to Congress

Although contemporary presidents have not gained much leverage over Congress by controlling its sessions, they have derived substantial power by virtue of their constitutional duty to report to Congress on the state of the nation and to recommend legislation they deem necessary. Since the Budget and Accounting Act of 1921 and the Employment Act of 1946, Congress has required that presidents annually submit messages to it that explain and justify their budget and that report on the condition of the economy. The State of the Union message, the budget message, and the economic report enable presidents to set the congressional agenda by laying before Congress a comprehensive legislative program. These mandatory messages offer an assessment of the nation's problems and announce the president's goals and priorities; the messages are also efforts to enlist the force of public opinion behind those priorities. Special messages emphasizing specific problems and proposing bills to deal with them complete the definition of the president's domestic program. (Chapter 8 examines the development of that program.)

Individual members of Congress still introduce a multitude of bills independently of the president, but the chief executive is in a position to dominate the congressional agenda. In the twentieth century, members of Congress came "almost routinely to demand that the president—not their own party leaders— develop new policies and programs" to deal with the complex problems the nation faced.[45] Occasionally, there have been efforts to return this power to Congress. During the first Bush administration, the Democratic majority in Congress advanced proposals in areas that the president did not address, such as civil rights and immigration. Speaker Newt Gingrich tried to do much the same for Republicans following their 1994 victory, when Clinton's 1995 State of the Union address provided few specific legislative proposals and adopted a defensive posture toward the conservative agenda.[46] But these efforts to replace presidential leadership with a congressionally generated agenda floundered. Clinton reemerged as a legislative force in 1996 by taking advantage of the unpopularity of Republican tactics that closed the government and by adopting much of the Republicans' agenda.[47] Thus, both recent efforts to wrest the agenda-making power from the president were short-lived. In the first months of his presidency in 2001, George W. Bush worked closely with Republican congressional leaders to fashion a common agenda that would take advantage of the then-unified party government.

The Veto Power

The Constitution establishes a major legislative role for presidents by requiring their approval of measures passed by Congress (Article 1, Section 7, Paragraph 2). Within ten days (Sundays excepted) after a bill or joint resolution is presented to the White House, the president must either (1) sign it into law; (2) disapprove or veto it and return it to the house of Congress in which it originated along with a message explaining this action; or (3) take no action on it, in which case it becomes law without the president's signature at the end of ten days. If Congress adjourns within that ten-day period and the president does not sign a measure awaiting action, then it does not become law and the president has exercised a "pocket veto." The president's action is final because adjournment prevents a measure from being returned to Congress for reconsideration and a possible override.

The veto is the president's ultimate legislative weapon; it carries the weight of two-thirds of the members of each house of Congress since that is what it takes to overturn a veto. In his classic treatise, *Congressional Government,* Woodrow Wilson noted the importance of the veto even at a time when Congress dominated the national government: "For in the exercise of his power of veto, which is, of course, beyond all comparison, his most formidable prerogative, the President acts not as the executive but as a third branch of the legislature."[48]

Andrew Jackson adopted a broad interpretation of the veto power, one giving him the right to reject legislation on the basis of its wisdom, merit, or equity as well as on constitutional grounds.[49] Modern presidents (since 1933) have espoused this "tribunative" view of the veto and have used it frequently.

One study of presidential veto messages associated with important legislation from 1933 to 1981 found that presidents gave five general reasons for vetoing legislation, listed here in order of importance: unwise on policy grounds (by far the most numerous); lack of fiscal soundness; unconstitutionality; administrative unworkability; and to protect the executive against legislative encroachment.[50] Another researcher reported that "the categories of and reasons for presidential vetoes are remarkably similar from president to president," largely because they are protecting the prerogatives of their office from Congress.[51]

The data in Table 5-2 demonstrate a much more extensive use of the veto by Presidents Roosevelt, Truman, and Eisenhower than by presidents who have served since 1961. The data also show that from 1961 through 1995 Democratic presidents vetoed fewer bills than did the Republicans. Of course, Democrats controlled Congress throughout much of that time—the Senate from 1961 through 1980 and 1987 through 1994, and the House from 1961 through 1994. President Clinton exercised no vetoes during the 103d Congress, controlled by his own party, "the first time since the 32d Congress (1851–1852) and the administration of Millard Fillmore that an entire Congress served without prompting a presidential rejection."[52] All of Clinton's thirty-seven vetoes occurred during the Republican-controlled Congresses of 1995–2000.

The effect of the veto power on policy is both negative and positive. It is negative by nature; once used, it signifies an impasse between the president and Congress, and prior policy is unchanged. Sometimes presidents find that the veto is the best means of emphatically communicating their intentions to Congress. Ford's sixty-six vetoes, for example, were his way of conveying his social and economic policy preferences to a liberal Democratic Congress. The positive aspect of the veto lies in its use as a bargaining tool to "shape, alter, or deter legislation."[53] By threatening to exercise the veto—a threat made credible only by actual use—presidents can define the limits of their willingness to compromise with Congress. They can state in advance what they will and will not accept, thereby reducing the likelihood of a showdown over a bill. Selective and sensitive use of the threat to veto can be a means of avoiding or of reconciling conflict with Congress. For example, in 1989–1991, President George Bush frequently threatened to veto bills as a way to "stimulate serious bargaining."[54] This

Table 5-2   Presidential Vetoes of Bills, 1933–2001

President	Regular vetoes	Pocket vetoes	Total	Number of vetoes overridden	Percentage of vetoes overridden
FDR (1933–1945)	372	263	635	9	1.4
Truman (1945–1953)	180	70	250	12	4.8
Eisenhower (1953–1961)	73	108	181	2	1.1
Kennedy (1961–1963)	12	9	21	0	0.0
Johnson (1963–1969)	16	14	30	0	0.0
Nixon (1969–1974)	26	17	43	7	16.3
Ford (1974–1977)	48	18	66	12	18.2
Carter (1977–1981)	13	18	31	2	6.5
Reagan (1981–1989)	39	39	78	9	11.5
G. Bush (1989–1993)	29	17	46	1	2.2
Clinton (1993–2001)	37	0	37	2	5.4

Sources: U.S. Senate Library, *Presidential Vetoes, 1789–1976* (Washington, D.C.: Government Printing Office, 1977) and *Presidential Vetoes, 1977–1984* (Washington, D.C.: Government Printing Office, 1985); *1985 Congressional Quarterly Almanac,* "Vetoes Cast by President Reagan," 6; *1988 Congressional Quarterly Almanac,* "Vetoes Cast by President Reagan," 6; *Congressional Quarterly Weekly Report,* Dec. 19, 1992, "President Bush's Vetoes," 3925–3926; "Six Bill Vetoed," *Congressional Quarterly Weekly Report,* Dec. 14, 1996, 3386; "Versatility with the Veto," *CQ Weekly,* Jan. 6, 2001, 52–54.

may have been the goal of his son, President George W. Bush, when he confronted a version of the "patients' bill of rights" passed by the Democratic-controlled Senate in June 2001. Part of a general effort the president hoped to support, the bill had specific provisions he found unacceptable.

The decision to veto, the override attempt, and the success of the veto and the override all depend on the "political environment (e.g., stage of the electoral cycle) and the political resources of the president," concluded one study of vetoes between 1945 and 1980.[55] Public support, another feature of the political environment, was critical for the success of vetoes and congressional overrides. However, dependence on public support places the president in a catch-22 situation: as support declines, use of the veto increases, but so does the likelihood of an override.[56] The strategic incentive for the president is to act decisively so as to form partisan or ideological factions on initial passage of the legislation. Timing also enters strategic calculations: the use or threat of a veto is more effective early in the administration. Another strategic consideration is the choice of issues. A social welfare bill, for example, imposes more demands on resources than, say, a government management measure.[57]

Presidents do not veto bills on the basis of purely subjective judgments or random advice. Rather, they rely on a systematic procedure, begun during Franklin Roosevelt's administration, for the analysis of enrolled bills (those that have passed both houses of Congress) once they are "received" (that is, once they have arrived at the White House).[58] The Legislative Reference Division of the Office of Management and Budget immediately solicits reactions to a measure

Table 5-3   OMB and Lead Agency Recommendations and Presidential Action on Enrolled Bills, January 1969–June 1976

Pattern of advice	Approval by president (percent)
OMB approval/lead agency approval	96
OMB approval/lead agency disapproval	95
OMB disapproval/lead agency approval	65
OMB disapproval/lead agency disapproval	35

Source: Stephen J. Wayne, Richard L. Cole, and James F. C. Hyde Jr., "Advising the President on Enrolled Legislation," *Political Science Quarterly* 94 (summer 1979): 310.

from the pertinent departments and agencies and from the budget examiners in the OMB program divisions that have jurisdiction over the bill. Recommendations and supportive rationales for presidential action on the legislation are due from the agencies and examiners within forty-eight hours. Legislative Reference collates the materials and prepares for the president a memorandum that summarizes the features of the legislation, reviews agency reactions, and states OMB's recommendations. Research has shown that a favorable OMB recommendation almost ensures that the president will sign a bill. A negative recommendation, however, is more of a danger signal, and the president and his staff will examine closely the recommendation of the "lead" agency in the federal bureaucracy. When OMB and the agency with the primary responsibility disagree, the president is likely to sign the bill. OMB disapproval carries more weight, however, than disapproval by the lead agency (see Table 5-3).

The goals of Nixon and Ford, two Republican presidents facing an opposition Congress, were "to rule and win."[59] That they withstood more than three-fourths of the efforts of Congress to override their vetoes indicates that they were quite successful. The enrolled bill process was an important advisory mechanism in their exercise of the veto power.

The President's Informal Legislative Influence

In 1960, Richard Neustadt startled students of the presidency when, in his now celebrated treatise *Presidential Power,* he asserted that the formal powers of the president amounted to little more than a clerkship. The Constitution, Neustadt argued, placed the president in a position of mostly providing services to other participants in national politics. "Presidential power," Neustadt declared, "is the power to persuade."[60] As the preceding examination of the president's formal legislative powers suggests, this is frequently the case in presidential relations with Congress. It is not enough for presidents to present a legislative program to Congress; they also must persuade congressional majorities to enact each statutory component of that program. To do so, presidents employ mostly informal rather than formal methods of influence. These informal legislative tools can be used to exert both indirect and direct pressure on Congress. Presidents may engage in bargaining, arm-twisting, and confrontation as general modes of working with Congress, which are discussed at the end of this section.

Indirect Influence

Presidents attempt to influence Congress indirectly through appeals to the public and by enlisting the support of interest groups. A careful presidential appeal, usually launched with a major public address, can generate pressure that causes Congress to act. The tactic is less likely to succeed when public opinion is divided and there is substantial opposition to the president's position. Presidents also are more likely to use popular appeals successfully in a crisis that appears to require congressional action. However, presidents must make selective use of such appeals. Congress may object to having the president too frequently "going over its head" to the people. In doing so the president attacks, directly or by implication, the wisdom and the motives of Congress and its members.

George W. Bush used his first televised address to a joint session of Congress on February 27, 2001, to launch an aggressive, campaign-style strategy to win support for his major legislative proposals. The administration had already displayed impressive organization by focusing in successive weeks on education, religious faith-based charities, and tax cuts, critical elements of the Bush program. Moreover, it carefully developed talking points for Republican members of Congress so the party message would be in harmony.[61] In the immediate aftermath of his speech (which offered a striking contrast to Clinton's speeches in its brevity and emphasis on broad themes rather than policy specifics), Bush visited states where he had run well in 2000 and where key Democratic votes were located—Arkansas, Florida, Georgia, Iowa, Louisiana, Nebraska, North Dakota, Pennsylvania, and South Dakota. The president left no doubt that he wanted those supporters attending the rallies to contact their representatives in Washington. As the president's spokesman explained, "Every day, in every way, whether it's at the White House or it's in travel, the president looks at how to get his plan across to the voters so voters can get their message to the Senators and congressmen."[62] The result of this carefully choreographed effort, of course, was a major victory on the tax-cut bill.

Marshaling the support of interest groups has become increasingly important to presidents in their efforts to apply leverage on Congress. Since the mid-1960s, interest groups have grown in number and in the scope of their efforts to shape national policy. Proliferation and intensification of interest group activities stem in part from the declining role of parties as mechanisms for linking public opinion with public policy and in part from the increased participation of citizens in national policy politics. Interest groups facilitate this participation and take an active part in policymaking through informal alliances with congressional committees and administrative agencies.[63] Presidents find it helpful, if not necessary, to obtain the backing of interest groups before moving on major legislation, and the national officers and federal relations directors of important groups often are consulted in the process of formulating such legislation. (Presidential liaison with interest groups is examined in chapter 8.)

Direct Influence

Presidents use two informal tools in their direct efforts to persuade members of Congress. They may grant or withhold services and amenities they have at their disposal as rewards for support or sanctions for lack of it, and they may become personally involved in the legislative process. Presidents vary greatly in their skills at exploiting these resources.

Favors. Bestowing or denying favors to members of Congress gives presidents a measure of leverage. Such favors may be given directly to an individual member or to important people in his or her constituency, or the favor may be of benefit to the constituency itself.[64] Favors given as rewards to individual members of Congress include appointments with the president and other high-ranking officials; letters or telephone calls from the president expressing thanks for support on important bills; campaign assistance in the form of cash contributions from the party's national committee, a presidential visit to the constituency, or a presidential endorsement; the opportunity to announce the award of federal grants to recipients in the constituency; invitations to be present at bill-signing ceremonies, to attend White House social functions, and to accompany the president on trips; and White House memorabilia such as pens, cuff links, and photographs. Favors for influential congressional constituents include appointments, appearances by administration officials at organization meetings, invitations to social functions, mailings on important occasions such as anniversaries, memorabilia, and VIP treatment such as White House mess privileges. To some extent, all members of Congress share in such benefits, but the president's supporters have readier access to them and feel more comfortable asking for them than do others.

The most important constituency-related rewards are jobs and projects. There are jobs at all levels of the federal government that are filled by appointment rather than through the civil service. Congressional recommendations by members of the president's party greatly influence the selection of U.S. district court judges, U.S. attorneys, U.S. marshals, customs collectors for ports of entry, and a variety of lesser positions. Projects often regarded as rewards for support include military installations; research and administrative facilities; public works such as buildings, dams, and navigational improvements to rivers and harbors; government contracts with local firms; grants to local governments and educational institutions; and the deposit of federal funds in banks. Presidents cannot direct projects exclusively to their supporters, but they can exercise discretion whenever possible. As some federal activities are reduced in size, eliminated, or turned over to state governments, their potential for use as bargaining chips necessarily declines.

Involvement in the Legislative Process. As accomplished politicians, presidents can help themselves by becoming personally involved in the legislative process, but this requires knowledge and skill that are products of their political background, experience, and leadership style. To turn participation in the legislative process to an advantage, a president should have knowledge of Congress and the Washington community, a sense of timing, a willingness to consult with congressional leaders and to give them notice in advance of major actions, sensitivity to the institutional prerogatives of Congress and to the personal and political needs of its members, and a balance between firmness and flexibility in resolving differences with Congress.

No president has ever possessed all of these skills, nor is one likely to do so. By most accounts, however, Lyndon Johnson exhibited more of them than any other modern president and made the most effective use of his involvement in the legislative process. Johnson believed that constant, intense attention by presidents and their administration was necessary to move their legislative program through Congress.[65] Johnson's success in persuading Congress to enact the unfinished agenda of President Kennedy's New Frontier program and his own Great Society bills in 1964 and 1965 makes his approach to Congress a good example for study. It should be noted, however, that Johnson's legislative triumphs were aided in no small measure by contextual factors for which he could not claim much credit. In the aftermath of the Kennedy assassination, public support for the New Frontier measures was high, and Johnson's landslide victory in the 1964 election also brought him large Democratic majorities in the House and the Senate.

Johnson grounded his legislative strategy in intimate knowledge of Congress as an institution and of its most influential members.[66] He knew whom to approach on specific issues and how to approach them. Johnson also placed considerable emphasis on proper timing. He waited to send bills to Congress until the moment seemed right for the maximum support and least opposition. He sent bills singly rather than in a package so that opposition would not develop automatically around several measures at once. In addition, Johnson took care to consult with important senators and representatives in formulating legislation. Before sending a bill to Congress, the president and his top aides would hold a briefing for congressional leaders to explain the bill's features. Cabinet secretaries were made responsible for the success of legislation in their areas, and the White House coordinated their efforts. Finally, when crucial votes were approaching on Capitol Hill, Johnson made intense personal appeals to the members whose votes served as cues for others and to members who were identified as uncommitted or wavering. Johnson's goal was to build congressional coalitions in support of his proposals. Through an analysis of head counts, used by Johnson's congressional liaison office to track House members' positions on bills over time, Terry Sullivan found that the Johnson administration built coalitions not just by mobilizing friends, but even by "converting hard core opponents."[67]

When the Vietnam War changed the political context, Johnson's approach to congressional relations was less effective. The president lost much of his touch

President Lyndon B. Johnson included Dr. Martin Luther King, Jr. at the ceremony to commemorate the signing of the Voting Rights Act of 1965, one of the administration's major legislative accomplishments and a landmark of the civil rights movement.

with Congress as he became increasingly involved in foreign policy matters and as the momentum of the Great Society gave way to the unpopularity of the war. The loss of forty-eight Democratic seats in the House of Representatives in the 1966 congressional elections also adversely affected Johnson's ability to push bills through Congress. Overall, however, presidents would be well advised to emulate the successful Johnson: gain detailed knowledge of Congress, respect its constitutional prerogatives, remain sensitive to the personal and constituency needs of its members, and create the organizational and political capacity to build coalitions.

Despite making little personal effort to court Congress, Richard Nixon enjoyed modest legislative success early in his administration. His relations with Congress turned sour, however, when he challenged the Democratic majority directly by impounding, or refusing to spend, appropriated funds and by claiming substantial executive privilege under which administration officials refused to provide information to congressional committees. Nixon's successor, Gerald Ford, had intimate knowledge of Congress, like Johnson, and he worked diligently to maintain good relations with its leaders. But as he confronted large, assertive Democratic majorities in both houses, his success was limited.

President Carter's inability to create a supportive climate in relations with the Hill is often cited as a reason for the limited success of some of his major legislative goals, such as welfare reform and a comprehensive energy conservation program. In contrast, President Reagan's congenial manner and relaxed style helped establish a generally positive, nonhostile attitude within Congress toward his legislative program. This appears to have been an important factor in the passage of tax-reform legislation in 1986. At critical points during the 99th Congress, the tax bill seemed doomed, only to be resurrected as members responded to presidential appeals for what supporters termed an equitable tax system.[68]

But a congenial climate with Congress may be unrelated to presidential success. The first President Bush, a former member of the House, knew many members of Congress well and maintained close contact with them. But, through the end of his third year, Bush had prevailed on fewer congressional roll calls than had his predecessors at similar points in their first terms.[69]

Although President Clinton lacked Washington experience, and most Democrats in Congress had not served with a president of their own party, he had a close and cooperative relationship with the Democratic leadership during the 103d Congress (1993–1994).[70] Clinton's legislative achievements were substantial. In both 1993 and 1994, he won on 86.4 percent of the floor votes in Congress on which he took a position.[71] The list of major legislation enacted was impressive: his economic program, which included a major deficit reduction; family and medical leave legislation; reauthorization and revision of the Elementary and Secondary Education Act; expansion of Head Start; motor-voter legislation; national service legislation; the Brady gun control bill; a comprehensive anticrime bill; the North American Free Trade Agreement (NAFTA); and legislation extending and expanding the General Agreement on Tariffs and Trade (GATT). He failed, however, to secure passage of bills to reform health care and welfare. Even though he was productive legislatively and attempted to address seriously the problems of declining middle-class incomes and economic dislocation that stemmed from changes in the U.S. economy and the globalization of markets, he received no political benefit from the voters in 1994.[72] Clinton's initially congenial relations with Congress were a distant memory by the time of the impeachment hearings, and his high first-year success rate on floor votes had hit a record low in 1995 at 36.2 percent.[73] Clinton's experience demonstrates that presidential congeniality cannot compensate for philosophical differences and partisan divisions.

Modes of Presidential–Congressional Relations

In their relations with Congress, presidents follow certain modes or patterns of behavior: bargaining, arm-twisting, and confrontation. As befits a relationship among professional politicians, bargaining is the predominant mode. Occasionally, the president bargains directly with members of Congress whose support is regarded as essential to the passage of a bill. In May 1981, for example, the Reagan administration agreed to revive a costly program to support the price of sugar in exchange for the votes of four Democratic representatives from Louisiana (where sugar is a key crop) on a comprehensive budget reduction bill.[74]

Presidents usually try to avoid such explicit bargains because they have limited resources available to trade, and the desire among members for these resources is keen. Moreover, Congress is so large and congressional power so decentralized that it is not possible for presidents to bargain extensively over most bills. In some instances, the president may be unable or unwilling to bargain. Fortunately, much presidential–congressional bargaining is implicit. Rather than a quid pro quo exchange of favors for votes, implicit bargaining involves generalized trading in which tacit exchanges of support and favors occur.

If bargaining does not result in the approval of their legislative proposals, presidents may resort to stronger methods such as arm-twisting, which involves intense, even extraordinary, pressure and threats. In one sense, arm-twisting is an intensified extension of bargaining, but it entails something more—a direct threat of punishment or retaliation if the member's opposition continues. Lyndon Johnson was perhaps the most frequent practitioner of arm-twisting among modern presidents. When gentler efforts at persuasion failed, or when a previously supportive member opposed him on an important issue, Johnson resorted to tactics such as deliberate embarrassment, threats, and reprisals. In contrast, President Eisenhower was most reluctant to pressure Congress. Arm-twisting is understandably an unpopular presidential tactic and, if used frequently, creates resentment and hostility. Still, judicious demonstration that there are costs associated with sustained opposition or desertion by normal supporters strengthens a president's bargaining position.

Presidents who are unable to gain support for their proposals through bargaining and arm-twisting may adopt a confrontational strategy in dealing with Congress. Confrontation might consist of appeals to the public, direct challenges to congressional authority, assertion of presidential prerogative, or similar tactics. President Nixon confronted Congress often and more sharply than any other modern president. Disdaining the role of legislative coalition builder, Nixon saw himself instead as deserving of congressional support by virtue of his election mandate and his constitutional position as chief executive. The most visible confrontation occurred between 1971 and 1973, when he challenged congressional spending decisions that were at variance with his budget proposals by impounding more than $30 billion that Congress had appropriated. Nixon also claimed Congress could not question thousands of executive branch officials or have access to routine documentary information.

A strategy of confrontation is unlikely to result in sustained congressional responsiveness to presidential initiatives. Congress has constitutional prerogatives and constituency bases of support that enable it to resist presidential domination. The imperatives for cooperation between the two branches are so great that most presidents try to avoid confrontations with Congress and enter them only when the constitutional integrity of the presidency is at issue.

To oversee this system of bargaining and negotiation, President Eisenhower established in the White House an Office of Legislative Affairs, staffed by knowledgeable specialists who lobbied legislators in behalf of the administration's program. Every administration since has maintained such a unit. Although some administrations have made subtle changes in assignments and techniques, the activities have become largely institutionalized in the Washington community, reflecting a clear set of expectations about how staff members will conduct the job. With such a staff in place, there is continuity in legislative-executive relations and a reduction in the variation resulting from presidents' individual abilities and skills.[75] Under George W. Bush, Nicholas E. Calio, a Washington lobbyist who held the same position at the conclusion of the earlier Bush administration, initially headed the office.[76]

Explaining Presidents' Legislative Success

If all presidents approach Congress with the same formal powers and informal tools of influence and use well-established staff arrangements to oversee the day-to-day relations, what accounts for the success or failure of their legislative efforts? Studies have identified at least six factors that affect presidents' ability to achieve their legislative goals: their partisan and ideological support in Congress, their popular support, their style in dealing with Congress, the contexts in which they must operate, cyclical trends in presidential–congressional relations, and the content of their domestic program. It is not possible to assess the relative importance of each factor thoroughly, but all of them have come into play since 1933, when FDR inaugurated the modern legislative presidency. The first five factors will be examined here; the sixth, in chapter 8.

Congressional Support

Presidents' support in Congress depends heavily on the size and cohesiveness of their party's strength there. George Edwards has shown that from 1961 through 1986, three Democratic and three Republican presidents consistently received strong support on roll call votes from the congressional members of their parties.[77] John Kessel notes that presidents' partisans have recently provided higher levels of support: from 1953 through 1980, presidents received support 66 percent of the time from their fellow partisans in the House and Senate, and that level rose to 75 percent from 1981 through 1996.[78] Edwards and Jon Bond and Richard Fleisher have found, however, that support may vary by issue. Republican presidents receive stronger support overall on foreign policy legislation than on domestic policy issues, primarily because of increased backing from liberal Democrats on foreign issues.[79]

It is interesting to note that partisan support for presidents in Congress apparently owes little to the storied effect of presidential coattails. The ability of presidents to transfer their electoral appeal to congressional candidates of their parties declined steadily from 1948 to 1988.[80] Even in 1984, when President Reagan won a landslide victory over the Democratic candidate, Walter Mondale, the measurable coattail effect was weak, though it was stronger than in 1980 and 1988.[81] Edwards attributes the decline in the power of coattails to increased split-ticket voting, the reduced competitiveness of House seats, and the electoral success of incumbents since 1952. The consequences of the reduced coattail effect are the loss of presidential leverage with Congress and greater difficulty for presidents in winning congressional approval of their major legislative proposals.

Because presidents cannot rely on full support from the members of their own party, they must build coalitions by obtaining support from some members of the opposition.[82] Coalition building is especially important when the opposition controls one or both houses of Congress—which has been the situation for most presidents since 1969. Several factors other than party membership influence congressional voting decisions, including constituency pressures, state and regional loyalty, ideological orientations, and the influence of interest groups.[83] On many occasions, presidents have received crucial support from the opposition. Eisenhower, for example, successfully sought Democratic votes on foreign policy matters; Republicans contributed sizable pluralities to the enactment of civil rights legislation in the 1960s; conservative Democrats, mainly from the South, often supported the domestic policy proposals of Nixon and Ford; conservative Democrats in the House were essential to Reagan's 1981 legislative victories; Clinton depended heavily on Republican support for the passage of NAFTA and GATT; and George W. Bush received critical, though limited, support from Democrats on his tax-reduction and education-reform proposals.

In summary, congressional support for the president is built primarily on fellow partisans, but party affiliation is seldom by itself a sufficient basis for the enactment of the president's legislative program. Constituency, regional, and ideological pressures reduce the number of partisan backers, and the president must try to attract support from members of the opposition party on the basis of their ideological orientations and their constituency and regional interests. Thus, a president's legislative success "is mainly a function of the partisan and ideological makeup of Congress."[84]

Popular Support

The prestige, or popular support, of presidents also affects congressional response to their policies. It has been widely observed that a popular president enjoys substantial leeway in dealing with Congress, and a president whose popularity is low or falling is likely to encounter considerable resistance. Bond and Fleisher argue, however, that popular support is only marginally related to presidential success on congressional floor votes.[85] Similarly, Edwards finds that public approval is a background resource that provides presidents with leverage but not control over Congress.[86]

Although presidential popularity is clearly, if marginally, related to congressional support for the president's legislative program and can be used as a tool of influence, it cannot be easily manipulated. There are factors, such as the erosion of popular support over time and the condition of the economy, over which the president has no control.[87] What presidents can do is to take advantage of their popularity when it is high to influence congressional opinion, as Johnson did in 1964 and 1965 and Reagan did in 1981 and, to a lesser extent, in 1985 and 1986 (after which his popularity plummeted because of the Iran-contra affair). Presidents can also appeal to the public beyond party lines for support.[88] To the extent that they succeed in building popular support, presidents can strengthen their support in Congress, if their style in dealing with Congress enables them to exploit it.

Presidential Style and Legislative Skills

The president's style in dealing with Congress has long been considered an important determinant of legislative success. Presidential style in congressional relations encompasses the degree to which presidents are accessible to members of Congress, their interactions with and sensitivity to the members, and the extent of their involvement in the legislative process.[89]

Modern presidents have varied greatly in their accessibility to members of Congress. Johnson and Ford were usually available to members and leaders alike without great difficulty, whereas Nixon was remote and inaccessible most of the time. Kennedy and Reagan frequently sought contact through telephone calls. The senior George Bush maintained a wide range of congressional friends and acquaintances but was criticized for not consulting enough with influential party and committee leaders. During his first two years, Clinton was so accessible and made such efforts to cultivate personal relationships with members of Congress that his effectiveness may have been impaired.[90] That accessibility lessened when he was working with an assertive Republican majority and with Democrats who distanced themselves from a president whom they regarded as a political liability. George W. Bush met with a broad cross-section of representatives and senators during his first months in office (more than ninety members in his first week in office alone, including many Democrats)[91] as he tried to set a non-confrontational tone in the nation's capital. Although accessibility on demand is not feasible because of the pressures on a president's time, it enhances congressional support if members know they can reach the president on matters of great importance to them. Accessibility to congressional leaders of both parties is particularly important if the president is to work effectively with Congress.

It is not clear how much presidents' interpersonal relations influence congressional support, but they are a distinctive part of a chief executive's style and affect the disposition of leaders and members toward the president. If nothing else, presidential popularity with members of Congress can improve relations even when there are sharp differences over issues. If the president has strained personal relations with many representatives and senators, sustained congressional support will be difficult to achieve even when the president's party has a majority, and many members share his goals.

Similarly, presidential involvement in the legislative process varies. Johnson, Ford, Kennedy, and Reagan all maintained a close interest in the course of legislation, and Johnson even actively directed its progress on occasion. In contrast, Nixon, Eisenhower, and Carter were more detached and had less interest in building congressional coalitions. George Bush displayed a varied pattern of interest in the progress of legislation, ranging from detachment to active engagement during his four years, as during the negotiations over the 1991 budget. Clinton developed a reputation for making concessions so early in legislative negotiations that he drew criticism for making it "too easy" for his opponents,[92] suggesting that he was not an effective legislative tactician. George W. Bush appears to delegate most of these decisions to the experts in his administration, relying more heavily on the advice and assistance of his vice president than have most of his predecessors. Unlike most vice presidents, Dick Cheney has an office on both the Senate and House sides of the Capitol building. Known briefly as the "fifty-first senator" because of his critical role in casting the tie-breaking vote before the Republicans lost the Senate majority, Cheney attends weekly Republican policy meetings in both the House and the Senate and regularly makes himself available to listen to congressional concerns. As Sen. Susan Collins, R- Maine, told the *New York Times*, "When I convey my views to the vice president, it's equivalent virtually to the president."[93]

Conventional wisdom holds that presidents' legislative skills are a major determinant of congressional support for their program, but empirical analyses provide little support for that argument. According to Edwards and other scholars, presidential legislative skills are effective at the margins of congressional coalition building and not at the core.[94] Presenting a somewhat different argument, Mark Peterson states that presidents have some, but not unlimited, control over the timing, priorities, and size of their legislative programs. By clearly establishing their priorities and carefully adjusting their "ambitions to fit the opportunities of the day," he concludes, presidents can be perceived as successful leaders of Congress.[95] If nothing else, these analyses should caution observers of the presidency against uncritical acceptance of personalized explanations of presidential success in Congress and encourage the search for other influences.

Contextual Factors

Most students of presidential–congressional relations agree that contextual factors over which the president has virtually no control—such as the structure of American political institutions and processes, public opinion, the alignment of political and social forces, economic and social conditions, and long-term trends in the political system—are more important than legislative skills as determinants of congressional decisions. For example, the cultural context of American politics is a source of frustration for presidents attempting to influence Congress. Edwards posits that phenomena such as extremely high and often contradictory public expectations of presidential performance, individualism, and skepticism of authority are powerful constraints on presidential leadership.[96] Bond and

Fleisher argue that Congress-centered variables, such as the partisan and ideological predispositions of members and leaders, which are determined by the outcome of the last election, are of greater importance than presidency-centered variables in explaining presidential influence in Congress.[97]

Taking a middle position between Edwards's presidency-centered analysis and the Congress-centered perspective of Bond and Fleisher, Peterson provides the most comprehensive and extensive analysis of contextual factors affecting presidential success in Congress. He identifies four contexts that shape congressional action on presidential programs: (1) the "pure context," which includes the "institutional properties" of Congress, political parties, and interest groups and over which the president has little influence and no control; (2) the "malleable context," which consists of "dynamic" political conditions resulting from electoral cycles and economic conditions and over which the president has "greater but unpredictable influence" and no control; (3) the "policy context"—a context the president can influence and to some extent control by making "strategic choices" in developing an agenda—which includes the consequence of various proposals for the political system, the relative importance of proposals for presidential policy goals, and the controversiality of proposals; and (4) the "individual context," which includes personal attributes, such as style and skills, and the choices the president makes concerning the organization of the presidency for the exercise of influence that distinguish the president and the administration.[98]

However one defines and classifies the contexts that affect the president's influence or success in Congress, it is important to recognize that they function to provide both constraints upon and opportunities for the exercise of presidential leadership. To a considerable extent, the president can do little to alter most of these contexts. What a president can do is take maximum advantage of the opportunities they present. In doing so the chief executive can act as a facilitator but not as a director who focuses change.

Cyclical Trends

Long-term cyclical fluctuations in presidential and congressional power also appear to affect the fate of specific presidential programs. The inauguration of FDR in 1933 marked the beginning of a period of presidential ascendancy that lasted until Nixon became enmeshed in the Watergate scandal. During that time, Congress made extensive delegations of power to the president and to executive branch agencies, presidents assumed responsibility for legislative leadership, Congress acquiesced in presidential domination of foreign and military policy, and the public looked to the presidency more than to Congress to solve the nation's problems.[99] The president and Congress clashed often during that period, but the dominant trend was one of presidential aggrandizement. When conflict occurred, Congress usually took defensive stands against presidential assertiveness.

In 1973, Congress moved to reassert its constitutional prerogatives after being angered over the conduct of the war in Southeast Asia and President Nixon's assertion of budget impoundment powers and executive privilege. Seizing the opportunity afforded by Nixon's preoccupation with Watergate and the plunge in public support, Congress enacted the War Powers Resolution of 1973, the Budget and Impoundment Control Act of 1974, and the National Emergencies Act of 1976.[100] These statutes were the major elements in a congressional resurgence designed to restrain presidential power. In 1974, the House Judiciary Committee approved three impeachment charges against President Nixon, who resigned on August 9 before the House could act on them. Nixon's two immediate successors, Gerald Ford and Jimmy Carter, had to deal with a resurgent Congress intent on curbing the uses of presidential power and retaining the constitutional parity with the president that it regained, at least partially, in the 1970s. This period of congressional resurgence was marked by increased skepticism of claims for presidential prerogative, careful scrutiny of presidential proposals, demands for more extensive consultation of congressional leaders by the White House, and more exacting senatorial confirmation hearings on presidential appointments.

During the Reagan presidency, Congress was more willing to accept presidential policy leadership and less assertive in insisting on its institutional prerogatives. The presidential–congressional relationship did not, however, return to the conditions that prevailed under the "imperial presidency" mentioned in chapter 1.[101] President Reagan had generally friendly relations with Congress despite sharp differences over policy, such as the budget deficit, and over presidential powers, such as impoundments and deferrals of appropriated funds. Reagan's relationship with Congress bent, but did not break, in 1987 following Democratic successes in the 1986 congressional elections and as a consequence of public disenchantment with his detached leadership, which was revealed by the Iran-contra affair as resting on too much delegation of presidential authority.

Both Presidents Bush and Clinton had stormy relationships with Congress over the budget. In the fall of 1990, Bush became embroiled in a protracted battle with leaders and members from both parties over the deficit in the budget for 1991. In October, a bipartisan plan negotiated by the administration with congressional leaders was rejected by a coalition of very liberal Democratic and very conservative Republican House members. Amid bitter exchanges within both parties, a compromise was reached. But just as that battle came to a close, most congressional Democrats and some Republicans sharply questioned Bush's handling of the Persian Gulf crisis and pressed him for a congressional vote of approval before initiating military action against Iraq. Although the administration insisted that it had authority to initiate such action on its own, Congress passed a resolution authorizing the use of U.S. forces to implement UN resolutions calling on Iraq to leave Kuwait or face economic sanctions and, if necessary, military action. Clinton's struggle was far more bitter and protracted, setting the stage for the impeachment controversy that followed. Clinton's battle with Congress over the 1996 budget escalated to new extremes with the two government shutdowns. The remainder of 1996 proved to be a temporary, elec-

tion-year truce that provided new grist for postelection congressional investigations of Clinton–Gore fund-raising abuses. Conflict between the president and
Congress escalated to new heights in 1998–1999 with the impeachment inquiry.
The problem confronted by George W. Bush was with moderates, mostly within
his own party. Despite Bush's espousal of a more inclusive approach to working
with Congress that would rest on cooperation with Democrats, moderates in his
own party felt excluded. The defection of Senator Jeffords was the most extreme
case. In a closely balanced Congress, those in the middle become objects of
appeal from both sides and often wield the decisive power.

Conclusion

The experiences of recent presidents in their relations with Congress provide
a few lessons. These presidents have found, or at least should have found, that
success is not automatic. It requires consultation before and during legislative
consideration and a willingness to negotiate and bargain with Congress. Coordination of legislative proposals between the White House and the executive
departments and agencies is most helpful. More important, cooperation between
the president and congressional leaders and between the institutional presidency
and Congress is essential. The constitutional separation of powers does not allow
the two branches to operate independently of each other; rather, it requires that
they exercise their shared powers jointly.[102]

The president's relationship with Congress takes place within the framework
of the constitutional separation of powers. That framework requires cooperation
but ensures conflict. This has been true during the more than 200 years that the
Republic has operated under the Constitution. The Framers sought to prevent
tyranny by establishing a balance between executive and legislative power.
However, the concept of balance entails a static relationship, whereas the relationship that has existed between the president and Congress has been continually in flux. First one branch has expanded its authority; then the second branch
has reasserted its prerogatives, recaptured lost powers, and acquired new ones.
The cycle of institutional aggrandizement, decline, and resurgence reflects certain strengths and weaknesses in the presidency and Congress and the respective
abilities of both branches to respond to social forces, economic conditions, and
political change.

The need for presidential–congressional cooperation is clear, but there are few
ways of obtaining it other than through consultation involving persuasion and
bargaining. Presidents cannot command congressional approval of their proposals any more than Congress can direct presidents in the exercise of their constitutional powers. The threat of government stalemate is always present, and
more often than not policy is an unsatisfactory compromise of presidential and
various congressional viewpoints.

Clearly, the presidential–congressional relationship is a dynamic one. It varies
according to contextual factors, cycles of presidential and congressional assertive-

ness, and the leadership skills and styles of individual presidents. Changes occur in the relationship, sometimes quickly and dramatically, as since the 1980s with the presidencies of Ronald Reagan, Bill Clinton, and George W. Bush. As the United States moves through its third century, the relationship between the president and Congress will be characterized—as it is today—by the stability provided by the Constitution as well as by adaptations to social, economic, and political change.

NOTES

1. Alissa J. Rubin, "Congress Readies Budget Bill for President's Veto Pen," *Congressional Quarterly Weekly Report*, November 18, 1995, 3512.

2. Alfred Hill, "The Shutdowns and the Constitution," *Political Science Quarterly* (summer 2000): 274. Also see Peri E. Arnold, "Clinton and Institutionalized Presidency," in *The Postmodern Presidency*, ed. Steven E. Schier (Pittsburgh: University of Pittsburgh Press, 2000), 28–31.

3. Starr also investigated the firing of White House employees in the travel office ("Travelgate"), the potential abuse of FBI files by the Clinton White House ("Filegate"), and the suicide of White House counsel Vincent J. Foster.

4. Carl M. Cannon, "So Very, Very Tired," *National Journal*, February 6, 1999, 318–322.

5. "Mr. Ruff for the Defense," editorial, *New York Times*, January 20, 1999, A30.

6. Arnold, "Clinton and the Institutionalized Presidency," 31.

7. Evan Thomas, "Acquittal: The Inside Story," *Newsweek*, February 22, 1999, 24–31; Kirk Victor and Carl M. Cannon, "Promise and Peril," *National Journal*, January 23, 1999, 170–175.

8. The results of the 2000 congressional elections: House Republicans 221, House Democrats 212, Independents 2, with one voting with each party caucus; Senate Republicans 50, Senate Democrats 50. The Senate tie produced a Democratic-controlled Senate for three weeks while Vice President Gore voted with the Democrats, followed by Republican control after inauguration day, when Vice President Cheney voted with the Republicans.

9. Susan Crabtree, "Bush's Charm Offensive Suffers Slight Setback," *Roll Call*, February 5, 2001; Mark Lacey, "Bush to Attend Democratic Caucuses," *New York Times*, January 27, 2001, A11; David E. Sanger and Alison Mitchell, "Bush, the Conciliator, Meets with Democrats," *New York Times*, February 3, 2001, A10.

10. James P. Pfiffner, *The Strategic Presidency* 2d ed. rev. (Lawrence: University Press of Kansas, 1996), ix. For a full discussion of the "cycle of decreasing influence" that underlies the need to "move it or lose it" at an administration's outset, see Paul C. Light, *The President's Agenda: Domestic Policy Choice from Kennedy to Reagan*, rev. ed. (Baltimore: Johns Hopkins University Press, 1991), 36–37.

11. Richard E. Cohen and David Baumann, "The GOP's Drive to Deliver," *National Journal*, May 12, 2001, 1402–1403. Ultimately, five Democrats supported the Bush budget plan, which included a large tax cut. The partisan conflict was intense, however, with Vice President Cheney casting two tie-breaking votes to keep the budget on track.

12. David E. Sanger, "President's Signature Turns Broad Tax Cut, and a Campaign Promise, into Law," *New York Times*, June 8, 2001, A18.

13. Frank Bruni and David E. Sanger, "Bush Defends His Stance Despite Stinging Defection," *New York Times*, May 25, 2001, A18; Katharine Q. Seelye and Adam Clymer, "Senate Republicans Step Out and Democrats Jump In," *New York Times*, May 25, 2001, A1.

14. Transcript of James M. Jeffords's announcement, *New York Times,* May 25, 2001, A18.

15. Richard L. Berke, "A Question of Governing from the Right," *New York Times,* May 25, 2001, A1.

16. Others had suggested that the honeymoon ended when Bush initiated a hard-hitting campaign in early March 2001 to secure passage of the tax-cut proposal. Jeffrey Bell, "Keep Up the Tough Talk, Mr. Nice Guy," *Washington Post,* March 4, 2001, B1.

17. Stephen J. Wayne, *The Legislative Presidency* (New York: Harper and Row, 1978), 8–12.

18. Theodore Roosevelt, *Autobiography* (New York: Macmillan, 1913), 292.

19. Woodrow Wilson, *Constitutional Government in the United States* (1908; reprint, New York: Columbia University Press, 1961).

20. Richard E. Neustadt, "The Presidency and Legislation: The Growth of Central Clearance," *American Political Science Review* (September 1954): 641–670.

21. Richard E. Neustadt, "The Presidency and Legislation: Planning the President's Program," *American Political Science Review* (December 1955): 980–1018; Wayne, *The Legislative Presidency;* Larry Berman, *The Office of Management and Budget and the Presidency* (Princeton: Princeton University Press, 1979); Light, *The President's Agenda.*

22. Samuel P. Huntington, "Congressional Responses to the Twentieth Century," in *The Congress and America's Future,* ed. David B. Truman (Englewood Cliffs, N.J.: Prentice-Hall, 1965), 23.

23. Ronald C. Moe and Steven C. Teel, "Congress as Policy-Maker: A Necessary Reappraisal," *Political Science Quarterly* (fall 1970): 443–470; John R. Johannes, *Policy Innovation in Congress* (Morristown, N.J.: General Learning Press, 1972); Gary Orfield, *Congressional Power: Congress and Social Change* (New York: Harcourt Brace Jovanovich, 1975).

24. In the Senate, the Republicans had a 53–47 majority. In the House, the 192 Republicans, who voted together on the major elements of President Reagan's economic legislation in a remarkable display of cohesion, were joined by a sizable bloc of conservative southern Democrats called the "Boll Weevils." In both chambers, Republicans and conservative Democrats maintained voting cohesion that enabled the majorities to enact the Reagan program.

25. For example, Clinton's budget proposals in 1993 passed by a single vote in both the House and the Senate without any support from Republicans. Barbara Sinclair, "Trying to Govern Positively in a Negative Era," in *The Clinton Presidency: First Appraisals,* ed. Colin Campbell and Bert A. Rockman (Chatham, N.J.: Chatham House, 1995), 121. Also see Barbara Sinclair, "The President as Legislative Leader," in *The Clinton Legacy,* ed. Colin Campbell and Bert A. Rockman (Chatham, N.J.: Chatham House, 2000), 72–83.

26. Bert A. Rockman, "Entrepreneur in the Political Marketplace: The Constitution and the Development of the Presidency" (paper presented at the annual meeting of the American Political Science Association, San Francisco, August 30–September 2, 1990), 26–27.

27. Charles O. Jones, *The Presidency in a Separated System* (Washington, D.C.: Brookings, 1994), 16.

28. Alexander Hamilton, John Jay, and James Madison, *The Federalist Papers* (New York: Modern Library, 1938), 335–337.

29. Lawrence C. Dodd, "Congress and the Quest for Power," in *Congress Reconsidered,* ed. Lawrence C. Dodd and Bruce I. Oppenheimer (New York: Praeger, 1977), 298–302.

30. James L. Sundquist, *The Decline and Resurgence of Congress* (Washington, D.C.: Brookings, 1981).

31. David S. Cloud, "Republicans Pushing the Envelope with Confrontational Approach," *Congressional Quarterly Weekly Report,* August 5, 1995, 2331–2334.

32. Thomas E. Mann, "Elections and Change in Congress," in *The New Congress,* ed. T. E. Mann (Washington, D.C.: American Enterprise Institute, 1981).

33. Roger H. Davidson and Walter J. Oleszek, *Congress and Its Members,* 4th ed. (Washington, D.C.: CQ Press, 1994), 63.

34. Among the leading critics of divided government are James L. Sundquist, "Needed: A Political Theory for the New Era of Coalition Government in the United States," *Political Science Quarterly* (winter 1988–1989): 613–635; Lloyd N. Cutler, "To Form a Government," *Foreign Affairs* 59 (fall 1980): 126–143; Cutler, "Now Is the Time for All Good Men," *William and Mary Law Review* 30 (fall 1989): 387–402; and Michael L. Mezey, *Congress, the President, and Public Policy* (Boulder: Westview, 1989).

35. Gary W. Cox and Samuel Kernell, "Conclusion," in *The Politics of Divided Government,* ed. Gary W. Cox and Samuel Kernell (Boulder: Westview, 1991), 242–243. Also see Matthew D. McCubbins, "Government on Lay-Away: Federal Spending and Deficits under Divided Party Control," in *The Politics of Divided Government,* 113–153.

36. David R. Mayhew, *Divided We Govern: Party Control, Lawmaking, and Investigations, 1946–1990* (New Haven: Yale University Press, 1991), 198.

37. Morris Fiorina, *Divided Government* (New York: Macmillan, 1992), 107, 108.

38. Ibid., 111.

39. Ibid., chap. 6.

40. Davidson and Oleszek, *Congress and Its Members,* chaps. 3–5; David R. Mayhew, *Congress: The Electoral Connection* (New Haven: Yale University Press, 1974).

41. Davidson and Oleszek, *Congress and Its Members,* chap. 1.

42. The main components of the Great Society were the Economic Opportunity Act of 1964, which launched a "war on poverty"; the Civil Rights Act of 1964; the Voting Rights Act of 1965; the Elementary and Secondary Education Act of 1965; and the Medicare Act of 1965.

43. This discussion follows Sinclair, "Trying to Govern Positively," 91–119.

44. Juliet Eilperin, "Bush to Woo Democratic Rank-and-File," *Washington Post,* January 22, 2001, A1.

45. Sundquist, *The Decline and Resurgence of Congress,* 143.

46. David S. Cloud, "Lack of New Proposals Reflects New Dynamic on the Hill," *Congressional Quarterly Weekly Report,* January 28, 1995, 259–260; Donna Cassata, "Swift Progress of 'Contract' Inspires Awe and Concern," *Congressional Quarterly Weekly Report,* April 1, 1995, 909–912.

47. Carroll J. Doherty, "Clinton's Big Comeback Shown in Vote Score," *Congressional Quarterly Weekly Report,* December 21, 1996, 3427–3428.

48. Woodrow Wilson, *Congressional Government* (1885; reprint, New York: Meridian, 1956), 53.

49. Joseph E. Kallenbach, *The American Chief Executive* (New York: Harper and Row, 1966), 354.

50. Richard A. Watson, "Reasons Presidents Veto Legislation" (paper presented at the annual meeting of the American Political Science Association, Chicago, September 3–6, 1987), 6, 7.

51. Albert C. Ringelstein, "Presidential Vetoes: Motivations and Classifications," *Congress and the Presidency* (spring 1985): 52–53.

52. Mark A. Peterson, "The President and Congress," in *The Presidency and the Political System,* 6th ed., ed. Michael Nelson (Washington, D.C.: CQ Press, 2000), 476.

53. Robert J. Spitzer, *The Presidential Veto: Touchstone of the American Presidency* (Albany: State University of New York Press, 1988), 100–103.

54. Janet Hook, "Avalanche of Veto Threats Divides Bush, Congress," *Congressional Quarterly Weekly Report,* Sept. 22, 1990, 2991. Hook cites an OMB spokeswoman as stating that the Bush administration had issued 120 veto threats since January 1989.

55. David W. Rohde and Dennis M. Simon, "Presidential Vetoes and Congressional Response: A Study of Institutional Conflict," *American Journal of Political Science* (August 1985): 307.

56. Ibid., 425.

57. Ibid.

58. Stephen J. Wayne, Richard L. Cole, and James F. C. Hyde Jr., "Advising the President on Enrolled Legislation," *Political Science Quarterly* 94 (summer 1979): 303–318.

59. Ibid., 316.

60. Richard E. Neustadt, *Presidential Power: The Politics of Leadership* (New York: Wiley, 1960), 10.

61. Dave Boyer, "White House, GOP on Hill in Harmony," *Washington Times*, February 14, 2001, A1. On the speech, see Dan Balz, "President Begins His Toughest Sell," *Washington Post*, February 28, 2001, A1.

62. Ari Fleischer as quoted by Scott Shepard, Cox News Service, March 4, 2001. Also see Mike Allen, "It's Campaign 2001: President Hits the Trail to Pitch Tax, Education Plans," *Washington Post*, March 2, 2001, A6.

63. Theodore J. Lowi, *The End of Liberalism*, 2d ed. (New York: St. Martin's Press, 1979); Randall B. Ripley and Grace A. Franklin, *Congress, the Bureaucracy, and Public Policy*, 5th ed. (Pacific Grove, Calif.: Brooks/Cole, 1991).

64. Joseph A. Pika, "White House Office of Congressional Relations: A Longitudinal Analysis" (paper presented at the annual meeting of the Midwest Political Science Association, Chicago, April 20–22, 1978).

65. Lyndon B. Johnson, *Vantage Point* (New York: Holt, Rinehart and Winston, 1971), 448; Doris Kearns, *Lyndon Johnson and the American Dream* (New York: Harper and Row, 1976), 226.

66. George C. Edwards III, *Presidential Influence in Congress* (San Francisco: Freeman, 1980), 117–120.

67. Terry Sullivan, "Headcounts, Expectations, and Presidential Coalitions in Congress," *American Journal of Political Science* (August 1988): 567. Elsewhere, Sullivan demonstrates that head counts are a valuable presidential tool for signaling congressional supporters and for obtaining information from them. "Explaining Why Presidents Count: Signaling and Information," *Journal of Politics* (August 1990): 939–962.

68. Jeffrey H. Birnbaum and Alan S. Murray, *Showdown at Gucci Gulch* (New York: Random House, 1987), 40–41, 94–95, 118, 169–171.

69. Chuck Alston, "Bush's High Public Standing Held Little Sway on Hill," *Congressional Quarterly Weekly Report*, December 28, 1991, 3751.

70. Sinclair, "Trying to Govern Positively," 96–100.

71. Steve Langdon, "Clinton's High Victory Rate Conceals Disappointments," *Congressional Quarterly Weekly Report*, December 31, 1994, 3619.

72. Sinclair, "Trying to Govern Positively," 121.

73. Jon Healey, "Clinton Success Rate Declined to a Record Low in 1995," *Congressional Quarterly Weekly Report*, January 27, 1996, 193.

74. Laurence L. Barrett, *Gambling with History* (Garden City, N.Y.: Doubleday, 1983), 334.

75. The most thorough study of this staff unit is by Kenneth Collier *Between the Branches: The White House Office of Legislative Affairs* (Pittsburgh: University of Pittsburgh Press, 1997). Also see the discussion in John H. Kessel, *Presidents, the Presidency, and the Political Environment* (Washington, D.C., CQ Press, 2001), 30–52.

76. Frank Bruni, "Returning to Action as Bush's Lobbyist to Congress," *New York Times*, February 12, 2001, A16.

77. George C. Edwards III, *At the Margins: Presidential Leadership of Congress* (New Haven: Yale University Press, 1989), chap. 3.

78. Kessel, *Presidents, the Presidency, and the Political Environment*, 26.

79. Edwards, *At the Margins*, 68–69; Jon R. Bond and Richard Fleisher, *The President in the Legislative Arena* (Chicago: University of Chicago Press, 1990), 171–175.

80. Gary C. Jacobson, *The Electoral Origins of Divided Government* (Boulder: Westview, 1990), 80–81.

81. Gary C. Jacobson, *The Politics of Congressional Elections*, 3d ed. (New York: HarperCollins, 1992), 161–162.

82. Sullivan, "Headcounts, Expectations, and Presidential Coalitions in Congress," 573–582.

83. John W. Kingdon, *Congressmen's Voting Decisions* (New York: Harper and Row, 1981); Aage R. Clausen, *How Congressmen Decide* (New York: St. Martin's Press, 1973).

84. Bond and Fleisher, *The President in the Legislative Arena*, 221.

85. Ibid., 182.

86. Edwards, *At the Margins*, 124–125.

87. John E. Mueller, *War, Presidents and Public Opinion* (New York: Wiley, 1973).

88. Samuel Kernell, *Going Public: New Strategies of Presidential Leadership*, 2d ed. (Washington, D.C.: CQ Press, 1993), chap. 1.

89. Wayne, *The Legislative Presidency*, 166.

90. Elizabeth Drew, *On the Edge* (New York: Simon and Schuster, 1994), 54, 266.

91. Mark Lacey, "Bush to Attend Democratic Caucuses," *New York Times*, January 27, 2001, A11.

92. Drew, *On the Edge*, 266. For a more positive review of Clinton's personal effectiveness, see Pfiffner, *The Strategic Presidency*, 180.

93. Lizette Alvarez and Eric Schmitt, "Cheney Ever More Powerful As Crucial Link to Congress," *New York Times*, May 13, 2001, A1, A16.

94. Edwards, *At the Margins*, 211. Also see Bond and Fleisher, *The President in the Legislative Arena*, 219; Bert A. Rockman, *The Leadership Question: The Presidency and the American Political System* (New York: Praeger, 1984), 214.

95. Mark A. Peterson, *Legislating Together: The White House and Capitol Hill from Eisenhower to Reagan* (Cambridge: Harvard University Press, 1990), 267.

96. Edwards, *At the Margins*, 8–15.

97. Bond and Fleisher, *The President in the Legislative Arena*, 220–234.

98. Peterson, *Legislating Together*, 92–94, chaps. 4 and 5.

99. Arthur M. Schlesinger Jr., *The Imperial Presidency* (Boston: Houghton Mifflin, 1973).

100. Sundquist, *The Decline and Resurgence of Congress*.

101. In the second edition of *The Imperial Presidency* (Boston: Houghton Mifflin, 1989), Schlesinger maintains that Reagan moved two-thirds of the way toward restoring the imperial presidency. He met two of Schlesinger's "tests"—extensive presidential war making and heavy reliance on secrecy—but Reagan did not direct his powers against administration critics (451, 457).

102. This is the central theme of Peterson's *Legislating Together*, in which he advocates a "tandem institutions" perspective on presidential–congressional relations.

SUGGESTED READINGS

Bond, Jon R., and Richard Fleisher. *The President in the Legislative Arena*. Chicago: University of Chicago Press, 1990.

Cox, Gary W., and Samuel Kernell, eds. *The Politics of Divided Government*. Boulder: Westview, 1991.

Edwards, George C., III. *At the Margins: Presidential Leadership of Congress*. New Haven: Yale University Press, 1989.

Fiorina, Morris. *Divided Government.* New York: Macmillan, 1992.

Fisher, Louis. *Constitutional Conflicts between Congress and the President.* 3d ed. Lawrence: University Press of Kansas, 1991.

Mayhew, David R. *Divided We Govern: Party Control, Lawmaking, and Investigations, 1946–1990.* New Haven: Yale University Press, 1991.

Peterson, Mark A. *Legislating Together: The White House and Capitol Hill from Eisenhower to Reagan.* Cambridge: Harvard University Press, 1990.

Shull, Steven A., ed. *The Two Presidencies: A Quarter-Century Assessment.* Chicago: Nelson-Hall, 1991.

Spitzer, Robert J. *President and Congress: Executive Harmony at the Crossroads of American Government.* New York: McGraw-Hill, 1993.

___. *The Presidential Veto: Touchstone of the American Presidency.* Albany: State University of New York Press, 1988.

Sundquist, James L. *The Decline and Resurgence of Congress.* Washington, D.C.: Brookings, 1981.

Thurber, James A., ed. *Divided Democracy: Cooperation and Conflict between the President and Congress.* Washington, D.C.: CQ Press, 1991.

___. *Rivals for Power: Presidential–Congressional Relations.* Washington, D.C.: CQ Press, 1996.

Wayne, Stephen J. *The Legislative Presidency.* New York: Harper and Row, 1978.

6   EXECUTIVE POLITICS

AMERICANS COMMONLY THINK OF THE president as the "chief executive" of the federal government, held responsible for its many activities and responsibilities. If government fails to meet popular expectations, the president takes the blame. Indeed, when President Jimmy Carter explained his administration's failure to fulfill some of its major campaign promises by saying that he had learned there were certain things that government could not do, his critics suggested that it was time to replace him with someone who could make government work. But Carter's problems were not isolated. Most modern presidents have encountered difficulties in their efforts to direct the executive branch. John F. Kennedy lamented the inertia of the State Department, and Ronald Reagan made his campaign attack on an overgrown federal bureaucracy one of the enduring themes of his presidency. Recent presidents proposing to harness the potential of government to deliver much-needed services must overcome the

Leading members of the Bush foreign policy team—Secretary of Defense Donald Rumsfeld, Secretary of State Colin Powell, and National Security Adviser Condoleezza Rice—must develop a strong personal rapport in order to function effectively during times of crisis.

cynical belief that bureaucracy is the problem, not the solution; thus, Bill Clinton's proposal to solve the nation's health care problems fell victim to the charge that it would create a bloated federal bureaucracy. Richard Rose, who has studied the president as a manager, has remarked that the "president's title of chief executive is a misnomer; he can more accurately be described as a nonexecutive chief."[1] The essence of Rose's argument is that, even within the executive branch, presidential powers of command are limited and that a president's success as an administrator depends to a great extent on the ability to win the trust of others. Thus, presidents confront an enormous challenge. The public both expects presidents to produce results and is unsure of government's role, not wanting it to become too intrusive. Even if the president is successful, therefore, the results may not be fully appreciated.

This chapter examines the president's responsibilities as chief executive and the factors that affect administrative performance. It opens with a discussion of the president's executive role and an examination of that role's constitutional, legal, and administrative foundations. Then it explores the president's relationships with the executive branch and the cabinet. After establishing that the president's powers of command over the units of the executive branch are limited, the chapter analyzes the formal powers and managerial tools that modern presidents have available to them in discharging their administrative duties.

The President as Executive

The president's executive role is grounded in ambiguous language found in Article II of the Constitution, where "the executive power" is vested in the president, who is directed to "take care that the laws be faithfully executed." The president may also "require the opinion, in writing, of the principal officer in each of the executive departments" and "grant reprieves and pardons." Modern presidents have tended to interpret these constitutional provisions broadly and have derived from them substantial additional powers. In addition to these constitutionally based powers, presidents have received extensive delegations of statutory authority from Congress.

All presidents confront a paradox. On the one hand, they enjoy considerable formal legal powers and head a vast, complex military and civilian bureaucracy. On the other hand, they have a limited ability to direct that bureaucracy toward the achievement of the administration's policy objectives and program goals. Understanding that paradox requires considering the constitutional relationship of the presidency to the legislative and judicial branches of government and the nature of the federal bureaucracy and the president's relationship to it.

In administration as in so many other areas, presidents require the cooperation of Congress and the judiciary but frequently find themselves in conflict with these other branches of government. Only Congress can authorize government programs, establish administrative agencies to implement the programs, and appropriate funds to finance them. However, presidents find that congressional cooperation may be difficult to obtain because presidents and members of Congress have different constituency and institutional perspectives regardless of party loyalties. There are also occasions when the exercise of presidential power must be acceptable to the judiciary. In short, presidential power is not self-executing and it is subject to restraint.

Although called "the executive branch," the federal bureaucracy is really the creation of the legislative branch. There are fourteen cabinet departments and scores of special agencies that constitute the federal bureaucracy, with a total workforce of more than four million civilian and military employees. When Congress establishes such federal departments and agencies, it is responding not only to presidential needs and requests, but also to demands and pressures from constituency forces, interest groups, and the general public. The result is that the structure of the federal bureaucracy is not hierarchical; rather, it tends to reflect the political fragmentation and committee jurisdictions of Congress. In sharp contrast to a widely held image, presidents do not look down upon subordinate administrative units from a position at the apex of a pyramid of authority. Instead, they confront a complex and confusing array of departments and agencies with varying degrees of independence from the president.

In addition, the career civil servants who staff bureaucratic units constitute a permanent federal government. They respond to demands from interest groups and to direction from congressional committees as well as to presidential leadership. Most modern presidents have entered office believing, or soon becoming convinced, that they cannot take the support and loyalty of the bureaucracy for granted but must constantly strive to earn both.[2]

Moreover, the vastness and scope of the federal bureaucracy, as measured by expenditures or numbers of employees, further contribute to the difficulty of the president's executive role. As the functions of the federal government expanded from the New Deal onward, the task of defining objectives and coordinating their achievement has grown increasingly difficult for presidents.

The president's task as the nation's chief executive is much more, therefore, than issuing commands. Nor is the job mainly that of finding ways to bring a large complex bureaucracy under operational control. Rather, the president must secure congressional cooperation while suppressing the executive branch's natural tendencies toward conflict with the legislative branch and must give direction to the bureaucracy so that it will help accomplish the administration's goals.

The President and the Executive Branch

Presidents need help in managing the federal bureaucracy. Originally, FDR expanded the White House staff and created other units in the Executive Office of the President for just this purpose—to help him define objectives, convert them into operating programs, allocate resources to the agencies that administer the programs, and coordinate the implementation of programs within the federal government and among federal, state, and local governments. Such staff units are meant to be extensions of a president's eyes, ears, and designated agents. In addition, political executives are expected to assist the president: department secretaries and agency administrators appointed by the president outside the civil service are charged with directing the work of the career employees, coordinating the operations of their component bureaus, and developing and maintaining links with other federal departments and agencies and with state and local governments. Presidents quickly discover, however, that the reality of their relations with the federal bureaucracy bears little resemblance to the idealized vision just described. For example, Joseph Califano, a former presidential aide and cabinet officer, has observed that "smaller federal agencies and numerous bureaus within large departments respond to presidential leadership only in the minds of the most naive students of government administration."[3]

Tension between the president, presidential agents, and the bureaucracy has been present in every modern administration. It exists, at least in part, because of what Hugh Heclo has identified as the distinction between "political leadership in the bureaucracy" and "bureaucratic power."[4] The direction and effectiveness of the political leadership presidents provide depend on the personality, leadership style, and values of each one as well as on external events and conditions. In contrast, bureaucratic power is relatively permanent and does not depend on personalities and transitory political and environmental factors. It is a power that belongs to the career civil servants who compose the permanent government. How the government performs, Heclo suggests, "can be thought of as the product of political leadership times bureaucratic power."[5]

At least five general factors contribute to bureaucratic power and shape the pattern of presidential-bureaucratic relations: the size, complexity, and dispersion of the executive branch; bureaucratic inertia and momentum; the personnel of the executive branch; the legal position of the executive branch; and the susceptibility of executive branch units to external political influence. Major consequences of the interaction of these factors are presidential frustration and a pattern of policymaking that often is sharply at odds with the norm of democratic accountability; it is a system that obscures rather than clarifies those responsible for a policy and a decision.

Size, Complexity, and Dispersion of the Executive Branch

The scope of federal government activities has exploded since 1933, tremendously increasing the number of agencies and the range of programs the agencies administer. The size of the budget and the number of federal employees indicate the magnitude of the operations. The federal budget for 2001 was $1.853 trillion, and there were more than 2.7 million civilian and 1.4 million active duty military employees. These employees oversee domestic programs that reach into every community in the nation and touch the lives of individuals from birth to death. Considerations of national security extend U.S. military and foreign policy activities around the world. It is hardly surprising that providing leadership and direction to the federal bureaucracy is a difficult task. It would be so even if the president could command prompt and unquestioning obedience from subservient departments and agencies.

The multiplicity of agencies and programs creates an additional obstacle to effective political leadership in the executive branch. The complexity that results from overlapping jurisdictions leads in some cases to duplication of efforts and in other cases to contradictory efforts. Presidents must be coordinators. When they define goals for a policy area, they most often deal not with single administrative units but with many. In outdoor recreation, for example, the Forest Service (a unit of the Agriculture Department), the National Park Service (a unit of the Interior Department), and the Army Corps of Engineers all maintain facilities for public use. Or consider the use of land owned by the federal government. Policies of the Forest Service and the Interior Department's Bureau of Land Management are sometimes in sharp conflict. Another example involves the difficult trade-off between energy and environmental policies, which was experienced acutely in the 1970s and is quickly becoming a hotly contested political issue of the new millennium. Efforts to conserve energy and reduce foreign oil imports are often in conflict with attempts to reduce air and water pollution or preserve clean beaches and pristine forests. At times, the Department of Energy and the Environmental Protection Agency appear to be working at cross purposes. For example, substituting U.S. coal for oil reduces dependence on imported oil but increases problems of maintaining air quality.

The great size of the federal bureaucracy means its activities are widely dispersed. Presidents, their aides, and their principal political appointees are at the center of government. The people who operate programs, deliver services to individuals, and regulate the conduct of businesses and other organizations are at the periphery. These people, almost all of them civil servants, are there when a new president and staff take office, and they will be there after the political executives depart. They know their programs and the pitfalls involved in administering them. They control the human and material resources needed to implement programs successfully. Their position, at the point of delivery "where programs meet people," is the source of much of their power.[6]

Bureaucratic Inertia and Momentum

Like a great ocean-going vessel, bureaucracies can neither stop quickly nor turn sharply. Instead, bureaucratic inertia means it is hard to get a new government activity started, and, once it is under way, it is even more difficult to stop or significantly redirect it. In short, "bureaucracies at rest tend to stay at rest and bureaucracies in motion tend to stay in motion."[7] Much of this inflexibility arises because of organizational routines—prescribed operating procedures that have worked successfully in the past—or interest group efforts.

The momentum of ongoing programs especially frustrates presidents. Government commitments are reflected in public laws, the amount of money allocated for those activities in annual appropriations, and the number of civil service and military employees who carry out the activities.[8] By the mid-1990s, mandatory expenditures constituted more than 60 percent of the government's budget. The principal mandatory items included interest on the national debt; entitlement programs such as Social Security, Medicare, and Medicaid; federal retirement and veterans' benefits; food stamps; and unemployment compensation. Even the discretionary portion of the budget is highly resistant to cuts because of support from groups that benefit from those expenditures. Presidents can influence the shape of the federal budget, but major changes usually require several years to be implemented. From one year to the next, presidents tend to be limited to incremental changes.

But presidents, with their fixed term of office, are often impatient to make changes. The incremental adjustments that are possible through annual budgeting hardly seem adequate given the usual scope of presidential objectives and the time available. The time perspective of the bureaucracy is much different. Members of the permanent government can afford to be patient. In the budget process, they fight to maintain their "base," which is their current appropriation, and to add as large an increment to it as possible.[9] Over time, small annual increases are transformed into large permanent gains. Bureaucratic momentum thus works to the advantage of the permanent government and acts as a constraint on presidents who try to counter it. President Reagan and his successors tried to overcome the effects of incremental budgeting by means of a top-down process that restricted total government spending and forced agencies and their congressional and interest group supporters to accept cuts or limited growth.[10] This was not exclusively a Republican initiative. Bill Clinton scored political points when he grandly announced that "the era of big government is over" during his 1996 State of the Union message. He was also reflecting his own commitment to cut spending and slow the rate of programmatic growth, steps needed to balance the federal budget. (The reasons for these efforts are discussed in chapter 9.)

The large number of career federal employees also commits the president to maintaining ongoing programs. Major reductions in personnel or redirection of their activities are economically and politically costly. People will oppose actions that threaten to deprive them of their jobs or that require them to move, undergo additional training, or reduce their sense of security and importance. Most presidents can make only modest adjustments in the size and mission of the federal workforce. President Clinton was somewhat more successful in this regard than other modern presidents. In September 1993, Vice President Al Gore presented to Clinton the final report of the National Performance Review, a task force commissioned to "reinvent government." In endorsing that report, Clinton pledged the elimination of 252,000 federal jobs over a five-year period. The reductions eventually totaled more than 300,000 at the end of seven years.[11]

Bureaucratic Personnel

Presidents must depend on both political and career officials to operate the federal bureaucracy. Until 1883, when the Pendleton Act created the federal civil service, there was no distinction between the two groups. Presidents could theoretically appoint all members of the federal bureaucracy, a "spoils system" of tangible rewards for those loyal party members who had supported the election winner. This is the origin of the saying "to the victors belong the spoils." But with the creation and expansion of the civil service system, presidential control of government personnel declined, and the characteristics and roles of appointed and career officials became more distinctive, often hindering presidential direction of programs. The political executives—those still appointed by the president and charged with directing the careerists—are a weak substitute for the old patronage-based system and constitute what Hugh Heclo has called a "government of strangers."[12] Aside from cabinet officers, a few important subcabinet appointees, and the heads of major independent agencies, these political executives are largely unknown to the president and to one another. Only in a loose sense do they constitute a presidential team able to provide direction for the bureaucracy.

Selection of the cabinet secretaries involves the president directly and traditionally in an attempt to build support for the administration by including representatives of various constituencies in the party and the country.[13] Thomas Cronin maintains that presidents sometimes appoint personal friends to especially important cabinet departments because of the close counseling relationship involved.[14] In his study of cabinet appointments from 1861 to 1984, Jeffrey Cohen found modest support for Cronin's thesis about pretenure ties between presidents and cabinet members.[15] Selection of other political executives is also affected by multiple and often conflicting pressures, such as loyalty to the president, party membership, technical competence, the wishes of the cabinet member under whom the appointee will serve, and the demands of congressional members, interest groups, and state and local party leaders.

When done with care and planning, recruiting people to serve in an administration has the potential to be an instrument of control over policy, a tool of administrative management, and an important component of presidential relations with Congress, interest groups, and political parties. Consequently, it is a highly political process. Presidents since Eisenhower have used personnel staffs located in the White House to run the appointment process for them. The process is always chaotic at the start of a new administration because of the large number of positions to be filled, pressures for jobs from campaign workers and party members, and uncertainty about how to proceed. The number of inquiries from job seekers can be crushing, reaching nearly 1,500 a day in recent cases.[16] Eventually the search becomes fairly systematic, and presidential personnel staffs have come to serve modern presidents well.[17] Over time, centralization of appointment decisions in the Presidential Personnel Office has increased presidential control and bureaucratic responsiveness, but there have been unintended and costly consequences of this process. As Thomas Weko points out, it permits job seekers, interest groups, members of Congress, and campaign contributors to press their claims directly on the White House staff, transferred into the White House conflicts that once were waged outside of it, provoked conflict between the appointments staff and the administrative units, and diminished the importance of program considerations.[18]

The process also depends on an active president who provides sustained support for the selection of appointees. Ronald Reagan excelled in this regard, whereas Richard Nixon's lack of interest contributed to his inability to establish effective control over the executive branch. The Reagan White House exercised tight control over the recruitment of political executives, filling sensitive positions with individuals loyal to the president and committed to his ideology. Cabinet members were not permitted to conduct independent searches for subcabinet officials and ideological affinity became the primary criterion for appointment. Prospective appointees were screened for policy views, political and personal backgrounds, and, if considered necessary, expertise. Although it took the Reagan administration a long time to get its political executives in place (it took the next two administrations, Bush's and Clinton's, even longer), the result was tighter control over the executive branch and greater cohesion within it than other modern presidents have been able to achieve.[19]

Bill Clinton's experience illustrates the difficulty that presidents encounter. The Clinton personnel operation had almost 300 employees during the transition and more than100 in the Presidential Personnel Office in March 1993. The objective of the operation was to create a competent staff for the new administration that also responded to the claims and demands of campaign workers and contributors and represented the diverse blocs, movements, and constituencies that had brought electoral victory. The operation's political success was reflected in the diversity of the appointees, recruited to reflect EGG, or "ethnicity, gender and geography."[20] However, its preoccupation with diversity, ethical concerns, and a series of botched nominations resulted in a slowed pace of appointments that brought sharp criticism from Congress, constituency groups within the Democratic Party, and the media. Clinton's personnel staff "found it extraordinarily difficult to meet the demands from contemporary electoral politics, *and* to ensure that . . . political appointments were used to achieve presidential control of the bureaucracy."[21]

Because the outcome of the 2000 election long remained in question, George W. Bush's search for personnel got off to a late start. But there were other sources of delay as well. At the hundred-day mark in the administration, Bush was well behind the record of the Reagan and Clinton administrations in getting appointees in place. With 488 top appointments to make, Bush had announced 177 candidates, but only 60 names had been submitted to the Senate and, of those, only 29 had been confirmed. This meant that "in nine of the fourteen cabinet departments, the secretary [was] the only senior policy-maker who [had] been confirmed."[22] Candidates were delayed by the need to fill out extensive questionnaires, complete financial disclosure forms, and undergo background investigations. Other administrations also encountered these hurdles, but with each new administration the delays have grown longer. Clay Johnson, Bush's chief talent scout, hoped to get the full subcabinet in place by August 2001, accepting the inevitable delays of a laborious process.[23]

The political executives chosen through the presidential appointment process often are amateurs in the precarious world of Washington politics. They lack the political knowledge and substantive skills needed to provide effective leadership in their jobs. They quickly discover their dependence on top-level career executives and lower-ranking civil servants for the information and advice needed to serve the president effectively. That support is only obtained by paying a price, however, in the form of loyalty to the agency and support for its programs within the administration, before Congress, and with the public. Members of the president's team suddenly find themselves striking a balance between the often conflicting claims of the White House and of the agencies they lead. It is generally conceded that it takes twelve to eighteen months for political executives to master their jobs. Their average tenure, however, is only two years. The high rate of turnover makes it difficult to develop teamwork within departments and agencies. Cabinet secretaries are continually adapting to new assistants, and people on the same administrative level barely get to know one another. One result is that expectations and roles are in flux, and there are problems of coordination and control.

Political executives, who look upward to the president for support and direction and downward to the permanent government for support and services, are imperfect instruments for presidential control of the bureaucracy. They can best serve the president by winning the trust of the careerists who make up the permanent government, but to do so they find it expedient to maintain a considerable degree of independence from the White House.

Conflicts between the White House and the career executives arise for understandable reasons. The relatively secure tenure of upper-level civil servants (as contrasted with the expendability and shorter tenure of political executives) allows them to take a more gradual approach to resolve problems and to pursue their objectives obliquely and by indirection because such a strategy is less likely to generate political opposition. In contrast, political executives, urged on by the White House, tend to pursue their goals quite directly and to see virtue in conflict. Careerists also try to avoid becoming identified with a political party or a political appointee. The civil servant must remain politically neutral to remain a civil servant; hence, he or she is cautious about political involvement. Political executives, many of whom are unfamiliar with the ways of the bureaucracy, often mistake such caution for opposition or disloyalty. This point of view is reinforced by the high value that career executives place on maintaining their relationships with clientele group representatives, congressional members and staff, and individuals outside the Washington community who are involved in or knowledgeable about their agency's programs. Maintaining good relations with these political forces is also important for political executives but might be viewed from the White House as examples of disloyalty.

To correct perceived deficiencies in the career service and to increase presidential control over the higher civil service (those in GS-16 and higher positions), the Carter administration engineered the passage of the Civil Service

Reform Act (CSRA) of 1978. The CSRA established the Senior Executive Service (SES), a professional managerial corps of career civil servants, whose members are eligible for financial bonuses. It also increased the ability of political executives to transfer career officials within and between agencies and to raise the number of noncareerists in the SES and lower positions.[24] Another provision of the CSRA replaced the three-person bipartisan Civil Service Commission with the single-headed Office of Personnel Management (OPM), which gave the president more control over the career service. Reagan's first director of the OPM, Donald J. Devine, aggressively implemented a partisan style of leadership.[25] Neither of Reagan's immediate successors, George Bush and Bill Clinton, used politicization of the career service as extensively as Reagan did to direct the executive branch.

Legal Arrangements

The ambiguous legal position of the executive branch is the fourth factor that affects a president's control over the bureaucracy. All departments and agencies are established by Congress and derive their authority to operate from statutes. Presidents do not enter into contracts, initiate projects, or make grants. Their subordinates do so, but not in response to presidential directives. It is true that presidents act through subordinates, but they do so principally through persuasion because of the nature and source of their legal authority and that of their subordinates.

Although the Constitution charges presidents with responsibility for executing the laws, their legal position as chief executive is somewhat unclear because Congress has—with presidential approval—delegated authority to and imposed duties directly on various administrative officials. In some cases, such as independent regulatory commissions and the Federal Reserve Board, presidents have no formal power to direct agency actions or set agency policy. Their influence upon these units is based on presidential budgetary and appointment powers and on persuasive abilities. For cabinet members, heads of independent agencies, and other political executives with operating authority to whom Congress has directly delegated power, the situation is ambiguous. As chief executive the president, by virtue of the "take care" clause of the Constitution, can command the decisions of subordinates. In doing so, however, the president risks confrontation with Congress and with the clientele groups and individuals affected by the administrative units involved. In addition, the Supreme Court long ago ruled that the president must not interfere with the performance of a "purely ministerial" duty that does not involve the exercise of discretion or judgment.[26] Nor may the president prevent the execution of the law by subordinates.

Congress has provided administrative officials with broad delegations of discretionary authority because legislation can seldom be drafted in sufficient detail to cover all contingencies that might arise. Congress also has made vague and general grants of power because it is politically advantageous for legislators to shift difficult and potentially unpopular decisions to the bureaucracy. The Supreme

Court has approved the delegation of legislative authority to the executive branch with the proviso that the delegations be accompanied by clear statutory guidelines.[27] However, the Court's insistence on specific statutory standards has seldom been followed by Congress or by the lower courts.[28] The standards the Court uses have tended to be vague and unspecific, such as "just and reasonable rates," "excess profits," and "the public interest, convenience, and necessity." In spite of judicial review of the fairness of administrative procedures and judicial reference to the legislative history of statutes as found in congressional committee hearings and reports and floor debates in Congress, administrative officials retain substantial discretionary authority that complicates the president's task of controlling the bureaucracy.

Susceptibility to External Influence

The federal bureaucracy is susceptible to forces outside of individual departments, agencies, and bureaus because American political parties are unable to provide administrative units with political support and to link party programs with the pursuit of presidential policy goals. Presidential administrations lack internal policy cohesiveness and instead depend on the president's personal leadership to hold them together. In the face of external criticism and pressure, executive branch units are unable to find much support within the administration. Demands on the president are extensive, his energy and attention are not unlimited, and he tends to conserve his political resources for high-priority objectives.

If presidential support for an agency is lacking, the agency must look elsewhere for help in maintaining its authority, funding, and personnel. It turns to the public, especially to the individuals and groups who are affected by its programs, and it turns to Congress, particularly to the committees or subcommittees with jurisdiction over the agency's legislative authorizations and appropriations.

The regulations that agencies promulgate and enforce, or the benefits and services they deliver, provide the basis for the development of enduring ties between them and their clientele groups. An agency without a well-organized clientele is in a precarious position. Clientele groups can publicize an agency's accomplishments and defend it against attack. In exchange, the agency administers its programs with a manifest concern for the interests of the clientele. The agency consults with clientele group officials and with individual notables who are attentive to its activities. Such outsiders often are invited to participate in agency decision making. They do so by serving on advisory councils and panels and through informal personal contacts. Agencies seldom perform acts such as drafting guidelines and regulations or awarding grants without extensive external participation and consultation. There is also a two-way flow of personnel between agencies and their clientele organizations. These mutually beneficial relations are characteristic of most domestic policy areas in the federal government.

Washington has countless examples of these relationships. The National Education Association (NEA) and several other education interest groups provide support and protection to the Department of Education in exchange for access and information. The NEA led the congressional effort to elevate the former U.S. Office of Education to departmental status in 1979 and the battle to prevent the abolition of the fledgling department during the Reagan administration. Over the years, several Department of Education political executives have found employment with the NEA and other education interest groups after leaving the government. On occasion, those lobbies have helped to recruit or have provided personnel to staff the agency.

Agencies also find it easy and convenient to develop strong ties to the congressional committees or subcommittees with which they deal. Committee members usually receive immediate attention and preferential treatment from agency personnel. Congressional requests for consideration on appointments and grants, suggestions concerning program administration, and inquiries on behalf of constituents are quickly acknowledged. Congressional influence with the agencies strengthens the committee members in their constituencies.[29] Bureaucrats use their connections with congressional committee members to effect changes in their statutory authority and gain favorable treatment during budget negotiations. Agencies may use their committee ties to obtain more funds than the president has recommended for them or to modify their activities in a way that is not fully in accord with presidential preferences.

Agencies are not, however, totally resistant to presidential directives, nor is it in their interest to be so. Agencies frequently need presidential support and attention. Moreover, they often find that their interests coincide with those of the president. Agencies and the president need each other to accomplish their goals. If the true test of presidential power is the president's power to persuade, one of the best measures of an agency's strength is the degree to which a president must "bargain with it in order to secure its cooperation."[30]

The President and the Cabinet

Most modern presidents have come to office announcing their intent to make more extensive use of the cabinet as a collective decision-making body than the previous incumbent did. The media and academics have generally applauded such pledges. Yet, with the exception of Dwight Eisenhower, presidents have not used their cabinets as vehicles of collective leadership. Moreover, they have experienced strained relationships with many individual cabinet members.

This gap between expectation and experience suggests that there is a widespread lack of understanding of the cabinet on the part of the public and most political leaders. In point of fact, the Constitution places executive authority, ultimately, in the president alone. The notion of collective or collegial leadership—typically found among cabinet members in parliamentary systems, who share leadership responsibility—is incompatible with constitutional reality and inconsistent with American practice. The president is not first among equals; he is explicitly "number one," the person in charge. Cabinet members are presidential appointees, and they serve at the president's pleasure. There is no obligation to consult them as a group or to act according to their wishes. The cabinet has no formal constitutional or legal standing. It exists by custom, and presidents are free to use it as little or as much as they see fit. Bill Clinton, for example, met with his entire cabinet only twice from the beginning of 1998 to May 1999.[31]

The fact that the cabinet has seldom been a high-level decision-making body does not mean that it lacks political significance. Cabinet members are the principal spokespersons for administration policy on Capitol Hill and throughout the nation. They are also the top political executives expected to provide direction for those federal commitments deemed so important as to warrant cabinet-level status. Management tasks are perhaps becoming increasingly important to cabinet members as their service in the job has become longer. Whereas the average tenure of cabinet members in the Nixon administration was 1.73 years, the service of Clinton's cabinet members was 3.36 years by the middle of 1999, the culmination of a six-administration trend of lengthening service.[32] Finally, cabinet composition has great symbolic value as a means of representing major social, economic, and political constituencies in the highest councils of the administration.[33] Newly elected presidents try to select cabinet members whose presence will unify those constituencies behind the new administration.

While political experience, group identification, and technical expertise are important, there is no dominant criterion for selecting cabinet members. However, Nelson Polsby found in a study of the Nixon and Carter cabinets that presidents tend initially to select cabinets that are broadly representative and whose members can speak for clientele groups and party constituencies.[34] This observation characterized George W. Bush's initial cabinet appointments as well (see Table 6-1). There had been much speculation following the 2000 presidential election that Bush would nominate a number of Democrats to his cabinet as a way of recognizing the narrowness of his victory and broadening his base of support, but only Norman Mineta, secretary of transportation and a holdover from the Clinton cabinet where he served as secretary of commerce, has this distinction.

In general, presidents face constraints in selecting cabinet members. Appointees to head some departments, such as Agriculture, generally must be acceptable to clientele groups. In choosing the secretaries of defense and of the Treasury, presidents may give special weight to the candidates' expertise and experience. Generalist administrators, however, often are named to head the Departments of Commerce, Health and Human Services, Housing and Urban Development, and Transportation.

Presidents often try to use the cabinet as a decision-making body early in their administrations, but most of them eventually abandon the effort and come to rely heavily on the White House staff instead.[35] They find that most cabinet members are concerned primarily with issues that affect their departments and with their personal relationships with the president. There is often competition between cabinet members for the president's attention, and personality clashes within the

Table 6-1 George W. Bush's Initial Cabinet Appointees, by Criteria of Appointment

Position	Political experience	Clientele or ethnic group identification	Technical expertise	Pretenure friendship
Inner Cabinet				
Defense secretary				
Donald H. Rumsfeld	✓		✓	
Attorney general				
John Ashcroft	✓			
Secretary of State				
Colin Powell	✓	✓	✓	✓
Treasury secretary				
Paul H. O'Neill	✓			✓
Outer Cabinet				
Agriculture secretary				
Ann M. Veneman	✓	✓	✓	✓
Commerce secretary				
Don Evans	✓			✓
Education secretary				
Rod Paige		✓	✓	
Energy secretary				
Spencer Abraham	✓			
Health and Human Services secretary				
Tommy G. Thompson	✓			
Housing and Urban Development secretary				
Mel Martinez	✓	✓		✓
Interior secretary				
Gale A. Norton	✓	✓	✓	
Labor secretary				
Elaine L. Chao	✓	✓		
Transportation secretary				
Norman Y. Mineta	✓	✓	✓	
Veterans Affairs secretary				
Anthony J. Principi	✓		✓	
Cabinet-level positions				
EPA administrator				
Christine Todd Whitman	✓	✓		✓
OMB director				
Mitchell E. Daniels Jr.	✓			
UN ambassador				
John Negroponte			✓	
U.S. trade representative				
Robert B. Zoellick	✓			✓

cabinet are not infrequent. Under these circumstances, cabinet meetings are unsatisfactory devices for focused, analytical discussion of major issues. At best they can serve as forums for informal discussion of issues and problems and for the exchange of information. The crucial factor limiting the role of the cabinet is the absence of any integrating force within the administration other than the president. The weakness of political parties in the governing process and the presidency's preeminent constitutional and political position combine to make the president the only source of cohesion and policy coordination. Individual cabinet members feel loyal to the president *and* to the permanent governments within their departments. These conflicting loyalties inhibit the development of an informal sense of unity and purpose, without which the cabinet cannot realize its potential as a formal advisory body and policymaking mechanism.[36]

Presidents frequently have developed strong, positive relationships with individual cabinet members and, through them, with their departments, but there is no guarantee that this will happen. A personality conflict between the president and a cabinet member or antipathy on the part of the White House staff can prevent such a development. There is a tendency in most administrations for one or two cabinet members to stand out and to develop close ties with the president. During Reagan's second term, Attorney General Edwin Meese III and Secretary of the Treasury James A. Baker III enjoyed considerable leeway to pursue their own agendas without aggressive interference from the White House staff, provided they did not conflict with the president's ideological precepts.[37] In the first Bush administration, James Baker (State), Robert A. Mosbacher (Commerce), and Nicholas F. Brady (Treasury), all old friends of the president, enjoyed high standing with him.[38] In contrast to the general pattern, no single member dominated the Clinton cabinet. Treasury secretaries Lloyd Bentsen and Robert Rubin enjoyed independent stature because of their political and business experience, respectively. Despite a heavy emphasis on teamwork, Clinton's cabinet did not work effectively as a unit, but its members, acting individually in Washington and throughout the country, were good advocates for the administration's policy goals.[39] At the outset of George W. Bush's administration, observers of the Washington power game were impressed with the influence of Vice President Dick Cheney, whose broad responsibilities and access provided him with more apparent clout than any of the cabinet members. This was especially pronounced after Bush publicly contradicted public positions of Secretary of State Colin L. Powell and Environmental Protection Agency Administrator Christine Todd Whitman during the first hundred days of the administration. A lingering question was whether the new president would rely more heavily on his White House staff or his cabinet secretaries to provide direction for policy.[40]

Whatever the variations in relations between individual presidents and their cabinet members, there has been a tendency for modern presidents to develop close ties with the heads of the Departments of State, Defense, Treasury, and Justice. Cronin refers to these as the "inner cabinet" departments because their activities and responsibilities are of the highest priority—national security, the condition of the economy, civil rights, and the administration of justice—and because they cut across the concerns of the public and all members of Congress. These matters tend to dominate the president's time and attention.[41] Inner cabinet members, therefore, almost always have direct, frequent, and continuing contact with the president.

The heads of the other departments—Agriculture, Commerce, Education, Energy, Health and Human Services, Housing and Urban Development, Interior, Labor, Transportation, and Veterans Affairs—constitute the "outer cabinet."[42] Their departments have more sharply focused activities. Outer cabinet members, subjected to strong clientele and congressional pressures, find themselves acting as advocates for those interests within the administration.[43] Frequently, those pressures conflict with the president's broader priorities.

Because of the diversity and scope of department activities and the particular orientations of some cabinet members, presidents generally have looked to sources other than the cabinet for policy advice. Presidents have additional sources of advice for priority policy areas in the Executive Office of the President. Since its creation in 1947, the National Security Council (NSC) and its staff have been used extensively by presidents to coordinate the making and execution of foreign and military policy (*see chapter 10*). In the important areas of economic policy, presidents work closely with the chair of the Council of Economic Advisers, the director of the Office of Management and Budget (OMB), the secretary of the Treasury, and the chair of the Federal Reserve Board (*see chapter 9*). In the domestic policy areas, which involve primarily the outer cabinet departments, domestic policy staffs and OMB have provided assistance to the president in policy formulation (*see chapter 8*), and cabinet committees, interagency committees, and policy councils have been employed to coordinate policymaking and implementation.

Cabinet committees, which are usually appointed on an ad hoc basis to handle specific problems, can focus quickly on them and attempt to develop solutions. The committees' usefulness for long-term monitoring of policy implementation is limited, however, by other demands on their members and by the tendency of their operations to become routine and to lose flexibility. Interagency committees, which operate mostly at the agency and subcabinet levels, may achieve a measure of coordination, but their work is often hampered by competition between agencies and by a lack of status and visibility.

Presidents also have used policy councils to highlight particular problems. Before the Reagan administration, most policy councils, other than the NSC, had more symbolic value than operational utility to presidents in their management of the executive branch. In his first term Reagan invested heavily in the cabinet council approach. He established seven councils in addition to the NSC: commerce and trade, economic affairs, energy and natural resources, food and agriculture, human resources, legal policy, and management and administration. The theory behind the cabinet council system was that issues would move upward through the full cabinet to the president for decision. Over time, it became apparent that the system was unduly cumbersome, and for his second term, Reagan reduced the number of cabinet councils to two. The remaining councils—the Economic Policy Council and the Domestic Policy Council—had more clearly defined jurisdictions and lines of authority. Despite the later changes, Reagan's cabinet council system is given high marks for "fostering the sense that policy development was a team operation between the cabinet officers and the White House."[44]

President George Bush continued to utilize the Economic Policy Council and the Domestic Policy Council, but with apparently limited effectiveness. Early in 1992, amid reports of "squabbling over domestic policy and rivalries among policy makers," Secretary of Transportation Samuel Skinner replaced John Sununu as White House chief of staff and Secretary of Agriculture Clayton Yeutter was named to the new post of counselor for domestic policy and charged with "centralizing what had been a diffuse policy-making apparatus."[45] Yeutter was not effective in managing domestic policy and left the White House in August 1992.

Clinton began his presidency with three policy staff units in the White House: the National Economic Council, the Domestic Policy Council, and the Office of Environmental Policy, headed by a presidential assistant or deputy assistant.[46] In addition, there were three high-level individuals with access to the president: the senior adviser for policy development, Ira Magaziner; the senior adviser for policy and strategy, George Stephanopoulos; and the first lady, Hillary Rodham Clinton, who chaired the task force that developed the administration's health care reform proposal. The fragmentation of advice that this structure produced reflected Clinton's desire to be at the center of an informal, collegial policymaking process, which he ran like a continuous seminar.[47] With respect to selling and implementing his policy choices, however, Clinton preferred a more formal structure.[48]

George W. Bush retained the Domestic Policy Council and the National Economic Council as coordinating units at the outset of his administration and staffed each with trusted assistants.[49] But the administration also relied heavily on ad hoc task forces to work on particular policy problems. For example, Vice President Cheney headed the group that designed a national energy policy, and a second group was formed to review military preparedness. Thus, early in Bush's presidency, it was difficult to determine how his administration would choose to conduct business.

Presidential Control of the Bureaucracy

The preceding analysis of presidential relations with the cabinet and the bureaucracy highlights the obstacles that presidents encounter in seeking to control policymaking and implementation. Presidents are not, however, without resources for this effort. They have substantial powers granted by the Constitution, delegated by Congress, and derived from the nature of their office. The most important are the powers to appoint and remove subordinates, to issue executive orders, and to prepare the annual federal budget and regulate expenditures.

Appointment and Removal

The essential powers for presidential control of the bureaucracy are the powers to appoint and remove subordinate officials. As critical as these powers are to the president's executive responsibilities, however, they are subject to limitation by Congress.[50] The Constitution gives the president broad powers of appointment (Article II, Section 2, Paragraph 2), but it makes high-ranking officials subject to senatorial confirmation, and it authorizes Congress to vest the appointment of lower officials in the president, in department heads, or in the courts. Congress determines whether the Senate must confirm an appointment to a position. There were about 1,200 full-time positions in the federal bureaucracy subject to Senate confirmation at the outset of George W. Bush's term in office.[51] The president's personal imprint will be on each of these positions. The Senate can also narrow the president's discretion in making appointments by establishing detailed qualifications for various offices. Congress cannot, however, give itself the power to appoint executive officials.[52] Neither can it force the president to make an appointment to a vacant position.[53] The president's appointive powers also are constrained by political considerations and practices such as senatorial courtesy, whereby senators effectively have veto power over certain administrative and judicial appointments from their home states.

The Senate generally has given presidents considerable leeway in the appointment of top-level political executives. But confirmation is not automatic, and the Senate has used rejections to express disapproval of specific individuals or of particular practices.[54] Since the Watergate scandal of 1972–1974, the Senate has tended to be more careful and procedurally consistent in examining the backgrounds, qualifications, and relevant policy views of presidential nominees. However, the confirmation process has "become more tedious, time-consuming, and intrusive for the nominees," a situation exacerbated by interparty conflict.[55] For example, the Senate finally confirmed Richard C. Holbrooke as U.S. permanent representative to the United Nations in August 1999 after a fourteen-month odyssey that included two federal ethics investigations, four hearings conducted by the Senate Foreign Relations Committee, and "holds"—objections to a nominee that delay action—placed by several Republican senators in an effort to wrest concessions from the administration on matters unrelated to the nomination. The prospects of such a tortuous and contentious process causes candidates to withdraw from consideration or decline invitations to serve.[56] George W. Bush, already delayed in staffing his administration, faced the prospects of even slower progress after the Senate majority changed from Republican to Democrat in June 2001.

The Constitution also empowers the president to make appointments when the Senate is in recess. Such appointments must be confirmed by the end of the Senate's next session, but in the interim the appointee continues to serve. Senators often object to recess appointments to high-level positions because they feel inhibited from thoroughly examining people who have already begun their duties. Congress now remains in session most of the year, which suggests presidents would have fewer opportunities to make recess appointments. But President Clinton made extensive use of acting appointments after Republicans gained control of the Senate in 1995 and he encountered problems getting nominees approved. Temporary appointments became long running, a controversial exercise of this constitutional power. For example, the head of the Justice Department's Criminal Division served on an acting basis for two and a half years without even being nominated. Walter E. Dellinger III served as solicitor general—the federal government's lead lawyer before the Supreme Court—for more than fourteen months without ever having his name submitted for Senate approval because a major battle was expected.[57] One of the most contentious cases focused on Bill Lann Lee, whose nomination as assistant attorney general for civil rights was bottled up in the Senate Judiciary Committee on three different occasions because of his allegedly liberal policy views, though a recorded vote was never taken for fear of antagonizing Asian American voters. Lee served in an "acting" capacity and was renominated by Clinton on two other occasions in an attempt to force Senate action. His service far exceeded the 120-day limit that Congress set for such appointments in the 1980s, but successive administrations have asserted great freedom in extending "acting" appointments indefinitely.[58]

The removal power is the logical complement of the appointment power. The ability to remove subordinate officials on performance or policy grounds is fundamental to presidential control of the executive branch. Without the removal power, the president cannot be held fully responsible for the actions of subordinates or for the failure of departments and agencies to achieve presidential objectives. The Constitution is silent, however, concerning the removal of executive officials other than through impeachment, a cumbersome process that is limited to instances of "bribery, treason, and other high crimes and misdemeanors."

Presidents have clashed with Congress over the removal power. The post–Civil War conflict between President Andrew Johnson and Congress over Reconstruction policy involved the removal power. In 1867, Congress brought impeachment proceedings against Johnson for violating the Tenure of Office Act, which it had passed over his veto. That statute authorized all persons appointed with the advice and consent of the Senate to continue to hold office until the president appointed and the Senate confirmed a successor. President Johnson tried to remove Secretary of War Edwin Stanton without permission, thus triggering the impeachment effort. Although Johnson survived the impeachment trial by one vote, the issue of the removal power remained unresolved. (Congress repealed the Tenure of Office Act in 1887.)

The Supreme Court dealt directly with the removal power in a decision involving a challenge to President Woodrow Wilson's summary removal of a postmaster.[59] The Court invalidated an 1876 law that required senatorial consent for the removal of postmasters. It held that the Constitution gave the president the removal power and that Congress could not place restrictions on its exercise. Nine years later, however, the Court upheld the provisions of the Federal Trade Commission Act that limited the grounds for removal of its members.[60] The Court ruled that the president's unqualified power of removal is limited to "purely executive offices" and that Congress may prescribe conditions for the removal of officials performing "quasi-legislative" and "quasi-judicial" functions.

However, the Court has not clarified fully the meaning of these terms. One of the
instances of the removal power occurred in August 1981, when
an fired 11,400 striking members of the Professional Air Traffic
anization. A U.S. court of appeals upheld the action, interpreting
e of the president's obligation to enforce a statute prohibiting
l employees.[61]

re are some statutory and judicial restrictions on the removal
limits remain somewhat undefined. Moreover, presidents may
informal means to force officials from office for reasons other
use. Presidents can call publicly for an official's resignation, or
authority they have delegated to an official as a means of indi-
and lack of confidence. Secretary of Defense Les Aspin resigned
om the White House staff in November 1993, following the
1993 of eighteen U.S. servicemen who were part of a United
ing force in Somalia. Prior to that incident, Aspin had rejected
military for additional equipment for the peacekeepers.[62]

s

iterpretation of separation of powers, the president has no
direct legislative authority. From the beginnings of the Republic, however, presidents have issued orders and directives on the basis of Article II. Most modern
presidents have followed Theodore Roosevelt's "stewardship" theory of executive power (*see chapter 1*), which holds that Article II confers on them inherent
power to take whatever actions they deem necessary in the national interest
unless prohibited from doing so by the Constitution or by law. Executive orders
have been a primary means of exercising this broad presidential prerogative
power. "They are presidential edicts, legal instruments that create or modify
laws, procedures, and policy by fiat."[63] Particularly in the twentieth century,
executive orders helped push "the boundaries of presidential power by taking
advantage of gaps in constitutional and statutory language that allow them to fill
power vacuums and gain control of emerging capabilities."[64]

It is generally recognized that to have the force of law, executive orders must
find their authority in the Constitution or in an act of Congress. As noted, the
Supreme Court has upheld delegations of legislative power to the executive
branch provided Congress establishes "intelligible" standards to guide administrative officials in the exercise of their authority.[65] In reviewing challenges to
statutory delegations, however, the Court has consistently adopted a presump-
tion in favor of statutes authorizing executive action by order or rule.

Historically, presidents have used a variety of unilateral instruments to
accomplish their goals, including executive orders, directives, memoranda,
proclamations, policy instructions, and interpretations of congressional intent.
Reliance on such strategies is especially prominent in crucial policy areas such as
civil rights, economic stabilization, and national security,[66] or when conflict with
Congress means action cannot be accomplished through legislation. In the realm

of civil rights, Franklin Roosevelt established a Fair Employment Practices Commission in 1943 to prevent discriminatory hiring by government agencies and military suppliers. In 1948, Harry S. Truman ended segregation in the armed forces by executive order. In March 1961, shortly after taking office, John Kennedy issued a sweeping order creating the Equal Employment Opportunity Commission and giving it broad enforcement powers. Lyndon Johnson went even further, requiring by executive order preferential hiring of minorities by government contractors.

Franklin Roosevelt established broad precedents for the use of executive orders to achieve economic stability and a number of his successors have followed suit. During World War II, he issued executive orders to establish the Office of Price Administration (OPA) and the Office of Economic Stabilization and to give them extensive powers over prices, wages, and profits. The OPA also rationed scarce consumer goods such as meat, butter, sugar, shoes, automobile tires, and gasoline. As a basis for his actions, Roosevelt cited his responsibility as president to respond to the "unlimited emergency" created by the war. The Emergency Price Control Act of 1942 provided retroactive statutory endorsement for the establishment of the emergency agencies and the measures implemented by them. In 1970, in the face of persistent inflation, Congress passed the Economic Stabilization Act, which authorized the president to issue orders that would control wages and prices, but with few criteria to guide these actions. On August 15, 1971, President Nixon issued an executive order imposing a ninety-day freeze on nonagricultural wages and prices and establishing the Cost of Living Council to administer the controls. A subsequent order, issued October 15, extended the controls and established additional machinery to aid in administering them. A legal challenge to the statute, as an unconstitutional delegation of unbridled authority, failed before a U.S. district court.[67]

Presidents also have used executive orders in pursuit of national security. In 1942, for example, Roosevelt ordered the internment of all persons of Japanese ancestry living in the Pacific coastal states, 70,000 of whom were U.S. citizens. The Supreme Court upheld this massive deprivation of basic civil liberties on the basis of the commander-in-chief clause.[68]

Executive orders have long played a major role in presidential policymaking but have been used to varying degrees. President Carter made the heaviest use of executive orders among the past six administrations, and presidents since 1981 have made less use of them than have their three predecessors (see Table 6-2). There is some disagreement in the literature over whether presidents confronted by a Congress controlled by the opposition party will make heavier use of executive orders. For example, year-to-year totals show that Clinton's use of executive orders actually declined rather than increased when he confronted a hostile Republican Congress after 1995, though he may still have used executive orders as a way to make progress on major policy initiatives.[69] In his exhaustive study of executive orders, Kenneth Mayer traces the pattern of their use from 1936 through 1995 and concludes that the issuance of orders "rises and falls in

Presidents have made extensive use of executive orders to accomplish a wide range of policy goals. Franklin Roosevelt issued one of the most controversial orders in 1942 when more than 110,000 Japanese Americans living on the West Coast were relocated to internment camps around the nation.

response to significant events."[70] For example, the onset of war triggers new administrative arrangements and new regulations governing economic controls and wartime mobilization, just as peace requires their removal. The focus of executive orders has also changed over time. There was a significant rise in the incidence of orders dealing with executive branch administration, foreign affairs, and domestic policy during the period of 1936–1999.[71] Finally, Democrats make more use of executive orders than Republicans, more orders are issued at the end of a term and when the president's public support is low than under the opposite conditions, and more orders are issued when the president's party is in the congressional majority, a counterintuitive finding.[72]

Unilateral presidential action, however, can be reversed. During the Korean War, the Supreme Court invalidated Truman's seizure of the steel industry on the grounds that he had not used the machinery established in the Taft-Hartley Act of 1947 to avert a strike.[73] More recently, we have the example of a successor president reversing an action of his predecessor. President Clinton issued an

Table 6-2   Executive Orders, 1969–2001

President/years in office	Total executive orders issued by administration	Executive orders per year
Richard Nixon (1969–1974)	346	62.9
Gerald R. Ford (1974–1977)	169	67.6
Jimmy Carter (1977–1981)	320	80
Ronald Reagan (1981–1989)	381	47.6
George Bush (1989–1993)	166	41.5
William J. Clinton (1993–2001)	364	45.5
George W. Bush (2001–)	24	NA

Source: "Executive Orders Disposition Tables, April 13, 1945–July 31, 2001," *Presidential Documents on NARA Web Sites,* Aug. 3, 2001, National Archives and Records Administration, *Federal Register,* www.nara.gov/fedreg/eo.html.

executive order, shortly after taking office, to reverse a Bush administration policy that he had criticized in the campaign. He ended the prohibition against doctors at federally funded clinics providing advice and information about abortions.[74] In turn, George W. Bush reversed this order during his first week in office and reinstated his father's policy.

From 1932 until 1983, Congress exerted a measure of control over executive lawmaking through use of the legislative veto. Provisions added to certain statutes gave Congress the power to review and reject executive orders or administrative regulations authorized by the legislation. The legislative veto took various forms. It allowed disapproval of regulations by concurrent resolution or by simple resolution of either house or by action of a committee of either house. In its most common form, the legislative veto required that the proposed action lie before Congress for a specified period—usually sixty or ninety days—during which either chamber could disapprove it. The president's reorganization authority, which Congress first authorized in 1939, carried such a procedure. Other major statutes that contained a form of legislative veto include the War Powers Resolution of 1973, the Budget and Impoundment Control Act of 1974, the Federal Elections Campaign Act of 1974, and the National Emergencies Act of 1976. In all, more than 250 statutes provided for some type of legislative veto before the Supreme Court declared it unconstitutional in 1983.

In *Immigration and Naturalization Service v. Chadha,* the Court held the one-house legislative veto provision of the Immigration and Nationality Act to an unconstitutional breach of the separation of powers.[75] The Court reasoned that the veto involved "the exercise of legislative power" without "bicameral passage followed by presentment to the President," that is, such actions were not subject to presidential concurrence or veto. Initial reaction to the decision was that it was not a definitive ruling and that somehow Congress would find a way statutorily to control executive branch lawmaking.[76] Although the Court threw out past practices, Congress has required agencies to obtain approval from the appropriations committees before taking specified actions and used informal agreements with agencies to achieve the same goal.[77]

Congress has also employed the joint resolution of approval before an executive action can be taken.[78] For example, the Reorganization Act Amendments of 1984 provide that a presidentially prepared reorganization plan submitted to Congress cannot take effect unless approved by a joint resolution within ninety days. This provision places the burden on the president rather than on Congress, and the president has only a specific number of days in which to act. In effect, the joint resolution of approval works like a one-house legislative veto: if either house refuses to approve an action, it cannot be taken. The major disadvantage of the device for Congress is that it requires much time, and extensive use of it would threaten the congressional agenda with legislative gridlock.

Presidents and Money

Presidents have substantial financial powers, delegated by Congress, which they use in their efforts to control the bureaucracy. The most important of these is the power to formulate the budget, which controls the amount of spending by federal departments and agencies. It also establishes the president's spending priorities, sets the timing of program initiatives, and distributes rewards to and imposes sanctions on executive branch units.[79] By controlling the total amount of the budget, the president can attempt to influence the performance of the economy (*see chapter 9*).

Presidential use of the executive budget was a twentieth-century development. The enormous increase in expenditures during World War I, and the task of managing the sizable national debt that resulted, convinced Congress of the need for an executive budget. The Budget and Accounting Act of 1921 made the president responsible for compiling department and agency estimates and for submitting them annually to Congress in the form of a budget. The statute established the Bureau of the Budget (BOB), located in the Treasury Department, to assist the president in assembling and revising these estimates. The departments and agencies were prohibited from submitting their requests directly to Congress as they had done previously.

The initial emphasis in the development of the federal budget process was on the control of expenditures and the prevention of administrative abuses.[80] The focus of the budget was on objects of expenditure, that is, the personnel, supplies, and equipment needed to operate each agency. During the New Deal period, in the 1930s, the emphasis shifted from control to management. The budget was seen as a means of evaluating and improving administrative performance. The focus of the budget also shifted from objects of expenditure to the work and activities of departments and agencies. The transfer of BOB in 1939 from the Treasury Department to the new Executive Office of the President symbolized the management orientation. BOB was to become the president's management arm. A decade later, upon recommendation of the Hoover Commission, the government adopted a performance budget organized by functions and activities rather than by line items representing objects of expenditure.

The most recent stage in the development of budgeting is its orientation toward planning. This emphasis attempts to link annual budgeting, geared to the appropriations process in Congress, to long-range planning of government objectives. The focus is on the relationship of long-term policy goals to current and future spending decisions. The limited success of the planning orientation is reflected in the rapid arrival and departure of budgeting systems, such as the program planning budgeting system (PPBS) and zero-base budgeting (ZBB).[81] The budgeting process, as it had developed by the early 1970s, embodied all three orientations—control, management, and planning—but it was least effective as a planning device.

The limitations of the executive budget as an aid to presidential decision making stem from the incremental nature of the traditional budget process and from restrictions and conditions imposed by Congress. Budgeting is inherently incremental because it is done annually. The budget cycle forces the president and Congress to act according to a timetable that stretches from twenty-two months before the start of the fiscal year (October 1) through the ensuing year. Decision makers in Congress and the bureaucracy are concerned primarily with how large an increase or decrease will be made in a department's or an agency's budget. For fifteen years, from 1982 to 1997, huge federal deficits accompanied by strong public resistance to tax increases caused presidential and congressional budget decisions to be focused primarily on reducing spending. But emergence of a budget surplus in 1998 ushered in a debate between Republicans and Democrats over the need for tax cuts. Republicans finally won the struggle in 2001, when George W. Bush engineered a massive tax cut to be spread over eleven years. But when the threat of deficits emerged in mid-2001, questions again arose about the capacity of government to plan effectively. (*See chapter 9 for further details.*)

Congress makes its own budget decisions and is not bound by the president's requests. It limits total spending through resolutions proposed by the budget committees in each house. Although the congressional budget total is usually fairly close to the president's, the priorities in the two budgets often differ sharply. In the 1970s, Congress quarreled bitterly with Nixon and Gerald Ford over spending for domestic programs, and as already noted, in the 1980s it squared off with Reagan over the size of the deficits in his proposed budgets and the role of spending cuts and tax increases in reducing them. In the early 1990s, Congress continued these battles with George Bush.

Bill Clinton encountered the constraints imposed by deficit politics when he attempted to use his first budget as a vehicle for policy change.[82] Although Congress narrowly (with no Republican support) accepted most of his five-year plan (1994–1998) to reduce the deficit by almost $500 billion, it embarrassed Clinton by rejecting a $16 billion package to stimulate the economy.[83] In 1995, the first Republican-controlled Congress in forty years ignored the administration's budget, which did not contain proposals for eventually eliminating the deficit, and adopted a budget resolution that projected a balanced budget in fiscal year 2002. Nearly two years of budget battles ensued, not resolved until a 1997 agreement was reached on how to balance the budget.[84] George W. Bush, in contrast, found a cooperative Congress controlled by his own party during the first half of 2001 and secured passage of a massive tax cut. After Democrats became the Senate majority, however, there was a high likelihood of reentering an era of budget conflict.

In addition to budgeting, presidents have certain discretionary spending powers that increase their leverage over the bureaucracy. They have substantial nonstatutory authority, based on understandings with congressional appropriations committees, to transfer funds within an appropriation and from one program to another. The committees expect to be kept informed of such "reprogramming" actions.[85] Fund transfer authority is essential to sound financial management, but it can be abused to circumvent congressional decisions. In 1970, for example, Nixon transferred funds to support an extensive unauthorized covert military operation in Cambodia. Nevertheless, Congress has given presidents and certain agencies the authority to spend substantial amounts of money on a confidential basis, the largest and most controversial of which are for intelligence activities.

Presidents also have exercised some measure of expenditure control through the practice of impounding or returning appropriated funds to the Treasury. Since George Washington, presidents have routinely impounded funds as a means of achieving savings when actual expenditures fall short of appropriations.[86] They also have withheld funds when authorized or directed to do so by Congress for purposes such as establishing contingency reserves or imposing a ceiling on total expenditures. Presidents from FDR through Lyndon Johnson also impounded some of the funds that Congress had added, over their objections, for various programs. Although such actions often drew congressional criticism, they did not lead to confrontation because they occurred infrequently and were generally focused on expenditures for specific programs or projects. Congress recognized that circumspect use of impoundments helped its members to resist strong pressures for increased spending.[87]

Impoundment became a major constitutional issue during the Nixon administration. Sweeping impoundments in domestic program areas, especially agriculture, housing, and water pollution control, led to charges that the president arbitrarily and illegally had substituted his spending priorities for those of Congress. What distinguished the Nixon impoundments from those of earlier administrations was their "magnitude, severity, and belligerence."[88] Specifically, Nixon's impoundments differed from those of other presidents in several ways: they involved larger amounts; some were made in direct violation of explicit congressional instructions to spend the funds; some were designed to terminate entire programs rather than individual projects; and some were directed at appropriated funds that had not been included in the president's budget proposals. Moreover, Nixon claimed constitutional rather than statutory authority for impoundment.[89] He used impoundments as the primary weapon in a battle with Congress over domestic spending priorities. He did not bargain or negotiate over them but imposed his priorities by fiat.

Nixon's actions resulted in lawsuits to compel release of the funds; most of the suits were decided against the president on statutory grounds. Congress also passed the Budget and Impoundment Control Act of 1974. The Antideficiency Act of 1950 had limited the purposes of impoundments to establishing contingency reserves and the saving of money that otherwise would be wasted. The 1974 statute established procedures for congressional review by requiring that the president report all impoundments to Congress. Proposals to rescind appropriated funds, that is, to return them to the Treasury, must be approved by both houses within forty-five days. Proposals to defer spending to the next fiscal year can be disapproved by either house.

The Supreme Court's ruling invalidating the legislative veto affected congressional power to control impoundments. (Since the 1974 legislation called for approval of rescissions by both houses, *Chadha* did not invalidate that procedure.) But the only way left for Congress to overturn a deferral of funds is to pass a bill or joint resolution. Because such a measure is subject to presidential veto, the president's deferral power is strengthened. Congress's most effective way to circumvent a possible veto is to attach a rider canceling the deferral to an appropriation bill that the president feels compelled to sign in order to keep the involved agencies operating. But riders are a cumbersome device. When Reagan began to defer sizable amounts ($5.4 billion for fiscal 1986) in his second term as a means of reducing spending on programs he opposed, Congress found itself without a viable means of controlling the deferrals.[90]

In 1996, Bill Clinton was the beneficiary of the Republican Party's promise in its 1994 election manifesto, the Contract with America, to establish a line-item veto for the president's use in fighting the budget deficit, a power that many governors enjoy at the state level. Bill Clinton was the first and probably last president to enjoy this power. The Line-Item Veto Act authorized the president to cancel specific spending items or tax breaks rather than veto an entire appropriation bill only when the budget was in deficit. Ultimately, this statute was invalidated in a 1998 Supreme Court decision[91] but not before Clinton invoked the authority eighty-two times.

Presidential Management of the Bureaucracy

In addition to their formal powers, modern presidents have relied on managerial tools in their ongoing efforts to coordinate and direct executive branch operations. Three major tools—staffing, reorganization, and planning—have been employed with mixed results. The limited success of presidential efforts to manage the federal bureaucracy more effectively stems primarily from the political character of the administration of the executive branch. The president must rely more on persuasion than command to achieve objectives. This is not to argue that the public sector is inhospitable to modern management techniques, but to suggest that political forces significantly affect their use.[92]

Staffing

Unquestionably, staffing is crucial to presidential management of the bureaucracy. As discussed in chapters 1 and 4, the institutionalized presidency has grown steadily as presidents have turned to staff support as a means of directing the executive branch and of fulfilling the many roles required of the officeholder. The functions of presidential staff in program implementation and of the cabinet in advising the president have varied in recent administrations, but the tendency has been toward reliance on a strong, sizable, and centralized White House staff to protect the political interests of presidents, to act as their principal policy advisers, and to direct (as opposed to monitor and coordinate) the implementation of presidential priorities by the bureaucracy.

Critics of this structure argue that it has undercut the advisory potential of the cabinet, narrowed the president's perspective on policy choices, and inhibited effective and responsive bureaucratic performance. Stephen Hess cautions that reliance on a centralized White House staff has been "self-defeating."[93] Experience under Nixon and Reagan supports this view. Yet, Ford and Carter both tried a decentralized model of White House staffing and abandoned it in favor of hierarchical arrangements.

President George Bush adopted the hierarchical model of White House organization at the start of his administration in 1989. His chief of staff, former New Hampshire governor John Sununu, maintained tight control over White House operations, at times with a heavy hand. He functioned as the guardian of the president's political interests, serving as Bush's link to conservatives, and he often appeared to have set the administration's course on domestic social policy issues. In these roles, he was the target of considerable congressional and media criticism.[94] As that criticism extended to Sununu's ostentatious use of White House "perks," such as taking a White House car and chauffeur to attend a New York stamp auction, he became a political liability to the president. Bush replaced Sununu in late 1991. Samuel Skinner, the new chief of staff, brought in several new people and ran the office less despotically than his predecessor, but experienced difficulty in asserting and maintaining control.[95]

The Clinton White House reflected the leadership style of a highly intelligent, energetic, enthusiastic, and enormously self-confident president who lacked self-discipline, assumed large numbers of personal responsibilities, had difficulty focusing his goals and managing his efforts, and was reluctant to delegate tasks to others.[96] Clinton entered office with no plan for organizing the White House and proceeded to staff it largely with consultants who had worked on his campaign and friends and political associates from Arkansas.[97] The chief of staff, Thomas F. McLarty III, was a public utility executive Clinton had known since childhood. The initial staff lacked the Washington experience and political stature that might have prevented damaging early missteps such as the botched nominations of Zoe Baird and Kimba Wood to be attorney general, the conflict with Congress over ending discrimination against gays in the military, and the defeat of the economic stimulus bill. Corrective efforts were taken, but in January 1994, journalist Burt Solomon still described the Clinton White House as "amorphously organized," characterized by a "muddled management structure" that did business through a "snarl of networks."[98]

McLarty was replaced in June 1994 by Leon Panetta, the director of OMB, who brought some much-needed order to the Clinton White House. Panetta and his successors, Erskine Bowles and John Podesta, established control over the flow of communications and personal access to the president.[99] A greater degree of centralization and formal organization proved to be an operational necessity to counteract Clinton's lack of discipline. Clinton also demonstrated the ability to recognize his failings and take corrective action. White House staff personnel at the start of Clinton's second term were more pragmatic and less ideological and had more Washington experience than their first-term counterparts.[100] This reflected the modest centrist agenda on which Clinton had successfully campaigned.

George W. Bush is most likely to follow a modified version of the "spokes-in-a-wheel" White House structure that was so successful during Reagan's first term. In this model, a limited number of aides have access to a president who freely delegates responsibilities. Reagan had three key advisers; it is still unclear how many spokes Bush will utilize. Two key Bush advisers held positions in previous White Houses: Vice President Cheney was chief of staff for Ford, and Andrew Card, the new chief of staff, was deputy chief in the earlier Bush administration. This base of White House experience helped in creating a smoothly functioning staff system that drew high praise during its initial months in office. In striking contrast to his immediate predecessor, Bush appears to be a "disciplined delegator," who will draw upon the services of his able aides from the outset.[101] Critics, however, raise the same questions as they did about Reagan and, even earlier, Eisenhower. When presidents delegate, observers ask, "who's really in charge?" For critics, it seemed that Vice President Cheney was exercising more responsibility than his constitutional superior, an issue fueled by several health crises experienced by the vice president during the first months of the administration.[102]

Since the Reagan administration, the presidency has become increasingly centralized and politicized. Terry Moe defends these developments as an inescapable consequence of the extensive expectations that impinge upon the presidency.[103] A similar conclusion emerged from a 1986 symposium featuring eight former White House chiefs of staff (or their functional equivalents) who served presidents from Eisenhower through Carter. In their view, "the demands for activism and the requirements of self-reliance encourage presidents to look favorably upon the kinds of services provided by a rationalized White House run by a strong chief."[104]

Reorganization

It has been almost an article of faith among political leaders and public administration theorists that executive reorganization can increase presidential power over the bureaucracy. Johnson, Nixon, and especially Carter had strong convictions that the performance of the executive branch could be improved and the bureaucracy brought to heel through changes in administrative structure. However, Johnson's efforts were nonconsequential, and Nixon's were interrupted by his resignation from office. By most accounts, the results of Carter's reorganization efforts—by far the most extensive—were modest.[105]

Organizational structure and administrative arrangements are significant because they reflect values and priorities and because they affect access to decision makers. The location and status of an administrative unit—as a department, an independent agency, or a component of a department—symbolize the importance of its goals and the interests it serves. Administrative arrangements also can contribute to or frustrate the achievement of accountability to Congress and the public. Reorganizing, however, does not necessarily result in increased efficiency of operation, greater program effectiveness, or enhanced public accountability. This is true because there is no ideal form for a government agency or a consistent set of prescriptions for organizing the executive branch. One set of standard prescriptions tends to centralize authority, and another tends to disperse it. More important, the most profound consequences of organizational change are not in the "engineered realm of efficiency, simplicity, size, and cost of government"; rather, they lie in the areas of "political influence, policy emphasis, and communication of governmental intentions."[106] For example, the placement of the Occupational Safety and Health Administration in the Department of Labor rather than in the Department of Health, Education, and Welfare led to an initial focus of regulations on mechanical rather than on biological hazards in the workplace. Experience has shown that although the rationale for reorganization is couched in the rhetoric of economy and efficiency, the crucial factors in decisions to reorganize are power, policy, and symbolic significance.

In 1939, Congress authorized presidents to propose executive reorganization plans that take effect after sixty days unless disapproved by both houses. When extending that authority in 1949, Congress allowed either house to disapprove such plans. Congress continued to renew the reorganization authority with little change until 1973, when it was allowed to lapse in the conflict with Nixon over his efforts to centralize control of the executive branch. In 1977, Carter requested and received renewal of the authority with provision for veto by either house. Neither Reagan, Bush, nor Clinton displayed any interest in using the reorganization power to enhance presidential control of the executive branch.

Carter's reorganization achievements exceeded those of his immediate predecessors and of his successors but fell far short of the thorough restructuring of the executive branch and reduction in the number of agencies he had promised. Congress passed legislation that established new cabinet Departments of Energy and of Education and allowed five reorganization plans to take effect. Carter and his staff were unprepared for the jurisdictional conflicts that accompanied congressional consideration of reorganization proposals.[107] The president also lacked a well-conceived, comprehensive strategy that could be defended on political grounds. For Carter, the principal goal of reorganization was the fulfillment of campaign commitments. What was lacking was an understanding of reorganization as a means of redistributing influence and redirecting policy. The Carter experience indicates that reorganization has its uses, but they are more in the realm of policy and politics than management improvement.

The Clinton administration ignored reorganization in favor of the personnel reductions called for in Vice President Gore's *National Performance Review Report,* along with the report's recommendations to cut red tape, enhance customer satisfaction, empower employees, and eliminate unneeded functions. The Gore report represented a sharp break with the administrative management paradigm that had dominated presidential efforts to manage the bureaucracy since the Brownlow Committee report of 1937. That philosophy, which the reports of the Hoover Commission (1949) and the Ash Council (1971) also embodied, "emphasized the need for democratic accountability of departmental and agency officers to the President and his central management agencies and through these institutions to the Congress."[108] In its stead, the Gore report embraced the entrepreneurial management paradigm made popular by David Osborne and Ted Gaebler in their book *Reinventing Government.*[109] They call for a "cultural and behavioral shift in the management of government" from a bureaucratic to an entrepreneurial government. In their view, public agencies are entrepreneurial organizations competing in a market environment in which success is determined by the degree of customer satisfaction. Clinton's reinvention effort evolved over time and in two later phases shifted attention to reducing government's cost and then to attacking complex problems, such as finding ways to create and maintain "safe communities," a highly complex issue for government to tackle.[110] Clinton's departure from administrative orthodoxy sparked extensive discussion among academics,[111] but in the short run, few conclusions can be drawn about Clinton's novel strategy. The experience is certain to influence later thinking about the range of strategies presidents might consider.

Planning

Aaron Wildavsky defined planning as "current action to secure future consequences."[112] Foresight in anticipating problems and developing solutions to them is the essence of effective planning. One of the hallmarks of successful corporate management has been long-range planning, but the federal government has not had a high degree of success in this area. Planning is applicable to all major activities of the government—national security, economic affairs, human resources, and natural resources—and the nation has "paid a heavy price" for the government's failure "to take adequate account of the future."[113] In the early

1950s, for example, experts were warning of the eventual depletion of domestic oil sources, yet only after the oil embargo of 1973–1974 did the government begin to develop an energy policy that looked to the future. When oil again became plentiful in the 1980s, the United States abandoned that policy because it was politically unpopular, so the problem persisted into the next millennium, where it again confronts decision makers with difficult choices.

The reasons for the limited success of planning by the federal government lie in the nature of the planning process and its relationship to politics. Planning is a rational process. It operates on the assumption that objectives are known and accepted. The task is to select the best means appropriate to the achievement of the desired ends. Planning decisions are made comprehensively, that is, "as if a single mind were supporting a single set of preferences."[114] Conflict and disagreement do not interfere because the planners know what is desired. However, public planning, like all other planning, takes place in an uncertain world. Planners do not have adequate knowledge of the future, and their predictions often are fallible.

In addition to the intellectual limitations of all planning, public planning is limited by politics. Public planners do not have the power to command acceptance of their choices. Public choices are made on the basis of the preferences of individuals and groups through a process of bargaining and compromise. The agreements reached in the process of political decision making determine the objectives of public planners. There is no correct result because political preferences are continually changing. As a consequence, political planners make accommodations to social forces. They shorten their time frames (usually extending them no further into the future than the next election), thus reducing the need for prediction, and offer their plans as proposals or suggestions rather than as directives. The result is that political factors tend to dominate planning, and planning tends to blend with regular political decision making.

Presidents have engaged in long-range planning with only limited success. As noted, attempts to combine annual budgeting with comprehensive planning through the program planning budgeting system and zero-base budgeting have not succeeded. Introduced throughout the government by President Johnson in 1965, PPBS used cost-benefit calculations to choose between alternative programs and formulate long-range objectives. ZBB, a project of President Carter, compared the effects of alternative funding levels on long-term objectives within a single program. Both approaches entailed comprehensive attempts to relate spending decisions to long-range consequences. Each required extensive amounts of information and analyses that were never integrated with budget decisions. Thus, bureau and agency officials did not find it worthwhile to take either process seriously. A fatal defect of both PPBS and ZBB was neglect of the hard political choices involved in the budget process. Nor was Congress supportive of either device.

President Nixon introduced a similar technique that focused on goals, called management by objectives (MBO), to strengthen his oversight of the executive branch. He directed twenty-one departments and agencies to prepare rank-order lists of their principal objectives. After the Office of Management and Budget reviewed the lists, the president approved objectives for each reporting unit. These presidential objectives then became the standard for monitoring the performance of the units. MBO differed from the planning process of PPBS and ZBB in that it focused first on immediate objectives, then on intermediate objectives that could be achieved in a fiscal year, and finally on long-term goals.[115] MBO was primarily useful within departments and agencies for routine oversight of agreed-on actions. It helped to spot problems, and it facilitated communications between the departments and OMB. What it could not do was aid in the choice between objectives. In this respect, it was outside the political process and the concerns of the president.

MBO lapsed into disuse under Carter. Aside from ZBB, Carter's major planning effort was to require agencies to use a multiyear framework in planning their budget requests. The objective was to integrate planning with the budget cycle. Other than to continue multiyear budgeting, Reagan demonstrated little interest in planning. He appeared to believe that domestic policy planning was socialistic and incompatible with a free market economy. Reagan's immediate successor, George Bush, although neglecting domestic policy planning, was committed to and actively involved in foreign and defense policy planning. Generally, these areas have been more successful than domestic policy planning, and future presidents will always need to engage in national security planning. Clinton had an intense interest in domestic and economic policy and an understanding of planning. His proposals for reforming health care and the welfare system included planning that linked them to the five-year deficit reduction that was integral to the 1994 budget. But Clinton exhibited little by way of planning after the Republicans assumed control of Congress in 1995. Moving toward a balanced budget then became the overriding concern. In the administration's terminal years, creating a legacy was more important than planning.

With a heavy emphasis on pursuing legislative victories during its early months in office, the administration of George W. Bush did not demonstrate much attention to planning, with the notable exception of developing a coherent energy policy. Just two weeks into the new administration, Bush named Vice President Cheney to head a task force that released its recommendations on May 17, 2001, after meeting largely in secret. The administration's proposals primarily focused on ways to increase the supply of energy rather than conserve its use—encouraging oil and natural gas exploration, building electric transmission infrastructure, encouraging use of coal, and supporting nuclear power generation.[116] But the complex plan encountered enormous resistance in the face of electric outages in California, rising gas prices, and concerns about environmental protections. And questions arose whether an "energy industry that put its financial backing solidly behind Bush's election has received a plan that offers support for every major form of energy production and distribution."[117] Even more difficult tasks of planning would lie ahead.

Conclusion

Can the president lead the executive branch? Many of the studies discussed in this chapter raise doubts about the issue.[118] Although presidents have substantial formal powers and managerial resources, all chief executives wrestle with the problem of controlling their own branch of government. Their capacity to direct its many departments and agencies in the implementation of presidential policies is limited by bureaucratic complexity and fragmentation, conflict between the presidency and the bureaucracy, external pressure and influence on the bureaucracy, and the extreme difficulty of establishing an effective management system within the government.

Important milestones in this effort can be found throughout the twentieth century. Roosevelt created the Executive Office of the President in 1939, providing his successors with a critical group of presidential loyalists and policy experts independent of bureaucratic pressures. Johnson's enthusiastic endorsement of the program planning budgeting system in 1966 started a series of experiments in using the budget as a planning instrument. Nixon's centralization of decisions in the White House is a strategy others have emulated. Carter established the potential as well as the limits of using reorganization as a management tool, and his sponsorship of the Civil Service Reform Act of 1978 created a new cadre of presidential allies in the civil service.

Ronald Reagan came closest to assembling these instruments of control into a coherent administrative strategy, a consensus that prevails even two decades after he assumed office.[119] Reagan's centralized control of appointments fashioned a relatively unified "team" by making ideological compatibility with his goals the principal criterion for selection. Reagan also used cabinet councils as a means to link the White House staff with the cabinet officials in directing policy efforts. Most important, Reagan used the budget to enforce presidential spending priorities on departments and agencies. In the face of strong pressures to reduce spending, Reagan reversed the traditional pattern of budget preparation from the bottom up, in which agencies attempt to protect their bases, and instituted top-down budgeting, with presidential and OMB decisions being determinative.[120] Finally, Reagan attempted to accomplish policy change administratively wherever possible. This involved establishing procedures for review of regulations by OMB, diminishing the intensity of regulatory enforcement, and reinterpreting agency functions and relations with clientele in accordance with the administration's ideology.[121]

Nonetheless, Reagan encountered substantial difficulties. Interest groups and Congress present major external obstacles to presidential control and direction. Reagan overcame these to some extent by virtue of his temperament, leadership style, and perhaps most important, his limited, well-defined agenda, which tried to curtail rather than expand the role of government. Yet his detached, "laid back" administrative style was a major factor leading to the most difficult event of his presidency, the Iran-contra scandal. Reagan's approach to his executive responsibilities should indicate to future presidents that leadership of the president's own branch is a difficult task at best and that there is no way to accomplish it that will ensure effectiveness and please everyone involved.

Each president faces anew the challenges of asserting control. Reagan's successes did not extend to his successors, though they did provide guidance for future efforts. No doubt, George W. Bush and his White House aides will be attentive students.

NOTES

1. Richard Rose, "Government against Subgovernments: A European Perspective on Washington," in *Presidents and Prime Ministers*, ed. Richard Rose and Ezra N. Suleiman (Washington, D.C.: American Enterprise Institute, 1980), 339.

2. James P. Pfiffner challenges this viewpoint and maintains that presidents tend to overestimate the opposition they will get from the bureaucracy. See Pfiffner, "Political Appointees and Career Executives: The Democracy-Bureaucracy Nexus in the Third Century," *Public Administration Review* (January–February 1987): 57–65.

3. Joseph A. Califano Jr., *A Presidential Nation* (New York: Norton, 1975), 23.

4. Hugh Heclo, *A Government of Strangers* (Washington, D.C.: Brookings, 1977), 7.

5. Ibid.

6. Richard Rose, *Managing Presidential Objectives* (New York: Free Press, 1976), 160.

7. Francis E. Rourke, *Bureaucracy, Politics, and Public Policy*, 3d ed. (Boston: Little, Brown, 1984), 32.

8. Rose, *Managing Presidential Objectives*, 13–20.

9. Aaron Wildavsky, *The New Politics of the Budgetary Process*, 2d ed. (New York: HarperCollins, 1992), 87–88.

10. David A. Stockman, *The Triumph of Politics: Why the Reagan Revolution Failed* (New York: Harper and Row, 1986).

11. Paul C. Light, *Thickening Government: Federal Hierarchy and the Diffusion of Accountability* (Washington, D.C.: Brookings, 1995), 32–33.

12. Heclo, *A Government of Strangers*.

13. Jeffrey E. Cohen, *The Politics of the U.S. Cabinet: Representation in the Executive Branch, 1789–1984* (Pittsburgh: University of Pittsburgh Press, 1988), chaps. 3, 4.

14. Thomas E. Cronin, *The State of the Presidency*, 2d ed. (Boston: Little, Brown, 1980), 282.

15. Cohen, *The Politics of the U.S. Cabinet*, 136–139.

16. James P. Pfiffner, *The Strategic Presidency*, 2d ed. (Lawrence: University Press of Kansas, 1996), 57.

17. G. Calvin Mackenzie, *The Politics of Presidential Appointments* (New York: Free Press, 1981).

18. Thomas J. Weko, *The Politicizing Presidency: The White House Personnel Office, 1948–1994* (Lawrence: University Press of Kansas, 1995), 149–151, 157.

19. Richard P. Nathan, *The Administrative Presidency* (New York: Wiley, 1983), 74–76.

20. Joel D. Aberbach, "A Reinvented Government, or the Same Old Government?" in *The Clinton Legacy*, ed. Colin Campbell and Bert A. Rockman (New York: Chatham House Publishers, 2000), 120.

21. Weko, *The Politicizing Presidency*, 100, 101–102, 102–103.

22. "At the 200-Day Mark, Presidential Appointments Process Again Bogs Down," Presidential Appointment Initiative, Brookings Institution, April 2001, www.appointee.brookings.org/news/100days_pressrelease.htm.

23. Clay Johnson interviewed by James A. Barnes, "Selecting the Players," *National Journal,* June 23, 2001, 1874–1876.

24. Mark W. Huddleston and William W. Boyer, *The Higher Civil Service in the United States: Quest for Reform* (Pittsburgh: University of Pittsburgh Press, 1996); Edie N. Goldenberg, "The Permanent Government in an Era of Retrenchment and Redirection," in *The Reagan Presidency and the Governing of America,* ed. Lester M. Salamon and Michael S. Lund (Washington, D.C.: Urban Institute Press, 1984), 381–404.

25. Chester A. Newland, "A Midterm Appraisal—The Reagan Presidency, Limited Government and Political Administration," *Public Administration Review* (January–February 1983): 15–16.

26. *Kendall v. United States,* 37 U.S. (12 Pet.) 524 (1838).

27. *Panama Refining Co. v. Ryan,* 293 U.S. 338 (1934); *Schechter Poultry Co. v. United States,* 295 U.S. 495 (1935).

28. Louis Fisher, *Constitutional Conflicts between Congress and the President,* 3d ed. (Lawrence: University Press of Kansas, 1991), 98; Theodore J. Lowi, *The End of Liberalism,* 2d ed. (New York: Norton, 1979), chap. 5.

29. Morris P. Fiorina, *Congress: Keystone of the Washington Establishment,* 2d ed. (New Haven: Yale University Press, 1989).

30. Rourke, *Bureaucracy, Politics, and Public Policy,* 74.

31. Carl M. Cannon, "The Old-Timers," *National Journal,* May 22, 1999, 1387.

32. Ibid., 1388. The average tenure of cabinet members for the past six administrations based on data from Shirley Ann Warshaw reported in *National Journal* was Nixon 1.73 years, Ford 2.04, Carter 2.47, Reagan 3.27, Bush 2.52, Clinton 3.36.

33. Cohen, *The Politics of the U.S. Cabinet,* 173–176.

34. Nelson W. Polsby, "Presidential Cabinet-Making Lessons for the Political System," *Political Science Quarterly* (spring 1978): 15–25.

35. Pfiffner, *The Strategic Presidency,* 41–42, 65–66; Stephen Hess, *Organizing the Presidency,* 2d ed. (Washington, D.C.: Brookings, 1988), 200; Shirley Anne Warshaw, *Powersharing: White House–Cabinet Relations in the Modern Presidency* (Albany: State University of New York Press, 1996) 228–233.

36. Richard F. Fenno Jr., *The President's Cabinet* (New York: Vintage Books, 1959), 132.

37. Ronald Brownstein and Dick Kirschten, "Cabinet Power," *National Journal,* June 28, 1986, 1582–1589.

38. Burt Solomon, "A Cabinet Member Gets the Boot . . . And More Turnover Seems Likely," *National Journal,* December 22, 1990, 3098–3099.

39. James A. Barnes, "Like His Home-State Razorbacks . . . Clinton's Cabinet Plays to Win," *National Journal,* April 9, 1994, 852–853. Also see Warshaw, *Powersharing,* 198–227.

40. Lizette Alvarez and Eric Schmitt, "Cheney Ever More Powerful as Crucial Link to Congress," *New York Times,* May 13, 2001, A1. On the general operation of the administration, see John F. Harris and Dan Balz, "Conflicting Image of Bush Emerges," *Washington Post,* April 28, 2001, A1. Also see Alexis Simendinger, "Stepping into Power," *National Journal,* January 27, 2001, 246–248.

41. Cronin, *The State of the Presidency,* 270–272.

42. Ibid., 282–285.

43. Cohen, in *The Politics of the U.S. Cabinet,* finds a distinction between the older and the newer outer departments based on "the importance of interests in creating the department and on the complexity of its interest group environment" (144). The older departments—Agriculture, Commerce, Labor, and Interior—were created in response to demands from single interests that continue to provide them with some protection from presidential control. The newer departments tend to operate in

"more complex interest group environments" that may result in "intradepartmental conflict among advocates of the competing interests" (138, 139).

44. Warshaw, *Powersharing,* 167.

45. Andrew Rosenthal, "Sununu's Out and Skinner Is In, but White House Troubles Persist," *New York Times,* February 11, 1992, Al, A13. Also see Burt Solomon, "Bush's Renovated Inner Circle Has a Bit of a Reaganesque Look," *National Journal,* February 8, 1992, 346–347.

46. John Hart, *The Presidential Branch: From Washington to Clinton,* 2d ed. (Chatham, N.J.: Chatham House, 1995), 91.

47. Margaret C. Hermann, "Advice and Advisers in the Clinton Presidency: The Impact of Leadership Style," in *The Clinton Presidency: Campaigning, Governing, and the Psychology of Leadership,* ed. Stanley A. Renshon (Boulder, Colo.: Westview, 1995), 157.

48. Ibid., 159.

49. Margaret La Montagne, who served as an adviser to Governor Bush in Texas, was named director of the Domestic Policy Council, and Lawrence Lindsey, a campaign adviser, became director of the National Economic Council. See *National Journal,* June 23, 2001, 1889, 1894.

50. Fisher, *Constitutional Conflicts,* chaps. 2, 3.

51. Committee on Governmental Affairs, United States Senate, *Policy and Supporting Positions* (Washington, D.C.: Government Printing Office, 2000), also known as the "plum book." In a fuller discussion, Bradley H. Patterson and James P. Pfiffner, "The White House Office of Presidential Personnel," *Presidential Studies Quarterly* 31 no. 3 (September 2001) 420. Patterson and Pfiffner identify 1,125 full-time positions subject to confirmation, including 185 ambassadors, 94 district attorneys, 94 U.S. marshals, 15 in international organizations, and 4 in the legislative branch.

52. *Buckley v. Valeo,* 421 U.S. 1 (1976).

53. In 1973, President Nixon named Howard J. Phillips acting director of the Office of Economic Opportunity (OEO), an agency that Nixon planned to dismantle. Phillips began to phase out its programs and withhold funds from it. Sen. Harrison A. Williams, D-N.J., took legal action to force Nixon either to submit Phillips's name to the Senate for confirmation or to stop dismantling the OEO. A U.S. court of appeals ruled that Phillips was illegally holding office and enjoined him from further actions. See James P. Pfiffner, *The President, the Budget, and Congress: Impoundment and the 1974 Budget Act* (Boulder, Colo.: Westview, 1974), 116–117. The decision did not settle the issue though the effort was thwarted.

54. Three notable examples are the Senate's rejection of former senator John Tower, R-Texas, to be secretary of defense in 1989, its long delay in acting on the nomination of Dr. Henry Foster Jr. to be surgeon general of the United States, and its narrow support in 2001 for former senator John Ashcroft, R-Mo., to become attorney general. Tower had antagonized several of his former colleagues during his service in the chamber and was objectionable to many Democratic senators because of his hawkish views. Foster, a distinguished obstetrician and gynecologist, became a political football in the debate over abortion. The White House Personnel Office, in an inexplicable blunder, neglected to ask Foster if he had ever performed abortions until after the president announced the nomination on February 2, 1995. When Foster gave three different answers and explained them as due to a faulty memory, abortion opponents made the nomination a cause célèbre, and Sens. Robert Dole and Phil Gramm, both Republican presidential hopefuls, tried to outdo each other in their opposition to the nomination by threatening to keep it from coming to a vote in the Senate. The abortion issue then became entwined with Foster's credibility. Following confirmation hearings at which Foster performed very credibly, the Senate Labor and Human Resources Committee on May 24, 1995, approved the nomination by a 10–8

vote. A successful Republican filibuster prevented the nomination from coming to an up or down vote of the full Senate. John Ashcroft was a vehemently outspoken opponent of abortion whom Democrats suspected would not enforce the laws. After a surprisingly bitter debate, unusual in that senators seldom criticize one of their own, the full membership confirmed Ashcroft by a vote of 58–42.

55. Christopher J. Deering, "Damned if You Do and Damned if You Don't: The Senate's Role in the Appointment Process," in *The In-and-Outers*, ed. G. Calvin McKenzie (Baltimore: Johns Hopkins University Press, 1987), 119. Also see G. Calvin McKenzie, ed., *Innocent until Nominated* (Washington, D.C.: Brookings, 2001).

56. Anthony Lake withdrew from consideration as nominee to head the CIA in March 1997 after concluding that he would be subjected to endless delays and partisan criticism. Juliana Gruenwald, "Tenet Appears Likely to Win Confirmation as CIA Chief," *Congressional Quarterly Weekly Report*, March 22, 1997, 712–714. On the Holbrooke nomination, see Philip Shenon, "Holbrooke Nomination Passes One Hurdle but Faces Another," *New York Times*, July 1, 1999, A6; Philip Shenon, "Let's Slow Down on Holbrooke's Case, Lott Says," *New York Times*, July 23, 1999, A9; Eric Schmitt, "When Nomination Turns to Wrangling to Impasse," *New York Times*, July 28, 1999, A16; Miles A. Pomper, "Holbrooke Confirmed as U.N. Envoy," *CQ Weekly*, August 7, 1999, 1961–1962.

57. Kirk Victor, "Executive Branch End Run," *National Journal*, May 16, 1998, 1112–1114.

58. On the Lee nomination, see Aberbach, "A Reinvented Government," 124–126; Richard L. Berke and Steven A. Holmes, "In Confirmation Delays, a New G.O.P. Strategy," *New York Times*, November 11, 1997, A14; John M. Broder, "While Congress Is Away, Clinton Plays with Idea of an End Run," *New York Times*, November 24, 1997, A12; Dan Carney, "Battle over Lee Could Escalate with Recess Appointment," *Congressional Quarterly Weekly Report*, November 29, 1997, 2955; David Byrd, "Affirmatively Acting," *National Journal*, March 6, 1999, 612–616.

59. *Myers v. United States*, 272 U.S. 52 (1926).

60. *Humphrey's Executor v. United States*, 295 U.S. 602 (1935).

61. Fisher, *Constitutional Conflicts*, 79.

62. Elizabeth Drew, *On the Edge: The Clinton Presidency* (New York: Simon and Schuster, 1994).

63. Kenneth R. Mayer, *With the Stroke of a Pen: Executive Orders and Presidential Power* (Princeton: Princeton University Press, 2001), 4.

64. Ibid., 223.

65. *J.W. Hampton and Co. v. United States*, 276 U.S. 394 (1928).

66. For excellent discussions of presidential use of executive orders in the areas of information secrecy and intelligence organization as well as in civil rights, see Mayer, *With the Stroke of a Pen*, chaps. 5, 6.

67. *Amalgamated Meat Cutters v. Connally*, 337 F. Supp. 737 (1971).

68. *Hirabayashi v. United States*, 320 U.S. 581 (1943); *Korematsu v. United States*, 323 U.S. 214 (1944).

69. For an interpretation that Clinton relied more heavily on such instruments after the Republicans controlled Congress, see Aberbach, "A Reinvented Government," 128; and Alexis Simendinger, "The Paper Wars," *National Journal*, July 25, 1998, 1732–1739. Some reports confuse distinctions among the different forms of unilateral presidential action rather than adhering to the definition of executive orders maintained by the National Archives and Records Administration.

70. Mayer, *With the Stroke of a Pen*, 70.

71. Ibid., Table 3.3, 82.

72. Ibid., 102.

73. *Youngstown Sheet and Tube Co. v. Sawyer,* 343 U.S. 579 (1952).

74. Lawrence R. Jacobs and Robert Y. Shapiro, "Public Opinion in Clinton's First Year: Leadership and Responsiveness," in *The Clinton Presidency,* 201.

75. *Immigration and Naturalization Service v. Chadha,* 462 U.S. 919 (1983).

76. Joseph Cooper, "Postscript on the Congressional Veto," *Political Science Quarterly* (fall 1983): 427–430; Barbara Hinkson Craig, *The Legislative Veto: Congressional Control of Regulation* (Boulder, Colo.: Westview, 1983), 139–150; Fisher, *Constitutional Conflicts,* 152.

77. Fisher, *Constitutional Conflicts,* 150–152.

78. Louis Fisher, "Judicial Misjudgments about the Lawmaking Process: The Legislative Veto Case," *Public Administration Review* (November–December 1985): 709–710.

79. Richard M. Pious, *The American Presidency* (New York: Basic Books, 1979), 256–257.

80. Allen Schick, "The Road to PPB: The States of Budget Reform," *Public Administration Review* (December 1966): 243–258.

81. Wildavsky, *The New Politics of the Budgetary Process,* 436–440.

82. Allen Schick, *The Federal Budget: Politics, Policy, Process* (Washington, D.C.: Brookings, 1995), 2–4.

83. Bob Woodward, *The Agenda: Inside the Clinton White House* (New York: Simon and Schuster, 1994).

84. Daniel J. Palazzo, *Done Deal? The Politics of the 1997 Budget Agreement* (Chatham, N.J.: Chatham House, 1999).

85. Louis Fisher, *Presidential Spending Power* (Princeton: Princeton University Press, 1979), chap. 4.

86. Ibid., 148.

87. Vivian Vale, "The Obligation to Spend: Presidential Impoundment of Congressional Appropriations," *Political Studies* (1977): 508–532.

88. Fisher, *Constitutional Conflicts,* 196.

89. Pfiffner, *The President, The Budget, and Congress,* 40–44.

90. Jonathan Rauch, "Power of the Purse," *National Journal,* May 24, 1986, 1261.

91. William J. Clinton, President of the United States, et al., Appellants v. City of New York, et al. (1998). The case can be found at supct.law.cornell.edu/supct/html/97-1374.25.html.

92. Peri Arnold concludes his authoritative study of "the managerial presidency" by observing that "no modern president has fully managed the executive branch." He further argues that the "managerial conception of the presidency is untenable" because it "places impossible obligations on presidents" and creates unrealistic "public expectations of presidential performance." Peri E. Arnold, *Making the Managerial Presidency: Comprehensive Reorganization Planning, 1905–1980* (Princeton: Princeton University Press, 1986), 361–362.

93. Hess, *Organizing the Presidency,* 230–231.

94. Jack W. Germond and Jules Witcover, "Bush Left with Little Room for Error," *National Journal,* December 22, 1990, 3104.

95. Rosenthal, "Sununu's Out and Skinner Is In."

96. Fred I. Greenstein, "Political Style and Political Leadership: The Case of Bill Clinton," in *The Clinton Presidency,* 141.

97. Ibid., 142.

98. Burt Solomon, "Drawn and Redrawn . . . The Lines in the West Wing Get Blurrier," *National Journal,* January 15, 1994, 134; and "Crisscrossed with Connections . . . West Wing Is a Networker's Dream," *National Journal,* January 29, 1994, 256–257.

99. Burt Solomon, "Clinton's New Taskmaster Takes Charge," *National Journal,* August 6, 1994, 1872.

100. Todd S. Purdum, "The Ungreening of the White House Staff," *New York Times,* December 22, 1996, E10.

101. Alexis Simendinger, "Stepping into Power," *National Journal,* January 27, 2001, 247.

102. Stuart Rothenberg, "There's No Question about Who's in Charge at Bush's White House," *Roll Call,* March 26, 2001, www.rollcall.com.

103. Terry M. Moe, "The Politicized Presidency," in *The New Direction in American Politics,* ed. John E. Chubb and Paul E. Peterson (Washington, D.C.: Brookings, 1985), 235–271.

104. Samuel Kernell, "The Creed and Reality of Modern White House Management," in *Chief of Staff: Twenty-Five Years of Managing the Presidency,* ed. Samuel Kernell and Samuel L. Popkin (Berkeley: University of California Press, 1986), 228.

105. John R. Dempsey, "Carter Reorganization: A Midterm Appraisal," *Public Administration Review* (January–February 1979): 74–78; Arnold, *Making the Managerial Presidency,* chap. 10.

106. Herbert Kaufman, "Reflections on Administrative Reorganization," in *Setting National Priorities: The 1978 Budget,* ed. Joseph A. Pechman (Washington, D.C.: Brookings, 1977), 403.

107. Dempsey, "Carter Reorganization," 75.

108. Ronald C. Moe, "The 'Reinventing Government' Exercise: Misinterpreting the Problem, Misjudging the Consequences," *Public Administration Review* (March–April 1994): 112.

109. David Osborne and Ted Gaebler, *Reinventing Government: How the Entrepreneurial Spirit Is Transforming the Public Sector from Schoolhouse to State House, City Hall to Pentagon* (Reading, Mass.: Addison-Wesley, 1992), 111.

110. Donald F. Kett, *Reinventing Government: A Fifth Year Report Card,* Center for Public Management Report 98–1 (Washington, D.C.: Brookings Institution, September 1998).

111. In "The 'Reinventing Government' Exercise," Ronald Moe argues that Clinton's effort substitutes results for processes and amounts to abandonment of public law as the basis of political accountability (112). The political scientist James Q. Wilson doubts whether in the era of big government "political accountability can any longer be equated with presidential power." James Q. Wilson, "Reinventing Public Administration," *P.S.: Political Science and Politics* (December 1994): 671. The famed management consultant Peter Drucker called for a new theory that "asks what the proper functions of government might be and could be . . . [and] what results government should be held accountable for." Peter Drucker, "Really Reinventing Government," *Atlantic Monthly* (February 1995): 61.

112. Aaron Wildavsky, *Speaking Truth to Power* (Boston: Little, Brown, 1979), 120.

113. Fred V. Malek, *Washington's Hidden Tragedy* (New York: Free Press, 1978), 129.

114. Wildavsky, *Speaking Truth to Power,* 129.

115. Rose, *Managing Presidential Objectives,* chap. 6.

116. Peter Behr, "Energy Plan to Fuel Long Fight; at Issue Is Environmental Cost of Plentiful, Cheaper Power," *Washington Post,* May 15, 2001, A9.

117. Peter Behr, "Bush Places His Bet on Energy Industry," *Washington Post,* May 18, 2001, E1.

118. See, for example, Arnold, *Making the Managerial Presidency;* Colin Campbell, *Managing the Presidency: Carter, Reagan, and the Search for Executive Harmony* (Pittsburgh: University of Pittsburgh Press, 1986); and Rose, *Managing Presidential Objectives.* Also see Walter Williams, *Mismanaging America: The Rise of the Anti-Analytic Presidency* (Lawrence: University Press of Kansas, 1990).

119. Nathan, *The Administrative Presidency.*

120. Allen Schick, "The Budget as an Instrument of Presidential Policy," in *The Reagan Presidency and the Governing of America*, 113.

121. Lester M. Salamon and Alan J. Abramson, "Governance: The Politics of Retrenchment," in *The Reagan Record*, ed. John L. Palmer and Isabell V. Sawhill (Cambridge, Mass.: Ballinger, 1984), 97; Joseph A. Pika and Norman C. Thomas, "The President as Institution Builder: The Reagan Case," *Governance* (October 1990): 444–447.

SUGGESTED READINGS

Arnold, Peri E. *Making the Managerial Presidency: Comprehensive Reorganization Planning, 1905–1980.* Princeton: Princeton University Press, 1986.

Campbell, Colin. *Managing the Presidency: Carter, Reagan, and the Search for Executive Harmony.* Pittsburgh: University of Pittsburgh Press, 1986.

Cohen, Jeffrey E. *The Politics of the U.S. Cabinet: Representation in the Executive Branch, 1789–1984.* Pittsburgh: University of Pittsburgh Press, 1988.

Cronin, Thomas E. *The State of the Presidency.* 2d ed. Boston: Little, Brown, 1980.

Fisher, Louis. *Constitutional Conflicts between Congress and the President.* 3d ed., rev. Lawrence: University Press of Kansas, 1991.

Hart, John. *The Presidential Branch: From Washington to Clinton.* 2d ed. Chatham, N.J.: Chatham House, 1995.

Hess, Stephen. *Organizing the Presidency.* 2d ed. Washington, D.C.: Brookings, 1988.

Light, Paul C. *Thickening Government: Federal Hierarchy and the Diffusion of Accountability.* Washington, D.C.: Brookings, 1995.

Mayer, Kenneth R. *With the Stroke of a Pen: Executive Orders and Presidential Power.* Princeton: Princeton University Press, 2001.

Nathan, Richard P. *The Administrative Presidency.* New York: Wiley, 1983.

Pfiffner, James P. *The Strategic Presidency.* 2d ed. Lawrence: University Press of Kansas, 1996.

___. *The Managerial Presidency.* 2d ed. College Station: Texas A&M University Press, 1999.

Warshaw, Shirley Anne, *Powersharing: White House–Cabinet Relations in the Modern Presidency.* Albany: State University of New York Press, 1996.

Weko, Thomas J. *The Politicizing Presidency: The White House Personnel Office, 1948–1994.* Lawrence: University Press of Kansas, 1995.

7 JUDICIAL POLITICS

Controversy over how to count contested ballots in Florida led to court cases that culminated in Bush v. Gore. *Canvassing board members, such as Judge Robert Rosenberg of Broward County, worked long and hard during their manual recount of those disputed ballots.*

HIGH DRAMA GRIPPED THE NATION ON December 12, 2000, when a 5–4 majority of the U.S. Supreme Court ruled that the manual recounts ordered by the Florida Supreme Court to determine the outcome of the contested presidential election between George W. Bush and Al Gore could not proceed. By calling a halt to the recounts, the Court effectively decided the outcome of the election: the original (and some said flawed) machine-tabulated results that gave Bush a razor-thin margin of victory would stand. The ruling precluded further challenges by Gore, who argued that the machines failed to count the ballots of many voters who had intended to vote for him.[1]

In all, seven of the Court's nine members agreed that Florida's "clear intent of the voter" standard governing manual recounts violated the equal protection clause of the U.S. Constitution because it was too imprecise.[2] Different counties could use different standards to determine voter intent, thereby leading to "arbitrary and disparate treatment" of members of the Florida electorate. In other words, identical ballots could lead to one person's vote being counted in one county but not another (depending upon whether or not such things as a "hanging," a "dimpled," and a "pregnant" chad were thought to reveal the clear intent of the voter). The Court majority's per curiam decision—an unsigned opinion used either when the conclusion reached by the Court is so straightforward that no extended discussion is needed or (as in this case) when the Court is so fragmented that it can only reach agreement on the narrow result announced—held that this lack of a uniform standard for counting ballots did not provide "sufficient guarantees of equal treatment" and that the recount therefore violated the one-person, one-vote principle set forth by the Court in 1960s voting rights cases such as *Reynolds v. Sims* and *Gray v. Sanders*.[3]

Nonetheless, the seven members of the Court who joined the per curiam decision remained bitterly divided about whether such a violation could be overcome and whether a "safe harbor" deadline imposed by Congress in an 1887 law precluded recounts after that deadline (which happened to be the same day that the Supreme Court issued its ruling). The safe harbor deadline guarantees that a state's election results are binding on Congress if the state produces a conclusive result at least six days prior to the date when the electors are scheduled to meet (*U.S. Code,* vol. 3, sec. 5), which in 2000 was December 18.

Of the seven members of the Court who joined the per curiam decision, five voted to call a halt to the recounts. This five-person majority (William Rehnquist, Sandra Day O'Connor, Antonin Scalia, Anthony Kennedy, and Clarence Thomas—all of whom had been appointed by either Ronald Reagan or the first President George Bush) concluded that the safe harbor deadline was binding and that no recounts could take place after that date. As they put it, *U.S. Code,* vol. 3, sec. 5, "requires that any controversy or contest that is designed to lead to a conclusive selection of electors be completed by December 12."[4] According to these five, since it was already December 12, efforts to establish uniform standards that would not violate equal protection were fruitless because there would be no time to proceed with a recount. A slim 5–4 majority therefore ruled that recounts could not proceed and that the original machine counts already certified by the Florida secretary of state be considered official.

Bush v. Gore is a very complicated decision that produced four separate dissents: each dissenting judge (Stephen Breyer, Ruth Bader Ginsburg, David Souter, and John Paul Stevens) wrote one and was joined by one or more of the other three on various points within the dissents. Two of these dissents came from justices who had recognized a potential equal protection problem and actually joined part of the per curiam decision (Souter, appointed by President Bush, and Breyer, appointed by President Clinton). Souter and Breyer broke ranks from the other five justices who had joined the per curiam decision and dissented because they felt that the equal protection violation could be corrected by establishing a uniform standard for determining the clear intent of the voter and that recounts should then continue. Both Souter and Breyer insisted that the majority's emphasis on a rigid deadline for counting votes was misplaced. They dismissed, in Souter's dissent, the deadline issue as "not serious" because "no State is required to conform to sec. 5 if it cannot do that (for whatever reason); the sanction for failing to satisfy the conditions of sec. 5 is simply loss of what has been called its 'safe harbor.' And even that determination is to be made, if made anywhere, in the Congress."[5] Souter and Breyer therefore concluded that there "is no justification for denying the State the opportunity to try to count all the disputed ballots now."[6] As Souter put it, "Unlike the majority, I see no warrant for this Court to assume that Florida could not possibly comply with this [equal protection] requirement before the date set for the meeting of electors, December 18."[7]

The remaining two members of the Court who had not joined the per curiam decision (Stevens, appointed by Gerald R. Ford, and Ginsburg, appointed by President Clinton) agreed with Souter and Breyer that the five-person majority had misinterpreted section 5 and thereby established an artificial deadline. Both agreed that the recounts should proceed. All four dissenters agreed that the Supreme Court should not have accepted the case for review.[8] As Justice Ginsburg wrote: "The extraordinary setting of this case has obscured the ordinary principle that dictates its proper resolution: Federal courts defer to state high courts' interpretations of their own state law. This principle reflects the core of federalism."[9]

Ginsburg and Stevens differed from the other two dissenters, however, by rejecting the view that the existing recount procedure violated equal protection. That is why neither Ginsburg nor Stevens joined the per curiam decision. As Ginsburg put it, "I cannot agree that the recount adopted by the Florida court, flawed as it may be, would yield a result any less fair or precise than the certification that preceded that recount."[10] Even Breyer, who had recognized a potential equal protection violation and joined the per curiam decision, admitted in his dissent (joined by Ginsburg and Stevens) that the majority's remedy "harms the very fairness interests the Court is attempting to protect."[11] Justice Stevens explained why: the majority's decision to stop the recount "effectively orders the disenfranchisement of an unknown number of voters whose ballots reveal their intent—and are therefore legal votes under state law—but were for some reason rejected by ballot-counting machines."[12]

E. Joshua Rosenkranz, president of the Brennan Center for Justice at New York University's School of Law, made a similar argument. He said that the majority never acknowledged that "the biggest disparity among Florida voters resulted from using different kinds of voting machines from one county to another. Voter A casts his or her vote easily, simply and reliably, based on the latest optical scanning technology," he explained, "while his neighbor, Voter B, cast his or her vote on an archaic, dysfunctional, error-prone voting machine. By some estimates, Voter B's vote was up to 10 times as likely to be thrown out as Voter A's. What's more, the error-prone machines were more likely to be used in communities of color: just the sort of inequality *Baker v. Carr* was designed to fix."[13]

Indeed, Justice Stevens argued that if the majority really wanted to apply equal protection as rigidly as it seemed to claim, it should also call into question a wide range of other accepted practices, such as "Florida's decision to leave to each county the determination of what balloting system to employ" (since some ballots led to more "undercounts" than others).[14] The majority, however, claimed that its use of equal protection was confined only to this particular recount in this particular case.[15] As Rosenkranz put it, this caveat transformed the majority's "apparent love affair with political equality" into "just a one-night stand"[16]—an embrace of equal protection designed to achieve a political outcome that the majority favored.

Reasonable men and women can disagree about which of the positions articulated by the various justices in *Bush v. Gore* is correct. Nonetheless, a variety of factors led many people to repeat the argument that the Court's decision was driven more by politics than by legal reasoning. Most legal observers were surprised that the Supreme Court agreed to hear the case in the first place, since judicial restraint usually precludes review of this type of "political question"— especially before the issue has been exhausted in the political arena.

The 5–4 split in *Bush v. Gore* also helped to create the impression that the decision was politically motivated: the Court's more conservative members voted in the majority to stop the recount and the more liberal members dissented. The reasoning used by the justices reinforced the image of political motivation. Justices on both sides seemed to alter their positions to arrive at their results. Members of the majority who normally embraced states' rights and who usually deferred to state court interpretations of state law seemed all too eager to intervene. Dissenters, who were typically more critical of states' rights, now seemed converted to the cause.

Many commentators were particularly distressed by the majority's equal protection claim, arguing that it seemed to fly in the face of the Court's precedents. Even some of Bush's own lawyers thought it was a weak argument when they first considered raising it.[17] As legal theorist Ronald Dworkin has written, the equal protection clause was designed to protect against discrimination: "it condemns not any difference in the way a state's law treats different citizens, but only certain distinctions that put some citizens, in advance, at a disadvantage against others." Dworkin went on to explain why the "clear intent of the voter" standard governing the recount did not violate equal protection:

Voters who indent a chad without punching it clean through run a risk that a vote they did not mean to make will be counted if they live in a county that uses a generous interpretation of the "clear intent" statute; or they run a risk that a vote they meant to make will be discarded if they live in a county that uses a less generous interpretation. But since neither of these risks is worse than the other—both threaten a citizen's power to make his or her vote count—the abstract standard discriminates against no one, and no question of equal protection is raised.[18]

In a stinging portion of his dissent in *Bush v. Gore,* Justice Stevens (joined by Ginsburg and Breyer) emphasized that the Court should not have agreed to hear the case and argued that its decision to do so had undermined its legitimacy. "It is confidence in the men and women who administer the judicial system that is the true backbone of the rule of law," he wrote. "Time will one day heal the wound to that confidence that will be inflicted by today's decision. One thing, however, is certain. Although we may never know with complete certainty the identity of the winner of this year's presidential election, the identity of the loser is perfectly clear. It is the Nation's confidence in the judge as an impartial guardian of the rule of law."[19]

Never before had the Supreme Court so directly determined the outcome of a presidential election through one of its rulings. Backlash against the Court was swift and harsh. Democrats chided the majority's ruling as a blatantly political, conservative activist decision. Thousands of angry letters poured into the Supreme Court. Several members of the Supreme Court bar (those who are eligible to argue cases before the Court) resigned in protest—a response that court officials had not seen before. Reports claimed that the case had polarized law clerks for the justices: those for the more liberal justices were said to be "dismayed at the court's role in the case," while clerks for the more conservative justices viewed the majority's ruling as "one of integrity" and were angered by the criticism of the Court.[20] When Justices Kennedy and Thomas appeared before a congressional committee on March 29, 2001, Rep. Jose E. Serrano, D-N.Y., told them that his constituents—most of whom were black or Latino—were "angry, bitter, and disenchanted" by *Bush v. Gore.*[21] Kennedy and Thomas defended the ruling, as had Chief Justice William Rehnquist in a public speech on January 1, 2001.

One of the most novel responses to *Bush v. Gore* came from Yale law professor Bruce Ackerman, who suggested that the Senate should refuse to confirm any of the new President Bush's Supreme Court nominees because of the ruling. "In our democracy," he wrote,

there is one basic check on a runaway Court: presidential elections. And a majority of the justices have conspired to eliminate this check. The Supreme Court cannot be permitted to arrange for its own succession. To allow this president to serve as the Court's agent is a fundamental violation of separation of powers. It is one thing for unelected judges to exercise the sovereign power of judicial review; it's quite another for them to insulate themselves yet further from popular control. When sitting justices die or retire, the Senate should refuse to confirm any nominations offered up by President Bush.[22]

When George W. Bush entered office, most Court observers believed that during his presidency he would have the opportunity to appoint at least two or three justices to the Supreme Court. In January 2001, John Paul Stevens was eighty years old and had served on the Court since 1975. Although appointed by a Republican (Gerald Ford), Stevens had become a solid member of the Court's more liberal block. William Rehnquist was seventy-six years old and a leader of

Given its power of judicial review, the Supreme Court has the authority to decide important issues of public policy—ranging from the outcome of the 2000 presidential election to abortion rights. From left to right (seated): Antonin Scalia, John Paul Stevens, William Rehnquist, Sandra Day O'Connor, Anthony Kennedy, and (standing): Ruth Bader Ginsburg, David Souter, Clarence Thomas, and Steven Breyer.

the conservative wing of the Court. He had been appointed as an associate justice by Richard Nixon in 1972 and elevated to chief justice by Ronald Reagan in 1986. Sandra Day O'Connor, though only seventy, was also viewed as eager to leave the Court to spend more time with her husband, who faced health problems. A centrist, O'Connor—the first woman to serve on the Supreme Court—had been appointed by Reagan in 1981. In addition to potential Supreme Court appointments, Bush entered office with eighty vacant seats to fill on federal trial and appellate courts. Because federal judges have life tenure, presidents have an opportunity to use judicial appointments to shape judicial policymaking for years to come. As such, these appointments are very important. Because they require Senate confirmation, they can also be very contentious—as we shall see in the next section.

This chapter examines the basic relationship between the president and the federal courts. The first section analyzes the most important influence the president exerts over these courts: the power, with the consent of the Senate, to appoint their members. The chapter next explores other means by which the chief executive affects the business of the courts, and, finally, it examines the reverse situation: how the federal courts, and the Supreme Court in particular, influence the actions of the president.

Presidential Appointment of Federal Judges

Perhaps the greatest impact the president can have on the courts is the selection of federal judges who share the administration's policy goals. These judges include not only the nine justices who currently sit on the U.S. Supreme Court, but also more than 800 additional judges who sit on lower federal courts. (States have their own independent court systems.) The Constitution established (and requires) one Supreme Court. It authorized (but did not require) Congress to create lower federal courts. Congress created lower courts almost immediately through the Judiciary Act of 1789, and that system has grown and evolved since then. All federal judges are nominated by the president, confirmed by the Senate, and once appointed serve "during good Behaviour." In other words, they have life tenure subject to impeachment or resignation. This means that once they are on the bench, federal judges can influence judicial policymaking for years to come. This is no small matter since judges rule on such controversial issues as abortion, affirmative action, school prayer, and the rights of criminal defendants.

One might think that impartial judges who objectively apply the law according to set standards of interpretation should all arrive at the same "correct" outcome in cases that come before them. In practice, however, there are very different views among judges about how to interpret legal texts. Moreover, judges are human beings who are influenced, at least in part, by their backgrounds, personal beliefs, and judicial philosophies. As a result, different judges can—and do—reach different conclusions when confronted with the same case (*Bush v. Gore* is just one of many examples of this). Therefore, presidents work hard to nominate judges with a similar judicial philosophy. Interest groups—well aware of the impact that judges can have on policy—also take keen interest in these nominees. So, too, does the Senate, which has the power to confirm or reject nominees.

Selection of Lower Federal Court Judges

There are two basic types of lower federal courts: trial courts (called U.S. district courts) and appellate courts (called U.S. courts of appeals).[23] These are distinct from state courts. The fact that the United States has an overlapping system of state and federal courts can be confusing, especially since each state structures its court system differently than other states. The result is that we have fifty-one court systems in this country: one at the federal level and one for each of the fifty states. State courts usually hear cases involving state law, while federal courts hear cases involving federal law. Sometimes a single action can provoke cases in both state and federal law. Timothy McVeigh, for example, violated federal law when he blew up the federal building in Oklahoma City and was tried in federal court. But he could also have been tried in state court for violating state law against murder. Moreover, cases involving state law that begin in state court can sometimes be appealed to federal court. This happens only when a case involves a *federal question*. A federal question exists if a state law is alleged to violate federal law, a U.S. treaty, or the U.S. Constitution. It can also exist if police or prosecutors are alleged to have violated the constitutional rights of a criminal defendant. A person convicted in state court because of evidence gathered from an unreasonable search and seizure or a coerced confession, for example, could appeal to federal court. If there is no federal question, however, the highest state court remains the court of last resort. The manner of selecting state court judges varies from state to state and is completely unrelated to federal judicial selection.

U.S. district courts are where federal criminal and civil cases originate and where trials are held. Each of these courts has jurisdiction over a geographic area called a district. Each district falls within the boundary of a single state, and, by tradition, judges who come from that state staff a district's courts.[24] Every state has at least one district. Those with heavier caseloads have more than one, and Congress occasionally adds new districts to accommodate increased caseloads. Since district courts are the point of entry to the federal judicial system, they hear more cases than any other kind of federal court. There are also more of them than any other kind of federal court: currently more than 600 judges staff ninety-four courts.

The courts of appeals are intermediate appellate courts between the district courts and the Supreme Court. Each has jurisdiction over a geographic area called a circuit, made up of several districts. There are twelve regional circuits: one for the District of Columbia and eleven numbered circuits covering the rest of the country. Unlike districts, the numbered circuits have jurisdiction over several states (the First Circuit, for example, covers Maine, Massachusetts, New Hampshire, and Rhode Island). The circuit courts hear appeals from the trial courts and decide whether or not the trial court made a legal error in trying the case. In other words, courts of appeals answer questions of *law* rather than questions of *fact*. Unlike proceedings in the district courts, there are no witnesses, no testimony, and no jury. Judges on the courts of appeals base their rulings on written legal arguments called briefs and on oral arguments presented by lawyers representing each side of the case. A panel of three judges usually hears appeals. A majority vote of the panel is necessary to overturn a lower court ruling, and the court of appeals issues a written opinion explaining its ruling.

Only about one-sixth of the litigants from the district courts appeal, so the caseload for the courts of appeals is significantly less than the caseload of the district courts. Despite the fact that they hear fewer cases than the district courts, the courts of appeals are very influential because of their power to set important precedents that are binding on the lower courts in their circuit. Since the U.S. Supreme Court accepts such a minuscule number of cases from the courts of appeal for review, the courts of appeals are effectively the court of last resort in more than 99 percent of the cases that come before them.[25] As such, appointments to the courts of appeals are especially important.

In theory, the appointment process for these lower federal courts is the same as for the Supreme Court: the president nominates and the Senate either confirms or rejects. In practice, presidents have traditionally had less control over the selection of these lower federal court judges than over the selection of Supreme Court justices. This is especially true at the district court level because of a practice called "senatorial courtesy." Senatorial courtesy has existed as an informal rule since the early days of George Washington's administration. It means that members of the Senate (out of courtesy) will generally refuse to confirm people to federal positions who do not have the support of the senators from the state where the vacancy exists.

Senatorial courtesy was formally institutionalized in the 1940s through the development of the so-called blue slip procedure.[26] Both of the senators from the state where the vacancy occurs (regardless of party affiliation) receive a letter from the chairman of the Senate Judiciary Committee asking for advice about the nominee. Enclosed is a form, printed on blue paper, where such advice can be offered. Although senators may put their support or opposition in writing and return the form, it is understood that failure to return the blue slip amounts to a veto that will prevent committee hearings on the nominee—a de facto invocation of senatorial courtesy that usually blocks the nomination.[27]

There is debate about what role should be played by those home-state senators who are *not* of the president's party. During certain periods, only blue slip vetoes from senators of the president's party could block a nomination.[28] During others, either home-state senator, regardless of party, could block the nomination. According to David O'Brien, the latter interpretation prevailed until the 1970s. It hardly mattered, though, since the overwhelming majority of nominees were confirmed (98 percent between 1951 and 1962) with only perfunctory review by the Senate.[29] Still, the threat of invoking the blue slip influenced the types of judges nominated. For example, threats by southern Democrats to block liberal nominees during the Kennedy and Johnson administrations in the 1960s led to the appointment of more conservative judges in the South than might otherwise have been the case.

Sen. Edward Kennedy, D-Mass., chairman of the Senate Judiciary Committee in 1979–1981, weakened the veto power of the blue slip—largely to help President Jimmy Carter bypass potential opposition to his more liberal nominees from fellow southern Democrats. Kennedy said that a blue slip veto would no longer preclude hearings on a nominee, but no attempt to invoke such a veto occurred during his tenure.[30] Sen. Strom Thurmond, R-S.C., continued Kennedy's practice under his tenure as chair of the Judiciary Committee, probably because a fellow Republican (Ronald Reagan) controlled the White House. A weakened veto power would make it more difficult for home-state Democrats to block Republican nominees.

Then, during the last six years of the Clinton administration (when a Democrat controlled the White House and Republicans controlled the Senate), Republican Senate Judiciary Committee chairman Orrin Hatch of Utah routinely allowed blue slips from home-state Republicans to prevent hearings on many Democratic nominees put forward by the president. This amounted to a strengthening of the veto power of the blue slip because it allowed home-state senators who were *not* of the same political party as President Clinton to block his nominees. Once George W. Bush became president in 2001, however, Hatch abruptly shifted gears and sought to weaken the power of the blue slip. Now that Democrats were in the same position that Republicans had been in when Clinton controlled the White House, Hatch wanted to discount the veto power of home-state Democrats, saying that support of a home-state Republican should overcome opposition of a home-state Democrat. The *New York Times* called Hatch's turnabout both ironic and audacious, since Republicans had for six years "routinely obstructed" President Clinton's judicial nominations and were now trying to remove the possibility that Democrats could do the same.[31] Not surprisingly, Senate Democrats reacted with fury to Hatch's proposal. Sen. Charles E. Schumer, D-N.Y., wrote a letter of protest signed by all nine Democrats on the Judiciary Committee and supported by all fifty Senate Democrats.[32] Before the issue could be resolved, Republican senator Jim Jeffords of Vermont defected from the Republican Party, thus throwing control of the Senate to the Democrats. Sen. Patrick Leahy, D-Vt., took over as Judiciary Committee chairman. Leahy indicated that he would enforce the blue slip rule, thus allowing home-state Democrats to block President Bush's Republican nominees.[33]

An outgrowth of senatorial courtesy and the blue slip is that presidents turn to home-state senators for advice about whom to nominate. Home-state senators of the same party as the president are the most influential, although some presidents have also sought at least some advice from home-state senators of the opposition party (even when they do so, presidents very rarely appoint judges of the opposing party). Especially in the early part of our history—when communication was slow and difficult, and the president was literally more isolated and removed from the various states than today—that practice made sense. It assumed that home-state senators were better able to select qualified individuals than the president because they knew more about the existing pool of candidates. Over time, however, senators came to treat district court appointments as a form of patronage. Former attorney general Robert F. Kennedy went so far as to call it "senatorial appointment with the advice and consent of the senate."[34]

G. Alan Tarr has pointed out that senatorial courtesy has influenced the type of individuals who are appointed to district courts. Because these appointments have long served as a form of political patronage for home-state senators of the president's political party, it is not surprising that roughly 95 percent of all district court judges appointed during the past hundred years have come from the same political party as the appointing president. Tarr also notes that "district court judges have usually 'earned' their positions by active party service in their state prior to appointment."[35]

As an attempt to ensure the quality of these judges, the American Bar Association (ABA) created its Standing Committee on Federal Judiciary in 1946 to review the qualifications of all federal judicial nominees.[36] Republicans on the Senate Judiciary Committee embraced the ABA's role—partly to block some of President Harry Truman's Democratic nominees. When Republican president Dwight D. Eisenhower entered office in 1953, he established a formal link between the White House and the ABA. The ABA would review the qualifications of all potential nominees before the president nominated anyone.

By the 1980s, however, Republicans had come to view the ABA with suspicion. Once a conservative organization, the ABA had become more liberal over time. Republicans were especially angry that four of the fifteen members of the ABA's standing committee rated Ronald Reagan's failed Supreme Court nominee Robert Bork "not qualified" in 1987. In March 2001, President George W. Bush severed the White House link with the ABA—something his father had threatened to do in 1991. In a letter to ABA president Martha W. Barnett, White House counsel Alberto R. Gonzales (who is on the list of potential Bush Supreme Court nominees) wrote: "We will continue to welcome suggestions from all sources, including the ABA. The issue at hand, however, is quite different: whether the ABA alone—out of the literally dozens of groups and many individuals who have a strong interest in the composition of the federal courts—should receive advance notice of the identities of potential nominees in order to render prenomination opinions on their fitness for judicial service."[37] When Democrats took control of the Senate in June 2001, however, they reinstated a role for the ABA by promising not to hold hearings on Bush's judicial nominees until the Senate Judiciary Committee received their ABA ratings. Democrats insisted that the ABA ratings validate a nominee's professional qualifications and feared that Bush's attempt to bypass the ABA was part of an effort to appoint more ideologically extreme judges to the bench. They also pointed to the fact that many of the White House lawyers assigned to judicial selection in the Bush administration were affiliated with the conservative Federalist Society. The Federalist Society had long opposed the ABA's role in rating nominees.[38] Formed in 1982 in response to the perception that liberal ideology dominated law schools and the legal profession, the Federalist Society "has become a major source of conservative legal thinking, and a clearinghouse for the selection of conservative law clerks, government political appointees, judges, and other key policymaking spots in the Bush administration."[39]

In what some people see as an attempt to appoint more ideological judges, presidents in recent years have exerted greater control over the selection of lower federal court judges—especially those for the courts of appeals. The control began, ironically, as a part of President Carter's efforts to institute merit selection of federal judges. In 1977, by executive order, Carter created the Circuit Court Nominating Commission. The commission diminished the role of senators in the selection of courts of appeals judges by taking control of the screening process for nominees. Under the new system, the commission would submit a short list of qualified nominees to the president, who would then nominate someone from that list.[40] Carter also urged senators to create, voluntarily, nominating commissions to advise him on the selection of district court judges from their states. By 1979, senators from thirty-one states had created such commissions.[41] The changes were made to help ensure that the awarding of judgeships was based on qualifications and not used merely as a form of political patronage for senators.

Despite Carter's emphasis on merit in judicial selection, his appointments remained partisan: over 90 percent of his district court appointments and just over 82 percent of his appeals court appointments were of fellow Democrats.[42] Carter also considered affirmative action to be an important criterion for judicial selection. He made a deliberate effort to place women, African Americans, and Hispanics on the federal judiciary—appointing more of each than had been placed on the bench by all previous presidents combined.[43]

Ronald Reagan transformed the selection process when he took office in 1981. He abolished Carter's commission system and seized control of the selection process as part of an effort to screen nominees to ensure that they reflected his administration's ideology. He created the President's Committee on Federal Judicial Selection, staffed by representatives of the White House and the Justice Department, to conduct the screening—which included extensive interviews of all leading candidates. Sheldon Goldman called it "the most systematic judicial philosophical screening of candidates ever seen in the nation's history."[44] Reagan attorney general Edwin Meese III bluntly said the appointments were meant to "institutionalize the Reagan revolution so it can't be set aside no matter what happens in future presidential elections."[45] By the time he left office, Reagan had set a new record for the number of lower federal judges appointed: 290 district court judges and 78 appeals court judges.[46] George Bush, who had served as Reagan's vice president before becoming president in 1989, appointed almost 200 additional federal judges during his four years as president.

Presidents Carter, Reagan, and Bush had all benefited from legislation that significantly expanded the number of federal judges. President Clinton did not. During Clinton's eight years in office, Congress created only 9 additional seats—as compared with 85 under Bush, 85 under Reagan, and 152 under Carter.[47] Clinton also faced a Senate controlled by opposition Republicans during his last six years in office. In 1997, Republican senators orchestrated an unprecedented slowdown of the confirmation process to protest what they called Clinton's "activist" (liberal) nominees. Such charges may have reflected partisan hyperbole more than fact. Studies suggest that Clinton's nominees were actually quite moderate. This was true even of those nominees confirmed before Republicans took control of the Senate.[48] Clinton's appointees also had the highest ABA ratings of the past four presidents.[49]

As a result of the Republican slowdown, one in ten seats on the federal judiciary were vacant by the end of 1997. Twenty-six seats had remained empty for more than eighteen months, and one-third of the seats in the Ninth Circuit were empty. In March 1997, House majority whip Tom DeLay, R-Texas, even suggested that congressional Republicans should begin efforts to impeach liberal federal judges.[50] Such tactics provoked outcries. Even Chief Justice William

Rehnquist, a conservative appointed by Reagan, criticized the Senate for its slowdown in his annual State of the Judiciary address. "The Senate is surely under no obligation to confirm any particular nominee," Rehnquist said, "but after the necessary time for inquiry, it should vote him up or vote him down."[51]

In part because of Rehnquist's criticism, Senate Republicans backed away from their slowdown, and the backlog of vacancies eased in 1998. But the delay tactics returned in 1999 and continued through the rest of the Clinton presidency. By then, Republicans hoped to delay confirmation until a Republican president was elected. They were especially concerned with appeals court appointments. In 2000, the Senate confirmed only 39 of 81 judicial nominees put forward by Clinton (an additional two nominees withdrew). Nominations of 42 judicial candidates remained unconfirmed when Clinton left office in January 2001—38 of them had never even received a judiciary committee hearing.[52]

Despite the slowdowns and the lack of new judicial seats to fill, Clinton appointed 378 judges during his eight years in office. By the end of Clinton's second term, the number of his appointees serving on the courts narrowly surpassed the number of Reagan–Bush appointees still serving by a margin of 42.7 percent to 40.7 percent.[53] Even more than Jimmy Carter, Clinton diversified the bench through these appointments. He appointed 111 women and 62 African Americans: more of each than Ford, Carter, Reagan, and Bush combined had appointed in nineteen years (see Table 7-1).[54] Nonetheless, Republicans had the opportunity to make significant inroads when George W. Bush took office in 2001. By the end of his second month in office, Bush already had 94 judicial vacancies to fill (including 28 on appellate courts).[55] Bush assigned White House counsel Alberto Gonzales an active role in judicial selection. In the first two months of the Bush presidency, Gonzales interviewed some 50 potential nominees to fill those vacancies.[56] The Bush administration was eager to fill them quickly while Republicans still (with the tie-breaking vote of Vice President Cheney) held marginal control of the Senate. They especially feared that the ninety-eight-year-old Republican senator from South Carolina, Strom Thurmond, might die or resign because of ill health before the 2002 elections. If that happened, the Democratic governor of South Carolina would name a replacement. None of Bush's judicial nominees were confirmed, however, before Senator Jeffords defected from the Republican Party and threw control of the Senate to the Democrats in June 2001. Suddenly, Bush's nominees were in for much closer scrutiny than they would have been under a Republican-controlled Senate.[57]

Selection of Supreme Court Justices

The president clearly dominates the process of selecting members of the Supreme Court. Despite the constitutional admonition that the Senate offer "advice and consent" on presidents' nominees, the extent to which presidents seek advice from senators on whom to nominate is minimal. A rare exception came in 1874, when President Ulysses S. Grant formally sought the advice of Senate leaders before nominating Morrison Waite to be chief justice.

Table 7-1   Race, Ethnicity, and Gender of all Federal Judicial Appointments, by Administration (Nixon to Clinton)

President	Total appointments	Male	Female	White	African American	Hispanic	Asian	Native American	Arab American
Clinton (1993–2001)	378	267 (70.6%)	111 (29.4%)	285 (75.4%)	62 (16.4%)	24 (6.3%)	5 (1.3%)	1 (.26%)	1 (.26%)
G. H. W. Bush (1989–1993)	192	156 (81.2%)	36 (18.8%)	172 (89.6%)	11 (5.7%)	8 (4.2%)	1 (0.5%)	0	0
Reagan (1981–1989)	378	347 (91.8%)	31 (8.2%)	356 (94.2%)	7 (1.9%)	13 (3.4%)	2 (0.5%)	0	0
Carter (1977–1981)	258	217 (84.1%)	41 (15.9%)	202 (78.3%)	37 (14.3%)	16 (6.2%)	2 (0.8%)	1 (0.4%)	0
Ford (1974–1977)	65	64 (98.5%)	1 (1.5%)	59 (90.8%)	3 (4.6%)	1 (1.5%)	2 (3.1%)	0	0
Nixon (1969–1974)	227	226 (99.6%)	1 (0.4%)	218 (96%)	6 (2.6%)	2 (0.9%)	1 (0.4%)	0	0

Source: Alliance for Justice, "Judicial Selection Project: Annual Report 2000," http://www.afj.org/jsp/report2000.

While presidents have only recently come to appreciate and take full advantage of their ability to influence judicial policymaking through *lower* federal court appointments, they have long recognized the importance of Supreme Court appointments. Through its power of judicial review, the Court has the authority—when a legitimate case or controversy is brought before it—to review actions of the other branches of government and the states (as in *Bush v. Gore*), and to strike down those that violate the Constitution.

The Supreme Court's Power of Judicial Review. First used by the Court in *Marbury v. Madison*, 5 U.S. 137 (1803), the Supreme Court's unenumerated power of judicial review is an important part of our system of checks and balances. It serves as a way of policing the actions of other governmental actors and ensuring that they are acting in accordance with the Constitution. It prevents temporary legislative majorities from invading the rights of minorities and keeps strong-willed presidents from thwarting the Constitution. It is, in other words, a protection against "tyranny of the majority" and other abuses of power by government officials.

But there are also dangers associated with judicial review. After all, it is up to a simple majority of the Court to determine what the Constitution means and whether a governmental action violates it. This may seem like an easy task, but it is not. Many provisions of the Constitution are notoriously vague and ambiguous. As a result, they are susceptible to different interpretations. As we saw in chapter 1, the ambiguity of Article II has led to considerable disagreement over the scope of presidential power. Such ambiguity extends to many other important provisions of the Constitution. For example, what does "equal protection" mean? "Unreasonable searches and seizures"? "Cruel and unusual punishment"? The First Amendment says that Congress shall make no law abridging freedom of speech. But what is "speech"? Does it include libel? Campaign contributions? False advertising? Obscenity? Advocacy to overthrow the government? Flag burning? Nude dancing? These questions have all come before the Court. Reasonable people disagree about how to answer them.

The real danger of judicial review lies in the possibility that a majority of the Court might take advantage of the Constitution's ambiguities to impose its own will. Under the guise of upholding the Constitution, five unelected judges could choose to impose policies that they support and nullify those that they do not. Judges from both ends of the political spectrum are susceptible to that temptation. Some say that is what happened when a conservative majority on the Court struck down government attempts to regulate business in the early twentieth century,[58] or when a liberal majority in the 1960s and 1970s used an unenumerated "right of privacy" to strike down state laws that banned abortion and the use of contraceptives.[59]

Even when the Court is doing its best to apply the Constitution fairly and accurately, answers to many constitutional questions remain a matter of judgment. It is precisely for that reason that Supreme Court appointments are so important. Decisions reached by the Court are of vital interest to the president because they affect presidential programs, the operation of the entire political system, and the functioning of U.S. society in general. Presidents realize that they can affect those decisions through their appointments to the Court. Therefore, they usually take great care in the people they nominate.

Nominee Qualifications. Generally speaking, there are three broad categories of qualifications that presidents and their aides take into account when screening nominees: professional, representational, and doctrinal.[60] Surprisingly, the Constitution contains no specific qualifications for being a Supreme Court justice. This stands in stark contrast to the very specific constitutional qualifications for the president, senators, and members of the House of Representatives.[61] Since federal law has not mandated specific qualifications either, it "is legally possible, though scarcely conceivable, that a non-citizen, a minor or a non-lawyer could be appointed to the Court."[62]

There may be no legally mandated qualifications, but there are qualifications that are important. Among them are a nominee's *professional* experience. Although President Bush severed the official relationship between the White House and the American Bar Association in 2001, the ABA ratings of nominees continue to be an important barometer for senators and the public to gauge the professional merits of a nominee. As noted earlier, Democrats vowed not to hold hearings on Bush's nominees without ABA ratings when they regained control of the Senate in June 2001. The ABA bases its ratings largely on the nominee's professional qualifications. So, too, do others who assess whether an individual is fit to serve on the Supreme Court. Thus, while not required by the Constitution, every justice who has served on the Supreme Court has been a lawyer, and high professional standards have been an important criterion when selecting and confirming nominees.[63]

In addition to being trained as lawyers, all justices have devoted their professional lives primarily to the practice or teaching of law (as opposed to other types of public service). Moreover, all but one justice previously held public office—often one associated with the courts, such as district attorney. Several, though, had never served as a judge before (including John Marshall, Felix Frankfurter, and Earl Warren). An analysis of the prior occupations of Supreme Court justices reveals that they have come principally from four types of positions: twenty-one had held federal office in the executive branch, twenty-seven had been judges of a lower federal court, twenty-one had been judges of a state court, and twenty-five had been attorneys in private practice. Elected officials also have served on the nation's highest bench, including one president (William Howard Taft), six U.S. senators, two members of the House of Representatives, and three state governors.[64]

Representational qualifications are also an important concern when presidents screen candidates. These include the partisan affiliation of potential nominees and the geographic region they represent, as well as such factors as their race, gender, and ethnicity. With rare exceptions, presidents appoint justices from their own political party. Early in the nation's history, geographic balance was also a major consideration for presidents when deciding upon a nominee. This was especially true because Supreme Court justices then had the onerous responsibility of "riding circuit"—traveling around the country to preside over appeals in lower federal courts of a particular circuit that they were assigned to. Prior to the Civil War, presidents tried to have at least one justice from each of the circuits. By 1891, though, Congress had abolished the requirement of circuit riding, thus doing away with the most important need for geographic balance. Still, some effort is made to represent different parts of the country on the Supreme Court. Occasionally, a president tries to use a Supreme Court appointment to curry favor with a particular region of the country. Thus, both Herbert Hoover and Richard Nixon tried to appoint southerners to the Supreme Court as a way to build electoral support in the South for reelection.[65]

More recently, religion, race, gender, and ethnicity have become important representational concerns. Although the Court has historically had a distinctly white, male, Protestant bias, a "Catholic seat" has existed by tradition since 1836, as has a "Jewish seat" since 1916 (although the latter remained vacant from 1969 to 1993). In 2001, there were five Protestants, two Catholics, and two Jews sitting on the Court. Since 1967, there has always been an African American on the Court, and since 1981 at least one woman (Reagan had made the appointment of a woman a campaign promise in 1980). Both Bush and Clinton gave serious consideration to appointing the first Hispanic to the Court, and many predict that George W. Bush will follow through (probably with the appointment of White House counsel Alberto Gonzales). Such an appointment would help to build electoral support among the increasingly large Hispanic population in key electoral states such as California, Florida, and Texas.

Doctrinal qualifications refer to the perception that a nominee shares the president's political philosophy and approach to public policy issues. This is especially important given the Court's power to interpret the Constitution and exercise judicial review. As noted above, some presidents, such as Ronald Reagan, have made doctrinal considerations a central part of their screening process. Although Reagan's appointment of Sandra Day O'Connor was driven largely by representational concerns, he was careful to select a woman who fit his doctrinal qualifications. His later elevation of William Rehnquist to chief justice, his appointments of Antonin Scalia and Anthony Kennedy, and his unsuccessful nominations of Robert Bork and Douglas Ginsburg were motivated largely by doctrinal considerations. On the Court, Rehnquist and Scalia are part of a core conservative block that Kennedy and O'Connor frequently join.

In contrast, Bill Clinton was somewhat less concerned with doctrinal representation. Although applauded for their representational impact, Ruth Bader Ginsburg and Stephen Breyer actually drew some criticism from liberal Democrats who were distressed that the first Democratic president since Lyndon Johnson with the opportunity to fill vacancies on the Court (Carter made no appointments) picked candidates with moderate, mainstream rather than activist, liberal constitutional views. Both justices, of course, were Democrats who were more liberal than Reagan's nominees. But in the interest of avoiding a confirmation battle in the Senate, Clinton selected experienced and moderate federal appeals court judges rather than ideologues to fill his Supreme Court vacancies. Ginsburg and Breyer had strong support from both liberals and conservatives on the Senate Judiciary Committee and went on to win easy confirmation.

The Clinton appointments indicate that doctrinal considerations can have different implications for presidents. A president's concern may not be to pack the court with justices who will pursue particular policies, but rather to appoint persons whose general philosophy is similar to the president's own and reflects the mood of the country. When Bush entered office in 2001, observers speculated that he would revert to more systematic doctrinal considerations similar to those used by Reagan.

Initial Screening and Selection. As David Yalof points out, different presidents go about screening and selecting potential Supreme Court nominees in different ways. Even within a single administration, Yalof identifies a variety of factors that influence the president's initial selection process. These include (1) the timing of the vacancy, (2) the composition of the Senate, (3) the public approval of the president, (4) attributes of the outgoing justice, and (5) the realistic pool of candidates available to the president.[66] If the vacancy occurs early in their term, presidents are usually in a stronger position politically than if the vacancy occurs at the end of their term. On the other hand, if the vacancy occurs shortly before their reelection campaign, or toward the end of their last term, presidents may be more limited in the type of nominee that they can send to the Senate and may feel compelled to nominate a more moderate, consensus candidate. The same is true if the opposition party controls the Senate (a common phenomenon in recent years) or if a president's approval ratings are low. Choice of a successor may also be more limited if the outgoing justice represents a particular religious or demographic group, or if presidents feel that a particular region of the country needs representation on the Court. And, obviously, presidents are limited by the available pool of candidates. For example, presidents may find it difficult to find a nominee that fits the precise mix of professional, doctrinal, and representational concerns that they would like.

Since 1853, the Justice Department has had formal responsibility for collecting applications and recommendations of potential nominees, who also undergo a background check by the Federal Bureau of Investigation, a unit of the Justice Department. Historically, the attorney general (the head of the Justice Department) played the primary role in this process. As Yalof notes, however, the growth and bureaucratization of both the White House and the Justice Department have led to the emergence of specialized staff units assigned to vet potential nominees.[67] The Office of White House Counsel, created as part of the president's personal staff during the Truman administration, now plays an important role—as does the chief of staff and other White House officials. In the early part of George W. Bush's administration, Alberto Gonzales led the search for all federal judges.

In some administrations, overlapping responsibilities between the White House and the Justice Department have led to internal power struggles over what type of judges to nominate. This happened during the Reagan administration. When Justice Lewis Powell resigned from the Supreme Court in 1987, Attorney General Meese and other Justice Department officials pushed for a staunchly conservative nominee: Robert Bork. On the other hand, White House counsel Arthur B. Culvahouse and Chief of Staff Howard Baker both pushed for a moderate consensus nominee. The Justice Department won, but the Senate went on to defeat the Bork nomination in one of the most contentious confirmation battles in recent history.[68]

Of course, many people have a desire to influence the nomination decision. The *legal community* is particularly eager to influence the selection process. This community includes professional organizations such as the ABA. Clearly the ABA's ratings can have an influence on how nominees are perceived by the public and the Senate. Other legal groups, as well as individual lawyers, also participate in the selection process. They may suggest nominees to the president or announce their evaluations of the person the president nominated. Coalitions of lawyers sometimes sign letters of support for, or of opposition to, specific nominees. Even Supreme Court justices themselves occasionally participate in the process by recommending a potential nominee to the president or even lobbying publicly for a candidate. Chief Justice William Howard Taft (1921–1930) was particularly active in that regard. More recently, Chief Justice Warren Burger suggested the nomination of Harry Blackmun in 1970 and Sandra Day O'Connor in 1981.[69]

Interest groups also lobby for and against the selection of nominees. As early as the 1880s, interest groups recognized how directly the Supreme Court could affect them and began taking an active interest in the Senate confirmation of nominees.[70] They also began to lobby presidents before nominations were announced.[71] Nowadays, they take very public stances on nominations—often before vacancies on the Supreme Court occur. Thus, the National Abortion and Reproductive Rights Action League sent a letter from Kate Michelman, the group's president, to millions of households in April 2001 warning: "You and I need to be prepared to oppose George W. Bush's nominees to the Supreme Court. It could happen next week. It could happen next month." But when it does, she wrote, a Bush nominee could "strangle reproductive freedom for many years to come."[72]

Senate Confirmation. Once nominated by the president, a candidate to the Supreme Court must be confirmed by the Senate. This requires a simple majority vote. Of the 149 nominations to the Supreme Court since 1789, the Senate has voted to outright reject only 12. It effectively rejected 10 others, either by voting to "postpone" consideration of the nominee or by taking no action at all. In such cases, the nomination died at the end of the Senate session. In addition, presidents have withdrawn 5 nominations in the face of certain Senate defeat. Combined, that amounts to 27 failed nominations (see Table 7-2). (Two other nominations were withdrawn on a technicality. Another nominee died after being confirmed, and 7 others declined their seat after Senate confirmation.)

Despite an overall acceptance rate of 81.6 percent, the failure rate of Supreme Court nominees (18.4 percent) is the highest for any appointive post requiring Senate confirmation.[73] Five nominations have failed just since 1968. This is a reflection of the concern for the profound effect that Supreme Court appointments can have on public policy.

Confirmation is also a test of presidential strength. "Weak" presidents—those who are unelected, those who face a Senate controlled by the opposition, and those in their terminal year in office—are statistically less likely to secure confirmation of their Supreme Court nominees. The unusually long period of divided government in recent years (with the White House controlled by one party and the Senate by another) has added to the contentiousness of confirmation battles. From 1969 through 2000, different parties controlled the Senate and the White House for twenty out of thirty-two years. Divided government returned again in June 2001, when Democrats regained control of the Senate. On average, confirmation rates drop from 87.9 percent when the same party controls the White House and the Senate to only 54.5 percent during periods of divided government.[74] Ongoing public policy debates over such controversial issues as race and

Table 7-2   Failed Supreme Court Nominees

Nominee and year of nomination	President and party	Composition of Senate	Action
John Rutledge, 1795	Washington (F)	19 F, 13 DR	Rejected 14–10
Alexander Wolcott, 1811	Madison (DR)	28 DR, 6 F	Rejected 24–9
John J. Crittenden, 1828	J. Q. Adams (NR)	28 J, 20 NR	Postponed 23–17
Roger B. Taney, 1835	Jackson (D)	20 D, 20 W	Postponed 24–21
John C. Spencer, 1844	Tyler (W)	28 W, 25 D	Rejected 26–21
Reuben H. Walworth, 1844[a]	Tyler (W)	28 W, 25 D	Postponed 27–20
Edward King, 1844[b]	Tyler (W)	28 W, 25 D	Postponed 29–18
Edward King, 1844	Tyler (W)	28 W, 25 D	Withdrawn
John M. Read, 1845	Tyler (W)	28 W, 25 D	No action
George W. Woodward, 1845	Polk (D)	31 D, 25 W	Rejected 20–19
Edward A. Bradford, 1852	Fillmore (W)	35 D, 24 W	No action
George E. Badger, 1853	Fillmore (W)	35 D, 24 W	Postponed 26–25
William C. Micou, 1853	Fillmore (W)	35 D, 24 W	No action
Jeremiah S. Black, 1861	Buchanan (D)	36 D, 26 R	Rejected 26–25
Henry Stanbery, 1866	A. Johnson (R)	42 U, 10 D	No action
Ebenezer R. Hoar, 1869	Grant (R)	56 R, 11 D	Rejected 33–24
George H. Williams, 1873	Grant (R)	49 R, 19 D	Withdrawn
Caleb Cushing, 1874	Grant (R)	49 R, 19 D	Withdrawn
Stanley Matthews, 1881	Hayes (R)	42 D, 33 R	No action
William Hornblower, 1893	Cleveland (D)	44 D, 38 R	Rejected 30–24
Wheeler H. Peckham, 1894	Cleveland (D)	44 D, 38 R	Rejected 41–32
John J. Parker, 1930	Hoover (R)	56 R, 39 D	Rejected 41–39
Abe Fortas, 1968	Johnson (D)	64 D, 36 R	Withdrawn
Clement Haynsworth, 1969	Nixon (R)	58 D, 42 R	Rejected 55–45
G. Harrold Carswell, 1970	Nixon (R)	58 D, 42 R	Rejected 51–45
Robert H. Bork, 1987	Reagan (R)	55 D, 45 R	Rejected 58–42
Douglas Ginsburg, 1987	Reagan (R)	55 D, 45 R	Withdrawn

Source: John Anthony Maltese, *The Selling of Supreme Court Nominees* (Baltimore: Johns Hopkins University Press, 1995), 3.

Note: F is Federalist, DR is Democratic Republican, NR is National-Republican, D is Democrat, W is Whig, R is Republican, J is Jacksonian, and U is Unionist. Tyler, Fillmore and Andrew Johnson were not elected.

[a]Reuben Walworth's nomination was later withdrawn.

[b]Edward King was nominated twice.

abortion—something that journalist E. J. Dionne has called a "cultural civil war"[75]—have also contributed to intense confirmation battles. Interest groups fan the flames through their efforts for and against nominees.

Interest groups led the opposition to all of the nominees who were rejected by the Senate or forced to withdraw in the twentieth century. John J. Parker, a southern court of appeals judge nominated by Herbert Hoover in 1930, fell victim to the combined opposition of the American Federation of Labor and the National Association for the Advancement of Colored People (NAACP), who viewed him as antilabor and racist. Labor and the NAACP again joined forces to defeat two Nixon nominees: Clement Haynsworth, a federal court of appeals judge from South Carolina, in 1969, and G. Harrold Carswell, a federal court of appeals judge from Florida, in 1970.[76] Lyndon Johnson's nomination of Abe Fortas to be chief justice in 1968 was bitterly attacked by conservative groups because of his liberal decisions in obscenity cases and suits concerning the rights of the accused in criminal proceedings.[77] A major effort by civil rights, women's, and other liberal groups contributed to the defeat in 1987 of Reagan's nomination of Robert Bork, a controversial conservative federal appeals court judge.[78]

Sometimes other problems are involved. Some people considered Fortas's acceptance of a legal fee from a family foundation and his advising President Johnson on political matters to be unethical activities for a justice of the Supreme Court.[79] Haynsworth was criticized for ruling on cases in which he had a personal financial interest. Much of the opposition to Carswell from members of the bar, particularly law professors, stemmed from his perceived lack of professional qualifications. Sen. Roman Hruska, R.-Neb., Carswell's leading supporter in the Senate, made the situation even worse when he tried to make the nominee's mediocrity a virtue by saying on national television that mediocre people needed representation on the Supreme Court. Suddenly, Carswell was a national joke. This, coupled with some shockingly racist statements that Carswell had made when running for public office ("I believe the segregation of the races is proper and the only practical and correct way of life in our states," and "I yield to no man . . . in the firm, vigorous belief in the principles of white supremacy, and I shall always be so governed"), doomed Carswell's nomination.[80]

Active involvement by interest groups in every Supreme Court confirmation process dates back only to the 1960s or so. Although organized interests attempted to block Senate confirmation of a Supreme Court nominee as early as 1881, their success in blocking the confirmation of three nominees in three years (Fortas, Haynsworth, and Carswell in 1968, 1969, and 1970, respectively) marked a turning point. Since then, interest groups have taken an active stand on virtually all Supreme Court nominees, although their involvement accelerated dramatically with the Bork nomination in 1987. Starting with that nomination, interest groups moved beyond testifying at confirmation hearings and mobilizing their members to lobby their senators, to a full-fledged public relations offensive, including the use of television, radio, and print ads, coupled with mass mailings and the use of phone banks to sway public opinion. They also attempted to influence reporters and editorial writers through the use of press briefings and fact sheets that they aggressively distributed.

The increased role of interest groups corresponded with the increased visibility of Senate Judiciary Committee hearings and floor votes on nominees. Prior to the twentieth century, the confirmation process was shrouded in secrecy. The Senate Judiciary Committee held hearings behind closed doors and rarely even kept records of its proceedings. As the *New York Times* wrote in 1881, the "Judiciary Committee of the Senate is the most mysterious committee in that body, and succeeds better than any other in maintaining secrecy as to its proceedings."[81]

At that time, the committee usually deliberated without hearing from any witnesses. Interest groups seldom participated in this phase of the process (none testified until 1930), and no nominee appeared before the committee until Harlan Fiske Stone in 1925. Nominees actually thought it improper to answer any questions and maintained almost complete public silence. When a reporter from the New York *Sun* asked Louis Brandeis about his nomination in 1916, Brandeis quickly replied: "I have nothing to say about anything, and that goes for all time and to all newspapers, including both the *Sun* and the moon."[82] Presidents, too, maintained almost complete public silence about their nominees. When the full Senate finally voted on a nominee, it almost always did so in closed session and often with no roll call vote. This secrecy played an important part in minimizing the role of interest groups and others who had an interest in the outcome of a nomination. So, too, did the fact that senators then were not popularly elected, but chosen by state legislators. This undermined the potent threat of retaliation against senators now enjoyed by the electorate (a power on which interest groups can capitalize).

All this changed in the twentieth century. The passage of the Seventeenth Amendment to the Constitution in 1913 provided for the direct election of senators, and Senate rules changes in 1929 opened floor debate on nominations. Public opinion now mattered in a very direct way to senators—they were dependent upon it for reelection. Thus, they began to use public Judiciary Committee hearings as a way of both testing and influencing public opinion. Since 1981, Judiciary Committee hearings have been broadcast live on television for the entire world to see. The emergence of the modern "public presidency" (*see chapter 3*) also led to greater involvement by presidents in promoting their nominees. As specialized staff units developed in the White House, they, too, came to be used as a way to secure support for nominees and thereby increase the likelihood of Senate confirmation. Today, the Office of Communications, the Office of Public Liaison, the Office of Political Affairs, and other staff units are all used in this manner.[83]

Even if successfully confirmed, judicial appointees may fail to vote the way the president had hoped. Ronald Reagan and his immediate successor, George Bush, appointed six justices to the Supreme Court with the avowed hope of overturning *Roe v. Wade,* 410 U.S. 113 (1973), the controversial abortion rights decision. Nonetheless, three of those appointees went on to uphold *Roe.*[84] Dwight D. Eisenhower later lamented his appointment of Earl Warren as chief justice because of his liberal voting record on the bench, and Harry Truman—never one to mince words—was furious when Tom Clark, who had been Truman's attorney general, did not vote on the Supreme Court as the president had hoped. "I don't know what got into me," Truman later fumed. "He was no damn good as Attorney General, and on the Supreme Court . . . it doesn't seem possible, but he's been even worse. He hasn't made one right decision that I can think of. . . . It's just that he's such a dumb son of a bitch."[85] Despite White House chief of staff John Sununu's prediction to President Bush that David Souter would be a "home run" for conservatives, Souter actually went on to be one of the most liberal members of the Rehnquist court. The heightened screening of judicial nominees minimizes such "mistakes," but no one can completely predict the behavior of individuals once they sit on the Court.

Other Presidential Influences on the Federal Courts

Although the appointment of federal judges is the most important method by which the president affects the courts, there are other ways to influence their activities. The first is through the solicitor general, an official that Robert Scigliano calls "the lawyer for the executive branch."[86] The second is through legislation that affects the operation of the Supreme Court—a means Congress, too, has tried to use to its advantage and the president's disadvantage. The third is through the enforcement of court decisions.

Role of the Solicitor General in the Appellate Courts

The solicitor general, an official appointed by the president with the advice and consent of the Senate, plays an important role in setting the agenda of the federal appellate courts. First, the solicitor general determines which of the cases the government loses in the federal district courts will be taken to the courts of appeals. Second, of the cases the government loses in the lower courts, the solicitor general decides which to recommend that the Supreme Court hear. Unlike the courts of appeals, which must take cases properly appealed to them, the Supreme Court chooses the cases it hears.[87] The Supreme Court is more likely to take cases proposed by the solicitor general than by other parties.

Once the Supreme Court accepts a case involving the federal government, the solicitor general decides the position that the government should take and argues the case before the Court. Thus, "the Solicitor General not only determines whether the executive branch goes to the Supreme Court but what it will say there."[88] And what it says there usually advances the policy goals of the incumbent president.[89] Moreover, the solicitor general's influence is not restricted to cases in which the federal government itself is a party. He or she also decides whether the government will file an amicus curiae (friend of the court) brief supporting or opposing positions by other parties who have cases pending before the Court.

Amicus filings by the solicitor general increased dramatically in the twentieth century. Steven Puro, who analyzed the briefs filed from 1920 through 1973, found that 71 percent occurred in the last twenty years of that period.[90] He concluded that whether by its own initiative or as a result of an invitation from the Supreme Court, the federal government participated as amicus in almost every major domestic question presented before the Court since World War II. Particularly prominent is the government entrance into the controversial issues of civil liberties, civil rights, and the jurisdiction and procedures of the courts.

When the federal government becomes involved in a case before the Supreme Court, it is usually successful. Scigliano's analysis of Court opinions chosen at ten-year intervals beginning in 1800 shows that the United States has consistently won 62 percent or more of its litigation there. Its record as amicus is even more impressive. Puro found that in the political cases he examined, the federal government supported the winning side in almost 74 percent of its appearances. An analysis of race discrimination employment cases from 1970 to 1981 showed that the government won 70 percent of the cases in which it was a direct party and 81.6 percent of those in which it filed amicus briefs.[91]

Much has been written about why solicitors general are so successful in their appearances before the Supreme Court. Kevin McGuire argues that it really boils down to one thing: litigation experience.[92] They are the prototypical "repeat player." Solicitors general or members of their staff argue far more cases than any other party, including any law firm in the country.[93] Thus, they develop a great deal of expertise in dealing with the Court. This expertise translates into high quality briefs and an intimate understanding of the workings of the Court. Solicitors general may also build up credit with the Court because they help the justices manage their caseload by holding down the number of government appeals. Christopher Zorn also notes that amicus filings by the solicitor general "are highest when both the administration and the Court share similar policy preferences, and drop off substantially when those preferences diverge." Zorn concludes that, like other litigants, "the solicitor general appears to explicitly take into account the probability that his position will be received favorably by the Court when formulating his litigation strategies."[94]

The Reagan administration used the solicitor general's office particularly aggressively to promote its conservative policy agenda.[95] In tandem with Reagan's appointments to both the Supreme Court and the lower federal courts, this "other campaign" led by Solicitor General Rex Lee entailed efforts to persuade the Supreme Court to change previous "liberal" rulings on matters such as abortion, prayer in the public schools, busing, affirmative action, the rights of the accused in criminal cases, and federal-state relations.[96] Lincoln Caplan argued that this marked a shift away from the solicitor general's traditional posture of restraint to a posture of aggressively pushing the Court to take cases that advanced the administration's social policy agenda. The result, according to Caplan, was a temporary loss of the Supreme Court's trust in the solicitor general's presentation of facts and interpretation of the law.[97] Succeeding presidents did not continue such an aggressive use of the solicitor general's office.

Solicitors general serve an average length of two years in their post. They can be fired by the president, but they can also be rewarded with an even more prestigious position. Franklin Roosevelt elevated two of his solicitors general, Stanley Reed and Robert Jackson, to the Supreme Court. Likewise, Lyndon Johnson elevated Thurgood Marshall. In the first half of 2001, some observers speculated that George W. Bush might do the same with his solicitor general, Theodore Olson, who successfully argued Bush's case before the Supreme Court during the contested 2000 presidential election, although Democrats vowed to fight such a nomination. Once Democrats took control of the Senate in June 2001, the prospects of an Olson nomination diminished.

Legislation Affecting the Supreme Court

The president also can affect the actions of the Supreme Court through legislation. Presidential authority to propose bills to Congress and to work for their adoption, as well as the power to oppose measures favored by members of Congress and, if necessary, to veto them, means that the president can influence legislation affecting the Court. At the same time, Congress can pass legislation concerning the Court that threatens the president's own power.

In 1937, Franklin Roosevelt became actively involved in trying to get Congress to exercise its power to expand the size of the Supreme Court. The power to establish the size of the Supreme Court is left up to Congress by the Constitution, and Congress has changed the size of the Court several times. Historically, though, Congress has done so without prompting from the president. Sometimes it has even altered the size of the Court in an effort to thwart a particular president. For example, in the latter days of the John Adams administration, the lame-duck Congress—still controlled by the Federalists—passed the Judiciary Act of 1801. That act reduced the number of justices from six to five in an attempt to prevent the incoming president, Democratic-Republican Thomas Jefferson, from appointing a replacement for ailing justice William Cushing. (Since justices have life tenure, the size of the Court would not actually decrease until a justice left the bench.) Not surprisingly, the Democratic-Republicans quickly repealed the 1801 law and restored the number of justices to six when they took control of Congress later that year. In 1807, the Democratic-Republican Congress increased the number of justices to seven to accommodate population growth in Kentucky, Tennessee, and Ohio. Thus, the Federalists' attempt to thwart President Jefferson failed, and he went on to name three justices, including Thomas Todd to occupy the new seat created in 1807. (Ironically, Cushing recovered and lived until 1810; his successor was named by James Madison, not Jefferson.)

Congressional manipulation of the size of the Court so as to affect presidential appointments also occurred in the 1860s. The 1863 Judiciary Act expanding the Court from nine to ten members enabled Abraham Lincoln to appoint Stephen J. Field, who subsequently supported the president on war issues. Shortly thereafter, the Radical Republicans, who controlled Congress, passed legislation reducing the number of justices to prevent Lincoln's successor, Andrew Johnson, from naming justices they feared would rule against the Reconstruction program. Soon after Ulysses S. Grant was inaugurated in March 1869, the size of the Court was again expanded; this expansion, plus a retirement, enabled Grant to appoint Justices William Strong and Joseph P. Bradley. Both voted to reconsider a previous Supreme Court decision, *Hepburn v. Griswold,* that had declared unconstitutional the substitution of paper money for gold as legal tender for the payment of contracts.[98] The new decision validated the use of "greenbacks" as legal tender.[99] The three successive changes in the size of the Court within a six-year period brought the results that Congress desired.

Roosevelt's 1937 "Court packing" proposal was different from these earlier examples because of his aggressive efforts to promote congressional action. Frustrated by the invalidation of much of the early New Deal legislation (between January 1935 and June 1936 the Court struck down eight separate statutes), Roosevelt proposed legislation in early 1937 that would permit him to appoint one justice, up to six in number, for each sitting member of the Court who failed to retire voluntarily at age seventy. Buoyed by his landslide electoral victory in 1936, and confident that the Democrat-controlled Congress would follow his lead, Roosevelt announced the proposal at a press conference without consulting with members of Congress. Samuel Kernell points to it as an early, failed attempt at "going public."[100] Although FDR contended that the additions were necessary to handle the Court's caseload, it was patently clear that his real purpose was to liberalize the Court. The proposal stimulated violent opposition from members of the bar, the press, and many of Roosevelt's political supporters in Congress who were angered that they had not been consulted about the plan. At this point, Justice Owen J. Roberts, a centrist who had been aligned with four conservative colleagues in striking down New Deal legislation, began to vote with the other four justices to uphold the legislation—thus giving FDR the new majority he had been seeking. The unpopularity of Roosevelt's proposal, Justice Roberts's mitigating action (which observers dubbed "the switch in time that saved nine"), and the sudden death of Majority Leader Joseph Robinson of Arkansas, who was leading the president's effort in the Senate, resulted in Congress's failure to adopt the Court-packing plan. Kernell calls it "FDR's most stunning legislative failure in his 12 years in office."[101] Yet Roosevelt won the legal battle anyway. Once Roberts switched his vote, conservative members—now in dissent—began to leave the Court. By the time he died, Roosevelt had managed to appoint all but one of the nine justices of the Supreme Court and thus secure a Court majority willing to uphold his policies.

In addition to its power to change the size of the Supreme Court, Congress can also pass legislation altering the appellate jurisdiction of the Court.[102] Presidents could conceivably introduce such legislation—which could take away the power of the Supreme Court to hear appeals in specific types of cases—just as Roosevelt introduced legislation with regard to the size of the Court. As recently as the 1980s, Sen. Jesse Helms, R-N.C., introduced legislation to take away the Supreme Court's appellate jurisdiction to hear cases involving school prayer. (Helms was angered that the Court had declared state-sponsored prayer in public schools a violation of the establishment clause requirement of a separation between church and state.) Helms's effort failed, and presidents have not joined in efforts to secure passage of such jurisdiction-stripping proposals.

Presidents have been more willing to urge Congress to propose constitutional amendments to overturn Supreme Court rulings, and to lobby for the passage of legislation that might undermine existing rulings. Republican presidents Reagan and George H. W. Bush both sought to overturn *Roe v. Wade* by pressuring Congress to propose a constitutional amendment outlawing abortion. Although unsuccessful in this effort, both presidents signed legislation that limited use of federal funds for abortions and made access to abortions more difficult. Bush also supported a constitutional amendment to overrule a controversial Supreme

Court decision, *Texas v. Johnson,* 491 U.S. 397 (1989), that permitted flag burning as a form of protected symbolic speech. When the Supreme Court struck down the Gun Free School Zones Act in *United States v. Lopez,* 514 U.S. 549 (1995), President Clinton strongly criticized the Court and ordered Attorney General Janet Reno to come up with other ways to keep guns out of school.[103]

Enforcement of Court Decisions

Although the federal courts have the authority to hand down decisions on cases within their jurisdiction, they have no independent power to enforce their decisions. Lacking both the power of the purse and of the sword, the Supreme Court depends upon the executive branch to enforce its rulings. Thus, President Eisenhower called out federal troops in 1957 to enforce court-ordered school desegregation in Little Rock, Arkansas. The order was an outgrowth of the Supreme Court's landmark *Brown v. Board of Education* ruling that overturned the "separate but equal" doctrine of *Plessy v. Ferguson.*[104]

Sometimes less forceful action by the president helps to bring about compliance with Supreme Court rulings. For instance, President Kennedy, in a June 1962 press conference, publicly supported the Supreme Court's controversial ruling in *Engel v. Vitale,* which banned state-sponsored prayer in public schools, thus setting an example for others to follow.[105] Presidents also set an example by complying with court orders aimed at them. Thus, immediately after the Supreme Court held in 1952 that President Truman's seizure of the steel mills was unconstitutional, the president ordered the mills restored to private operation.[106] Likewise, President Nixon complied with the Court's 1974 ruling in *United States v. Nixon* that he turn over to a federal district court tapes of his conversations with executive aides.[107] That action produced evidence of the president's involvement in the Watergate affair, led to the House Judiciary Committee's impeachment vote against him, and ultimately resulted in Nixon's resignation.

Nonetheless, presidents have sometimes defied—or threatened to defy—the Court. The fear that President Jefferson's secretary of state, James Madison, would (with the president's blessing) defy a court order to deliver commissions that would result in the seating of Federalist judges probably influenced John Marshall's opinion in *Marbury v. Madison.* Thus, Marshall gave the Jefferson administration what it wanted—it did not force delivery of the commissions— but did so by creating the power of judicial review. More blatantly, President Lincoln once ignored a federal court ruling that declared his suspension of habeas corpus unconstitutional.[108] But Lincoln's response remains an exception to the rule, for chief executives usually have enforced court decisions, even when they would have preferred not to do so.

Judicial Oversight of Presidential Action

Through its power of judicial review, the Supreme Court has the ability to invalidate presidential actions. This is a significant check on presidential power, although it is one that has been used quite infrequently. The Founders originally left open the question of who had the final power to interpret the Constitution. If, as Thomas Jefferson contended, each branch has the authority to interpret the Constitution as far as its own duties are concerned, then the president would be the judge of the constitutionality of executive actions. As a result of *Marbury v. Madison,* though, the Supreme Court has the power to make the final judgment on such matters. Although *Marbury* was decided in 1803, the Supreme Court did not declare a presidential action unconstitutional until after the Civil War.

Of the forty-two people who have served as president,[109] only a handful have been the objects of major Supreme Court decisions invalidating their actions. Even when invalidating a specific presidential action, the Court has often endorsed a broad reading of presidential power. For example, the Court, as previously noted, invalidated President Truman's seizure of steel mills during the Korean War.[110] Truman argued that government seizure to keep open the steel mills (which were involved in a labor dispute that threatened to shut them down) was essential to the war effort. But in seizing the mills, Truman ignored the provisions of the Taft-Hartley Act that permitted the president to obtain an injunction postponing for eighty days a strike that threatened the national safety and welfare. Instead, he issued an executive order seizing the steel mills, based on his authority under the Constitution and U.S. law and as commander in chief. The steel companies protested the seizure as unconstitutional, and the case went to the Supreme Court.

By a 6–3 vote, the Court invalidated the president's seizure. Although six justices voted against the specific action in question, seven justices (the three dissenters plus four of the justices in the majority) explicitly recognized that presidents have a range of "inherent" power to take actions not explicitly authorized by the Constitution. The three dissenters said that power was broad enough to cover Truman's seizure of the mills. The other four justices who recognized some degree of inherent power stressed that such power is not absolute, and that it was not broad enough to cover a situation such as this where the president went against the will of Congress. Thus, even though the case invalidated an action taken by a specific president, it set a precedent that actually *expanded* presidential power through the Court's recognition of inherent power.

Similarly, a unanimous Supreme Court in *United States v. Nixon* ruled against President Nixon's refusal to surrender subpoenaed White House tapes to Watergate special prosecutor Leon Jaworski.[111] In refusing to surrender the tapes, Nixon had claimed the existence of an "executive privilege" relating to private conversations between the chief executive and his advisers. While the Court rejected Nixon's specific claim of privilege, it nonetheless recognized for the first time that the principle of executive privilege did have constitutional underpinnings. As with *Youngstown,* the Court ruled against a specific exercise of presidential power while at the same time expanding the general scope of presidential power.[112]

The Supreme Court has been especially deferential to presidential power in the realm of foreign affairs. In *United States v. Curtiss-Wright Export Corp.,* 299 U.S. 304

(1936), the Court recognized that presidents have a wider degree of discretion in foreign affairs than they do in domestic affairs. Justice George Sutherland went so far as to call the president "the sole organ of the federal government in the field of international relations."[113] Similarly, the Court has recognized that presidents have broad power to respond to military emergencies and wage war even in the congressional absence of war. In *The Prize Cases*, 67 U.S. 635 (1863), the Supreme Court recognized President Lincoln's power to impose a military blockade on southern ports—an act of war—even though Congress had not yet actually declared war. During World War II, the Court upheld broad executive power to impose the forced relocation of Japanese Americans and others of Japanese ancestry to federal detention centers.[114] More recently, the Court upheld the power of the president to seize Iranian assets during the Iran hostage crisis of the 1970s and use them as a bargaining chip to help free American hostages.[115]

In addition to establishing general parameters of presidential power, Supreme Court decisions can have significant repercussions on the fate of particular presidents. Two such decisions had a particular bearing on Bill Clinton. Had it not been for a 1988 ruling upholding (over the lone dissent of Antonin Scalia) the constitutionality of the independent counsel law, and a unanimous 1997 ruling that allowed a sexual harassment lawsuit against the president by Paula Jones to proceed while he was still in office, Clinton might have been spared the independent counsel investigation by Kenneth Starr and the impeachment trial brought about as a result of the Monica Lewinsky scandal.[116]

Conclusion

The relationship between the presidency and the judiciary is a very important one. On the one hand, the judiciary has the power to hand down rulings that have a direct effect on presidents and their policies. On the other, presidents can influence the federal courts through the power to nominate judges to serve on them. Both have long-term consequences. Supreme Court rulings are not easy to overturn. Those based on the Constitution can only be overruled by the Court itself or through the passage of a constitutional amendment. The president's power to appoint can also be far-reaching. Federal judges, unlike members of Congress and the political appointees of the executive branch, serve for life. That fact all but guarantees that the judicial nominees of George W. Bush will be closely scrutinized and, in all likelihood, hotly contested.

NOTES

1. *Bush v. Gore*, 121 S. Ct. 525 (2000). Among the many accounts of the Supreme Court's role in the 2000 election, the most thorough is Howard Gillman, *The Votes That Counted: How the Court Decided the 2000 Presidential Election* (Chicago: University of Chicago Press, 2001).

2. The Florida legislature had provided for this standard by law. Florida Statute 101.5614(5): "No vote shall be declared invalid or void if there is a clear indication of

the intent of the voter as determined by the canvassing board." A majority of states (including Texas) followed a similar standard (see footnote 2 of Justice Stevens's dissent in *Bush v. Gore,* 540). Ironically, the Florida Supreme Court may have failed to try to clarify that standard (by telling counties exactly how to identify the "clear intent" of the voter) because the U.S. Supreme Court had already chastised the Florida court for imposing its own interpretation of Florida law in *Bush v. Palm Beach Canvassing Board,* 121 S. Ct. 471 (2000) (see Justice Breyer's dissent in *Bush v. Gore,* 551, for a discussion of this).

3. *Bush v. Gore,* 530, 531. *Reynolds v. Sims,* 377 U.S. 533 (1964); *Gray v. Sanders,* 372 U.S. 368 (1963).

4. *Bush v. Gore,* 533 (two of the seven members who joined the per curiam opinion, Breyer and Souter, dissented on that particular point).

5. *Bush v. Gore,* Justice Souter's dissent (joined by Breyer, Stevens, and Ginsburg), 543.

6. Ibid., 546.

7. Ibid., 545.

8. Ibid., 542. They also made it clear that they thought the Court should not have reviewed *Bush v. Palm Beach County Canvassing Board,* 121 S. Ct. 471 (2000), either. In that case, the U.S. Supreme Court first reviewed the Florida Supreme Court's ruling allowing manual recounts. The U.S. Supreme Court vacated and remanded the decision in a per curiam decision, instructing the Florida Supreme Court to clarify its basis for requiring the recounts by demonstrating that its decision was based on Florida state law. The Florida Supreme Court did so and proceeded to order the recounts that were stopped in *Bush v. Gore.*

9. *Bush v. Gore,* Justice Ginsburg's dissent, 549.

10. Ibid., 550.

11. *Bush v. Gore,* Justice Breyer's dissent, 552.

12. *Bush v. Gore,* Justice Stevens's dissent, 541.

13. E. Joshua Rosenkranz, "High Court's Misuse of the Past," *National Law Journal,* January 15, 2001, A20. *Baker v. Carr,* 369 U.S. 186 (1962), though confined to jurisdictional issues, held that the Supreme Court could hear cases involving reapportionment, thus allowing court challenges to the drawing of legislative districts on the grounds that they deprived citizens of equal protection. It led to the "one person, one vote" principle articulated the next year in *Gray v. Sanders,* 372 U.S. 368 (1963).

14. *Bush v. Gore,* Justice Stevens's dissent, 541.

15. "Our consideration is limited to the present circumstances, for the problem of equal protection in election processes generally presents many complexities." *Bush v. Gore,* 532.

16. Rosenkranz, "High Court's Misuse of the Past," A20.

17. David Von Drehle et al., "In Florida, Drawing the Battle Lines," *Washington Post,* January 29, 2001, A1. See also Gillman, *The Votes That Counted.*

18. Ronald Dworkin, " 'A Badly Flawed Election': An Exchange," *New York Review of Books,* February 22, 2001, 9.

19. *Bush v. Gore,* Justice Stevens's dissent, 542.

20. Joan Biskupic, "Election Still Splits Court," *USA Today,* January 22, 2001, 1A.

21. Charles Lane, "Two Justices Defend Court's Intervention in Florida Dispute," *Washington Post,* March 30, 2001, A13.

22. Bruce Ackerman, "The Court Packs Itself," *The American Prospect,* February 13, 2001, online edition.

23. In addition to the district courts and the courts of appeals, there are several specialized courts. These include the U.S. Court of International Trade and the U.S. Court of Federal Claims.

24. The District of Columbia and U.S. territories, such as Guam, also have district courts.

25. G. Alan Tarr, *Judicial Process and Policymaking,* 2d ed. (New York: West/ Wadsworth, 1999), 40.

26. David M. O'Brien, *Judicial Roulette* (New York: Priority Press, 1988), 70.

27. Howard Ball, *Courts and Politics: The Federal Judicial System,* 2d ed. (Englewood Cliffs, N.J.: Prentice-Hall, 1987), 199.

28. Ibid., 199–200.

29. Joel Grossman, *Lawyers and Judges: The ABA and the Politics of Judicial Selection* (New York: Wiley, 1965), 168, 170.

30. O'Brien, *Judicial Roulette,* 71.

31. "Doing Business in the Senate," editorial, *New York Times,* June 19, 2001, A22.

32. Thomas B. Edsall, "Democrats Press Bush for Input on Judges," *Washington Post,* April 28, 2001, A4. See also "Blocking Judicial Ideologues," editorial, *New York Times,* April 27, 2001, A24.

33. Jonathan Ringel, "Gearing Up to Vote on Court Nominees," *The Recorder,* June 18, 2001, 3.

34. O'Brien, *Judicial Roulette,* 33.

35. Tarr, *Judicial Process,* 75.

36. Sheldon Goldman, *Picking Federal Judges: Lower Court Selection from Roosevelt through Reagan* (New Haven: Yale University Press, 1997), 86; see also Grossman, *Lawyers and Judges,* chap. 3.

37. Quoted in Neil A. Lewis, "White House Ends Bar Association's Role in Screening Federal Judges," *New York Times,* March 23, 2001, A13. For a recent scholarly assessment of the ABA's ratings, see Susan Brodie Haire, "Rating the Ratings of the American Bar Association Standing Committee on Federal Judiciary," *Justice System Journal* 22, no. 1 (2001): 1–17.

38. Thomas B. Edsall, "Federalist Society Becomes a Force in Washington; Conservative Group's Members Take Key Roles in Bush White House and Help Shape Policy and Judicial Appointments," *Washington Post,* April 18, 2001, A4.

39. Thomas B. Edsall, "Liberals Form Counter to Federalist Society," *Washington Post,* August 1, 2001, A5.

40. Larry C. Berkson and Susan B. Carbon, *The United States Circuit Judge Nominating Commission: Its Members, Procedures, and Candidates* (Chicago: American Judicature Society, 1980).

41. Alan Neff, *The United States District Judge Nominating Commissions: Their Members, Procedures, and Candidates* (Chicago: American Judicature Society, 1981).

42. Harry P. Stumpf, *American Judicial Politics,* 2d ed. (Upper Saddle River, N.J.: Prentice Hall, 1998), Tables 6-2 and 6-3, 180–183.

43. Goldman, *Picking Federal Judges,* 282; Stumpf, *American Judicial Politics,* 183.

44. Sheldon Goldman, "Reagan's Judicial Legacy: Completing the Puzzle and Summing Up," *Judicature* 72 (April–May 1989): 319–320.

45. Quoted in O'Brien, *Judicial Roulette,* 61–62.

46. Goldman, *Picking Federal Judges,* Tables 9.1 and 9.2. The total number of federal judicial appointments with life tenure rises to 372 if you include Reagan's four Supreme Court appointments. It rises slightly higher if you include his appointment of non–Article III judges who staff specialized courts and do not have life tenure.

47. Alliance for Justice Judicial Selection Project, "2000 Annual Report," 3. Available online, www.afj.org/jsp.

48. Ronald Stidham, Robert A. Carp, and Donald Songer, "The Voting Behavior of President Clinton's Judicial Appointees," *Judicature* 80 (July–August 1996): 16–20. See also Alliance for Justice Judicial Selection Project, "2000 Annual Report," 4–5;

Sheldon Goldman and Elliot Slotnick, "Picking Judges Under Fire," *Judicature* 82 (May–June 1999): 265–284; Nancy Scherer, "Are Clinton's Judges 'Old' Democrats or 'New' Democrats?" *Judicature* 84 (November–December 2000): 151–154.

49. Goldman and Slotnick, "Picking Judges Under Fire," 282.

50. Michael Kelly, "Judge Dread," *New Republic*, March 31, 1997, 6.

51. John H. Cushman Jr., "Senate Imperils Judicial System, Rehnquist Says," *New York Times*, January 1, 1998, A1.

52. Alliance for Justice Judicial Selection Project, "2000 Annual Report," 5.

53. Ibid., 2.

54. Ibid., 1. For a thorough discussion of Clinton's judicial legacy, including his record on diversity, see Sheldon Goldman et al., "Clinton's Judges: Summing Up the Legacy," *Judicature* 84 (March–April 2001): 228–254.

55. "ABA a Key Player on Federal Bench," editorial, *Chicago Sun-Times*, March 27, 2001, 31.

56. Bennett Roth, "Change in Judicial Appointments Signaled by Bush; Clinton Nominees Are Pulled," *Houston Chronicle*, March 21, 2001, A1.

57. William Glaberson, "In New Senate, New Scrutiny of Judicial Nominees," *New York Times*, May 30, 2001, A20.

58. For example, *Lochner v. New York*, 198 U.S. 45 (1905).

59. *Roe v. Wade*, 410 U.S. 113 (1973); *Griswold v. Connecticut*, 381 U.S. 479 (1965). See Robert H. Bork, *The Tempting of America* (New York: Free Press, 1990), for a criticism of both lines of cases.

60. Robert Scigliano, *The Supreme Court and the Presidency* (New York: Free Press, 1971), chap. 4.

61. For a comprehensive discussion of the Framers' debate on qualifications, see Michael Nelson, "Qualifications for President," in *Inventing the American Presidency*, ed. Thomas E. Cronin (Lawrence: University Press of Kansas, 1989).

62. Joel B. Grossman and Stephen L. Wasby, "The Senate and Supreme Court Nominations: Some Reflections," *Duke Law Journal* (August 1972): 559, note 8.

63. Though all Supreme Court justices have been lawyers, not all have had law school degrees. Law schools as we know them did not exist in the early part of the nineteenth century, and a majority of the lawyers learned the profession through apprenticeship rather than law schools into the early part of the twentieth century. See David M. O'Brien, *Storm Center: The Supreme Court in American Politics*, 5th ed. (New York: Norton, 2000), 34.

64. Ibid., 34.

65. See John Anthony Maltese, *The Selling of Supreme Court Nominees* (Baltimore: Johns Hopkins University Press, 1995), chaps. 4, 5.

66. David Alistair Yalof, *Pursuit of Justices: Presidential Politics and the Selection of Supreme Court Nominees* (Chicago: University of Chicago Press, 1999), 4–5.

67. Ibid., 7, 12–13.

68. Ethan Bronner, *Battle for Justice: How the Bork Nomination Shook America* (New York: Norton, 1989), 29–36; Mark Gitenstein, *Matters of Principle: An Insider's Account of America's Rejection of Robert Bork's Nomination to the Supreme Court* (New York: Simon and Schuster, 1992), 28–37.

69. Lawrence Baum, *The Supreme Court*, 6th ed. (Washington, D.C.: CQ Press, 1998), 31–35.

70. Scott H. Ainsworth and John Anthony Maltese, "National Grange Influence on the Supreme Court Confirmation of Stanley Matthews," *Social Science History* 20 (spring 1996): 41–62.

71. For early examples of this, see Maltese, *The Selling of Supreme Court Nominees*, 47–49, 53.

72. Quoted in Robin Toner, "Interest Groups Set for Battle on a Supreme Court Vacancy," *New York Times,* April 21, 2001, A1.

73. P. S. Ruckman Jr., "The Supreme Court, Critical Nominations, and the Senate Confirmation Process," *Journal of Politics* 55 (August 1993), 794. If you include the two nominations withdrawn on a technicality, the failure rate rises to 19.5 percent.

74. Maltese, *The Selling of Supreme Court Nominees,* 5.

75. E. J. Dionne, "A Town Hall Meeting: A Process Run Amok—Can It Be Fixed?" *ABC News Nightline,* American Broadcasting Company (ABC), October 16, 1991.

76. For extensive case studies of all three of these nominations, see Maltese, *The Selling of Supreme Court Nominees,* chaps. 1, 4, 5.

77. It should be noted that Associate Justice William Rehnquist's nomination for chief justice in 1986 was attacked by liberal groups because of his alleged insensitivity to the rights of minorities and women. He was ultimately confirmed, but the thirty-three votes against him were the most ever cast against a confirmed justice up to that point.

78. For thorough accounts of the role of interest groups in the Bork nomination, see Patrick B. McGuigan and Dawn M. Weyrich, *Ninth Justice: The Fight for Bork* (Washington, D.C.: Free Congress Foundation, 1990); and Michael Pertschuk and Wendy Schaetzel, *The People Rising: The Campaign Against the Bork Nomination* (New York: Thunder's Mouth Press, 1989).

79. Robert Shogan, *A Question of Judgement: The Fortas Case and the Struggle for the Supreme Court* (New York: Bobbs-Merrill, 1972).

80. Maltese, *The Selling of Supreme Court Nominees,* 14, 16.

81. "The Electoral Count," *New York Times,* January 30, 1881.

82. Quoted in Alpheus Thomas Mason, *Brandeis: A Free Man's Life* (New York: Viking, 1946), 467.

83. See Maltese, *The Selling of Supreme Court Nominees,* for thorough accounts of all of these developments.

84. *Planned Parenthood of Southeastern Pennsylvania v. Casey,* 505 U.S. 833 (1992).

85. Quoted in David M. O'Brien, *Storm Center: The Supreme Court in American Politics,* 5th ed. (New York: Norton, 1993), 84.

86. Scigliano, *The Supreme Court and the Presidency,* chap. 6. See also Lincoln Caplan, *The Tenth Justice: The Solicitor General and the Rule of Law* (New York: Random House, 1987); Rebecca Mae Salokar, *The Solicitor General: The Politics of Law* (Philadelphia: Temple University Press, 1992).

87. The Supreme Court's discretion has changed some over time. Since 1988, that discretion is almost absolute. Cases now come to the Supreme Court almost exclusively by way of a writ of certiorari. To grant "cert" (agree to hear a case), four of the nine justices must vote to accept review. See Craig R. Ducat, *Constitutional Interpretation,* 7th ed. (Belmont, Calif.: West, 2000), 31.

88. Scigliano, *The Supreme Court and the Presidency,* 172.

89. Christopher Zorn, "Information, Advocacy, and the Role of the Solicitor General as Amicus Curiae" (working paper, Emory University, 1999), 1.

90. Steven Puro, "The United States as Amicus Curiae," in *Courts, Law, and Judicial Processes,* ed. S. Sidney Ulmer (New York: Free Press, 1981), 220–230.

91. Scigliano, *The Supreme Court and the Presidency,* chap. 6; Puro, "The United States as Amicus Curiae"; Karen O'Connor, "The Amicus Curiae Role of the U.S. Solicitor General in Supreme Court Litigation," *Judicature* 66 (December–January 1983): 261.

92. Kevin T. McGuire, "Explaining Executive Success in the U.S. Supreme Court," *Political Research Quarterly* 51 (June 1998): 522.

93. This situation is to be contrasted with the paucity of experience attorneys general have before the Court: traditionally, they argue only one case before their

term is over. For an interesting account of Robert Kennedy's first appearance before the Court two years after he became attorney general, see Victor Navasky, *Kennedy Justice* (New York: Athenaeum, 1980), chap. 6.

94. Zorn, "Information, Advocacy, and the Role of the Solicitor General as Amicus Curiae," 9. For a discussion of similar strategy by other litigants, see Donald Songer, Charles M. Cameron, and Jeffrey A. Segal, "An Empirical Test of the Rational-Actor Theory of Litigation," *Journal of Politics* 57 (November 1995): 1119–1129.

95. Caplan, *The Tenth Justice.*

96. Elder Witt, *A Different Justice* (Washington, D.C.: Congressional Quarterly, 1986), chaps. 6, 7.

97. Caplan, *The Tenth Justice,* 79–80, 255–256.

98. *Hepburn v. Griswold (First Legal Tender Case),* 8 Wall. 506 (1870).

99. *Knox v. Lee, Parker v. Davis (Second Legal Tender Case),* 12 Wall. 457 (1871).

100. Samuel Kernell, *Going Public,* 2d ed. (Washington, D.C.: CQ Press, 1993), 110.

101. Ibid.

102. For a useful review of this power, see Gerald Gunther, "Congressional Power to Curtail Federal Court Jurisdiction: An Opinionated Guide to the Ongoing Debate," *Stanford Law Review* 36 (1984): 895. The most famous Supreme Court case involving this issue is *Ex Parte McCardle,* 74 U.S. 506 (1869).

103. Stumpf, *American Judicial Politics,* 429.

104. *Brown v. Board of Education,* 347 U.S. 483 (1954); *Plessy v. Ferguson,* 163 U.S. 537 (1896).

105. Stumpf, *American Judicial Politics,* 429. *Engel v. Vitale,* 370 U.S. 421 (1962).

106. *Youngstown Sheet and Tube Co. v. Sawyer,* 343 U.S. 579 (1952).

107. *United States v. Nixon,* 418 U.S. 683 (1974).

108. *Ex parte Merryman,* 17 F. Cases 144 (1861).

109. Although George W. Bush is our forty-third president, Grover Cleveland counted as both the twenty-second and the twenty-fourth president.

110. *Youngstown Sheet and Tube Co. v. Sawyer.* For a thorough history of the case, see Maeva Marcus, *Truman and the Steel Seizure Case: The Limits of Presidential Power* (Durham: Duke University Press, 1994).

111. *United States v. Nixon,* 418 U.S. 683 (1974).

112. For accounts of executive privilege, see Raoul Berger, *Executive Privilege: A Constitutional Myth* (Cambridge: Harvard University Press, 1974); Mark J. Rozell, *Executive Privilege: The Dilemma of Secrecy and Democratic Accountability* (Baltimore: Johns Hopkins University Press, 1994).

113. For a discussion of this, see Lee Epstein and Thomas G. Walker, *Constitutional Law for a Changing America: Institutional Powers and Constraints,* 4th ed. (Washington, D.C.: CQ Press, 2001), 248–250.

114. *Korematsu v. United States,* 323 U.S. 214 (1944). For an account of this, see Peter Irons, *Justice at War: The Story of the Japanese-American Internment Cases* (New York: Oxford University Press, 1983).

115. *Dames & Moore v. Regan,* 453 U.S. 654 (1981).

116. *Morrison v. Olson,* 487 U.S. 654 (1988); *Clinton v. Jones,* 520 U.S. 681 (1997). For a discussion of the Lewinsky scandal, see Mark J. Rozell and Clyde Wilcox, eds., *The Clinton Scandal and the Future of American Government* (Washington, D.C.: Georgetown University Press, 2000).

SUGGESTED READINGS

Abraham, Henry. *Justices, Presidents, and Senators: A History of U.S. Supreme Court Appointments from Washington to Clinton.* 4th ed. Lanham, Md.: Rowman and Littlefield, 1999.

Baum, Lawrence. *The Supreme Court*. 7th ed. Washington, D.C.: CQ Press, 2001.

Bronner, Ethan. *Battle for Justice: How the Bork Nomination Shook America*. New York: Norton, 1989.

Caldeira, Gregory, and John Wright. "Lobbying for Justice." *American Journal of Political Science* 42 (April 1998).

Caplan, Lincoln. *The Tenth Justice: The Solicitor General and the Rule of Law*. New York: Random House, 1987.

Epstein, Lee, and Thomas G. Walker. *Constitutional Law for a Changing America: Institutional Powers and Constraints*. 4th ed. Washington, D.C.: CQ Press, 2001.

Gerhardt, Michael J. *The Federal Appointments Process: A Constitutional and Historical Analysis*. Durham: Duke University Press, 2000.

Gillman, Howard. *The Votes That Counted: How the Court Decided the 2000 Presidential Election*. Chicago: University of Chicago Press, 2001.

Goldman, Sheldon. *Picking Federal Judges: Lower Court Selection from Roosevelt through Reagan*. New Haven: Yale University Press, 1997.

Goldman, Sheldon, et al. "Clinton's Judges: Summing Up the Legacy." *Judicature* 84 (March–April 2001).

Maltese, John Anthony. *The Selling of Supreme Court Nominees*. Baltimore: Johns Hopkins University Press, 1995.

O'Brien, David M. *Judicial Roulette*. New York: Priority Press, 1988.

Salokar, Rebecca Mae. *The Solicitor General: The Politics of Law*. Philadelphia: Temple University Press, 1992.

Yalof, David Alistair. *Pursuit of Justices: Presidential Politics and the Selection of Supreme Court Nominees*. Chicago: University of Chicago Press, 1999.

8   THE POLITICS OF
DOMESTIC POLICY

BILL CLINTON IN 1992 WAS THE FIRST
president since FDR to win election with a
campaign that focused almost exclusively
on domestic problems. In fact, one of Clinton's sharpest criticisms of his predecessor,
President George Bush, was that Bush had
neglected serious social and economic
conditions in the United States while concentrating on foreign policy. Clinton
appeared to be undaunted by the conventional wisdom, in vogue since the end of
World War II, that regarded domestic policy as the black hole of presidential politics. Although Clinton became much more
active in foreign policy in his second term
(continuing his attempts to negotiate a
Middle East peace settlement almost to the
very end of his presidency), George W.
Bush and Al Gore both concentrated on
domestic issues in the 2000 presidential
campaign.

Upon taking office, presidents do confront a vast array of domestic problems,
issues, and demands for government

*President Clinton proposed and
implemented AmeriCorps, a domestic
version of the Peace Corps, to
encourage Americans of all ages and
backgrounds to engage in community
service. Here he joins a graduating
class of AmeriCorps on August 9,
1999.*

284

action. Already in operation are numerous complex and costly programs that compete for limited funds. Many of them enjoy the support of powerful interest groups and congressional leaders. Whatever the administration does (or fails to do) in response to public demands is likely to cost the president political support.

Presidents face a congested public policy agenda that results from interrelatedness, overlapping, and layering of issues.[1] Many political scientists have classified public policy for analytical purposes, but the most widely used classification scheme, or typology, is Theodore Lowi's division of policies into distributive, regulatory, and redistributive categories.[2] He based his categories on who the policies affect, ranging from individuals to the entire society, and the likelihood that the government will have to exercise coercion to implement the policy.

Distributive policies have the most diffused impact. They affect specific groups of people and provide individualized benefits. They have low visibility, produce little conflict, and are not likely to require the application of coercion. Examples of distributive policies include agricultural price supports, public works projects, and research and development programs. *Regulatory* policies affect large segments of society and involve the application of coercion. Although regulatory issues tend to be highly technical, they often are quite visible and controversial. Examples include pollution control, antitrust, and occupational safety and health. *Redistributive* policies have the broadest impact on society. They involve the transfer of resources (wealth and income) from some groups to others. They require coercion, are highly visible, and usually are accompanied by social or class conflict. Examples of redistributive policies include Social Security and tax reform.

Lowi argued that the type of policy determines the focus and behavior of political actors. Distributive policy politics involves limited presidential and extensive congressional participation and decision making that relies heavily on logrolling—the mutual exchange of support for legislation. Regulatory policy politics produces moderate presidential and substantial congressional interest and involvement, with frequent conflict between the president and Congress. Redistributive policy politics often is fraught with ideological disputes and presidential-congressional conflict. Presidents tend to be most involved with redistributive policy issues. This is the case whether the government is seeking to expand or limit the scope of its activities.

Steven Shull has used Lowi's policy typology to examine presidential and congressional roles in domestic policy formation. He found that there were "some differences in presidential and congressional behavior . . . along lines anticipated by the 'theory,'" and that "modest empirical distinctions" existed among the three policy categories.[3] The principal problem with Lowi's typology is the difficulty in making it operational for purposes of measurement. The problem arises because an issue may change its designation over time, starting out, for example, as a redistributive issue and becoming distributive. This is what happened to Title I of the Elementary and Secondary Education Act of 1965, a program of federal assistance to local school districts for economically disadvantaged children. As a new program, it sparked controversy because of its redistributive effects, but over time it became a routinized distribution of federal funds that was part of the established structure of school finance. In other words, Lowi's categories are not fixed in time. Shull concluded that Lowi's typology is not as useful as substantive classification based on policy content.

John Kessel has broken down domestic policy into areas involving social benefits, civil liberties, natural resources, and agriculture.[4] Each area entails a specific type of politics and its own temporal pattern, both of which have implications for presidential participation. The politics of social benefits, such as housing and Social Security retirement, involves the allocation of resources. Thus, it is similar to Lowi's distributive and redistributive categories. Presidents use the distribution of social benefits to build public support. Thus, they tend to pay most attention to social benefits as they approach reelection; afterward, if they are successful, they are much less concerned with these benefits. Civil rights involve a pattern of politics that is regulatory and highly sensitive because of differing conceptions of fairness. Presidents are most likely to act on civil rights issues immediately after their election, both because these issues are highly controversial and because campaign promises must be fulfilled. The politics of natural resources, which includes environmental protection, is primarily regulatory, and agriculture mostly involves allocation. The temporal patterns in natural resource and agricultural policy politics are a function of long-range developments and entail limited presidential participation.

Whether one approaches domestic policy using Lowi's analytical typology or Kessel's substantive classifications, it is clear that as a practical matter presidents can become fully involved with only a small number of problems and issues. The Lowi and Kessel approaches suggest that in domestic policy, presidents tend to focus on matters such as maintaining the financial integrity of the Social Security system, reforming welfare, and dealing with major civil rights proposals. They do not take up all major redistributive, social benefit, and civil rights issues, and may consciously avoid some that may involve enormous financial or political costs. They are unlikely to become bogged down with routine distributive policies or with the technicalities of economic and social regulation. Jimmy Carter harmed himself politically when he tangled with Congress over eighteen water projects he regarded as unnecessary. Other presidents have been content to leave the distribution of "pork barrel" projects to Congress. Although George W. Bush initially vowed to slash such pork in half (from $16 billion in fiscal 2001 to $8 billion under his proposed budget), he backed off in the summer of 2001 to avoid a fight with Congress. In Bush's transportation spending bill alone, the House of Representatives had added some 900 local pork barrel projects. Proposed spending for local projects mushroomed in other areas as well. For example, Bush had proposed an allocation of $300,000 for rebuilding beaches in Brevard County, Florida, but Congress proposed $8.5 million. Budget Director Mitchell E. Daniels Jr. conceded in July 2001 that such increases were "an acceptable cost of doing business" with Congress.[5]

The range and complexity of domestic problems and issues produce a policy congestion that makes coordination the essential presidential function in this area. Coordination has been complicated, however, by the interrelatedness of domestic, economic, and national security policy. If, on the one hand, presidents attempt to coordinate specific policies through simplification—say, by proposals to balance the budget or reorganize the bureaucracy—they encounter the opposition of powerful forces mobilized around those policy issues. Ronald Reagan's 1982 proposals to move toward a balanced budget by reducing Social Security cost-of-living allowances provide an excellent example. Opposition from the senior "gray lobby" and most members of Congress quickly stymied the idea.

If, on the other hand, presidents fail to coordinate complex policies effectively, they risk loss of popular and congressional support as well as having to deal with interest group opposition. This happened early in Clinton's first term when he lost control of his health care proposal. Lack of coordination in selling the proposal to Congress and the public allowed opponents to pick apart bits and pieces of the plan. As cracks appeared, opponents took control of the agenda, thereby dooming the president's proposal.

The Domestic Policy Process

The domestic policy process consists of actions that culminate in the development and presentation of legislative proposals to Congress, the issuance of executive orders, and the preparation and submission of annual budgets. There is a cyclical regularity to much of the policy process because annual events—such as the State of the Union, budget, and economic messages—define the broad outlines of the president's program.[6] (Although these events occur at approximately the same time each year, the full cycles last longer than a year. The budget for the fiscal year beginning on October 1, 2001, for example, had its origins in the budget review process conducted in the spring of 1999.) Formal events for proposing policy, like the president's annual submission of the budget, are supplemented by the emergence of policy proposals at other times during the year. Such proposals may emerge due to unexpected events or because of other forces coming from outside the White House itself. Thus, Sen. John McCain, R-Ariz., pushed campaign finance reform in 2001, even though it was an issue the White House would have preferred not to have on the agenda.

Policy Streams

The process of setting the president's domestic policy agenda can be understood as the convergence in the White House of three tributary streams: the first identifies *problems and issues* requiring attention; the second produces *proposed solutions* to the problems; and the third carries the *political factors* that establish the context for policymaking. According to John Kingdon, these three streams operate largely, but not absolutely, independently of one another. Problems and solutions develop separately and may or may not be joined, and political factors may change regardless of whether policymakers have recognized a problem or whether a potential solution is available.[7]

The First Stream: Problems and Issues. Problems and issues move on to the president's domestic policy agenda either because their seriousness and high visibility make it impossible to avoid them or because of presidential initiative. Examples of unavoidable problems that force the president to react include such matters as energy shortages, a failing economy, high rates of inflation and unemployment, the emergence of acquired immune deficiency syndrome (AIDS) as a major threat to public health, and the problems resulting from increased drug abuse. Other times, presidents act more proactively by adding items that they believe are instrumental to the achievement of their goals.

Once enough important people, inside and outside the government, begin to think that something should be done about a certain problem or issue, it is likely that the president will react by adding that item to the administration's domestic agenda.[8] This pressure may occur as a consequence of changes in economic and social indicators, such as rates of inflation, unemployment, energy costs, infant mortality, and students' scores on various standardized tests. Influential decision makers in the presidency, the bureaucracy, Congress, the private sector, and state and local governments routinely monitor changes in a large array of indicators. Whether these changes add up to a problem is a matter of interpretation. That interpretation takes place in the context of the symbolic significance of the matter, the personal experiences of the president and the other decision makers with it, and the relationship of the subject to other problems and issues.

The president and other decision makers may be moved to recognize a condition as a compelling problem because of a "focusing event," such as a disaster or a crisis. For example, the near meltdown of a reactor at the Three Mile Island power plant in western Pennsylvania in March 1979 thrust nuclear safety to the forefront of the domestic agenda after safety proponents had struggled for years with little success to gain recognition for this issue. More recently, the California energy crisis of 2001, coupled with rising energy prices in the rest of the country, focused nationwide attention on energy policy.

On occasion, presidents have no choice but to deal with a problem, even though they may prefer not to do so. The 1992 riots in Los Angeles forced a reluctant George Bush to propose legislation to aid the damaged city, while events in Somalia, Haiti, and Bosnia forced Bill Clinton to devote more attention than he wished to foreign policy. Similarly, the collision of a U.S. Navy surveillance aircraft with a Chinese F-8 interceptor over the South China Sea in April 2001 and the subsequent detention of the U.S. flight crew by the Chinese government forced George W. Bush to focus attention on the diplomatic standoff.

Some problems and issues remain on the agenda through successive presidential administrations. Feasible solutions may not have been found, solutions may have been tried unsuccessfully, or the problem may have been "solved" only to reemerge in a different form. Health care exemplifies such an issue. Harry S. Truman proposed a comprehensive national health insurance program in

1945 as an additional Social Security benefit.[9] The American Medical Association and major business associations successfully attacked the proposal as "socialized medicine." Both John F. Kennedy and Lyndon B. Johnson advanced proposals for national health insurance, and in 1965, Congress responded partially with Medicare, a health insurance plan for Social Security retirees age sixty-five and over. Since then, pressures have continued for a plan that would provide universal coverage. In the 1970s, it received support from Richard M. Nixon and Jimmy Carter, as opinion polls showed that a majority of the population favored some kind of national health insurance program. During the recession in the early 1990s, health care reform became a salient issue as millions of workers either lost or feared losing health insurance along with their jobs. In 1991, Harris Wofford, an unknown Pennsylvania Democrat, defeated a popular Republican ex-governor and former U.S. attorney general, Richard Thornburg, in a special Senate election by advocating health care reform. Bill Clinton made the need for health care reform one of the central issues in his 1992 presidential campaign, and it became one of the principal goals of the domestic policy agenda in his first two years, although it failed to pass Congress. Health care remained an important issue, however, and Democrats introduced a "patients' bill of rights" when they regained control of the Senate in June 2001. The plan—long opposed by Republicans—would regulate the managed health care industry and give patients the power to sue their HMOs for denial of coverage. Even President Bush seemed ready to accept some form of the plan.

At other times, presidents have broader discretion to determine which problems and issues to emphasize. In such cases, three goals affect their selection of problems and issues to address: reelection (for a first-term president); historical achievement; and a desire to shape public policy in accordance with their beliefs.[10] Presidents vary in the emphasis they place on these goals. Nixon's willingness to propose innovative policies for welfare reform and revenue sharing, even at the expense of alienating some of his conservative supporters, reflected his concern with historical achievement.[11] As he approached his reelection campaign, Carter shifted from making agenda decisions on the basis of his beliefs to making them on the basis of politics. Reagan consistently defined domestic policy in terms of his conservative ideology, even at the risk of electoral disadvantage. The first President Bush drew frequent criticism for his limited, largely reactive domestic agenda that "intrigued some in Washington less for what it contained . . . than for what it ignored."[12] Clinton's initial agenda reflected his desire to implement substantial domestic policy reforms in accordance with his centrist strategy as a New Democrat. After the Republican victory in the 1994 congressional elections, Clinton scaled down and modified his agenda with a view toward his 1996 reelection campaign. Much of his second term was consumed with the Monica Lewinsky scandal and his impeachment trial in the Senate.

The Second Stream: Solutions. Once a problem or an issue has been recognized, the availability of a solution becomes an important determinant of whether it will rise to a high position on the president's agenda.[13] Solutions take several forms, ranging from *direct actions*, such as legislative proposals or executive orders, to *symbolic actions*, such as appointment of a study commission or a task force, to *no action* at all. Problems can have several solutions, and a single solution can be applied to more than one problem. Some solutions attach themselves naturally to a problem, or they may be consciously selected from among competing alternatives. Most solutions that are coupled with problems on the president's agenda come from ideas generated outside the presidency. This is due, in part, to time constraints facing executive advisers and the relatively small size of the institution of the presidency in relation to the policymaking environment as a whole. Aside from the presidency, the principal sources of policy ideas are Congress, the bureaucracy, interest groups, universities, think tanks (research institutes), and state and local governments. Within the presidency, the president's campaign promises (such as George W. Bush's pledge to cut taxes) are a source of policy proposals and a benchmark for evaluating externally generated ideas.[14] In addition, the president's domestic policy staff may develop new ideas once the president is in office.

Many of the ideas that emerge as proposed solutions to problems on the president's agenda have been circulating among members of "issue networks" that develop around clusters of related problems and issues. Issue networks are simply groups of individuals and organizations that support particular policy positions. Such networks might consist of members of Congress and their legislative aides, bureaucrats, interest groups, the media, scholars and other experts in research organizations, and representatives of state and local government. Together they promote specific ideas and proposals, such as campaign finance reform, energy policy, and a patients' bill of rights. Issue networks are motivated by their participants' desire to advance their personal and organizational interests and to influence public policy in accordance with their values. Network participants study, analyze, and discuss problems and solutions among themselves, and they attempt to inform and influence the major decision makers in government, the most important of whom is the president.

The process by which policy ideas develop, advance, and either succeed or fail to gain acceptance is often lengthy and generally diffused. John Kingdon describes it as a "policy primeval soup" in which ideas are continually bumping into one another and either surviving, dying, combining, or emerging into new forms.[15] Those ideas that do manage to become incorporated into a president's specific policy proposal are evaluated according to three criteria: economic, political, and technical feasibility.

The *economic feasibility*, or cost, of a potential solution is especially important, as demands for federal expenditures far outweigh the government's capacity to supply the necessary funds. Few proposals for major new spending programs are likely to survive in an era of resource constraints. Proposals to restrain or reduce spending are more attractive to a president struggling to control the budget deficit. A proposal's *political feasibility* is determined initially by its compatibility with the values and interests of other important decision makers, particularly in

Congress. Ultimately, a proposal must gain the acquiescence, if not the acceptance, of the public. The *technical feasibility* of a proposal—the question of its workability—does not receive as much attention as its economic and political costs. Some ideas—such as proposals for welfare reform that maintain reasonably high payments, reduce inequities between recipients in different states and between recipients and the working poor, and do not increase the cost to the government—are economically and politically very attractive but unworkable in practice. Presidents Nixon and Carter made this discovery, much to their dismay, after the failure of their major efforts to achieve welfare reform.[16]

Similar problems plagued the Clinton administration and the Republican leaders of the 104th Congress as they sought to develop a mutually acceptable welfare reform bill in 1995. Both sides wanted legislation that would reduce welfare dependency with no increase in the budget. Not only were such goals incompatible, but Clinton and the Republicans disagreed fundamentally over the means to achieve them.[17] Twice, in December 1995 and January 1996, Clinton vetoed Republican bills that ended welfare as a federal entitlement by turning it over to the states, but then in August 1996 he signed a compromise bill.[18] Such conflict among the three criteria is always present. Budget costs may rule out a proposal that is politically and technically feasible, such as rapid cleanup of toxic waste sites. Or political costs may prevent acceptance of a workable proposal that is compatible with a tight budget, such as freezing Social Security cost-of-living increases. Eventually, a short list of presidential proposals emerges from a multitude of potential solutions.

The Third Stream: Political Factors. The last of Kingdon's metaphor of three policymaking streams is the tributary that carries political factors.[19] Such factors affect the setting and implementation of the president's agenda and include the national mood, the balance of political forces, and events within the government.

The *national mood* is a somewhat amorphous phenomenon that is difficult to define. It is not identical with public opinion, nor can it be ascertained through survey research. It is perhaps best described as the perception among important decision makers that a consensus exists or is building in the country among various attentive publics and political activists for specific government policies. Politicians sense the national mood in suggestions, requests, and other communications from interest groups, state and local government officials, corporate executives, and politically active citizens; in news media coverage of events; and in editorial commentary. The national mood also reflects the influence of social movements such as civil rights, environmentalism, and family values. Without a favorable national mood, major new policies—such as health care reform during the Clinton administration or George W. Bush's proposal to drill for oil in the Arctic National Wildlife Refuge as part of a broader plan of energy independence—are not likely to be adopted. In short, the national mood is a reflection of the politically relevant climate or temper of the times.

Considerably more concrete than the national mood is the extent of consensus and conflict that determines the *balance of political forces*. The prospects for adoption of a proposed policy change depend on the balance of organized interests and other forces, but assessing the balance on any issue is largely a matter of informed guesswork. The complex pattern of pluralistic political forces and the fragmentation of government authority combine to provide a strong advantage to the *opponents* of policy change. Often, heavy political costs are associated with even raising an issue for consideration, let alone obtaining adoption of a proposal. This is particularly the case with existing government programs, most of which have powerful clientele groups that stand ready to defend their programs. Clientele interests, in triangular alliances with agencies that administer the programs and congressional subcommittees with jurisdiction over the programs, engage in bargaining and logrolling to maintain and enhance the programs. To overcome the natural inertia of the government, a strong constituency for political change must be mobilized; otherwise a proposal will encounter much difficulty. For example, the Carter administration's efforts to enact a national energy policy were unsuccessful despite widespread shortages of fuels until compromises made the proposal acceptable to the oil industry and consumer interests. More recently, Clinton's proposal for health care reform failed due to strong opposition from a variety of special interests that tipped the balance of political forces against the proposed change. Campaign finance reform stalled in Congress in the summer of 2001, not because of interest group opposition, but because many of those voting on the proposal thought it would go against their own interests.

Events within government are the third major political factor that shapes the president's policy agenda. Election outcomes can produce fundamental changes in the agenda. The 1980 election, which brought Ronald Reagan to the presidency and gave the Republicans control of the Senate for the first time in a quarter of a century, was such an event. An ideologically defined, conservative agenda replaced the liberal agenda that had been in effect since the New Deal. Similarly, the 1994 election, in which the Republicans captured control of both houses of Congress for the first time in forty years, profoundly reshaped President Clinton's domestic agenda. Much of the revised agenda consisted of defensive reactions to Republican proposals to curtail affirmative action and regulatory policies affecting the environment, occupational health and safety, and business and financial practices, and to achieve major cost savings in Medicare. Moreover, this new agenda did not include health care reform, and the welfare reform proposal was conservatively fashioned to compete with Republican plans. Although Clinton won reelection in 1996, Republicans retained control of Congress. Despite initial cooperation in implementing policy, divided government continued to limit the president's ability to implement his domestic policy proposals—especially after the Monica Lewinsky story broke in early 1998 and the impeachment proceedings began. Although George W. Bush campaigned in the 2000 election as a moderate Republican who was "a uniter, not a divider," his actions during his first hundred days—a traditional testing period—as president signified a major shift to the right. That shift, coupled with Bush's failure to reach out to the moderate wing of his own party, led Vermont senator James M. Jeffords to defect from the Republican Party—an action that gave Democrats control of the Senate in June 2001.[20] Suddenly, the president confronted an entirely new policy environment—one in which it would be much more difficult to enact a staunch conservative agenda.

Jurisdictional matters are another intragovernmental development that may affect agenda setting. Disputes over bureaucratic and committee turf often delay or prevent action, although jurisdictional competition occasionally may accelerate consideration of a popular issue. In addition, a proposal may be structured so that it will be handled by a committee or an agency that is favorably disposed to it.

In sum, the most significant domestic policy action is likely to occur when the national mood and election outcomes combine to overcome the normal inertia produced by the balance of political forces and the fragmentation of government authority among numerous bureaucratic and congressional fiefdoms. Once items begin to rise on the agenda, however, organized political forces attempt to shape policy proposals to their advantage or to defeat the proposals outright.

Resources and Opportunities

Successful policy leadership results from advancing appropriate solutions to specific problems under favorable political circumstances. Not all policy proposals can receive presidential attention and consideration. Some are not compatible with a president's overall objectives and ideology, but many otherwise acceptable proposals never become part of the president's agenda because limited presidential resources cannot be wasted on them. Quite simply, presidents must establish priorities.[21] This is accomplished through what political scientist Paul Light calls a "filtering process" that maintains an orderly flow of problems and solutions to the president and merges them to produce policy proposals. The objectives of the process are to control the flow of items so that important problems, issues, and alternatives receive attention without overloading the president and to ensure that policy proposals have been formulated with due regard to relevant political factors. There are two filters through which problems and solutions pass as they are melded into presidential decisions: resources and opportunities.

Resources: Political Capital. One of the most important resources for a president is political capital. This is the reservoir of popular and congressional support with which newly elected presidents begin their terms. As they make controversial decisions, they "spend" some of their capital, which they seldom are able to replenish. They must decide which proposals merit the expenditure of political capital and in what amounts. Reagan, for example, was willing to spend his capital heavily on reducing the role of the federal government, cutting taxes, and reforming the income tax code, but not on antiabortion or school prayer amendments to the Constitution. Material resources determine which proposals for new programs can be advanced and the emphasis to be placed on existing programs.

Bill Clinton's initial political capital was not sufficient to enact his ambitious agenda.[22] Although he won a clear electoral college victory and had a 6 percent vote margin over incumbent president George Bush, he received only 43 percent of the popular vote because of the third-party candidacy of Ross Perot. Immediately after the election, the Republican Senate leader, Bob Dole, pointedly claimed to speak for the 57 percent of the electorate who had opposed Clinton. Although Clinton's victory temporarily ended twelve years of divided government, the potential for ending presidential-congressional stalemate over domestic policy was diminished with the simultaneous Republican gain of ten seats in the House of Representatives. Congressional Republicans, no longer constrained by loyalty to their own president, were free to oppose Clinton in order to discredit his leadership. Moreover, the centrist New Democrat stance that Clinton adopted to win election was not shared by a majority of congressional Democrats, who were considerably more liberal. Finally, the damage to Clinton's image done in the campaign by allegations of sexual misconduct and his avoidance of military service in the Vietnam War reduced the public's trust and support of him. These factors limited the capital that Clinton could spend on advocating potentially controversial domestic policies.

George W. Bush also entered office with limited political capital. He lost the popular vote in the 2000 presidential election to Al Gore and took power only after a protracted dispute over which candidate had won Florida's electoral votes. Moreover, he faced the highest disapproval rating of any incoming president since polling began (25 percent according to the Gallup Poll).[23] By June 2001, Bush's Gallup disapproval rating had climbed to 35 percent.[24] Through his first hundred days in office, Bush enjoyed marginal Republican control of the Senate (although it was split 50–50, Vice President Dick Cheney—in his constitutional role as president of the Senate—had the power to break all ties in favor of the Republicans). President Bush secured passage of a sweeping tax cut in May, but that victory was overshadowed by the news that Democrats had regained control of the Senate. The return to divided government would make passage of future Bush initiatives more difficult.

Interestingly, Bush did not act as though he had only limited political capital when he entered office. Instead, he proceeded confidently, acting as though he had a mandate for his conservative agenda. "I know the value of political capital," Bush said just before his inauguration, "how to earn it and how to spend it."[25] He attempted to earn additional capital by proceeding swiftly with a few key proposals that seemed to enjoy broad support, like his tax cut and education reform. But he may have gone too far when he also pushed forward with more controversial proposals such as his faith-based initiative, missile defense program, and plan to drill for oil in the Arctic National Wildlife Refuge. He further angered environmentalists and European allies with his handling of the global

Protesters in Lansing, Michigan, object to President Bush's 2001 tax-cut proposal on the grounds that it will benefit the rich at the expense of working families. Bush secured congressional passage of the tax cut the following month.

warming issue, and Vice President Cheney may have misread the national mood when he seemed to dismiss the role of energy conservation in the administration's push for energy independence.

Some critics felt that President Bush was pursuing a more conservative agenda than his tentative mandate allowed, a decision that, as previously noted, alienated Republican moderates and led Senator Jeffords to become an Independent. Having lost control of the Senate to the Democrats, Bush reached out to moderate Republicans and softened some of his rhetoric. Although the media played up his administration's initial missteps,[26] and his Gallup approval rating fell to 51% by early September 2001 (a six-point drop from when he entered office), Bush's political capital was at least temporarily replenished by the outpouring of public and congressional support in the wake of terrorist attacks on the World Trade Center and the Pentagon.

Opportunities. In addition to resources, Light argues that presidents need opportunities to formulate the agenda. These opportunities are often described metaphorically as windows: they open for a while and then close. They may be scheduled or unscheduled. Scheduled opportunities to shape the agenda occur in conjunction with the annual cycle of presidential messages to Congress (State of the Union, budget, and economic report), the congressional calendar, and action-forcing deadlines, such as renewals of program authorizations. An administration's greatest opportunity to set the agenda occurs during January and February, when Congress begins a new session and presidents deliver their messages, and in August and September, when Congress returns from recess and earlier proposals can be replaced or modified.[27] Unscheduled opportunities occur as the result of focusing events or changes in political conditions, such as the balance of power shift in the Senate. Both scheduled and unscheduled windows of opportunity eventually close, some sooner than others. An opportunity is more likely to be seized and an issue given a high place on the president's agenda when problems, solutions, and political factors come together.[28] Without a viable solution and in the absence of favorable political conditions, a problem has a limited chance of moving up on the agenda. For instance, popular support for biomedical research is substantial, but the slow pace of development of treatments and cures for diseases such as cancer limits presidential attention to the issue.

Opportunities also fluctuate as a presidential term progresses. In a president's first year in office, Congress and the public have high expectations of policy change based on campaign promises and the election mandate. Opportunities tend to be at their peak during the so-called honeymoon period of a new administration. In the second and fourth years of a president's term, concern focuses increasingly on the forthcoming election campaign, and policy opportunities decline. The third year frequently is regarded as crucial, for the administration is by then experienced, mature, removed from immediate electoral pressures, and anxious to make its mark.[29] Opportunities are most likely to be exploited effectively then and in the first year of a president's second term—assuming there is one. Because a second term is also a final term, the president's "lame-duck" status tends to restrict further policy opportunities. The effects of lame-duck status on presidential initiatives are especially notable following the midterm congressional election in a president's second term.

There are conflicting patterns in the progression of opportunities as presidents move through their term. On the one hand, as they acquire experience and expertise, they become more effective and thus increase their policy opportunities. On the other hand, as their congressional and popular support declines through the term, they lose opportunities. Light describes these as cycles of increasing effectiveness and declining influence.[30] It is ironic that as presidents become more skilled at finding opportunities, they become less able to utilize them.

The Domestic Policy Environment

The most outstanding characteristic of the domestic policy environment is its complexity. Myriad actors—individuals, groups, and other government institutions and agencies—all pursue a seemingly incalculable range of objectives and protect countless interests. Although presidential power is limited, the president is better situated than anyone else to give direction and bring some degree of coordination to the domestic policies of the U.S. government.

The fragmentation of political power and influence that is the hallmark of the U.S. political system is the product of a heterogeneous and pluralistic society and of constitutional arrangements designed to produce deliberate rather than expeditious government decision making. Nowhere is the fragmentation of power more apparent and more profound than in the domestic policy environment.

Interest Groups

Outside the government, thousands of interest groups constantly seek to influence policy. They range from organizations that are concerned with the full range of the government's activities, such as Americans for Democratic Action, to those that focus on a single issue, such as the National Rifle Association (NRA), which is dedicated to preventing the adoption of strict gun control legislation. Interest groups are concerned not only with virtually every government program that distributes benefits to individuals and organizations and regulates their conduct but also with possibilities for new programs. Simply stated, the objectives of interest groups are to secure the adoption of policies that are beneficial to their members and to prevent the adoption of policies they view as harmful to them. Interest groups operate in all sectors of domestic policy—agriculture, civil rights, social welfare, and natural resources. They include organizations that represent business; labor; the professions; consumers; state and local governments and their subdivisions; public officials; social groupings based on age, sex, race, religion, and shared attitudes and experiences; and groups that present themselves as protectors of the unorganized public interest. In sum, interest groups represent every aspect of society and help to convey our myriad interests to policymakers. Within the national government, interest groups attempt to exert influence directly on Congress, the bureaucracy, the courts, and the presidency. As we saw in chapter 3, presidents responded to the increasingly important role of interest groups by assigning individual White House aides the responsibility for maintaining liaison with them in such policy areas as civil rights, education, and health. This eventually led to Nixon's establishment of the Office of Public Liaison. Interest groups have also attempted to exert influence indirectly, principally by endorsing and making campaign contributions to presidential and congressional candidates and by urging their members to bring pressure to bear on the White House and on their representatives in Congress.

It is difficult to measure the effectiveness of interest group influence on public policy because there are multiple points of access to government decision makers; numerous groups usually seek to influence a particular policy or set of related policies; and powerful forces other than interest groups also are at work. Nonetheless, there is widespread belief that the growth in interest group activity since 1965 has contributed substantially to the rise of federal spending on domestic programs and the expansion of federal regulation into noneconomic areas, such as consumer protection, product safety, and occupational safety and health.[31] The demands of interest groups, often asserted as a matter of "right" and defended on grounds of fairness or improving quality of life, have strained the fiscal capacity of the federal government and created new conflicts in society.

Mancur Olson, an economist, has argued that societies with large numbers of powerful "distributional coalitions" (his term for interest groups) have experienced unsupportably high public spending and little or no economic growth as a consequence of the political influence of such groups. The groups press for public benefits for their members even though the result may be disadvantageous to the entire community. According to Olson, unless an interest group encompasses most of the population, there is "no constraint on the social cost such an organization will find it expedient to impose on the society in the cause of obtaining a larger share of the social output for itself."[32] To a substantial extent, domestic policy politics has become the pursuit of narrow group interests, even at the expense of the general public interest, which is usually unorganized, unarticulated, and difficult to identify or define. The president is better situated, in terms of political resources, than anyone else to define, enhance, and defend the public interest. That is the president's principal challenge in the domestic policy area. Harry Truman was fond of saying that his job was to act as a lobbyist for the American people, most of whom are not represented by lobbyists.

Separation of Powers and Federalism

The pattern of interest group activity traditionally has been described as "policy subgovernments," mutually beneficial triangular relationships among interest groups, administrative agencies, and congressional subcommittees. Subgovernments, and the more open and amorphous issue networks that cut across and intersect with them, contribute to the fragmentation of power and influence in the domestic policy environment. That fragmentation is enhanced by constitutional arrangements that divide power among the branches of government and between the national and state governments and also by the internal structures of Congress and the federal bureaucracy. The constitutional design—which established a system of 'separated sharing powers'—was created to prevent the abuse of power.[33]

The Framers invented federalism as a means of resolving the seemingly insoluble conflict between advocates of a consolidated system of government and the proponents of state sovereignty. Their ingenious compromise, which artfully avoided establishing a precise boundary between national and state powers, has been adapted to the needs of the times by successive generations of political leaders. The current system of federalism still leaves primary responsibility for most basic government services in the hands of the states and their local subdivisions. These services include public education, public health, public safety, and construction and maintenance of streets, roads, and highways. The federal government has programs that help finance state and local activities in these and other areas, and it exerts a substantial degree of influence on them by virtue of its grant and regulatory programs. Still, most of the federal government's domestic policy activity does not entail direct federal administration.

Presidential leadership in domestic policy requires that the president persuade, bargain with, and cooperate with Congress, federal administrators, and state and local officials. In these relationships, the president has limited power to command and must rely instead on personal skills as a political leader—principally persuasion and bargaining—to achieve goals.

The structure of authority in Congress has varied over time with a prevailing tendency toward fragmentation. The reforms of the early 1970s, while strengthening somewhat the majority party leadership in the House, provided individual members with extensive opportunities to influence policy.[34] Consequently, Congress often found it difficult in the following decades to give direction to public policy, and presidents encountered problems in their relations with Congress. Unlike their predecessors in the late 1950s and 1960s, presidents from the mid-1970s to the early 1990s could not easily negotiate agreements with top party leaders and one or two influential chairs in each house and be confident that those agreements would prevail in floor voting. Rather, the presidents had to deal separately, in each chamber, with several committee chairs, subcommittee chairs, and party leaders. Agreements reached at one stage in the legislative process often came undone later.

The congressional environment changed dramatically following the Republican takeover in 1994. In the House, the new majority leadership under Speaker Newt Gingrich, R-Ga., imposed tight discipline on Republican members and committee chairs, who were eager to implement a conservative policy revolution.[35] Party government not seen since the first decade of the twentieth century seemed to have returned, at least for the time being. Although the new Senate was predictably less disciplined, its Republican majority demonstrated considerable unity given the disruptiveness of the presidential candidacies of Majority Leader Bob Dole and Phil Gramm of Texas. Though the conservative revolution did not occur during the Clinton administration, the right was heartened with the election of George W. Bush in 2000. However, tight discipline and a push for a conservative agenda appears to have ended up hurting congressional Republicans as evidenced by Senator Jeffords's defection and pointed complaints from other party members who felt excluded. Sen. John McCain said, "Tolerance of dissent is the hallmark of a mature party, and it is well past time for the Republican party to grow up."[36]

The effects of extensive congressional fragmentation on the president's involvement in domestic policy have been mixed. Congress has been unable to counterbalance the presidency by providing alternative policy leadership, but at the same time, presidents have found it increasingly difficult to lead Congress. Congressional influence has been extensive, if only in a negative sense, because of its inertia and its ability to resist presidential direction. Whether this condition will change with increased centralization of authority and purpose on the part of the congressional majority remains to be seen.

Fragmentation of a different sort characterizes the federal bureaucracy. As noted in chapter 6, an independent power exists in the bureaucracy that is based in career civil servants, who constitute a permanent government. The members of the permanent government have professional and agency loyalties and close ties to the interest groups who constitute their clientele and to the congressional subcommittees with jurisdiction over their appropriations and the legislation that authorizes their programs. Subgovernments and issue networks comprise members of the permanent government and complicate presidential control of policy development and implementation in or by the bureaucracy. In addition, the fragmentation resulting from the size and complexity of the federal bureaucracy creates enormous problems of management and policy coordination for the president.

The Domestic Policy Apparatus

The need for presidential coordination in domestic policy has been recognized for some time. The principal effort to enable presidents to provide the necessary coordination was the development of a domestic policy staff apparatus in the Executive Office of the President. The domestic policy staff evolved slowly, in conjunction with the development of the president's legislative role (*see chapter 5*). This was an evolutionary process that relied initially on the Bureau of the Budget (BOB) and later saw the establishment of a separate staff to formulate and implement domestic policy.

BOB: Central Clearance and Legislative Program Planning

From the early nineteenth century until the creation of the Bureau of the Budget in 1921, the president's role in domestic policy formulation was ad hoc and unorganized.[37] In its first year of operation, the BOB required that all agency legislative proposals for the expenditure of federal funds be submitted to it before being sent to Congress. Those proposals that the BOB determined were not in accord with the president's financial program were not sent forward, and agencies were to inform Congress if pending legislation had been found not in accord. This procedure, known as "central clearance," was expanded during Franklin Roosevelt's administration to cover the substantive content of proposed legislation. The procedure's original function, as stated above, was to ensure that legislative proposals of various departments and agencies were compatible with the president's overall program goals.[38] Over time, central clearance acquired additional functions, including supervising and coordinating executive branch legislative initiatives, providing a clear indication to congressional committees of the president's position on proposed legislation, and making various administrative units aware of one another's goals and activities.

Beginning in 1947, the BOB's domestic policy role expanded to include participation in developing the president's legislative program.[39] The bureau's Legislative Reference Division worked directly with Truman's White House staff in reviewing agency recommendations and integrating them in a comprehensive legislative program. The addition of responsibilities to formulate policy involved BOB personnel in the pursuit of the president's political goals, a development that may later have resulted in questions about its ability to provide professional staff services to the president. Moreover, in the 1960s, as the BOB became deeply involved in program planning, White House staff played a larger role in the clearance process, and the line between clearance and legislative planning became more and more blurred.[40]

When Dwight D. Eisenhower came into office, he was initially unprepared to submit a legislative program to Congress but quickly recognized that he was expected to do so. The centralized clearance and planning processes lodged in BOB were compatible with Eisenhower's penchant for systematic staff operations, and he continued to employ them throughout his administration. The principal distinction between him and his predecessor in this regard was that Eisenhower attached a lower priority to new domestic policy proposals. Central to the process of legislative programming as it developed by 1960 were annual submissions of legislative proposals by departments and agencies. Items that were not enacted in one year were introduced in the next. The result was a highly routinized process that was nearly impervious to new ideas. This system was suitable for Eisenhower's limited domestic policy initiatives, but the next presidents—John F. Kennedy and Lyndon B. Johnson—overcame the rigidities and bureaucratic domination of the BOB-based program planning process by obtaining ideas and suggestions from nongovernment sources.[41]

Task Forces and Study Commissions

The mechanism used by Kennedy and Johnson for gathering policy advice was the task force, a group consisting of experts from inside and outside the government. Before his inauguration, Kennedy appointed several such groups to advise him on the major issues and problems facing the new administration. The reports of these task forces, and of a number of others appointed after Kennedy took office, provided the basis for much of his New Frontier program.[42]

Although Kennedy remained eager for new ideas and suggestions, he did not rely heavily on outside sources of advice after the initial round of task forces. Instead, he turned primarily to his cabinet for suggestions. Johnson appointed a set of task forces in the spring of 1964 with the specific mission of developing a distinctive program for his administration. Johnson's task forces were made up of outsiders, and they operated in secret. He was so pleased with their reports, which furnished much of the form and substance of his Great Society program, that he made task forces a regular part of his program development process. The White House staff coordinated the task force operations, and the BOB integrated the proposals into the annual legislative program. Johnson favored the task force process because it largely avoided the tortuous task of bargaining with departments and agencies and because it was not adulterated by bureaucratic, congressional, and interest group pressures.[43] He used the device so extensively, however—in 1967 alone at least fifty task forces were preparing reports—that it became routinized and lost the informality and flexibility that had made it so valuable for developing new proposals.

The presidents who followed Johnson made little use of task forces. (Nixon appointed fourteen task forces during his campaign, but their suggestions did not figure prominently in his initial legislative proposals.) Instead, they relied on more formal advisory bodies, such as commissions and White House conferences, to study issues and problems and to gather outside recommendations. Presidential commissions are broadly representative bodies that often are appointed to defuse highly sensitive issues. In September 1981, for example, President Reagan appointed the National Commission on Social Security Reform to develop a solution to a crisis in Social Security funding. Although the commission did not solve the crisis, it provided "cover" under which the principals, Reagan and House Speaker Thomas P. O'Neill, D-Mass., worked out a compromise.[44] As one of his first official actions, President Clinton appointed the Task Force on National Health Care Reform to develop the administration's proposed legislation within a hundred days.[45] Headed by the first lady, Hillary Rodham Clinton, and the senior adviser for policy development, Ira Magaziner, the task force consisted of 500 experts from inside and outside government who divided themselves into thirty-four groups and operated secretly. The unprecedented size of the task force, its cumbersome secret process, and Hillary Clinton's role in it made it a target for criticism well before it finished its work. Five months after the deadline, the unwieldy body produced a 1,350-page proposal for a Health Care Security Act. The delay in developing the proposal postponed congressional consideration of it until 1994, when it became caught up in election year politics. The proposal's "complexity, high cost, and obtrusive bureaucracy made it an easy target for Republicans" and contributed to the failure of Congress to enact it.[46]

Because of the representative character of presidential commissions, their reports often blur critical issues. This occurs in consequence of their efforts to obtain consensus. Or commissions may make findings and suggestions that embarrass the president, as did the 1970 report of the Scranton Commission, which blamed campus unrest on President Nixon.

White House conferences bring together groups of experts and distinguished citizens for public forums held under presidential auspices. Their principal function is to build support among experts, political leaders, and relevant interests for presidential leadership to deal with the problems at issue. Neither White House conferences nor presidential commissions have served as the basis for major legislative proposals, but they have given legitimacy to certain presidential undertakings.

Domestic Policy Staffs

Since Johnson, presidents have used domestic policy staffs in the Executive Office of the President and a politicized Office of Management and Budget (OMB) to develop legislative programs. Nixon established the Domestic Council in 1970 as part of a reorganization of the presidency, in which the Bureau of the Budget was renamed the Office of Management and Budget. The Domestic Council comprised the president, the vice president, the attorney general, and the secretaries of Agriculture, Commerce, Housing and Urban Development, Interior, Labor, Transportation, Treasury, and Health, Education and Welfare, as well as the director and deputy director of OMB. The Domestic Council was to be a top-level forum for discussion, debate, and determination of policy analogous to the National Security Council (NSC) (*see chapter 10*). Like the NSC, the Domestic Council had a staff of professionals and support personnel. Headed by John Ehrlichman, the presidential assistant for domestic policy, the staff dominated Nixon's domestic policymaking process during the last two years of his first term, 1971–1972.[47]

The Domestic Council conducted its activity through work groups headed by one of six assistant directors. These groups prepared working papers for the president, evaluated departmental proposals for legislation, and participated in drafting presidential messages to Congress and preparing supportive materials for specific legislative proposals. In addition to assisting the president in formulating policy proposals, the Domestic Council also advocated, monitored, and evaluated policy.[48] This arrangement, in effect, made Ehrlichman the president's general agent for domestic policy. Under him, the Domestic Council centralized control over domestic policy in the White House. The president's interests, as defined and expressed by Ehrlichman, took precedence over the interests of departments and agencies, as conveyed by cabinet members and agency heads.

The council's domination of domestic policy did not survive Ehrlichman's departure from the White House in April 1973.[49] The influence of the staff was clearly a function of Ehrlichman's status with the president. Under Ehrlichman's successor, Kenneth Cole, the Domestic Council became more of a service unit, and OMB resumed many of the functions of planning legislative programs.

In addition to the development of a presidential staff for domestic policy, Nixon also effected a major transformation in OMB by using it for political purposes. The OMB director became indistinguishable from other high-level presidential assistants, and a layer of political appointees, called "program assistant directors," was placed above OMB's career staff. Nixon's politicization of OMB reduced its ability to serve the institutional needs of the presidency as an impartial professional staff agency.[50]

President Ford used OMB to facilitate the unusual transfer of power from Nixon to himself after Nixon's resignation, and he relied on it to help plan and coordinate programs in a more traditional and less partisan manner than Nixon had. Initially, Ford intended to give the Domestic Council a major planning role by making Vice President Nelson Rockefeller its chair. However, Rockefeller never became Ford's general agent for domestic policy. The long delay in congressional confirmation of Rockefeller's appointment and his conflict with White House chief of staff Donald Rumsfeld appear to have prevented such a development.[51] The council's staff director, James Cannon, a Rockefeller appointee, never gained influence with Ford, who sought advice from a wide range of sources, including OMB, several cabinet members, and the Economic Policy Board, which was established in 1974 as a result of Ford's concern with economic policy problems (*see chapter 9*). That emphasis partly explains why Ford seldom used the Domestic Council for policy planning. Indeed, by the fall of 1976, the council no longer participated in legislative programming, and the staff was engaged in diverse activities such as answering presidential mail, preparing policy option memoranda, drafting presidential statements on legislation, and helping to explain the president's program to Congress.[52]

President Carter abolished the Domestic Council shortly after taking office, but he retained a domestic policy staff headed by one of his top aides, Stuart Eizenstat. In some respects, Eizenstat and his staff acquired a policymaking role that resembled that of Ehrlichman and the Domestic Council in the Nixon administration. However, Eizenstat and the domestic policy staff did not dominate the domestic policy process, and they functioned more in the role of "effective administrator and of contributing advisor."[53]

Ronald Reagan, who came to office with a set, ideologically defined policy agenda and a strong commitment to cabinet government, created a new policy apparatus. The principal units were OMB, the Office of Policy Development (OPD), and seven cabinet councils. OMB's domestic policy involvement was especially crucial during Reagan's first year in office (1981), when the prime objective of drastically reducing the role of the federal government was linked to a budget reduction strategy that was implemented through use of the congressional budget process (see chapter 9). OMB director David Stockman was the principal architect of the first substantial rollback of the government's domestic programs since the New Deal.

The OPD was the Reagan administration's equivalent of Carter's domestic policy staff. Headed by a presidential assistant for policy development, the OPD worked through cabinet councils, which had jurisdiction over economic affairs, commerce and trade, human resources, natural resources and environment, food and agriculture, legal policy, and management and administration.[54] The councils' members included appropriate cabinet and subcabinet officers and personnel from OMB and the White House staff. Each council had a secretariat composed of department and agency representatives and used working groups to provide expertise and to analyze issues.

The OPD/cabinet council system did not, however, become the directing force for domestic policy. Other factors, particularly the president's long-range objectives and budget pressures, determined the agenda from the beginning of the administration. Reagan's domestic policy apparatus worked out "details secondary to the president's fixed view of government."[55] In other words, it performed an administrative rather than an advisory role.

Developments in the first year of Reagan's second term resulted in a further diminution of the OPD/cabinet council system. The newly appointed White House chief of staff, the former Secretary of the Treasury Donald Regan, moved quickly to bring the three major policy areas—economics, national security, and domestic policy—under his control. The number of cabinet councils was reduced from seven to two: Economic Affairs and Domestic Policy. (The National Security Council, a statutory body, remained as it was.) Secretary of the Treasury James Baker and Attorney General Edwin Meese III chaired the economic and domestic policy councils, respectively. The OPD was reduced in size, and its director reported to Regan. In addition to simplifying and reducing the size of the OPD–cabinet council system, Regan centralized authority over domestic policy in his office. However, the two remaining cabinet council chairs, Meese and Baker, enjoyed substantial autonomy to pursue policy projects of their own choosing. By early 1986, Regan had gained control of all access to the president with respect to domestic policy not under the purview of the two cabinet councils.

The diminished domestic policy apparatus of Reagan's second term reflected a shift in the administration's orientation from changing policies to defending them. Having accomplished most of his initial domestic agenda, principally curtailment of the growth of federal agencies and a reduction in spending on them, Reagan concentrated his energies on national security and economic policy objectives. The domestic policy apparatus under Reagan was at least partially deinstitutionalized.

The same condition continued under Reagan's vice president and successor, President George Bush.[56] The assistant to the president for economic and domestic affairs, Roger Porter, a former Harvard professor, directed the Office of Policy Development. The OPD and the White House Office of Cabinet Affairs provided staff support for the Domestic Policy Council and the Economic Policy Council. However, major issues usually bypassed the cabinet council system and were resolved by Chief of Staff John Sununu or the budget director, Richard Darman. Sununu's self-defined role was to protect the conservative integrity of the administration against those who urged the president to pursue more politically pragmatic options, while Darman functioned as a nonideological guardian of the budget and advocate of economic growth. Both intervened frequently on low-level issues. However, some cabinet members, such as Secretary of Housing and Urban Development Jack Kemp and Secretary of Transportation Samuel Skinner, took the lead in developing major domestic legislative proposals and pushing them in Congress.[57]

The domestic policy process during the first two years of the Clinton administration was frequently frenetic and uncoordinated.[58] The Domestic Policy Council did not meet regularly. Development of health care reform, the principal initiative, was the responsibility of the large task force headed by First Lady Hillary Clinton and Ira Magaziner. Cabinet members, such as Health and Human Services Secretary Donna Shalala, did not play a major role in developing initiatives.

Although formally lodged in a Domestic Policy Council chaired by a high-level presidential assistant, the policy process was operationally centered in the president himself. Clinton, with his intense interest in domestic policy, presided over numerous wide-ranging and intensive meetings with his advisers that shifted back and forth between various policy alternatives. There was no single individual, such as the chief of staff, or group comparable to Reagan's Legislative Strategy Group responsible for resolving disputes, imparting coherence and practicality to the many proposals, and moving them forward to Congress in a timely manner. Clinton resisted delegating such authority to others. Despite his intellectual brilliance and energy, however, he was unable to "ringmaster" the domestic policy process effectively on his own.[59]

Then the Republicans won control of both houses of Congress in the 1994 midterm elections. (Although Republicans had controlled the Senate as recently as 1986, they had not controlled the House of Representatives since 1954.) The new Republican majority largely controlled policymaking through most of 1995, and for a time the "Republican revolution" seemed to live up to its name.[60] Then came the notorious budget battle of 1995–1996, when Republicans pushed for sharp cuts in entitlement programs. President Clinton reasserted himself, exercised his first veto in response to the proposed cuts, and rallied opposition to the Republican plan. House Speaker Newt Gingrich refused to compromise, and the stalemate led to government shutdowns, which the public blamed on the Republicans. In the end, President Clinton won the political battle.

Paul J. Quirk and William Cunion have noted that the government shutdowns led to a new phase of Clinton's domestic presidency. It began in January 1996 and ran through the eruption of the Monica Lewinsky scandal in early 1998. It was marked by an unusual degree of cooperation between Clinton and the Republican majority in Congress, leading to a "notable amount of significant legislation," including a major overhaul of the welfare system.[61] With the help of political strategist Dick Morris, Clinton followed a centrist strategy of "triangulation." He finally seemed to master the art of domestic policymaking. But cooperation and policy output came to halt in 1998 and 1999 with the Lewinsky scandal and the ensuing impeachment of the president.

In contrast to Clinton's frenetic style, George W. Bush's domestic policy process was highly structured during his first hundred days. Unlike any president before him, Bush came to office with a master's degree in business administration (which he had earned from Harvard's Business School). He surrounded himself with high-level advisers who not only had experience in government but also had experience as chief executive officers of major businesses. Many observers predicted that Bush would be "the chairman of the board of the world's biggest conglomerate"—a leader who would delegate to his "cabinet of experienced CEOs."[62]

The strength of the business model that Bush embraced was its efficiency. In addition, Bush instilled discipline in his staff and insisted on punctuality. Like Reagan, he concentrated his efforts during his first months in office on implementing a few key issues—notably the tax cut, which he secured passage of in May 2001. However, Bush's first months in office suggested that he would be less willing to delegate than Reagan had been. And some pundits began to question whether Bush's business model would ultimately prove to be flexible enough for the demands of Washington.[63] Only time would tell.

Modern Presidents and Domestic Policy

Modern presidents have varied greatly in the extent of their interest and involvement in domestic policy. Franklin Roosevelt was preoccupied with domestic policy during his first two terms (1933–1941) as he orchestrated the development, enactment, and implementation of the New Deal, which encompassed the most extensive set of social and economic reforms in U.S. history. The New Deal's immediate stimulus was the Great Depression, but it was also a response to the effects of urbanization and industrialization.

Roosevelt's approach to domestic policy was pragmatic. He tried a wide range of policies. Those that did not work were quickly discarded. Those that proved successful were incorporated in a greatly expanded role for the federal government, which assumed positive responsibilities for individual, corporate, and general welfare that went far beyond the traditional negative functions of safeguarding public health, safety, and morals. Among the most prominent legacies of the New Deal are the Social Security system; unemployment compensation; support of agricultural prices; insurance of bank deposits; extensive public works projects such as the Grand Coulee Dam in Washington state and the Tennessee Valley Authority; and federal regulation of securities exchanges, communications, and energy. During his final years in office (1941–1945), FDR devoted himself almost exclusively to national security policy, as "Dr. Win the War" took over from "Dr. New Deal."

Roosevelt's successor, Harry Truman, was deeply involved with national security from the start of his presidency, even though his interests and experience lay in the area of domestic policy. In his first term (1945–1949), Truman offered few domestic policy initiatives, for he was occupied first with ending the war, then with the transition from war to peace and with difficulties in dealing with America's wartime ally the Soviet Union. Following his upset reelection victory in 1948, Truman proposed a comprehensive set of domestic policy reforms called the Fair Deal. The Fair Deal agenda included national health insurance and federal aid to education and expanded agricultural price supports. Little of the Fair Deal was implemented, however, as the cold war intensified and the United States became involved in the Korean War (1950–1953).

Truman's successor, Dwight Eisenhower, a general and World War II hero, was a conservative who had no desire to expand the federal government's role in the life of the nation. He did not, however, attempt to repeal any of the New Deal reforms. His administration (1953–1961) was marked by economic expansion and stabilization in international affairs, and punctuated by recessions in 1954 and 1958. Among Eisenhower's major domestic policy accomplishments were the passage of legislation authorizing construction of the Interstate Highway System; the National Defense Education Act in 1958, a direct response to the Soviet success in launching the first earth satellite; and limited civil rights bills in 1957 and 1960.

Domestic policy innovation and expansion of federal programs were a central objective of John Kennedy (1961–1963) and Lyndon Johnson (1963–1969). Kennedy developed and submitted to Congress his extensive domestic policy agenda, the New Frontier, which included most of the unfinished agenda of the Fair Deal plus proposals for expanded civil rights legislation.

At the time of Kennedy's assassination, in November 1963, Congress was considering several pieces of New Frontier legislation. Johnson moved quickly and effectively in 1964 to secure passage of much of the Kennedy agenda, including the Vocational Education Act, the Higher Education Act, and the Civil Rights Act of 1964. In addition, Johnson launched the War on Poverty, featuring the Economic Opportunity Act of 1964, which established the Office of Economic Opportunity. In his 1964 election campaign, Johnson proposed additional domestic reforms under the rubric the Great Society. The year 1965 witnessed the largest outpouring of new domestic policy legislation since the New Deal. Congress passed the Elementary and Secondary Education Act, the Voting Rights Act, and legislation authorizing Medicare, Medicaid, and the model cities program aimed at urban renewal. The Departments of Housing and Urban Development and Transportation were established. Hundreds of new federal grant-in-aid programs for state and local governments were implemented. Johnson's zealous pursuit of domestic policy goals gave way, however, to international concerns. The Vietnam War occupied his attention in his last two years in office (1967 and 1968). Funds for Great Society programs were restricted before many of them could be fully implemented as the costs of the war consumed an increasing portion of the federal budget. Opposition to the war in the United States and from abroad led Johnson to retire from public life rather than seek reelection.

Richard Nixon, who succeeded Johnson in 1969, offered an innovative proposal to reform the welfare system, which Congress ultimately rejected. He also considered a variety of suggestions for reforming the financing of public education. Perhaps his principal domestic policy accomplishment was the establishment of federal revenue sharing with state and local governments. Nixon's major achievements, however, were in the realm of national security policy, where his primary interests lay.

Nixon's successor, Gerald Ford, was a moderate Republican who confronted a liberal Democratic Congress in the wake of Watergate. Although he did much to restore trust in the presidency, he was unable to convince Congress to follow his lead on domestic policy. Perhaps his greatest influence on domestic policy came in the form of *blocking* congressional action. In only twenty-nine months in office, Ford cast sixty-six vetoes. Only twelve of his vetoes were overridden.

Jimmy Carter, a moderate in a largely liberal party, presented a wide range of domestic policy proposals during his administration. He struggled with Congress over a national energy policy; the legislation that eventually passed was a watered-down compromise. He was unable to obtain passage of his proposal for welfare reform, and he temporized at length before proposing a national health insurance plan. Carter was an active president in domestic policy, but he achieved few of his major objectives.

Reagan campaigned successfully for the presidency in 1980 with the most radically conservative proposals for domestic policy since before the New Deal. Reagan's stated purpose was no less than to institute a "new American Revolution." The essentials of that revolution in domestic policy were defined in terms of Reagan's conservative ideology. Except for the armed forces and support for law enforcement, the role of the federal government would be drastically curtailed. There would be a massive devolution of federal programs to state and local governments. The reduction in federal spending for domestic programs would provide the resources for an overdue military buildup, made necessary by the threat posed by the Soviet Union, and for a substantial cut in income taxes. Reagan further believed that the tax cut would stimulate an economic expansion that would generate enough revenue to bring the federal budget into balance. Finally, he was committed to drastic reductions of federal regulation of the economy, the environment, and the workplace.

The foundation of Reagan's domestic policy goals was an unswerving belief in the viability of a free market as the means of rationally and efficiently allocating resources and maximizing productivity. Allowing the free market to operate would increase material well-being and enhance individual freedom. Reagan's domestic policy objectives were long range. He was not interested in the details of specific programs. What was done in domestic policy had to be compatible with the long-term goals that flowed from his ideological frame of reference. Pragmatic adjustments and compromises with individuals and interests who did not share his ideology were to be avoided at all costs. In this respect, Reagan stood in sharp contrast to his predecessors from FDR to Carter.

The domestic policy agenda of Reagan's successor, George Bush, was characterized by its limited scope and the absence of a clear vision of American society.[64] A major theme for domestic policy—"empowerment" of individuals by means such as allowing public housing residents to buy their homes and giving parents greater freedom in choosing schools for their children—did not emerge until late in the second year of his administration.[65] Taking office at a time "ripe for inaction" (the public supported neither further reductions in the size of government nor major new domestic programs), the nonideological Bush devoted most of his energy to national security issues.[66] Moreover, budget constraints created by the massive deficits of the Reagan years permitted very little opportunity for policy initiatives.

In spite of the lack of a comprehensive domestic policy agenda, the Bush administration was not without several major legislative achievements.[67] These included a bailout for the financially devastated savings and loan industry, the first major revision of the Clean Air Act in a decade, a bill establishing rights for the disabled, a sweeping child care bill, and revision and reauthorization of federal housing programs. One close observer remarked that "in many domestic policy fields, Bush has done better than his Administration's phlegmatic reputation suggests."[68]

Bill Clinton entered office committed to be a domestic policy president. His extensive agenda was centrist, or New Democrat, in its ideological orientation. Determined to "hit the ground running" and avoid the early missteps that had plagued the Carter administration, Clinton's first hundred days were notable for some easy early victories, a costly defeat, and indications of difficulties ahead.[69] The easy wins came with enactment of Clinton's campaign proposal for a National Service program and leftover measures from the Bush years: the Family and Medical Leave Act, the Motor Voter Registration law, and the Brady handgun registration bill. The defeat resulted from Clinton's effort to fulfill a campaign pledge to end discrimination against gays and lesbians in the armed forces. The announcement that this would be accomplished by an executive order—as Truman had ended racial discrimination in the military—met with strong opposition from the chairman of the Joint Chiefs of Staff, Gen. Colin Powell, and other high-ranking military officers and from many members of Congress, including Sen. Sam Nunn, D-Ga., chairman of the Armed Services Committee. In the face of such opposition and strongly negative media and public reaction, Clinton retreated and negotiated a compromise "don't ask, don't tell" policy that pleased no one. The debate over the issue hurt Clinton politically because it "raised doubts about the strength of his leadership," disappointed one of his important support groups, and identified him with an unpopular and openly liberal cause.[70]

That Clinton would encounter difficulties in securing the enactment of his domestic agenda became apparent early in 1993, when Congress rejected his economic stimulus proposal. His economic program, embodied in the 1994 congressional budget resolution and the subsequent reconciliation bill, passed narrowly with no Republican support in either the House or the Senate (see chapter 9). Although the legislation fulfilled the campaign commitment to reduce the budget deficit substantially, a tax increase (on business and the wealthy) was necessary to make the legislation work.

Clinton's major domestic policy achievements in 1993 and 1994 were accomplished with difficulty and did not receive wide popular approval or media recognition. Two important bills designed to enhance competitiveness and expand export markets by liberalizing foreign trade—the North American Free Trade Agreement (NAFTA) in 1993 and the General Agreement on Tariffs and Trade (GATT) in 1994—passed over the opposition of organized labor and a majority of House Democrats. The $30 billion crime prevention bill passed in August 1994 with the support of forty-two House Republicans after nearly being defeated by a coalition of the Black Caucus and conservatives opposed to the ban on assault weapons.

The bipartisan support that was essential to these achievements did not materialize for health care reform, the centerpiece of Clinton's domestic agenda.[71] In addition, powerful interest group opposition arose after the introduction of the legislation, which was detailed, complex, and not easily understood. In Congress, the committee process broke down as three House and two Senate committees were unable to resolve the substantive and political problems with the legislation. None of the House committees and only one Senate committee, Finance, was able to report a bill. The Democratic leadership in each chamber was unable to fashion a compromise that stood a chance of passage, and no floor votes were taken. (Clinton's threat in January 1994 to veto any bill that did not provide for universal coverage was an obstacle to developing a bipartisan compromise.)

Kingdon's policy-streams model provides a useful framework for analyzing the demise of health care reform.[72] Two problems secured the issue's place on the agenda—rapidly increasing costs and uneven access. On balance, political conditions favored action. However, as is the case with any redistributive policy legislation, there was potential for interest group opposition. Moreover, favorable public opinion could be moved (as it subsequently was), and public opposition to additional taxes to finance reform and the budget deficit constrained the alternatives. The greatest difficulties occurred in the solutions stream. None of the three primary alternatives—a single-payer national health insurance system run by the federal government, a system of managed competition, and incremental changes in current insurance arrangements—could muster a majority among the advocates of reform. Consequently, the administration and Democratic congressional leaders were unable to build a consensus "among the advocates and specialists around a particular package of policies."[73]

In the second half of Clinton's term, the Republican leadership in Congress seized and dominated the domestic policy agenda. With considerable success, Clinton fought Republican efforts to finance massive tax cuts at the expense of Medicare, end affirmative action, and cripple regulatory programs. In an action that was essential to his reelection strategy to run as a centrist, he kept his 1992 campaign promise to "end welfare as we know it." On August 22, 1996, despite misgivings, he signed a compromise bill that had the support of almost all congressional Republicans and half of the Democrats.

As shown in the past several decades, the relationship of modern presidents to domestic policy can be understood in terms of a cyclical theory of politics and policy.[74] Domestic political change in the twentieth century took place in recurring cycles of "electoral politics and governmental response" that focused on the presidency. At the center of each cycle was a "presidency of achievement" marked by legislation that altered "the role of the federal government in American society."[75] Three conditions are required for a presidency of achievement to occur: "an empowering election, leadership skill, and ideas."[76] During the twentieth century, each presidency of achievement usually was preceded by one or more presidencies of "preparation" and followed by one or more presidencies of "consolidation" in which the reforms were rationalized and legitimized. Although the cycle of preparation, achievement, and consolidation is recurring, it is not inevitable.[77]

In terms of this theory, Roosevelt was a president of achievement, even though a presidency of preparation did not precede him, because the system-threatening crisis of the Great Depression disrupted the cycle. Truman's was a "presidency of stalemate" in which he sought to "set off a new round of achievement in the face of a strong public disposition for consolidation."[78] Eisenhower was "the quintessential president of consolidation," who brought stability and order to the changes initiated under Roosevelt's New Deal.[79] Kennedy served to prepare the way for Johnson's presidency of achievement—the Great Society—which was consolidated under Nixon. Ford fell outside the cycle with a "presidency of stasis," characterized by confusion regarding policy problems and solutions.[80] Carter's was a presidency of preparation for Reagan's achievements. Carter's rhetoric and some of his actions involving deregulation, scaling back the size and scope of domestic programs, and strengthening the military foreshadowed the achievements of Reagan's conservative "revolution."[81] George Bush consolidated the changes implemented under Reagan and thus fits nicely into the cycle.

Clinton took office with an ambitious agenda; the accomplishment of that agenda would have stamped him as a president of achievement. But with the exceptions of 1996 and 1997, he never really controlled the domestic policy process. He did achieve a balanced budget (indeed, a surplus) for the first time since 1969, but both he and Congress were distracted for much of his second term by the Lewinsky scandal and the impeachment battle. His problematical election mandates in 1992 and 1996 (he failed to get 50 percent of the popular vote in either election), his unfocused and primarily tactical skills (especially in the first term), his desire to please, and finally his battle to survive impeachment weakened his leadership. Although he had ideas in abundance, political, institutional, and economic factors limited their applicability to the solution of policy problems.

Conclusion

Presidents approach the task of making domestic policy with varying amounts of resources and differing policy opportunities. Their domestic policy leadership depends to a large extent on their effectiveness in using the available resources to exploit existing opportunities and create new ones. They are most apt to do this effectively when the three components of the policy stream—problems, solutions, and politics—converge. A president's ability to bring these three tributary streams together is one indication of effective policy leadership.

Successful policy leadership requires that presidents spend their resources carefully and exploit opportunities skillfully. To do so presidents must pay particular attention to four strategic factors: goals, priorities, timing, and costs and benefits.

Modest, flexible *goals* usually are easier to achieve than those that are extensive and ideologically derived. So, too, are goals that enjoy substantial support among the public and policymaking elites. In establishing their goals, presidents take such considerations into account along with their values and beliefs. A primarily pragmatic set of objectives tends to be easier to accomplish than one that is ideologically derived. It is less likely, however, to have an impact on society than a more visionary and comprehensive set of objectives. In some circumstances, ideological goals may be highly appropriate. For example, Ronald Reagan initially struck a responsive note in Congress and the public with his unabashedly conservative domestic program. Presidents are free to be as pragmatic or as ideological as they wish in establishing their goals. However they decide, the mix they choose affects their policy leadership.

Closely related to goals, *priorities* also affect policy leadership. Presidents who clearly define their priorities generally have been more successful than those who have not done so because the policy process can handle only a few major issues at a time, even though many contend for attention. If a president does not indicate preferences, other participants will pursue their own objectives, possibly to the detriment of the president's. Nor is it realistic for presidents to expect that all of their goals will receive consideration to the exclusion of those of other participants. In this respect a comparison between Carter and Reagan is instructive. Carter developed a lengthy domestic agenda and insisted that all of his goals were vitally important to the nation and deserving of enactment. Congress responded by taking its time in dealing with Carter's program and by pursuing many of its own objectives. Some of Carter's goals, such as welfare reform and national health insurance, were never adopted; others, such as a national energy policy, were passed in greatly modified form after extensive delay and bargaining. Many congressional Democrats complained that Carter failed to provide them with direction and guidance for his domestic proposals. In contrast, Reagan made his priorities clear at the beginning of his administration, and he continued to do so. Congress had little doubt about which goals Reagan considered vital, and on which he would spend political capital, and which goals were less important to him. Cutting domestic spending, strengthening national defense, and reducing and reforming taxes took precedence over balancing the federal budget, ending legalized abortion, and restoring school prayer.

Timing, the third strategic consideration in successful policy leadership, is crucial to effective exploitation of opportunities. If opportunities are missed, they may be lost indefinitely. Good timing also involves taking advantage of the regular policy and electoral cycles. Proposals submitted at appropriate times in those cycles have greater likelihood of adoption. Proposals also can be withheld until conditions are ripe for their submission. A proposal that has limited support can be moved to the top of the agenda and pushed successfully as the result of a disaster, a crisis, or some other focusing event. Presidents who are able to time the presentation of proposals to coincide with favorable events and conditions are more likely to be effective policy leaders than those who lack such a sense of timing. Two presidents whose timing of domestic proposals was effective were Franklin Roosevelt during the first hundred days of the New Deal, when the Great Depression provided the rationale for a comprehensive set of economic recovery and reform laws, and Lyndon Johnson, who in early 1964 used the shock of the Kennedy assassination to secure passage of the Civil Rights Act. In contrast, Bill Clinton's poor timing of his health care reform and welfare reform proposals contributed to their failure.

Finally, successful policy leadership requires that presidents be attentive to the *costs and benefits* of raising problems for consideration and posing solutions to them. As presidents decide which problems and issues to emphasize, they focus on political benefits. They select agenda items according to the prospective electoral, historical, and programmatic benefits of the times.[82] When presidents select solutions for problems they are addressing, their emphasis is on costs.[83] Political costs, assessed in terms of congressional, electoral, bureaucratic, and interest group support, enter their calculations at each stage of the process. Increasingly, presidents and other actors have tended to view political costs in terms of avoiding blame and claiming credit for the outcomes.[84]

Economic costs have sharply limited the alternatives in recent years as budget pressures have mounted. These pressures force presidents to make hard choices, such as whether to support new programs and which existing programs to emphasize, maintain, or reduce. Technical costs and questions of workability also enter the selection of policy alternatives.

No prescription or formula can guarantee that a president will provide successful domestic policy leadership, in part because some problems, such as the high unemployment rate among African American men, are very difficult to solve, or solutions for them do not exist. Another reason for the absence of a workable formula is that conditions constantly change. Some problems may be solved only to reemerge in a new form; others may decline in importance. Solutions that are viable today may not be so a few years hence, or solutions may have unanticipated consequences or side effects that become problems in their own right. Political conditions, such as the popular mood or control of Congress, are in flux, so strategies may have to be modified frequently. Because many of the requirements of successful policy leadership are not fixed, what worked well for one president may be only partially useful to those who come later.

Even presidents who take office committed to concentrating their energies on domestic policy encounter extensive frustrations. They may enjoy some initial successes, as did Reagan; but the difficulties of accomplishing additional objectives eventually increase, and the sharing of power with Congress, the bureaucracy, and organized interests becomes ever more burdensome. The natural tendency is for presidents to turn their attention to national security or economic policy. In these areas, the challenges are more immediately threatening to the general welfare; the constraints on a president's ability to act, although very real, are not as frustrating; and successful policy leadership appears less elusive.

NOTES

1. The concept of "issue congestion" was developed by Hugh Heclo, "One Executive Branch or Many?" in *Both Ends of the Avenue,* ed. Anthony King (Washington, D.C.: American Enterprise Institute, 1983), 26–58.

2. Theodore J. Lowi, "American Business, Public Policy, Case Studies, and Political Theory," *World Politics* (July 1964): 677–715.

3. Steven A. Shull, *Domestic Policy Formation: Presidential-Congressional Partnership?* (Westport, Conn.: Greenwood Press, 1983), 155; Steven A. Shull, "Change in Presidential Policy Initiatives," *Western Political Quarterly* (September 1983): 497.

4. John H. Kessel, *Presidential Parties* (Homewood, Ill.: Dorsey, 1984), 112–115.

5. Jonathan Weisman, "Bush to Accept Budget 'Pork,'" *USA Today,* July 10, 2001, A1.

6. Kessel, *Presidential Parties,* 68–69.

7. The policy-stream metaphor borrows from Paul Light, "The Presidential Policy Stream," in *The Presidency and the Political System,* ed. Michael Nelson (Washington, D.C.: CQ Press, 1984), 423–448; and John W. Kingdon, *Agendas, Alternatives, and Public Policies,* 2d ed. (New York: HarperCollins, 1995), 85–86.

8. This discussion follows Kingdon, *Agendas,* chap. 5.

9. This discussion of the development of the health care issue follows B. Guy Peters, *American Public Policy: Promise and Performance,* 3d ed. (Chatham, N.J.: Chatham House, 1993), 230–235.

10. Paul Light, *The President's Agenda: Domestic Policy Choice from Kennedy to Reagan,* 3d ed. (Baltimore: Johns Hopkins University Press, 1991), chap. 3; and Light, "Presidential Policy Stream," 427–428.

11. Ironically, Nixon's preoccupation with the judgment of history helped to cut short his presidency. He consistently explained the installation of the secret taping system in the Oval Office as motivated by his desire to have a complete and accurate record for use by historians. That taped record provided the "smoking gun" that led the House Judiciary Committee to vote the impeachment charges that prompted his resignation in August 1974.

12. Burt Solomon, "Bush Plays Down Domestic Policy in Coasting toward Reelection," *National Journal,* March 30, 1991, 752–753.

13. Kingdon, *Agendas,* 142–143.

14. Jeff Fishel, *Presidents and Promises: From Campaign Pledge to Presidential Performance* (Washington, D.C.: CQ Press, 1984).

15. Kingdon, *Agendas,* 131.

16. Vincent J. Burke and Vee Burke, *Nixon's Good Deed: Welfare Reform* (New York: Columbia University Press, 1974); Laurence E. Lynn Jr. and David deF. Whitman, *The President as Policymaker: Jimmy Carter and Welfare Reform* (Philadelphia: Temple University Press, 1981).

17. Jack W. Germond and Jules Witcover, "On Welfare, It's Politics as Usual," *National Journal,* August 5, 1995, 2021.

18. "Social Policy," *Congressional Quarterly Weekly Report,* November 2, 1996, 3148–3149.

19. This discussion is based on Kingdon, *Agendas,* chap. 7.

20. Richard L. Berke, "Balance of Power: A Question of Governing from the Right," *New York Times,* May 25, 2001, A1.

21. This discussion follows Light, "The Presidential Policy Stream," 440–446.

22. Paul J. Quirk and Joseph Hinchcliffe, "Domestic Policy: The Trials of a Centrist Democrat," in *The Clinton Presidency: First Appraisals,* ed. Colin Campbell and Bert A. Rockman (Chatham, N.J.: Chatham House, 1995), 264–267.

23. David W. Moore, "Initial Job Approval for Bush at 57 percent, but Highest Disapproval of Any President since Polling Began," Gallup Poll release, February 6, 2001, www.gallup.com.

24. Gallup poll conducted June 8–10, 2001. An ABC News/*Washington Post* poll conducted May 31–June 3, 2001 found a disapproval rating of 40 percent. Both the Gallup and the ABC News/*Washington Post* polls found an approval rating of 55 percent. For these and other polls, go to www.govspot.com and click on "Polls/opinion."

25. Quoted in Ron Fournier, "Bush's Test: To Unite the Great Divide," *Pittsburgh Post-Gazette*, January 21, 2001, A9.

26. For example, Richard L. Berke and Frank Bruni, "Crew of Listing Bush Ship Draws Republican Scowls," *New York Times*, July 2, 2001, A11.

27. Light, "The Presidential Policy Stream," 444–445.

28. Kingdon, *Agendas*, 194–195.

29. Kessel, *Presidential Parties*, 60.

30. Light, *The President's Agenda*, 36–38.

31. Harold Wolman and Fred Tietlebaum, "Interest Groups and the Reagan Presidency," in *The Reagan Presidency and the Governing of America*, ed. Lester M. Salamon and Michael S. Lund (Washington, D.C.: Urban Institute Press, 1985), 299–301.

32. Mancur Olson, *The Rise and Decline of Nations* (New Haven: Yale University Press, 1982), 44.

33. Richard E. Neustadt, *Presidential Power and the Modern Presidents: The Politics of Leadership from Roosevelt to Reagan* (New York: Free Press, 1990), 29.

34. Leroy Rieselbach, *Congressional Reform: The Changing Modern Congress* (Washington, D.C.: CQ Press, 1994); Roger H. Davidson, ed., *The Postreform Congress* (New York: St. Martin's Press, 1992).

35. Donna Cassata, "Republicans Bask in Success of Rousing Performance," *Congressional Quarterly Weekly Report*, April 8, 1995, 986, 988, 990; Jennifer Babson, "Armey Stood Guard over Contract," *Congressional Quarterly Weekly Report*, April 8, 1995, 987; and Adam Clymer, "House Party: With Political Discipline It Works Like Parliament," *New York Times*, August 6, 1995, E6.

36. CNN Breaking News, May 24, 2001 (11:01 a.m.), Transcript #01052405V00.

37. Lester M. Salamon, "The Presidency and Domestic Policy Formulation," in *The Illusion of Presidential Government*, ed. Hugh Heclo and Lester M. Salamon (Boulder: Westview Press, 1981), 179.

38. Richard E. Neustadt, "The Presidency and Legislation: The Growth of Central Clearance," *American Political Science Review* (September 1954): 641–670; Robert S. Gilmour, "Central Clearance: A Revised Perspective," *Public Administration Review* (March–April 1971): 150–158.

39. Richard E. Neustadt, "The Presidency and Legislation: Planning the President's Program," *American Political Science Review* (December 1955): 980–1018; Larry Berman, *The Office of Management and Budget and the Presidency* (Princeton: Princeton University Press, 1979), 42–43; Stephen J. Wayne, *The Legislative Presidency* (New York: Harper and Row, 1978), 103–105.

40. Gilmour, "Central Clearance"; Berman, *The Office of Management and Budget*.

41. Norman C. Thomas and Harold L. Wolman, "The Presidency and Policy Formation: The Task Force Device," *Public Administration Review* (September–October 1969): 459–471.

42. Texts of the reports were published in *New Frontiers of the Kennedy Administration* (Washington, D.C.: Public Affairs Press, 1961).

43. Lyndon B. Johnson, *The Vantage Point* (New York: Holt, Rinehart and Winston, 1971), 326.

44. Paul Light, *Artful Work: The Politics of Social Security Reform* (New York: Random House, 1985), 232.

45. Quirk and Hinchcliffe, "Domestic Policy," 274–275.

46. Ibid., 275.

47. Raymond J. Waldman, "The Domestic Council: Innovation in Presidential Government," *Public Administration Review* (May–June 1976): 260–268.

48. Margaret Jane Wyszomirski, "The Roles of a Presidential Office for Domestic Policy: Three Models and Four Cases," in *The Presidency and Policy Making*, ed. George

C. Edwards III, Steven A. Shull, and Norman C. Thomas (Pittsburgh: University of Pittsburgh Press, 1985), 134.

49. John Helmer and Louis Maisel, "Analytical Problems in the Study of Presidential Advice: The Domestic Council Staff in Flux," *Presidential Studies Quarterly* (winter 1978): 52–53.

50. A sharp debate rages over politicization of OMB and the institutionalized presidency generally. Berman, in *The Office of Management and Budget*, argues that politicization has damaged, if not destroyed, the capacity of OMB to serve the institutional needs of the presidency in a professional manner. In contrast, Terry Moe in a seminal essay, views politicization as a logical (indeed necessary) institutional development resulting from the extensive and steady growth of "expectations surrounding presidential performance." See "The Politicized Presidency," in *The New Direction in American Politics*, ed. John E. Chubb and Paul E. Peterson (Washington, D.C.: Brookings, 1985), 269.

51. Wyszomirski, "The Roles of a Presidential Office," 136–137.

52. Wayne, *The Legislative Presidency*, 123.

53. Wyszomirski, "The Roles of a Presidential Office," 140.

54. For an extended description of the OPD/cabinet council system, see Chester A. Newland, "Executive Office Policy Apparatus: Enforcing the Reagan Agenda," in *The Reagan Presidency*, 153–159. Martin Anderson, who was Reagan's first director of the OPD, provides a participant's perspective on the cabinet councils in *Revolution* (New York: Harcourt Brace Jovanovich, 1988), chap. 19.

55. Ibid., 160.

56. This discussion follows Colin Campbell, "The White House and the Presidency under the 'Let's Deal' President," in *The Bush Presidency: First Appraisals*, ed. Colin Campbell and Bert A. Rockman (Chatham, N.J.: Chatham House, 1991), 210–212.

57. Julie Rovner, "On Policy Front, Home Is Not Where Bush's Heart Is," *Congressional Quarterly Weekly Report*, February 2, 1991, 292.

58. This discussion follows Colin Campbell, "Management in a Sandbox," in *The Clinton Presidency*, 77–80.

59. Ibid., 79.

60. Paul J. Quirk and William Cunion, "Clinton's Domestic Policy: The Lessons of a 'New Democrat,'" in *The Clinton Legacy*, ed. Colin Campbell and Bert A. Rockman (New York: Chatham House, 2000), 208.

61. Ibid., 210–211.

62. David E. Sanger, "Trying to Run a Country Like a Corporation," *New York Times*, July 8, 2001, sec. 4, 1.

63. Ibid.

64. Paul J. Quirk, "Domestic Policy: Divided Government and Cooperative Presidential Leadership," in *The Bush Presidency*, 73–76.

65. Burt Solomon, " 'Empowerment,' Whatever It Is, Powers Ahead in Policy Circles," *National Journal*, December 12, 1990, 3046–3047; Solomon, "Power to the People?" *National Journal*, January 26, 1991, 204–209.

66. Quirk, "Domestic Policy," 73; Kenneth T. Walsh, "George Bush's Idea-free Zone," *U.S. News and World Report*, January 14, 1991, 34–35.

67. Rovner, "On Policy Front," 292–293; Burt Solomon, "Grading Bush," *National Journal*, June 8, 1991, 1331–1335.

68. Solomon, "Grading Bush," 1331.

69. This discussion follows Quirk and Hinchcliffe, "Domestic Policy," 267–268.

70. Ibid., 268.

71. This discussion follows Alissa J. Rubin, "Overhaul Issue Unlikely to Rest in Peace," *Congressional Quarterly Weekly Report*, October 1, 1994, 2797–2801.

72. This discussion follows Kingdon, *Agendas,* 217–221.

73. Ibid., 221.

74. Erwin C. Hargrove and Michael Nelson, *Presidents, Politics, and Policy* (New York: Knopf, 1984); Michael Nelson, "The Presidency: Clinton and the Cycle of Politics and Policy," in *The Elections of 1992,* ed. Michael Nelson (Washington, D.C.: CQ Press, 1993), 125–152.

75. Nelson, "The Presidency," 126.

76. Ibid., 145.

77. Ibid., 128.

78. Hargrove and Nelson, *Presidents, Politics, and Policy,* 68.

79. Ibid., 72.

80. Ibid., 68.

81. Ibid., 81–83.

82. Light, *The President's Agenda,* 71.

83. Ibid., 134–136.

84. R. Kent Weaver, *Automatic Government: The Politics of Indexation* (Washington, D.C.: Brookings, 1988), chap. 2.

SUGGESTED READINGS

Baumgartner, Frank R., and Byron D. Jones. *Agendas and Instability in American Politics.* Chicago: University of Chicago Press, 1993.

Fishel, Jeff. *Presidents and Promises: From Campaign Pledge to Presidential Performance.* Washington, D.C.: CQ Press, 1984.

Hargrove, Erwin C., and Michael Nelson. *Presidents, Politics, and Policy.* New York: Knopf, 1984.

Kessel, John H. *Presidents, the Presidency, and the Political Environment.* Washington, D.C.: CQ Press, 2001.

Kingdon, John W. *Agendas, Alternatives, and Public Policies.* 2d ed. New York: HarperCollins, 1995.

Light, Paul C. *Artful Work: The Politics of Social Security Reform.* New York: Random House, 1985.

____. *The President's Agenda: Domestic Policy Choice from Kennedy to Clinton.* 3d ed. Baltimore: Johns Hopkins University Press, 1999.

Lynn, Laurence E., Jr., and David deF. Whitman. *The President as Policymaker: Jimmy Carter and Welfare Reform.* Philadelphia: Temple University Press, 1981.

Quirk, Paul J., and William Cunion. "Clinton's Domestic Policy: The Lessons of a 'New Democrat.'" In *The Clinton Legacy,* ed. Colin Campbell and Bert A. Rockman. New York: Chatham House, 2000.

Shull, Steven A. *Domestic Policy Formation: Presidential-Congressional Partnership?* Westport, Conn.: Greenwood Press, 1983.

____. *The President and Civil Rights Policy: Leadership and Change.* Westport, Conn.: Greenwood Press, 1989.

Sundquist, James L. *Politics and Policy: The Eisenhower, Kennedy, and Johnson Years.* Washington, D.C.: Brookings, 1968.

Warshaw, Shirley Anne. *The Domestic Presidency: Policy Making in the White House.* Boston: Allyn and Bacon, 1996.

9 THE POLITICS OF ECONOMIC POLICY

During the Great Depression, Franklin Roosevelt used radio broadcasts from the White House, known as "fireside chats," to persuade the public to support his unprecedented economic policies.

ECONOMIC ISSUES DOMINATED THE 1992 presidential election campaign and most of the following decade. Polls indicated that the public blamed President George H. W. Bush and his administration for the 1991–1992 recession. Bush insisted that the economy was fundamentally sound and that recovery from the recession had begun. The Democratic candidate, Bill Clinton, charged that Bush had indeed neglected the economy and focused his campaign on economic issues. A sign stating, "It's the Economy, Stupid," hung on the wall of his national campaign headquarters.[1] Clinton promised to end the recession, ensure long-run prosperity through investments in human capital and physical infrastructure, and reduce the substantial federal budget deficit. That year's independent candidate, Ross Perot, stressed the importance of ending the deficit and reducing the expanding national debt. The electorate responded by choosing Clinton while giving Perot

319

19 percent of the vote. Not surprisingly, the deficit and other economic issues dominated Clinton's first two years in office. Quite surprisingly, however, Clinton got only modest credit for presiding during a period of record economic growth with low inflation that coincided with a near-miraculous transformation in the annual budget from a $290 billion deficit in 1992 to a $69.2 billion surplus in 1998. Although Clinton enthusiasts hailed this turnaround as a great achievement, many analysts saw it as the product of luck and the efforts of Alan Greenspan, chairman of the Federal Reserve Board. As one pair of analysts concluded, "the bounty of the 1990s resulted less from Clinton's personal stewardship of prosperity than from his willingness to follow the learned advice of others and, more fundamentally, from economic forces beyond his control."[2]

Clinton's attentiveness to economic matters was not new. Presidents have been concerned about the condition of the economy since the early years of the Republic. Some who confronted serious economic adversity, such as Martin Van Buren in 1837, Ulysses S. Grant in 1873, Grover Cleveland in 1893, Theodore Roosevelt in 1907, and Warren G. Harding in 1921, did little more than ride out the storm. The electorate, however, reacted by denying reelection to Van Buren and by inflicting sizable losses on the president's party in the midterm congressional elections of 1838, 1874, and 1894. In fact, the existence of a relationship between business cycles and election results was known long before Edward Tufte's precise empirical analysis of the phenomenon.[3] Only since the 1930s, however, have presidents attempted to control business cycles through public policy, and the public has come to expect them to do so.

This chapter examines the president's economic policy responsibilities and activities. It begins by distinguishing between actions designed to manage the entire economy (macroeconomic policy) and those meant to control specific aspects of the economy (microeconomic policy). The primary focus of the chapter is on macroeconomic policy. The chapter reviews presidential efforts to manage the economy from 1933 to 2001 and then describes the politics of macroeconomic policymaking. Next we analyze how the president makes economic policy and the ways in which presidents since Dwight D. Eisenhower have handled the problem of coordinating economic policy. The chapter concludes with an assessment of the congressional role in macroeconomic policymaking.

Macroeconomic Policy

Management of the entire economy by the government is known as **macroeconomic policy,** and the government has two principal tools to use: fiscal policy and monetary policy. Using fiscal policy, the government tries to regulate the level of the nation's economic activity by varying taxes and public expenditures. A policy of increasing spending and reducing taxes aims to expand the economy; one of decreasing spending and increasing taxes aims to contract it. A budget deficit (when spending exceeds tax revenues) stimulates economic activity, whereas a budget surplus (when tax revenues exceed spending) slows the economy. The president and Congress jointly make fiscal policy. They determine expenditures through budgeting and appropriations, and they establish taxes through legislation. Monetary policy refers to a government's efforts, through its central bank (in the United States, the Federal Reserve System), to regulate economic activity by controlling the supply of money—currency and credit. An independent agency, the Board of Governors of the Federal Reserve System, makes monetary policy. Although fiscal policy and monetary policy constitute distinct realms of policymaking, administrations seek to coordinate them.

Since the Great Depression of the 1930s, the goals of macroeconomic policy have remained constant: to hold down the rate of inflation, to establish and maintain full employment, and to achieve a steady rate of economic growth. However, policymakers have pursued these goals through alternative theories: classical conservative economics, Keynesianism, monetarism, and supply-side economics.

Conservative economic theory lost credibility during the Great Depression when the administrations of Herbert Hoover and Franklin D. Roosevelt (at the outset) stressed balancing the budget and failed to restore confidence in the economy and produce the desired upturn. Both presidents had sought to balance the budget by reducing government spending and even raising taxes despite mounting unemployment. FDR quickly discovered that emergency spending and loan programs provided relief and produced a measure of recovery. The ideas of John Maynard Keynes, a British economist whom Roosevelt met in 1934, offered an explanation for why fiscal stimulus is effective and eventually provided a rationale for deficit spending. Keynes argued that an economic decline is caused by a drop in private demand for goods and services. Government could stimulate demand by increasing its own expenditures or increasing those of consumers by reducing taxes. The temporary deficits created by fiscal stimulation would be financed by government borrowing and repaid during periods of hyperactivity in the economy. FDR did not fully accept Keynesian ideas until a sharp recession followed his attempt to return to a balanced budget in 1937. Eventually the economy's recovery following mobilization during World War II, which was supported by government spending, provided most economists with empirical validation of Keynes's basic theories. Conservative economics, however, retained its hold on many political leaders, such as Eisenhower, who made balanced budgets their goal and regarded fiscal stimulation of lagging demand as an emergency measure.

While Keynesianism was establishing itself as the new orthodoxy, another theory emerged to challenge it. The monetarists, under the leadership of the economist Milton Friedman, held that the key to maintaining economic stability lay not in stimulating demand but in limiting the growth rate of the money supply to no more than the growth rate of the economy. Inflation occurs, monetarists claim, when the money supply expands too rapidly. The only remedy for inflation is a painful contraction in the money supply. Monetarists hold that fiscal policy and the size of budget deficits are subordinate to monetary policy and the growth rate of the money supply, which for them constitute the basic means of managing the economy.

Monetarism gained adherents as the limitations of Keynesianism became apparent during the 1970s. Keynesian theory has an inflationary bias—its primary defect as a macroeconomic theory. Decisions on taxing and spending are made by the president and members of Congress—politicians concerned with reelection—and not by professional economists. Consequently, it has proved easier in practice to increase spending and cut taxes, the Keynesian prescription for expansion, than to cut spending and increase taxes, the theory's remedy for inflation. In the 1970s, when inflation became the nation's leading economic problem, political decision makers were unwilling to impose the Keynesian solution. They feared the electoral consequences of reducing government spending and raising taxes when their constituents were struggling to make ends meet. Although the inflationary bias of Keynesianism is a political defect rather than a weakness in the theory itself, this bias nevertheless has made it less attractive than other theories as a guide to policy.

Monetarism, whatever its theoretical merits and limitations, offered a politically palatable way to control inflation through the autonomous Federal Reserve Board, known as the Fed, which reduces inflation by contracting the money supply. Political officeholders can blame the consequences of monetary contractions, such as high interest rates and rising unemployment, on the Fed and its amorphous supporters: "Wall Street" investing interests and the banks. But monetarism also became politically unattractive when efforts to control inflation proved painful during the late 1970s. By the early 1980s a new theoretical approach, supply-side economics, had emerged and been embraced by President Ronald Reagan.

Essentially supply-side economics is an amalgam of Keynesianism and monetarism.[4] Supply-siders endorse strict monetary restraint as the means to control inflation, but they also believe, unlike pure monetarists, that fiscal policy can be used to achieve macroeconomic policy objectives. The supply-siders assert, however, that the Keynesians misdirect government efforts. Instead of stimulating demand through higher spending and tax cuts for consumers, the supply-siders seek to stimulate supply through tax cuts that provide incentives to encourage investments and productivity, which in turn increase the supply of goods and services. Increasing the supply of goods and services stimulates the demand for them. That is, the additional jobs that are created ultimately fuel consumer buying, though the focus of the policy is producers, not consumers. Supply-siders are not disturbed by budget deficits resulting from tax-cut incentives. They believe an expanded economy will not be inflationary and eventually will generate enough revenues at lower rates of taxation to balance the budget.

Supply-side economics draws sharp criticism from both liberals and conservatives who doubt the validity of assumptions on which the theory rests. Liberals charge that it is another version of the discredited "trickle down" approach to economic policy, under which tax advantages for the affluent are justified on the grounds that they eventually lead to prosperity for all. Conservatives fear that supply-side tolerance of budget deficits will lead to excessive rates of inflation and will erode confidence in the monetary system. Although critics would like supply-side policies to work, they do not believe that they can. Experience since 1981 with a massive cut in federal income taxes, phased in over several years and based on supply-side reasoning, supports their pessimism. The economy steadily expanded during the 1980s and 1990s, but a balanced budget was not achieved until 1998, when there was a modest surplus. The Democrats, whose willingness to raise taxes in 1993 helped increase government revenues, claimed credit for this accomplishment. But when signs of an economic slowdown emerged in late 2000, the issue of tax cuts reemerged during the presidential campaign, and after a new administration was in place, Republicans passed a dramatic tax reduction at the urging of President George W. Bush. This new effort provided another opportunity to observe how the federal budget would be affected by supply-side policies in the long run.

For nearly two decades, federal policymakers were forced to rely more heavily on monetary policy than on fiscal policy to manage the economy. In the face of large and persistent deficits, there was little room to increase spending or reduce taxes, actions that would have further expanded the deficit. Moreover, Republicans and Democrats disagreed vehemently over the level and purposes of government spending and the structure of taxes—who pays how much. In this intractable setting, monetary policy instruments became the only viable alternative for macroeconomic management.[5] Although the appearance of budget surpluses seemed to breathe new life into fiscal policy, this revival would prove short-lived if the Bush tax cuts adopted in 2001 were so large that the federal government once again began to run a deficit.

Microeconomic Policy

Microeconomic policy is a term used to describe government regulation of specific economic activities; it also encompasses antitrust policy, which is designed to prevent business monopolies and stimulate competition. Microeconomic policies focus on specific industries or on economic practices in several industries. They are designed to affect directly the infrastructure of the economy and only indirectly its overall performance. Modern presidents generally have paid less attention to microeconomic than to macroeconomic policy, largely because its impact is more narrowly focused. Most presidents, however, have on occasion endorsed specific microeconomic policies or used microeconomic policy tools to achieve macroeconomic or other policy goals. President Reagan, for example, strongly supported deregulation and privatization to reduce the role of government and strengthen the free market. Greater reliance on the market, he believed, would lead to a more productive economy.

Before the Great Depression, presidents were involved exclusively with microeconomic policy and did not regard overall management of the economy as a primary policy responsibility. To preserve competition in the market, Theodore Roosevelt and William Howard Taft vigorously enforced the Sherman Anti-Trust Act of 1890—Roosevelt with great fanfare and Taft with quiet effectiveness. Woodrow Wilson persuaded Congress to establish an independent regulatory agency, the Federal Trade Commission, with extensive authority to regulate anticompetitive and unfair business practices. Roosevelt, Taft, and Wilson believed that the federal government should act to correct imperfections in the operations of the free market economy.

During the New Deal, Franklin Roosevelt endorsed legislation that established or strengthened independent regulatory agencies: the Securities and Exchange Commission, the Federal Power Commission, the Federal Communications Commission, the Civil Aeronautics Board (CAB), and the National Labor Relations Board. These agencies received broad grants of authority to regulate the interstate aspects of specific industries, such as trade in stocks and bonds, electric power and natural gas, broadcasting and wire communications, and air transportation, as well as economywide activities such as labor-management relations. FDR's use of microeconomic policy was characterized by a pragmatic search for techniques of government intervention that would improve the operation of certain economic sectors or lead to an improvement in the overall health of the economy. Policies that worked were retained; those that failed were abandoned.

FDR's successors varied in their use of microeconomic policies. Presidents Harry S. Truman, Eisenhower, John F. Kennedy, and Lyndon B. Johnson accepted the legitimacy of government regulation of economic activity that had been established by 1940, including antitrust policy. They differed mainly in the intensity with which they enforced regulations and in their willingness to use certain microeconomic policy tools.

Beginning in the late 1960s and continuing into the 1970s, Congress passed a new set of statutes expanding federal regulation of economic activity as a way to achieve noneconomic goals, such as a cleaner physical environment, safer automobiles and other consumer products, and a higher degree of safety and health in the workplace. Presidents initially approved the new regulatory activities, but as their economic costs became apparent, Richard Nixon and Gerald R. Ford raised questions about the appropriateness of federal regulation in general. A deregulatory movement gained support, endorsed by Ford and Jimmy Carter. Ford assigned overall responsibility for deregulation to a member of the Council of Economic Advisers (CEA) and issued an order that required agencies to analyze the impact of their actions on inflation. Carter established the Regulatory Analysis Review Group, chaired by a CEA member, with responsibility for reviewing new rules and regulations with potential economic costs of $100 million or more. There is little evidence, however, that these actions reduced the volume of new regulations or the economic impact of regulation on industry.[6] Carter also supported legislation that deregulated the airline and trucking industries. (The CAB ceased to function at the end of 1984, but the Interstate Commerce Commission continued to regulate railroads.)

Reagan promised in his 1980 election campaign to reduce substantially the amount of federal regulation; he argued that regulation was a primary cause of the decline of productivity in the economy. Reagan established the Task Force on Regulatory Relief, headed by Vice President George Bush, to analyze the economic effects of existing and proposed regulations. This task force prepared the way for the establishment, in the Office of Management and Budget (OMB), of the Office of Information and Regulatory Affairs to review proposed agency regulations, a unit that continued into the twenty-first century. Reagan also issued two executive orders, numbers 12291 and 12498, mandating that all major regulations be subjected to cost-benefit analysis, authorizing the OMB director to delay the implementation of regulations, and requiring each agency annually to prepare a regulatory program that specified all regulatory actions in progress and those planned for the future. These changes ensured continued presidential influence over the regulatory process. The Reagan administration employed a three-pronged administrative strategy that substantially reduced the effectiveness of regulation.[7] First, the administration used OMB review procedures to kill or to slow the issuance of regulations. Second, it reduced the intensity of regulatory enforcement. Third, Reagan appointees changed their agencies' orientation from confrontation to cooperation as a way to achieve compliance.

President Bush did not change the regulatory review process that Reagan established with his two executive orders. Like Reagan, he involved his vice president in an antiregulation effort. Dan Quayle chaired the Council on Competitiveness, which had broad authority to intervene in drafting federal regulations. However, Bush's regulatory policy differed markedly from that of his predecessor. Whereas Reagan implemented a regulatory reform agenda based on his conservative ideology, Bush had no holistic vision for regulatory reform, nor did he continue Reagan's opposition to social regulation—especially occupational safety and environmental protection. Bush gave stronger support to economic regulatory policy, and he appointed moderates to regulatory positions, in sharp contrast to Reagan's practice of naming conservative appointees, who were philosophically opposed to regulations.[8]

Regulatory policy initially was not a major concern of the Clinton administration. Its legislative proposals extended the existing regulatory philosophy. Following their takeover of Congress in 1995, the Republicans introduced legislation designed to provide relief from environmental regulation to businesses and individuals.[9] The bills restricted the authority of federal agencies to issue regulations by requiring justification of proposed rules through cost-benefit and risk analyses. Also, they made it easier for parties likely to be subject to regulations to challenge them before they were issued.[10] President Clinton responded by threatening to veto any legislation that greatly relaxed environmental regulation, and he adopted a strong defensive posture regarding efforts to weaken and relax federal regulation generally.

During the early months of his administration, George W. Bush triggered fears among environmentalists, organized labor, and consumer advocacy groups that he would seek to overturn regulations deemed harmful by business. The administration declared a sixty-day delay while it reviewed new rules approved by the departing president during his final days in office. These included rules to lower the level of arsenic in drinking water, ban road construction and limit logging on sixty million acres of federal forests, require higher efficiency for air conditioners, reduce diesel exhaust in the air, and reduce repetitive-motion injuries in the workplace.[11] Some rules were reversed, grabbing the headlines and allowing critics to suggest that Bush would favor business interests, but the administration's actions were sufficiently mixed that a coherent approach to economic regulation was not yet evident. Although it was clear that OMB's regulatory review would apply stringent cost-benefit criteria to proposed regulations, initial assessments suggested that the administration would be forced to act with greater moderation and in a less probusiness manner than had first been assumed.[12]

In all modern presidential administrations, microeconomic policies have been secondary to macroeconomic policy. Microeconomic policies, such as vigorous antitrust enforcement or support for deregulation, can be used to achieve macroeconomic policy goals and to highlight the theoretical rationale for administration policy, but microeconomic policies cannot replace fiscal and monetary policies as the primary means by which presidents discharge their responsibility for the health of the nation's economy.

Presidents and the Economy: 1933–2001

The president's role as manager of the economy dates from FDR's New Deal with its commitment to use the federal government's power to bring about recovery from the Great Depression. Keynesian economics and its prescription of increased government spending to compensate for inadequate private spending for investment and consumption provided a theoretical justification for government intervention. Ultimately, it was not the New Deal reforms or recovery programs that ended the depression but the huge increase in government spending during World War II. All of the nation's unused productive capacity—capital facilities and human resources—were mobilized to achieve victory, and government borrowing financed much of that mobilization.

After the war Congress passed the Employment Act of 1946, committing the U.S. government to maintain "maximum employment, production, and purchasing power." This act translated into law the widespread expectation, developed during the Roosevelt administration, that the government would guarantee to the fullest extent possible a prosperous economy. It also made the president primarily responsible for providing economic policy leadership, although it furnished him with few new tools for the task. It created the CEA and an accompanying staff to provide professional analysis and advice, and it required the president to report annually to Congress on the condition of the economy and to offer proposals for improving or maintaining its health. Ultimate power over the president's economic proposals, however, remains with Congress.

From the end of World War II until the late 1960s, presidents and Congress fought with each other over economic policy. Truman struggled unsuccessfully with Congress over its desire to reduce wartime taxes, but he was somewhat more effective in controlling the inflation that resulted from spending for the Korean War. Eisenhower's conservative policies tended to prevail over the plans of a Democratic Congress to increase domestic spending. The Eisenhower administration was marked by two recessions, in 1954 and 1958, with a period of economic expansion between them. The Kennedy-Johnson administration fully embraced Keynesian theory, and a 1964 income tax cut had the desired effect of expanding the economy and increasing revenues. It was thought that economic forecasting and management of the economy had developed to the point where fine-tuning of unemployment and the inflation rate was possible.[13]

In 1966, however, economic conditions began to change. Vietnam War expenditures rose rapidly, the deficit increased, and President Johnson shifted his focus from economic expansion to economic restraint. Congress resisted Johnson's requests for higher excise taxes, and for political reasons he refrained from asking for income tax increases. He feared that Congress would refuse the request and that in the course of congressional debate embarrassing questions would be raised about the war and its cost. With a congressional election scheduled in 1966, he was unwilling to risk debate and defeat. By the time Johnson had requested additional income taxes and Congress had approved a temporary 10 percent income surtax, the economy had begun a prolonged inflationary period that drastically changed the conditions that had been relatively stable since 1946. (The first twenty-five years of the post–World War II period had been characterized by an inflation rate of approximately 3 percent a year, an unemployment variance between 4 percent and 8 percent, and sustained growth in the gross domestic product.)

Presidents since Johnson have had to contend with a changing and increasingly intractable economy. Inflation rates crept upward into double digits in the late 1970s and early 1980s before declining, unemployment remained high by postwar standards into the mid-1990s, and the federal budget ran a deficit every year between 1970 and 1997 (see Table 9-1). Underlying these developments have been systemic factors beyond the control of the government: the increased dependence of the economy on foreign sources of raw materials, especially oil; the growing interdependence of the U.S. economy with those of other industrial democracies; the declining productivity of the U.S. economy in relation to foreign competition; the growth and maturation of domestic social welfare programs based on statutory entitlements; and a commitment to improve the quality of the physical environment even at substantial cost to economic growth and productivity.

Richard Nixon was the first president to encounter this changing economic environment. His response was twofold. He consistently pursued the classical conservative course of attempting to counter inflation by pushing Congress for reductions in federal spending to balance the budget. In addition, Nixon took the

Table 9-1   Inflation, Unemployment, and Federal Budget Deficits/Surpluses, 1970–2000

	Inflation[a]	Unemployment[b]	Deficit/surplus[c]
1970	5.7%	4.9%	$–2.84
1971	4.4	5.9	–23.03
1972	3.2	5.6	–23.37
1973	6.2	4.9	–14.91
1974	11.0	5.6	–6.14
1975	9.1	8.5	–53.24
1976	5.6	7.7	–73.73
1977	6.5	7.0	–53.66
1978	7.6	6.6	–59.19
1979	11.3	5.8	–40.73
1980	13.5	7.1	–73.84
1981	10.3	7.6	–78.98
1982	6.2	9.7	–127.99
1983	3.2	9.6	–207.82
1984	4.3	7.5	–185.39
1985	3.6	7.2	–212.33
1986	1.9	7.0	–221.25
1987	3.6	6.2	–149.77
1988	4.1	5.5	–155.19
1989	4.8	5.3	–152.48
1990	5.4	5.6	–221.23
1991	4.2	6.8	–269.36
1992	3.0	7.5	–290.40
1993	3.0	6.9	–255.11
1994	2.6	6.1	–203.28
1995	2.8	5.6	–164.01
1996	3.0	5.4	–107.51
1997	2.3	4.9	–21.99
1998	1.6	4.5	+69.19
1999	2.2	4.2	+124.41
2000	3.4	4.0	+166.69[d]

[a] Percent increase in the consumer price index.

[b] Percent of the civilian noninstitutional population sixteen years of age or over.

[c] In billions of dollars.

[d] Estimated.

Sources: *Statistical Abstract of the United States,* Tables 532, 643, 768, www.census.gov/prod/www/statistical-abstract-us.html. Table 532 contains estimated data on 2000 budget surplus. For data on deficits in the years 1971–1974 and 1976–1979, see Office of Management and Budget, *Budget of the United States Government, Fiscal Year 2002,* www.whitehouse.gov/omb/budget/fy2002/hist.pdf. For 2000 data on inflation and unemployment, see "USA Statistics in Brief," www.census.gov/statab/www.brief.html.

extraordinary step, for a conservative Republican, of freezing prices and wages in August 1971. The imposition of wage and price controls is an extreme measure, for through it the president suspends the normal operation of market forces. Although Roosevelt and Truman imposed controls during World War II and the Korean War, Nixon has been the only president to do so in peacetime. He acted under authority that Congress delegated to the president in the Economic Stabilization Act of 1970, which it passed over his strong objections. The wage and price freeze experience during 1971–1973 suggests that peacetime wage and price controls are at best a temporary means of curbing inflation and that they can quickly become a political liability unless their impact is moderated—Nixon did not suffer the political consequences in 1972, but congressional Republicans did.

Upon taking office in August 1974, President Ford assumed that the principal economic problem confronting the United States was inflation, and he pushed to cut federal spending. Almost before his anti-inflation campaign was launched, however, economic conditions changed, and Ford spent his last year as president combating a recession that contributed to his electoral defeat in 1976. Ford's successor, Jimmy Carter, fared little better. Carter initiated an antirecession program of increased federal spending and tax cuts to stimulate business investment. The economy responded almost too quickly, and Carter was confronted with surging inflation rates that reached double digits during his last two years in office.

Perhaps Carter's most important decision affecting the economy was his naming of Paul Volcker as chairman of the Federal Reserve Board in 1979. Volcker's appointment reflected Carter's disenchantment with the ability of Keynesian theory to provide solutions to the problem of stagflation, a combination of a stagnant economy and rising prices. Essentially a monetarist, Volcker moved quickly to curb inflation by restraining the growth of the money supply. Although Carter did not fully abandon Keynesianism, he gave monetarism a prominent role in macroeconomic policymaking for the first time.

The rate of inflation did not respond quickly to Volcker's efforts to tighten the money supply, but interest rates on consumer loans rose sharply. These developments undoubtedly contributed to Carter's defeat by Ronald Reagan in the 1980 election. One of Reagan's campaign pledges was to restore vitality to the economy through a revolutionary program of major reductions in taxing and spending. Congress responded positively to Reagan's initiatives in 1981 by enacting the largest income tax cut in U.S. history and by reducing domestic spending in nonentitlement programs. Congress also supported Reagan's proposals for a major defense buildup, projected over five years from 1981 through 1986.

The results of the Reagan administration's macroeconomic policies were mixed. The major accomplishment—credit for which must be given to the Fed— was the curtailment of inflation, which fluctuated between annual rates of 1.9 to 4.3 percent from 1983 through 1988. Also, in 1983 the economy began a sustained period of growth that lasted through 1990. Before that growth spurt, however, the United States experienced the most severe recession since World War II, with unemployment rising to 10.75 percent in the fourth quarter of

1982. In spite of the prosperity achieved since 1982, unemployment did not drop below 5 percent until fifteen years later.

On the negative side, the Reagan administration's macroeconomic policies produced massive federal budget deficits. The deficits grew rapidly through a conjunction of forces: the recession of 1982 caused revenues to fall and triggered automatic countercyclical spending (such as unemployment compensation); the tax cuts and increased defense spending authorized in 1981 became effective, reducing revenues and increasing some expenditures. The result was a large structural, or permanent, deficit as the increases in federal revenues promised by supply-side advocates failed to materialize and Congress refused to provide sizable additional cuts in nondefense spending. Finally, interest payments rose quickly to pay for government borrowing needed to close the gap between spending and revenues. From $990 billion in 1980, the debt rose to $3.1 trillion ten years later.[14] Net interest payments became one of the fastest growing items in the federal budget, an obstacle to reducing the deficit and a constraint on spending for other purposes.

The deficits proved embarrassing to President Reagan because they violated traditional conservative values of fiscal restraint. But ironically the deficits also brought political advantage to the Reagan administration. The unprecedented deficit spending put money in the pockets of American consumers, creating additional demand that in turn stimulated the economy and served as the basis for the sustained recovery from the 1981–1982 recession. That recovery was crucial to Reagan's 1984 reelection victory, for voters concluded that his economic policies had worked quite well. That Reagan had become a practitioner of Keynesian demand management on a grand scale was immaterial to him and his supporters. The deficits also provided Reagan with an effective argument for restraining the growth of nondefense spending.

George H. W. Bush's victory in the 1988 presidential election was an endorsement of the status quo. The country was prosperous and not at war. The only economic policy mandate Bush received derived from his pledge that there would be "no new taxes." Like Reagan, Bush promised to eliminate the budget deficit by reducing spending. He kept his promise not to raise taxes until October 1990, when he faced the prospect of an enormous deficit that would trigger automatic budget cuts. His administration negotiated a budget deal with Congress that would balance the budget by 1996, a goal overcome by unanticipated expenditures for the Persian Gulf War and the costs of bailing out failed savings and loan institutions insured by the federal government.[15] The deficits for fiscal 1991 ($269.36 billion) and 1992 ($290.40 billion) were the highest ever in U.S. history. The recession that began in late 1990 and continued into 1992 meant Congress could not cut spending or raise taxes, thus impeding administration and congressional efforts to curb the deficit.

The 1992 election gave a clear indication of voter dissatisfaction with the condition of the economy, but it produced no general agreement on economic policies. This was due in part to Bill Clinton's lack of a clear electoral mandate—he received only 43.3 percent of the vote—and in part to the candidate's failure to provide concrete proposals for deficit reduction out of fear of antagonizing the voters. "While concerned about ending deficits, the voters [were] even more concerned with preventing the spending cuts and tax increases necessary to accomplish that goal."[16] During the campaign, Clinton promised an economic stimulus package and a middle-class tax cut; deficit reduction was a distant concern. This plan began to change on December 3, 1992, during his first meeting with Fed chair Alan Greenspan, who argued that the key to prosperity was convincing Wall Street that the new administration was committed to reducing the budget deficit.[17]

President Clinton moved quickly to address economic problems. His economic program, unveiled on February 17, 1993, contained three parts: deficit reduction; long-term investments in research, education and training, and physical infrastructure; and short-term spending to stimulate the economy. By a single vote in each chamber, Congress narrowly passed legislation (called a reconciliation bill) that reduced the deficit by $496 billion over five years, mainly through tax increases on the wealthy; the investment spending proposals were severely reduced or deferred; and a Senate filibuster mounted by Republicans killed the stimulus package. Economic conditions improved quickly under Clinton but not fast enough to avoid devastating losses in the 1994 congressional midterm elections. Unemployment dropped from about 7 percent at the time of the 1992 election to around 6 percent in 1994 and 4.5 percent in 1998. Inflation was moderate at 2.9 percent in his first term and dropped to 2.0 percent in 1997–1998. The economy, which grew at a healthy annual rate of almost 4 percent in 1994,[18] averaged 2.6 percent throughout his first term and 3.9 percent in 1997–1998.[19] As a result of the 1993 deficit reduction package and a stronger than anticipated economic performance, the budget deficit fell from nearly $300 billion in 1992 to almost $108 billion by 1996[20] and turned the corner with a modest surplus in 1998. This goal was reached in just one year, five years earlier than anticipated in the budget agreement reached between Clinton and congressional Republicans in 1997.[21]

Evaluated in terms of these conventional indicators, Clinton's economic policies succeeded, but he received delayed political rewards. In the 1994 congressional elections, regarded as a referendum on Clinton's overall performance, the voters handed the Democratic Party a stunning defeat as the Republicans regained control over Congress for the first time in forty years. No Republican legislator had voted for the economic package, and the Democrats were branded as the party of high taxes. During the 1996 election and by the end of his term, however, Clinton's contributions to national prosperity seemed to underlay his reelection and the strong public support he received even in the midst of the impeachment controversy (see chapter 5).

Ultimately "Clinton's fiscal policy served as a laboratory for a change in economic thought." Rather than relying on government deficits to stimulate economic activity, Clinton sought "balanced budgets—or better yet, surpluses—

[which] are believed to hold down interest rates, free capital for the private sector and reassure investors about long-term economic stability."[22] Thus, the conventional Keynesian strategy for pursuing an expansionary fiscal policy was turned on its head. Ironically this challenge to traditional economic thinking may have laid the groundwork for George W. Bush's initial economic success.

Approval of a massive tax cut at the outset of the Bush administration cast into doubt whether a key feature of the Clinton legacy—budget surpluses large enough to pay off the accumulated national debt and maintain solvency for the big-ticket programs of Social Security and Medicare—would survive. Clinton was almost too successful. When estimates of future surpluses grew to $5.6 trillion over ten years, arguments against tax cuts were undermined.[23] Congressional Republicans had passed a tax cut bill in 1999 only to have it vetoed by Clinton, with the president justifying his action as a way to save Social Security and Medicare. Bush surprised most observers when he made the tax cut a centerpiece of his campaign for president because the polls did not show great public support for the idea. Despite the Democrats' resistance, Al Gore, their candidate for president in 2000, felt compelled to propose a $500 billion cut of his own during the campaign.

Uncertainty prevailed about what the $1.35 trillion tax cut over eleven years would mean for the economy. Much like Ronald Reagan's tax cuts in the 1980s, Bush's cut would restrain nondefense government spending and possibly stimulate economic growth through lower interest rates, as occurred under Clinton. But Reagan's tax cuts occurred over three years; the decade-long Bush plan was far more complicated, with some cuts phased in and others phased out throughout the decade, corresponding to the size of the anticipated surplus along the way. One goal was to ensure that Social Security and Medicare funds would not be needed to cover annual government expenses—that they would stay secure in the "lockbox" that politicians had pledged to observe. However, critics pointed out that in any given year, because of a slowdown in the economy, revenue projections could be off and the lockbox would have to be opened. Even further complicating matters, baby boomers would begin retiring in 2011, starting a long-anticipated drain on Social Security resources and increasing health care costs just when the surplus picture became even blurrier.[24] To supply-siders, lower tax rates appeared to lead to the kind of sustained economic growth needed to finance seniors' retirement and additional health care costs. To Keynesians, however, the confidence in projected surpluses seemed ill advised. Nevertheless, Bush used classic Keynesian arguments—the need to combat the economic slowdown in 2001 by stimulating consumer demand—to sell his supply-side tax cut.[25] The administration seemed to be populated by economic opportunists, not ideologues.

The foundation was set for future political fireworks. When it was discovered in early summer 2001 that the projected surplus for fiscal year 2001 might have been too optimistic, Democratic leaders were preparing their answer to the question, "who blew the surplus? Bush spent it on a tax cut that was too large, was based on economic forecasts that were too cheerful, and will ultimately come at the expense of popular programs such as Medicare and Social Security."[26] But the budget arguments remained detailed and difficult for the public to follow. The original surplus projected for fiscal year 2001 was $275 billion, and that was reduced to $219 billion in July because of declining revenues. However, when one removed the surplus for Social Security and Medicare (the lockbox), only $92 billion remained, of which $74 billion would go for the tax cut in the first year, leaving a modest $18 billion surplus to cover additional spending in areas like defense. This working margin shrank even further in early September when revised projections from the Congressional Budget Office suggested that the administration would need $9 billion of Social Security funds in 2002 and close to $20 billion in 2003 to meet its spending goals. Democrats hoped to reopen the tax-cut issue and pin any blame for renewed deficits on Bush.[27] But these highly partisan budget debates were ended, or possibly delayed, by the terrorist attacks on the World Trade Center and the Pentagon on September 11 (*see chapter 10*). Surplus Social Security funds would be tapped to meet emergency needs that were likely to grow rapidly.

The Politics of Macroeconomic Policymaking

Presidents do not make macroeconomic policy in a vacuum solely according to economic theories. Their decisions in this crucial area are intensely political and are affected by consideration of other policy goals (including microeconomic policy), electoral politics, interest group politics, and bureaucratic politics among institutional participants in the policymaking process. In a very real sense the United States has a political economy, and the nation is an economic polity. The president is the focal point of the relationships involved in both of these entities.

Policy Politics

The achievement of macroeconomic policy goals is affected by, and has an effect on, other policy goals. National security policy objectives, for example, often have a profound impact on economic policy. In the 1980s the widely held consensus that U.S. military strength had declined compared with that of the Soviet Union resulted in substantial increases in defense spending beginning in fiscal year 1982. These increases, however, were a major obstacle to efforts to balance the budget. A decade later, the end of the cold war between the United States and the Soviet Union in late 1991 precipitated a budget struggle over the disposition of the "peace dividend" that congressional Democrats believed should result from the reduction of tensions. In the October 1990 budget agreement between President Bush and Congress, any reductions in either defense or discretionary domestic spending were to be devoted to reducing the deficit. And as a final example, in 1995 President Clinton battled over defense spending with the new Republican majority in Congress, the latter charging that the level of spending proposed in his 1996 budget sacrificed "necessary modernization and development" of weapons and equipment to fiscal considerations.[28] A similar battle between Congress and President George W. Bush threatened to break out in late 2001 over increased defense spending, but Congress was likely to support major increases in the face of a war on terrorism.

Over the same twenty-year period, budget-balancing efforts in domestic programs conflicted with commitments made to Social Security beneficiaries, welfare recipients, retired federal employees, and numerous other groups served by federal programs. In addition, the macroeconomic goals of economic growth, increased productivity, and full employment often appeared to be at odds with regulatory policies designed to improve environmental quality, enhance occupational safety and health, increase the safety of automobiles and other consumer products, and protect consumers against a variety of unfair business practices. Fiscal policy frequently served as the arena for resolving such trade-offs.

Electoral Politics

Macroeconomic policy has important implications for electoral politics. It has long been recognized that presidential administrations and congressional majorities manipulate fiscal policy to produce short-term improvements in economic conditions to enhance their party's election prospects. They may adjust the timing and location of benefits to achieve this end, making policies that amount to marginal adjustments rather than fundamental restructuring of the economic system.

Presidents do not automatically avoid hard political choices and cave in to election pressures from party and special constituencies.[29] Ronald Reagan remained firm throughout his presidency in his commitment to the 1981 income tax cut based on supply-side theory, even though it meant proposing and defending record peacetime budget deficits (of around $200 billion) that were anathema to his conservative supporters. George Bush adhered to his 1988 campaign pledge not to raise taxes until the budget agreement with Congress in October 1990. He reluctantly agreed to tax increases of $146 billion as part of a five-year, $496 billion deficit reduction package. (Opponents attacked him for breaking that pledge in the 1992 election campaign, and he expressed regret at having done so.) In response to congressional pressures from Republicans and conservative Democrats and to advice from his economic advisers, Bill Clinton abandoned his campaign promise of a tax cut for the middle class and settled for half of the major investments in human resources and infrastructure that were key elements in his proposed 1993 economic program. His final package included deficit reduction achieved through $240 billion in tax increases and $246 billion in spending cuts, both of which had significant political implications.[30]

Interest Group Politics

In making economic policy, presidents and Congress also are subjected to pressures from several important interest groups, including business, labor, agriculture, the financial community, state and local governments, and foreign governments. The effect of these interests on policy varies according to the issues and the current economic conditions in the United States and elsewhere.

Business and labor interests are the most organized and thoroughly entrenched. Businesses use umbrella organizations, such as the Chamber of Commerce of the United States and the National Association of Manufacturers, to exert influence, as well as industry-based trade associations like the Automobile Manufacturers Association and the American Gas Association. Individual companies, especially large corporations, also try to shape policy to their liking. Businesses usually concentrate their lobbying on microeconomic policies that specifically affect their operations but may also be concerned about inflation, tax burdens, and interest rates, areas of macroeconomic policy. Organized labor encompasses the giant AFL-CIO (American Federation of Labor and Congress of Industrial Organizations) and a host of independent unions. Its position on macroeconomic policy issues is usually in sharp contrast to that of business. Labor supports fiscal stimulation of the economy in periods of recession and opposes the use of monetary restraints to curb inflation. It is typically not unduly disturbed by budget deficits and is much more worried by unemployment than by inflation. Like business, labor takes great interest in microeconomic policy directly affecting its interests, including regulation of labor-management relations and regulations in behalf of occupational safety and health.

Agricultural interest groups, though shrinking in membership, remain quite diverse. The American Farm Bureau Federation and the National Grange support conservative policies, while the National Farmers Union and the National Farmers Organization take much more liberal stances. Regardless of their ideology, farm organizations tend to oppose monetary policies that result in high interest rates because the use of credit is an essential feature of farm management.

The financial community consists of two principal components, the securities exchanges, or Wall Street, and banks and other financial institutions. (Wall Street and financial institutions buy and sell "paper"—government and private financial obligations—and bonds, the longer-term securities.) Wall Street registers its reactions to monetary and fiscal policies in the prices of corporate stocks traded on the major stock exchanges. Movements of stock market indicators, such as the Dow Jones index of thirty leading industrial stocks, often reflect the degree of investor confidence in administration policies. Bond prices move upward or downward inversely with interest rates and thus reflect monetary policy shifts; interest paid on short-term government and commercial paper also fluctuates as monetary policy changes. Administrations seek to have their policies favorably received by Wall Street and by major banks and other leading financial institutions. A vote of "no confidence" by the financial community in the government's economic policies makes the administration vulnerable to criticism by political opponents and weakens its popular support. As in the broader business world, members of the financial community tend to support conservative fiscal policies and monetary restraint to control inflation. They fear large deficits, whether due to high spending levels or sizable tax cuts.

With the advent of the Great Society domestic programs in the mid-1960s, state and local governments became vitally interested in macroeconomic policy. The federal government is a source of funding for a wide range of state and local programs in areas such as education, welfare and social services, housing and urban development, transportation, and health care. In addition, states and their local subdivisions received unrestricted federal revenue-sharing funds from 1972 through 1987. Consequently, many state and local governments, both collectively—through national associations, such as the U.S. Conference of Mayors—and individually—through the efforts of members of Congress—have exerted pressure to maintain the flow of federal funds, even though this goal could be accomplished only at the expense of larger and potentially inflationary budget deficits.

Presidents Reagan and Bush sought a major reordering of federal fiscal responsibilities, hoping to reduce state and local dependence on federal funding. This effort failed to accomplish its most revolutionary goals, but it triggered a rethinking of federal aid and its implications for macroeconomic policy.[31] In the face of mounting budget deficits in 1993 and 1994, Republicans and conservative Democrats opposed Clinton's infrastructure spending, a central component of his economic program. These activities, his opponents argued, were more appropriate for state and local governments to fund. Conservatives also demanded that financial responsibility for major redistributive programs be shifted to the states. In 1995 the Republican majority in Congress proposed ending entitlement status for welfare (Aid to Families with Dependent Children) and Medicaid, changes to be accomplished by converting federally funded programs, which were accompanied by extensive federal rules and regulations, to programs giving block grants to states. States would be freed from most federal controls, but funding would be fixed and would not increase as demands for services expanded. The proposed changes would have saved about $200 billion. Initially Clinton opposed these changes by vetoing two Republican versions, but in 1996 he compromised with the Republicans. Much to the dismay of many Democrats, welfare, but not Medicaid, lost its entitlement status and became a block grant program.[32]

Presidents and their administrations are constrained to some degree by the effect of economic policy decisions on the economies of other countries. Foreign governments have an intense interest in U.S. macroeconomic policy. Friendly governments—the European Community, Japan, and Saudi Arabia—favor a dollar that is neither overvalued nor undervalued and a healthy U.S. economy with full employment and a low inflation rate. If the dollar is weak, the value of much of their international currency reserves declines, and their goods are less competitive in U.S. markets. If the dollar is too strong, their investment capital migrates to the United States, and the high competitiveness of their products in U.S. markets threatens to provoke trade restrictions. When unemployment in the United States rises, the major market for their goods contracts. When interest rates are higher in the United States than in Europe or Japan, investment capital moves to the United States. Consequently, foreign governments press

U.S. administrations to keep the exchange value of the dollar from fluctuating widely and to hold down interest rates.

Presidents do not respond to all interest group constituencies, and the constituencies whose support they do seek vary in importance to them. In no case, however, do presidents make macroeconomic policy decisions without regard to some interest groups, which are major features in the politics of economic policymaking.

The Economic Subpresidency

In discharging the role of economic manager, chief executives seek to meet popular and elite expectations that their actions will result in a prosperous economy. Presidents must develop and implement policies and build support for those policies in the public and in the Washington community. To accomplish these complex and demanding tasks, they need information, advice, and administrative assistance to focus energy on major issues, integrate the policies of their administrations, take account of all-important interests, and maintain the administration's cohesion. This advice and assistance is provided by a set of specialized organizations located in the presidency and in the executive branch, organizations that James Anderson and Jared Hazleton call "the economic subpresidency." All those who are engaged in making, defining, communicating, and implementing economic policy decisions, "whether they act personally or as part of an institution," are part of this policymaking system.[33] How presidents use the economic subpresidency varies across administrations and with economic conditions, but this system is central to policymaking and presidential management of the economy. Staff members serve in one of four major administrative units—the CEA, OMB, the Treasury Department, or the Fed—or on various intragovernmental committees and councils. Leading members of these units over the last five decades are listed in Tables 9-2 through 9-5.

The Council of Economic Advisers

The Council of Economic Advisers has three members who are appointed by the president and subject to Senate confirmation, plus a small staff of approximately thirty-five, divided evenly between professional economists and support personnel. Traditionally most CEA members and professional staffers have had extensive experience in business or government. The CEA's chair (see Table 9-2) is responsible for administering the council, hiring staff, representing the CEA on other government councils and committees, and reporting to the president. He or she establishes the council's orientation according to the president's overall objectives. The chair's relationship with the president largely determines the CEA's influence in shaping economic policy.

The CEA has no operational responsibility but serves entirely in a staff capacity. It gathers information, makes economic forecasts, analyzes economic issues, and prepares the annual *Economic Report of the President,* presented to Congress. It

Table 9-2   Chairs of the Council of Economic Advisers, 1953–2001

President	Chair	Years
Eisenhower	Arthur F. Burns	1953–1956
	Raymond T. Saulnier	1956–1961
Kennedy	Walter W. Heller	1961–1963
Johnson	Walter W. Heller	1963–1964
	Gardner H. Ackley	1964–1968
	Arthur M. Okun	1968–1969
Nixon	Paul W. McCracken	1969–1971
	Herbert Stein	1972–1974
Ford	Herbert Stein	1974
	Alan Greenspan	1974–1977
Carter	Charles L. Schultze	1977–1981
Reagan	Murray L. Weidenbaum	1981–1982
	Martin Feldstein	1982–1984
	Beryl Sprinkel	1986–1988
H. W. Bush	Michael J. Boskin	1989–1993
Clinton	Laura D. Tyson	1993–1994
	Joseph E. Stiglitz	1995–1997
	Janet L. Yellen	1997–1999
	Martin Baily	1999–2001
G. W. Bush	R. Glenn Hubbard	2001–

Sources: John H. Kessel, *Presidents, the Presidency, and the Political Environment* (Washington, D.C.: CQ Press, 2001), chap. 5; and "The Decision Makers," *National Journal*, June 23, 2001.

provides the president with expert economic advice, though on occasion CEA members act as public spokespersons for the president. The council usually has not brokered agreements among conflicting parties or coordinated policymaking within the administration, although its members tend to reflect the theories and policy views of the president. In general Democratic presidents have had Keynesian CEA members, and Republicans have selected classical conservative and monetarist economists. Reagan, for example, appointed a conservative economist to chair the CEA at the start of his presidency and added a monetarist and a supply-sider. All three were committed to free trade, reduced government spending, a balanced federal budget, and limited federal intervention in the economy.

The CEA's relationship with presidents is a function of how they perceive the need for economic expertise and whether they share basic interests and values with CEA members. Given a need and common ground, the council may play an important role in economic policymaking. Its expertise enhances presidential policies, and its analyses and forecasts acquire political significance through association with the presidency. However, the council can do only what the president asks and allows it to do.

The relationships of Presidents Carter and Reagan to the CEA illustrate the range of uses that can be made of the council and the extent of its influence on policy. Charles Schultze (1977–1981) chaired Carter's CEA and had served as director of the budget under President Johnson. Schultze played a major role in shaping the Carter administration's economic policies, and the CEA was at the center of the economic subpresidency. In contrast, the two CEA chairs in Reagan's first term, Murray Weidenbaum (1981–1982) and Martin Feldstein (1982–1984), were overshadowed by the budget director, David Stockman, and Secretary of the Treasury Donald Regan, neither of whom was an economist. The CEA was such a peripheral part of the economic subpresidency during Reagan's first term that when Feldstein returned to the faculty of Harvard in July 1984, the president delayed appointing a successor for almost a year. The council's professional staff shrank in size, and rumors circulated in Washington that Reagan wanted to abolish the unit. He finally named Beryl Sprinkel (1986–1988), a supply-side economist who had served for four years as undersecretary of the Treasury for monetary affairs, as chair in April 1986. Sprinkel rebuilt the council's staff and moved it back into the mainstream of the economic subpresidency.[34]

Under President Bush the CEA played a more significant role with respect to the deficit than it did under Reagan. Its chair, the monetarist economist Michael Boskin (1989–1993), enjoyed the president's confidence and often acted as a spokesperson for the administration. President Clinton appointed Laura D'Andrea Tyson (1993–1994) of Stanford University, who was an expert on trade policy and not a professional macroeconomist, to chair his CEA. But when Tyson became chair of another White House coordinating unit—the National Economic Council—in 1995, three others succeeded her as CEA chair: Joseph Stiglitz (1995–1997), Janet Yellen (1997–1999), and Martin Baily (1999–2001). The rapid turnover is one indicator that the CEA may not have played an important role in Clinton policymaking.

The council's forecasts help to set the boundaries of the president's legislative program and budget proposals. It is to the president's advantage for the council to approach its advisory task deductively, fitting program pieces together within the framework of his overall objectives. As Paul McCracken (1969–1971), the former CEA chair under President Nixon, observed, "An economic adviser does his most effective work when he is positioned to look at the general interest."[35] The council's contribution to policymaking is, then, primarily conceptual and not in the realm of implementation or coordination. This is the reality that confronts George W. Bush's CEA chair, R. Glenn Hubbard (2001–), most recently a professor of economics and business at Columbia University, who had served in the Treasury Department under President Bush's father.[36]

The Office of Management and Budget

Presidents receive economic advice of a different sort from the roughly five hundred employees in the Office of Management and Budget. Whereas the CEA's primary concern is controlling the business cycle and achieving sustained economic growth, OMB's major focus is allocating resources to federal administrative agencies and their programs through the annual preparation of the pres-

Table 9-3   Directors of the Budget Bureau/Office of
Management and Budget, 1953–2001

President	Director	Years
Eisenhower	Joseph M. Dodge	1953–1954
	Rowland R. Hughes	1954–1956
	Percival F. Brundage	1956–1958
	Maurice Stans	1958–1961
Kennedy	David E. Bell	1961–1962
	Kermit Gordon	1962–1963
Johnson	Kermit Gordon	1963–1965
	Charles E. Schultze	1965–1968
	Charles J. Zwick	1968–1969
Nixon	Robert P. Mayo	1969–1970
	George P. Shultz	1971–1972
	Casper Weinberger	1972–1973
	Roy L. Ash	1973–1974
Ford	Roy L. Ash	1974–1975
	James P. Lynn	1975–1976
Carter	Bert Lance	1977
	James T. McIntyre	1978–1981
Reagan	David Stockman	1981–1986
	James C. Miller III	1986–1988
H. W. Bush	Richard G. Darman	1989–1993
Clinton	Leon E. Panetta	1993–1994
	Alice Rivlin	1994–1996
	Franklin D. Raines	1996–1998
	Jacob J. Lew	1998–2001
G. W. Bush	Mitchell E. Daniels Jr.	2001–

Sources: John H. Kessel, *Presidents, the Presidency, and the Political Environment* (Washington, D.C.: CQ Press, 2001), chap. 5; and "The Decision Makers," *National Journal*, June 23, 2001.

ident's budget. Its institutional bias is toward holding down spending. It is the principal instrument through which the president fashions the expenditure component of fiscal policy. In addition, OMB provides economic forecasts to the president and acts as a "legislative and regulatory gatekeeper" by conducting detailed policy analysis of proposed bills and agency rules.[37]

The Office of Management and Budget was originally a presidential staff agency (known as the Bureau of the Budget) comprising an elite group of government careerists devoted to serving the presidency, whoever the particular president might be. Since President Nixon reorganized it in 1970, OMB has been more actively involved than before in serving the political needs of the president. Beginning in the Nixon administration, OMB directors (see Table 9-3) have participated in developing presidential policies and in building support for them. The budget has become as much a political weapon as a managerial tool or an instrument of fiscal policy.

The politicization of OMB and the political use of the budget were never more apparent than during the Reagan administration and David Stockman's tenure as budget director (1981–1986). Stockman dominated federal budgeting in a manner unknown before him. He centralized the executive budget process in OMB and involved himself extensively in the congressional budget proceedings through direct negotiations and bargaining with congressional committees.

Under Stockman's successor, the economist James C. Miller III (1986–1988), OMB continued to serve Reagan's political interests, but much less visibly. During the Bush presidency OMB was a major player in the economic subpresidency. Its director, Richard Darman (1989–1993), and the White House chief of staff, John Sununu, were the principal negotiators with Congress concerning fiscal policy. (Darman dealt primarily with spending and Sununu with taxes.) OMB also became the dominant agency for economic forecasting.

The budget remained the main instrument for achieving the president's policy goals during the Clinton administration. Clinton named Leon Panetta (1993–1994), chair of the House Budget Committee, as his first OMB director. Panetta was a "deficit hawk" (a strong advocate for deficit reduction) and a Democratic loyalist who possessed parliamentary acumen and budgetary expertise.[38] He played an important role in shaping Clinton's 1993 economic plan and selling it to Congress. When Panetta became Clinton's chief of staff in June 1994, the economist Alice Rivlin (1994–1996) became OMB's director. Rivlin had served previously as director of the Congressional Budget Office and was even more hawkish on the deficit than Panetta. Their presence "ensured that deficit reduction would command considerable attention" as the administration shaped economic policy.[39] Rivlin was succeeded by Franklin D. Raines (1996–1998) and Jacob Lew (1998–2001). George W. Bush chose as OMB director Mitchell E. Daniels Jr. (2001–), a lawyer with political experience on Capitol Hill and in the Reagan White House but not in budget-related positions.[40]

The Treasury Department

The third institutional participant in the economic subpresidency is the Treasury Department, which is responsible for collecting taxes, managing the national debt, controlling the currency, collecting customs, and handling international monetary affairs, including management of the balance of payments and the value of the dollar in relation to other currencies. With more than 140,000 employees, it is the primary government source of information on revenues, the tax system, and financial markets. It also takes the lead in developing tax bills and steering them through Congress.[41]

The primary concerns of the Treasury Department traditionally have been the adequacy of revenues, the soundness of the dollar, and the cost of financing the debt. To finance the debt, the department has advocated either low interest rates or a balanced budget. Since 1951, however, it has opposed easy credit and usually has acted as a restraint on expansionary fiscal policies. Before the Reagan administration, a situation in which high interest rates accompanied a large deficit was anathema to the institutional interests of the Treasury. Its position altered substantially under President Reagan and Donald Regan (1981–1985),

342   THE PRESIDENT AND PUBLIC POLICY

Table 9-4   Secretaries of the Treasury, 1953–2001

President	Secretary	Years
Eisenhower	George M. Humphrey	1953–1957
	Robert Anderson	1957–1961
Kennedy	C. Douglas Dillon	1961–1963
Johnson	C. Douglas Dillon	1964–1965
	Henry H. Fowler	1965–1968
	Joseph W. Barr	1968–1969
Nixon	David M. Kennedy	1969–1971
	John B. Connally	1971–1972
	George P. Shultz	1972–1974
	William E. Simon	1974
Ford	William E. Simon	1974–1977
Carter	W. Michael Blumenthal	1977–1979
	G. William Miller	1979–1981
Reagan	Donald T. Regan	1981–1985
	James A. Baker III	1985–1988
	Nicholas F. Brady	1988–1989
H. W. Bush	Nicholas F. Brady	1989–1993
Clinton	Lloyd M. Bentsen	1993–1994
	Robert E. Rubin	1995–1999
	Lawrence H. Summers	1999–2001
G. W. Bush	Paul H. O'Neill	2001–

Sources: John H. Kessel, *Presidents, the Presidency, and the Political Environment* (Washington, D.C.: CQ Press, 2001), chap. 5; and "The Decision Makers," *National Journal*, June 23, 2001.

secretary of the Treasury during Reagan's first term (see Table 9-4). An avowed believer in supply-side economics, Regan argued that temporary deficits resulting from tax-cut incentives would lead ultimately to economic growth, expanded revenues, and balanced budgets. He opposed efforts to reduce the deficit by raising taxes. He was much more concerned with the supply of money in the domestic economy than with the exchange value of the dollar. Regan's successor as secretary of the Treasury, James A. Baker III (1985–1988), concentrated heavily on exchange rate problems.

Secretary of the Treasury Nicholas Brady played a marginal role in the economic subpresidency under President George Bush. As noted, Darman and Sununu dominated administration negotiations on fiscal policy. One veteran White House observer and analyst suggests that the "patrician" Brady was no match for the "pit bull approach of his two economic policy colleagues."[42]

President Clinton's first two secretaries of the Treasury, Lloyd Bentsen (1993–1994) and Robert Rubin (1995–1999), were central participants in the economic subpresidency. By appointing Bentsen, a moderate Democrat with business experience who chaired the Senate Finance Committee, Clinton sought to reassure the business community.[43] The appointment of Rubin, a Wall Street investment banker who first served in the Clinton administration as chair of the National Economic Council (see discussion later in the chapter), accomplished a similar purpose. Both men were deeply involved in shaping the 1993 economic

Table 9-5   Chairs of the Federal Reserve Board,
1951–2001

President	Chair	Years
Eisenhower	William McC. Martin	1951–1961
Kennedy	William McC. Martin	1961–1963
Johnson	William McC. Martin	1963–1969
Nixon	William McC. Martin	1969–1970
Nixon	Arthur F. Burns	1970–1974
Ford	Arthur F. Burns	1974–1977
Carter	Arthur F. Burns	1977–1978
Carter	G. William Miller	1978–1979
	Paul A. Volcker	1979–1981
Reagan	Paul A. Volcker	1981–1987
Reagan	Alan Greenspan	1987–1989
H. W. Bush	Alan Greenspan	1989–1993
Clinton	Alan Greenspan	1993–2001
G. W. Bush	Alan Greenspan	2001–

Sources: John H. Kessel, *Presidents, the Presidency, and the Political Environment* (Washington, D.C.: CQ Press, 2001), chap. 5; and "The Decision Makers," *National Journal*, June 23, 2001.

program.[44] Lawrence Summers, a Rubin protégé as deputy secretary, served as secretary from 1999 to 2001. George W. Bush selected Paul H. O'Neill (2001–) as Treasury secretary, a ten-year veteran of OMB who later worked for International Paper before becoming CEO of Alcoa Aluminum.[45]

Organizationally the Treasury Department is divided between large units with major line responsibilities, such as the Internal Revenue Service, and policy-related units, such as the office of the undersecretary for monetary affairs. The policy-related units, located in the office of the secretary, never have provided coordination of economic policy for an administration, although the potential exists for them to do so.[46]

The Federal Reserve Board

The Federal Reserve Board is an independent agency charged with responsibility for regulating the money supply and the banking system. Its seven members are appointed by the president to fourteen-year terms with the consent of the Senate. The president designates one member of the board to act as its chair for a four-year term, but the chair, an important source of institutional influence, often serves beyond that limit, as shown in Table 9-5. The Fed has three ways of controlling the money supply: the rediscount rate, reserve requirements, and open-market operations.

The rediscount rate is the interest rate charged commercial banks to borrow from the Federal Reserve. An increase in the rediscount rate tightens the availability of credit because it forces banks to charge more to their borrowers. Reserves are liquid assets that banks hold to meet demands for ready cash from their depositors. The Federal Reserve requires commercial banks belonging to it to maintain a certain percentage (usually ranging from 10 percent to 20 percent)

Alan Greenspan, originally appointed Chairman of the Federal Reserve Board by Ronald Reagan in 1987, provides great continuity to the "economic subpresidency" and wields enormous influence over the direction of the United States economy.

of their deposit liabilities in the form of cash in their vaults or on account with the regional reserve bank for this purpose. A reduction in the reserve requirement increases the amount of money banks may loan to their borrowers, whereas an increase in the reserve requirement decreases the availability of bank credit.

Although neither the president nor Congress can tell the Fed how to conduct monetary policy, the board traditionally has been responsive to political pressures. One critic charges that the Fed has shown far greater responsiveness to political timing than to cyclical fluctuations in the economy. He maintains that the formal independence of the Fed is a myth and that its policies are designed primarily to maintain its internal cohesion and reduce its external vulnerability.[47]

Although independent, the Fed is a ready target for politicians in adverse economic conditions. Depending on circumstances, the inflation resulting from expansionary monetary policy or the stagnation and unemployment caused by restrictive policy can draw fire. During the Clinton administration, members of Congress and Wall Street frequently criticized the Fed for raising interest rates at the first sign of inflation and reducing them too slowly, but relations between the president and the Fed chair, Alan Greenspan, were generally cordial. Clinton twice reappointed Greenspan (1996 and 2000) to the post he first assumed in 1987 under Ronald Reagan. The strongest clash between the Clinton administration and the Fed occurred in 1994 when Greenspan, with help from the banking industry, torpedoed a Treasury Department proposal to create a Federal Banking Commission that would have consolidated bank regulation in a single agency.[48] The proposal would have combined the responsibilities shared by the Fed, the Treasury Department's Office of the Comptroller of the Currency and its Office of Thrift Supervision, and the independent Federal Deposit Insurance Corporation.

Presidents and Economic Policy Coordination

The independence of the Fed, the operational needs and organizational interests of the Treasury Department, and the institutional perspectives of other departments and agencies have led presidents to seek various ways of coordinating economic policy. For reasons explained in chapter 6, the cabinet has not been a satisfactory vehicle for collective leadership. Instead, presidents have developed a variety of intragovernmental councils and committees designed to provide a cohesive macroeconomic policy and to integrate it with other policy objectives. Most of these entities failed to survive the administrations of their creators, for subsequent presidents sought mechanisms more compatible with their own operating styles. However, a brief review of these undertakings reveals common patterns in their approaches and indicates the essential requirements for a minimal amount of coordination.

Probably the most significant development for macroeconomic policymaking occurred under President Kennedy with the creation of the "troika," an informal committee consisting of the chair of the CEA, the secretary of the Treasury, and the director of the budget. The troika's original purpose was to coordinate economic forecasting, but it quickly became a mechanism for developing cooperation within the economic subpresidency in formulating fiscal policy. This arrangement stood in contrast to President Eisenhower's sharply focused groups, which, although they met often, were too numerous to bring about effective coordination. When joined by the chair of the Fed to coordinate monetary policy, the group has been known as the "quadriad." These participants have a "mutual interest in cooperation, not in their legal independence from each other. For an administration's economic policy to succeed, the Fed should pursue a parallel monetary policy" and vice versa.[49]

Working with staff support from the CEA, the Treasury Department, OMB, and occasionally the Fed, the troika/quadriad has helped many presidents formulate macroeconomic policy in a rapid, adaptive manner with some measure of protection from political and bureaucratic pressures. Not all presidents have made extensive use of the troika, but it is a natural institutional grouping that continues to operate, with the Treasury Department assuming responsibility for revenue estimates, OMB generating estimates of federal expenditures, the CEA forecasting economic trends, and the Fed (when involved) projecting money supply requirements.

Under Lyndon Johnson, the troika operation became regularized, and it emerged as the principal mechanism for the development of fiscal policy advice and alternatives.[50] President Nixon was uncomfortable with attempts to make policy by cabinet-level committees and designated Secretary of the Treasury John Connally (1971–1972) in early 1971 as his economic "czar," with responsibility for making major decisions. Connally dominated the troika, but his successor as Treasury secretary, George Shultz (1972–1974), operated in a more collegial manner. At the start of his second term, in January 1973, Nixon made Shultz assistant to the president for economic affairs and named him to chair a new cabinet-level coordinating body, the Council on Economic Policy. Shultz, working through interdepartmental committees, became the dominant figure in making and expounding economic policy for the Nixon administration.

Shultz's more inclusive machinery ushered in a series of presidential experiments with coordinating councils, a series of "troika plus" groups. Gerald Ford used the Economic Policy Board (EPB), which operated in a formal and structured way to coordinate domestic and foreign economic policies. The secretary of the Treasury chaired the EPB, which also included the secretaries of labor, commerce, and state, the chair of the CEA, the director of OMB, and the assistant to the president for economic affairs. The latter official also directed the small EPB staff, housed in the Executive Office of the President. Departments and agencies provided information, analysis, and expertise. Roger Porter, who served as executive secretary to the EPB throughout its existence, has described it as providing systematic advice to the president by exposing him to competing arguments "in a group discussion that permitted exchange and argument among the advocates before the president."[51]

President Carter replaced the EPB with the Economic Policy Group (EPG), cochaired by the secretary of the Treasury and the chair of the CEA. The EPG was a large, unwieldy body. It had no staff, was accessible to a wide range of interested officials, and was not organized as a formal advisory body to the president. Attempts to focus its work led to the creation of a steering committee, chaired by the secretary of the Treasury and including the usual suspects—the chair of the CEA, the director of OMB, and the presidential assistants for domestic affairs and for national security affairs. However, its operations remained so unstructured that it was unable to coordinate even minor policy initiatives.[52]

President Reagan replaced the Economic Policy Group with the Cabinet Council on Economic Affairs (CCEA). Like its predecessor in the Nixon administration, the CCEA was a forum for discussion of issues and alternatives. Porter, veteran of the Ford system, was its secretary and informally coordinated its operations. The council served to establish consensus within the administration. In addition to the council, the troika met regularly to coordinate economic forecasting. But coordination efforts did not ensure that struggles for influence would disappear. The major participants in these battles were Treasury Secretary Donald Regan, OMB Director David Stockman, and White House assistants James Baker and Edwin Meese. The administration had clearly defined macroeconomic policy goals: to reduce the role of the federal government in the U.S. economy, thus reducing taxes and spending, and to increase productivity, savings, and investment, thus ensuring vigorous and sustained economic growth and full employment. There was, however, sharp disagreement over the means to that end. That conflict reflected competition among classical conservative, monetarist, and supply-side theories and focused on the significance of federal budget deficits. The winners in the conflict were Regan and Meese—the supply-side advocates. Stockman was the principal loser.[53]

President Bush continued the advisory group, renaming it the Economic Policy Council. Porter once again managed its activities, with the help of his staff in the Office of Policy Development, and served as assistant to the president for economic and domestic affairs.[54] However, the council met irregularly and did not establish an effective roundtable process for preparing issues for presidential decision. Nor did the troika, which fell into disuse during Reagan's second term, reacquire its former importance. The struggle for influence centered on the OMB director, Richard Darman, and the chief of staff, John Sununu, but no single individual or group had responsibility for defining for the economic subpresidency how policies were to be integrated.

Given the high priority that President Clinton placed on economic issues during the 1992 campaign, it is not surprising that he was deeply involved in making economic policy. One of his first acts was to establish a National Economic Council (NEC) to coordinate domestic and international economic policies in a way similar to the National Security Council's coordination of foreign and military policymaking.[55] Operating with a professional staff of twenty, the NEC's first chair, Robert Rubin, established an open, collegial, and nonhierarchical process that incorporated a wide and balanced range of economic considerations into the issue recommendations sent to the president.[56] The NEC's effectiveness became apparent during the 1993 budget battles; cabinet members worked through the budget and refrained from infighting and leaks that had plagued previous administrations.[57] All was not well, however, because Clinton's economic advisers frequently clashed with his political advisers, who had managed his campaign. These conflicts concerned the primary focus of the administration's economic program and were fought both within the presidency and publicly.[58] The economic advisers stressed the importance of deficit reduction and the impact of policy on financial markets. The political advisers wanted to emphasize the populist issues that had helped to elect Clinton.[59] Rubin emerged as the dominant economic adviser and continued in that role after becoming secretary of the Treasury. His successor at the NEC, Laura Tyson, was unable to parlay coordination into influence, but Gene Sperling, the next director, was more successful in doing so.[60]

President George W. Bush's director of the NEC, Lawrence Lindsey, brought an especially rich foundation of personal experience to the position. A former member of the Board of Governors of the Federal Reserve System, Lindsey served on the CEA's staff under Reagan and was a special White House assistant in the administration of George H. W. Bush. As George W. Bush's economic adviser during the 2000 presidential election, Lindsey also was expected to enjoy the president's confidence.[61]

As in other areas of policy, the nation is heavily dependent on presidents' attitudes, values, and operating styles for economic leadership. Congressionally established advisory mechanisms, such as the CEA, are helpful, and presidents can take other measures to assist them in identifying issues and achieving policy coordination; but advisory staffs and coordinating mechanisms provide no guarantee that the president will adopt effective policies or achieve his objectives. There is, moreover, an important check on presidential economic policymaking—Congress's power over taxing, spending, and the monetary system.

The Congressional Role in Macroeconomic Policy

Most of the executive branch agencies and processes that involve macroeconomic policy and the president's economic role were established by statute: the Federal Reserve Act of 1914, the Budget and Accounting Act of 1921, and the Employment Act of 1946. Traditionally Congress has dealt with economic policy through separate consideration of tax legislation and annual appropriations. Tax bills have entailed redistributive issues—that is, questions of who bears the burdens and which special interests will secure favorable provisions, or "loopholes." The congressional tax-writing committees (House Ways and Means and Senate Finance) have jealously guarded their powers and been unwilling to propose new tax legislation that did not accommodate special interests. The 1986 tax reform act departed substantially from traditional revenue legislation that contains numerous advantages and benefits for a wide range of interests. The two tax-writing committees responded positively to President Reagan's call for simplification and reform of the federal tax code, though many observers have argued that additional simplification is needed.[62] Appropriations decision making, centered in the House and Senate Appropriations Committees, traditionally focuses on incremental changes in budget requests of departments and agencies. The politics of the budget process is a highly stylized game in which the institutional participants play specific roles. The primary consideration in Congress is the amount of increase or decrease in each agency's base, which is the previous year's appropriation. The total level of expenditures is the sum of the thirteen major appropriations bills passed annually.[63]

Congress does not attempt consciously to shape fiscal policy through its taxing or spending legislation. Rather, its money decisions are the product of its fragmented authority structure, as reflected in the multiplicity of powerful committees and subcommittees, the weakness of its party organizations, and the strong constituency orientation of its members because of their constant concern with reelection.

Although the Budget and Accounting Act of 1921 required the president to prepare an annual budget and a comprehensive plan for spending, and although the Employment Act of 1946 required an annual economic report that projected revenues and expenditures in light of economic forecasts, Congress imposed no such requirements on itself. Fiscal policy was whatever remained of the president's program after it emerged from "a piecemeal and haphazard legislative process."[64] The inability of Congress to participate rationally on an equal basis with the presidency in shaping fiscal policy led to conflict during the Nixon administration when federal spending became a politically significant issue. Spending grew rapidly in response to previously enacted statutory "entitlements" that could not be disregarded without revising the original authorizing legislation. Entitlements include Social Security benefits; federal retirement, farm price support, and welfare payments; and food stamps. Most entitlement payments to individuals increase automatically with the cost of living.[65] The problem was compounded by "off-budget" spending through loan guarantees and tax credits. This was the beginning of runaway budget deficits, which burgeoned from 1971 to 1997 as spending on entitlements and other mandatory programs grew four times faster than did spending in discretionary areas.[66]

Nixon challenged Congress to curb spending; when it did not do so, he frequently vetoed spending bills and made extensive use of impoundment. The primary response of Congress to this controversy with Nixon and to frustration over its inability to shape policy was the Budget and Impoundment Control Act of 1974, which created a procedure for handling impoundments. More important, that statute established a congressional budget process, created House and Senate Budget Committees, and provided Congress with independent staff support for macroeconomic forecasting and budget analysis in the form of the Congressional Budget Office.

Central to the congressional budget process in its present form are the budget resolution and the reconciliation legislation.[67] The budget resolution must be approved by both House and Senate but does not require the president's signature. As such it does not have the force of law, but it serves as the vehicle for changes in budget policy, allocates available money to congressional appropriations committees, and may activate reconciliation legislation. The extent to which the budget resolution changes budget policy, as opposed to reflecting existing policies, determines its importance. Usually the budget resolution is merely the means by which Congress organizes its action, but on three occasions it has set in motion major changes in fiscal policy. Presidents Reagan (in 1981) and Clinton (in 1993), each with sharply different objectives, used the congressional budget process to change taxing and spending policy. In 1995 Republican congressional leaders used the budget process to impose far-reaching policy changes that Clinton strongly opposed.

Each budget resolution contains totals for revenues, expenditures, the deficit or surplus, and the national debt for the next fiscal year. Congress must adhere to these totals as it makes taxing and spending decisions. The budget resolution also contains target totals for the next four fiscal years and allocations of new budget authority for the next year to the major areas of federal spending—for example, defense, agriculture, and interest on the national debt.[68] It may also include reconciliation instructions.

Reconciliation is the process that Congress uses "to bring revenue and spending under existing law into conformity with the levels set in the budget resolution."[69] It proceeds in two stages. First, Congress incorporates in the budget resolution binding instructions to specific committees—those that have jurisdiction over revenues and mandatory spending programs—to recommend statutory changes that will achieve the spending and revenue levels set in the resolution. Next, the House and Senate enact the committees' recommendations in a reconciliation bill. Reconciliation is an optional process that has tended to be used when either the president's budget or Congress seeks a multiyear deficit reduction agreement. Reconciliation legislation has become the major means of reducing the deficit. The 1995 reconciliation bill stalled in January 1996 after a protracted battle between President Clinton and Congress over how to achieve a balanced budget by 2002. Although not far apart on the amount of savings needed, they disagreed fundamentally over spending priorities and the congressional insistence on removing entitlement status from Medicaid and welfare.

The creation of the congressional budget process did not substantially change "the established process in Congress for raising and spending money."[70] Nor did it make Congress more fiscally responsible. What the congressional budget process did produce was a change in executive-legislative budget relationships.[71]

The increased centralization of budgetary decision making in Congress enhanced the legislative branch's ability to influence presidential budget policies while providing the president with greater leverage over congressional budget decisions. Congress and the president became, as Allen Schick put it, "more interdependent: each [was] more vulnerable than before to having its budget preferences blocked or modified by the other."[72]

From 1981 onward, Congress was locked in protracted conflict with Presidents Reagan, Bush, and Clinton over fiscal policy and the deficit. The same could hold true for George W. Bush. Reagan and Bush attempted to control the deficit through spending cuts and resisted tax increases, while Congress fought to protect pork barrel projects that benefited its constituencies and entitlements and other programs that enjoyed wide popular or strong interest group support. Clinton won congressional support for his five-year deficit reduction package in 1993 but then waged intense budget battles with a Republican-controlled Congress during his final six years in office. Although George W. Bush won congressional support during his first months in office, the stage was set for protracted battles over implementation of his tax cuts and spending priorities. It was not clear how budget issues would play with the public. Cutting the budget deficit proved not to be a winning election issue in recent years, as Bush found out in 1992, Clinton in 1994, and Gore in 2000. Perhaps cutting taxes would prove to be more successful for George W. Bush in 2002 and 2004.

Conclusion

Can the president bring order and cohesion to macroeconomic policy? Can the presidency serve as the instrument for effective management of the economy? Such questions have become increasingly important since 1970 as the U.S. economy has matured, interdependence with other economies has increased, and the ability to raise productivity, sustain economic growth, and keep inflation and unemployment at acceptably low levels has faltered from time to time. Clearly the challenge that macroeconomic policy poses to presidents is of continuing importance. Presidents face formidable obstacles and problems as they respond to that challenge.

Three major obstacles confront presidents in the performance of their economic policymaking role: expectations are inordinately and unrealistically high, they have limited authority to meet those expectations, and the base of knowledge on which they act is often limited and unreliable. The problem of unrealistic expectations is not peculiar to macroeconomic policy. Modern presidents have tended to make sweeping promises to be elected, and the American people have developed a deep faith that a strong, capable president can provide solutions to their most pressing problems.

As presidents try to develop policies that will meet popular expectations, they encounter problems. Bush discovered as the recession of 1991 dragged into 1992 that the public is impatient for tangible results and that the pressure for actions that can provide a "quick fix" is great. Approaching elections heighten the search for measures that will produce immediate results. Also, fulfillment of one set of expectations, such as curbing inflation, may lead to unwelcome consequences, such as increased unemployment and high interest rates that dampen other expectations. Pressure for action is usually strong, and the popular bias against inaction runs deep; yet inaction may be the most prudent course to follow. In short, exaggerated popular expectations that the president will manage the economy effectively may limit his capacity to do so. Even an ostensibly healthy economy may not eliminate or ease the apprehensions of the public, as Clinton discovered in 1994 when many voters, "driven by perceptions of job insecurity and sluggish wage growth," were concerned about the future of the economy and their family finances in the midterm elections.[73]

In striving to meet the unrealistic expectations of a public eager to place its trust in executive leadership, presidents discover that their authority to act is limited. In the area of macroeconomic policy three factors restrict presidential ability to act: congressional prerogatives, the independence of the Federal Reserve Board, and the absence of coordinating power within the executive branch. Presidents must collaborate with Congress in making fiscal policy. Their success depends on congressional responsiveness to their leadership, to their effectiveness as communicators and persuaders. They do not have independent authority to increase or reduce taxes or spending.

Monetary policy is equally confining because of the independence of the Fed. The only resources the president has available to influence the Fed are persuasion and the periodic opportunity to appoint new members to the board and to designate its chair. Although presidents have regularly exerted pressure on the Fed, and it has taken political factors into consideration, there is no assurance that monetary policy will be compatible with fiscal policy or that it will not impede the achievement of other policy objectives. As John Kessel concludes, "presidents are in the position of having only partial control (shared power in fiscal policy, only power to persuade in monetary policy) over blunt instruments that only sometimes lead to the desired economic results."[74]

Economics provides a shaky foundation for recommending policies that directly affect the operation of the entire economy. Economic forecasting is an inexact science and is subject to considerable margins of error. The validity of the projections of the Council of Economic Advisers, the Office of Management and Budget, the Treasury Department, and the Federal Reserve Board depends on the assumptions that underlie them and on the quality and quantity of information available. The assumptions vary with the institutional orientation of the agency making the forecast, the theories of the economists on the agency's staff, and political pressures on the agency. The Fed's assumptions, for example, reflect the influence of monetarism; OMB's, a traditional concern with budget balancing. As Stockman's account of his tenure as OMB director indicates, there is pressure on forecasters to resolve budget problems by adopting best-case or "rosy" scenarios of economic performance.[75] If the assumptions underlying a forecast prove wrong, then policies based on the forecast may lead to unanticipated outcomes. For example, the record deficits incurred during his administration initially caught President Reagan by surprise because he enthusiastically accepted OMB's rosy scenario.

The nation has moved from a conservative consensus on economic policy in the 1920s and early 1930s to a Keynesian consensus in the 1950s and 1960s to a lack of consensus in the 1980s, 1990s, and beyond. Policies have shifted from Nixon's imposition of wage and price controls to Reagan's embrace of supply-side theory, Bush's pragmatism, and Clinton's emphasis on long-term growth and investment in human capital. Despite all these changes, presidents still lack the capacity to control the economy even though rapidly changing economic conditions, in the United States and elsewhere, would seem to require a maximum amount of adaptiveness. The president's ability to respond to new situations, such as a sudden, large increase in the price of oil, is limited. Institutional arrangements, both statutory and constitutional, restrict the president's actions and dictate that he rely primarily on persuasion to accomplish his objectives. Moreover, experience with different processes for economic policymaking and coordination suggests that the internal structure of the presidency has little effect on policy outcomes in this area. Beyond economic conditions, over which the president has little control, the factors that appear to affect economic policymaking and outcomes most substantially are the president's ideology and leadership.

NOTES

1. John P. Frendreis and Raymond Tatalovich, *The Modern Presidency and Economic Policy* (Itasca, Ill.: Peacock Publishers, 1994), 300.

2. Raymond Tatalovich and John Frendreis, "Clinton, Class, and Economic Policy," in *The Postmodern Presidency: Bill Clinton's Legacy in U.S. Politics,* ed. Steven E. Schier (Pittsburgh: University of Pittsburgh Press, 2000), 41–42. Also see the review of Clinton's accomplishments by Paul J. Quirk and William Cunion, "Clinton's

Domestic Policy: The Lessons of a 'New Democrat,' "in *The Clinton Legacy,* ed. Colin Campbell and Bert A. Rockman (Chatham, N.J.: Chatham House, 2001), 214–216.

3. Edward R. Tufte, *Political Control of the Economy* (Princeton: Princeton University Press, 1978).

4. A. James Reichley, "A Change in Direction," in *Setting National Priorities: The 1982 Budget,* ed. Joseph A. Pechman (Washington, D.C.: Brookings, 1981), 236–240.

5. John H. Kessel, *Presidents, the Presidency, and the Political Environment* (Washington, D.C.: CQ Press, 2001), 150–151.

6. Alan Stone, *Regulation and Its Alternatives* (Washington, D.C.: CQ Press, 1982), 262.

7. Lester M. Salamon and Alan J. Abramson, "Governance: The Politics of Retrenchment," in *The Reagan Record,* eds. John L. Palmer and Isabel V. Sawhill (Washington, D.C.: Urban Institute Press, 1984), 47.

8. Marshall R. Goodman, "A Kinder and Gentler Regulatory Reform: The Bush Regulatory Strategy and Its Impact" (paper presented at the annual meeting of the Midwest Political Science Association, Chicago, April 1991).

9. David S. Cloud, "Industry, Politics Intertwined in Dole's Regulatory Bill," *Congressional Quarterly Weekly Report,* May 6, 1995, 1219–1224; and Bob Benenson, "GOP Sets the 104th Congress on New Regulatory Course," *Congressional Quarterly Weekly Report,* June 17, 1995, 1693–1697.

10. David S. Cloud, "Dole's Bill: An 'Aggressive' Position," *Congressional Quarterly Weekly Report,* May 6, 1995, 1221.

11. James A. Barnes, "Is Bush Poisoning His Well?" *National Journal,* April 14, 2001, 1120–1121; and Eric Pianin, "Administration Revisits Forest Lands Rules; Paper Industry, Western Governors Want Protective Regulation Scaled Back," *Washington Post,* July 7, 2001, A2.

12. Eric Pianin and Mike Allen, "Clinton Forest Rules to Stand," *Washington Post,* May 4, 2001, A1; Cindy Skrzycki, "OMB to Revisit Costs, Benefits of Rules," *Washington Post,* May 29, 2001, E1; Amy Goldstein, "'Last-Minute' Spin on Regulatory Rite: Bush Review of Clinton Initiatives Is Bid to Reshape Rules," *Washington Post,* June 9, 2001, A1; Marilyn Geewax, "Bush Proving to be No Radical When It Comes To Regulation," Cox News Service, June 13, 2001; and Juliet Eilperin, "GOP Won't Try to Halt Last Rules By Clinton: Hill Power Shift Forces Retreat on Spring Plans," *Washington Post,* July 30, 2001, A1.

13. Walter W. Heller, *New Dimensions in Political Economy* (New York: Norton, 1966).

14. Jackie Calmes, "The Voracious National Debt," *Congressional Quarterly Weekly Report,* March 24, 1990, 896.

15. George Hager, "Deficit Shows No Gain from Pain of Spending Rules," *Congressional Quarterly Weekly Report,* July 20, 1991, 1963. Bush also encountered shortfalls in revenues arising from "technical reestimates" and higher projected spending for Medicaid.

16. Frendreis and Tatalovich, *The Modern Presidency,* 314.

17. Richard W. Stevenson, "The Wisdom to Let the Good Times Roll," *New York Times,* December 25, 2000, A1.

18. "Administration Economic Assumptions," *Congressional Quarterly Weekly Report,* February 11, 1995, 430; and John R. Cranford, "White House Sees Solid Growth Leading to 'Soft Landing,'" *Congressional Quarterly Weekly Report,* February 11, 1995, 412.

19. Clinton's term averages can be found in Tatalovich and Frendreis, "Clinton, Class, and Economic Policy," Table 1, 44. Unemployment data can be found in Harold W. Stanley and Richard G. Niemi, *Vital Statistics on American Politics 1999–2000* (Washington, D.C.: CQ Press, 2000), Table 11-10.

20. George Hager, "Time Is Ripe for Agreement but Gridlock Dies Hard," *Congressional Quarterly Weekly Report,* November 16, 1996, 3280–3281.

21. Daniel J. Palazzolo, *Done Deal? The Politics of the 1997 Budget Agreement* (Chatham, N.J.: Chatham House, 1999). Palazzolo contends that the process of moving toward a balanced budget was fifteen years in the making, stretching back to 1982.

22. Stevenson, "The Wisdom to Let the Good Times Roll," A12.

23. Glenn Kessler, "Bush Tax Cut Pares Government's Role," *Washington Post*, May 21, 2001, A1.

24. Ibid.

25. Beginning in December 2000, President-elect Bush and Vice-President-elect Cheney expressed concerns about an economic slowdown, a potential recession. Such warnings may have been an effort to inoculate the new administration against criticism for poor stewardship of the economy or to sell the president's tax-cut proposals as a way to stimulate a sagging economy. This campaign of "talking down" the economy in itself became controversial. See John Maggs, "The Power of Negative Thinking," *National Journal*, April 14, 2001, 1086–1091. For supply-side criticisms of the Bush plan, see John Maggs, "Tax Cuts Now, and Later," *National Journal*, April 14, 2001, 1094. For a review of the many ills that Bush claimed the tax cut would cure, see Dana Milbank, "The Cut That Heals All Ills; President Bush's Miracle Tax Tonic," *Washington Post*, May 16, 2001, C1.

26. John F. Harris and Glenn Kessler, "Dwindling Surplus Helps Hill Rekindle Blame Game," *Washington Post*, July 9, 2001, A1.

27. Ibid.

28. Pat Towell, "Conflict Looms over B-2 and F-22 As Bill Heads to House Floor," *Congressional Quarterly Weekly Report*, July 29, 1995, 2292.

29. Paul E. Peterson and Mark Rom argue that presidents have little incentive to "manipulate the economy for either electoral or partisan reasons." In their view presidents can best achieve their diverse objectives through economic policies that maintain a balance between inflation and steady economic growth with minimal rates of unemployment. See "Macroeconomic Policymaking: Who Is in Control?" in *Can the Government Govern?*, ed. John E. Chubb and Paul E. Peterson (Washington, D.C.: Brookings, 1989), 149.

30. George Hager and David S. Cloud, "Democrats Tie Their Fate to Clinton's Budget Bill," *Congressional Quarterly Weekly Report*, August 7, 1993, 2122–2129.

31. David R. Beam, "New Federalism, Old Realities: The Reagan Administration and Intergovernmental Reform," in *The Reagan Presidency and the Governing of America*, ed. Lester M. Salamon and Michael S. Lund (Washington, D.C.: Urban Institute, 1984), 440; and Paul E. Peterson, *The Price of Federation* (Washington, D.C.: Brookings, 1995), 69.

32. Peri Arnold, "Clinton and the Institutionalized Presidency," in *The Postmodern Presidency*, 26–28.

33. James E. Anderson and Jared E. Hazleton, *Managing Macroeconomic Policy: The Johnson Presidency* (Austin: University of Texas Press, 1986), 14.

34. Dick Kirschten, "Sprinkel Finds a Better Market for Advice in Second Reagan Term," *National Journal*, March 22, 1986, 714–715. According to Reagan CEA member William Niskanen, Feldstein's assumption of a public role destroyed his effectiveness. His successor, who had no ties to academia, was "comfortable with a short leash" and thus more effective. See William A. Niskanen, *Reaganomics* (New York: Oxford University Press, 1988), 295, 296.

35. Paul W. McCracken, "Reflections on Economic Advising" (paper presented at the Princeton University Conference on Advising the President, Princeton, N.J., October 31, 1975), 4.

36. For a brief profile, see *National Journal*, June 23, 2001, 1896.

37. Joseph A. Davis, "Policy and Regulatory Review: Growth in Legislative Role Sparks Concern in Congress," *Congressional Quarterly Weekly Report*, September 14, 1985, 1809.

38. M. Stephen Weatherford and Lorraine M. McDonnell, "Clinton and the Economy: The Paradox of Policy Success and Political Mishap" (paper presented at the annual meeting of the American Political Science Association, Chicago, August 31–September 3, 1995), 21.

39. Ibid., 28.

40. For a brief profile, see *National Journal*, June 23, 2001, 1905.

41. Anderson and Hazleton, *Managing Macroeconomic Policy*, 27.

42. Colin Campbell, "The White House and the Cabinet under the 'Let's Deal' President," in *The Bush Presidency: First Appraisals*, ed. Colin Campbell and Bert A. Rockman (Chatham, N.J.: Chatham House, 1991), 211.

43. Frendreis and Tatalovich, *The Modern Presidency*, 56.

44. Weatherford and McDonnell, "Clinton and the Economy," 20–21.

45. For a brief profile, see *National Journal*, June 23, 2001, 1987.

46. Colin Campbell, *Managing the Presidency: Carter, Reagan and the Search for Executive Harmony* (Pittsburgh: University of Pittsburgh Press, 1986), 123–135. Also see Kessel, *Presidents, the Presidency, and the Political Environment*, 127–129.

47. Ibid., 120.

48. Paul Starobin, "One-Two Punch," *National Journal*, April 2, 1994, 768–883.

49. Kessel, *Presidents, the Presidency, and the Political Environment*, 138.

50. Anderson and Hazleton, *Managing Macroeconomic Policy*, 83.

51. Roger B. Porter, *Presidential Decision Making: The Economic Policy Board* (New York: Cambridge University Press, 1980), 176.

52. Campbell, *Managing the Presidency*, 138.

53. David A. Stockman, *The Triumph of Politics: Why the Reagan Revolution Failed* (New York: Harper and Row), 1986.

54. Campbell, " 'Let's Deal' President," 210.

55. Frendreis and Tatalovich, *The Modern Presidency*, 70.

56. Paul Starobin, "The Broker," *National Journal*, April 16, 1994, 878–883.

57. Weatherford and McDonnell, "Clinton and the Economy," 21.

58. Bob Woodward, *The Agenda: Inside the Clinton White House* (New York: Simon and Schuster, 1994).

59. Weatherford and McDonnell, "Clinton and the Economy," 39.

60. Kessel, *Presidents, the Presidency, and the Political Environment*, 143; Tatalovich and Frendreis, "Clinton, Class, and Economic Policy," 47; and Stevenson, "The Wisdom to Let the Good Times Roll," A13.

61. For a brief profile, see *National Journal*, June 23, 2001, 1894–1895.

62. Jeffrey H. Birnbaum and Alan S. Murray, *Showdown at Gucci Gulch: Lawmakers, Lobbyists, and the Unlikely Triumph of Tax Reform* (New York: Random House, 1987).

63. Each year Congress passes thirteen major appropriations bills that finance the government operations conducted by departments and agencies. The appropriations do not include entitlement programs, such as Social Security, Medicare, and Medicaid, or interest on the national debt.

64. James L. Sundquist, *The Decline and Resurgence of Congress* (Washington, D.C.: Brookings, 1981), 199.

65. R. Kent Weaver, *Automatic Government: The Politics of Indexation* (Washington, D.C.: Brookings, 1988).

66. Palazzolo, *Done Deal?*, 20.

67. This discussion follows Allen Schick, *The Federal Budget: Politics, Policy, Process* (Washington, D.C.: Brookings, 1995), chap. 5.

68. Schick defines budget authority as "legislation that enables an agency to incur obligations. Obligations occur when agencies take any action . . . that commits the government to the payment of funds." Ibid., 19.

69. Ibid., 82.

70. Allen Schick, "The Evolution of Congressional Budgeting," in *Crisis in the Budget Process: Exercising Political Choice*, ed. Allen Schick (Washington, D.C.: American Enterprise Institute, 1986), 8.

71. Ibid., 15.

72. Ibid.

73. Alfred J. Tuchfarber, Stephen E. Bennett, Andrew E. Smith, and Eric W. Rademacher, "The Republican Tidal Wave of 1994: Testing Hypotheses About Realignment, Restructuring, and Rebellion" (paper presented at the annual meeting of the American Political Science Association, Chicago, August 31–September 3, 1995), 20–21.

74. Kessel, *Presidents, the Presidency, and the Political Environment*, 151.

75. Stockman, *The Triumph of Politics*, 97–98, 329–332.

SUGGESTED READINGS

Anderson, James E., and Jared E. Hazleton. *Managing Macroeconomic Policy: The Johnson Presidency*. Austin: University of Texas Press, 1986.

Collender, Stanley E. *Guide to the Federal Budget: Fiscal 2000*. Washington, D.C.: Brookings Institution Press, 1999. Published annually.

Fisher, Louis. *Presidential Spending Power*. Princeton: Princeton University Press, 1975.

Frendreis, John P., and Raymond Tatalovich. *The Modern Presidency and Economic Policy*. Itasca, Ill.: Peacock Publishers, 1994.

Kessel, John H. *Presidents, the Presidency, and the Political Environment*. Washington, D.C.: CQ Press, 2001.

Kettl, Donald F. *Leadership at the Fed*. New Haven: Yale University Press, 1986.

Mills, Gregory B., and John L. Palmer, eds. *Federal Budget Policy in the 1980s*. Washington, D.C.: Urban Institute Press, 1984.

Niskanen, William A. *Reaganomics*. New York: Oxford University Press, 1988.

Palazzolo, Daniel J. *Done Deal? The Politics of the 1997 Budget Agreement*. Chatham, N.J.: Chatham House, 1999.

Pfiffner, James P., ed. *The President and Economic Policy*. Philadelphia: Institute for the Study of Human Issues, 1986.

Porter, Roger B. *Presidential Decision Making: The Economic Policy Board*. New York: Cambridge University Press, 1980.

Schick, Allen. *The Capacity to Budget*. Washington, D.C.: Urban Institute Press, 1990.

____. *The Federal Budget: Politics, Policy, Process*. Rev. ed. Washington, D.C.: Brookings, 2000.

Stein, Herbert. *Presidential Economics: The Making of Economic Policy from Roosevelt to Reagan and Beyond*. 2d rev. ed. Washington, D.C.: American Enterprise Institute, 1988.

Stockman, David A. *The Triumph of Politics: Why the Reagan Revolution Failed*. New York: Harper and Row, 1986.

Tufte, Edward R. *Political Control of the Economy*. Princeton: Princeton University Press, 1978.

Wildavsky, Aaron. *The New Politics of the Budgetary Process*. 2d ed. New York: HarperCollins, 1992.

10 THE POLITICS OF NATIONAL SECURITY POLICY

To comply with national security policies instigated by the Reagan administration, the U.S. Air Force dismembered B-52 bombers, which were then left for ninety days so that Russia could confirm the destruction with satellite photos.

NATIONAL SECURITY POLICY USUALLY reflects long-term geopolitical conditions in the world. Examples are the alliance of the United States with other nations in NATO, the North Atlantic Treaty Organization; the postwar conflict between the United States and the Soviet Union following World War II; the intractability of religious and cultural differences in the Balkans, the Middle East, Northern Ireland, and elsewhere. Seldom do single events serve as dramatic turning points that reshape the direction of policy, but millions of people were convinced that their lives and U.S. foreign policy were permanently altered by the events of September 11, 2001, when a series of terrorist attacks fully or partially destroyed two symbols of American power in the world: the twin towers of the World Trade Center in New York City and the Pentagon, headquarters of the U.S. military, just across the Potomac River from Washington, D.C.

In a coordinated attack, three airliners carrying large fuel supplies were hijacked by small groups of men who then sacrificed their own lives and those of the passengers by flying the planes directly into their targets. A fourth aircraft, presumably headed for Washington, D.C., crashed before reaching its goal, the attack apparently foiled by the efforts of passengers aboard the plane. Millions witnessed the second attack on the World Trade Center on live television, the fireball and crumbling towers becoming searing images in their collective memory. For days the nation's normal life seemed suspended as attention focused on stories of emergency evacuations, reports of heroic rescue efforts, the search for missing loved ones, and the expanding investigation. Nearly 6,000 persons died in the two incidents. In the aftermath, the economy was seriously disrupted with the stock exchanges closed for four days and the air transportation system shut down, eventually resuming operation at severely reduced levels.

Only the surprise Japanese attack on Pearl Harbor, in December 1941, that led to American involvement in World War II had a similar galvanizing effect on the nation. Before the week was over, President George W. Bush secured congressional approval of an emergency appropriation of $40 billion for disaster relief and increased preparedness. Congress also approved by near unanimous votes of 98–0 in the Senate and 420–1 in the House a resolution authorizing the president to use "all necessary and appropriate force against those nations, organizations, or persons he determines planned, authorized, committed or aided the terrorist attacks . . . or harbored such organizations or persons."[1] National unity and patriotic fervor prevailed on Capitol Hill where partisan conflict and recrimination had been building in the expected battle over budget priorities. In a vast outpouring of solidarity, people throughout the nation attended religious services and nondenominational ceremonies, gave blood, donated money, and flew the American flag out of remembrance and support for those who had died or suffered losses. It almost seemed as though the nation was reluctant to return to normal as the government prepared a response.

Indeed, the administration recognized how dramatically these events had altered its direction and focus. President Bush, in a news conference held two days after the attacks, acknowledged that "this is now the focus of my administration. We will be very much engaged in domestic policy, of course. I look forward to working with Congress on a variety of issues. But now that war has been declared on us, we will lead the world to victory."[2]

Mobilizing public support for a war effort and fashioning a multilateral, international response became the principal concerns of an administration that had been forced to scramble on the day of the attacks. On September 11, President Bush had been in Florida at an event designed to build support for his education program when he learned of the attacks. He returned to Washington by way of military installations in Louisiana and Nebraska only after the situation had stabilized and the danger of attempts on the White House and *Air Force One*, his plane, had been resolved. In his prime-time address to the nation that evening, Bush quietly reassured the American people that everything was being done to help the injured, continue the federal government's operations without interruption, and find those responsible for the attacks. In the following days his rhetoric escalated to a virtual declaration of war against the enemies of civilization. The United States was about to launch a sustained assault against a very different kind of enemy in hopes of eradicating terrorism. Despite the initial outpouring of national and international support, there could be little doubt that difficult times lay ahead in maintaining the levels of unity needed for success both at home and abroad.

A war on terrorism was a far cry from the national security challenges that dominated most of the last half of the twentieth century. Following World War II, the United States and the Soviet Union were the dominant countries in world affairs. Cast in the role of adversaries, they led two armed camps of nations—one democratically governed, the other ruled by Communist Party dictatorships. The industrial democracies and the communist bloc coexisted in an uneasy peace, maintained in part by the threat of mutual nuclear annihilation. At the same time, each power grouping actively courted the support of the "uncommitted" developing countries, nations of the so-called third world. These countries, most of which faced enormous economic and social problems, varied in their orientations toward Washington and Moscow.

Superimposed on the basic pattern of U.S.-Soviet competition was the twentieth-century technological revolution in communications, transportation, and weaponry, which had the effect of shrinking the world and making the risks of military confrontation greater than ever. In addition, the United States grew more economically dependent on other countries, especially suppliers of basic raw materials, such as oil. In an environment characterized by military precariousness and economic interdependence, national security policy—foreign affairs and military policy—claimed most of the president's attention. No chief executive could focus primarily and indefinitely on domestic policy. Sooner or later, presidents found themselves caught up with national security issues.

Modern presidents from Franklin D. Roosevelt to Bill Clinton—and now George W. Bush—have been drawn almost irresistibly to concentrate on national security policy rather than domestic policy. The reasons for this predictable emphasis across administrations were at least twofold: first, the crucial importance of the United States in the international community; and second, the political advantages that presidents normally derived from devoting much of their energy to national security.[3]

Ronald Reagan came into office in 1981 committed to bringing about a conservative revolution in domestic and economic policy but found himself drawn toward national security policy issues. His successor, George Bush, was preoccupied with foreign and military policy from the start of his administration and only reluctantly turned his attention home when the economy faltered and his reelection campaign approached. In that campaign, Bill Clinton successfully attacked Bush for neglecting the health of the economy and serious domestic problems and promised that, if elected, he would concentrate on them. Much to his dismay, Clinton discovered upon taking office that the end of the cold war brought new conflicts and still greater uncertainty to international affairs. Like his predecessors, Clinton eventually had to involve himself extensively with foreign policy, at least in part due to his political needs during the 1998–1999 impeachment controversy. As he prepared to leave office, Clinton seemed consumed by the desire to produce a long-evasive Middle East peace settlement.

During his initial hundred days in office, George W. Bush dealt primarily with domestic policy. An unexpected crisis in relations with China provided a reminder that foreign policy frequently intrudes unexpectedly on the national agenda. But the terrorist attacks of September 2001 and the subsequent "war on terrorism" were likely to become the defining moments for his presidency and help determine whether he could be reelected to a second term in office.

This chapter examines the president's role in making and directing national security policy. It reviews the major concepts and issues that have dominated national security policy since World War II. It then defines the essential national security policymaking problem as one in which the president is both the solution and the problem. Finally, the discussion turns to (1) the relationship between the president and Congress with respect to national security and (2) the problem of organizing an effective policymaking system for national security.

Issues in National Security Policy: Search for a New Consensus

For more than two decades, from the end of World War II until March 1968, America's principal national interest was clear-cut: military containment of communism. But when the North Vietnamese Tet offensive precipitated Lyndon Johnson's decision to end the escalation of American involvement in the Vietnam War, the broad consensus undergirding U.S. national security policy began to disintegrate. Until Tet, a succession of presidents from both political parties had consistently pursued the doctrine of containment, and differences of opinion within the policymaking elite and in the mass public were accommodated by compromises. Bipartisan support for the consensus in Congress gave presidents a free hand in formulating and implementing foreign and military policies. The only effective constraints imposed on presidential actions were the boundaries of the consensus, which began to break up in 1968, when it became apparent that containment could be preserved only through an indefinite, limited war in Vietnam or greatly expanded U.S. involvement that carried risks of conflict with the Soviet Union.

Even after the United States failed to "contain" communism in Vietnam, presidents continued to employ single, overarching concepts to build domestic political support for their national security policies. They found that "selling programs to Congress and the American people in the postwar era was always made easier if they could be clothed in one garment."[4] Détente, human rights, the "evil empire," the "new world order," engagement, and enlargement have emerged as successors to containment, but none has proved to be the core of an enduring national consensus. It remains to be seen whether responding to a terrorist attack will provide the sustained political support that has been missing for so long.

In 1972 and 1973, President Nixon told the American people that a policy of *détente* would ease, if not end, the precarious Soviet-American tensions of the cold war. Détente was to be implemented through actions such as cultural exchanges, increased trade between the two countries, and negotiations to limit strategic nuclear weapons. Established attitudes and behavior patterns are not easy to change, however, and Nixon and his successor, Gerald Ford, found it convenient to seek support for their policies by citing threatening Soviet actions in various parts of the world, such as Africa, Latin America, and the Middle East.

Jimmy Carter effectively campaigned on the pledge, which he reaffirmed at the outset of his administration, that morality, manifested in universal commitment to the defense of *human rights*, would be the cornerstone of U.S. foreign policy. However, Carter's human rights focus failed to provide the basis for a new consensus because it was not consistently applied. The United States found it easier to protest and threaten to take action against human rights violations in countries not vital to its interests, such as the Soviet Union and its allies, than in those that were vital, such as South Korea and South Africa. Indeed, misguided application of the human rights doctrine hastened the downfall of the shah's friendly but authoritarian government in Iran and contributed to the establishment of the equally oppressive, but virulently anti-American, Islamic republic of Ayatollah Ruhollah Khomeini. Furthermore, the United States did not have the capacity to enforce the doctrine against powerful violators.

Reagan took office proclaiming belligerently that his administration's framework for national security policy was continued opposition to and competition with the Soviet Union, which he once called "the evil empire."[5] In practice, however, his anti-Soviet stance was less than doctrinaire—strong rhetoric was combined with restrained conduct. In other words, he said one thing and did another. In November 1981, for example, Reagan offered to cancel plans to place additional land-based intermediate-range missiles in West Germany and in several other North Atlantic Treaty Organization (NATO) countries in exchange for the withdrawal of comparable Soviet SS-20 missiles from Eastern Europe and the western part of Russia. Negotiations to limit nuclear weapons and curtail the arms race, although initially unsuccessful, eventually produced the Intermediate Range Nuclear Forces Treaty, the first arms reduction agreement of the cold war, a singular achievement—but not one consistent with a strategic vision based on superpower conflict.

Further undercutting Reagan's ability to construct a new consensus were the persistent questions posed by journalists and political critics about the administration's interpretation and explanation of its actions and the president's knowledge of the details of events. Many observers questioned who was in charge—the president or his aides in the State Department, the Central Intelligence Agency (CIA), and the National Security Council (NSC). These questions seemed fully justified when the administration's foreign policy surged out of control with the disclosure of the Iran-contra affair.[6] In November 1986, the administration acknowledged that it had sent arms to Iran but stated that only a small number of obsolete weapons had been involved. It maintained that the shipments were designed to establish contact with and encourage moderate elements in Iran. Reagan refused to acknowledge that selling arms to Iran had been an error, and he vigorously denied that there had been any explicit exchange of arms for hostages, although each hostage's release had been preceded by an arms shipment. The seriousness and complexity of the affair snowballed in late November 1986, when the president acknowledged, through Attorney General Edwin Meese, that profits from the arms sales ($10 million–$30 million) had been diverted to the Nicaraguan contras through a numbered Swiss bank account. This was a direct violation of the Boland amendment, adopted by Congress in 1984, which prohibited use of government funds to support covert operations against the government of Nicaragua. Reagan claimed he had not been fully informed about the matter.

The selling of arms to Iran in apparent exchange for American hostages called into question the commitment of the United States to resisting terrorism and isolating countries, such as Iran, that support terrorism. It also undermined the U.S. position of neutrality in the seven-year war between Iran and Iraq and damaged its relations with moderate Arab states such as Saudi Arabia. Several members of Congress charged that the arms sales apparently violated laws requiring "the administration to report on covert operations and other diplomatic and military operations overseas."[7] (The president exempted himself from the legislation and the embargo against arms sales to Iran that had been in effect since the 1979–1980 hostage crisis by formally making a finding, on January 17, 1986, that the sales were necessary to national security.)

Questions about Reagan's competence in managing foreign policy focused on his detached administrative style, which entailed extensive delegation and a disdain for factual details. His supporters explained that he took care of "the big picture" and left the rest to subordinates. Until late 1986, this approach seemed to serve him effectively. The Iran-contra affair emboldened critics to point out that regardless of how little Reagan might have known he was accountable for the actions of his administration. The operation of the foreign policy process, especially the role played by the NSC staff, contributed a great deal to Reagan's political difficulties and did little to protect him from foreign policy mistakes.

In contrast to Reagan, his successor, George Bush, was a hands-on president deeply engaged in the formulation and implementation of national security policy. He concerned himself with its details and participated actively in negotiations with foreign leaders. In addition, he approached foreign policy with a pragmatic, rather than ideological, orientation. All of this resulted, however, in the criticism that his administration's foreign policy was purely tactical and lacked a strategic design.[8] The "new world order" that Bush announced following the collapse of communism in Russia and throughout Eastern Europe was unable to sustain a national consensus, in part because its meaning remained unclear.

In general, the Bush administration's national security policies met with popular approval, although the administration's refusal to retaliate against the government of China for the June 1989 Tiananmen Square massacre of students pressing for democratic reforms drew sharp criticism. Many members of Congress questioned the administration's conduct of relations with Panama and Iraq, where close U.S. ties with undemocratic leaders began to unravel and produced military action. But, for the most part, the public remained supportive. Bush continued the policies of the late Reagan years but with greater flexibility and adaptiveness.[9] He provided "a kind of competent Reaganism" and "restore[d] professionalism to the conduct of foreign policy."[10] In the Persian Gulf War, in 1991, for example, Bush skillfully mobilized domestic and world opinion behind the most effective international coalition since World War II. He demonstrated the ability of the United States to project its power far from its home base. However, by not removing Iraqi president Saddam Hussein from power and bringing peace and stability to the Middle East, the United States failed to realize fully the fruits of victory and created problems for Bush's successor.

Despite its success, the Bush foreign policy was essentially reactive. Its major initiatives—the invasion of Panama and the Gulf War—were responses to crises. The absence of a strategic framework led to an emphasis on individual problems and to policies that lacked cohesion. While Bush spoke grandly of a new world order, he gave little indication of its shape and dimensions. His administration was unable to develop a strategic design for the post–cold war world or a replacement for the Soviet threat as the unifying force that held the NATO countries and Japan together. Moreover, the absence of a strategic focus for national security left the Bush administration with little sense of how to counter calls for isolationism or to cope with the increasing impact of international factors on the domestic economy.

During Bill Clinton's first term, the national security policies of his administration drew extensive criticism from foreign policy analysts as "ad hocracy," reflecting a confusion of means and ends unresolved by a central vision or overarching conceptual framework.[11] From the outset it expressed a wide array of high-minded goals, including the expansion of democracy and human rights; the alleviation of disease, hunger, and poverty; growing globalization as free markets proliferated within states and free trade grew between them; and control of weapons of mass destruction. Frequently, however, the administration encountered difficulty translating these goals into workable policies in specific instances, such as the failed effort at nation building in Somalia, the intervention to restore democracy in Haiti, the early uncertainty about policy in Bosnia, and inaction in the face of genocide in Rwanda. Clinton's administration also vacillated between multilateralism and unilateralism as means to achieve its ends, sometimes acting alone and at other times refusing to act unless allies joined in the effort.

The first extensive statement of the administration's strategy, which appeared in July 1994, identified three central themes: domestic renewal, engagement abroad to enlarge market democracies, and multilateralism as a primary mode of operation.[12] Domestic purpose provided the dominant orientation for the national security policy: market democracies would be extended ("enlargement") and threats contained ("engagement") in order to achieve renewal at home.[13] Two of Clinton's biggest foreign policy successes—enactment of legislation implementing the North American Free Trade Agreement (NAFTA) and renewing and expanding the General Agreement on Tariffs and Trade (GATT)—were justified as improving the American economy. By 1998, however, there had been important shifts in the Clinton administration's official statements. Defending the nation from terrorism, drug trafficking, and crime, as well as from weapons of mass destruction, became more prominent goals than advancing market economies. There was also recognition that managing the international financial markets was a critical task, an appropriate goal given the widespread impacts of financial crises in Mexico and Asia.[14] But the new statement of goals still lacked a unifying statement of purpose.

In its application, the Clinton administration's actions were often replete with indecision, inconsistencies, and policy reversals and frequently seemed to be formulated in response to domestic political interests and pressures rather than guided by any inner logic. In no case were these difficulties more apparent than with respect to the civil war in Bosnia. As a presidential candidate, Clinton had criticized the Bush administration for not taking action to end the fighting. As president, he initially advocated lifting the embargo on arms to the Muslim-led government forces and supporting them with air strikes against their Serbian opponents. After sharp criticism from France and Great Britain, contributors of most of the troops to a United Nations peacekeeping force, he abandoned "lift and strike" in favor of working through NATO and the United Nations. Clinton agreed, in November 1995, to commit U.S. ground forces to participate in a NATO peacekeeping force to enforce a settlement to the conflict agreed to by the warring Serbs, Croats, and Muslims. This action encountered sharp domestic criticism from the Republican-dominated Congress and the media, and polls showed little support for military involvement in Bosnia.

In fact, the Clinton administration never clearly resolved the question of when military power could appropriately be employed, despite having done so more frequently than any of its four predecessors (see Table 10-1). President Clinton, often criticized for avoiding military service, ordered U.S. forces into action in Bosnia, Haiti, Somalia, Iraq, Afghanistan, Sudan, and Kosovo. Public opinion was firmly behind none of these efforts and played a major role in the abrupt end of several, including the humanitarian mission of U.S. forces in Somalia after eighteen servicemen were killed fighting the forces of a local warlord. Similarly, public opinion was reluctant to see the United States become deeply involved in reestablishing a democratic government in Haiti or to intervene to stop the killing in Rwanda. Criticism from congressional conservatives was persistent; House Republicans, for example, rejected a resolution in April 1999 authorizing American participation in the air war against Yugoslavia that had already started on March 24 and lasted for thirty-eight days. Although the Clinton administration was able to accomplish important parts of its global eco-

Table 10-1   Presidential Use of Force Reported in Compliance with the War Powers Resolution, 1969–2001

President/term	Times complied with War Powers Resolution
Nixon (1969–1974)	0
Ford (1974–1977)	4
Carter (1977–1981)	1
Reagan (1981–1989)	14
G. H. W. Bush (1989–1993)	7
Clinton (1993–2001)	58
G. W. Bush (2001–)	4[a]

Source: Richard F. Grimmet, "War Powers Resolution: Presidential Compliance." *CRS Issue Brief for Congress*, Congressional Research Service, Library of Congress, September 20, 2001, http://www.house.gov/markgreen/crs.htm.

[a]Through September 20, 2001.

nomic agenda with the help of congressional Republicans who supported passage of NAFTA and GATT, other administration initiatives were rejected, including renewal of fast-track negotiating authority to conclude trade agreements.[15] Even the administration's major international financial achievements were difficult: when Congress refused to approve a $50 billion assistance package for Mexico, Clinton was forced to use unilateral executive authority; refurbishing the International Monetary Fund's financial resources after the Asian crisis occurred only after a year-long delay.

A persistent subject of disagreement—and some would say administration confusion—was U.S. policy toward China. In early 1993, Clinton informed China that unless it significantly improved its human rights record he would not renew most-favored-nation status for it a year later. (The granting of this status assures a country that it will receive the same tariff concessions that are extended to all other states.) When the deadline arrived without appreciable improvements in human rights, Clinton extended the status, rationalizing that so much was at stake economically that ending it would do more harm than good. The original "get tough" position on China disappeared entirely during the president's state visit to Beijing in June 1998, when Clinton sought to "normalize" relations by discussing areas of disagreement with his hosts but at the same time finding opportunities for "constructive engagement." Modest concessions had been made by China on human rights and nuclear nonproliferation prior to the visit, but the principal Chinese goal was to be admitted to the World Trade Organization, a multilateral entity established in the 1994 GATT agreement. Republican critics of Clinton's China policy stressed examples of Chinese espionage in stealing nuclear weapons secrets, efforts to influence the 1996 presidential election with illegal campaign contributions, the failure of China to live up to nuclear nonproliferation promises, and continued human rights violations.[16]

In early 2001, China proved to be the central international problem of George W. Bush's fledgling administration when an American airplane conducting an electronic surveillance mission over the South China Sea collided with a Chinese military jet and was forced to land on Chinese territory. The American crew was held incommunicado for several days while the two nations—a superpower and a potential superpower—sorted through their options and negotiated a settlement. The major question in these negotiations was whether the United States would apologize for causing the death of the Chinese pilot and violating Chinese territory without permission. A carefully phrased statement allowed the United States to express "regret" without a formal apology, allowing both the administration and the Chinese government to save face.[17] Shortly after this incident, Bush abandoned longstanding American ambiguity about its commitment to defend Taiwan, an island nation that China claimed as a province, by "proclaiming that the United States would use its full military might to defend Taiwan against military attack." He also expanded weapons sales to Taiwan, pushed a missile defense system implicitly targeted at China, and suspended two-way talks between the United States and Chinese military establishments.[18] From the Chinese perspective, the new administration appeared intent on making the two nations' relationship more competitive than cooperative. The Bush administration subsequently sought to reverse field and denied that policy had changed, but the damage had been done.

China policy was the most dramatic of several signals that the Bush administration would emphasize traditional security concerns more than the economic globalization that lay at the heart of Clinton's world view. After an election campaign that had emphasized domestic issues—education, tax cuts, and health care—the new administration did not rush forward to articulate a strategic framework or to construct a new foreign policy consensus, though it did make a number of departures. Russia was publicly criticized for technology and weapons sales to Iran and China, and fifty Russian diplomats were sent home as punishment for spying; negotiations with North Korea on an agreement to halt its missile development program were put on hold; the administration angered Japan and European allies by rejecting the Kyoto treaty on global warming; and the administration looked for a way to get out of the Balkans. To some, this added up to an administration position of "New Realism" that was reminiscent of Reagan's first administration but with clearer commitments and tougher negotiating positions.[19] Allies were concerned about the growing tendency toward "unilateralism" they could discern in administration actions—the tendency to impose American preferences even in the face of strong objections.

Terrorism posed both an opportunity and a threat to the new administration's search for a strategic consensus. By the fall of 2001, budget forecasts of declining revenues and a slowing economy led many Democrats to question whether the nation could afford increased expenditures for defense as the administration had proposed in its budget for fiscal year 2002. In the immediate aftermath of the terrorist attacks, Congress was quite willing to appropriate additional funds for some purposes, but voices were raised questioning whether additional spending for a missile defense system (another administration initiative that harkened back to the Reagan years) any longer made sense. The real threat suddenly appeared to be not North Korea or Iraq—the rogue states likely to develop nuclear-tipped missiles—but the loosely linked terrorist organizations that could rely on stealth, secrecy, and low-tech weapons. The growing terrorist threat made it more likely, however, that intelligence spending would increase. Spending reductions after the cold war had severely reduced the capacity for human intelligence (that is, spying), a place where increases might make a difference in preventing future terrorist attacks. Launching a "war on terrorism," therefore, was likely to have consequences for the larger debate over the nation's defense needs. It was unclear whether the Bush administration would be able to provide an overarching framework for dealing with both traditional and nontraditional sources of threat, and the nation could expect a battle for scarce dollars between proponents of missile defense and those in favor of intelligence spending. Moreover, the widespread dislocations in the investment and financial communities caused by the attack on the World Trade Center should have reminded policymakers of the effects of globalism, a perspective far more prominent in the Clinton than in the Bush administration. Thus, far from offering an easy answer to the problem of developing a strategic consensus, the terrorist attacks may have added to the complexity of the task.

Perhaps we should not be surprised that successive administrations have not succeeded in developing widespread public support for a strategic consensus. Articulating a new foreign policy requires taking positions on scores, if not hundreds, of difficult issues, something politicians are reluctant to do.[20] Moreover, from an American perspective, the international environment is full of contradictory pressures and has become more and more unmanageable. With the disappearance in 1991 of the Soviet Union as one of the world's two superpowers, the number of regional and communal (ethnic, religious, tribal) conflicts has proliferated. China aspires to become a great power and other nations, such as Iraq, hope to become regional powers. There are also history-laden animosities that have now come to the surface, particularly in the Balkans, where the United States and its NATO allies intervened in Bosnia and Kosovo.

"Security" has also taken on new meanings with threats arising from uncontrolled immigration, international drug dealers, and, most dramatically, international terrorists. These threats may have become just as pressing as those from ambitious nation-states. In marked contrast to the cold war era, the new international agenda is heavily—some argue predominantly—economic, raising issues that intermingle with domestic social and macroeconomic policy matters. This further complicates the president's efforts to present national security policy in terms of an overarching framework. New issues broaden the range of interest groups seeking to exert leverage on policies that deal with natural resources, managing the international monetary system, marketing U.S. agricultural products overseas, and pursuing an international trade policy that adds, rather than subtracts, jobs at home. Because these issues have immediate and powerful effects on important domestic constituencies, they require negotiations with powerful interests at home and abroad. In addressing such problems, presidents no longer enjoy the discretion or broad support that was accorded them in foreign and military policy at the height of the cold war.

The National Security Policymaking Problem

When the Soviet Union collapsed in 1991, and with it the threat posed by international communism, isolationist forces long dormant in the United States reawoke to challenge the dominant internationalism of the post–World War II era. This development made any prospect of a national security policy built on a broad consensus beyond reach in the foreseeable future. Isolationism and the end of bipartisan congressional support for administration policies—a result, as noted earlier, of the Vietnam War (1965–1973)—have made the need for effective international leadership in the United States all the more critical. Such leadership is complicated, however, by the governmental structure established in the Constitution—separate institutions sharing power—which creates continuing tension between the president and Congress over the control of national security policy. Edward S. Corwin observed that the Constitution "is an invitation to struggle" between the two branches "for the privilege of directing American foreign policy."[21] Although the struggle continues, and power over foreign policy is divided, the president has played the dominant role in shaping national security policy through most of the nation's history. Presidential advantages of unity, secrecy, and dispatch are especially compelling during periods of crisis and potential conflict.

Dependence on presidential leadership carries risks, however. The idiosyncrasies of individual presidents' operating styles and personalities can be sources of uncertainty and noncohesiveness in policy and can exacerbate the institutional tensions between Congress and the president. (To some extent this happened during the Iran-contra affair.) The nation needs in its national security policy "institutions that provide continuity" and "structures and processes that promote coherence."[22] The problem is that if institutions, structures, and procedures respond to the short-term needs and whims of individual presidents, discontinuity in policy is likely to multiply. National security policymaking presents the United States with a circular and seemingly inescapable problem: the country depends on the president for central policy leadership, born of constitutional arrangements and operational imperatives, but this produces discontinuity in policy and a lack of cohesiveness that result from a policymaking system geared to presidential domination.

The President, Congress, and National Security

The powers of the federal government in international affairs are "inherent, plenary, and exclusive."[23] They are not granted expressly by the Constitution; rather they derive from the nation's existence as a sovereign entity in the international community. To say that the national power over international affairs is inherent means that it does not depend on an affirmative grant of power in the Constitution. The exclusive and plenary character of that power means that it cannot be exercised by the states or anyone else and that its exercise is not limited by the reserved powers of the states.

The Constitution, however, is ambiguous in its assignment of the power to control foreign relations. Both the president and Congress have formal constitutional powers in this area, indicating that the Founders intended control to be shared. In a 1793 debate with James Madison in the *Gazette of the United States,* Alexander Hamilton argued that direction of the nation's foreign policy is inherently an executive function.[24] Madison's position—that since the power to declare war is vested in Congress, presidential powers in this regard are merely instrumental—has not been borne out by subsequent events. Longstanding usages and the practical aspects of the conduct of foreign relations have combined to make the president *the sole organ* of the United States in the conduct of its external affairs. Negotiations and communications with other governments have been, from the early years of the Republic, a presidential monopoly.

Congress, however, has retained considerable ability to influence the substantive content of the foreign and defense policies that the president implements. Policies developed by the president cannot remain viable for long without congressional support in the form of implementing legislation and appropriations. Nevertheless, throughout most of U.S. history the president has been and is today the "most important single factor in the determination of American foreign policy."[25] The reasons can be understood, at least in part, through examination of the powers of the president and Congress in national security matters.

The Powers of the President

In addition to the inherent powers of the executive derived from the involvement of the United States in the international community, the president's powers over national security stem from two sources: formal powers granted by or implied from specific constitutional provisions and powers delegated to the executive branch by Congress. The president's dominant national security policy role is based on a relatively modest constitutional foundation: the power to receive ambassadors and ministers, the power to negotiate treaties, designation as commander in chief of the armed forces, the general grant of executive power, and the clause enjoining the president to "take care that the laws be faithfully executed." Operationally, these provisions result in four major areas of presidential authority over national security: recognition and nonrecognition of other governments; making, implementing, and terminating international agreements; the appointment of personnel to conduct foreign and military policy; and the use of military force as a means of achieving policy goals.

Recognition and Nonrecognition of Foreign Governments. Article II, Section 3, of the Constitution grants the president power to "receive Ambassadors and other public Ministers"—in essence, authority to recognize foreign governments. Because foreign diplomats are accredited to the president, the decision whether to receive them and thus recognize their governments is exclusively the president's. By implication, the chief executive can also refuse to grant that recognition or withdraw it.

Traditionally, under international law, governments grant recognition to other governments provided the latter are stable, have effectively established their authority, and are meeting their international obligations. Recognition allows the United States to express its approval or disapproval of foreign regimes. This weapon is particularly effective when exercised by a nation as powerful and influential as the United States. Other nations may alter their conduct at the prospect of U.S. recognition and the threat of its withdrawal. The leverage gained through use of the recognition power is limited, however, and is lost once recognition is granted or relations are broken.

Some well-known instances involving use of the recognition power illustrate its value as well as its limitations. After the Russian Revolution in 1917–1918, the United States refused to recognize the communist government of the Soviet Union on the grounds that it had obtained power illegally, expropriated foreign-owned property without compensation, and oppressed its citizens. Although the disapproval of the Soviet regime implied through nonrecognition did not end, FDR established diplomatic relations with the Soviet Union in 1933; he believed that practical considerations made recognition advantageous to the United States. In contrast, immediately following the proclamation of the new state of Israel in 1948, President Harry Truman granted it recognition (despite strong opposition within the State Department), making the United States the first nation to do so. The support of the United States has been vital to the survival of Israel ever since.

When a communist regime took power in China in 1949 after a revolutionary struggle, the United States refused to recognize it, instead regarding the nationalist government on the island of Taiwan as the legitimate government of China. Not until 1979 did the United States establish diplomatic relations with the People's Republic of China (PRC) and withdraw recognition from Taiwan. Recognition was made possible by a relaxation of ideological rigidity by the Chinese regime, U.S. acceptance of the regime as the legitimate government of China, and mutual awareness of the policy and economic advantages that would accrue to each nation. At the same time, however, the United States did not recognize PRC sovereignty over Taiwan. The Carter administration's policies toward the two Chinas encountered challenges in Congress but were eventually upheld. Similarly, reestablishing normal relations with Vietnam in July 1995 risked renewed bitterness and resentment on the part of those who had supported the war and many of those who had fought in it. Opponents criticized President Clinton's action as self-serving—he had avoided military service in the war (1965–1973). In its defense, the administration argued that it sought to achieve economic gain for both countries and an end to the internal debate that had divided this country for thirty years.

Although presidents are legally free to exercise the recognition power on their own, political prudence dictates that they take congressional views and public opinion into consideration, effectively limiting the range of presidential discretion.

International Agreements. The Constitution provides a second influential presidential power in foreign affairs: the authority to conduct negotiations with other nations that result in treaties or binding executive agreements. The constitutional basis for the treaty-making power is found in Article II, Section 2, which declares that the president "shall have power, by and with the Advice and Consent of the Senate, to make treaties, provided two thirds of the Senators present concur." The authority to make executive agreements is not mentioned explicitly, but its constitutionality is "universally conceded."[26] That authority may be implied from the president's function as the nation's official organ for the conduct of foreign relations or as a convenient means of implementing a recognized executive power, such as the commander-in-chief power and the "take care" clause of the Constitution.[27] In addition, executive agreements may be concluded pursuant to provisions of valid treaties and of existing legislation.

Treaties require Senate approval, but executive agreements do not. The Senate's own members limited its role in the treaty-making process in 1789, when they set a precedent by refusing to advise George Washington on provisions of a treaty under negotiation. The Senate may, however, amend or attach reservations to treaties submitted for its approval. Amendments change the content of a treaty and thus require additional negotiations with the foreign nation; reservations merely clarify the Senate's understanding of the treaty's provisions. The requirement of a two-thirds vote for approval gives the Senate substantial leverage over the executive in the treaty-making process, something presidents can sidestep through executive agreements.[28] Nonetheless, Congress and the media may regard some issues as so important that presidents must pursue the additional political legitimacy that a treaty provides.

The dramatic change in the relative importance of executive agreements and treaties can be seen in Table 10-2. By the late nineteenth century, agreements concluded in the previous fifty years slightly outnumbered treaties. That ratio widened over the next fifty-year period (1889–1939), then exploded during the period 1939–1989, when 11,698 new executive agreements were concluded as opposed to only 702 treaties. Congress repeatedly has expressed its disapproval of the use of executive agreements in lieu of treaties, but the only limitation it has imposed, in the Case-Zablocki Act of 1972, is to require that the legislature be notified of all such agreements. Although Congress is free to take action against executive agreements to which it objects, it has been unable to impose effective limits on the president's power to make them.[29] Interestingly, as Table 10-3 shows, the ratio of executive agreements to treaties changed markedly under Clinton compared to that of his immediate predecessors, mainly because of the unusually large number of trade treaties concluded during his adminis-

Table 10-2 Treaties and Executive Agreements Concluded by the United States, 1789–1989

Period	Treaties	Executive agreements
1789–1839	60	27
1839–1889	215	238
1889–1939	524	917
1939–1989	702	11,698
Total	1,501	12,880

Source: *Treaties and Other International Agreements: The Role of the U.S. Senate,* Congressional Research Service, Library of Congress, January 2001, Table II-1. Report submitted to the Committee on Foreign Relations, U.S. Senate, 106:2, Senate print 106-71.

tration. It would be premature, however, to see this as the altering of a longer term trend.

Why use treaties at all? Presidents are compelled by domestic political considerations to submit international agreements for Senate approval as treaties. Approval by the Senate gives an international agreement a degree of legitimacy that otherwise would be lacking. For instance, President Carter chose to submit to the Senate as a treaty the agreement providing for gradual termination of U.S. control of the Panama Canal. Carter apparently knew that such action would be difficult to defend publicly in any case, and avoidance of Senate approval could impose unacceptable political costs on his administration. For similar reasons, Carter submitted the second Strategic Arms Limitation Talks (SALT) agreement to the Senate as a treaty even though approval was unlikely.

Table 10-3 International Agreements, 1969–2001

President/Term	Executive agreements	Treaties	Ratio
Nixon (1969–1974)	1,116	180	14.2:1
Ford (1974–1977)	677	99	25.6:1
Carter (1977–1981)	1,169	148	17.9:1
Reagan (1981–1989)	2,840	125	22.7:1
Bush (1989–1993)	1,350	67	20.2:1
Clinton (1993–2001)	1,870[a]	197[a]	9.5:1

Source: *Treaties and Other International Agreements: The Role of the U.S. Senate,* Congressional Research Service, Library of Congress, January 2001. Data from Table II-2. Report submitted to the Committee on Foreign Relations, U.S. Senate, 106:2, Senate print 106-71.

[a]Through 2001.

On several occasions, however, modern presidents have taken important action through executive agreements, knowing that Congress was unlikely to support a treaty: in 1940, Franklin Roosevelt exchanged fifty "overage" destroyers for ninety-nine-year leases on bases in British possessions in the Western Hemisphere; in 1973, the United States and North Vietnam ended hostilities and exchanged prisoners of war through an executive agreement; and in 1981, the United States and Israel negotiated an agreement for strategic cooperation in the Middle East.

The decision to designate an international agreement as a treaty is the president's, based on political rather than legal grounds.[30] But Congress is not without influence, especially if the agreement is not self-executing. In other words, if a treaty or an executive agreement requires legislation or an appropriation for its implementation, Congress can require the executive to take note of its views. During the Clinton administration, two important agreements, NAFTA and GATT, required legislation to become effective. In considering the legislation, Congress conducted an extensive debate over the merits and demerits of the agreements. Clinton had to seek the support of congressional Republicans because a majority of Democrats—fearing negative consequences for U.S. jobs—opposed both bills. Congress has no constitutional duty to implement a treaty or an executive agreement. Moreover, even though treaties and executive agreements have the force of law, they cannot contravene specific provisions of the Constitution.

Although the president's power to negotiate international agreements is subject to political and constitutional limitations, the power to terminate such agreements is not. Clearly, the president can cancel an agreement that did not receive Senate approval, but the Constitution is silent about whether approval of the Senate is required to terminate a treaty. The Supreme Court ruled in 1979 that the president could unilaterally abrogate a defense treaty with Taiwan that was part of the agreements establishing diplomatic relations between the United States and the People's Republic of China.[31] Since the 1970s, presidents also have expanded their power in the treaty area through reinterpretation. The Reagan administration provides the best example: in 1985, it broadened the terms of the 1972 Anti-Ballistic Missile (ABM) Treaty, over the objections of the Senate and the Soviet Union, to accommodate development of the strategic defense initiative.[32] President George W. Bush announced in May 2001 that he would proceed with development and deployment of an antimissile defense system and hoped to establish a "new framework" with Russia that was likely to take the form of an executive agreement rather than a new or amended ABM treaty.[33] It was later revealed that the Bush administration was considering a radical departure from the past—abandoning all strategic weapons treaties in order to maximize flexibility in making nuclear force decisions.[34] It remains to be seen how Congress, U.S. allies, and Russia will respond to this fundamental change in longstanding strategic policy.

Appointments. As noted in chapter 6, the power to appoint subordinates is an important part of presidential control over policy. It is a power that the president shares with the Senate, however, in naming high-ranking officials. Although the general considerations affecting presidential appointments also apply to national security policymakers, specific concerns in this sphere warrant attention.

The most important appointments affecting national security are the positions of secretary of state, secretary of defense, director of central intelligence, and the president's assistant for national security affairs. With these appointments, the president indicates the direction and orientation of the foreign and military policy of his administration. The appointment of the secretary of state is significant for procedural and substantive reasons. The choice of a well-known figure with definite policy views—such as the selection of Gen. George C. Marshall by President Truman, John Foster Dulles by President Dwight D. Eisenhower, and Gen. Alexander Haig by President Reagan—reflects the intention to rely heavily on the secretary for advice and guidance. The choice of a relatively unknown individual, such as President Kennedy's designation of Dean Rusk and President Nixon's selection of William P. Rogers, indicates that the president intends to play the dominant role in foreign policy formulation and to relegate to the secretary the management of the foreign affairs bureaucracy. President Clinton's selection of Warren M. Christopher, a soft-spoken lawyer with a reputation as a shrewd negotiator, appeared to indicate that the president, in keeping with his campaign focus, did not intend to emphasize foreign policy or to involve himself extensively with it. The reversal of the importance Clinton placed on foreign policy was signaled at the beginning of his second term when he named Madeleine K. Albright to replace Christopher. As UN ambassador (1993–1996), Albright had acquired a reputation for firmness and strong policy views. George W. Bush's selection of Gen. Colin L. Powell, broadly implied throughout the 2000 election campaign, communicated the president's intention to assemble an experienced and respected group of foreign policy advisers.

The appointment of the secretary of defense also indicates the president's plans for the department. Kennedy's choice of Robert S. McNamara, the president of the Ford Motor Company, signified the president's determination to make the armed forces more efficient through application of modern management techniques. Clinton reinforced the idea that he intended to leave most national security matters to subordinates when he named a highly regarded defense intellectual, Rep. Les Aspin, D-Wis., as secretary of defense. Again, in 2001, George W. Bush's selection of Donald Rumsfeld, a senior Republican with extensive Washington experience and a reputation for being a hard-driving manager, made it clear that Bush would assemble a star-studded team of national security advisers.

The position of director of central intelligence involves managing the CIA and coordinating the activities of the intelligence community.[35] The directorship was often politically controversial during the cold war because of charges that the

CIA and other intelligence agencies had engaged in covert activities designed to assassinate foreign political leaders and overthrow foreign governments. Critics also charged the CIA with ineffective intelligence work, such as the failure to anticipate the Iranian revolution of 1978–1979 and Iraq's invasion of Kuwait in 1990. CIA directors have tended to be either intelligence professionals, such as William Colby and Robert Gates, or experienced politicians, such as George H. W. Bush and William Casey. The latter, Reagan's first CIA director, apparently played a major role in the Iran-contra affair. His involvement could not be proved, however, because he became ill with cancer and died before the congressional investigation into the affair.[36] Casey's successor was FBI director William Webster, a former federal judge. Reagan appointed him to remove the aura of illegality and scandal that Casey's freewheeling activities had cast upon the agency. In 1988, President Bush's first nominee to head the CIA was Robert Gates, whose nomination drew substantial opposition in the Senate because of his connection with the Iran-contra affair. After lengthy hearings and floor debate, the Senate confirmed Gates, 64–31, in November 1991.[37] President Clinton's replacement for Gates, R. James Woolsey, a former army officer, attracted little notice until 1994, when the nation was shocked by a revelation that a sensitive CIA operative, Aldrich Ames, had been a Soviet mole for nine years.[38] Although Woolsey was not personally responsible for the Ames affair, he was held accountable for the agency's ineffectiveness and resigned in early 1995.[39] George W. Bush held over Clinton's final CIA director, George J. Tenet, a move designed to enhance continuity that John F. Kennedy had also taken four decades earlier when he retained Allen Dulles as director of the CIA and Richard Nixon had done when he kept Richard Helms in the post. In the aftermath of the World Trade Center and Pentagon attacks of September 2001, some members of Congress questioned whether Tenet should be retained as director, but Vice President Cheney publicly provided him with a strong vote of confidence.

In making high-level executive and diplomatic appointments, the president must be attentive to senatorial attitudes and concerns, although the Senate normally defers to presidential choices even in the face of doubts about the competence of the nominee. Reagan's nomination of William P. Clark, a longtime political associate and California Supreme Court justice, as deputy secretary of state brought strong criticism from the press and several senators when Clark revealed a dreadful lack of knowledge of foreign affairs during his confirmation hearing before the Foreign Relations Committee. Nevertheless, the committee recommended his approval, and the Senate complied.[40]

One of the most important national security appointments, that of the national security assistant, is not subject to Senate approval. Over the years McGeorge Bundy, Henry Kissinger, Zbigniew Brzezinski, and Colin L. Powell have held this potentially powerful post. In 2001 George W. Bush named Condoleeza Rice to the position. The president also is free to designate personal representatives to conduct negotiations or perform specific missions without the requirement of confirmation. President Carter used distinguished career diplomats Ellsworth Bunker and Sol Linowitz to negotiate with the governments of Panama and several Middle East countries, respectively. Prominent Democratic statesman W. Averell Harriman served as a roving ambassador without portfolio under several presidents, beginning with FDR.

The appointment power is essential to presidential control of direction and implementation of foreign and military policy. It is a means whereby presidents can shape both the conduct and the content of policy. Presidents enjoy wide latitude in exercising the power, but they must be sensitive to the limits imposed by international and domestic politics and by the Senate.

The Use of Military Force. The Constitution states, "The President shall be Commander in Chief of the Army and Navy of the United States" and of the state militia when it is called into federal service (Article II, Section 2). It does not, however, define the nature of the president's powers and duties as commander in chief. In fact, extensive powers pertaining to the use of military force are found in Article I, the legislative article. Most important, Congress is empowered to declare war. Constitutionally, then, the power to use military force is shared between Congress and the president. Historical practice, however, has resulted in a vast expansion of presidential authority to use force at the expense of the powers of Congress. The dominance of the president in this regard has been almost total in wartime; in times of peace, Congress has partially reclaimed the ground it lost. Nonetheless, the result has been the continual aggrandizement of presidential power.[41]

The war powers of the president are sweeping and have their basis in the Constitution, in statutory delegations of authority by Congress, and in judicial interpretations. The constitutional foundation of the president's war powers was laid early in the Civil War when Abraham Lincoln married the commander-in-chief clause to the "take care" clause.[42] As discussed in chapter 1, Lincoln used the resulting war powers to justify a wide range of actions to suppress the rebellion. These included activation of state militias, expenditure of appropriated funds for unauthorized purposes, suspension of the writ of habeas corpus in militarily insecure areas, and the imposition of a naval blockade of Confederate ports. The Supreme Court upheld the legality of the blockade in the *Prize Cases,* in which it declared that the president had a duty to defend the nation by appropriate means, including military action.[43] The refusal of the Court to overturn any of Lincoln's actions until after the war set a precedent of judicial deference that would be followed in future wars.

Lincoln's actions demonstrated that the war powers of the president extend far beyond mere military command. During World War II, the president's powers as commander in chief expanded exponentially under FDR. Among other things, Roosevelt ordered the internment of all persons of Japanese ancestry, including both naturalized and native-born U.S. citizens, who were residing in the Pacific Coast states. The Supreme Court acquiesced in this deprivation of basic civil liberties.[44] Roosevelt also created, by executive order, emergency agencies, such as the War Labor Board, and endowed them with sweeping regulatory powers and accompanying sanctions. In his most dramatic assertion of the war power, on September 7, 1942, FDR demanded that Congress repeal certain sections of the Emergency Price Control Act that constrained his powers during the national emergency. If Congress did not act by October 1, he threatened to act on his own authority. Congress responded as the president wished, thus avoiding a constitutional showdown.

Congress has further contributed to the development of the president's war powers through extensive delegations by statute. As discussed in chapter 1, during World War I, Congress enacted laws that authorized the president to regulate, requisition, and purchase a wide range of materials and products, to prohibit exports, to license trade, to censor international communications, to regulate enemy aliens in the United States, and to seize and operate the railroads. These powers were expanded during World War II through passage of legislation such as the Lend-Lease Act, which authorized the procurement and leasing of war materials to countries regarded as vital to the defense of the United States; the Emergency Price Control Act, which established the Office of Price Administration and authorized it to fix prices and ration a wide range of goods and services; and a host of other statutes. Many congressional delegations of authority to the president were open-ended and not revised or withdrawn until passage of the National Emergencies Act of 1976.

In short, once war is declared, presidential powers are vast. To ensure national survival, whatever the president says must be done is done without regard to constitutional considerations and with the acquiescence, if not full approval, of the Supreme Court and Congress. Some leading constitutional scholars have charged that the Constitution is suspended in wartime and the president becomes a de facto dictator.[45]

The president's power to use military force in peacetime, or even in periods of undeclared war, is less clear-cut. Although the Supreme Court has been reluctant to resolve questions in this area, Congress has been more assertive of its prerogatives. However, the president still has substantial responsibilities and concomitant powers to protect American lives and property abroad, discharge international obligations, and preserve national security. Constitutional language is vague, and statutory enactments are an incomplete guide to the exercise of this authority.

Following World War II, Congress and the president were united in the commitment to contain communism. The most sensitive issue during the cold war was the authority of the president to commit U.S. troops to fight abroad. On several occasions between 1945 and 1965, presidents sent U.S. forces into combat or placed them in situations that could easily lead to combat.[46] These included the Korean War, the dispatch of four divisions to Western Europe as a permanent commitment to NATO, Eisenhower's responses to Chinese pressures on Taiwan and to increased tensions in the Middle East, the 1965 intervention in the Dominican Republic, as well as the Vietnam War.

Vietnam produced the most extensive and controversial instances of presidential war making in the post–World War II era. Beginning with Truman, presidents made commitments of military aid and provided military advisers to the government of South Vietnam. By the end of 1963, more than 16,000 military advisers were in that country, many of them actively participating in combat although not formally authorized to do so. In August 1964, the Johnson administration reported a confrontation in the Gulf of Tonkin between a North Vietnamese gunboat and a U.S. destroyer. At Johnson's request, Congress passed the Gulf of Tonkin Resolution, which authorized the president to "take all necessary steps including use of armed force" to assist nations belonging to the Southeast Asia Treaty Organization (to which the United States was a signatory) in defense of their freedom. On the authority of the Constitution, the Southeast Asia Treaty, and the Gulf of Tonkin Resolution, Johnson ordered a vast increase in the strength of U.S. forces in Vietnam; by late 1967, they exceeded 500,000. He also authorized military commanders to conduct air raids against military targets in North Vietnam.[47] President Nixon extended the scope of military operations even while trying to negotiate an end to U.S. involvement in the war. In 1970, he ordered a covert invasion of Cambodia and the bombing of Laos to destroy enemy supply and staging areas, and in December 1972, he authorized the bombing of the North Vietnamese capital city of Hanoi and the major port city of Haiphong. These actions were taken without consulting Congress.

Initially, Congress backed administration efforts to contain communism in Southeast Asia through the use of military force. As the war dragged on, however, popular support began to wane, a widespread domestic protest movement began to take shape, and opposition to U.S. policy rose abroad from the country's allies and from developing nations. Many members of Congress questioned the wisdom and the legality of placing the decision to use military force entirely in the president's hands. As long as presidential use of force appeared to be successful, congressional opposition was minimal; but when the use of force appeared to be failing, or the risks increased and the costs in popular support became too great, Congress reasserted its constitutional authority to participate as an equal partner with the president in determining where and under what conditions the United States would wage war.

Americans remain sensitive to the experience with war powers during the Vietnam years. Although Congress overwhelmingly endorsed President Bush's request for authority to wage war on terrorism in September 2001, there was concern lest this be another Gulf of Tonkin resolution providing the president with a "blank check" to take whatever action he deemed necessary. As a result, the resolution included explicit reference to the War Powers Resolution and the need to observe its provisions.

The Assertion of Congressional Powers

Congress has substantial constitutional powers that enable it to claim parity with the president in shaping national security policy. As noted above, the Senate is directly involved in the treaty approval process and the confirmation of appointments; congressional action in the form of authorizations and appropriations is necessary to implement all presidential decisions that are not self-executing; and the power to declare war rests solely with Congress and implies a congressional prerogative over the use of military force. However, operational realities and a bipartisan foreign policy consensus led to presidential domination of national security policy during the cold war.

The failure of the Vietnam War—labeled by critics as a "presidential war"—ended, at least temporarily, Congress's deference to White House domination of national security policy. During the 1970s, Congress limited presidents' ability to wage undeclared war, reduced unrestrained use of executive agreements, restored the treaty as the principal means of making international agreements, reassessed its sweeping delegations of authority to presidents in past wars and emergencies, and curbed secrecy and covert activities in the conduct of foreign and military affairs.

The most important congressional attempt to reclaim powers lost or given to the executive was the War Powers Resolution of 1973. Passed over Nixon's veto, House Joint Resolution 542 provided that the president might commit the armed forces to combat only in the event of a declaration of war, specific statutory authorization, or a national emergency created by an attack on the United States or its armed forces. The resolution urged the president to consult with Congress in "every possible instance" before committing forces to combat abroad, and it required consultation after such commitment. Specifically, it required a written report to Congress within forty-eight hours of a commitment and required ending the commitment within sixty days unless authorized by Congress. The commitment could be extended for thirty additional days if the president certified to Congress that military conditions required continued use of the forces to ensure their safety. Finally, it stated that, through use of a concurrent resolution that would not be subject to presidential veto, Congress might order the disengagement of U.S. forces before the end of the first sixty days.[48]

The effectiveness of the War Powers Resolution as a congressional means of controlling presidentially initiated military action is unclear. Presidents had submitted eighty-eight reports under the resolution through September 2001 (see Table 10-1).[49] In only one of these, the rescue of the *Mayaguez,* a merchant ship that had been seized by Cambodian gunboats in 1975, did the president trigger the sixty-day clock. President Ford submitted four reports, Carter one, Reagan fourteen, George Bush seven, Clinton fifty-eight, and George W. Bush four through September 2001. Since its passage, all presidents have regarded the War Powers Resolution as an unconstitutional encroachment on their powers, and their reports have carefully avoided any acknowledgment of its constitutionality. In addition, they have been able to circumvent the intent of the resolution by not activating the sixty-day clock, by stating that they were reporting "consistent with the War Powers Resolution," and by holding that merely informing Congress meets the resolution's requirement of consultation. The position of the executive has been consistent across administrations, while Congress has been unable to formulate a "unitary position or statement of institutional interest."[50] Nor has Congress challenged the president by starting the sixty-day clock. Congress considered triggering the clock in 1983, in legislation involving the multinational force in Lebanon, but ultimately authorized U.S. participation in the force for eighteen months. This was done after an agreement was reached with the White House.[51]

President Bush's actions during the Persian Gulf War of 1990–1991 are typical of how presidents deal with the War Powers Resolution.[52] Before sending U.S. armed forces to the gulf in response to Iraq's August 2, 1990, invasion of Kuwait, Bush notified congressional leaders of the planned deployment on August 8. The next day, he sent the Speaker and the president pro tem a letter in which he stated that the report was "consistent with" the War Powers Resolution. During the next six months, there was a massive buildup of U.S. forces in the gulf area, the United States and Iraq exchanged bellicose threats, and the United Nations adopted a resolution imposing a deadline for Iraq to withdraw from Kuwait. At no point, however, did either the president or Congress begin the sixty-day countdown. Rather, the president argued that he had the authority to force Iraq to leave Kuwait without congressional approval. Nevertheless, on January 8, 1991, one week before the UN deadline, Bush asked Congress to approve a joint resolution authorizing the use of force. Congress did so four days later by votes of 52–47 in the Senate and 250–183 in the House.[53] When Bush signed the resolution, he reasserted his position that the War Powers Resolution was unconstitutional. The resolution approved on January 12, 1991, has been recognized as the functional equivalent of a declaration of war. Whether Bush weakened his position, that he already had the authority to initiate hostilities, is an unanswered question.

The effect of the War Powers Resolution on the constitutional roles of the president and Congress in making decisions about war and peace is unclear. At the very least, the legislation was a symbolic victory for Congress, serving notice that sustained military commitments outside the country could no longer be made by presidential fiat but required congressional approval and, by implication, popular support. I. M. Destler observed, "It is hard to conceive of a formula better crafted to balance the need for presidential capacity to respond quickly to foreign emergencies and the need—as a matter of right *and* effective policy—for democratic judgment on the deployment of troops in combat."[54]

However, most commentary on the War Powers Resolution has been negative. There is "growing consensus" that it "has not worked as Congress envisioned."[55] Presidents have neither consulted Congress in "any meaningful manner" nor have they sought to make the law work by invoking its provisions.[56] Instead, they have sought to circumvent it. For its part, Congress has been unwilling to challenge presidential nonresponsiveness to the War Powers Resolution, and the courts have been unwilling to intercede until it does so.[57]Michael Glennon summarized the effectiveness of the resolution: "Whatever congressional intent underlay the War Powers Resolution, any expectation that its pro-

During the Persian Gulf crisis and war in 1990–1991, George H. W. Bush (shown sharing Thanksgiving dinner with U.S. troops in Saudi Arabia) skillfully mobilized domestic and international support before using American forces against the Iraqi army.

cedures would actually lead to collective legislative-executive judgment in the war-making process was mistaken."[58] Presidential evasion, congressional acquiescence, and judicial deference have combined to accomplish this result.[59]

Can anything be said in defense of the War Powers Resolution? Congress is certainly aware of its deficiencies, as is evidenced by extensive hearings on it, frequent proposals for its amendment, and the efforts of some Republican members in 1995 to restrict U.S. support for and participation in multilateral peacekeeping operations.[60] If the resolution is so fatally flawed and revision has not been possible, why has it not been repealed?[61] The reason may be that the resolution suits congressional purposes. It "allows Congress the luxury of being politically comfortable with its decisions regarding a military action while providing a convenient forum for criticizing the President."[62] Congress can use the War Powers Resolution to force the president to end an unpopular military operation, or it can criticize presidential failure to comply with the procedural requirements of the resolution when public opinion is supportive or divided. Either way, Congress cannot lose.[63] From this perspective, the War Powers Resolution constrains presidential war making by forcing presidents to take it into account and to recognize the possibility, albeit distant, of congressional action. The resolution reminds presidents that, under the Constitution, they share with Congress the crucial decision to lead the nation into war. That Congress has not vigorously applied the War Powers Resolution or buttressed it by denying funding for military action does not mean it is of little consequence.

Tightening its language and subjecting it to Supreme Court interpretation could clarify the ambiguities surrounding the resolution, but neither Congress nor the president so far has been willing to take such action, perhaps because the outcome is uncertain. Citing as precedent the history of presidential war making, the Court could sustain the resolution. Or, noting that since it was forced on the presidency at a time of institutional weakness, it "undercuts the legitimacy of the executive branch," and thus the Court might choose to overturn it.[64]

Increased congressional participation in national security decision making may not be constitutionally mandatory, but it has become necessary on political grounds. It is somewhat ironic, however, that Congress's desire to share in making national security policy and increased knowledge and competence on the part of individual members and expanded committee staffs have not been accompanied by congressional capability to assume the added responsibility.[65] Congressional reforms during the 1970s, especially in the House, and additional changes in the 1980s further fragmented power and made it more difficult for Congress to speak authoritatively with one voice. The proliferation of subcommittees and the growing interdependence of domestic and foreign policy issues have added to the number of congressional participants in national security policy matters. Congressional staffs have grown in size and influence so that they, too, are drawn into negotiations between the branches. These developments, along with expanded pressures from interest groups and other domestic constituencies, make more elusive the achievement of interbranch consensus.

The difficulty that Congress currently faces in assuming a more active and constructive role in national security policy should not obscure its positive contributions. Among other things, Congress has curbed unrestrained presidential war making; it has forced reconsideration of extensive if not excessive overseas commitments and imposed caution on assuming new obligations; it has broadened the popular base of U.S. foreign policy; and it has instituted more careful scrutiny of agencies involved in national security. Following the exposure of the Iran-contra affair, Congress moved through its relevant committees to find the facts so that responsibility could be affixed and recommendations made for changes in procedures. In sum, Congress has expanded the base of legitimacy for foreign and military policy.

The constitutional "invitation to struggle" is still present. Congress has open to it alternative approaches for developing its national security policy role in today's complex international environment. At times it will be tempted to revert to the pattern of acquiescence in presidential domination that prevailed from World War II until 1973. On other occasions, Congress may be tempted to take matters into its own hands, because of popular pressures or distrust of the president's policies and capabilities. A third path is that of collaboration tempered by a sense of constitutional and political responsibility to be constructively critical.

A fourth path—all-out conflict—nearly erupted during the impeachment of President Clinton in December 1998. Congressional outrage nearly boiled over on the eve of the scheduled House vote on articles of impeachment. Clinton ordered an air attack on Iraq after learning of Iraq's continued failure to cooperate with UN weapons inspectors responsible for overseeing Iraq's disarmament after the Persian Gulf War. The impeachment vote was delayed for several days but not without extensive questioning of the president's motives in launching an attack that had been delayed numerous times in the past, including a month earlier. Several Republican leaders publicly spoke out against the action and expressed doubts about the president's credibility. Editorials wondered whether he was "risking lives to cling to power."[66] Even before this incident, the president's role as foreign policy leader had been highlighted throughout most of 1998. Kosovo had become a constant problem, and the administration devoted considerable effort to fashioning a common NATO plan, which was announced on January 29, 1999, the day after the Senate's failed vote on removal of the president. Similarly, Clinton's dramatic visit to China took place in June 1998, an opportunity for the president to showcase his knowledge, skill, and charm. More generally, however, the most effective way for Clinton to respond to "scandal-related attacks on himself was to seek the shelter of the presidency's gravity and responsibilities," reminding the country of just how important it was that he continue doing his job.[67] Thus, impeachment imposed enormous strains on the delicate institutional relationships essential for effective policy.

Organizing and Managing National Security

Beyond dealing with the constitutional issues and political considerations involved in national security policy, the president also confronts a formidable administrative task: organizing the presidency and the executive branch for the formulation and implementation of policy and managing the processes that have been established. The organizational task entails establishing and changing structures and processes. As the Iran-contra investigation revealed, a lax approach to these tasks can be costly.

One of the soundest observations on these problems came from the Commission on the Organization of the Government for the Conduct of Foreign Policy (the Murphy Commission). It opened its 1975 report with the observation that "good organization does not insure successful policy, nor does poor organization preclude it."[68] The commission went on to assert, however, that organizational arrangements have a continuing and powerful impact on the content of public policy and the effectiveness with which it is implemented.[69] Organization determines the level of government (national, state, or local) and the agency that will deal with a problem. Government organization performs three primary functions: it "creates capabilities" for performing tasks that are beyond the reach of individuals; it "vests and weighs particular interests and perspectives" by increasing or reducing the probability of their inclusion in decision making; and it "legitimates decisions" by ensuring that relevant parties are consulted and that decisions are made by proper authorities.[70]

Although there is no specific model to which national security organization must conform, two considerations are paramount: organization must be capable of adapting to changing events and conditions, and it must be able to accommodate the operating style of the presidents, whose constitutional roles make them the focal point of the policymaking process. Congress has enacted legislation—the National Security Act of 1947 was the most far-reaching—establishing organizational units to aid presidents in the conduct of national security policy. The principal units are the National Security Council and its staff, the departments of State and Defense, the joint chiefs of staff, and the Central Intelligence Agency. Though Congress has established these staffing units, it cannot prescribe how presidents will employ them. How they choose to manage staff, cabinet, and independent agencies is a matter totally at their discretion.

Although the National Security Council, which is the basic structure for the management of national security affairs, has remained substantially unchanged since its creation in 1947, presidents have used it in various ways. Congress established the council in response to the pressures of the cold war and in reaction, at least in part, to the administrative confusion that often characterized Franklin Roosevelt's freewheeling approach to management.

The experience of presidents since Truman substantiates Alexander George's observation that chief executives, upon taking office, must define their role in the national security policymaking system before they can design and manage the roles and relationships of other major participants in it.[71] According to conventional wisdom, the basic choice every president must make is whether to manage the system through the secretary of state and the State Department, as Truman did, or to centralize it in the White House, as Nixon did, with the national security assistant playing the major role. Failure to decide on either approach is likely to result in confusion over policy goals and lack of cohesion in policy implementation, as was the case with Clinton.

Having come to office committed to focus on the economy and domestic problems, as noted above, Bill Clinton paid little attention to the organizational and operational aspects of the national security process during his first term. He staffed the major positions with "brokers and bureaucrats" and reserved the important decisions for himself.[72] Neither the national security assistant and the NSC staff nor the secretary of state and the State Department were clearly in charge. The result was a series of ad hoc reactions to crises, problems, and domestic pressures.

Clinton's second term was different, if not demonstrably better. Foreign policy became more prominent, a common pattern for second-term presidents who are intent on leaving a legacy by looking for success abroad. And Clinton did a great deal of just that, logging the most trips and the most miles of any president in history.[73] He also shuffled his aides by bringing Madeleine Albright into State

Figure 10-1   Presidential Management Styles and National Security Assistant's Roles

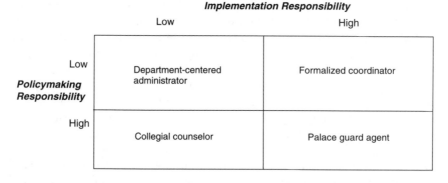

Source: Cecil V. Crabb Jr. and Kevin V. Mulcahy, *American National Security: A Presidential Perspective* (Pacific Grove, Calif.: Brooks/Cole, 1991), 189.

and William Cohen into Defense. Albright seemed to take the lead in defining a clearer strategic direction, and the administration engaged in sustained efforts to bring peace to the Middle East and the Balkans, regions of traditional animosities that have defied generations of diplomatic effort. Organizationally, the most important Clinton departure was creation of the National Economic Council (NEC), a structure designed to coordinate economic strategy much the way the National Security Council has done for military and foreign policies. Under its first director, Robert Rubin, the NEC became an important player in economic policymaking, both domestic and international. Clinton enhanced the importance of economic issues in foreign policy by insisting that the treasury secretary, the head of the NEC, and the director of the Office of Management and Budget attend NSC meetings.[74]

Cecil Crabb and Kevin Mulcahy have developed a typology for analyzing presidential management of national security that is based on responsibility for policymaking and for implementation of policy.[75] They have identified four presidential management styles—department-centered, formalized, collegial, and palace guard—with accompanying roles for the national security assistant—administrator, coordinator, counselor, and agent (see Figure 10-1). Presidents, such as Truman, who have limited interest in the formation and implementation of foreign policy, deputize the secretary of state to act and speak for them (while making final decisions themselves), and rely primarily on the State Department for analysis and implementation have a *department-centered* style. The national security assistant, in the corresponding role of administrator, acts primarily as a high-level staff aide who supervises the advisory process and facilitates the presentation of views to the president. He or she does not act independently or function as a primary policy adviser. Adm. Sidney Souers, Truman's executive secretary for the National Security Council, functioned in this capacity.

Dwight Eisenhower looked to the national security bureaucracy—the Departments of State and Defense and the intelligence community—for policy recommendations, carefully examined a wide range of proposals and plans, and retained control over policymaking and implementation. He exemplifies the *formalized* management style. His national security assistant, Robert Cutler, functioned as a coordinator, whose principal task was to facilitate the making of national security policy by defining options and managing the flow of ideas and information. A coordinator also reviews policy, but the president and the secretary of state make the final decisions. Although no subsequent president has fully followed Eisenhower's management example, some academics still praise its advantages while others criticize its lack of flexibility.[76]

The *collegial* management style, typified by Kennedy and Johnson, involves an informal national security process. In this model, the president operates with ad hoc working groups, tends to distrust the national security bureaucracy, and seeks to centralize decision making in the White House, with the NSC staff performing independent analysis and policy review functions. The counselor role of the national security assistant, exemplified by McGeorge Bundy under Kennedy and Walt Rostow in the Johnson administration, entails a close personal relationship with the president in which the assistant is a major policy adviser and acts to safeguard the president's interests. Clinton's ad hoc management of national security policy most closely approximated the collegial style. The role of his national security assistants, Anthony Lake and later Sandy Berger, was to keep foreign policy from overshadowing the president's focus on economic and domestic affairs while not appearing weak and ineffectual.[77]

In the *palace guard* management style, associated with Richard Nixon, the president centralizes policymaking in the White House and maintains a tight rein on implementation. The State Department and other units of the national security bureaucracy are "virtually excluded" from an active policymaking role and "relegated" to implementing the decisions of the president and the national security assistant.[78] Nixon's national security assistant, Henry Kissinger, acted as the president's agent. In that capacity, he directed the policymaking process, served as the president's closest policy adviser, and on occasion actively implemented policy by conducting negotiations with foreign governments.

Crabb and Mulcahy argue that experience since 1947 reveals that neither the administrator nor the agent roles for the national security assistant are to be recommended. The administrator role is likely to be ineffective unless the president and the secretary of state are capable, hands-on administrators. The agent role carries the risk that national security assistants may go into business for themselves, acting without presidential knowledge or approval as Reagan claimed was the case with Adm. John Poindexter and his assistant, Lt. Col. Oliver North, in the Iran-contra affair. By implication, Crabb and Mulcahy suggest that the president adopt either the collegial management or formalized style for national security. Whether presidents choose the coordinator or counselor role for their national security assistant should be determined by their management style. The president also must exercise care to select a national security assistant whose personality is compatible with the designated role.[79] Jimmy Carter encountered considerable difficulty in managing national security because of conflict and competition between Cyrus Vance, the secretary of state, and Zbigniew Brzezinski, the national security assistant. At least part of the problem stemmed from Carter's apparent failure to recognize that Brzezinski was an ambitious, assertive individual more suited to the role of agent than that of administrator, which Carter apparently wished him to play.

Reagan, who vacillated in establishing a preferred management style and in defining the national security assistant's role, experienced trouble formulating a coherent foreign policy and implementing it effectively. That six individuals served as national security assistant during the Reagan administration highlights the instability in the president's management of national security. These problems became most evident during Reagan's second term, when turmoil prevailed in the relationship between Secretary of State George Shultz and the NSC staff. One national security assistant, Robert McFarlane, acted as a policy advocate rather than as an honest broker coordinating policymaking by departments and agencies, and he even carried out special missions for the president. Mulcahy describes the system as a "collegial arrangement for the management of foreign affairs with the White House acting as umpire."[80] An unanswered question is whether any conceivable system for managing foreign policy could have overcome Reagan's deliberate disengagement from policymaking and his lack of interest in and concern with policy implementation.

As noted earlier, George Bush was a hands-on president, concerned with details and actively involved in negotiations with foreign leaders. Bush's collegial management style prescribed a counselor's role for Brent Scowcroft, his national security assistant, who organized the national security process in a manner that most resembled Lyndon Johnson's.[81] He made little use of a formal process to identify and analyze options and relied instead on a small group of intimate advisers. There was little evidence of conflict within Bush's national security inner circle, and it received high marks for its cohesiveness and competence.[82]

Bill Clinton's participation in the national security policymaking process during his first term was episodic and nonsystematic.[83] In the early going, no one else was authorized to speak with a strong and forceful voice for the administration.[84] The result was haphazard decision making and the appearance of weakness and inconstancy in policy, an early image that Clinton was unable to overcome.

President George W. Bush's challenge will be to harmonize many powerful voices. At the outset of his administration, it was difficult to determine how the national security team would function. With several high-visibility, assertive personalities in cabinet positions (such as Donald Rumsfeld and Colin Powell), a palace guard style seemed least likely. A collegial style could emerge, as much the product of Vice President Cheney's considerable influence as that of Condoleeza Rice, the national security assistant. Perhaps the most likely style is a variation of the formalized system established by Eisenhower that accommodates strong cabinet secretaries within a White House–centered staff system. Such a system would also be consistent with the president's preference to delegate extensively but reserve final judgment for himself. As in all other administrations, the product would be a combination of the president's personal style, the qualities of the principal advisers assembled to help him, and the president's confidence in their advice.

Internal struggles are inevitable, and Washington observers watch for such policy divisions. Secretary of Defense Rumsfeld provided an early example when he appeared to adopt a unilateral policy to punish China in response to its downing a U.S. spy plane. The Pentagon announced that exchanges between the United States and the Chinese military would be fully suspended, a position that had been rejected in Security Council discussions. Rumsfeld was later forced to retreat from the policy, but it led to speculation about whether a major rift was developing between "hard-liners" in the Pentagon and "doves" in the State Department, with the NSC staff being divided.[85] Similarly, speculation persisted on whether Bush would seek advice from his father, the former president, whose international experience was far greater than his son's.[86]

The Bush team functioned smoothly during its first real test, the terrorist attack on the World Trade Center and the Pentagon. Both President Bush and Secretary of State Powell were out of town at the time of the attack, but they returned to Washington to become central figures in fashioning the national response. Under the danger of further attacks, Vice President Cheney and National Security Adviser Rice coordinated initial responses from the Presidential Emergency Operations Center, a nuclear attack shelter in the basement of the White House. This twenty-first century attack was met with twenty-first century government organization: the president remained in contact with the White House team throughout the crisis by secure telephone and even convened a teleconference meeting of the National Security Council. Upon his return to Washington, the president met regularly with the NSC and coordinated action with the FBI and the Transportation Department, as well. In short, the system appeared to work smoothly, reaching several critical decisions about both tactics and strategy and projecting an image of calm determination after a jittery first day.[87]

Conclusion

National security is the president's most important substantive policy responsibility, presenting major and complex problems of leadership and management. For the nation, the effectiveness of foreign and military policy in preserving and protecting its sovereignty and independence is of paramount interest. To a large extent, that interest stands or falls on every president's performance. Presidents must interpret and exercise their powers within constitutional and statutory limits. It is imperative that they consult with Congress, because to be effective they must have congressional cooperation. Yet, operational realities require that presidents be accorded ample latitude to act independently and often secretly. Tensions inevitably arise between Congress and the president over national security policy, although Barbara Hinckley suggests that the conflict between them is primarily symbolic and is staged to convince the public that both institutions are alert and active and that policymaking is democratic.[88] However, the tasks involved are primarily executive in nature, and executive control of foreign and military policy persists in spite of Congress's major constitutional role.[89] The Constitution and political prudence require "shared power and balanced institutional participation" as norms in national security decision making.[90]

Perhaps the most important lesson in this regard is that since 1945 most of the nation's successful foreign policies—the Truman Doctrine, the Marshall Plan, NATO, the Panama Canal treaty, arms control, and the Persian Gulf War—"have been adopted by Congress and the people after meaningful debate."[91] For the most part, the major failures—FDR's Yalta agreements with Stalin, the Bay of Pigs invasion, the Vietnam War, and the Iran-contra affair—have been initiated and implemented unilaterally by presidents.

Presidents also discover that resolution of national security issues must be coordinated with the handling of domestic and economic concerns because policy domains increasingly overlap and solutions cannot be compartmentalized. Presidents no longer can fashion national security policies without regard to domestic political and economic pressures; they need flexibility in action and to protect their personal political stakes. The principal institutional means that modern presidents have used to manage national security—a White House-centered national security system directed by a national security assistant heading a professional NSC staff—has served this purpose, but often at the expense of long-range continuity and cohesion in policy. The alternative organizational strategy—a State Department-centered system with the secretary of state playing a dominant policymaking and advisory role—has attracted support from some students of national security policy and from political outsiders as a means of obtaining the desired degree of continuity and integration. Presidents since Eisenhower, however, have found such an arrangement unsuitable to their style of operation.

In the emerging international system, the United States remains the world's major power. Its people and the rest of the world are deeply affected by the policy preferences, personality, and operating style of its presidents. The statecraft they employ and how they view and exercise national power will critically affect the shape of that system.

NOTES

1. "Authorization for Use of Military Force," Joint Resolution adopted September 14, 2001, *Washington Post,* September 15, 2001, A4.

2. Remarks of George W. Bush in a news conference September 13, 2001, as reported by eMediaMillWorks, www.washingtonpost.com.

3. The "two presidencies" thesis holds that presidents enjoy relatively greater success with Congress in foreign than in domestic policy. According to Terry Sullivan,

modern Republican and Democratic presidents have had approximately equal success with foreign policy proposals, but Democratic administrations have done better with domestic policy because of their party's longtime domination of Congress. See Sullivan, "A Matter of Fact: The 'Two Presidencies' Thesis Revitalized," in *The Two Presidencies: A Quarter Century Assessment,* ed. Steven A. Shull (Chicago: Nelson Hall, 1991), 143–157. On the rise of partisan and ideological bickering over foreign policy issues in Congress during the 1990s, see James M. McCormick, Eugene R. Wittkopf, and David M. Dana, "Politics and Bipartisanship at the Water's Edge: A Note on Bush and Clinton," *Polity* 30 (fall 1997): 133–149.

4. James Chace, "Is a Foreign Policy Consensus Possible?" *Foreign Affairs* (fall 1978): 30.

5. Strobe Talbot, *The Russians and Reagan* (New York: Vintage Books, 1984).

6. The most comprehensive and informative account of the Iran-contra affair is by Theodore Draper, *A Very Thin Line: The Iran-Contra Affairs* (New York: Hill and Wang, 1991). For the perspective of two participants in the congressional hearings, see William S. Cohen and George J. Mitchell, *Men of Zeal* (New York: Viking, 1988). The role of the CIA and its director William Casey receive careful attention by Bob Woodward in *Veil: The Secret Wars of the CIA, 1981–1987* (New York: Simon and Schuster, 1987). Also essential to a full understanding of Iran-contra is the report of the Tower Commission (John Tower, Edmund Muskie, and Brent Scowcroft). President's Special Review Board, *Report of the President's Special Review Board* (Washington, D.C.: Government Printing Office, 1987).

7. John Felton, "Secret Weapons Sale Stirs Up Legal Questions," *Congressional Quarterly Weekly Report,* November 22, 1986, 2929.

8. Terry L. Deibel, "Bush's Foreign Policy: Mastery and Inaction," *Foreign Policy* (fall 1991): 20–22; Steven V. Roberts, "The Second Sin of George Bush," *New Leader,* March 11–15, 1991, 3.

9. Daniel P. Franklin and Robert Shepard, "Analyzing the Bush Foreign Policy." Paper presented at the annual meeting of the American Political Science Association, Washington, D.C., August 29–September 1, 1991, 2–3.

10. Deibel, "Bush's Foreign Policy," 3–4.

11. David C. Hendrickson, "The Recovery of Internationalism," *Foreign Affairs* (September–October 1994): 26–43. For similar criticisms, see Richard N. Haas, "Paradigm Lost," *Foreign Affairs* (January–February 1995): 43–58 and Larry Berman and Emily O. Goldman, "Clinton's Foreign Policy at Midterm," in *The Clinton Presidency: First Appraisals,* eds. Colin Campbell and Bert A. Rockman (Chatham, N.J.: Chatham House, 1995), 290–324.

12. William J. Clinton, *A National Security Strategy of Engagement and Enlargement* (Washington, D.C.: Government Printing Office, 1994).

13. Berman and Goldman, "Clinton's Foreign Policy," 302–303.

14. William J. Clinton, *A National Security Strategy for a New Century* (Washington, D.C.: The White House, October 1998). For commentary, see Emily O. Goldman and Larry Berman, "Engaging the World: First Impressions of the Clinton Foreign Policy Legacy," in *The Clinton Legacy,* eds. Colin Campbell and Bert A. Rockman (New York: Chatham House, 2000); and James M. McCormick, "Clinton and Foreign Policy: Some Legacies for a New Century," in *The Postmodern Presidency: Bill Clinton's Legacy in U.S. Politics,* ed. Steven E. Schier (Pittsburgh: University of Pittsburgh Press, 2000).

15. Every president since Gerald Ford had enjoyed authority to negotiate trade agreements and have them considered by Congress following a procedure that limits amendments and sets a deadline for action. This authority lapsed in 1993 and was extended for a period into 1994. Clinton proposed its continuation on several occasions but confronted opposition in the House, where it died in 1998 with Democrats overwhelmingly opposing him. See Raymond Tatolovich and John Frendreis, "Clinton, Class and Economic Policy," in *The Postmodern Presidency,* 49–50.

16. Carl M. Cannon, "First Denials, Then Spin," *National Journal,* May 29, 1999, 1467–1468; Miles Pomper, "The China Policy Syndrome: U.S. Struggles to See Clearly," *CQ Weekly,* March 13, 1999, 625–626; Editorial, "China Without Illusions," *New York Times,* March 14, 1999, A14.

17. John Maggs, "Reading Tea Leaves," *National Journal* May 19, 2001, 1486.

18. James Kitfield, "The New World Disorder," *National Journal* May 19, 2001, 1476.

19. Ibid., 1474–1481. Also see James Kitfield, "In Foreign Policy, Bush II Is Like Reagan I," *National Journal,* March 31, 2001, 963–965.

20. See the comments of Lee Hamilton, former member of the House, D-Ind., as reported by Charlie Cook, "China Crisis Halts Slide of Bush's Poll Ratings," *National Journal,* April 21, 2001, 1186.

21. Edward S. Corwin, *The President: Office and Powers,* 4th ed. (New York: New York University Press, 1957), 171.

22. Ibid.

23. Joseph E. Kallenbach, *The American Chief Executive* (New York: Harper and Row, 1966), 485.

24. Corwin, *The President,* 179.

25. Ibid., 185.

26. Ibid., 213.

27. Ibid.; Kallenbach, *The American Chief Executive,* 502.

28. The treaty-making process entails three distinct stages: negotiation, Senate approval, and ratification by the president. Contrary to popular understanding, the Senate does not ratify a treaty—it approves the treaty negotiated by the president. The president may refuse to sign, that is, to ratify, a treaty approved by the Senate, either because of amendments or reservations or because it was negotiated by a previous administration.

29. Cecil V. Crabb Jr. and Pat M. Holt, *Invitation to Struggle: Congress, the President, and Foreign Policy,* 4th ed. (Washington, D.C.: CQ Press, 1992), 6.

30. Harold Hongju Koh argues, however, that Congress should create by statute its own procedures for determining when international agreements should be submitted to the Senate for approval. See Koh, *The National Security Constitution: Sharing Power after the Iran-Contra Affair* (New Haven: Yale University Press, 1990), 195.

31. *Goldwater v. Carter,* 444 U.S. 996 (1979). Although the Court based its decision on the recognition of foreign governments, the case has been interpreted as authorizing unilateral presidential breaking of treaties in accordance with their terms.

32. Koh, *The National Security Constitution,* 43.

33. David E. Sanger and Steven Lee Myers, "Bush Seeks Missile Shield Along with Nuclear Cuts; Calls '72 Treaty Outdated," *New York Times,* May 2, 2001, A1.

34. Michael R. Gordon, "U.S. Weighing Future of Strategic Arms Pacts," *New York Times,* May 9, 2001, A1.

35. The intelligence community consists of the Central Intelligence Agency; the National Security Agency; the Bureau of Intelligence and Research in the Department of State; the Defense Intelligence Agency; the intelligence offices of the army, navy, air force, and marine corps; and intelligence offices in the departments of Energy and Treasury. Crabb and Holt, *Invitation to Struggle,* 25.

36. Woodward, *Veil,* chap. 25.

37. Pamela Fessler, "Gates Confirmed to Lead CIA into Post-Soviet Era," *Congressional Quarterly Weekly Report,* November 9, 1991, 3291–3292.

38. Aldrich Ames was the Soviet branch chief of the CIA's counterintelligence group. From 1985 through 1993, he sold sensitive information, including the names of the entire network of spies that the United States had established in the Soviet Union during the cold war, to the KGB. Most of those agents were executed. For accounts of the Ames case, see Tim Weiner, David Johnson, and Neil A. Lewis,

Betrayal (New York: Random House, 1995); and David Wise, *Nightmover* (New York: HarperCollins, 1995).

39. Donna Cassata, "Congress Jumps to CIA's Aid in Its Quest for Identity," *Congressional Quarterly Weekly Report,* January 7, 1995, 41–42.

40. Clark subsequently proved to be a quick learner and a person of great administrative ability. Within a year, he was receiving praise from many of his former critics.

41. Corwin, *The President,* chap. 6; Arthur M. Schlesinger Jr., *The Imperial Presidency* (Boston: Houghton Mifflin, 1989), chaps. 1–7.

42. Corwin, *The President,* 229.

43. *Prize Cases,* 67 U.S. (2 Black) 635 (1863).

44. *Korematsu v. United States,* 323 U.S. 214 (1944).

45. Clinton Rossiter, *Constitutional Dictatorship: Crisis Government in Modern Democracies* (New York: Harcourt, Brace, 1963).

46. Such actions have numerous precedents, including Jefferson's dispatch of the navy to stop the Barbary pirates from seizing U.S. merchant ships and holding their crews for ransom, and Theodore Roosevelt's contribution of U.S. Marines to the international expeditionary force that put down the Boxer Rebellion in China in 1904.

47. Larry Berman, *Planning a Tragedy: The Americanization of the War in Vietnam* (New York: Norton, 1982). For a comparative analysis of how Eisenhower and Johnson dealt with pressures to intervene militarily in Vietnam, see John P. Burke and Fred I. Greenstein, *How Presidents Test Reality: Decisions on Vietnam, 1954 and 1965* (New York: Russell Sage Foundation, 1989).

48. The Supreme Court's decision in *Immigration and Naturalization Service v. Chadha,* 462 U.S. 919 (1983), which held that the legislative veto was unconstitutional, made this provision inoperative. Congress subsequently substituted a joint resolution for the concurrent resolution; however, the former is subject to a presidential veto.

49. Richard F. Grimmett, "War Powers Resolution: Presidential Compliance," *CRS Issue Brief for Congress,* Congressional Research Service. Library of Congress, Washington, D.C., March 21, 2001.

50. Robert A. Katzman, "War Powers: Toward a New Accommodation," in *A Question of Balance: The President, Congress, and Foreign Policy,* ed. Thomas E. Mann (Washington, D.C.: Brookings, 1990), 55.

51. Ibid., 66.

52. Joshua Lee Prober, "Congress, the War Powers Resolution, and the Secret Political Life of 'a Dead Letter,' " *Journal of Law and Politics* 7 (1990): 177–229.

53. Carroll J. Doherty, "Bush Is Given Authorization to Use Force Against Iraq," *Congressional Quarterly Weekly Report,* January 12, 1991, 65–70.

54. I. M. Destler, "The Constitution and Foreign Affairs," *News for Teachers of Political Science* (spring 1985): 16.

55. Katzman, "War Powers," 35; Thomas M. Franck, "Rethinking War Powers: By Law or by 'Thaumaturgic Invocation'?" *American Journal of International Law* 83 (1989): 768.

56. John M. Hillebrecht, "Ensuring Affirmative Congressional Control Over the Use of Force: Two Proposals for Collective Decision Making," *Stanford Journal of International Law* 26 (1990): 511.

57. See *Lowry v. Reagan,* 676 F. Supp. 333 (D.D.C. 1987), and *Dellums v. Bush,* 752 F. Supp. 1141 (D.D.C. 1990). In *Lowry,* the district court rejected the request of 110 members of Congress that it issue a declaration that President Reagan was required to file reports under the War Powers Resolution concerning two incidents in the Persian Gulf. The court held that it could not act because Congress had not acted on the issue. In *Dellums,* the court rejected the request of 45 Democratic members of Congress that it enjoin President George Bush from conducting military operations in the

Persian Gulf without a declaration of war by Congress. The court held that the issue was not ripe for decision because a majority of Congress had not sought relief and the executive had not committed itself to a course of action that made war imminent.

58. Michael J. Glennon, *Constitutional Diplomacy* (Princeton: Princeton University Press, 1990), 102–103.

59. Koh, *The National Security Constitution.*

60. Dick Kirschten, "A Contract's Out on U.N. Policing," *National Journal,* January 28, 1995, 231–232.

61. On June 7, 1995, the House rejected, by a 217–201 vote, a proposal by Rep. Henry Hyde, R-Ill., to repeal the War Powers Resolution. Carroll J. Doherty, "House Approves Overhaul of Agencies, Policies," *Congressional Quarterly Weekly Report,* June 10, 1995, 1655.

62. Prober, "Congress, the War Powers Resolution," 229.

63. Ibid., 223–226, 229.

64. Destler, "The Constitution and Foreign Affairs," 15.

65. James L. Sundquist, *The Decline and Resurgence of Congress,* (Washington, D.C.: Brookings, 1981), 270.

66. William Safire, "On Impeachment Eve," *New York Times,* December 17, 1998, A31. On the comments of Senate Majority Leader Trent Lott and House Whip Tom Delay, see R. W. Apple Jr., "No Reservoir of Credibility," *New York Times,* December 17, 1998, A1, A15. On the air attacks more generally, see Francis X. Clines and Steven Lee Myers, "Biggest Attack Since '91 War—Britain Gives Support," *New York Times,* December 17, 1998, A1, A15.

67. Peri E. Arnold, "Bill Clinton and the Institutionalized Presidency," in *The Postmodern Presidency,* 35.

68. *Report of the U. S. Commission on the Organization of the Government for the Conduct of Foreign Policy* (Washington, D.C.: Government Printing Office, 1975), 1.

69. Also see Burke and Greenstein, *How Presidents Test Reality,* esp. chap. 13.

70. Graham T. Allison and Peter Szanton, "Organizing for the Decade Ahead," in *Setting National Priorities: The Next Ten Years,* ed. Henry Owen and Charles Schultze (Washington, D.C.: Brookings, 1976), 232–233.

71. Alexander L. George, *Presidential Decisionmaking in Foreign Policy: The Effective Use of Information and Advice* (Boulder: Westview, 1980), 146.

72. Burt Solomon, "When It Comes to Geopolitics . . . Who's Painting the Big Picture?" *National Journal,* March 5, 1995, 550–551.

73. Emily O. Goldman and Larry Berman, "Engaging the World," 228.

74. Ibid., 244. For additional discussion of the National Economic Council, see Raymond Tatalovich and John Frendreis, "Clinton, Class and Economic Policy," in *The Postmodern Presidency,* 2000.

75. Cecil V. Crabb Jr. and Kevin V. Mulcahy, *American National Security: A Presidential Perspective* (Pacific Grove, Calif.: Brooks/Cole, 1991), chap. 9. The discussion relies on Crabb and Mulcahy.

76. See most recently the following minidebate: Fred I. Greenstein and Richard H. Immerman, "Effective National Security Advising: Recovering the Eisenhower Legacy," and Arthur Schlesinger Jr., "Effective National Security Advising: A Most Dubious Precedent," *Political Science Quarterly* 115 (fall 2000): 335–351.

77. Elizabeth Drew, *On the Edge* (New York: Simon and Schuster, 1994), 28, 138.

78. Crabb and Mulcahy, *American National Security,* 189–190.

79. Ibid.

80. Kevin V. Mulcahy, "The Secretary of State: Foreign Policymaking in the Carter and Reagan Administrations," *Presidential Studies Quarterly* (spring 1986): 296.

81. Burt Solomon, "Making Foreign Policy in Secret May Be Easy, but It Carries Risks," *National Journal,* January 12, 1991, 90–91.

82. Larry Berman and Bruce W. Jentelson, "Bush and the Post–Cold-War World: New Challenges for American Leadership," in *The Bush Presidency: First Appraisals,* ed. Colin Campbell and Bert A. Rockman (Chatham, N.J.: Chatham House, 1991), 99–103.

83. Solomon, "When It Comes to Geopolitics"; Solomon, "Clinton's Fast Break on Cuba . . ." Or Foreign Policy on the Fly, *National Journal,* September 3, 1995, 2044–2045. On the early Clinton record, see Bruce W. Nelan, "The No-Guts, No-Glory Guys," *Time,* November 22, 1993, 48–50 and Bert A. Rockman, "Leadership Style and the Clinton Presidency," in *The Clinton Presidency,* 352–355.

84. Mortimer B. Zuckerman, "The Limits to Leadership," *U.S. News and World Report,* September 12, 1994, 96.

85. John Maggs, "Reading Tea Leaves," *National Journal* May 19, 2001, 1488–1489.

86. Jane Perlez, "Fatherly Advice to the President on North Korea," *New York Times* June 10, 2001, A1.

87. David E. Sanger and Don Van Natta Jr. "In Four Days, a National Crisis Changes Bush's Presidency," *New York Times,* September 16, 2001, A1.

88. Barbara Hinckley, *Less than Meets the Eye: Foreign Policy Making and the Myth of the Assertive Congress* (Chicago: University of Chicago Press, 1994), 175, 193.

89. Paul E. Peterson, "The International System and Foreign Policy," in *The President, the Congress, and the Making of Foreign Policy,* ed. Paul E. Peterson (Norman: University of Oklahoma Press, 1994), 12–14.

90. Koh, *The National Security Constitution,* 207.

91. Stephen E. Ambrose, "The Presidency and Foreign Policy," *Foreign Affairs* (winter 1991–1992): 136.

SUGGESTED READINGS

Berman, Larry. *Planning a Tragedy: The Americanization of the War in Vietnam.* New York: Norton, 1983.

Burke, John P., and Fred I. Greenstein. *How Presidents Test Reality: Decisions on Vietnam, 1954 and 1965.* New York: Russell Sage Foundation, 1991.

Crabb, Cecil V., Jr., and Pat M. Holt. *Invitation to Struggle: Congress, the President, and Foreign Policy.* 4th ed. Washington, D.C.: CQ Press, 1992.

Crabb, Cecil V., Jr., and Kevin V. Mulcahy. *American National Security: A Presidential Perspective.* Pacific Grove, Calif.: Brooks/Cole, 1991.

Draper, Theodore. *A Very Thin Line: The Iran-Contra Affairs.* New York: Hill and Wang, 1991.

Fisher, Louis. *Congressional Abdication on War and Spending.* College Station: Texas A&M University Press, 2000.

———. *Presidential War Power.* Lawrence: University Press of Kansas, 1995.

George, Alexander L. *Presidential Decisionmaking in Foreign Policy: The Effective Use of Information and Advice.* Boulder: Westview, 1980.

Glennon, Michael J., and J. William Fulbright. *Constitutional Diplomacy.* Princeton: Princeton University Press, 1990.

Henderson, Philip G. *Managing the Presidency: The Eisenhower Legacy—From Kennedy to Reagan.* Boulder: Westview, 1988.

Henkin, Louis. *Constitutionalism, Democracy and Foreign Affairs.* New York: Columbia University Press, 1992.

Hinckley, Barbara. *Less than Meets the Eye: Foreign Policy Making and the Myth of the Assertive Congress.* Chicago: University of Chicago Press, 1994.

Johnson, Loch K. *Bombs, Bugs, Drugs, and Thugs: Intelligence and America's Quest for Security.* New York: New York University Press, 2000.

Koh, Harold Hongju. *The National Security Constitution: Sharing Power after the Iran-Contra Affair.* New Haven: Yale University Press, 1990.

Mann, Thomas E., ed. *A Question of Balance: The President, the Congress, and Foreign Policy.* Washington, D.C.: Brookings, 1990.

Peterson, Paul E., ed. *The President, the Congress, and the Making of Foreign Policy.* Norman: University of Oklahoma Press, 1994.

President's Special Review Board (Tower Commission). *Report of the President's Special Review Board.* Washington, D.C.: Government Printing Office, 1987.

Schlesinger, Arthur M., Jr. *The Imperial Presidency.* Rev. ed. Boston: Houghton Mifflin, 1989.

Spanier, John, and Steven W. Hook. *American Foreign Policy Since World War II.* 15th ed. Washington, D.C.: CQ Press, 2000.

11   GEORGE W. BUSH: TRANSITION TO POWER AND FIRST 180 DAYS

THE CIRCUMSTANCES SURROUNDING THE contested 2000 presidential election did not make the new president's transition to power an easy task. Uncertainty about who had won dogged both candidates from the early evening of election day (November 7). The television networks first declared Al Gore the winner at 7:48 P.M. EST—even before all polls were closed—based on exit surveys of voters leaving election precincts. By 10:00 P.M. the networks were forced to retract their declaration and announce instead that the election was too close to call. In the early morning hours of November 8, George W. Bush gained momentum. Shortly after 2:00 A.M. the networks began calling the election again—this time for Bush. Prompted by the networks' projections, Gore telephoned Bush to concede around 2:40 A.M., but almost immediately it appeared that the networks had erred again by prematurely calling the outcome. New returns showed that the election was

Chief Justice William Rehnquist swears in George W. Bush as the 43rd president on January 20, 2001.

still in doubt, and by 3:00 A.M. the networks had declared the race too close to call. The new returns, coupled with the realization that Florida law required an automatic machine recount when the election margin was so close, led Gore to telephone Bush a second time, shortly after 3:15 A.M., to withdraw his concession.[1] Those confounding hours paved the way for weeks of uncertainty about which of the two candidates would actually take office.

As discussed in the preceding chapters, the controversy centered on the state of Florida. A Bush victory in the electoral college depended on winning Florida's electoral votes, but his initial margin of victory in Florida's popular vote was only 1,768 votes. Florida law requires an automatic machine recount whenever a margin of victory is less than or equal to one-half of 1 percent of the vote cast, as was the case here.[2] Florida law also allows the candidates to request manual recounts in selected counties. Such counties are compelled to comply with a candidate's request by recounting a sample of the county (at least three precincts or 1 percent of the total vote cast).[3] If the manual recount of the sample indicates an error that could affect the outcome of the election, Florida law requires that the canvassing board "shall . . . manually recount all ballots" in that county.[4] Florida law further states that "no vote shall be declared invalid or void if there is a clear indication of the intent of the voter as determined by the canvassing board."[5] This last requirement caused trouble. Leaving a determination of voter intent to individual canvassing boards meant that different counties could establish different standards for deciding which votes counted (just as different counties used different types of ballots and ballot-counting devices). Trying to set standards for determining voter intent led to great debate in the following weeks.

Gore exercised his right to request manual recounts in four counties in south Florida where there were many reports of voting irregularities. Bush did not exercise his right to call for recounts. In the counties where Gore requested recounts, voters had registered their choices on paper punchcards. These ballots required voters to punch through and dislodge perforated disks (called "chads") on the cards. Machines could count only those punchcards whose chads had been completely dislodged. Florida's requirement that ballots showing "a clear indication of the intent of the voter" be counted proved especially difficult to implement in counties using these punchcards. Attempts to establish standards about which ballots counted led to fierce debate. For example, did a chad clinging to a punchcard by only one of its four corners signify a clear intent of the voter to punch out that chad and thereby cast a vote, even though the machine could not count it? What if the chad clung to two corners instead of just one? Or what if the chad was clearly indented but not detached from the punchcard at any point? Should these "hanging," "pregnant," or "dimpled" chads count? Which, if any, constituted "a clear indication of the intent of the voter"? Florida law compelled canvassing boards to confront such questions but set no uniform standard for answering them. As such, Florida law was similar to the laws of a majority of the rest of the states. Ironically a Texas bill signed into law by Gov. George W. Bush had established a lenient standard for determining the intent of the voter. The Texas standard would have counted almost all of the contested ballots that were rejected by machines in Florida, even though the Bush team argued against embracing such a lenient standard there.[6]

Confronted with the daunting task of determining voter intent, county boards labored long and hard to produce an accurate manual recount that complied with Florida law. By November 15 the statewide mechanical recount was completed, but manual recounts were still under way in three of the four contested counties. Based on the recount so far, Bush's lead had dwindled to only 327 votes. That day, before the manual recount could be completed, Katherine Harris—the Florida secretary of state and cochair of the Florida Bush campaign— intervened and stopped the recount. She construed Florida law to require that all nonabsentee ballot votes must be reported within one week of the election and refused to permit an extension to complete the manual recount that Florida law allowed.[7] Democrats charged that she had misconstrued the law for partisan reasons, and argued that if Florida law allowed a manual recount, it should surely allot time to complete it. Despite the outcry, Harris certified Bush the winner on November 18. With the addition of absentee ballots (themselves the object of contention because Republican officials had added missing information to some absentee ballot applications so that they could be counted), Bush's margin of victory stood at 930 votes.[8]

Democrats appealed to the Florida court system for a clarification of Florida law about the deadline that Harris had imposed. On November 21 a unanimous Florida Supreme Court held that Harris had misinterpreted Florida law and that manual recounts must continue. The court said that the statutory language about the deadline was ambiguous and contradictory and that it was more important to prevent the disenfranchisement of legal voters than to adhere to a rigid one-week deadline for counties to report votes.[9]

Just as Democrats had questioned whether Secretary of State Harris, as cochair of the Bush campaign, had been impartial, Republicans questioned whether the Florida Supreme Court—all of whose members had been appointed by Democratic governors—had been unbiased. The Bush team appealed the ruling to the U.S. Supreme Court, arguing that the Florida court's decision that the counting of all legal votes was more important than the one-week deadline for tallying votes had illegally changed election procedures after election day. The Gore team responded that the Florida court simply had done what all courts do: it had interpreted the law (which, in light of the statutes' ambiguous and contradictory wording, especially needed clarification by a court). A unanimous Supreme Court ruled on December 4 that the Florida court should more clearly explain the basis for its ruling, but it also concluded that so long as the Florida court demonstrated on remand that its decision was based strictly on Florida law, the decision could stand.[10]

In the meantime, Gore formally contested in Florida court the state's official election results as certified by Harris. He lost at the trial court level but won on appeal to the Florida Supreme Court on December 8. By a vote of 4 to 3, the

Florida court reinstated the votes from the manual recount that Harris had refused to accept and ordered a statewide recount of all "undervotes" (those ballots rejected by machines because a chad was not completely dislodged).[11] The court's ruling again reduced Bush's margin of victory—this time to only 154 votes. It began to look as if Gore might win after all. A statewide recount began but was halted by the U.S. Supreme Court with a stay issued December 9. In *Bush v. Gore,* decided December 12 and discussed at length in chapter 7, the Court stopped all further recounts. In so doing, it effectively declared that Bush had won the presidential election.[12]

The official count of the electoral votes came on January 6, 2001. Bush won by 271 electoral votes to Gore's 267. Gore, however, won the popular vote nationwide by a margin of nearly 540,000 votes. This total was almost five times John F. Kennedy's margin of victory over Richard Nixon in 1960 and some 30,000 votes more than Nixon's over Hubert Humphrey in 1968. Bush became only the fourth president in history to take office despite losing the popular vote (the others were John Quincy Adams in 1824, Rutherford B. Hayes in 1876, and Benjamin Harrison in 1888).

By the time the official count of electoral votes had taken place, it was only two weeks until inauguration day. One side effect of the lingering uncertainty about the outcome of the election was to make more difficult the transition to the Bush presidency.

The Truncated Transition

A normal transition to power proved impossible in the wake of the 2000 presidential contest because there was no clear winner until weeks after election day. The federal government provides funds and office space for presidents-elect to mount their transitions. In 2000 the government allocated $5.3 million in transition funds.[13] It also provided a two-story, ninety-thousand-square-foot office building in Washington, D.C., one capable of holding 540 people and equipped with three hundred computers and phones. The building even had its own zip code: 20270.[14] The General Accounting Office, however, refused to release the money or open the office space to either of the candidates until the outcome of the election had been resolved. This refusal was a problem for both candidates. After all, the transition period is an essential and—even under the best of circumstances—*small* window of opportunity to establish a new White House team and prepare an agenda for the critical first hundred days of the new administration.

James P. Pfiffner has emphasized that presidents must "hit the ground running" after they take the oath of office. As Pfiffner explains, presidents "want to take advantage of the 'mandate' from the voters and create a 'honeymoon' with Congress." Early victories in implementing their policy goals "may provide the 'momentum' for further gains. This desire to move fast is driven by the awareness that power is fleeting."[15] Likewise, Paul Light, as discussed in chapter 8, has argued that a president's "political capital" decreases over time. As political capital is expended, a president's influence and ability to accomplish his goals is diminished. That is why presidents are so eager to move quickly to implement their policy goals. Their eagerness to accomplish their goals, though, comes at a time when they and their staffs are new to their jobs and relatively inexperienced. Thus, Pfiffner notes that a president's "greatest opportunity to work his will comes when he has the least ability to do it effectively; this is what makes planning an effective transition so critical."[16] Quite simply, the ability to move quickly and effectively depends on a well-organized transition that gets key players in position in a timely way and sets the stage for early policy planning.

Without knowing the outcome of the election, and without federal funds and office space to help them, both candidates were hampered in their transition planning. A concern for public relations also limited the extent to which either Bush or Gore could proceed—at least publicly—with transition planning in the days immediately after the election. Choosing a cabinet and making other transition plans before being declared the winner could look presumptuous, even unseemly, but failing to do so could handicap the new administration. The task was particularly daunting for the Republicans because they had been out of power for eight years and had an estimated three thousand positions to fill.

On November 27, three weeks after election day, Dick Cheney—Bush's running mate and transition head—held a news conference to announce that the Bush team would open a privately funded transition headquarters in McLean, Virginia. As a result of Harris's certification of Bush as the winner of the Florida election, Bush had declared himself "president-elect." Although court rulings were still pending, Cheney chastised the Democrats for not conceding. "Vice President Gore and Senator Lieberman are apparently still unwilling to accept the outcome," he told reporters. "That is unfortunate in light of the penalty that may have to be paid at some future date if the next administration is not allowed to prepare to take the reins of government."[17]

In the coming week the Bush team moved forward with transition plans in a very public way. As ABC News reported, the tactic was "both practical and strategic" in that Bush wanted "to create a sense of inevitability about his accession to the White House."[18] In an interview with the *Washington Post* on January 11, 2001, Bush explained his motives: "I thought it was important that people know that I was beginning to think about putting a White House staff together. Dick [Cheney] and I were meeting all the time about the Cabinet. I wanted to show movement, I wasn't trying to say I am the president."[19] On November 28 Gore announced that *both* he and Bush, "in the interests of the nation," should proceed with transition planning and activities. While Cheney and retired general Colin Powell prepared to meet with Bush to discuss transition plans, Gore met with his running mate, Sen. Joseph Lieberman of Connecticut, and his transition director, Roy Neel.[20] By December 7 Bush was able to declare: "When it comes to a White House staff, I've pretty much made up my mind on who should serve," although he said that official announcements of staff and cabinet appointments would not come until the election dispute had been resolved.[21] That resolution came with the Supreme Court's decision in *Bush v. Gore* on December 12 and with Gore's concession on December 13. The Bush team received the keys to the official government transition offices from the General Services Administration at a news conference on December 14. On January 20, 2001—the same day Bush was sworn in as president—the Senate confirmed seven of Bush's fourteen cabinet appointments, including Colin Powell as secretary of state and Donald Rumsfeld as secretary of defense.

Considering the circumstances, the Bush transition went smoothly—more smoothly, in fact, than Bill Clinton's, which got off to a remarkably slow start after the 1992 election. Clinton took six weeks to make *any* appointments, and it took a full ten months after he was sworn in for all of his appointees to be confirmed by the Senate.[22] Taking a different approach, Bush seemed to have his major appointments lined up within four weeks of election day, although he held back any cabinet announcements until December 16—three days after Gore conceded and just under six weeks after the election.

If Clinton's transition stood out for its problems, Bush's did so for its discipline in the face of major obstacles.[23] Part of the problem for the Clinton transition team came from the inexperience of Clinton and his aides, most of whom had never before served in government. In contrast, Bush had witnessed his father's transition first hand and was surrounded with aides who had a great deal of government experience. He also benefited from the leadership of Dick Cheney, who had participated in five transitions (Nixon's in 1969, Ford's in 1974, Reagan's in 1981, and George H. W. Bush's in 1989). That experience paid off. Despite a mild heart attack just two weeks after election day, Cheney played an active role as head of the transition team. He knew the importance of a good transition. "The quality of a transition has a direct bearing on the quality of the administration that follows it," he told reporters.[24] He also knew that time was of the essence. Thus, behind-the-scenes transition planning had started immediately after election day. That is why, when the Bush team got the keys to the transition office, the president-elect was ready to name most of his cabinet members. Extensive work had already been done on lower-level appointments as well, although the sheer number of appointments that had to be confirmed by the Senate (about one thousand in all) meant that many departments would be working with bare-bones staff for some time to come. Still, despite all the obstacles in its path, the Bush team managed its time more efficiently and effectively than Clinton had.

David Gergen, himself a veteran of many Republican transitions who went on to serve in the Clinton White House, said in an interview with ABC News that the Bush team was "the most disciplined, most focused" of any since Reagan.[25] This helped it to avoid the most serious mistakes associated with transitions. According to Charles O. Jones, these mistakes include: (1) failing to establish leadership, (2) mismanaging time and opportunity, (3) misjudging or mishandling appointments, and (4) failing to relate properly with Congress.[26] Avoiding pitfalls in all of these areas, Bush received high marks. He reached out to members of both parties in Congress, managed his time effectively, and established leadership of the transition effort from the start.

Although several of Bush's nominees came under fire—notably his choice of John Ashcroft for attorney general—the only nomination that was derailed was that of Linda Chavez to be labor secretary, and none was clearly mishandled. Bush did expend a good deal of political capital to secure Senate confirmation of Ashcroft, but in the end the appointment helped to solidify his conservative base. The Chavez withdrawal was due to Chavez herself rather than to mishandling by the Bush team. Chavez had withheld damaging information from the new administration: an illegal Guatemalan immigrant, Marta Mercado, had lived in her home for two years. During that time Chavez paid Mercado to perform household chores. In doing so, Chavez may have violated federal laws against harboring and employing undocumented immigrants. The real problem, however, stemmed from the fact that Chavez not only had withheld this information but also had been at the forefront of efforts to derail Bill Clinton's nomination of Zöe Baird to be attorney general in 1993. Chavez had opposed Baird because she had hired an illegal immigrant as a nanny and had failed to pay Social Security taxes for her.[27] At that time Chavez was sharply critical of Baird in public appearances. "I think most of the American people were upset . . . that she hired an illegal alien," Chavez said of Baird on the PBS *McNeil/Lehrer NewsHour.* "That was what upset them more than the fact that she did not pay Social Security taxes."[28] When Chavez herself came under attack in 2001 for actions similar to Baird's, she decried the "game of search and destroy" that forced her to withdraw.[29] Despite the embarrassment, the Bush team cut its losses quickly with Chavez's withdrawal and nominated another woman for the post, Elaine Lan Chao.

In the end, Bush was praised for the diversity of his cabinet and other high-level appointments (see Figure 11-1). Clinton had made diversity a high priority when making appointments—so much so that it became an overriding (and ultimately distracting) theme of his transition.[30] Bush achieved diversity with less fanfare. Clinton initially had appointed women or minorities to eight of fourteen cabinet positions: four women, three African Americans, and one Hispanic.[31] Bush also named eight women or minorities to the cabinet: three women, two African Americans, one Hispanic, and two Asian Americans (had Chavez not withdrawn, he would have had two Hispanics and one Asian American in the cabinet). In addition, he appointed Condoleeza Rice, an African American woman, to the key post of national security adviser and Christine Todd Whitman as head of the Environmental Protection Agency.[32] He also fulfilled his promise to name a Democrat to the cabinet—Norman Mineta as transportation secretary—and appeased both the moderate and conservative wings of his party with his other appointments.

Despite a successful transition, many observers continued to have low expectations for a Bush presidency. Could a president who came to power without winning the popular vote and after the bitter contest for Florida's electors really

Figure 11-1   The Bush cabinet

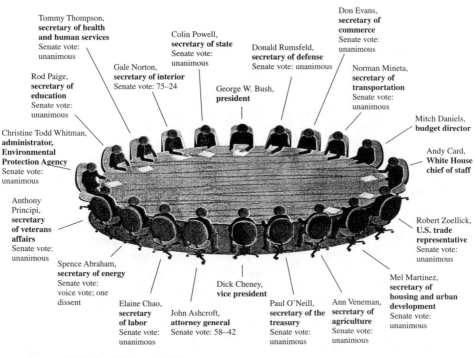

Tommy Thompson, **secretary of health and human services** Senate vote: unanimous

Colin Powell, **secretary of state** Senate vote: unanimous

Donald Rumsfeld, **secretary of defense** Senate vote: unanimous

Don Evans, **secretary of commerce** Senate vote: unanimous

Rod Paige, **secretary of education** Senate vote: unanimous

Gale Norton, **secretary of interior** Senate vote: 75–24

George W. Bush, **president**

Norman Mineta, **secretary of transportation** Senate vote: unanimous

Christine Todd Whitman, **administrator, Environmental Protection Agency** Senate vote: unanimous

Mitch Daniels, **budget director**

Andy Card, **White House chief of staff**

Anthony Principi, **secretary of veterans affairs** Senate vote: unanimous

Robert Zoellick, **U.S. trade representative** Senate vote: unanimous

Spence Abraham, **secretary of energy** Senate vote: voice vote; one dissent

Dick Cheney, **vice president**

Mel Martinez, **secretary of housing and urban development** Senate vote: unanimous

Elaine Chao, **secretary of labor** Senate vote: unanimous

John Ashcroft, **attorney general** Senate vote: 58–42

Paul O'Neill, **secretary of the treasury** Senate vote: unanimous

Ann Veneman, **secretary of agriculture** Senate vote: unanimous

Source: *USA Today*, February 1, 2001.

Note: Sitting around the table at a typical Bush cabinet meeting are 20 people. This illustration shows who they are, what they do, where they sit, and their confirmation vote.

bring the nation together and successfully lead it—especially when that president had as little government experience as Bush?

Taking the Reins: The First Hundred Days

Partly due to low expectations, Bush got off to a successful start in his first few weeks in office. The negative attention focused on outgoing president Bill Clinton—including concerns about his pardon of fugitive financier Marc Rich, criticism of his plans to rent expensive office space in New York City, and questions about the propriety of taking White House furniture and other gifts as he left town—also helped the new president.

Though not a great orator, Bush delivered a well-written inaugural address with poise. Inaugurations are an opportunity to bring the nation together and legitimize power relationships. Bush stressed the need for unity and civility as a way of healing the wounds of the election:

America, at its best, matches a commitment to principle with a concern for civility. A civil society demands from each of us good will and respect, fair dealing and forgiveness. . . . Civility is not a tactic or a sentiment. It is the determined choice of trust over cynicism, of community over chaos. And this commitment, if we keep it, is a way to shared accomplishment.[33]

As Bush turned to the task of governing, he followed the examples of John F. Kennedy and Ronald Reagan. Like Kennedy, Bush came to power after a controversial election and with no clear mandate, and he followed Kennedy's example of not letting these obstacles stand in his way. After his victory in 1960 Kennedy downplayed talk that he lacked a mandate. "The margin is narrow, but the responsibility is clear," Kennedy said. "There may be difficulties with Congress, but a margin of only one vote would still be a mandate."[34] Kennedy's rhetorical flourish rang especially true for Bush because he faced a Senate evenly divided between Democrats and Republicans. Bush knew all too well that he might have to rely on Vice President Cheney to cast tie-breaking votes in his constitutional role as president of the Senate. Thus, he made a special effort to reach out to Democrats on Capitol Hill. On February 2 Bush attended a private policy retreat of Senate Democrats—the first president to attend such a meeting held by members of the opposing party. Already he had met with more than one hundred Democratic members of Congress as part of a "charm offensive." Two days later he attended a House Democratic retreat. At the same time he followed Kennedy's lead and proceeded confidently as if he *did* have a mandate.

Bush also took a page from Reagan's playbook by planning a simple, clear-cut legislative agenda for his first hundred days. David Gergen, who played a major role in Reagan's transition (and went on to serve as his director of communications), prepared a study for Reagan that compared the first hundred days of every president since FDR. The evidence showed that successful presidents immediately established a clear and simple agenda. Those who did not set a clear-cut agenda, like Jimmy Carter, hurt themselves badly. Thus, Reagan's legislative agenda for 1981 focused on just four main issues.[35] Bush followed that example by focusing initially on a short list of priorities that included education reform, faith-based initiatives, tax cuts, and military preparedness (including a missile defense system).[36] The theme of his first week in office was education reform, followed by a week on each of the other issues.[37] Energy policy soon became a high priority as well, but it was clear that the tax-cut proposal would dominate the first hundred days. (*See chapter 9 for additional discussion of the tax cut.*)

Initially it seemed that there was not strong support for such a massive cut—especially given Democrats' insistence throughout the campaign that the cut would give too much to the rich and too little to those who most needed it. But a string of events helped Bush. His call for a tax cut in his inaugural address was the biggest applause line in the speech—a sign of the direction in which the political winds were blowing. On January 25 Federal Reserve chair Alan Greenspan reversed his prior stand on tax cuts and—to the dismay of Democrats—said that a substantial cut would promote economic growth. The statement undermined the Democrats' argument that a huge tax cut would deplete the budget surplus and ultimately threaten entitlement programs like Social Security.

Emboldened, Bush sent his tax cut proposal to Congress on February 8, before he had even unveiled his budget plan (which he did not release until April 9). Then, in his address to a joint session of Congress on February 27, the president deftly made his proposal of $1.6 trillion in tax cuts look like the compromise position. As discussed in chapter 3, Bush began by saying: "Some say my tax plan is too big." He knew that Democrats would interrupt to applaud (as they did). "Others say it is too small," he continued, giving Republicans a chance to respond with applause of their own. Aware that he had set himself up perfectly, Bush concluded: "I respectfully disagree. The plan is just right." That led to the biggest applause of all. The next day he set out on the first of a series of campaigns around the country to promote the tax cut and urge the American people to put pressure on Congress to pass it. "The surplus is not the government's money," he said. "The surplus is the people's money, and I'm here to ask you to join me in making that case to any federal official you can find."[38]

Republicans secured House passage of the tax plan on March 8 but in the process angered Democrats, who felt that Republicans were unwilling to compromise. House Minority Leader Richard Gephardt (D-Mo.) said that the way in which the Republicans had secured House passage of the plan proved that "bipartisanship is over."[39] The tax plan then moved to the Senate, where it faced stiffer opposition. Although Democratic senator Zell Miller of Georgia said that he would vote to support the tax cut—an important boost for Bush—the first hundred days passed without final action on the issue. Indeed, they passed without *any* major legislative victories.

In the opening days of the Bush administration, some pundits predicted—and many Democrats feared—that Bush would follow Bill Clinton's tactic of "triangulation": moving to the center and co-opting the opposition party's issues. Much of the centrist rhetoric in Bush's inaugural address and his first speech to a joint session of Congress suggested that strategy. His first fifty days in office were particularly successful—the closest he came to a true "honeymoon," culminating in House passage of the tax cut on the forty-eighth day. He had delivered an impressive address to Congress in February, media coverage was largely favorable, and his Gallup poll approval rating had risen from 57 percent when he first took office to 63 percent in a poll taken March 5–7. Democrats had reason to worry. Then came a series of distractions and missteps in March, accompanied by what many characterized as a swerve to the right on policy issues.

The first distraction came early that month, when Cheney was hospitalized for an "urgent" angioplasty to clear a blocked artery in his heart. Then the administration took a series of actions that gave credence to the charge that it was hostile to the environment. On March 13 Bush reversed his campaign pledge to require new power plants to reduce carbon dioxide emissions. To some, this date marked the end of the Bush honeymoon. The turnabout angered many moderate Republicans who had rallied to the pledge during the campaign, and made them question whether Bush was the moderate he had claimed to be. Suddenly other early actions taken by Bush—like his first policymaking act as president, an executive order banning U.S. aid to international groups that support abortion—were viewed in a new light. Rather than being seen as moves to appease the conservative wing of his party, they were seen as elements of Bush's true agenda. His reversal on carbon dioxide, his renunciation of the Kyoto treaty on global warming, and his eagerness to drill for oil in the Arctic National Wildlife Refuge not only angered environmentalists but also gave fuel to the argument that Bush was catering to the interests of big business (who had given so much money to his campaign).

The biggest misstep came on March 20, when the Bush administration revoked a regulatory action put in place by President Clinton that reduced the level of arsenic in drinking water. Symbolically the move was a disaster. How could the president support arsenic in the drinking water? "It is baffling—just baffling," said Senate Minority Leader Tom Daschle (D-S.D.). "We're going to have to put warning labels on water bottles."[40] Sen. Hillary Clinton (D-N.Y.) said that Bush's charm offensive had turned into a "harm offensive."[41] No matter that the action was apparently a bureaucratic decision by the Environmental Protection Agency, one that seemed to catch White House officials, who claimed they had not been sufficiently consulted about the decision, off guard.[42] It followed on the heels of other reversals of Clinton initiatives, including the repeal of workplace safety regulation. Democrats had multiple issues to attack the president with. "Five times in the last eight days a president who pledged compassionate conservatism has given us environmental disasters, public health threats, and special interest favors," intoned Sen. Dick Durbin (D-Ill.). "Ronald Reagan tried to tell us ketchup was a vegetable, [and] now George W. Bush is trying to tell us arsenic is a flavor enhancer in our drinking water."[43]

Bush's meeting with German chancellor Gerhard Schroeder on March 29 provided another opportunity for critics to highlight the administration's stand on global warming and its support for the controversial missile defense plan. European countries were distressed by both stands and angry at what was described as Bush's "Lone Ranger–style foreign policy—announce first, consult with allies later."[44] European nations also were concerned by the president's lack of experience in foreign affairs. When he departed from a prepared script on U.S.-Taiwanese relations in an interview on ABC's *Good Morning America* on April 25, he inadvertently "rewrote decades of careful ambiguity on U.S. help for Taiwan against China."[45] Asked if the U.S. had an obligation to defend Taiwan, Bush said: "Yes, we do, and the Chinese must understand that." Pushed on whether such a defense would be backed up by the full force of the U.S. military, Bush said the U.S. would do "whatever it took to help Taiwan defend herself."[46] Administration officials scrambled to clarify the president's remarks and assert that they signaled no change in policy.

On the domestic front, the introduction of a campaign finance bill that Bush opposed by Sen. John McCain, a fellow Republican from Arizona, also took the spotlight off the president's agenda. The Senate debated the plan for two weeks in March. As Bush attempted to steer attention back to his proposed tax cut, another distraction intervened: a diplomatic standoff with China over the collision of a U.S. navy surveillance plane and a Chinese fighter jet over the South China Sea on April 1. As discussed in earlier chapters, the Chinese jet crashed and the U.S. plane made an emergency landing in China. For eleven days media attention was riveted to the standoff. Would China release the U.S. crew? China eventually did. In the end Bush earned high marks for his handling of the crisis, but the administration again found itself off message.

As the press marked the end of the first hundred days, the administration downplayed its missteps, saying they were "part of the newness of governing."[47] Cheney and White House Chief of Staff Andrew Card went on the television talk shows to praise the president for bringing "civility" back to Washington. The president marked the occasion by hosting a lunch for more than two hundred members of Congress from both parties.[48] Media coverage was mixed. Stories noted the lack of legislative accomplishments but also gave the president high marks for the staff he had assembled. Most important, public opinion remained high: 62 percent approval, according to a Gallup poll taken April 20–22. Rather than judging the president after the first hundred days, White House officials suggested that the press use 180 days as its benchmark.

The Next Eighty Days

As the Bush administration moved through the month of May, it seemed to be gathering steam. The economic downturn had helped the administration build support for its proposed tax cut. Many began to see the cut as a way to help jump-start the economy. Although the president's original proposal had not provided immediate tax relief, modifications were made to allow refunds as soon as the legislation passed. On May 23 the Senate finally joined the House in approving Bush's tax cut by a vote of 62 to 38. Twelve Democrats joined all fifty Republicans in voting for a $1.3 trillion cut—slightly less than the $1.6 trillion that Bush had asked for. Although a conference committee still had to iron out differences between the House and Senate versions of the bill, it looked as if a tax cut would be ready for Bush's signature by the end of the week.[49] This achievement was a huge victory for the president.

News of the Senate action, though, was sidelined by a stunning development. James M. Jeffords, a moderate Republican senator from Vermont, planned to defect from his party and become an independent.[50] Though the Senate was evenly divided between Democrats and Republicans, Republicans had controlled the chamber since Bush had taken office because of Vice President Cheney's tie-breaking vote. Now, as a result of Jeffords's switch, Democrats would control the Senate. The shift meant more than just a Democratic majority. It meant a transfer of leadership from Senate Majority Leader Trent Lott (R-Miss.) to Senator Daschle and a corresponding shift to Democratic control of committees and committee assignments.[51] Suddenly the president's ability to implement his agenda seemed seriously undermined.[52]

Jeffords's defection and his justification for it triggered a renewed round of stories about Bush's policy swerve to the right. "I became a Republican not because I was born into the party," Jeffords explained, "but because of the kind of fundamental principles that . . . many Republicans stood for: moderation, tolerance, fiscal responsibility." But increasingly, he said, he found himself at odds with the party:

I understand that many people are more conservative than I am, and they form the Republican Party. Given the changing nature of the national party, it has become a struggle for our leaders to deal with me and for me to deal with them. Indeed, the party's electoral success has underscored the dilemma that I face within the party. In the past, without the presidency, the various wings of the Republican Party in Congress have had some freedom to argue and influence and ultimately shape the party's agenda. The election of President Bush changed that dramatically.[53]

Other moderate Republicans also sounded the alarm. Senator Olympia J. Snowe of Maine said that the defection "should be a wake-up call for our party's leaders that the voices of moderate Republicans must be welcomed and respected."[54] As noted in chapter 8, Senator McCain was even more pointed: "Tolerance of dissent is the hallmark of a mature party, and it is well past time for the Republican Party to grow up."[55] Although many blamed Lott for Jeffords's defection, the switch was an embarrassment to Cheney, who had served as the administration's chief liaison with the Senate.[56] He had attended the Senate Republican caucus's weekly meetings on a regular basis and according to one account was "the administration's chief negotiator and dealer" on Capitol Hill.[57] Yet, as the *New York Times* put it, Jeffords "got away without anyone in the administration noticing that he was heading out the door."[58]

Ever since Cheney's strong performance in the vice presidential debate against Sen. Joseph Lieberman in the 2000 election campaign and his key role in the transition, many had viewed Cheney as the power behind the throne in the Bush administration.[59] When he took office in January 2001, Cheney assumed more responsibilities than any previous vice president. He chaired the president's budget review board, thus assuming primary responsibility for the federal budget. He played a central (and unprecedented) role in national security policy, attending every major meeting of the National Security Council and being one of a select group that had a final say in national security policy. He chaired a task force that undertook a major review of U.S. energy policy and was a driving force behind a similar review of U.S. defense needs that was led by his friend and colleague Secretary of Defense Donald Rumsfeld.[60]

Cheney came to office with a great deal of experience in government. He had worked in the Nixon administration as a special assistant to Rumsfeld, who was then the director of the Office of Economic Opportunity. Rumsfeld went on to be a White House counsel to Nixon and later an assistant to President Gerald

Ford when Nixon resigned. Both times Rumsfeld moved, Cheney followed him. Under Ford, Rumsfeld served as secretary of defense, and Cheney became White House chief of staff. After Ford lost the 1976 presidential election, Cheney ran for Congress, winning a Wyoming House seat in 1978 that he held until 1989, when President George H. W. Bush named him secretary of defense. Cheney briefly contemplated a run for the presidency after Bush's defeat in 1992, but he decided instead to become the chief executive of Halliburton, a Fortune 500 energy services company specializing in the development of oil and gas production and known as the largest oil-drilling provider in the world.

George W. Bush relied heavily on this experience. Paul Light, who wrote a book about the vice presidency,[61] said that to compare Cheney with other vice presidents "is to diminish his real influence. He's really a chief of staff, the senior cabinet secretary, the chairman of the kitchen cabinet, the president's best friend and mentor, all rolled into one."[62] Even Ken Duberstein, Reagan's former chief of staff, noted the unparalleled influence, saying it was "the first time in our history we've had a president and a prime minister"—a suggestion that Bush was the titular leader but that Cheney was the real one.[63] But after the Jeffords defection, Cheney's luster began to wane. Again, a series of missteps compounded the situation.

President Bush's perceived shift to the right on policy, his stands on environmental issues, and the charge that he was catering to big business focused negative attention on Cheney. As one of the administration's chief policy architects, Cheney was seen as helping to push Bush to the right. With Jeffords's defection, some questioned that move. But most of the negative press centered on Cheney's role in developing the administration's energy policy and his close ties to the oil industry.

For some twenty years Cheney had touted the idea of drilling for oil in Alaska. Now, as head of the Bush administration's task force on energy policy, he served as a lightning rod for criticism of the idea. Critics also complained that Cheney, a former oil executive, had too much power over energy policy. They noted that when he left Halliburton to join the Republican ticket in 2000, the company had given him close to $20 million in cash and $10 million in stock options.[64] As head of the energy policy task force, "every decision that Mr. Cheney's team makes about access to new energy supplies will have a direct bearing on the company."[65] Cheney fueled the impression that his task force had received undue influence from the oil industry by refusing to disclose whom his group had consulted when writing its report on energy issues (such as domestic oil exploration).[66]

In June the General Accounting Office (GAO)—the investigative arm of Congress—launched an investigation into the task force and issued a "demand letter" instructing Cheney to disclose the information.[67] It was the first time since the creation of the GAO in 1921 that the office had issued such a letter to a vice president. The standoff pitted U.S. Comptroller General David M. Walker, head of the GAO and a Republican who had worked in the Reagan administration, against the White House. On August 3 Cheney refused to honor the demand letter, making it likely that the GAO would take legal action against him.[68] As Walker put it, Cheney's attorneys were "engaged in a broad-based, frontal assault on our statutory authority. We cannot let that stand."[69]

Energy policy and the GAO were not Cheney's only problems. He also had drawn criticism for holding a reception for hundreds of Republican donors at the vice president's residence—an action that drew comparisons with Bill Clinton's fund-raising tactics.[70] Then in late June he had another health scare. Doctors implanted a pacemaker equipped with a sophisticated defibrillator that could administer an electric shock to the heart if it went into a chaotic rhythm. It was Cheney's third major heart-related procedure since the November election.[71] This time news accounts did not make him sound quite as indispensable to the Bush administration as they had before.

At the same time, Bush's Gallup approval rating had dropped to a new low. A Gallup poll conducted June 28–July 1 showed the president's approval rating at 52 percent, ten points lower than his high in April and five points below his first approval rating on taking office. His disapproval rating was also high: 34 percent. Even fellow Republicans who normally were sympathetic to Bush began to express concern about the administration.[72] Other events also seemed to under-mine elements of the Bush agenda. Falling fuel prices dampened the urgency for some of the administration's energy proposals.[73] Talk of an energy crisis no longer rang true. Even California found itself facing a *surplus* of energy.[74] There was also increased talk that the federal budget surplus would not be as big as expected. Some predicted a return to deficits and a possible need for the gov-ernment to dip into the Medicare surplus.[75]

But as Congress moved toward its August recess, Bush achieved a few key vic-tories that helped him to secure his footing. On August 1 the Republican-con-trolled House passed his energy package (including a provision that would allow drilling in the Arctic National Wildlife Refuge).[76] The plan still had to be passed by the Senate—a more difficult prospect—but at least it had survived the first major hurdle. At the same time, the president struck a deal with Rep. Charlie Nor-wood (R-Ga.), a former dentist and the major architect of a patients' bill of rights that the president previously had threatened to veto. The compromise caught the bill's cosponsors by surprise. Both of the other House sponsors—Republican Greg Ganske of Iowa and Democrat John D. Dingell of Michigan—rejected the com-promise, deeming it worse than no legislation at all. But after bitter debate the House passed the measure on August 2 by a vote of 218 to 213.[77]

The White House negotiations with Norwood that led to the compromise, dis-cussions that were followed by Bush's surprise appearance in the White House briefing room with Norwood on August 1 to announce the deal, were viewed as a triumph for the president.[78] Days earlier Norwood's position had seemed irrec-oncilably at odds with the president's. Thus, as Dan Balz of the *Washington Post* put it, the deal "was the political equivalent of pulling a rabbit out of a hat for the president."[79] The bill still had to be reconciled with the version passed by the Senate—a potentially tough road—but Bush had managed to avoid what would have been a damaging defeat in the Republican-controlled House. In the fickle world of Washington opinion, Bush seemed to be in charge again.

Senate rejection on August 2 of Sheila Gall, Bush's nominee to head the Consumer Product Safety Commission, served as a reminder that the Democratic-controlled Senate would remain an obstacle for the president. Although the president's Gallup approval rating rose slightly to 56 percent in a poll conducted July 19–22, an ABC News/*Washington Post* poll released August 1 showed that 54 percent of the respondents felt that Bush did not understand "the problems of people like you."[80]

Still, as Congress recessed and the president prepared for his August vacation, the White House made the most of its victories. In a Rose Garden ceremony on August 3 to tout his accomplishments, Bush—surrounded by his cabinet—said: "Together with Congress, we're proving that a new tone, a clear agenda, and active leadership can bring significant progress to the nation's capital. We're ending deadlock and drift, and making our system work on behalf of the American people."[81] In fact, an analysis of roll-call votes released by Congressional Quarterly (CQ) the day before the president's remarks showed that partisanship had not decreased under Bush's watch and actually may have increased. Party unity votes in the Senate had risen from 48.6 percent in 2000 to 64.1 percent under Bush—the highest level in the six years that CQ had analyzed such votes. Party unity votes in the House also increased—from 43 percent in 2000 to 45.4 percent—a rate similar to those of previous years.[82]

But hovering behind the president's last-minute victories and his continued call for a "new tone" in Washington were the words of Richard Neustadt, who almost a half-century earlier had stressed the importance to presidential power of bargaining and persuasion.[83] Neustadt's admonition remained true, but as summer progressed, renewed divisiveness emerged as the budget surplus evaporated. In April the White House Office of Management and Budget had projected a $281 billion surplus for the fiscal year. By September it was predicting a surplus of only $158 billion—all but $1 billion of which was part of Social Security. It seemed inevitable that the government would have to dip into the Social Security surplus to pay for government programs. Suddenly everyone was asking who was responsible for losing the surplus. Amid the finger-pointing, a Gallup poll conducted September 7–10 showed the president's approval rating again slipping to a new low—this time down to 51 percent.[84] Media commentators questioned whether Bush could find a defining moment to legitimize his leadership and rally support for his policies.

Then, as the president promoted education reform in Florida on September 11, the biggest terrorist attack in U.S. history occurred in New York and the Washington area. Terrorists hijacked four U.S. passenger jets, crashing two into New York's World Trade Center and one into the Pentagon in Arlington, Virginia, across the Potomac River from the nation's capital. The fourth—presumably headed for a target in Washington—crashed in a rural part of Pennsylvania after the passengers tried to overpower the hijackers. The ensuing collapse of the trade

The moment that changed the Bush presidency: On the morning of September 11, 2001, White House chief of staff Andrew H. Card, Jr., informs the president that a second plane has struck the World Trade Center in New York.

center and the thousands of deaths caused by the terrorists galvanized the country and gave Bush his defining moment. He became, overnight, a war president.

"War has been waged against us by stealth and deceit and murder," Bush said September 14 in remarks at the National Cathedral observing the National Day of Prayer and Remembrance. "This nation is peaceful, but fierce when stirred to anger. This conflict has begun on the timing and terms of others. It will end in a way, and at an hour, of our choosing."[85] In his weekly radio address the next day the president stressed the enormity of what lay before him: "Victory against terrorism will not take place in a single battle, but in a series of decisive actions against terrorist organizations and those who harbor and support them. We are planning a broad and sustained campaign to secure our country and eradicate the evil of terrorism."[86]

President Bush's approval rating skyrocketed. A Gallup poll conducted September 13 showed it at 86 percent—up an astonishing thirty-five points in less than a week and only three points below the highest approval rating in Gallup history (89 percent for Bush's father during the Persian Gulf War). The Gallup Organization called it "the highest rally effect for any president in the past half century."[87] Congress also rallied around the president, showing a degree of unity unprecedented in recent memory. With only one dissenting vote in the House, Congress passed a joint resolution authorizing the president to "use all necessary and appropriate force" to respond to the terrorist attacks.[88] Congressional leaders of both parties said that they stood "shoulder-to-shoulder" with the president.

The event altered Bush's relationship with the rest of the world. The president who had seemed determined to focus on domestic problems and, in his first months in office, had sometimes been perceived as insensitive to U.S. allies, now had to build a worldwide coalition against terrorism.[89] In remarks to reporters on September 13, Bush acknowledged that the focus of his administration had changed—waging a war on terrorism was now his first priority.[90] In the immediate aftermath of the attacks, the world supported the United States. For the first time in its history, NATO invoked Article 5 of its charter, declaring that an attack on one member of the alliance would be considered an attack on all members. In other actions large and small, people around the world demonstrated their support for the United States: Palestinian leader Yasser Arafat gave blood, hundreds of thousands rallied at a candlelight vigil in Germany, and British officials played the "Star Spangled Banner" during the changing of the guard at Buckingham Palace.

In his remarks at the National Cathedral, Bush reminded his listeners that "adversity introduces us to ourselves." It also helped to re-introduce him to the nation. Until then, doubts had remained about the legitimacy of his election and even about his capacity to govern. But as R. W. Apple Jr. wrote in the *New York Times,* Bush's response to the national crisis helped to change that situation: "You could almost see him growing into the clothes of the presidency."[91] Of course, sustained leadership would be needed in the days ahead to reaffirm that newfound legitimacy. But as the president and his aides settled back to work, with Congress and the nation at least temporarily behind him—and with his political capital replenished—it seemed as if the next hundred days of his administration might count as his first.

Although the extent to which Bush ultimately would succeed or fail was not known, the newly declared war on terrorism reminded us that presidents cannot govern single-handedly. That much, at least, the Framers intended, and that much remains a constant of the otherwise changing and changeable presidency.

NOTES

1. CBS News issued an eighty-seven-page report on its Web site, www.cbsnews.com, that provided a detailed chronology of what happened at that network November 7–8. See Terry Jackson, "CBS Details Election Call Breakdown," *Miami Herald,* January 6, 2001, 20A. Among the growing number of accounts of that night is Jake Tapper, *Down and Dirty: The Plot to Steal the Presidency* (Boston: Little, Brown, 2001), 23–40.

2. Florida statute 102.141(4).

3. Florida statute 102.166(4).

4. Florida statute 102.166(5).

5. Florida statute 101.5614(5).

6. Gerald M. Pomper, "The Presidential Election," in *The Election of 2000,* ed. Gerald M. Pomper (New York: Chatham House, 2001), 129.

7. Florida statutes 102.111 and 102.112 seemed to contradict each other. The former said that county returns not received by the Department of State on the seventh day following the election "shall be ignored," though the latter said that they "may be ignored." Either interpretation could have validated Harris's decision to ignore returns from counties that had not completed manual recounts, although an argument could have been made that both provisions applied only to normal machine-tabulated results.

8. An extensive study by the *New York Times* showed that many flawed absentee ballots were counted and that Florida's counties were inconsistent in the standards they used to count the ballots—to the advantage of Bush. Thus, although "arbitrary and disparate treatment" that might have helped Gore (different standards for counting ballots in different counties) was decried by the Supreme Court, similar treatment that had helped Bush slipped by unchallenged. See David Barstow and Don Van Natta Jr., "How Bush Took Florida: Mining the Overseas Absentee Vote," *New York Times,* July 15, 2001, A1.

9. *Palm Beach Canvassing Board v. Harris,* SC00-2346, reprinted in *Bush v. Gore: The Court Cases and the Commentary,* ed. E. J. Dionne Jr. and William Kristol (Washington, D.C.: Brookings, 2001), 24–47.

10. *Bush v. Palm Beach Canvassing Board,* 121 S.Ct. 471 (2000), reprinted in *Bush v. Gore,* ed. Dionne and Kristol, 48–52.

11. *Gore v. Harris,* SC00-243, reprinted in *Bush v. Gore,* ed. Dionne and Kristol, 58–96.

12. For conflicting views about the Supreme Court's ruling in *Bush v. Gore,* see Alan M. Dershowitz, *Supreme Injustice: How the High Court Hijacked Election 2000* (New York: Oxford University Press, 2001); and Richard A. Posner, *Breaking the Deadlock: The 2000 Election, the Constitution, and the Courts* (Princeton: Princeton University Press, 2001).

13. Julia Campbell, "Power Struggle: Bush Pushes Forward with Transition Plans," abcnews.com, November 28, 2000.

14. "Taking the Reins: Bush Prepares for Transfer of Power," abcnews.com, December 14, 2000.

15. James P. Pfiffner, *The Strategic Presidency: Hitting the Ground Running,* 2d ed., revised (Lawrence: University Press of Kansas, 1996), 6.

16. Ibid., 7.

17. Campbell, "Power Struggle."

18. Peter Dizikes, "Full Speed Ahead," abcnews.com, December 5, 2001.

19. Interview with George W. Bush, "'I Realized It Could Be Trouble,'" *Washington Post,* February 4, 2001, A19.

20. "Transition Game," abcnews.com, November 29, 2000.

21. Peter Dizikes, "Waiting for the White House: Bush, Looking Ahead, Continues Transition Work," abcnews.com, December 7, 2000.

22. See Figure 4-1 in Charles O. Jones, *Passages to the Presidency: From Campaigning to Governing* (Washington, D.C.: Brookings, 1998), 95. See also Campbell, "Power Struggle."

23. Jones, *Passages to the Presidency,* 188.

24. Stephen Seplow, "Problems? Bush Has Plenty in His New Job," *Philadelphia Inquirer,* January 21, 2001, D1.

25. Interview with David Gergen, abcnews.com, March 9, 2001.

26. Jones, *Passages to the Presidency,* 175–176.

27. Christine Todd Whitman, Bush's nominee to head the Environmental Protection Agency, also had provided housing and money to an illegal immigrant couple

from 1986 to 1990 but had disclosed the information, apologized, and paid outstanding taxes on wages in 1993, when Zöe Baird came under fire.

28. Quoted in "Chavez Under Siege," abcnews.com, January 9, 2001.

29. "Chavez Withdraws," abcnews.com, January 10, 2001. Chavez implied, perhaps correctly, that Baird had sought cheap labor through her arrangement with an illegal immigrant, while Chavez had the well-being of her immigrant employee at heart.

30. Jones, *Passages to the Presidency,* 96.

31. Ibid., 212 n. 28.

32. Gregory Rodriguez, "Reflections of America," *Los Angeles Times,* January 14, 2001, M1.

33. For the full text of the speech, see the *New York Times,* January 21, 2001, A13.

34. Quoted in Carl M. Brauer, *Presidential Transitions: Eisenhower Through Reagan* (New York: Oxford University Press, 1986), 63.

35. Stephen J. Wayne, "Congressional Liaison in the Reagan White House: A Preliminary Assessment of the First Year," in *President and Congress: Assessing Reagan's First Year,* ed. Norman J. Ornstein (Washington, D.C.: American Enterprise Institute, 1982), 56.

36. Mark Halperin and Elizabeth Wilner, "Bush 100 Days Marked by Short List of Goals," abcnews.com, April 30, 2001.

37. "On the Homefront," abcnews.com, April 24, 2001.

38. Quoted in Mike Allen, "Bush Takes Tax Cut on the Road," *New York Times,* March 1, 2001, A10.

39. Quoted in ibid.

40. "Arsenic and Old Rules: Bush Rolls Back Clinton Arsenic Standards," abcnews.com, March 21, 2001.

41. "On the Homefront," abcnews.com, April 24, 2001.

42. Doyle McManus, "The First 100 Days: At 100 Days and Counting, Bush's Star on the Rise," *Los Angeles Times,* April 29, 2001, A1.

43. A. B. Stoddard, "Green Hornets: Democrats Hammer Bush on Environment," abcnews.com, March 22, 2001.

44. Keith B. Richburg, "After 100 Days, Europe Divided on Bush," *Washington Post,* April 29, 2001, A7.

45. Mary Dejevsky, "Bush Reaches 100th Day with Little to Proclaim," *The Independent* (London), April 30, 2001, 12.

46. "Bush Vows Taiwan Support, But Officials Say No Change in Policy," abcnews.com, April 25, 2001.

47. Karen Hughes quoted in McManus, "The First 100 Days," A1.

48. Dejevsky, "Bush Reaches 100th Day," 12.

49. David E. Rosenbaum, "Senate Approves Cut in Income Tax in Bipartisan Vote," *New York Times,* May 24, 2001, A1.

50. Alison Mitchell, "G.O.P. Senator Plans Shift, Giving Democrats Control in Setback for White House," *New York Times,* May 24, 2001, A1.

51. Philip Shenon, "Change in Parties Would Transform Powerful Panels," *New York Times,* May 24, 2001, A26.

52. Robin Toner, "Bush Agenda Now Faces Tough Sledding in Senate," *New York Times,* May 25, 2001, A19.

53. Transcript of Senator Jeffords's announcement, "'A Struggle for Our Leaders to Deal with Me and for Me to Deal with Them,'" *New York Times,* May 25, 2001, A20.

54. Quoted in Richard L. Berke, "A Question of Governing From the Right," *New York Times,* May 25, 2001, A1.

55. Ibid., A21.

56. Carter M. Yang, "Taking Control," abcnews.com, May 25, 2001. See also Frank Bruni, "While a Restless Senator Stirred, The Bush Team May Have Slept," *New York Times,* May 24, 2001, A1.

57. Martin Kettle, "Hidden Powerhouse of the U.S. Presidency: While George Bush Takes the Public Eye, Vice-President Dick Cheney Pulls the Washington Strings," *The Guardian* (London), April 28, 2001, 19.

58. Bruni, "While a Restless Senator Stirred," A1.

59. See, for example, Peter Preston, "The Man Who Is Really Running the U.S.A.," *The Observer,* December 17, 2000, 15.

60. Kettle, "Hidden Powerhouse," 19.

61. Paul C. Light, *Vice-Presidential Power: Advice and Influence in the White House* (Baltimore: Johns Hopkins University Press, 1984).

62. Quoted in Kettle, "Hidden Powerhouse," 19.

63. Ibid., 19.

64. Preston, "The Man Who Is Really Running the U.S.A.," 15.

65. Kettle, "Hidden Powerhouse," 19.

66. David E. Sanger, "Trying to Run a Country Like a Corporation," *New York Times,* July 8, 2001, sec. 4, 3.

67. "Energy Investigation: Cheney Task Force's Ties to Industry Questioned," abcnews.com, June 18, 2001.

68. Dana Milbank and Ellen Nakashima, "Cheney Rebuffs GAO's Records Request," *Washington Post,* August 4, 2001, A11.

69. Ellen Nakashima, "Can GAO Make Cheney Blink?" *Washington Post,* August 3, A17.

70. Michael Beschloss, "Money and Politics: Bush and Cheney Reopen the Debate Over Political Fund-Raising," abcnews.com, May 23, 2001.

71. David. E. Sanger, "Cheney's Doctors Expect to Implant Device for Heart," *New York Times,* June 30, 2001, A1.

72. Richard L. Berke and Frank Bruni, "Crew of Listing Bush Ship Draws Republican Scowls," *New York Times,* July 2, 2001, A11.

73. Joseph Kahn, "Drop in Fuel Price May Weaken Push for Energy Plans," *New York Times,* July 16, 2001, A1.

74. James Sterngold, "California's New Problem: Sudden Surplus of Energy," *New York Times,* July 19, 2001, A1.

75. Richard W. Stevenson, "Seeing Red, or Not," *New York Times,* July 13, 2001, A18.

76. Lizette Alvarez, "President's Plan on Energy Use Moves Forward," *New York Times,* August 2, 2001, A1.

77. David E. Rosenbaum, "How a Lawmaker Shifted Position on an Issue and Took a Majority with Him," *New York Times,* August 3, 2001, A18.

78. Dana Milbank and Juliet Eilperin, "On Patients' Rights Deal, Bush Scored with a Full-Court Press," *Washington Post,* August 3, 2001, A9.

79. Dan Balz, "Despite Wins, Bush Faces Battles Ahead," *Washington Post,* August 3, 2001, A1.

80. "Bush Approval Rating Stabilizes, But Poll Finds Reservations Remain," abcnews.com, August 1, 2001.

81. Quoted in Dana Milbank, "In the Rose Garden, Bush, Aides Revel in Their Successes," *Washington Post,* August 4, 2001, A4.

82. Milbank, "In the Rose Garden," A4.

83. Richard Neustadt, *Presidential Power* (New York: Wiley, 1960).

84. See www.gallup.com.

85. President George W. Bush, remarks at the National Cathedral, Washington, D.C., September 14, 2001. For the text of Bush's speech, see www.whitehouse.gov.

86. President George W. Bush, weekly radio address, September 15, 2001. For the text of the address, see www.whitehouse.gov.

87. David W. Moore, poll analysis, "Confidence in Leaders: Americans Rally Around Government Leaders in Wake of Terrorist Attacks," September 14, 2001. See www.gallup.com.

88. S.J. Res. 23. The lone dissenting vote came from Rep. Barbara Lee (D-Calif.), a pacifist. See Philip Shenon, "The Lone Voice: In One Vote, A Call for Restraint," *New York Times*, September 16, 2001, A6.

89. William Drozdiak, "Crisis Forces Shift in Policy as Bush Assembles Coalition," *Washington Post*, September 17, 2001, A9.

90. "Excerpts from President's Remarks on Investigation Into Attacks," *New York Times*, September 14, 2001, A18.

91. R. W. Apple Jr., "President Seems to Gain Legitimacy," *New York Times*, September 16, 2001, A6.

SUGGESTED READINGS

Brauer, Carl M. *Presidential Transitions: Eisenhower Through Reagan*. New York: Oxford University Press, 1986.

Burke, John P. *Presidential Transitions: From Politics to Practice*. Boulder, Colo.: Lynne Rienner, 2000.

Dershowitz, Alan M. *Supreme Injustice: How the High Court Hijacked Election 2000*. New York: Oxford University Press, 2001.

Jones, Charles O. *Passages to the Presidency: From Campaigning to Governing*. Washington, D.C.: Brookings, 1998.

Pfiffner, James P. *The Strategic Presidency: Hitting the Ground Running*. 2d ed., revised. Lawrence: University Press of Kansas, 1996.

Posner, Richard A. *Breaking the Deadlock: The 2000 Election, the Constitution, and the Courts*. Princeton: Princeton University Press, 2001.

RESULTS OF PRESIDENTIAL CONTESTS, 1912–2000

Year	Republican nominee (in *italics*) and other major candidates	Democratic nominee (in *italics*) and other major candidates	Election winner	Division of popular vote[a] (percent)	Division of electoral vote[b]
1912	William Howard Taft (incumbent president)	Woodrow Wilson (governor of New Jersey)	Wilson (D)	42–23	435–8
	Theodore Roosevelt[c] (former president)	James Champ Clark (representative from Missouri and Speaker of the House)			
1916	*Charles Evans Hughes* (justice, U.S. Supreme Court)	*Woodrow Wilson* (incumbent president)	Wilson (D)	49–46	277–254
	Elihu Root (former secretary of state)	None			
1920	*Warren G. Harding* (senator from Ohio)	*James Cox* (governor of Ohio)	Harding (R)	60–34	404–127
	Leonard Wood (general)	William McAdoo (former secretary of the Treasury)			
	Frank Lowden (governor of Illinois)	A. Mitchell Palmer (attorney general)			
	Hiram Johnson (senator from California)				
1924	*Calvin Coolidge* (incumbent president)	*John W. Davis* (former solicitor general)	Coolidge (R)	54–29	382–136
	Hiram Johnson (senator from California)	Alfred Smith (governor of New York)			
		William McAdoo (former secretary of the Treasury)			
1928	*Herbert Hoover* (former secretary of commerce)	*Alfred Smith* (governor of New York)	Hoover (R)	58–41	444–87
	Frank Lowden (governor of Illinois)	James Reed (senator from Missouri)			
		Cordell Hull (representative from Tennessee)			
1932	*Herbert Hoover* (incumbent president)	*Franklin D. Roosevelt* (governor of New York)	Roosevelt (D)	57–40	472–59
	Joseph France (former senator from Maryland)	Alfred Smith (former governor of New York)			
		John Garner (representative from Texas and Speaker of the House)			

Results of Presidential Contests, 1912–2000 *(Continued)*

Year	Republican nominee (in *italics*) and other major candidates	Democratic nominee (in *italics*) and other major candidates	Election winner	Division of popular vote[a] (percent)	Division of electoral vote[b]
1936	*Alfred Landon* (governor of Kansas) WIlliam Borah (senator from Idaho)	*Franklin D. Roosevelt* (incumbent president) None	Roosevelt (D)	61–37	523–8
1940	*Wendell Willkie* (Indiana lawyer and public utility executive) Thomas E. Dewey (U.S. district attorney for New York) Robert Taft (senator from Ohio)	*Franklin D. Roosevelt* (incumbent president) None	Roosevelt (D)	55–45	449–82
1944	*Thomas E. Dewey* (governor of New York) Wendell Willkie (previous Republican presidential nominee)	*Franklin D. Roosevelt* (incumbent president) Harry Byrd (senator from Virginia)	Roosevelt (D)	53–46	432–99
1948	*Thomas E. Dewey* (governor of New York) Harold Stassen (former governor of Minnesota) Robert Taft (senator from Ohio)	*Harry S. Truman* (incumbent president) Richard Russell (senator from Georgia)	Truman (D)	50–45	303–189
1952	*Dwight D. Eisenhower* (general) Robert Taft (senator from Ohio)	*Adlai Stevenson* (governor of Illinois) Estes Kefauver (senator from Tennessee) Richard Russell (senator from Georgia)	Eisenhower (R)	55–44	442–89
1956	*Dwight D. Elsenhower* (incumbent president) None	*Adlai Stevenson* (previous Democratic presidential nominee) Averell Harriman (governor of New York)	Eisenhower (R)	57–42	457–73
1960	*Richard Nixon* (vice president) None	*John F. Kennedy* (senator from Massachusetts) Hubert Humphrey (senator from Minnesota) Lyndon B. Johnson (senator from Texas)	Kennedy (D)	49.7–49.5	303–219
1964	*Barry Goldwater* (senator from Arizona) Nelson Rockefeller (governor of New York)	*Lyndon B. Johnson* (incumbent president) None	Johnson (D)	61–39	586–52

Results of Presidential Contests, 1912–2000 *(Continued)*

Year	Republican nominee (in *italics*) and other major candidates	Democratic nominee (in *italics*) and other major candidates	Election winner	Division of popular vote[a] (percent)	Division of electoral vote[b]
1968	*Richard Nixon* (former Republican presidential nominee) Ronald Reagan (governor of California)	*Hubert Humphrey* (incumbent vice president) Robert F. Kennedy (senator from New York) Eugene McCarthy (senator from Minnesota)	Nixon (R)	43.4–42.7	301–191
1972	*Richard Nixon* (incumbent president) None	*George McGovern* (senator from South Dakota) Hubert Humphrey (senator from Minnesota) George Wallace (governor of Alabama)	Nixon (R)	61–38	520–17
1976	*Gerald R. Ford* (incumbent president) Ronald Reagan (former governor of California)	*Jimmy Carter* (former governor of Georgia) Edmund Brown, Jr. (governor of California) George Wallace (governor of Alabama)	Carter (D)	50–48	297–240
1980	*Ronald Reagan* (former governor of California) George Bush (former director of Central Intelligence Agency) John Anderson (representative from Illinois)	*Jimmy Carter* (incumbent president) Edward M. Kennedy (senator from Massachusetts)	Reagan (R)	51–41	489–49
1984	*Ronald Reagan* (incumbent president) None	*Walter F. Mondale* (former vice president) Gary Hart (senator from Colorado)	Reagan (R)	59–41	525–13
1988	*George Bush* (vice president) Robert Dole (senator from Kansas)	*Michael Dukakis* (governor of Massachusetts) Jesse Jackson (civil rights activist)	Bush (R)	53–46	426–111
1992	*George Bush* (incumbent president) Patrick Buchanan (journalist)	*William Clinton* (governor of Arkansas) Paul Tsongas (former senator)	Clinton (D)	43–37	357–168
1996	*Robert Dole* (senator from Kansas) Patrick Buchanan (journalist)	*William Clinton* (incumbent president) None	Clinton (D)	49–41	379–159
2000	George W. Bush (governor of Texas) John McCain (senator from Arizona)	Al Gore (incumbent vice president) Bill Bradley (former senator)	Bush (R)	47.9–48.4	271–267

Note: The table begins with the year 1912 because presidential primaries were first held that year.

[a] Division of popular vote is between the Republican and Democratic nominees.

[b] Division of electoral vote is between the Republican and Democratic nominees.

[c] When the Republican convention failed to choose him as its nominee (selecting instead the incumbent president, William Howard Taft), former president Theodore Roosevelt withdrew from the party and created the Progressive Party. As the Progressive Party nominee, Roosevelt received 27 percent of the popular vote and 88 electoral votes.

APPENDIX B

PERSONAL BACKGROUNDS OF U.S. PRESIDENTS

President	Age at first political office	First political office / Last political office[a]	Age at becoming president	State of residence[b]	Father's occupation	Higher education[c]	Occupation
1. Washington (1789–1797)	17	County surveyor / Commander in chief	57	Va.	Farmer	None	Farmer, surveyor
2. Adams, J. (1797–1801)	39	Surveyor of highways / Vice president	61	Mass.	Farmer	Harvard	Farmer, lawyer
3. Jefferson (1801–1809)	26	State legislator / Vice president	58	Va.	Farmer	William and Mary	Farmer, lawyer
4. Madison (1809–1817)	25	State legislator / Secretary of state	58	Va.	Farmer	Princeton	Farmer
5. Monroe (1817–1825)	24	State legislator / Secretary of state	59	Va.	Farmer	William and Mary	Lawyer, farmer
6. Adams, J. Q. (1825–1829)	27	Minister to Netherlands / Secretary of state	58	Mass.	Farmer, lawyer	Harvard	Lawyer
7. Jackson (1829–1837)	21	Prosecuting attorney / U.S. Senate	62	Tenn.	Farmer	None	Lawyer
8. Van Buren (1837–1841)	30	Surrogate of county / Vice president	55	N.Y.	Tavern keeper	None	Lawyer
9. Harrison, W. H. (1841)	26	Territorial delegate to Congress / Minister to Colombia	68	Ind.	Farmer	Hampden-Sydney	Military
10. Tyler (1841–1845)	21	State legislator / Vice president	51	Va.	Planter, lawyer	William and Mary	Lawyer
11. Polk (1845–1849)	28	State legislator / Governor	50	Tenn.	Surveyor	U. of North Carolina	Lawyer
12. Taylor (1849–1850)	None	None [a]	65	Ky.	Collector of internal revenue	None	Military
13. Fillmore (1850–1853)	28	Stale legislator / Vice president	50	N.Y.	Farmer	None	Lawyer
14. Pierce (1853–1857)	25	State legislator / U.S. district attorney	48	N.H.	General	Bowdoin	Lawyer
15. Buchanan (1857–1861)	22	Assistant county prosecutor / Minister to Great Britain	65	Pa.	Farmer	Dickinson	Lawyer

Personal Backgrounds of U.S. Presidents *(Continued)*

President	Age at first political office	First political office / Last political office[a]	Age at becoming president	State of residence[b]	Father's occupation	Higher education[c]	Occupation
16. Lincoln (1861–1865)	25	State legislator / U.S. House of Representatives	52	Ill.	Farmer, carpenter	None	Lawyer
17. Johnson, A. (1865–1869)	20	City alderman / Vice president	57	Tenn.	Janitor-porter	None	Tailor
18. Grant (1869–1877)	None	None [a]	47	Ohio	Tanner	West Point	Military
19. Hayes (1877–1881)	36	City solicitor / Governor	55	Ohio	Farmer	Kenyon	Lawyer
20. Garfield (1881)	28	State legislator / U.S. Senate	50	Ohio	Canal worker	Williams	Educator, lawyer
21. Arthur (1881–1885)	31	State engineer / Vice president	51	N.Y.	Minister	Union	Lawyer
22. Cleveland (1885–1889) 24. (1893–1897)	26	Assistant district attorney / Governor	48	N.Y.	Minister	None	Lawyer
23. Harrison, B. (1889–1893)	24	City attorney / U.S. Senate	56	Ind.	Military	Miami of Ohio	Lawyer
25. McKinley (1897–1901)	26	Prosecuting attorney / Governor	54	Ohio	Ironmonger	Allegheny	Lawyer
26. Roosevelt, T. (1901–1909)	24	State legislator / Vice president	43	N.Y.	Business-man	Harvard	Lawyer, author
27. Taft (1909–1913)	24	Assistant prosecuting attorney / Secretary of war	52	Ohio	Lawyer	Yale	Lawyer
28. Wilson (1913–1921)	54	Governor / Governor	56	N.J.	Minister	Princeton	Educator
29. Harding (1921–1923)	35	State legislator / U.S. Senate	56	Ohio	Physician, editor	Ohio Central	Newspaper editor
30. Coolidge (1923–1929)	26	City councilman / Vice president	51	Mass.	Storekeeper	Amherst	Lawyer
31. Hoover (1929–1933)	43	Relief and food administrator / Secretary of commerce	55	Calif.	Blacksmith	Stanford	Mining engineer
32. Roosevelt, F. (1933–1945)	28	State legislator / Governor	49	N.Y.	Business-man, landowner	Harvard	Lawyer
33. Truman (1945–1953)	38	County judge (commissioner) / Vice president	61	Mo.	Farmer, livestock	None	Clerk, store owner
34. Eisenhower (1953–1961)	—	None [a]	63	Kan.	Mechanic	West Point	Military

Personal Backgrounds of U.S. Presidents *(Continued)*

President	Age at first political office	First political office / Last political office[a]	Age at becoming president	State of residence[b]	Father's occupation	Higher education[c]	Occupation
35. Kennedy (1961–1963)	29	U.S. House of Representatives / U.S. Senate	43	Mass.	Businessman	Harvard	Newspaper reporter
36. Johnson, L. (1963–1969)	28	U.S. House of Representatives / Vice president	55	Texas	Farmer, real estate	Southwest Texas State Teacher's College	Educator
37. Nixon (1969–1974)	34	U.S. House of Representatives / Vice president	56	Calif.	Streetcar conductor	Whittier	Lawyer
38. Ford (1974–1977)	36	U.S. House of Representatives / Vice president	61	Mich.	Businessman	U. of Michigan	Lawyer
39. Carter (1977–1981)	38	County Board of Education / Governor	52	Ga.	Farmer, businessman	U.S. Naval Academy	Farmer, businessman
40. Reagan (1981–1989)	55	Governor / Governor	69	Calif.	Shoe salesman	Eureka	Entertainer
41. Bush (1989–1993)	42	U.S. House of Representatives / Vice president	64	Texas	Businessman, U.S. senator	Yale	Businessman
42. Clinton (1993–2001)	30	State attorney general / Governor	46	Ark.	Car dealer	Georgetown	Lawyer
43. Bush, G. W. (2001–)	48	Governor / Governor	54	Texas	U.S. President	Yale	Businessman

[a] This category refers to the last civilian office held before the presidency. Taylor, Grant, and Eisenhower had served as generals before becoming president.
[b] The state is where the president spent his important adult years, not necessarily where he was born.
[c] Refers to undergraduate education.

APPENDIX C

THE CONSTITUTION ON THE PRESIDENCY

ARTICLE I

Section 3. ... The Vice President of the United States shall be President of the Senate, but shall have no Vote, unless they be equally divided.

The Senate shall chuse their other officers, and also a President pro tempore, in the Absence of the Vice President, or when he shall exercise the Office of President of the United States.

The Senate shall have the sole Power to try all Impeachments. When sitting for that Purpose, they shall be on Oath or Affirmation. When the President of the United States is tried the Chief Justice shall preside: And no Person shall be convicted without the Concurrence of two thirds of the Members present.

Judgment in Cases of Impeachment shall not extend further than to removal from Office, and disqualification to hold and enjoy any Office of honor, Trust or Profit under the United States: but the Party convicted shall nevertheless be liable and subject to Indictment, Trial, Judgment and Punishment, according to Law.

Section 7. ... Every Bill which shall have passed the House of Representatives and the Senate, shall, before it become a Law, be presented to the President of the United States; If he approve he shall sign it, but if not he shall return it, with his Objections to that House in which it shall have originated, who shall enter the Objections at large on their Journal, and proceed to reconsider it. If after such Reconsideration two thirds of that House shall agree to pass the Bill, it shall be sent, together with the Objections, to the other House, by which it shall likewise be reconsidered, and if approved by two thirds of that House, it shall become a Law. But in all such Cases the Votes of both Houses shall be determined by yeas and Nays, and the Names of the Persons voting for and against the Bill shall be entered on the Journal of each House respectively. If any Bill shall not be returned by the President within ten Days (Sundays excepted) after it shall have been presented to him, the Same shall be a Law, in like Manner as if

425

he had signed it, unless the Congress by their Adjournment prevent its Return, in which Case it shall not be a Law.

Every Order, Resolution, or Vote to which the Concurrence of the Senate and House of Representatives may be necessary (except on a question of Adjournment) shall be presented to the President of the United States; and before the Same shall take Effect, shall be approved by him, or being disapproved by him, shall be repassed by two thirds of the Senate and House of Representatives, according to the Rules and Limitations prescribed in the Case of a Bill.

ARTICLE II

Section 1. The executive Power shall be vested in a President of the United States of America. He shall hold his Office during the Term of four Years, and, together with the Vice President, chosen for the same Term, be elected, as follows. Each State shall appoint, in such Manner as the Legislature thereof may direct, a Number of Electors, equal to the whole Number of Senators and Representatives to which the State may be entitled in the Congress: but no Senator or Representative, or Person holding an Office of Trust or Profit under the United States, shall be appointed an Elector.

[The Electors shall meet in their respective States, and vote by Ballot for two Persons, of whom one at least shall not be an Inhabitant of the same State with themselves. And they shall make a List of all the Persons voted for, and of the Number of Votes for each; which List they shall sign and certify, and transmit sealed to the Seat of the Government of the United States, directed to the President of the Senate. The President of the Senate shall, in the Presence of the Senate and House of Representatives, open all the Certificates, and the Votes shall then be counted. The Person having the greatest Number of Votes shall be the President, if such Number be a Majority of the whole Number of Electors appointed; and if there be more than one who have such Majority, and have an equal Number of Votes, then the House of Representatives shall immediately chuse by Ballot one of them for President; and if no Person have a Majority, then from the five highest on the list the said House shall in like Manner chuse the President. But in chusing the President, the Votes shall be taken by States, the Representation from each State having one Vote; a quorum for this Purpose shall consist of a Member or Members from two thirds of the States, and a Majority of all the States shall be necessary to a Choice. In every Case, after the Choice of the President, the Person having the greatest Number of Votes of the Electors shall be the Vice President. But if there should remain two or more who have equal Votes, the Senate shall chuse from them by Ballot the Vice President.] [1]

The Congress may determine the Time of chusing the Electors, and the Day on which they shall give their Votes; which Day shall be the same throughout the United States.

No Person except a natural born Citizen, or a Citizen of the United States, at the time of the Adoption of this Constitution, shall be eligible to the Office of

President; neither shall any Person be eligible to that Office who shall not have attained to the Age of thirty five Years, and been fourteen Years a Resident within the United States.

In Case of the Removal of the President from office, or of his Death, Resignation, or Inability to discharge the Powers and Duties of the said Office,[2] the Same shall devolve on the Vice President, and the Congress may by Law provide for the Case of Removal, Death, Resignation or Inability, both of the President and Vice President, declaring what officer shall then act as President, and such Officer shall act accordingly, until the Disability be removed, or a President shall be elected.

The President shall, at stated Times, receive for his Services, a Compensation, which shall neither be increased nor diminished during the Period for which he shall have been elected, and he shall not receive within that Period any other Emolument from the United States, or any of them.

Before he enter on the Execution of his Office, he shall take the following Oath or Affirmation: — "I do solemnly swear (or affirm) that I will faithfully execute the Office of President of the United States, and will to the best of my Ability, preserve, protect and defend the Constitution of the United States."

Section 2. The President shall be Commander in Chief of the Army and Navy of the United States, and of the Militia of the several States, when called into the actual Service of the United States; he may require the Opinion, in writing, of the principal Officer in each of the executive Departments, upon any Subject relating to the Duties of their respective Offices, and he shall have Power to grant Reprieves and Pardons for Offenses against the United States, except in Cases of Impeachment.

He shall have Power, by and with the Advice and Consent of the Senate, to make Treaties, provided two thirds of the Senators present concur; and he shall nominate, and by and with the Advice and Consent of the Senate, shall appoint Ambassadors, other public Ministers and Consuls, Judges of the supreme Court, and all other officers of the United States, whose Appointments are not herein otherwise provided for, and which shall be established by Law: but the Congress may by Law vest the Appointment of such inferior Officers, as they think proper, in the President alone, in the Courts of Law, or in the Heads of Departments.

The President shall have Power to fill up all Vacancies that may happen during the Recess of the Senate, by granting Commissions which shall expire at the End of their next Session.

Section 3. He shall from time to time give to the Congress Information of the State of the Union, and recommend to their Consideration such Measures as he shall judge necessary and expedient; he may, on extraordinary Occasions, convene both Houses, or either of them, and in Case of Disagreement between them, with Respect to the Time of Adjournment, he may adjourn them to such Time as he shall think proper; he shall receive Ambassadors and other public

Ministers; he shall take Care that the Laws be faithfully executed, and shall Commission all the officers of the United States.

Section 4. The President, Vice President and all Civil Officers of the United States, shall be removed from office on Impeachment for, and Conviction of, Treason, Bribery, or other high Crimes and Misdemeanors.

ARTICLE VI

... This Constitution, and the Laws of the United States which shall be made in Pursuance thereof, and all Treaties made, or which shall be made, under the Authority of the United States, shall be the supreme Law of the Land; and the Judges in every State shall be bound thereby, any Thing in the Constitution or Laws of any State to the Contrary notwithstanding.

The Senators and Representatives before mentioned, and the Members of the several State Legislatures, and all executive and judicial Officers, both of the United States and of the several States, shall be bound by Oath or Affirmation, to support this Constitution; but no religious Test shall ever be required as a Qualification to any Office or public Trust under the United States.

AMENDMENT XII *(Ratified June 15, 1804)*

The Electors shall meet in their respective states and vote by ballot for President and Vice-President, one of whom, at least, shall not be an inhabitant of the same state with themselves; they shall name in their ballots the person voted for as President, and in distinct ballots the person voted for as Vice-President, and they shall make distinct lists of all persons voted for as President, and of all persons voted for as Vice-President, and of the number of votes for each, which lists they shall sign and certify, and transmit sealed to the seat of the government of the United States, directed to the President of the Senate; — The President of the Senate shall, in the presence of the Senate and House of Representatives, open all the certificates and the votes shall then be counted; — The person having the greatest number of votes for President, shall be the President, if such number be a majority of the whole number of Electors appointed; and if no person have such majority, then from the persons having the highest numbers not exceeding three on the list of those voted for as President, the House of Representatives shall choose immediately, by ballot, the President. But in choosing the President, the votes shall be taken by states, the representation from each state having one vote; a quorum for this purpose shall consist of a member or members from two-thirds of the states, and a majority of all the states shall be necessary to a choice. [And if the House of Representatives shall not choose a President whenever the right of choice shall devolve upon them, before the fourth day of March next following, then the Vice-President shall act as President, as in the case of the death or other constitutional disability of the President—][3] The person having the greatest number of votes as Vice-President, shall be the Vice-President, if such number be a majority of the whole number of Electors appointed, and if no person have a majority, then from the two highest numbers on the list, the Senate shall choose the Vice-President; a quorum for the purpose shall consist of two-thirds of the whole number of Senators, and a majority of the whole number shall be necessary to a choice. But no person constitutionally ineligible to the office of President shall be eligible to that of Vice-President of the United States.

AMENDMENT XX *(Ratified Jan. 23, 1933)*

Section 1. The terms of the President and Vice President shall end at noon on the 20th day of January, and the terms of Senators and Representatives at noon on the 3d day of January, of the years in which such terms would have ended if this article had not been ratified; and the terms of their successors shall then begin.

Section 2. The Congress shall assemble at least once in every year, and such meeting shall begin at noon on the 3d day of January, unless they shall by law appoint a different day.

Section 3.[4] If, at the time fixed for the beginning of the term of the President, the President elect shall have died, the Vice President elect shall become President. If a President shall not have been chosen before the time fixed for the beginning of his term, or if the President elect shall have failed to qualify, then the Vice President elect shall act as President until a President shall have qualified; and the Congress may by law provide for the case wherein neither a President elect nor a Vice President elect shall have qualified, declaring who shall then act as President, or the manner in which one who is to act shall be selected, and such person shall act accordingly until a President or Vice President shall have qualified.

Section 4. The Congress may by law provide for the case of the death of any of the persons from whom the House of Representatives may choose a President whenever the right of choice shall have devolved upon them, and for the case of the death of any of the persons from whom the Senate may choose a Vice President whenever the right of choice shall have devolved upon them.

Section 5. Sections I and 2 shall take effect on the 15th day of October following the ratification of this article.

Section 6. This article shall be inoperative unless it shall have been ratified as an amendment to the Constitution by the legislatures of three-fourths of the several States within seven years from the date of its submission.

AMENDMENT XXII *(Ratified Feb. 27, 1951)*

Section 1. No person shall be elected to the office of the President more than twice, and no person who has held the office of President, or acted as President, for more than two years of a term to which some other person was elected President shall be elected to the office of the President more than once. But this Article shall not apply to any person holding the office of President when this Article was proposed by the Congress, and shall not prevent any person who may be holding the office of President, or acting as President, during the term within which this Article become operative from holding the office of President or acting as President during the remainder of such term.

Section 2. This Article shall be inoperative unless it shall have been ratified as an amendment to the Constitution by the legislatures of three-fourths of the several States within seven years from the date of its submission to the States by the Congress.

AMENDMENT XXIII *(Ratified March 29, 1961)*

Section 1. The District constituting the seat of Government of the United States shall appoint in such manner as the Congress may direct:

A number of electors of President and Vice President equal to the whole number of Senators and Representatives in Congress to which the District would be entitled if it were a State, but in no event more than the least populous State; they shall be in addition to those appointed by the States, but they shall be considered, for the purposes of the election of President and Vice President, to be electors appointed by a State; and they shall meet in the District and perform such duties as provided by the twelfth article of amendment.

Section 2. The Congress shall have power to enforce this article by appropriate legislation.

AMENDMENT XXV *(Ratified Feb. 10, 1967)*

Section 1. In case of the removal of the President from office or of his death or resignation, the Vice President shall become President.

Section 2. Whenever there is a vacancy in the office of the Vice President, the President shall nominate a Vice President who shall take office upon confirmation by a majority vote of both Houses of Congress.

Section 3. Whenever the President transmits to the President pro tempore of the Senate and the Speaker of the House of Representatives his written declaration that he is unable to discharge the powers and duties of his office, and until he transmits to them a written declaration to the contrary, such powers and duties shall be discharged by the Vice President as Acting President.

Section 4. Whenever the Vice President and a majority of either the principal officers of the executive departments or of such other body as Congress may by law provide, transmit to the President pro tempore of the Senate and the Speaker of the House of Representatives their written declaration that the President is unable to discharge the powers and duties of his office, the Vice President shall immediately assume the powers and duties of the office as Acting President.

Thereafter, when the President transmits to the President pro tempore of the Senate and the Speaker of the House of Representatives his written declaration that no inability exists, he shall resume the powers and duties of his office unless the Vice President and a majority of either the principal officers of the executive department or of such other body as Congress may by law provide, transmit within four days to the President pro tempore of the Senate and the Speaker of the House of Representatives their written declaration that the President is unable to discharge the powers and duties of his office. Thereupon Congress shall decide the issue, assembling within forty-eight hours for that purpose if not in session. If the Congress, within twenty-one days after receipt of the latter written declaration, or, if Congress is not in session, within twenty-one days after Congress is required to assemble, determines by two-thirds vote of both houses that the President is unable to discharge the powers and duties of his office, the Vice President shall continue to discharge the same as Acting President; otherwise, the President shall resume the powers and duties of his office.

NOTES

1. The material in brackets has been superseded by the Twelfth Amendment.
2. This provision has been affected by the Twenty-fifth Amendment.
3. The part in brackets has been superseded by Section 3 of the Twentieth Amendment.
4. See the Twenty-fifth Amendment.

INDEX

CREDITS

58 *Gallup Report,* November 1988, pp. 6–7. © 1998 by the Gallup Reports; *The Gallup Poll Monthly,* November 1992, p. 9. Used by permission. **91** and **92** Samuel Kernell and Gary C. Jacobson, *The Logic of American Politics,* pp. 241 and 243. © 2000 by CQ Press. Reprinted by permission of the publisher. **99** Harold W. Stanley and Richard G. Niemi, *Vital Statistics on American Politics, 1999–2000.* © 2000 by CQ Press. Reprinted by permission of the publisher. **126** Reprinted by permission of Greenwood Publishing Group, Inc. Westport. Conn., from *The Leadership Question,* by Bert A. Rockman. © by Praeger Publishers, 2004. Fred I. Greenstein, *Personality and Politics,* p. 27. © 1975 by W. W. Norton. Used by permission of the author. **128** Harold W. Stanley and Richard G. Niemi, *Vital Statistics on American Politics 1999–2000,* Table 6–2, pp. 244–245. © 2000 by CQ Press. Reprinted by permission of the publisher. **130** Edward Pessen, *The Log Cabin Myth: The Social Backgrounds of the Presidents,* p. 68. © 1984 by Yale University Press, New Haven, Conn. Used by permission of the publisher. **187** Michael Nelson, ed., *Guide to the Presidency,* 2d ed., pp. 1698–1703. © 1996 by CQ Press. Reprinted by permission of the publisher. **188** Stephen J. Wayne, Richard L. Cole, James F. C. Hyde, "Advising the President on Enrolled Legislation," *Political Science Quarterly* Reprinted with permission from *Political Science Quarterly,* 94 (Summer 1979):310. **262** Alliance for Justice, "Judicial Selection Project: Annual Report 2000," http://www.afj.org/jsp/report2000. **268** John Anthony Maltese, *The Selling of Supreme Court Nominees,* p. 3, Table 1. © 1995. Reprinted by permission of the Johns Hopkins University Press. **338, 340, 342,** and **343** John H. Kessel, *Presidents, the Presidency, and the Political Environment,* chap. 5. ©2001 by CQ Press. Reprinted by permission of the publisher. **385** Cecil V. Crabb, Jr., and Kevin V. Mulcahy, *American National Security: A Presidential Perspective,* p. 189. © 1991 by Thomson Learning. Used by permission of the publisher.

PHOTOGRAPHS

1 The White House/Bill Fitz-Patrick; **4** Library of Congress; **9** Library of Congress; **30** National Archives; **33** AP/Wide World Photo; **75** Library of Congress; **103** MTV; **123** AP/Wide World Photo; **131** The White House; **170** AP/Wide World Photo; **192** Lyndon B. Johnson Library; **208** AP/Wide World Photo; **229** Farm Security Administration—Office of War Information Photograph Collection/Library of Congress; **249** AP/Wide World Photo; **254** AP/Wide World Photo; **284** AP/Wide World Photo; **295** AP/Wide World Photo; **319** National Archives; **344** AP/Wide World Photo; **357** Alex S. MacLean; **381** George Bush Library; **396** Scott J. Ferrell, Congressional Quarterly Inc; **412** Reuters.